WHAT *to* DRINK *with* WHAT *you* EAT

WHAT *to* DRINK *with* WHAT *you* EAT

THE DEFINITIVE GUIDE TO PAIRING FOOD WITH WINE,
BEER, SPIRITS, COFFEE, TEA—EVEN WATER—BASED ON
EXPERT ADVICE FROM AMERICA'S BEST SOMMELIERS

ANDREW DORNENBURG *and* **KAREN PAGE**
Photographs by MICHAEL SOFRONSKI

BULFINCH PRESS
New York • Boston • London

ALSO BY THE AUTHORS

Becoming a Chef

Culinary Artistry

Dining Out

Chef's Night Out

The New American Chef

The Flavor Bible

Copyright © 2006 by Andrew Dornenburg and Karen Page
Photography by Michael Sofronski

Bulfinch Press
Hachette Book Group
237 Park Avenue, New York, NY 10017
www.bulfinchpress.com

First Edition: October 2006
Sixth Printing, 2010

Bulfinch is an imprint of Little, Brown and Company. The Bulfinch name and logo are trademarks of Hachette Book Group, Inc.

Library of Congress Cataloging-in-Publication Data
Dornenburg, Andrew.
    What to drink with what you eat : the definitive guide to pairing food with wine, beer, spirits, coffee, tea — even water — based on expert advice from America's best sommeliers / Andrew Dornenburg and Karen Page.
        p. cm.
    Includes index.
    ISBN: 978-0-8212-5718-0 (hardcover)
    1. Cookery. 2. Wine and wine making. 3. Beverages. I. Page, Karen. II. Title.
TX714.D6755 2006
641.5 — dc22   2005036007

Design: Vertigo Design NYC
Jacket design by Wilcox Design

PRINTED IN SINGAPORE

For Susan Bulkeley Butler, author of the wonderful book *Become the CEO of You, Inc.*, for her inspiring motto

The flavor of a food almost always reveals the quality of a wine and exalts it. In turn, the quality of a wine complements the pleasure of a food and spiritualizes it.

— Luigi "Gino" Veronelli, wine critic (1926–2004)

CONTENTS

PREFACE

"The best way to have a good idea is to have a lot of ideas." —LINUS PAULING

"Life is the sum of all your choices." —ALBERT CAMUS

We researched and wrote this book for two simple reasons: 1) to serve as an idea-starter to help you consider a lot of ideas regarding what to drink with what you eat; and 2) to guide you to make even better choices when selecting a beverage, so that you have the potential to enjoy a peak experience every time!

To paraphrase Linus Pauling, we firmly believe that the more ideas you take into account, the more likely you are to have some good (or even great) ones from which to choose. And we agree with Albert Camus that the better your choices, the better your life. We hope that this book will improve your ideas and your choices — and, ultimately, your life.

In fact, *What to Drink with What You Eat* has the potential to be the most important book you read this year. After all, what other title can promise the opportunity to bring more pleasure into your life through something you already do three times a day? Our hope is to help you extend the realm of gastronomy at play in your daily life by encouraging you to explore a whole new world of offerings of wine, beer, cocktails, coffee, tea, and even water.

After considering a lot of different beverage ideas, what's the best way to winnow down your final choices? To maximize your pleasure (and that of your guests), you'll want to consider such factors as your (and their) personal beverage preferences, which we'll explore in Chapter 2. As you might be constrained by what you have on hand, we'll help you get ready for anything in Chapter 4. And you'll also want to think about what might best accompany whatever it is you're eating, which we delve into in Chapters 3, 5, and 6.

This book represents the better parts of two lifetimes of research. We've been collecting these guidelines and recommendations — and taste-testing as many of them as humanly possible — for more than two decades. Some have proven tried-and-true from our own personal experiences, as we've researched classic food and beverage pairings extensively — from oysters and Sancerre, to chocolate and tawny port — and put them to the test against our own palates. Others we discovered during the course of our travels and restaurant visits, often by putting ourselves into the hands of top sommeliers and chefs. (Who knew pan-seared venison with Arizona Zinfandel could be such a delicious match, as we learned at Janos in Tucson?) Still others were amassed over the years for our previous books through interviews with a virtual Who's Who of the food and beverage world. In fact, we started this research on compatible flavors in earnest when setting out to write our book *Culinary Artistry* over a decade ago, but space constraints precluded the inclusion of most beverages in that 400-plus-page reference.

However, the majority of the recommendations that comprise the more than fifteen hundred entries you'll find in the pages that follow came from the dozens of experts — including many of America's best sommeliers — we interviewed over the past few years. Collectively, these recommendations make up a virtual thesaurus of food and beverage pairing ideas.

Over the course of researching this book, we've had our eyes opened in delicious ways:

- *While we received enormous pleasure from a hundred-year-old Sauternes served to us with sautéed foie gras by the late chef Jean-Louis Palladin, we've also learned the joys of a simple bottle of Beaujolais on a summer afternoon picnic!*

- *Chef Marcus Samuelsson's New York restaurant, Riingo, surprised us with a delicious course that disproved the notion that red meat requires red wine, in the form of a trio of tartares (including beef) served with a glass of German Riesling.*

- *We tasted how well a French rosé played off pastrami from Katz's Delicatessen during the appetizer course of one of the most memorable wine tasting dinners we've ever attended, at Amy Sacco's restaurant, Bette, in New York.*

- *When we celebrated Valentine's Day over dinner with friends at Gilt this year, sommelier Jason Ferris delighted our table with a rare Tasmanian Pinot Noir that managed to pair beautifully with chef Paul Liebrandt's duck and steak dishes.*

But our food and beverage pairing compulsions started long before these instances — in Karen's case, in childhood. She remembers:

Some kids are picky eaters. Not me — I was an omnivore who would try anything once, from anchovies to chocolate-covered ants to duck blood soup.

I, on the other hand, was a picky *drinker*. Many kids would prefer to drink chocolate milk, hands-down, over regular milk. But I thought chocolate milk with a sandwich was gross — and found I could only drink it by itself or with the simplest of cookies, such as vanilla wafers.

On beautiful fall Sundays after church, my family would sometimes go for a drive to Yates Cider Mill in Rochester, Michigan, which is where I learned that nothing tastes better with freshly made doughnuts than just-as-fresh apple cider. Later, after getting to eat my share of ice cream as a waitress at an ice cream parlor, I discovered that the perfect palate refresher for a sundae was a glass of ice-cold water.

I first got to know wine, and especially Italian wine, while waitressing during college at Dave's Italian Kitchen in Evanston, where the restaurant's then-BYOB policy had me uncorking and serving countless bottles of Chianti Classico with chef Dave Glatt's pizza, and Soave Bolla to accompany his spaghetti with white clam sauce.

And I learned more about beer than most people who find themselves allergic to hops: My college boyfriend Larry was a fan of boutique beers who seriously considered opening his own brewery, so I not only tasted lots of Larry's home brews (made in a hallway closet), but also traveled with him to visit microbreweries from Maine to California. We even hosted British beer authority Michael Jackson in our apartment when he visited Chicago, so I found myself sampling — and falling for — my first lambic fruit beers (which I especially loved with, or instead of, dessert) in rather distinguished company.

A few years ago, over a casual lunch at Amy's Bread in New York City, I was so enamored with how my turkey sandwich was enhanced by the delicious sparkling cranberry juice called Fizzy Lizzy served there that I went home and wrote a fan email to founder Liz Marlin at the address on the label. I subsequently learned that her sparkling fruit juices were also served in top restaurants like Blue Hill at Stone Barns, spurring our interest in the matching of food with so-called "adult sodas."

Through my life-long passion for discovering new flavor marriages, I developed a special place in my heart for certain synergistic pairings, including:

- *Iron Horse Wedding Cuvée with chef Lydia Shire's potato-caviar pizza, served at our 1990 wedding at Boston's Biba.*

- *Fruit-flavored* agua frescas *with tacos at chef Mario Batali's favorite Tacqueria, San Jose #2 in San Francisco.*

- *The biodynamic wines that came alive with chef Ken Hnilo's organic cuisine at Gilbert's restaurant in Lake Geneva, Wisconsin.*

- *During our first trip to Spain in 2004, the Gran Colegiata Crianza with a dish of simple but perfect braised pork ribs in the tasting room of Bodegas Farina in Toro, which was one of the most astonishing combinations we've ever tasted.*

- *At chef Jean-Georges Vongerichten's Paris restaurant, Market, a passion fruit gelée that tasted sharp on its own yet was absolutely magical with our Alsatian Gewürztraminer.*

- *And just a few months later on a hot summer night in New York, sommelier Bikky Sharma served us a perfect chilled, off-dry white wine — also, in fact, an Alsatian Gewürztraminer: a 2002 Domaine Zind Humbrecht — to accompany our Indian dinner. The extraordinary pairing of this wine, with its essence of ripe melon, bananas, and other tropical fruit, with our spicy hors d'oeuvres and sweet scallops, has still not left our memories.*

Over the past couple of years, we've constantly consulted our unpublished manuscript — for the book you're holding — to make our own choices of what to drink: To celebrate the Chinese New Year this year, we ordered in Peking duck from our neighborhood Chinese restaurant. Looking up our experts' recommendations, we noticed that they were all fruity reds and whites — and remembering the unusually fruity Merlot we'd purchased the week before at a wine tasting in our neighborhood, we managed to make our own +2 pairing (the highest rating on our -2 to +2 scale) right on the spot.

We hope that this book serves as a delicious "idea starter" for your own memorable meals in the years to come. Scan the lists for ideas that make your mouth water and keep track of the pairings that you enjoy most.

You hold in your hands the collective wisdom of dozens of America's leading experts on the subject of food and beverage pairing. With it, we invite you to open your mind and your palate to the enormous pleasures available through the world of beverages. We hope it becomes a part of your way of life, and that you'll take a few seconds to refer to it daily to see how you can expand your horizons — and hopefully your pleasure — through what you drink.

We expect that, after reading this book, you will never be without an abundance of ideas — or delicious choices!

KAREN PAGE *and* ANDREW DORNENBURG

April 2006

ACKNOWLEDGMENTS

Great discoveries and improvements invariably involve the cooperation of many minds. — ALEXANDER GRAHAM BELL

Our heartfelt thanks to the gastronomes of history, whose experimentation led to the classic food and beverage pairings which have brought us so much pleasure — and to the dozens of sommeliers, chefs, and other experts carrying on this work who were so generous with their time when we sat down to interview them for this book (and then responded with patience to our seemingly endless stream of follow-up questions). We also give special thanks to all of the experts we've interviewed for our previous books whose insights have contributed immeasurably to our knowledge.

Thanks, too, for the contributions large and small of: Sebastian Beckwith of InPursuitOfTea.com; Joanna Breslin of Ana Mandara, Tobie Cancino, Mark Ellenbogen of Slanted Door, the French Pastry School in Chicago, Gary Jacob of Boyd Coffee Company, Mercedes Lamamie (New York) and Paloma Escorihuela (Spain) of the Trade Commission of Spain, Philippe Faure-Brac (for an extraordinary pairing dinner at Le Bistrot du Sommelier in Paris), Bouquet du Vin president Amy Meyer, transcriptionist Barbara Linder Millard, Michael Murray, copy editor and researcher Rosemary Newnham, Philip A. J. Nichols and Pamela Wallin of the Canadian Consulate, Sukey Pett, Herve This, and Charlie von Mueffling.

Our sincere thanks to Ann Balsamo, Carrie Bowden, Debi Bridges, Andria Chin, Elizabeth Denvir, Deborah DiClementi, Amy Ehrenreich, Lauren Falk, Georgette Farkas, Sam Firer, Sonia Fuller, Chris Gimbl, Rachel Hayden, Irene Holiastos, Jessica Jaffe, Kristine Keefer, Sean Lashley, Laura Lehrman, Chloe Mata, Tara McBride, Kristin Koca McLarty, Mimi Rice, Pierre Rougier, Heather Sherer-Berkoff, Sarah Waselik, Karen Wynn, and Melanie Young.

We'd like to thank our readers and friends who supported our CookbookRave effort, including Melissa Balmain, Kevin Barker, Dr. Jill Baron, Toni Boyle, Bill Bratton, Margaret Burdick, Susan Bulkeley Butler, Don Cogman, Leni Darrow, Blake Davis, Laura Day, Ruth Dondanville, Mark & Meredith Dornenburg, Robert Dornenburg, Michelle Fujita, Ashley Garrett, Elaine Gilde, Mark H. X. Glenshaw, Scott Green, Susan Greenberg, Lucie Grosvenor, Judith R. Haberkorn, Allison Hemming, Susan Hertzberg, Alan Jones, Rama Katkar, Evan Kleber, Rikki Klieman, Karen Kobelski, Laura Lau, Clement Lo, John Logan, Lee Logan, Lori Ludwig, Lynda Lyle, Dave Mabe, Susan Mabe, Brendan Milburn, Susan Miller, Paul Nicholson, Katherine Noesen, Jody Oberfelder, Kelley & Scott Olson, Jessica Page, Julie & Kevin Page, Cynthia & Jeff Penney, Laura Petersen, Lisa Prochazka, Juergen Riehm, Barry Salzman, Jim Shaw, Corinne Trang, Valerie Vigoda, Steve Wilson, Stephanie Winston, Clem & Sally Wood.

And our heartfelt thanks, too, to Bill Bratton & Rikki Klieman (for being two of the world's most incredible human beings and friends), Jason Binn and *LA Confidential*, Mitchell Burgess & Robin Green, photographer Howard Childs, Maria Cuomo Cole & Kenneth Cole, Gael Greene, Dr. Paul Greengard & Ursula von Rydingsvard, Larry Greifer, Linda Japngie, Richard Johnson, Eric & Tori Klein, Evan Lobel, Joan Luther, Kathy Reilly, Tammy Richards, Jimmy Rodriguez, Dawna Shuman, Andre Soltner, Addie & Gary Tomei, Richard Turley, and Suzanne Wickham-Beaird for their kindnesses.

We'd like to thank our friends and family whose love sustains us and who have long made coming together at the table with good food and drink such a pleasure for us. Special thanks are due to Laura Day, Samson Day & Adam Robinson (for lending us their home to work on this book and for Adam's serving as an editorial sounding board); Ashley Garrett & Alan Jones; Michael Gelb & Deborah Domanski; Gael Greene & Steven Richter; Cynthia & Jeff Penney, and Deborah Pines & Tony Schwartz.

We loved working with our gifted photographer, Michael Sofronski, who showed a keen eye for capturing the story within a shot. We give special thanks to his wife, Beth, and their son, Gavin, for sharing him with us, and to Susan Dey & Bernard Sofronski for first bringing his talents to our attention. We join Michael in thanking all the establishments (and people) which (and who) allowed him to capture such gorgeous photographs for this book: Amy's Bread, Artisanal (and Terrance Brennan), Beppe, Blue Hill at Stone Barns, Blue Smoke, Buttercup Bake Shop (and Jennifer Appel), Channing Daughters (and Allison Dubin), Eleven Madison Park, Fauchon (and Paul Constine), Fiamma, FineWaters.com, Inside (and Charleen Badman), Kai, Katz's (and Kenny Kohn), Lombardi's Pizza, Manley's Wine and Spirits (and Ramon Del Monte), Maremma (and Cesare Casella), Maxie (and Keishi Rikimaru), Pearl Oyster Bar, Relais & Châteaux House (and Daniel Boulud, Daniel Del Vecchio, Rachel Hayden, Brenda Homick, Patrick O'Connell, and Jean-Georges Vongerichten), Shake Shack, Solera, Union Square Cafe, Vino, Wild Edibles, and Zarela (and Zarela Martinez). And thanks to our models, including Tobie Cancino, Laura Day, Samson Day, Noah French, Brendan Milburn, Cynthia & Jeff Penney, Jocelyn Richardson, Adam Robinson, Valerie Vigoda, Alicia Wells, Rumer Willis, Steve Wilson, Lisa Wood, and Stacy Yoshioka.

Lastly and mostly, we'd like to thank Janis Donnaud — our smart, savvy literary agent who rivals the best sommeliers in being an extraordinary matchmaker — for connecting us with our new publisher. We reserve our biggest and most heartfelt thanks for all the talented people at Little, Brown and Bulfinch Press, especially our acquiring associate publisher Karen Murgolo (who managed the day-to-day miracle of making all our hard work on this book an enormous pleasure) and publisher Jill Cohen; Little, Brown publisher Michael Pietsch; Bulfinch publicists Matthew Ballast and Claire Greenspan; copyediting manager Peggy Freudenthal and copyeditor Deri Reed; production manager Denise LaCongo; subsidiary rights manager Jason Bartholomew; Bulfinch sales director Harry Helm and special sales director Suzanne Albert; editorial assistant Jim Schiff; the talented designers at Vertigo; YC Media publicists Kim Yorio and Aimée Bianca; and everyone else who helped to make this book the beautiful creation that it is. Karen adds a special thank you to Hachette Book Group USA deputy chairman and publisher, Maureen Egen for the pleasure of their unexpected lunch together in November 2005.

And Andrew insists on adding a special thank you to Karen, whose name may come second alphabetically on our books' covers, but whose vision for and contribution to all of our work together has been primary.

KAREN PAGE *and* ANDREW DORNENBURG

PHOTOGRAPHER'S ACKNOWLEDGEMENTS

I'd like to thank my wife, Beth, for loving and supporting me; Dad and Susan, for all their love and guidance; and my Mom, for watching over me. Thanks, too, to Gavin; to all the chefs we worked with for making their food look so good that all I had to do was push the button; and, last but not least, to Karen and Andrew, for giving me this opportunity.

MICHAEL SOFRONSKI

1 + 1 = 3:

Food and Beverage Pairing to Create a Peak Experience

It is impossible to live a pleasant life without living wisely and honorably and justly, and it is impossible to live wisely and honorably and justly without living pleasantly.

— EPICURUS, the fourth century B.C. philosopher whose ideas gave birth to Epicureanism, the enjoyment of (and highly refined taste in) fine food and drink

Enjoying good food and drink goes hand in hand with living a pleasant life. Your choices of what to eat and drink present you with an opportunity for pleasure, because the right beverage can bring greater enjoyment to whatever you're eating at breakfast, lunch, or dinner. Conversely, the wrong choice has the power to ruin the experience of a meal — three times a day! You can ensure greater pleasure in your life by making more informed choices.

Drink is inseparable from food. You've probably realized the glory of food and beverage pairing yourself countless times over the past few decades, whether through enjoying milk and cookies, beer and pretzels, or wine and cheese. If you're anything like us, just the idea of a freshly baked chocolate cupcake served with a tall glass of cold milk is enough to get your taste buds going — or maybe a dark chocolate dessert with a glass of tawny port is more your style. Either way, you're in for a lot of fun learning about other just-as-delicious combinations that have won our hearts.

What you drink can be seen as the final "seasoning" of any dish you're eating. Just as ill-matched flavorings (or *flavor enemies,* as we termed them in our book *Culinary Artistry*) can ruin a plate of food, drinking a beverage that's ill-suited to a dish can leave a bad taste in your mouth. Thus, beverages should be thought of as "condiments" that add the finishing touch to any dish. (You'd never put Tabasco sauce on ice cream. Why drink a tannic Cabernet Sauvignon with something sweet?) You can easily enhance your pleasure by avoiding common mistakes with your food and beverage pairings.

the POTENTIAL *of* FOOD *and* BEVERAGE PAIRING

As with anything you put in your body, you should think about what you consume. They should be things of quality and interest — because the dining experience is a moment when you've stopped all other activities, and it's a time to collect your thoughts, to be with yourself and your friends, and to share ideas. You should put interesting things on the table, both literally and figuratively — including interesting things to drink.
— DANIEL JOHNNES, beverage director, Daniel (NYC)

One of the greatest pleasures of gastronomy (which has been defined as "the science of gourmet food and drink") is the coming together of all aspects of the dining experience: great ambiance, service, food, and beverages — especially wine, which is the primary focus of this book. When what you're drinking melds with what you're eating, something magical takes place in your mouth, in terms of sheer sensory experience. The top restaurants in America celebrate food and beverage pairing as an indispensable aspect of creating dining experiences their guests will never forget. Chefs work with wine stewards — more commonly known as *sommeliers* — to come up with the perfect pairings, or "marriages," that will bring out the best of both the food and the beverage. Together, they seek to make the experience of both enjoyed together better than either would be on its own.

Daniel Boulud has been cited in our research for more than a decade as the virtual "gold standard" of American chefs; his four-star restaurant, Daniel, is considered by fellow chefs to be a New York City must-visit. When we asked him how he thought diners could best enjoy dining there, we assumed he would start by discussing the signature dishes he has worked on for years. However, he didn't once mention his celebrated bass wrapped in potato crust. Instead, he put the focus on *wine* as much as food, telling us how his tasting menu is built around matching the food and the wine:

> We might start with a Late Harvest Riesling or a sweet wine from the Loire Valley — and pair that with a terrine of foie gras and figs. This combination of food and wine creates a certain richness and privilege for the beginning of the meal. You want to start with it and be teased with it, then go on to drier and more serious wine. We might follow this with a lighter wine, like a Sauvignon Blanc, paired with vichyssoise, then build to larger flavors, like seafood paired with Chardonnay. Then we'd follow with a fish course paired with a white or a red wine, and then into the meat courses starting with a Rhône Valley wine, and then into Cabernet or Syrah, depending on the season . . .

Daniel Boulud's enthusiasm helped us to understand that pairing foods and beverages is truly at the heart of gastronomy, and that the world's most discriminating palates see food and drink as inseparable.

Anyone who's ever experienced a chef's tasting menu with paired beverages that was a true symphony of flavors understands that the best matches can create a peak experience. Great pairings are a natural high. In the 1960s and 1970s, a generation of Americans got their thrills from "sex, drugs, and rock 'n' roll." In the current era of celebrity chefs, it is great restaurants that now provide this generation with its (legal) peak experiences.

The classic pairings that often provide such peak experiences are gifts to us from the epicures of history who had the challenging task of first sampling countless combinations until realizing, "Hey — tomatoes taste great with basil!" and likewise, "Grilled steak is fabulous with red wine!" Time-honored pairings provide a benchmark to aim for with every meal.

Sampling great, classic food and beverage combinations can take you instantly on an exciting journey to another country (e.g., Italy, via hazelnut biscotti with Vin Santo) or even to another era (e.g., nineteenth-century France, via foie gras with a very old Sauternes). Serious food lovers will want to experience such classics for themselves — so why not start around the dinner table tonight?

WHY FOOD *and* BEVERAGE PAIRING *is* MORE *CHALLENGING* TODAY

The Sauternes-swigging Frenchmen of the 1800s drank Sauternes with just about everything, since only sweet wines could be made in the pre-refrigeration days of winemaking. They would be shocked and overwhelmed by the wine and other beverage choices we have today — much as just about everybody is these days. The problem today is that there are *so* many interesting beverages from which to choose that it can become overwhelming, not to mention confusing, and occasionally intimidating.

Food and beverages are increasingly diverse and complex. In North America, there's a wider array of choices than ever before of both foods (using ingredients and techniques from around the globe) and beverages (including wines, beers, sakes, waters, and more).

The old rules (e.g., "Drink white wine with white meat and fish, and red wine with red meat") and myths (e.g., "Red wine is better, more sophisticated, etc., than white wine and certainly more so than rosé") are no longer applicable — if they ever were — and have led some people to simply throw up their hands in frustration and settle for less than optimal pairings.

French food and wine came of age together and were designed to go together, resulting in classic combinations. However, with chefs today using global flavors and techniques only as starting points for their own creations, how is it possible to find the best beverage to accompany these dishes if they've only existed for an hour? The dawn of New American cuisine has changed the culinary landscape. In a typical week, the average American might eat dishes or flavors originating in seven different countries, from pizza to sushi to quesadillas. There are an increasing number of global flavors and techniques on the American table, as well as an increasing number of innovative dishes featuring new flavor combinations — all calling for new beverage choices.

Wine is now more accessible than ever — finally making its way into the mainstream of American culture via mega-retailers like Costco and Wal-Mart. However, as master sommelier Joseph Spellman points out, "Unfortunately, [mass retailers] are places with the least connectivity to food and wine — so most Americans are stuck without specialists to help them. We've put mom-and-pop wine stores out of business, and that is where the expertise really is, or was: in the specialist wine stores." Our hope is that this book can help to provide some sorely needed guidance.

MORE BEVERAGE CHOICES THAN EVER

Pairing food and drink is not as simple as it was twenty or thirty years ago, when it was primarily a matter of choosing between red and white wine, or between a wine from France or one from California. Sommeliers in fancy restaurants were the few concerned with food and beverage pairing and showcasing classic combinations. But today, you can enjoy that same pleasure in your own home every single night.

The era of FedEx can literally bring a world of beverages to your door, via online wine retailers and beer-of-the-month clubs — and even more possibilities for pleasure. Today on any given restaurant wine list, you might see wines from across the United States, from an Arizona Zinfandel to a Virginia Viognier. (As of 2002, there were wineries in all fifty states.) In addition to Old World wines from Europe, now you can find a huge array of wines from around the globe. The old popular varietals such as Chardonnay and Cabernet Sauvignon are changing, too, with oak levels rising and falling as often as hemlines — so you can't always assume that they'll taste exactly like the styles you've enjoyed in the past.

There are also more nonwine as well as nonalcoholic beverage options available. Alcohol is not as appropriate at certain times of day (e.g., morning), but why should you turn your palate off and settle for a less than optimal pairing just because it's breakfast time? Also, many people don't drink alcohol for health or other reasons, yet they also desire — and deserve — an optimal gastronomic experience. Therefore, instead of merely focusing on food and wine pairing, we decided to also include information about enjoying food with beer, sake, cocktails, coffee, tea, and even water.

While food and beverage pairing is an increasingly complicated topic, you don't have to be a wine (or beverage) geek to be able to enjoy it. You honestly don't need to know anything about where and how a wine was made to figure out if it pleases your palate or not. And you shouldn't be thrown off by terms like *residual sugar* or *terroir*, or bewilderingly specific point ratings of 95 or 76 for a particular wine. Those 100-point scale ratings that rate wines in a vacuum have next to nothing to do with how well those wines go with the foods you enjoy — or, for that matter, how well *you* enjoy those wines. After all, you already have a lifetime of food and beverage pairing under your belt, so don't make the mistake of thinking this involves too much effort. Have you ever enjoyed steak and red wine? Pizza and a Coke? A root-beer float with vanilla ice cream? Then you're already further along than you thought.

Why Sommeliers Do What They Do

Joe Catterson of Chicago's Alinea:

> More often than not, when we're serving people, we can give them great food and wine pairings that they've never experienced before at that level of nailing flavors, and enhance the experience of the food and the wine and the way they interact.

> I discovered a really interesting quote that coincided with my getting interested in taking the time and going to the trouble to match food and wine and to show people how effective it can be. I had stopped at the bookstore and picked up a book on wine that featured a line to the effect that, "For every dish, there is probably one perfect wine — but for most of us, life is too short to have to figure out what it is." It sort of struck me: "What kind of thing is *that* to write in a book? Isn't that exactly what my job is?"

> You need a person who takes the time to do this for everybody else whose life is too short. That's what *I* do.

Scott Calvert of the Inn at Little Washington:

> My approach to creating a pairing is much the same as a chef's to creating a dish. A chef will take a group of ingredients and alter their flavor profile by seasoning them. I do the same thing, only my "ingredients" are finished dishes and my "seasonings" are in a bottle.

WHY FOOD *and* BEVERAGE PAIRING *is* MORE *FUN* TODAY

"Never before has the consumer had such an opportunity to buy such great wines from all over the world, especially at the great prices you see today," attests Daniel beverage director Daniel Johnnes. Increased global competition has driven prices down, while both the quantity and the quality of wines and other beverages distributed in North America have increased in recent years — all of which is good news for "us epicures."

Of course it's possible to spend a lot of money on wine — thousands or even tens of thousands of dollars or more for a single bottle, if you wanted. However, there are fabulous wines and other beverages to be had for ten to fifteen dollars a bottle, if you know where to look for them (you'll find tips in Chapter 4).

"All the new wines on the market make food and beverage pairing more fun and more interesting," observes Jean-Luc Le Dû of Le Dû's Wines in New York. "This variety broadens our palates for even more wines to try with the increasing array of foods. Ten years ago, we were just starting to talk about newly available wines like Grüner Veltliner and New Zealand Sauvignon Blanc. However, the market has exploded since then, with more and more wines from Austria, such as Riesling, as well as red wines from Portugal."

Experts also mentioned Spain among the countries whose wine quality has improved, through everything from new production techniques to barrel aging. It has been considered a world-class producer for the past decade, and its wines offer some of the best values for the price. Italy was also cited for its growing reputation for quality.

"The quality of wine is getting better all over the world, even in the classic regions of France," says Le Dû. "It is a kick in the butt when wines have to compete on an international level, because they all have to be great."

CONCLUSION

There is magic in that distance between the food and the wine. The ideal match fills in that space. — DEREK TODD, sommelier, Blue Hill at Stone Barns (New York)

We've tapped the knowledge of some of America's leading palates, and synthesized their opinions so that you can be guided by consensus as well as well-informed opinion. The experts we interviewed are themselves guided by everything from history ("classic combinations"), to their first-hand professional experience at top restaurants, to their first-hand tasting experience on their nights off. We talked to, for example, Indian-born professionals about traditional beverages to enjoy with their native dishes and other ethnic food aficionados about their favorite accompaniments to dishes from other global cuisines.

Which magical combinations of food and wine will result in the greatest pleasure for *you*? Life is too short to try every combination for ourselves — especially the ones that have already been determined *not* to work. We can benefit from the wisdom of the ages, not to mention of the dozens of experts we interviewed, by taking advantage of their knowledge and experience, which are compiled and summarized in the pages that follow.

We hope that this book will help you live a more pleasurable life by bringing more enjoyment to every meal — whether you're cooking at home, ordering in, or dining out. You'll find just the perfect thing to drink with your roasted chicken, Thai curry, and Thanksgiving turkey in these pages. And you just might learn how to experience an old favorite combination in a new and better way — or discover the perfect midnight snack to go with your favorite Chardonnay.

Patrick O'Connell on "Overcoming Overwhelm" with Regard to Wine

Patrick O'Connell of the Inn at Little Washington in Virginia recognized twenty-five years ago that the subject of wine could be a little overwhelming — for guests and staff members alike. To counteract this, he took a simple approach with his employees and ended up creating a team of experts that made wine more accessible and enjoyable to guests as well.

In the early days, we had to deal with a lot of staff who had never been outside of this region [a rural area of Virginia, seventy-five minutes outside Washington] or county. Even though in our humble beginnings the wine list was not what it is today, it was still intimidating to them: It immediately set up all sorts of barriers. It was like a big wall that they couldn't go near because it was so confusing.

With regard to mastering cooking, I often recommend that people choose one dish and to make that dish over and over again until it becomes part of them. We used the same parallel with wine: Part of each staff member's "homework" was to choose one wine that they liked or felt they had an affinity toward. They had to buy a case of that wine, and then they had to learn everything they possibly

could about that wine and become the world's foremost expert on it.

At first they thought, "Yeah, right. I'm going to become the world's foremost expert . . ."

So they'd get their case of wine, and they'd be ever so proud. At first, it was just something to drink, and they'd start drinking it with everything. Then, they began to be a little more discriminating. They found they didn't like it at all when they drank it with X, Y, or Z. I remember one woman was drinking some kind of rosé with ice cream. She decided she did not like it.

Then, they would either call the winery if it was American, or write to it if it was European, and tell them about the project. The responses from the wineries were absolutely incredible. Our staff would come into meetings saying, "I was just talking to a woman at Sterling Vineyards today. She was so nice. When I told her about this project, she said, 'I'll send you all the labels of our wines and then I'll let you talk with the winemaker tomorrow afternoon. He'll tell you about the wine you've chosen and how we prepare the grapes.'"

The first benchmark was that they became the expert on the floor for that wine. If a guest asked anything about *their* wines, they'd fly to the table. The pride they had was clear — and of course each sounded like a genius, because they could talk about the grapes, the climate, the pebbles . . . whatever you wanted to know.

At one point, it got so extreme that our Polish manager asked, "Is it necessary that they speak to the guest about with whom the winemaker sleeps?" I said, "You're right — it's going a little far." But then after they felt that there was nothing left to learn about that wine and they really felt they had it, they could move on to other wineries and the same grape type. So, if they started with one Chardonnay, they could move to other Chardonnays. As they did that, there was no longer any intimidation about Chardonnay. The confidence that it built immediately provided a sense of security that wine was something that they could master.

Brian Duncan on Understanding Wine

"People think wine falls from outer space," wine director Brian Duncan of Chicago's Bin 36, a combination restaurant–wine store, has observed. "As an industry, we have done a poor job of removing the intimidation factor. The posters [of wine glasses filled with various fruit and flavoring agents] in our shop came from a desire to use every sense to get people to understand that wine is something familiar.

"I wanted to create visual impressions of wine that anyone can identify with. When a person sees a glass filled with a piece of caramel or peach or green apple, or a blade of grass, they can better understand those flavors. They used to hear people describe wine with those flavors and just thought they were being pretentious. But now I can say, 'Doesn't this wine smell like someone is mowing the lawn next door?' and they will say 'Yes!'"

Bin 36 features posters of wine glasses filled with the following representations of a particular wine's flavors and aromas:

Wine	Depicted by
BORDEAUX	berries, black currants, black cherries, cedar, plum, dark chocolate, oak
CHAMPAGNE AND SPARKLING WINE	green apple, lemon, citrus, cherries, strawberries, toast, biscuit
CHARDONNAY	apple, pear, citrus, melon, pineapple, peach, butter, honey, caramel, butterscotch, mixed spice
PINOT NOIR	raspberries, cherries, strawberries, cranberries, violets, roses, plum, chocolate
SAUVIGNON BLANC	fresh-cut grass, green apple, gooseberries, asparagus
SWEET/DESSERT WINES	honey, orange, pineapple, apricot, dried fig, raisins, hazelnuts
ALSATIAN VARIETALS (E.G., RIESLING)	peach, green apple, lychee nut, cinnamon
RHÔNE VARIETALS	dried fruit, blackberries, black currants, plum, smoke, pepper

the Pursuit *of* Pleasure

An Exploration of Sensory and Emotional Enjoyment

Pleasure is the starting point of every choice and of every aversion.

— EPICURUS

What is pleasure? Everybody can relate to the idea of the pleasure of eating or drinking something delicious. It's enjoying what we like (and avoiding what we don't).

However, pleasure is just as often a function of our emotional associations as it is of our physical sensations — and for this reason, there can be psychology as well as physiology at play when it comes to pairing beverages with food. As you'll see in Chapters 5 and 6, there are dozens of beverages that could go with any single dish. Therefore, it becomes an art form to balance what is "correct" for the dish (e.g., one of the recommended beverages) with what is correct for the guest (e.g., a selection from that list that is most likely to please someone as an individual).

It's a tricky art for restaurant sommeliers, and often involves assessing intuitively, or at least with great delicacy, a guest's likely price range, previous exposure to wine, palate, and willingness to experiment. This is often complicated by the difficulty many guests have in articulating their beverage preferences. "Guests always ask me what *I* would drink, and I joke, 'You don't want what I drink, because I have been in this business so long that you would be drinking some bizarre Blauburgunder from God-knows-where,'" says master sommelier Alpana Singh of Chicago's Everest. "Whereas *you* might enjoy a rich, buttery Chardonnay, *I* wouldn't get a kick out of that.'"

Chef Dan Barber of Blue Hill at Stone Barns in New York also makes an effort to assess guests' preferences to ensure them of an experience they'll enjoy. "It comes down to, 'How adventurous is the table?'" says Barber. "And it's typically the same for the food as for the wine. A table that is not going to be open to drinking rosé is also *not* going to be open to, say, lambs' brains. There are parallels."

So, before any discussion of the interaction of food and beverages on the tongue, we need to at least touch on their interaction in our heads — and how our thoughts and emotions are going to color those physical sensations. It's important to understand the lens through which we tend to view the world, so we can be aware of its influence on our perceptions and judgments.

Our hope is to encourage you to identify and develop your own preferences, while simultaneously moving beyond any unfounded biases to be able to enjoy a wider range of beverages. After reviewing the often broad array of beverages that can be enjoyed with the dishes and ingredients listed in this book (e.g., oysters), we hope you'll experiment with the full spectrum of pleasure that's possible (e.g., through such beverages as wine, Champagne, beer, stout, sake, and even cocktails).

ADVENTURERS *and* COMFORT SEEKERS

Of our desires, some are natural and necessary, others are natural but not necessary, and others are neither natural nor necessary, but due to groundless opinion.

— EPICURUS

As human beings, we are both "Adventurers" and "Comfort Seekers." While in general we may tend to live closer to one end of this spectrum than another, our mood and circumstances will influence which direction we lean at any given moment. When entertaining, we want to be as sensitive to our guests' preferences as a sommelier would be to a restaurant's diners.

Owner Steve Beckta of Beckta Dining & Wine in Ottawa believes that as a sommelier, it is almost *more* important to match a wine to a person than it is to match the wine to the food. "The most important part of being a sommelier is not your ability to taste, but your ability to empathize with the person who is in front of you," he argues.

During one of Beckta's regular talks at his alma mater, Algonquin College in Ottawa, where he completed its popular sommelier program, he tries to set students straight. "The first thing I tell them is, 'Great — you've just learned all these wonderful things about wine, and wine and food pairing. What you need to realize is that wine is, in fact, merely one component of hospitality and caring for people. It is a tool to use to make people happy.'

"With that statement, I've just crushed their entire idea of what wine is. They're thinking, 'No — wine is this great thing, and you're supposed to be championing the great thing!' But in truth, 'the great thing' is when you connect with someone over wine. It's not the wine in and of itself. It's simply the bridge over which you cross in order to do the thing you're really there to do, which is to connect with other people emotionally."

How do you use wine to please? Beckta paints a picture: "You've got these three big businessmen in. One says, 'I'm having lamb. He's having halibut. This guy over here is having scallops. We want the perfect wine that matches with all of them.' I say, 'OK — would you like me to choose different wines by the glass to go with each dish?' 'No, no — we want a bottle. We want something really special.'

"On one hand, if you look at the delicacy of the scallops and the richness of the halibut and the lamb, scientifically, there may be a bottle of wine that they 'should' have. But on the other hand, judging by the twelve things they've just told me, they're not going to like that at all. What they're going to love is a big-ass red from Australia. And their enjoyment is more important to me than getting the perfect wine and food match that they're not going to enjoy at all. So, I'm going to disregard what they ask for and give them the thing they have come here seeking, which is comfort. I'm going to respect that they are not looking to be outside of their comfort zone.

"But the next table that asks for the exact same recommendations will get different wines, because they just told me about their trip to a remote village in Thailand and that they just read Dostoevsky. They want to be out of their comfort zone. They want something they've never heard of before from a far, remote region that has more savory, more tart, more bitter, more aromatic qualities. They don't want luscious sweet fruit. They've done that and they've decided, 'No — that's not enough for me. I want more variety and adventure and excitement. I want to taste things that are different.'"

So, in such cases, the table of Comfort Seekers might be served a bottle of big, juicy Australian Shiraz, while the table of Adventurers is served individual glasses of Grüner Veltliner and Savennieres and another wine they've never heard of.

Lord knows we ourselves have been both Comfort Seekers and Adventurers on different occasions, from quite predictably ordering Iron Horse Wedding Cuvée — which was served at our wedding — on our anniversary whenever it's offered on the menu (an ultimate Comfort Seeker habit) to adventurously putting ourselves into the hands of our favorite sommeliers and letting them surprise us with blind tastings of "mystery" wines from around the world with our dinners (which are ultimately revealed after our often off-base but occasionally right-on guesses).

COMFORT AS A FAMILIAR COLOR

Sommeliers often pointed the finger at men as being the ultimate Comfort Seekers. "Guys are the worst," admits Brian Duncan of Bin 36. "They'll put their chests out and say, 'I only drink red wine,' as though I should give them a badge for passing up half the world of wine! I'm sorry — you don't get points for that, Buster."

Scott Tyree of Tru in Chicago agrees. "I saw a customer in for a business dinner looking at the list, and immediately knew he wanted a big red wine. So as he questioned me, I interjected, 'You prefer big, bold, rich, powerful, robust red wines,' to which he said, 'Yes!' enthusiastically," Tyree recalls. "We get a lot of people who equate big, bold, rich wine with 'good wine.' The first course of the meal was caviar — and big, bold Cabernet is not typically my choice for caviar. With that caviar, they drank red wine. That is where diplomacy comes in. It is not my place to say, 'No, you can't.'

"Dealing with a customer is like jazz: they throw a challenge at you, and you have to go with it and improvise a little. I never take it personally if someone doesn't agree with my wine choices," says Tyree. "There are a thousand choices that can work with a dish and this is simply what I am proposing."

COMFORT AS A FAMILIAR VARIETAL

When customers come in and order a bottle of wine that they had on a special day in their lives, what they want is to relive that experience — and not the wine they associate with it. What happens is that they will inevitably say, "This isn't how I remembered this wine . . ." Of course not — how could it be? In these cases, I'll recommend that customers try something new, to create a new experience and memory for themselves. — ERIC RENAUD, sommelier, Bern's Steak House (Tampa)

"It is staggering that roughly 70 percent of the wine consumed in the United States is domestic, and 80 percent of that is from California," observes Joshua Wesson of Best Cellars, a national wine store chain specializing in wines under fifteen dollars. "A further problem for some wine drinkers in breaking out of the box is that they look at wine selection like it is a zero-sum game. For example, they like Chardonnay, and therefore they don't like Riesling — or vice versa. Why can't you like *all* these wines? I don't understand the 'ABC' [anything but Chardonnay] crowd. I *love* Chardonnay! If you are a wine lover and hedonist, you are going to love Chardonnay. After all, it is just one color. If you are a painter, why would you just want one color on your palate? You'd want as many as possible, because you'd want to be able to *do* as much as possible. That's what getting to know and enjoy a variety of wines will let you do."

Richard Breitkreutz of New York's Eleven Madison Park restaurant agrees. "You need to taste and keep tasting," he says. "For example, you can imagine sticking your finger into a can of tomato sauce and licking it. Right now you already know what that tastes and smells like, because you've done it so many times before. You can imagine it. Wine would be the same thing if you exposed yourself to it more. Try lots of things and take good notes, and you'll develop more reference points.

"The most important thing about food and wine pairing is that, just like good jazz musicians need to spend time learning classical music before they can loosen up and start smearing notes, I would say the same is true for wine," he says, recommending, "Learn the classics, and then you can experiment."

COMFORT AS A FAMILIAR LABEL

In recognition of Comfort Seekers who find comfort in a familiar label, Alpana Singh of Everest says she likes to serve American classic wines on special occasions such as New Year's Eve and Valentine's Day. "I like to serve good ol' California wine that people are going to recognize, because the people who dine on these nights might only go out once a year, and this is a special occasion for them. I don't want to risk giving them something that they don't recognize and will never have again."

Despite the fact that the restaurant's chef (Jean Joho) and cuisine are both Alsatian, Singh had previously learned that on these nights, her customers weren't as comfortable being served Alsatian wines. "When I served all Alsatian wines, some people were a little overwhelmed. I would ask people if they liked the pairing and they were too intimidated to even respond. Instead, they made excuses like, 'I am not that sophisticated . . . ,' and I felt bad — and frustrated! Do you like it, or not? Don't tell me you are not sophisticated!

"The wine business is funny," muses Singh. "You would never walk into a car dealership and say 'You know what? I don't know anything about cars, so why don't you just pick one out for me? I am really not that sophisticated.' Fifty percent of the time when I tell people what I do, they will actually introduce themselves by saying, 'I am not that sophisticated about wine,' or 'I am not a connoisseur.' But when they add, ' . . . but I like to drink this,' I will tell them that the fact that they have a preference *makes* them a connoisseur!"

On New Year's Eve, Singh will serve wines such as magnums of Joseph Phelps Insignia, Mer Soleil Chardonnay, Caymans Conundrum, Newton unfiltered Chardonnay, Alsatian Crement (a sparkling wine), and Sauternes for dessert. "Some of our guests might say they are not sophisticated, but then they'll recognize all sorts of names, like Silver Oak, Sonoma Cutrer, Grgich Hill, Cakebread, Jordan, and Mondavi," she says. "What does make these wines special for me is that I feel like a proud American to be able to serve them. The Mondavis, Grgichs, and Martinis were pioneers before the insider cult California wines, and they set the stage. The reason I am even here is because someone named Mr. Martini decided to make wine in Napa Valley. It is sad that his wines can sometimes be forgotten on the more trendy wine lists, where Austrian wines are the new thing. So, on a night like New Year's Eve or Valentine's Day, it is nice for me to be able to pay homage to that history and tradition by going back to the standard bearers.

"I have 30 to 40 percent of these [American classic] wines on the list, and when someone orders one of those names I am happy that they are drinking wine. However, it's sometimes frustrating when we want to share other wines, and find ourselves wishing more people were willing to try something new," Singh admits. "Then, once they do, I know I have done my job if a person asks for the label — because it means I have created a new memory for them."

ENJOYING BEVERAGES ALL ALONG *the* COMFORT/ ADVENTURE SPECTRUM

Sampling new beverages is typically a low-risk proposition — with a high potential payoff. "I wonder why we often kill our little kid inside us?" muses Brian Duncan. "Where is that little kid who saw cotton candy for the first time and panted over it almost breathlessly? And where is the little kid in you when it comes to wine? Wine is a slow trip of discovery. You will be on that road for the rest of your life, so enjoy it! The worst that can happen is that you taste something you don't like — and you will never have to drink or buy it again."

Comfort Seekers looking to push themselves toward the more adventurous end of the spectrum might start small. If they love Cabernet Sauvignon, they might try some other reds — or a full-bodied, oaked white wine, or even a dark ale. For other ideas, see "If You Like This, You Might Also Like That," pages 16–17.

Our choice of beverage often depends on our mood. When we dine out, sometimes we want to "ride the roller coaster" with our arms up in the air, so we put ourselves into the sommeliers' hands so they can amuse and surprise us with their latest finds. Other times, we're more in the mood to hold hands and ride the ferris wheel — making us more likely to stick with ordering our favorite wine varietal or something from a favorite winemaker.

"SENSATIONAL" BEVERAGES

We must by all means stick to our sensations. — EPICURUS

Food and beverage pairing is all about listening to what your eyes and nose and mouth tell you. Too many people eat and drink without tasting a thing. Or they'll taste, but won't have the confidence to trust their perceptions of something as pleasurable or not. Your palate may be different from my palate, or the palate of your best friend, or the palate of the person recommending a wine — so learn to listen to *your* palate and to trust it. It won't lead you astray.

Since we've been drinking all our lives, it might seem a bit ridiculous to review the basics of how to taste a beverage — but many sommeliers assure us that it's not.

"For a lot of new wine drinkers, it is 'lips to throat' — and nothing happens," Brian Duncan observes. "I'll ask people to slow down, because then they'll get more out of the wine and develop an actual appreciation for what is special about it. I've found that getting people to take the time to really taste can change them for the rest of their food and wine experiences."

Appreciating quality can mean foregoing quantity. "When people go to Napa it is typically about, 'How many wines can I taste?' and 'How many wineries can I get to?'" says Duncan. "However, I was once leading a tasting in the [California sparkling wine producer] Schramsberg caves and whistled really loud and said, 'Hold it! This is how it is going to be done: Take the time to look at and smell what is in this glass.'"

Duncan wants people to get as much pleasure as he does out of the beverages he loves. "If you are not smelling your food and wine, you are cheating yourself. Eighty percent of what you taste is actually what you smell," he says. "By getting people to slow down, I am giving them 80 percent of their life back for free!"

HOW *to* TASTE WINE

Many sommeliers report pouring glasses of wine for guests in their restaurants who will immediately pick them up and take a big gulp.

Tru sommelier Scott Tyree says, "I want to shout, 'Wait!' By not taking the opportunity to stop to look at and smell the wine, they are missing out on a lot of pleasure."

Sommeliers recommend a three-step approach. First, stop and look. "Your first experience of wine is not going to be the flavor," says Tyree. "It will be looking at it and how beautiful it looks in the glass. That in itself can be a wonderful experience. Then, look at the texture and how it coats the glass."

Second, you'll want to give your glass of wine a whiff. "What are you smelling?" Tyree asks. "That is part of the experience and joy of drinking wine. You may not be able to identify guava, passion fruit, and specific exotic fruits, but you'll want to notice all the beautiful aromas coming out of the glass. You don't have to identify them — just acknowledge that they're there."

Third, it's time to give the wine a taste. "Hopefully, you'll taste luscious fruit and vibrant acidity," says Tyree. "Specifically, you don't want to taste anything off-putting, such as a vinegar-y or musty flavor. You don't have to be an expert to judge a wine. If it doesn't taste right to you, it's probably not — so ask the sommelier to taste a wine if you think it's suspect."

Over the course of tasting and retasting a wine, you may notice new aromas or flavors coming to light. Whatever your impressions are, they are correct: tasting wine is subjective and individual. So, don't be afraid of saying something stupid, or not having the right terminology to describe what you're experiencing. You can get tips on what to expect from a wine from a well-informed sommelier, who can certainly tell you what is typical of that varietal and/or of wines from that particular region. "It can be hard to focus on the wine in a dining setting, so as a sommelier I can explain what I was thinking when I selected the wine to go with the dish, and how I hoped that some of the flavors of the wine would mirror the flavors in the dish," says Tyree. "Hopefully the flavors will work together and nothing will clash in your mouth. It is as simple as that in food and wine pairing: we just want things to taste really good together."

If You Like This, You Might Also Like That

With input from Steve Beckta, Kathy Casey, Roger Dagorn, Hiromi Iuchi, Karen King, Ryan Magarian, Ron Miller, Garrett Oliver, Alpana Singh, Carlos Solis, Madeline Triffon, and other experts.

How can you best determine your taste in wine? Novices might want to gather a group of friends to taste a representative bottle of wine characterizing each of the six so-called noble grapes of French wine history, which are: 1) Cabernet Sauvignon, 2) Chardonnay, 3) Merlot, 4) Pinot Noir, 5) Riesling, and 6) Sauvignon Blanc.

Notice which individual wines you like best, as well as any tendencies (e.g., preferring one color to another, or lighter wines versus heavier wines, or drier wines versus fruitier wines).

Then, you'll be in an even better position to use the chart below to come up with new favorite beverages.

If you like . . .	You might also like . . .
CABERNET SAUVIGNON	Wine: Châteauneuf-du-Pape, Merlot, red Bordeaux or Burgundy, Shiraz / Syrah, Spanish reds (including Rioja), Zinfandel
	Beer: dark or pale ale
	Spirits: whiskey or brandy
CHAMPAGNE	Wine: sparkling wines like Asti, Cava, Moscato d'Asti, Prosecco, Sekt, sparkling Shiraz or Vouvray
	Beer: Lambic beer
	Sake: sparkling sake
CHARDONNAY	Wine: Chablis, Gewürztraminer, Meursault, Pinot Gris (Alsatian), Viognier, white Burgundy
	Beer: Good quality lager like Pilsner Urquell or Spaten
CHIANTI	Wine: Brunello, Châteauneuf-du-Pape, Pinot Noir, Priorat, Rioja, Sangiovese, Tempranillo
GEWÜRZTRAMINER	Wine: Pinot Gris (Alsatian), Riesling, Viognier
MERLOT	Wine: Beaujolais, red Bordeaux, Zinfandel
	Beer: dark ale, specifically Chimay Blue Label
MUSCATEL	Tea: Darjeeling
PINOT GRIGIO / PINOT GRIS	Wine: Albarino, Arneis, Fiano, Verdicchio
PINOT NOIR	Wine: Chinon, Grenache, Pinotage, red Burgundy, Ribera del Duero, Rioja, Sangiovese, Spätburgunder, Tempranillo, Toro
	Beer: porter
RED WINE	White wine: Roussanne
	Beer: ale
	Spirits: whiskey, rum, brandy
RIESLING	Wine: Albarino, Scheurebe, Txakoli
	Beer: Hoegaarten White Belgium beer

If you like . . .	You might also like . . .
SAUVIGNON BLANC	Wine: Albarino, Grüner Veltliner, Pouilly-Fumé, Sancerre, Txakoli
	Beer: India pale ale, Sierra Nevada pale ale
	Spirits: gin or vodka cocktail with citrus, a little sweetness, and an herb
SHERRY	Beer: Thomas Hardy's Ale
	Sake: Daikoshu (an aged sake)
	Tea: Keemun, classic Chinese black tea
SHIRAZ / SYRAH	Wine: Châteauneuf-du-Pape, Nero d'Avola, Priorat, Toro, Zinfandel
SWEETER WINE	Wine: Pinot Gris, Riesling Spätlese or Auslese, Moscato d'Asti
	Beer: Lambic Framboise and other fruit-flavored beer, Hoegaarden White Belgium beer
	Sake: sparkling and/or sweet sakes
WHITE WINE	Beer: lager
	Spirits: lighter spirits (vodka, gin), sparkling drinks
	Sake: most sakes

If you like California Cabernet Sauvignon, try Spanish wines. In Spain, they use American oak barrels. You get a lot of fruit, coconut, and dill. If I have someone ask me at the restaurant for a good Cabernet for around seventy dollars, with our mark-up, we can't do it. However, I can certainly offer them something similar in flavor and texture from Spain. — ALPANA SINGH, MS, Everest (Chicago)

You might be able to introduce Comfort Seekers to a very ripe Grenache from Châteauneuf-du-Pape. Or, you might introduce them to a northern Rhône Syrah that has some ripe qualities, but also has some savoriness, some herbaceousness, some spice, some diesel fuel qualities, and characteristics that are more challenging — while at the same time providing some of the comfort of that big, juicy thing. The question becomes, "How far out of the comfort zone do they want to play?" — STEVE BECKTA, owner, Beckta Dining & Wine (Ottawa)

Dark Belgian beers remind me of Burgundies, while older, stronger English beers are almost sherry-like. — GARRETT OLIVER, brewmaster, Brooklyn Brewery

TASTING: *the* NEXT LEVEL

As you become more experienced tasting wine, you may develop a sense of the wine's acidity, oak, texture, balance, and depth. In time, you may come to recognize particular varietals, regions, and even specific wines by aroma and taste.

Master sommelier Larry Stone has been credited with training and mentoring a number of America's top sommeliers. It was through his tutelage that several learned a rigorous approach to tasting and analyzing wine, including master sommelier Rajat Parr of Michael Mina in San Francisco, who confessed he didn't have things easy working under Stone.

"Larry is one of the best. He's the one who taught me — and he is great, but he's very demanding," remembers Parr. "At the restaurant, we always taste the wine before we serve it [which helps the restaurant identify any bottles of wine that might be corked or turned before they're served to guests]. He'd come up to me in the middle of service when I'm busy running around, and he'd hand me a quarter of an ounce of wine in a glass, so little you could barely smell it. He'd say, 'What is this?' I'd sputter, 'Larry, I'm busy!' He'd repeat, 'What is this?' And that's how I learned to blind taste. So now when I taste wine, I'm the quickest blind taster!"

Master sommelier Alan Murray of Masa's in San Francisco was mentored by both Stone and Parr. He remembers, "When I joined Rubicon [in San Francisco], Raj pushed me a lot. I would be in the middle of working a banquet on the third floor and he would run up to me and stick a wine in my hand. He would say '1983 Château Margaux' or just make me taste it blind, and run back down the stairs for service. He made sure I tasted wine.

"One night when I was still learning, he offered me a taste of wine. I said, 'Good, I haven't had this before.' He stopped and looked at me with a serious face and said, 'Yes, you have. I gave to you. That's it — I have no more wine for you, unless you remember what I give you.' That made my heart skip a beat and made me realize that I needed to remember every single wine I tasted. I understood that I could not develop my palate if I didn't pay attention.

"If you are not paying attention, you are doing something else. You need to discern whether it is a good bottle or not. Has it been stored properly? Is the wine 'showing,' or not showing? We will call each other up and ask other sommeliers whether they have tasted it recently."

If you want to taste multiple wines, keep it simple. Tasting two wines side by side will yield many lessons, and can be done easily any night of the week.

"The average person doesn't need to know much about *terroir* [which refers to the soil and other environmental factors that might be evident in a wine]," says Scott Tyree. "What they should focus on instead are the stylistic differences between Sauvignon Blanc from the Loire Valley which comes from a cool climate, versus Sauvignon Blanc from Napa Valley, which is not a cool climate. What are the differences — and what choices did the winemaker make? For example, taste a Sancerre next to a

Mondavi Fumé Blanc. You might notice that the Fumé has a dollop of oak, is higher in alcohol, and has more fruity than earthy flavors. Sancerre, on the other hand, will have higher acidity, maybe no oak at all, and lots herbal and grassy characteristics. Same varietal of wine, different climate. Then, you should remember those flavor profiles in coming up with the menu you are going to serve your friends."

While the best sommeliers have developed the ability to "taste without tasting" — that is, to call up in their memory the exact flavor and texture of a particular wine they might have tasted months or even years ago — all underscore the importance of actually tasting, and especially tasting wine with food. "At Union Square Cafe, we always had food with our wine tastings," says Karen King, the restaurant's first sommelier. "I think that really helped illustrate to the staff how food and wine change one another. These concepts are one thing to have in your mind. But until you experience them in your own body, you're not going to understand."

ENJOYMENT *is not* LIMITED *to* BOTTLES *with* CORKS

Endless shelves of beers, sakes, and other beverages from all around the world can seem just as intimidating as any wine shop — and learning to appreciate these beverages can be just as rewarding as learning about wine.

Some might turn up their noses to other beverages as somehow inferior to wine — but that's typically due to a simple lack of experience.

"What I have learned over time is that 'If you think your taste is better than other people's taste, you are almost certainly wrong,'" observes Garrett Oliver, brewmaster of Brooklyn Brewery. "People have good taste — but what they don't always have is exposure.

"Part of having taste is liking some things and not liking other things. If you liked everything you encountered — whether clothing, food, or drink — that would mean you have no taste, and that would be terrible. So, your goal is not to fall in love with everything you taste at a tasting. It is great if you do, but no big deal if you don't. For example, if you don't like the note of lychee in Gewürztraminer, or bitter beer, or dark-roasted beer, as long as you have tasted everything once and have your own taste, that's fine."

Oliver has found people to be very pleasantly surprised by their first encounters tasting truly well-crafted beers. "Every time we do a beer tasting, we open new doors into your food life," he says. "I compare it to music. If you are a lover of jazz, very possibly one day a person played you a John Coltrane or a Miles Davis record, and you said, 'Damn!' It is a very small thing, but on that day, the door swung open and you walked through. On the other side of that door was a better life, because you found something brand new to love and enjoy. That is the most powerful thing we can do in our business."

WHAT'S *YOUR* PLEASURE?

When sommelier Alpana Singh tries to understand what will please a particular table of guests, she believes there is nothing wrong with taking the gentle approach. "I start by asking, 'Do you like red or white wine? Dry or fruity? If they say they like fruity and are into Pinot Gris and Riesling, but find Viognier can get too sweet, I'll realize this person knows a lot and I can take a different approach. When I hear, 'I like dry,' which they will invariably repeat when I try to dig deeper, I will ask them, 'What have you had in the past that you really liked?' That takes away the jargon. Let's face it — we sommeliers have a funky way of talking: 'legs, body, fruits, banana, peaches, lychee, pineapple.' It is really hard to keep up!"

Remember, it's all about *your* pleasure and the pleasure of your guests.

So, what brings you pleasure? Adventure, or Comfort? Again, all of us are one or the other, depending on the occasion and our frame of mind. A strong Comfort Seeker who usually prefers to drink only white wines might find that their first trip to Italy spurs them to enjoy their first glass of Chianti with a plate of pasta with red sauce. Or a more moderate Comfort Seeker who typically enjoys the full spectrum of wines might find that a visit to a restaurant with Asian influences interests them in exploring the world of sake. A strong Adventurer might be open to any beverage at any time!

You should figure out what you like, so that when you eat in, you can choose beverages in line with your preferences — and when you eat out, you're able to communicate to a sommelier what your preferences are. They can then help you achieve the most pleasure through the wine or other beverages you drink to accompany your meal.

What should you tell a sommelier? You'll want to give them some sense of your palate, and a few clues to your individual likes and dislikes. For example, do you enjoy red and/or white wine? Do you prefer wines that are dry, off-dry, and/or sweet? Do you tend to like light-bodied and/or full-bodied wines? Do you enjoy sparkling wines with bubbles, or wines with a slight fizz (also known as *frizzante*)? Do you have a particular passion for wines from a specific part of the world, country, or region? Are you adventurous enough to try any sakes, spirits, or beers they might recommend?

It's all about knowing yourself and learning your palate, so you can bring the greatest pleasure to yourself and those you gather around your table.

CHAPTER THREE

Food *and* Beverage Pairing 101

Rules to Remember

Want to know the secret to pairing white wines? Think of a cool region wine with no oak on it — say, Sancerre, Pinot Grigio, or Tocai Friulano. Now, think of a lime. If you can put lime on your food, you can most likely pair it with an unoaked white wine. Ceviche and Sancerre is going to be a great pairing. Chicken in a béchamel sauce with Sancerre, probably not. Now, think of a white wine with oak on it — say, California Chardonnay. Think of it like butter. If a dish works with butter, it will work with the wine. Lobster with Chardonnay: a great pairing. Ceviche with Chardonnay: definitely not.

— GREG HARRINGTON, MS

Learning how to match specific beverages with particular dishes can take years of study. To become a sommelier, one must master advanced aspects of subjects ranging from biology to chemistry to geography and even geology. Luckily, you can acquire the impeccable taste of a master sommelier in a lot less time if you simply follow our shortcut rules in this chapter for addressing the most complex food and beverage pairing decisions. Chapters 5 and 6 will then provide you with "crib sheets" that will enable you to pair like a pro. If you're in a rush and all you're looking for are some ideas as to what to drink with dinner tonight, head straight to Chapter 5. Looking for ideas about what to serve with a special bottle of wine, beer, or sake, or another beverage? Turn directly to Chapter 6.

However, if you'd like to learn the guidelines used by some of America's leading sommeliers when deciding what to pair with what, you're likely to find this chapter of interest. We'll take you through some of their key methods for coming up with the perfect match — and share insights that can be useful to you when making your own matches. At the very least, this knowledge will enhance your enjoyment of the meal you serve, and who knows — you might just inspire your dinner guests with your newfound gastronomical erudition as you offhandedly comment on a pairing's regional or pH compatibility!

BEGIN *with the* END *in* MIND

The success of any pairing is measured by what happens when a sip of the beverage you're drinking interacts on your palate with the bite of food you've just eaten. When those sensations are jarring or otherwise unpleasant, you've stumbled upon a bad pairing. When those sensations are mildly or even wildly positive, you've got yourself a good match.

"My goal is for the wine to be like a 'wave' with the dish," says Stephane Colling, wine director of the restaurant The Modern at New York's Museum of Modern Art. "I want the wine to keep brushing up against different parts of the dish while both the dish and the wine maintain their own identity."

According to master sommelier Alan Murray of Masa's in San Francisco, any wine and food pairing will have one of three outcomes:

1. *The flavor of the food is more dominant than the flavor of the wine, and the wine takes a backstage.*
2. *The flavor of the wine dominates the food.*
3. *The food makes the wine taste better, and the wine makes the food taste better.*

"The last is the rarest of all outcomes, and the one I am always striving to achieve," says Murray. He easily could have been speaking for all sommeliers, who rhapsodize about those times when food and wine are in harmony — and each is the better for it.

Joe Catterson of Alinea in Chicago likes to let the wine set the stage for the food: "The thing I like most is bringing someone some wine to taste, and having that wine prime the palate for the dish to come." He also describes the peak experience possible when going back and forth between tasting a dish with a perfectly paired wine. "Sometimes the wine clears some of the flavors of the dish off the palate, replacing them with its own flavors. During the wine's 'finish' [the flavor left on your palate after swallowing], sometimes a particular flavor or two from the dish will pop back even stronger. That, to me, is really fascinating," he says.

Catterson remembers serving a pineapple-based dessert with an Austrian Late Harvest Sauvignon Blanc which did exactly that. "All of a sudden [with a sip of the wine], the pineapple flavor just came racing back on the palate," he recalls. "Sometimes when that happens, it's a flavor that wasn't obvious in the first place — even a primary flavor of the dish. So it makes you ask, 'Where was *that* before?' You're so intrigued that you have to go back and taste the dish again, and then retaste the wine." Personally, those are the moments we consider ordering seconds of both dessert and wine!

Such ethereal experiences, contrasted by occasional outrageously awful pairings, reflect the fact that there are different levels of success (or failure!) possible with any match. This is summarized in the five-point scale (+2 to -2, best to worst) commonly used in various guises:

Rating	Danny Meyer	Rocco DiSpirito	Max McCalman	Description
+2	😄	Ethereal	Perfect	The very best of all pairings.
+1	🙂		Positive	The majority of good pairings.
0	😐	Does No Harm	Neutral	
-1	🙁		Unpleasant	These are the worst of pairings, which we'll try to warn you away from in Chapters 5 and 6 by indicating what to AVOID.
-2	☹️	Train Wreck	Awful	

the BEST ROAD *to* TAKE *to* GET THERE

A Buddhist saying reminds us that different fingers point to the same moon. To become preoccupied with the finger is to miss the point.

Similarly, you always have different, equally valid ways of arriving at your ultimate destination: an ethereally delicious food and wine pairing. The particular route you take to get there matters little, while the destination is paramount. Since several different paths can lead you to a successful pairing, feel free to trust your instincts within these guidelines.

We interviewed dozens of America's most talented and experienced sommeliers. While there was consensus on several of the most important factors to consider, each sommelier had his or her own unique way of approaching the subject. For example:

- *Readers interested in geography and/or travel might be drawn to taking a regional approach to pairing food and beverages. Master sommelier Paul Roberts of the French Laundry and Per Se would weigh the importance of regionality (or, seeking out historical pairing precedents from a food or wine's native region) at about 75 percent. Regionality is his starting point for determining the context of a dish before going on to analyze other factors.*

- *Sensualists may want to dive into the sensory aspects of both food and wine, and their flavor components, textures, temperatures, etc. As beverage director Bernard Sun of Jean-Georges Management tells us, "The biggest key for food and wine pairing is to look at the relative weight of the food and wine you're pairing, along with their acid and sweetness levels. These are the three things that can make or break a match."*

- *Those preferring a scientific approach might want to emulate master sommelier Larry Stone of Rubicon, who uses his college science training to look at the chemistry of each pairing, analyzing the dish's and the wine's relative pH levels — acidity versus alkalinity, with a lower pH reflecting higher acidity and thus a tarter and crisper taste. You can then adjust dishes with either a pinch of salt or a squeeze of lemon to alter their pH to make them better matches with particular wines.*

We'll touch on each of these considerations, and more, in the pages that follow. As you study these principles, they'll provide you with touchstones to which you can refer when you make your own pairings.

Remember — this process is more of an art than a science. Each dish or beverage will have its own dominant characteristics, which you should use as starting points for narrowing down a selection of possible pairings. As master sommelier Greg Tresner of Mary Elaine's at the Phoenician points out, "When I see a dish, I just start tearing it apart — deconstructing its influences, what it's made of, and how it was made, so I'll have some idea what to pair with it."

Typically when pairing wine to a dish, you're aiming to narrow down your choice to a particular *varietal* or type of wine based on the grape, such as Chardonnay. Once you've selected the varietal, you'll further refine your selection to a specific style of that varietal for which a particular region (for example, California's Sonoma Valley versus France's Burgundy region) or winemaker (such as Sonoma-Cutrer) is known.

As Rubicon's Larry Stone advises, "The best thing to do is experiment. Taste food and wine together." Commenting on the success of his sommelier mentees Alan Murray and Rajat Parr, he says, "I didn't train them in my technique for matching food and wine, so I can't take any credit for their success. They are both really good tasters who like to cook and love wine. With the same focus, you too will succeed at food and wine pairing."

Tresner likens learning to pair food and wine with learning how to run a computer program: "Once you know how to do it, you don't even think about it anymore," he says. "Yet learning it drove you nuts!"

We'll try to keep the process a bit more sane — especially with our three simple rules:

RULE #1: *Think Regionally: If It Grows Together, It Goes Together*

RULE #2: *Come to Your Senses: Let Your Five Senses Guide Your Choices*

RULE #3: *Balance Flavors: Tickle Your Tongue in More Ways Than One*

That's all there is to it. Now, let's examine the rules in detail.

RULE #1: THINK REGIONALLY
If It Grows Together, It Goes Together

*People eat similar proteins all around the world. It's our job [as sommeliers] to fig-
ure out the region that inspired a dish, and then to find a wine to match.*

— PAUL ROBERTS, master sommelier, French Laundry (Napa) and Per Se (NYC)

*There is nothing better than a regional pairing with a regional dish. It is organic. I
see serving traditional pairings — like charcuterie with Riesling, and white asparagus with Muscat — as an added value to our guests. It is like a mini-vacation!*

— ALPANA SINGH, master sommelier, Everest (Chicago)

*If you are eating bouillabaisse in Nice and you open a bottle of Lafite Rothschild, it
will be a great experience simply because you are drinking Lafite! However, if you
were to open a bottle of Cassis Blanc that is neither fancy nor expensive, it would go
even better with the bouillabaisse . . . just as it would if you opened a bottle of
young, quaffable rosé with your sardines with fresh tomato and basil.*

— TIM KOPEC, wine director, Veritas (NYC)

When in Rome, do as the Romans do. Or, if you prefer, remember the professional chefs' motto "If it
grows together, it goes together."

According to our sommelier experts, thinking regionally — that is, pairing a dish with a beverage native to the same region — can take you at least 50 percent (and sometimes even 100 percent) of
the way to the perfect pairing. Many of the same basic ingredients (such as chicken) are eaten the
world over, with each region adding its own flavor profile (say, herbed and roasted chicken in France
or stir-fried and soy-sauced chicken in Asia), so pairing can be a matter of finding your grounding in
a specific longitude and latitude, and selecting a beverage from nearby.

Where did your meal originate? Italy? Spain? Japan? The red sauce of pizza and pasta pairs beautifully with Italian red wine, especially Chianti. Tapas shine with a dry sherry. Sashimi is sensational
with sake.

Classic pairings represent the wisdom of history. With such an extensive realm of ingredients and
an equally extensive realm of beverages from which to select, there's a nearly *infinite* number of possible food and beverage combinations to be tried. But it's not necessary to reinvent the wheel to come
up with many of the best pairings among them, because we can benefit from the chefs and wine
experts of history by paying attention to classic pairings which were already tried-and-found-true by
these gastronomes of years past. In Chapters 5 and 6, you'll find literally thousands of food and beverage combinations cited in our research that have stood the test of time.

Chef Craig Shelton of New Jersey's Ryland Inn believes there is a reason for a canon of classics, and for standing on the shoulders of others. He points out that if you look at a map of France and where Italy, Germany, and Spain attach to it, it's hard to think of a single grape that is not grown in that area. "So, if you just learn the basics of the cooking styles and wines of those regions — the major regions of France, and the primary regions of its neighboring countries — you'll largely have the work of food and wine pairing done for you," he argues. (You'll see that we've already done some of that work for you, in the sections on each country, below.)

Even at a restaurant with innovative cuisine such as Chicago's Alinea, sommelier Joe Catterson finds guidance in the classics. "Very often, if I look at a dish and its ingredients and realize that all of them say southern Italy to me, a southern Italian wine is a likely choice — and, very often, that pairing does work. When we had a dish with Parmesan cheese and Italian herbs on our menu, I started from Italy," he remembers. "Or, if you encounter an ingredient like eggplant, you ask yourself, 'In what cuisines do we find a lot of eggplant? What regions are we talking about?' Regionality gives you a starting point."

Karen King of The Modern finds that matching food with wine or other beverages from that region is a natural springboard for pairing. "I think it works a good 90 percent of the time," says King. "Just go to Italy: In every little region, they've been pairing the local dishes with their local wines for thousands of years. And everything I've had in Italy has tasted pretty darn good!"

It makes ultimate sense, then, that the wines of a region will naturally complement the foods from that region. Michael Flynn of Kinkead's in Washington, DC, says, "All you have to do is look at Alsace, for instance, where you have all these dishes from onion tarts to slow-cured meats and sausages that work well with dry and off-dry Riesling and Gewürztraminer — white wines that are essentially fruity. We know these pairings are tried and true."

Understanding regional pairings is such an important rule of thumb that sommelier Paul Roberts of the French Laundry and Per Se recommends that every time wine lovers buy another wine book, they should also pick up a cookbook from the same region. "You can live in a vacuum and say, 'I know a lot about the wines of Tuscany.' But if you don't know a lot about the *food* of Tuscany, who cares? You're just another wine geek. Wine knowledge must have context," he argues.

Regionality is behind the pairing of tomato sauce and Chianti, Camembert cheese and Calvados — even barbecue and iced tea. Daniel Johnnes, beverage director of Daniel, thinks that some of the best food-and-wine matches are in fact traditional dishes matched with wines from that region. "For example, I think that Rioja with a leg of lamb is a beautiful match, as is a Cabernet from Bordeaux, such as a Pauillac, with a leg of lamb," he says.

Then why would anyone ever want to pair a leg of lamb with anything else? In Johnnes's opinion, "Our palates — not to mention we as human beings — enjoy experimenting and trying new combinations. There are so many types of wine that I think sometimes you have to broaden the spectrum a little bit and say, 'Well, a Pauillac is the perfect match for this, but I want to try something different.' Maybe you'll say, 'I'd like to try this with a Côtes du Rhône or something with the same profile, something that has body and elegance.' I don't think you have to be limited."

Indeed, thinking regionally can open your mind to new possibilities, by being inspired by classic pairings from other parts of the world. "In America, we too often stick with the traditional pairing of [meat with] Bordeaux or Cabernet Sauvignon," Paul Roberts observes. "However, if you think about the classic pairings of Tuscany, you know that Sangiovese, whether [in the form of] Chianti Classico or Brunello, is great with meat. So when you have the opportunity to pair wine with a meat dish [here in the United States], you can serve Brunello instead. Those tasting it will say, 'Wow! I always drink Cabernet with my steak, but now I know about this great wine 'Brunello' from Tuscany!' And for your guests, it becomes this epiphany of an experience because they've never thought of that pairing before."

While thinking regionally is an excellent starting point, there are rare but notable exceptions. Cheese expert Max McCalman has observed that there are better matches for certain Spanish and Portuguese cheeses than their respective local wines. "Soil that is good for cheese production is not always good for wine production," McCalman observes. Because the animals are not grazing on the same soil as the grapes are grown in, there aren't the same kinds of synergies that can be found elsewhere.

Nonetheless, you will rarely go astray by starting your food-and-beverage pairing decisions by thinking regionally.

FRANCE

Understanding regional differences, even within a country, can take you a long way. Chef Daniel Boulud and sommelier Philippe Marchal point out that they serve French wines "North to South" in the tasting menus at four-star Daniel in New York City. Given France's climate, northern wines tend to be lighter-bodied whites, while more full-bodied red wines are produced as you move farther south.

Craig Shelton, chef-owner of the Ryland Inn in New Jersey, offers a general rule for understanding the cuisine of France: "If you were to draw a horizontal line across France somewhere below Lyon, you could generally say that everything above that line is cooked with butter and everything below that line is cooked with olive oil or duck fat."

Entire books are devoted to the foods and wines of France — but for the sake of giving beginners a place to start, here's a snapshot of its characteristic foods and beverages by region:

Region	Foods/Beverages
NORTHEAST: ALSACE/LORRAINE	game, pork, quiche, sauerkraut, sausage *off-dry white wines (Gewürztraminer, Riesling, Pinot Blanc)*
NORTHEAST: CHAMPAGNE	game, herring, sausage *beer, Champagne*
NORTH CENTRAL: ILE DE FRANCE/PARIS	urban melting pot of food *urban melting pot of wine and other beverages*
NORTHWEST: BRITTANY	crêpes, fish, oysters, seafood, shellfish *apple juice, cider, Muscadet*
NORTHWEST: LOIRE VALLEY	chèvre (goat cheese), game, pork, trout, wild mushrooms *fresh, crisp white wines, e.g., Pouilly-Fumé, Sancerre, Vouvray; Cabernet Franc*
NORTHWEST: NORMANDY	apples, Camembert cheese, cream *Calvados, cider*
SOUTHEAST: BURGUNDY	bacon, beef bourguignon, mustard *Chardonnay, Pinot Noir*

Region	Foods/Beverages
SOUTHEAST: DIJON	black currants, crayfish, gingerbread, mustard *Burgundy, kir (white wine with crème de cassis)*
SOUTHEAST: FRANCHE-COMTÉ	Bresse chickens, Comte and Morbier cheese *Vin Jaune (esp. with chicken); sweet Vin de Paille*
SOUTHEAST: LYON	beef, crayfish, onion soup, offal, pork *Beaujolais, Coteaux du Lyonnais*
SOUTHEAST: PROVENCE	basil, bouillabaisse, garlic, lamb, olive oil, seafood, tomatoes *rosé and red wines, esp. Bandol; Cassis*
SOUTHWEST: BASQUE	cod, ham, onions, peppers, tomatoes *Jurançon, Madiran*
SOUTHWEST: BORDEAUX	cèpes, lamb, oysters, pâté de foie gras, sausage, truffles *Cabernet, Cognac, Merlot, Sauternes, white Graves*
SOUTHWEST: GASCONY	duck, foie gras, goose, peppers, prunes, truffles *Armagnac, sweet Jurançon*
SOUTHWEST: PERIGORD	black truffles, duck, foie gras, mushrooms *red Cahors, sweet white Monbazillac*

ITALY

Given the overwhelming variety in a country like Italy, drinking regionally can help to ensure a good match. Italy has so many native varietals (not to mention regions), however, that it is a very difficult country to master, wine-wise.

"It's hard even for professionals to keep up," admits beverage director Bernard Sun of Jean-Georges Management. "The three most famous regions would be Piedmont, Tuscany, and Veneto. Piedmont has Barolo, Barbaresco, and the Nebbiolo grape. Tuscany is known for its Sangiovese grapes. Chianti made Tuscany famous, and then Brunello came up — but the Super Tuscans put the region even more on the map because they rival great Bordeaux and California Cabernets, taking the average price of a bottle of wine in the region from twenty dollars to sixty dollars. In Veneto, I think of light, crisp, and citrusy Pinot Grigio — and of Amarone."

Charles Scicolone of New York's I Trulli restaurant recalls a recent trip to Italy when several of the restaurants he visited urged him to drink the house wine: "Because it was the local wine, they felt it went better with the food than any other. And nine times out of ten, they were right."

Region	Foods/Beverages
NORTHEAST: E.G., VENETO	cured pork, risotto, seafood, sopressata *Amarone, Pinot Grigio, Prosecco, Trebbiano*
NORTHWEST: E.G., PIEDMONT	antipasto, pasta, polenta *Arneis, Barbaresco, Barbera, Barolo, Dolcetto, Moscato, Nebbiolo*
CENTRAL: E.G., TUSCANY	risotto, truffles *Sangiovese grapes (Brunello, Chianti, Super Tuscans), Trebbiano, Vernaccia*
SOUTH/ISLANDS: E.G., SICILY	pasta, pizza, sardines *Marsala, Nero d'Avola*

Joe Bastianich's Recommended Starter Case of Italian Wines

"Italy has seven hundred indigenous varietals of wine," says New York restaurateur Joe Bastianich. "It is a unique country because its socio-geodiversity is unlike any other in the world. For example, the southernmost point of Sicily is further south than the northern coast of Africa. And the northernmost point of Italy is well into central Alpine culture where people are speaking German in the mountains."

Given the daunting scale and scope of Italy and its wines, we asked Bastianich to recommend a case of Italian wine for readers looking to get started exploring Italian wines. He set the best possible criteria for a novice: "I would recommend inexpensive, *terroir*-driven wines."

Wine	Sample dishes that complement
Arneis	beef carpaccio
Barbera	game birds (e.g., squab)
Chianti	grilled steak
Dolcetto	baked white cardoon gratin with fontina
Montepulciano	stewed octopus with capers, olives, and tomato sauce
Moscato d'Asti	dessert, or on its own as dessert
Nero d'Avola	swordfish with capers and chickpea fritters
Prosecco	asparagus and boiled egg tremezzini [Italian sandwich]
Soave	polenta and Gorgonzola
Taurasi	monkfish in aqua pazza [spicy tomato sauce]
Tocai	prosciutto
Valpolicella	risotto with Gorgonzola

SPAIN

Each region of Spain has its own culinary culture, with great wines and great expression. Ron Miller, maître d'hotel of New York's Solera restaurant, says, "For example, in northern Spain, Albarino and the foods of the sea are perfectly matched. Here is a perfect example of 'what grows together, goes together.' The vineyards are on cliffs right along the sea, and the wines have a minerally quality to them with the freshness of the sea.

"Txacoli would be the same thing in the Basque country. It has crisp, apple-y style fruit, a little pear, minerally in the sense of shells and the sea. It is a volatile wine with high acidity, like Albarino. The crispness and zing at the end of these wines from the acidity is a palate refresher and is great with all types of seafood. This wine is a perfect match with the classic sauce of pil pil or with bacalao. Sidra is a cider that is from the Basque country and also good with seafood. You'll find seafood at all the cider houses.

In southern Spain, which is know for its fried foods, you'll find crisp, clean whites to cut the texture from frying. The roasted dishes featured in central Spain call for something with fuller body and weight, like amontillado or oloroso sherry. With the stewed dishes in Atlantic Spain, you want sherry, too — amontillo, oloroso, or fino. And finally, near the Mediterranean, rice dishes that feature seafood, like lobster, call for a bigger style of wine. Here, look for Spanish Viognier.

Region	Foods/Beverages
NORTH	seafood *Albarino*
BASQUE COUNTRY	bacalao, pil pil sauce, seafood *sidra (Spanish cider), Txakoli*
CENTRAL	roasted dishes *sherry (amontillado or oloroso)*
ATLANTIC	stewed dishes *sherry (amontillado, fino, or oloroso)*
SOUTH	fried foods *crisp, clean white wines*
MEDITERRANEAN	rice dishes with seafood, esp. lobster *Spanish Viognier*

GERMANY

Sommelier Daniel Johnnes tells us that Riesling is the only grape worth talking about in Germany. In a country with such an abundance of great beer, many would agree. Still, we wanted to take a slightly broader look at the country and the food associated with four of the most important of Germany's thirteen wine-growing regions:

Region	Foods/Beverages
MOSEL	buttery cheeses *Riesling*
PFALZ	pork, Emmenthaler cheese *Gewürztraminer, Müller-Thurgau, Riesling, Scheurebe*
RHEINGAU	game birds *Riesling, Spätburgunder*
RHEINHESSEN	cold meats *Riesling, Müller-Thurgau, Silvaner, sparkling wine*

Beer Sommelier Carlos Solis on Thinking Regionally

BELGIUM: These are my favorite beers in the world. They are "big" — very flavorful and in most cases high in alcohol. The flavors are pronounced with dried fruit, caramel, fig, raisins, toffee, and chocolate.

Pairings: game, pork, lamb, and Flemish stews cooked with beer the day before

GERMANY: Their Kölsch and pilsners are very refreshing and easy to drink, with a clean appearance and taste. Low in alcohol content, very defined toastiness, and low in bitter aftertaste.

Pairings: most spicy, condimented dishes such as those from Asian and Mexican cuisines; grilled meats; barbecue; pizza; grilled sausages

ENGLAND: Their beers are great examples of porters, stouts, and India pale ales, and some specialties, such as the original Thomas Hardy ale with its fine sherry taste — perfect for an after-dinner drink.

Pairings: I love their porters and stouts with dessert; they can stand well against a rich piece of chocolate cake, grandma's style puddings, most holiday desserts, and delicate chocolate-dipped strawberries.

UNITED STATES: American beers are pronounced in one single flavor: hops. American beers have gone wild with hops! They are very bitter and low in alcohol. Launching the beer renaissance of recent years, American microbrewers have gone wild with an array of styles from around the world. American microbrews range from light Kölsch and Lambic styles to Imperial stouts, Belgian-style triples, and double hop juice India pale ales. The Northwest microbreweries have become paradise for hops lovers and beer adventurers in this country.

Pairings: There are styles for every need depending on the occasion, from a weekend barbecue in the backyard to a formal sit-down dinner. My personal favorites are:

- pilsner styles with grilled meats and vegetables
- smoked porters and stouts with smoked salmon or oysters on the half-shell
- India pale ales with steamed mussels and clams; most pale ales and India pale ales are exceptionally good with seafood due to their high hop bitterness and flavors.

RULE #2: COME *to* YOUR SENSES
Let Your Five Senses Guide Your Choices

What sommeliers do is deconstruct: We take the most significant feature of a dish, and either compare or contrast it with the most significant feature of the wine. If you just look at a single ingredient, like the protein, you will miss the big picture. You will also miss the intricacy that is involved in breaking it down into its components and finding a wine that matches several elements — not just one — in the dish.

— ALPANA SINGH, master sommelier, Everest (Chicago)

The old adage, "Serve red wine with red meat, and white wine with white meat and fish," put the primary emphasis on the protein being served, which made sense at a point in time when food was simpler. Today, however, a dish's primary flavor driver is more likely to be its sauce or other seasonings, or even the cooking technique used to make it. It's important to take into consideration not only the featured ingredient of a dish — say, chicken — but also whether that chicken was simply poached for a salad, or marinated and barbecued.

The specific ingredients in a dish (primary ingredients, accent ingredients, seasonings such as herbs and spices, as well as any sauces), combined with the cooking techniques applied to them (which create its textures and temperatures) will help to drive the ideal pairing. The more you know about the food you're looking to pair to, the finer the distinctions you can make, allowing you to make the best possible matches.

For example, if you know that a dish has mushrooms in it, you might first think of the fact that red wine tends to complement mushrooms in general. If you know that the mushrooms are actually wild mushrooms, you'll have a sense of their having an even earthier quality. And if you learn that those wild mushrooms are chanterelles (which might lead you to an off-dry white wine) versus meaty porcini (which might suggest a big red wine), your wine selection can be further honed to match it.

We'll start by considering the "overall impression" given by such factors as a dish's weight, volume, and texture and temperature — which may well be driven by its most prominent ingredients, seasonings, and/or techniques.

WEIGHT

You need the weight of the wine to match the weight of the dish. If you have a very rich dish, you need a pretty rich wine that is full-bodied in style or at least very flavorful.

— SCOTT CALVERT, sommelier, the Inn at Little Washington (Virginia)

It's important first to get a sense of the dish's relative weight. Is it a light, medium, or heavy dish? Then, match the dish to an equally light-bodied, medium-bodied, or full-bodied wine.

Certain cooking techniques produce inherently lighter versus heavier results. Think of the difference, say, between a lightly poached dish versus a grilled dish versus one that has been braised for hours in a red wine sauce; each would likely call for an increasingly full-bodied wine.

In food and wine pairing, as in life, there is a season for all things. You wouldn't wear linen in winter — nor is that the best time to settle down with a chilled, light-bodied rosé. Likewise, heavy cashmere would be out of place at a summertime picnic — as would a very full-bodied Cabernet. You'll want to make sure that the wine you select is appropriate in weight given both the weight of the dish itself and the time of year it is being served.

Given that the best chefs tend to cook seasonally, you're especially likely to see different ingredients and cooking techniques employed at different times of year. It's just as natural to throw some shrimp or chicken on the barbecue during the warmest months (when no one wants to turn their ovens on!) as it is to braise, roast, and stew red meats during the coldest months. Lighter seafood or poultry will call for lighter-bodied wines, while those heavier meat dishes lend themselves better to fuller-bodied wines.

These days — with full-bodied oaky whites like Chardonnay easily able to knock out a light-bodied red like Pinot Noir — it's even more important to know something about a wine's weight than its color when pairing it with a particular dish. "While heavy reds still call for red meat, lighter reds like Pinot Noir are great with a heavier-weighted fish such as salmon," explains sommelier Bernard Sun. "A light Pinot Noir from Burgundy will even work with a white fish. White meats like chicken or veal can work with medium-bodied white or red wines. However, most seafood calls for light-bodied white wines."

How can you judge the weight of a liquid in a glass, such as wine? One clue is to pay attention to how others talk or write about it. Sometimes wines are referred to as *big*, which you can generally take to mean a fuller-bodied wine that's higher in alcohol, while a *softer*, or more delicate, wine would be one that's lighter-bodied and lower in alcohol.

The body of a wine is often correlated to its alcohol level (among other factors such as sweetness and tannin), so reviewing the percentage of alcohol that appears by law on every wine label can provide a clue. As a general rule, if it's less than 12 percent alcohol, it's likely to be a lighter-bodied wine, and if it's more than 13 or 14 percent, it's likely to be a fuller-bodied wine.

You can also simply *taste* the difference in weight, using a simple technique shared with us by Paul Roberts of the French Laundry and Per Se: Taste a wine, and see how the wine feels on the middle of your tongue. "If it's thin like water, think of it as light-bodied; if it's got the weight of whole milk, think of it as a full-bodied wine," Roberts told us. "And if it's somewhere in the middle, like 2-percent milk, it's likely a medium-bodied wine."

Using Roberts's analogy, we can think of:

LIGHT-BODIED WINES *such as Riesling (white) and Pinot Noir (red) as akin to water;*

MEDIUM-BODIED WINES *such as Sauvignon Blanc (white) and Merlot (red) as akin to 2 percent milk; and*

FULL-BODIED WINES *such as Chardonnay (white) and Cabernet Sauvignon (red) as akin to whole milk.*

"VOLUME"

The most important rule when pairing food and wine is to consider and address the flavor volume of the food and of the wine.

— STEVE BECKTA, owner, Beckta Dining & Wine (Ottawa)

In addition to considering a dish's weight, you'll also want to have a sense of the dish's overall intensity. As Steve Beckta phrases it, "If you were putting its flavor through a stereo speaker, how *loud* would it be? Delicate greens lightly dressed with lemon might be a 2 out of 10 on the flavor-volume scale, while a rib-eye steak topped with blue cheese might be a 10 out of 10."

Likewise, a delicate poached fish dish might be at a whisper, while a fish that's been rubbed in spices, grilled over mesquite, and served with a jalapeño salsa would be blaring. A whisper of a dish is better matched with an equally nuanced wine, while the latter needs a beverage that can stand up to all the noise. When a dish's acidity (as in salads and other sauces) or sweetness (as in desserts and fruit sauces) is at a high volume (loud!), your beverage choice needs to address (typically, by matching) those characteristics. For example, a mixed green salad with a tart vinaigrette would be well paired with an acidic Sauvignon Blanc.

Sommeliers who specialize in spicier cuisines face special challenges. Matt Lirette, sommelier at Emeril's New Orleans, has come up with general rules for balancing the heat of Creole-style seasoning — and to keep the "volume" of such dishes in balance. "One of the ways I deal with our food is to have a little residual sugar in the white wines," Lirette says, referring to the power of sweetness to temper hot and spicy flavors. "I also keep the alcohol levels low. With red wines, I find that tannin and alcohol amplify the heat in a dish. And as [bitter] tannin and salt don't work well together, either, I won't pair a tannic red with something salty, like prosciutto."

There's often a correlation between a dish's weight and its volume — but not always. Consider the following examples:

Weight/Volume	Dish
HEAVY/LOUD	grilled steak with blue cheese sauce
HEAVY/QUIET	buttered egg noodles
LIGHT/LOUD	chile peppers and bell peppers
LIGHT/QUIET	poached scallops

Like food, beverages have their own volume or intensity. "A vintage port could be a 10 out of 10 on the flavor-volume scale, whereas a light Sauvignon Blanc could be a 2," explains Steve Beckta. "You want dishes that can keep up with each wine, and where one does not dominate the other. You still want to be able to taste the wine while you're eating the food, and to be able to taste the food while you're drinking the wine. That way, they're complements to each other rather than being over-whelmed by one another."

What are the weight and volume of various popular wines? Consider the following examples:

Weight/Volume	Wine
FULL/LOUD	Cabernet Sauvignon
FULL/QUIET	Chardonnay, esp. with little or no oak
LIGHT/LOUD	Riesling
LIGHT/QUIET	Soave

Consider matching dishes and wines based on similar weight/volume profiles. In the instances above, they happen to match up nicely.

Considering Weight/Volume When Pairing

	Lighter/Quieter		Heavier/Louder
INGREDIENTS	fish	pork	beef
	shellfish	poultry	game
	vegetables	veal	lamb
TECHNIQUES	boiling	baking	braising
	poaching	sautéeing	grilling
	steaming	roasting	stewing
SAUCES	citrus/lemon	butter/cream	demi-glace
	vinaigrette	olive oil	meat stock
WINES	Pinot Grigio / Pinot Gris	Chardonnay	Cabernet Sauvignon
	Riesling	Merlot	Shiraz / Syrah
	Sauvignon Blanc	Pinot Noir	Zinfandel
	alcohol <12 percent	alcohol = 12–13 percent	alcohol > 13–14 percent
BEERS	lager	bock	brown ale
	pilsner	Oktoberfest	porter
	wheat beer	pale ale	stout
SAKES	most sake	aged sake	
SPIRITS	white (e.g., gin, vodka)		brown (e.g., bourbon, whiskey)
TEAS	green	oolong	black
COFFEES	light-roasted	medium-roasted	dark-roasted
WATERS	still	lightly sparkling	boldly sparkling

TEXTURE AND TEMPERATURE

A dish's texture and temperature will also have a bearing on its perfect pairing. Crispy dishes are often fried, calling for a bubbly beverage — such as Champagne or other sparkling wine, or beer — to refresh the palate. Rich dishes often play well off equally rich beverages: think of the combination of foie gras and Sauternes.

Just as we crave chilled dishes in summer and hot dishes in winter, so too do we especially appreciate cold beverages in hot weather and hot or room temperature beverages when the weather turns cold. The same roasted chicken that goes well with a Pinot Noir when served hot will pair even better with a chilled rosé when served cold on a picnic.

Cooking technique affects both the texture and temperature of a dish. Tuna can be served raw as sushi or hot off the grill, each with substantially different flavor, temperature, texture, and pairing implications (Champagne vs. Pinot Noir). Or, think of the difference between a cold and crunchy raw carrot and a hot carrot soup: Each would call for a different wine, the raw carrot seeking crispness and freshness in a wine (such as Sauvignon Blanc), while the soup seeks a wine with residual sugar to match its own (say, an off-dry Riesling).

RULE #3: BALANCE FLAVORS
Tickle Your Tongue in More Ways than One

Understanding the flavor components at play in a dish, and then comparing or contrasting those flavors, is the favored approach of David Rosengarten, editor in chief of DavidRosengarten.com, who championed this approach with coauthor Joshua Wesson in their 1989 book, *Red Wine with Fish*.

"What I came up with, through my years of experiments leading up to writing that book, was the notion that you just have to listen to your mouth. If I were to boil down all of food and wine pairing into one sound bite, it would be to think only about the components on the tongue," says Rosengarten. Think about the food as having the characteristics of sweetness, sourness, bitterness, and saltiness, and think about the wine as having sweetness, sourness, and bitterness. With the wine, you also want to consider the alcohol, oak, and tannin.

"Once you get comfortable with the framework of how these things play together, 99 percent of the time, you will have it!" Rosengarten promises.

Given the four basic taste components that the tongue can perceive (i.e., sweet, sour, bitter, salt), which are at play in the dish or beverage to which you're looking to match? Which dominate? Once you know where food and wine will land on your palate, you need to decide next which pairing will bring you the most joy.

THE WAY TO BALANCE: PAIR TO COMPARE, OR PAIR TO CONTRAST

Take your pick: compare or contrast. In the first instance, you'll pair a beverage with food that has similar taste or textural characteristics, savoring the similarities between the two. In the second, you'll purposely contrast the flavors of one with the other.

Both are valid approaches that we've enjoyed all our lives. "Take an Oreo cookie and a glass of milk — is there anything better?" laughs Paul Grieco of New York's Hearth. "You've got sweet and sweet, with the textures being rich and rich. An example of contrasts like pretzels and beer is when we finally left home and went to college: Salty and sour — man, you can just eat and drink that all night! You've got crunch and bubbles, so you've got some textural contrasts going on there, too, that pull the whole thing together."

However, comparing and contrasting each have their advantages — and disadvantages. Sommeliers such as Paul Roberts of the French Laundry and Per Se tend to play it safe by sticking with comparing foods and beverages due to the risks involved in attempting a successful contrast. "When you try to contrast, you run the risk of epiphany, but you also run the risk of falling flat on your face," he admits. "Unless I have the ability to try the dish and the wine together before serving them, I usually try to be very, very careful with the idea of contrast, simply because it runs the risk of a huge train wreck."

If you're unsure, then you're probably better off aiming to compare components rather than contrast them.

Principles of Balancing Taste Components of Food with Wine

Sweet foods
Compare: Pair savory dishes with sweet elements with wines that have a hint or more of sweetness.
Compare: Pair desserts with wines as sweet as, or sweeter than, the dessert.

Bitter foods
Compare: Pair bitter foods, from walnuts to grilled dishes, with tannic (bitter) wines.
Contrast: Counterbalance bitter foods with fruity, full-flavored wines.

Sour foods
Compare: Pair acidic foods with wines that are as acidic or more acidic.
Compare: Pair acidic foods with dry (not sweet) wines.

Salty foods
Contrast: Counterbalance salty foods with acidic wines.
Contrast: Counterbalance salty foods with bubbly beverages.
Contrast: Counterbalance salty foods with sweet wines.

Other Principles of Balancing Food and Wine

Weight

Compare: Pair lighter foods with lighter-bodied wines, and heavier foods with fuller-bodied wines.

Volume

Compare: Pair subtle dishes with equally nuanced wines.

Contrast: Counterbalance hot and/or spicy dishes with wines with a touch or more of sweetness.

Richness

Compare: Pair rich food with an equally rich or richer wine, typically from a warm region.

Contrast: Counterbalance fatty or oily foods with high-acid wines to cut through them.

Opulence

Compare: Pair grand dishes with grand wines.

Compare/Contrast: Pair modest dishes with more modest wines — although it can be fun to counterbalance a grand red with a simple hamburger!

Fruitiness / Earthiness

Pair fruity dishes with wines from New World regions. Pair earthy dishes with wines from Old World regions. How do you distinguish Old World from New World? If it had a king or a queen in the 1500s (e.g., France, Italy, Spain) it is Old World; and any place they sent explorers (e.g., United States) or prisoners (e.g., Australia) is New World.
— GREG HARRINGTON, master sommelier

Principles of Balancing Taste Components of Wine with Food

Acid is the ticket for matching with dishes, because it helps to move things along and to cleanse the palate. It's the most important thing in a wine. The Old World gets it right in terms of acidity levels almost every single time, and Riesling in particular serves this purpose exceptionally well.

— PAUL GRIECO, general manager, Hearth (NYC)

The best way to determine acidity is to ask yourself: How much does your mouth water after you taste it? Right underneath the tongue behind your lower lip is where you sense acid. The more acid, the more your mouth waters. The amount of salivation is the clue to acidity. Chablis is a high-acid style of wine and Gewürztraminer is a low-acid style. If you taste them side by side, you will notice the difference in how much your mouth waters.

— BERNARD SUN, beverage director, Jean-Georges Management (NYC)

Acidic wines (such as Champagne, Muscadet)
Compare: Pair high-acid wines with dishes with their own high acidity (e.g., salad with vinaigrette, pasta with tomato sauce).
Contrast: Counterbalance high-acid wines with fatty, oily, or rich foods (e.g., charcuterie, pâté, smoked salmon) to cut through the richness.
Contrast: Counterbalance high-acid wines with salty foods (e.g., caviar, oysters).

Tannic wines (such as Cabernet Sauvignon; note that as wines age, tannins soften)
Contrast: Counterbalance tannic wines with fatty dishes (e.g., well-marbled steak).
Compare: Pair tannic wines with bitter foods (e.g., grilled eggplant, walnuts).

Oaky wines (such as oaked Chardonnay)
Compare: Pair oaky wines with grilled dishes (e.g., grilled chicken).
Compare: Pair oaky, buttery wines with buttery and creamy dishes (e.g., lobster in cream sauce).

Sweet wines (such as off-dry to sweet Riesling or dessert wines)
Compare: Pair sweet wines with dishes with a touch or more of sweetness (e.g., fish with mango salsa, desserts).
Contrast: Counterbalance sweet wines with spicy dishes (e.g., Szechuan dishes).
Contrast: Counterbalance sweet wines with salty dishes (e.g., blue cheese).

WHEN STARTING *with the* BEVERAGE

When I'm coming up with a pairing for a bottle of wine, I always think first of all of the regions where that grape has prominence. Generally speaking, it tends to be Europe, so I'll think about the kinds of foods that are prepared in that region. I don't necessarily mean that people need to recreate a dish from the Black Forest if they're drinking Riesling. However, if you think about the types of foods and flavor combinations there, you can create a marriage that has some precedent and actually works. Geography comes first for me, at least as an inspiration.

— GEORGE COSSETTE, co-owner, Silverlake Wine (Los Angeles)

Say you've been given a gift of a bottle of wine and you are trying to determine what to eat with it. You'll want to do a little research to find out about its characteristics so you can plan ahead. Luckily, in the age of the Internet, help is just a Google search away.

Some of the clues include the wine's color, its origin (back to regionality!), the weight of the wine (and whether it's light-, medium-, or full-bodied), its age (as younger wines are likely to be bolder, and older wines more nuanced), its price (so you'll have a sense of it as an everyday wine, or something you'd like to save for a special occasion), and what sommeliers refer to as its structure: its levels of alcohol, acidity, sweetness, tannin, and oak.

A wine's structure is a function of the wine-making process, which is why so many wine books go deeply into the details of how tannic the grapes' skins are and how long they're left in contact with the wine (the longer they are, the more tannic the wine), or how much of the natural sugar in the grapes is allowed to convert into alcohol versus left as residual sugar (the more residual sugar, the sweeter the wine — although this may be balanced by other factors so that the wine does not necessarily taste sweet), or whether the wine was aged in oak and if so what kind of oak and for how long (the oakier the wine, the stronger the flavors of butter, vanilla, etc.).

While winemaker Christopher Tracy of Channing Daughters agrees that a wine's weight is more important than its color when making a pairing, he thinks next in importance is the level of tannin in red wines and the level of sweetness in white wines. "For instance, if you want to match a red wine with some light-fleshed fish or a vegetable dish or a light spring menu, you're not going to want a highly tannic, highly alcoholic, deeply colored red wine that's full-bodied. Instead, you're going to want something that is light in body, with very soft tannin that is not going to conflict," he says.

"On the other hand, if you're drinking a red wine with a lot of tannin and extracts [i.e., minerals] and color and body, you need to match that," says Tracy. "You need something that can help alleviate the astringency and bitterness and drying sensations from those things, which is why a leg of lamb or rib-eye steak is a classic match for a California Cabernet or a great Bordeaux."

Master Sommelier Joseph Spellman on the Importance of Understanding a Wine's Structure

In the French tradition, you would pair a high-acid wine with a high-fat food, such as a classic butter-based sauce. Your goal with the pairing would be to resolve the dish's high fat [by pairing it with a wine that would cut through its fat]. These days, however, you find many more dishes that have their own internal balance, because chefs love to balance their dishes with acids, salts, sugar, texture, and color. If a dish is perfect by itself, how do you choose a wine to make it better?

When you have enough acid from lemon juice or balsamic vinegar or any other element that is bringing the acidity to the dish, wine becomes redundant. Now it becomes a case of finding what flavors of the wine will envelop the whole dish. What wine will add some nuance to every flavor of the dish? What wine will help the acid, the texture, the length of flavor?

This approach is a very different way of thinking than in the past. Now, the structural points of the wine are more important than the aromatics or the flavors that we would have spent time on in the past. I think most people would agree that wine structure is the most important thing.

Structure is not something you can alter. It comes from the soil, the vines, and the energy the plant has absorbed over the period that the grapes have been ripening. Acid, alcohol, and tannin are very hard to mess with in the wine in a holistic way. That is part of the beauty of wine and why we have vintages, because you are going to get differences of structure every year.

COMING UP *with* "THE RIGHT ANSWER"

The good news is that there's rarely only one complementary pairing for a dish. Often, there are dozens, if not hundreds or more, possibilities!

This was highlighted to us in one of the single most instructive dinners we've ever enjoyed, with sommelier Belinda Chang selecting not one but *two* wines to accompany every dish of our tasting menu at the Fifth Floor restaurant in San Francisco. Often, one wine would complement the meat in the dish while the other played off the sauce — and it was fascinating to taste how each interacted with the same dish very differently. In his own take on giving customers different ways of enjoying each of chef David Waltuck's dishes at Chanterelle in New York City, master sommelier Roger Dagorn will offer both an Old World and a New World pairing for the dishes on the tasting menu.

On Bin 36's menu in Chicago, wine director Brian Duncan will offer two or more suggested pairings for each dish from Bin 36's extensive menu of wines by the glass. "It is rare that I will have a strong feeling of only one wine for a dish," Duncan explains. "What I like to do with a dish is something I call 'boxing': I will recommend both a white and a red with a dish, because each will do something different to it. It's like hitting it from two different sides: One will bring out flavors that the other won't."

CONCLUSION:
Are We Having Fun Yet?

Power has to be matched by power, and aroma matched with aroma.

— PIERO SELVAGGIO, owner, Valentino (Los Angeles)

If you've read this chapter instead of simply skipping to the "answers" in Chapters 5 and 6, you're likely to be most committed to the idea of experimenting with food and beverage pairing as a source of pleasure. Your exploration is likely to prove rewarding — both in terms of immediate pleasure, and in terms of the more educated palate you'll bring to every food and beverage pairing you encounter *next*.

Piero Selvaggio, owner of Los Angeles's Valentino restaurant, observes that you don't have to think too much about pairings to be able to enjoy them. "You can go with a classic pairing like steak and Cabernet Sauvignon and it is a fine match. It is expected, and it is safe. But it is the easy way out."

He explains, "If you are enjoying and analyzing what you are tasting, you will take a bite of food, then a sip of the wine, and roll it along your palate. When you slow down, you can experience what those sensations are like.

"Thinking more is key to enhancing the sophistication of your palate," argues Selvaggio. "With more knowledge, you can go to the next step and to a higher level of perception and experience.

"You experiment with food, you experiment with wine, and you experiment with both — then, you decide what is best and have an opinion. Your opinion is what pleases *you*," he says. "Remember, all the sensations we have from eating and drinking have to be satisfactory to *you* — as opposed to [wine expert] Robert Parker or someone else from whom you might have gotten an idea. They may have guided you to that wine or that pairing, but in the end, *you* are the ultimate judge."

Chef Patrick O'Connell on What You're Shooting For

[As Relais Gourmands' North American president], I'll go to these fabulous Relais & Châteaux international conferences featuring dinners by [top] chefs of that region. I love the idea of having a complete experience from the region — where you're eating food that you probably couldn't taste anywhere else, with a wine from just down the road — where the whole thing comes together and makes sense.

Often, it gets so intellectual in America. It becomes all about your brain instead of what you're feeling.

Personally, I don't like to be assaulted, startled, astonished, or knocked out by food and wine pairings so much as seduced by the whole experience. In other words, I tend to think it's a little like music: If you're aware of the individual components or parts, you're not losing yourself in it. For me, the epiphany has always been when I'm losing myself and being swept away by it.

A wine writer once told the story of how he'd had a great meal the night before. Someone had asked him, "What were you drinking with the main course?" and he replied, "I was having such a good time, I can't remember." I thought it was very refreshing to hear someone say that. I think it *should* be more like that, rather than people coming in and saying, "I had the most exquisite glass of 1964 Château whatever . . ." That can be sort of off-putting.

Of course, the writer would have remembered that pairing if it *wasn't* perfect, because people are more likely to remember an off-note. When someone sings really magnificently and they hit an off note, you remember it forever. But when anything is sung perfectly, it's just as it should be: "Of course." "Voilà!" Greatness often appears effortless.

A Conversation with Chef Daniel Boulud and Sommelier Philippe Marchal on the Order of a Menu

DANIEL BOULUD

DANIEL BOULUD: Some guests like to spend the evening with the waiters and the sommelier and to be educated and entertained. But most people want to spend the evening with their friends.

Before-Dinner Drinks

DANIEL BOULUD: Americans have a tendency to drink more alcohol before a meal than afterward. They will have three martinis but no digestif. Europeans will have a digestif instead. Europeans don't drink as much vodka as Americans. They will start with a glass of white wine or Champagne, and that is it.

Tasting Menus

DANIEL BOULUD: When you serve a tasting menu with wine pairings, it is a very disruptive process for the guests. Some guests have shared that, at other restaurants, between the waiters and the sommeliers and everything else, it becomes about the restaurant and "the show" — and not about them.

We try to be as professional and discreet as possible. If the guest wants more, we love to give it. If they want to know what Philippe thinks about Sauvignon Blanc and the winemakers, we have no problem — we go there with pleasure! We have to learn from the guest how much they want. It is a fine line to offer a lot, but not to cross the line from table to table.

Some guests just like red wine, and we don't throw them out! I think they are thinking like me sometimes: "Give me red, and I will be happy!"

As long as the customer orders good wine and has good taste in wine, I don't have a problem. I can respect someone who likes a particular style of wine and doesn't bother with the rest because they have found what makes them happiest.

We have so many customers who are strictly white Burgundy and red Bordeaux drinkers, and that is it! They don't want to be taken anywhere else, so we'd better surprise them nicely with what we have from those two regions in terms of vintages.

They are not blasé — they love their wine and they are specific as to why. It is not just about Montrachet; it is about drinking the best wine and vintages from that region.

The ideal wine and pairing menu is for a party of six to eight guests. That way, you can open a different bottle of wine for every course. You can choose special bottles that are unique.

Serving Wines from North to South

PHILIPPE MARCHAL: With wine, we start in the north [of France] and work south during a tasting. The wines of northern France get less sun, and are a little drier with more mineral notes, which work early on a menu. They also have less oak and more petrol on the nose. In the south, there is more sun, so the wines have more spice and bolder aromatics.

DANIEL BOULUD: The frame and the thinking of our wines is definitely France. The northern wines are fragile, delicate, and floral. With whites, we will also work north to south — from

Burgundy to upper Rhône, to Côte-Rôtie, to Hermitage, to Châteauneuf-du-Pape, then down to the Languedoc or Provence.

Moving Through the Courses

Foie Gras

DANIEL BOULUD: We start with foie gras or terrine — but we don't pair it with a Sauternes, which would be too much sweetness on the palate to start a meal. If we start with foie gras, we will serve a Quarts de Chaume, a Late Harvest Alsatian [white], a Vouvray, or Champagne.

PHILIPPE MARCHAL: I agree that a Sauternes is too sweet to start. What would you serve afterward? I also like a Late Harvest wine from Alsace, or a demi-sec from Vouvray. These wines have a little touch of dryness on the end.

DANIEL BOULUD: These wines work well with charcuterie and dishes with fruit condiments. If sweet wine plays a role in the middle of the meal, it just kills your palate. We serve a roasted foie gras sometimes at the end of the meal, and *then* we may pair it with an ice wine. We can accommodate a sweeter wine with hot foie gras than with a cold terrine — even if the French think Sauternes and foie gras is the ultimate!

PHILIPPE MARCHAL: At Daniel, we serve an eight- to ten-course meal. If you start with too heavy of a wine, in three courses, your palate will start to tire. You're done — it is too much.

Fish

PHILIPPE MARCHAL: With cured hamachi or marinated fluke, I will pair a New Zealand Sauvignon Blanc or something from the Loire Valley. I will serve a California Sauvignon Blanc if it has exotic fruit notes. I'll pair cannoli with lobster, spinach, and asparagus, with Pouilly-Fuissé, because it has enough minerality to match with the lobster and spinach.

DANIEL BOULUD: In a tasting, we will use a fish course to introduce red wine. We will serve a meatier fish like tuna with Bordelaise, truffles, and chanterelles, which can go with a Pinot Noir from Côte de Beaune or from Oregon.

Game or Game Birds

DANIEL BOULUD: Duck with cherries pairs with a Grenache from the southern Rhône that is on the spicy side. Gamier birds like duck or squab work well with Grenache, especially one that has a little age to it.

Meat

DANIEL BOULUD: For a red meat course, we will serve lamb or venison or beef, which may have a peppery or spicy reduction that goes with Syrah or American Cabernet Sauvignon.

Cheese

DANIEL BOULUD: With the cheese course, there are four ways to go, based on what the guest likes:

1. *White wine, such as an Alsatian Gewürztraminer, or a Sancerre or Pouilly-Fumé if guests are having goat cheese. White wine is a lighter, milder way to enjoy cheese.*

2. *Red wine. A Rhône wine that is rounded, like a Syrah, is my choice, because I am a Syrah man! When you drink a red wine, sometimes the tannins can kill the cheese. However, a wine with low tannin and rounded fruit with some age is good with cheese.*

3. *Sweet wine.*

4. *Port.*

PHILIPPE MARCHAL: With a creamy cheese like a triple crème, Champagne is wonderful. Its acidity makes it a great match.

Dessert

DANIEL BOULUD: With fruit desserts and especially exotic fruits with sweet spices, like vanilla or kaffir lime, we can be adventurous and go around the world with sweet wines.

PHILIPPE MARCHAL: In those cases, we will pour wines from Australia, South Africa, Germany, Canada, America, and Austria.

DANIEL BOULUD: In a sweet wine, you'll find complexity. We also like wines from the Languedoc, such as Muscat, as well as Italian Prosecco.

Chocolate

DANIEL BOULUD: In the summertime, we serve lighter chocolate desserts that incorporate fruits, especially berries. To pair with them, we will pour a young, fruity Banyuls.

PHILIPPE MARSHAL: I also pour Italian Vin Santo, which translates as Holy Wine. It is dry and aged five years, and I serve it slightly chilled.

DANIEL BOULUD: Port is good with some kinds of chocolate, but not all. If the dish has a dark, rich, buttery ganache with an intense flavor of chocolate, a vintage port works great.

White chocolate, milk chocolate, and dark chocolate that are light in flavor, like chocolate mousse, do *not* work with port. If you go too far, a very bitter dark chocolate will not work, either.

Banyuls has a nice toasty, nutty, not-too-sweet aspect that goes with a creamier chocolate dessert.

After-Dinner Drinks

DANIEL BOULUD: Now that people can't smoke anymore [inside New York restaurants, where it is illegal], we sell fewer after-dinner drinks. We used to sell a cigar and a couple of rounds of Cognac. I think we should put a couple of tables outside and roll our drink cart out there!

DANIEL BOULUD AND PHILIPPE MARCHAL: There are different preferences based on geography. Asians love Cognac, Armagnac, and whiskey. Europeans like a light eau de vie. The English like Calvados. Americans like Armagnac, Cognac, and grappa. And Italians, Spanish, and South Americans like grappa, too. It is cultural; Europeans, South Americans, and Asians are used to lingering after a meal.

White Wine with Meat? Red Wine with Fish?

I'd say 98 percent of pairing is protecting the food and the wine from each other.

— CRAIG SHELTON, chef-owner, the Ryland Inn (New Jersey)

When pairing food and wine, the most important thing to know is how to avoid being offensive.

— STEVE BECKTA, owner, Beckta Dining & Wine (Ottawa)

Would you ever serve white wine with red meat? "A rib-eye steak with Sauvignon Blanc — is it offensive? No," muses Steve Beckta. "However, you've basically just wasted the wine. You might as well be drinking alcoholic water, because you're not going to taste that wine at all."

White wine typically cannot stand up to red meat, and will be overpowered. So ran the conventional wisdom. The world of food and beverages, however, has changed. Whereas white wines used to be light and refreshing, and red wines more full-bodied and tannic, today you can find full-bodied, oaky (white) Chardonnays that could knock out a light-bodied (red) Pinot Noir any day.

Would you ever serve red wine with fish? "Tuna, which is a steak like fish, lends itself to red wine," attests sommelier Michael Flynn of Kinkead's in Washington, DC. "You could pair it with anything from a soft red like New World Pinot Noir to a Merlot or Zinfandel, or even an Old World earthier-style wine like a Châteauneuf-du-Pape or a southern Rhône Grenache."

However, classically red wine with white fish doesn't mix. "It's because the tannin reacts with the iodine in the seafood and makes everything taste tinny or metallic," explains Bernard Sun of Jean-Georges Management. "Red wine brings up the iodine, so if you drink it with shrimp, it will taste like it is out of a can."

Because of this, Michael Flynn of Kinkead's, which specializes in seafood cuisine and power-brokering guests, skews the wine list toward Pinot Noir, Barbera, Rioja, and Sangiovese-based Italian red wines. "If you're going to serve red wine, if you at least go with those fruit-forward red wines with softer tannins, you're getting into more familiar territory," he says.

Obviously, white wine goes with fish and white poultry. Chef Traci Des Jardins of San Francisco's Jardiniere points out the helpfulness of such classic guidelines: "Your broad-based guidelines include the fact that bigger Rhône wines and Cabernets and Bordeaux varietals lend themselves more obviously to big red meat, beef, and lamb."

Sure, but ever wonder why? Bernard Sun explains, "The reason red wine goes with red meat is because tannin is a protein and red meat is a protein. There are receptors in the back of your mouth that pick up protein/tannin as they come across the palate. Tannin gives your mouth the feel of drying up. It clogs up the receptors in the back of your palate. Red meat is also protein and clogs up those receptors. So the tannin in wine that dries up your mouth is not as dominant. Conversely, when red wine gets older, the proteins have a tendency to come together. These little molecules that you find in a young red become bigger clumps and chains of protein in an older red wine. These get so big that they become solid and turn into sediment that you find at the bottom of the bottle. In an older wine it is not that the tannin disappeared; it is just in a different form. This in turn makes the wine softer. It goes back to physics' 'matter neither creates or destroys' — tannin is still there, just in a different form."

White and Red Wine, by Body

While individual varietals can vary in body depending on the vintner or vintage, many have a tendency toward being light-, medium-, or full-bodied. While tasting the specific wine in question can allow you to make even better food pairings, using these general guidelines can give you a helpful starting point.

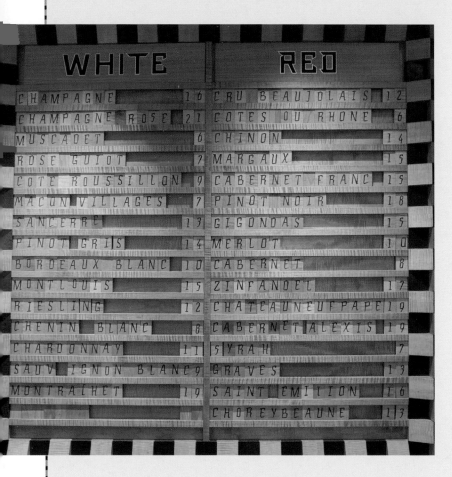

WHITE		RED	
CHAMPAGNE	16	CRU BEAUJOLAIS	12
CHAMPAGNE ROSE	21	COTES DU RHONE	6
MUSCADET	6	CHINON	14
ROSE GUIOT	7	MARGAUX	15
COTE ROUSSILLON	9	CABERNET FRANC	15
MACON VILLAGES	7	PINOT NOIR	18
SANCERRE	13	GIGONDAS	15
PINOT GRIS	14	MERLOT	10
BORDEAUX BLANC	10	CABERNET	8
MONTLOUIS	15	ZINFANDEL	17
RIESLING	12	CHATEAUNEUFPAPE	19
CHENIN BLANC	8	CABERNET ALEXIS	19
CHARDONNAY	11	SYRAH	7
SAUVIGNON BLANC	9	GRAVES	13
MONTRACHET	19	SAINT EMILION	16
		CHOREYBEAUNE	13

WHITE WINES: FROM LIGHT-BODIED TO FULL-BODIED*

LIGHT
Bordeaux, white
Chablis
Italian whites
Müller-Thurgau, German
MUSCADET
Orvieto
Pinot Blanc
Pinot Grigio
Prosecco
Riesling
Sauvignon Blanc
Soave
Verdicchio
VINHO VERDE

MEDIUM
Albarino
Bordeaux, white
Burgundy, white
Chablis, French
Champagne
Chardonnay (no oak)
Chenin Blanc
Gewürztraminer
Grüner Veltliner
Hermitage, white
Mâcon-Villages
Meursault
Pinot Bianco
Pinot Blanc, Alsatian
Pinot Gris

*If a varietal appears in more than one category, it's been known to fall into either. Listings appearing in **bold** are likely to fall into that category, and those in **BOLD CAPS** invariably fall into that category.

Pouilly-Fuissé
Pouilly-Fumé
Riesling, dry
Rioja, white
Sancerre
Sauvignon Blanc
Savennieres
Sémillon
Soave Classico
Sylvaner, Alsatian
Tocai Friulano
Vin Jaune
Vouvray

FULL
**BURGUNDY, WHITE, ESP.
GRAND CRU**
Chablis Grand Cru
**CHARDONNAY, OAKED, ESP.
CALIFORNIA AND
AUSTRALIA**
Chassagne-Montrachet
Condrieu
Côte de Beaune
Greco di Tufo
Mersault
PINOT GRIS, ALSATIAN
Puligny-Montrachet
Rhône, white wine
Scheurebe
VIOGNIER

RED WINES: FROM LIGHT-
BODIED TO FULL-BODIED*

LIGHT
Barbera
Bardolino
BEAUJOLAIS
Beaujolais-Villages
Burgundy, red
Cabernet Franc
Chianti
Chinon
Côte de Beaune
Côtes du Rhône
DOLCETTO
Gamay
Lambrusco
Pinot Noir, esp. inexpensive
Rioja Crianza
Rosé
Sangiovese
Tempranillo
Valpolicella

MEDIUM
Barbera
Beaujolais-Villages
Bordeaux, red
Brunello
Burgundy, red
Cabernet Franc
Cabernet Sauvignon
Cahors
CHIANTI CLASSICO
Chinon
Côte de Beaune
Côte de Nuits
Côte-Rôtie
Côtes du Rhône
Dolcetto
Graves
Malbec
Médoc

MERLOT
Montepulciano
Mouvèdre
Pinot Noir, esp. expensive
Pomerol
Pommard
Portuguese reds
Rioja Riserva
Saint-Émilion
Sangiovese
Shiraz / Syrah
Volnay
Zinfandel

FULL
Aglianico
Amarone
Bandol
Barbaresco
BAROLO
Bordeaux, red
Brunello
Burgundy, red, Grand Cru
CABERNET SAUVIGNON
Cahors
CHÂTEAUNEUF-DU-PAPE
Côte-Rôtie
Crozes-Hermitage
Hermitage
Madiran
Malbec, Argentinian
Merlot
Navarra
Petite Sirah
Pinotage, South African
**Rhône red wine and Rhône
blends**
Ribera del Duero
Rioja, Grand Riserva
SYRAH / SHIRAZ
ZINFANDEL

Fun with pH Levels When Making a Match

For the number-phobic, not to worry — you can certainly make great pairings *without* a PhD in chemistry! But here is some basic information you can use to make even more scientifically sophisticated pairings.

pH ranges from 0 (perfectly acidic) to 14 (perfectly alkaline). A pH of 7.0 is neutral (i.e., perfectly balanced between acidity and alkalinity). Water has an average pH of 7.0.

Most foods are acidic (i.e., <7.0), with the notable exceptions of such foods as egg whites (8.0), conch (a type of fish, 8.0), and baking soda (8.5).

A pH range of 3.0 to 3.4 is considered desirable for white wines, as is 3.3 to 3.6 for red wines.

For comparison's sake, orange juice typically come in around 3.5. A Coca-Cola web site lists Coke at 2.5 and Sprite at 3.2.

The pH level of lemon juice is 2.4, while the pH level of vinegar is 2.8.

How to use this information to make a better pairing:

If your wine is more acidic than the dish you're having with it, consider adding a squeeze of lemon or a drizzle of vinegar to the dish to balance the pairing.

If your dish is more acidic than your wine, consider adding salt (e.g., either from a salt shaker, or another salty element common to your dish's region of the world — say, soy sauce for an Asian dish, or anchovies for a Mediterranean dish) to balance the pairing.

Master sommelier Larry Stone told us:

If I know that a food has to go with a particular wine, I am familiar enough with cooking techniques that I can make a suggestion that will not radically change the chef's dish but will make it amiable to the wine that is being served.

That is a real problem when people talk about food and wine matching: They don't realize when the food is wrong. It is not necessarily that there is anything wrong with the dish per se; it is just that the *balance* of the dish is wrong, in that its level of acid is just wrong for the wine.

You can have a perfectly great dish, but paired with the wine, it is wrong. I once did a food and wine event with chef Rob Feenie, of Lumiere restaurant in Vancouver, who's a great chef. He had made a great soup that had an element of passion fruit, which can be fairly acidic. The soup for the event was already made, so it was not like we could take out any of the passion fruit. So I mentioned to Rob that if he added a little salt to it, it would lower the acidity and raise the pH of the dish to make it a better match with the wine. We added a tiny bit of salt, which radically changed the interaction between the wine and the soup.

The result? A terrific food and wine pairing. And kudos from guests!

CHAPTER FOUR

Selecting *and* Serving Beverages

Being Perfectly Prepared to Pour a Perfect Pairing

There are three "sly chameleon" wines that will go with just about everything except dessert: a 2001 Nepenthe Chardonnay from Australia, a 2001 Tavel dry rosé from Mordorée, and a 2000 Châteauneuf-du-Pape from Haut des Terres Blanches. These wines are compatible with all sorts of foods because they have fresh acidity; little, if any, oak; ripe, exuberant fruit; and soft, if any, tannin.

— MADELINE TRIFFON, MS, director of wine, Matt Prentice Restaurant Group (Detroit)

A single meal often comprises more than one beverage. A special dinner may start with aperitifs or cocktails, with bottled water on the table, moving into one or more wines with dinner, plus dessert wine with dessert, followed by after-dinner drinks, or coffee or tea — providing multiple food and beverage pairing opportunities.

If every pairing presents the prospect of a peak experience, how can you be best prepared to take advantage of this? For starters, the wider your choices of beverages on hand, the better your chances of being able to make a great pairing at every meal. This obviously goes beyond having a bottle each of red and white wine at the ready — so in Part I of this chapter, you'll find our experts' recommendations for a diverse case of wine to stock at home.

Just as important as selecting a beverage is serving it so you can enjoy it at its best: that is, at the optimal temperature and in optimal glassware. These factors play an even more vital role in your and your guests' enjoyment than you might have previously thought. It is just as easy to ruin an expensive wine through poor food pairings as it is through improper handling and serving. Conversely, an inexpensive wine served at the right temperature and in appropriate glassware can taste much finer. In Part II, you'll find expert tips on serving beverages to show them to their best advantage.

PART I: Beverages: Stocking Up

If the idea of "starting a wine cellar" is too intimidating, let's think of it instead as simply filling your wine rack, refrigerator, and cupboard with some wine, beer, water, tea, and coffee. We'll help to ensure that you'll have a choice of beverages around any time you're looking for one to accompany what you're eating.

WINE

For less than 1 percent of wine drinkers, enjoying wine is about buying fine wines to age in their cellars. "For the other 99 percent of us, it is about buying ten-dollar bottles of wine and drinking them soon thereafter," points out chef Rocco DiSpirito, who has his own Perfect Pairing Wine Club on Wine.com and hosted *Food Talk* on New York City's WOR Radio. "Some of my listeners are afraid to drink wine because they think if they can't spend thirty to fifty dollars a bottle, it won't be very good — and that if they're only able to spend ten dollars, they should buy beer instead."

DiSpirito finds himself constantly reminding people that there is "damn good wine" widely available for just ten dollars a bottle. "Ruffino Pinot Grigio is less than a hundred dollars a case, and it is great with Eli's Parmesan crackers. I am not kidding — it is an ethereal pairing," he enthuses. "Another great wine I love is Fife Rosé, which is only around ten dollars a bottle."

For the same price as an upscale coffeehouse drink, you can buy a bottle of one of the best beers in the world. For a few dollars more, you could take home a wonderful bottle of wine. One of the authors' favorite wines is Osborne Solaz, which is a Cabernet blend from Spain that is medium-bodied and full-flavored, and goes with a wide range of dishes. It is priced at less than nine dollars a bottle in New York City. At five glasses per bottle, it costs less than two dollars a glass to enjoy.

French wines in particular are perceived to be pricey. Before you panic when seeing red and white Burgundies among those recommended for your "starter case" of wines, we'll provide you with some assurances up front about their affordability.

FRENCH WINES: AN AFFORDABLE LUXURY

"People tend to think the wines of France are going to be too expensive and that those doors are closed," observes Best Cellars' Joshua Wesson. "However, that is simply not true. All of France is open to you. There is not any vaunted place in any part of the country where you could not buy good wine. In some places, you could buy tons of wine."

"C'est impossible!" we countered in response to Wesson's assertion. Setting a budget of the equivalent of fifteen dollars per bottle, we asked Wesson to take us to France. Off the top of his head, he took us on a virtual *Tour de France*, letting us know what kind of wine we could buy in each region:

ALSACE: *Pinot Blanc — a lovely bottle; or a fabulous sparkling wine or a stunning Sylvaner*

BEAUJOLAIS: *You could get a top cru Beaujolais (which is made from the region's best Gamay Noir grapes)*

BORDEAUX: *You could buy almost a third of the wines available in this region. Bordeaux has more producers than anywhere in France, and most are unsung and inexpensive. You could get Haut Médoc and satellite appellations of Saint-Emilion, as well as a ton of Bordeaux Supérieur.*

BURGUNDY: *A delicious bottle of either rouge or blanc, or a sparkling Crémant de Bourgogne, which is a lovely wine*

CAHORS: *You could buy a whole heap of the wine available here*

CHAMPAGNE: *A half-bottle of Champagne*

CÔTES DE PROVENCE: *A pretty good bottle of white or red*

CÔTE DU VENTOUX: *A lovely bottle*

GASCONY: *You could buy the whole region!*

LANGUEDOC: *Fifteen dollars will buy you two-thirds of the wine available in this region. Wherever your car breaks down in Languedoc, you could buy a bottle of wine. You could get an extraordinary Muscat.*

LOIRE VALLEY: *A top-drawer Muscadet or a sparkling wine*

MÂCON: *A stunning example*

PROVENCE: *A slayer rosé!*

RHÔNE: *A lovely white, red, or rosé*

SANCERRE: *A nice bottle of red or rosé*

POUILLY-FUMÉ: *A nice-entry level wine*

SAINT-VÉRAN: *A stunning one*

SOUTHWEST: *You can get almost everything*

VOUVRAY: *A pretty good bottle*

With this list, we conceded that Wesson had more than proved his point. We hope you'll remember that, if you want to try a French wine you read about in Chapter 5 or 6, cost shouldn't be an issue.

WINES TO HAVE ON HAND SO YOU'RE READY FOR ANY OCCASION

In Chapter 8, our experts share which wines they would not want to live without. We also asked some of them which wines *we* shouldn't live without. "You'll want to have a variety of wines on hand from lighter to heavy reds and whites — something for every situation and mood," recommends Jean-Luc Le Dû. With input from Le Dû and other sommeliers, we compiled a recommended "starter case" of wine. With these wines on hand, you can come home with just about anything from the store or take-out window, and be ready to open a bottle to fit your food and mood.

A RECOMMENDED "STARTER CASE" OF WINES TO HAVE ON HAND TO ASSURE YOURSELF OF A GREAT PAIRING ON MOST ANY OCCASION

1. RIESLING, GERMAN: *Our experts describe Riesling as the single most food-friendly white wine. Jean-Luc Le Dû points out that "Rieslings are held together by incredible acidity and they are amazingly well-balanced. They feel much drier than they actually are." Scott Tyree of Chicago's Tru recommends J.J. Prum from the Mosel, while sommelier Belinda Chang casts her vote for Donnhoff Schlossböckelheimer Kupfergrube Riesling Spätlese.*

2. PINOT NOIR / RED BURGUNDY: *Our experts describe Pinot Noir or red Burgundy as the single most food-friendly red wine. Kinkead's Michael Flynn tends to pair Oregon Pinots with red meat, and uses California Pinots as "crossover wines" for a table of guests eating both meat and fish. Chang reports, "Melville Pinot Noir from Santa Rita Hills is a cool little winery — and Gevrey Chambertin [red Burgundy] is pretty reasonable." Tyree recommends Eyrie Pinot Noir from Oregon, while Le Dû gives his nod to Côte de Nuits.*

3.   WHITE BURGUNDY / CHARDONNAY: *This versatile varietal has fans around the world. "Chardonnay is a very interesting grape, and number one would be white Burgundy from France. Number two would be Italy, and California is coming on strong because it is becoming more balanced and less oaky," says Le Dû. Chang is a fan of Ramonet Chassagne-Montrachet, while Tyree favors Puligny-Montrachet Domaine Leflaive.*

4.   CHAMPAGNE OR SPARKLING WINE *(e.g., Spanish Cava or Italian Prosecco): As Chang advises, "When in doubt, serve bubbly!" You'll be set for any special occasion that arises or to kick off any meal with a bottle of Champagne or other sparkling wine on hand — also a perfect match for fried or salty appetizers. Kinkead's Flynn observes that "rosé Champagne covers a whole lot of bases," while Chang attests that "Soter Beacon Hill Brut Rosé [sparkling wine] from Oregon's Willamette Valley goes with everything."*

5.   CABERNET SAUVIGNON: *You'll want a bottle of Cabernet on hand to accompany red meat dishes. As for the best source, Le Dû says, "It's a toss-up between hillside vineyards in California and Pomerol in France. There are also wonderful Cabernets made in Spain and Italy." Chang recommends: "Sequoia Grove Cabernet, at ten dollars a bottle. It is delicious, and I recommend it to all my friends who are getting married because it is so reasonably priced."*

6.   SHIRAZ / SYRAH: *This is another good bottle to have on hand to accompany earthier red meat dishes. Le Dû observes, "On a large-scale basis, Australia makes the best Shiraz in the world. On a vintage to vintage basis, from a small estate, you must look at the northern Rhône of France and Côte-Rôtie and Hermitage." Master sommelier Greg Harrington casts his vote for Syrah from Washington State: "I love it with grilled food, or hearty dishes with herbal or earthier sauces."*

7.   ROSÉ: *Rosé is an incredibly versatile wine that can take you from light to dark meats, and from the dinner table to a picnic. "Rosé is the Boutros Boutros-Ghali of wine," cracks Best Cellars' Joshua Wesson. "If you have a bottle each of bone-dry and off-dry rosé, there aren't many foods that wouldn't go with one or the other." Flynn points out that Spain makes "some wonderful rosé," where they're known as rosados.*

8.   GEWÜRZTRAMINER: *It's great to have a bottle of Gewürztraminer on hand to accompany everything from spicy foods to seafood to cheese. "If you don't know what wine to serve with any kind of fish or shellfish, just grab a Gewürztraminer," says chef Sandy D'Amato of Sanford restaurant in Milwaukee. Master sommelier Alpana Singh of Everest in Chicago reports, "We found in Alsace that everybody serves Gewürztraminer with their cheese."*

9.   SAUVIGNON BLANC, NEW ZEALAND: *Perfect for accompanying salads, vegetables, and seafood, New Zealand Sauvignon Blanc is described by Jill Gubesch, sommelier of Chicago's Frontera Grill, as her "go-to wine." "It has tropical fruit, like passion fruit and pineapple, but also bracing acidity, so it finishes dry," she says. "And it also has a voluptuousness that you don't find in any other style of Sauvignon Blanc."*

10. CHIANTI: *Charles Scicolone of New York's I Trulli describes Chianti Classico as "the perfect food wine." Veritas's Tim Kopec adds, "Pizza, and red sauce in general, are notoriously difficult to pair with wine — and present you with a perfect time to drink an inexpensive Chianti." It's equally perfect with tomato-sauced pasta.*

11. SHERRY: *One of our biggest surprises was to discover just how many fans Spanish sherry has, as expert after expert recommends it for its versatility in pairing with foods both as an aperitif as well as during (and even after) a meal. "I love sherry — it's so good with food," enthuses Karen King of The Modern. Kopec attests, "I'm fascinated by how well sherries go with foods as diverse as sardines, anchovies, almonds, roasted peppers, artichoke hearts, and even chocolates. What's more, you can buy a good bottle of sherry for fifteen dollars."*

12. MOSCATO D'ASTI: *You'll want a wine to have on hand to serve with dessert, and some of our experts refer to Moscato d'Asti as the single most versatile dessert wine around. Madeline Triffon calls Moscato d'Asti her "favorite all-purpose sweet wine."*

    BONUS BEVERAGE — HARD CIDER: *Joshua Wesson's vote for the single most food-friendly beverage goes to hard cider. "You could get three types of cider — dry, off-dry, and sweet — and they would go with almost everything you could ever imagine eating," says Wesson. "Cider is low in alcohol, and effervescent — and these two elements make a beverage more food friendly than one without them. That means cider can handle foods that are spicy, oily, sweet and sour, or salty. Cider goes brilliantly with all these foods. These characteristics make cider a perfect stunt double for beer. Beer doesn't have the ability to go as sweet — however, cider can. Cider is also higher in acid than beer, which gives the nod to cider."*

BEER

After tasting fifty to one hundred wines in a single day, a sommmelier's palate can get pretty beat up. That's when we need something soothing that is not aggressive — like a beer. Beer is low in acid, which is also why it goes so well with a lot of spicy food. — BERNARD SUN, beverage director, Jean-Georges Management

Even many of our wine-crazed sommeliers admit there are times when nothing but a beer will do! We turned to our experts for their recommendations of a versatile six-pack of beers that could take you through just about any pairing occasion. The list includes:

1. A QUAFFABLE BEER: *Anything you find easy to drink, whether a lager (as does Madeline Triffon) or a Tecate (as do Paul Roberts and David Rosengarten).*

2. PILSNER: *Pilsner is popular with our experts for pairing with everything from peanuts, hot dogs, and pizza to soft-shell crab sandwiches.*

3. WHEAT BEER: *This pairs well with everything from brunch to lunch (salads, sandwiches) to fried foods and spicier dishes.*

4. ALE: *Take your pick of an amber ale to accompany fried and salty foods, or a brown ale if steak is more your thing.*

5. BELGIAN LAMBIC BEER: *Standard versions can accompany anything from eggs to ceviche, while fruit-flavored versions (such as cherry or raspberry) can serve as dessert.*

6. STOUT: *Keep Guinness on hand if you're an oyster lover, or a chocolate or imperial stout if you have more of a sweet tooth (as they pair well with chocolate desserts).*

WATER

What kind of water would you like? Tap or bottled? Still or with bubbles? Choosing water is often one of the first decisions you're asked to make when dining out. At the four-star restaurant Alain Ducasse at the Essex House in New York City, the site of our own water epiphany, guests are asked about their preferences with regard to water's minerality and saltiness, and size of bubble. Waters are then selected to their taste from a silver basket of a half-dozen different waters.

Water plays an important role in any meal by continually cleansing and refreshing your palate. It takes on even greater importance if it is the only beverage being drunk. Despite being colorless and largely odorless, water is like any other beverage: If you line up a few side by side, you can definitely taste a difference.

Not all bottled waters are alike, and there are even finer distinctions to be made between merely "still" and "sparkling." FineWaters.com classifies bottled waters as one of five different styles, on a spectrum from still to bold:

STILL	no bubbles; flat
EFFERVESCENT	the tiniest bubbles
LIGHT	small bubbles
CLASSIC	medium-sized bubbles
BOLD	large, bold bubbles

The issue of sparkling versus still water depends on what you're eating. "The amount, size, or spacing of the bubbles is significant in matching water with food," advises Michael Mascha, founder of FineWaters.com. "With water, because there is not much aroma, mouthfeel becomes the most important thing. Perrier has a very large, bold bubble — it's like fireworks in your mouth. If it were paired with sushi, for example, it wouldn't work, given the subtlety of the fish. With sushi, still water or a water with very small bubbles would be a much better match."

Two indicators to look for on a water's label are its TDS and pH levels:

- *TDS stands for total dissolved solids. This number represents how much mineral content is left behind when the water evaporates. A higher TDS indicates higher mineral content and heavier taste. "The higher the TDS, the more body the water will have," explains FineWaters.com's Mascha. "Spa water from Belgium has a TDS of 33 which is almost like rain water (soft), and Apollinaris from Germany has a TDS of 2650, so it will have a much more substantial mouthfeel because of its (hard) mineral content."*

- *The other important thing to look for is a water's pH, which represents relative acidity or alkalinity. As with wines and other beverages, the scale ranges from 0 to 14, with a neutral pH being 7.0; beverages below that are acidic (sour), and above that are alkalinic (bitter). As an example, Perrier is 5.5, or slightly acidic.*

Below is a sampling of popular waters and their style, TDS, and pH levels, which can get you started in identifying your personal preferences.

A SAMPLING OF POPULAR WATERS (SORTED BY TDS LEVEL)

Brand (origin)	FineWaters.com Style	TDS	pH level
Voss (Norway)	still, effervescent	22	6.4
Spa (Belgium)	still	33	6.0
Font d'Or (Spain)	still	128	7.7
Fiji (Fiji)	still	160	7.5
Ty Nant (U.K.)	still, bold	165	6.8
Hildon (U.K.)	still, effervescent	312	7.4
Sole (Italy)	still, light	412	7.2
Perrier (France)	bold	475	5.5
Wattwiller (France)	still	889	7.6
San Pellegrino (Italy)	classic	1109	7.7

TEA

Tea is much more delicate than wine . . . The people who respond best to the intricacies of tea are people who enjoy wine.

— JAMES LABE, tea sommelier/owner, Teahouse Kuan Yin (Seattle)

As passionate as chefs can be about food and even wine, we found some to be just as passionate about tea. Patrick O'Connell of the Inn at Little Washington drinks only tea throughout his day. At the inn, he offers almost two dozen different teas during afternoon tea service. During the winter, he even keeps a healthy tea infusion warming on the stove for his kitchen crew. When traveling through the South, tea fanatic Sandy D'Amato of Milwaukee's Sanford Restaurant chooses where to eat by the quality of a restaurant's iced tea.

You need to select a tea that is right for what you are eating — but, happily, your lessons on pairing food with wine apply here, too, as pairing food with tea is very similar. Kai Andersen of New York's tea purveyor Ito En and its Manhattan restaurant Kai advises, "Start with white tea and light teas at the beginning of the meal, and then finish with oolong or black tea, which are stronger, at the end of the meal. With dessert, serve a floral or scented tea."

"If you are drinking a green tea, a dish with a lot of spice will overpower it," says Andersen. "Oolong, on the other hand, can stand up to spice very well. It clears your palate and aids digestion." James Labe adds, "Darjeeling can also stand up to spicy and acidic foods like lemon or a tomato curry, because it has a cleansing and refreshing quality on the palate."

RECOMMENDED TEAS TO STOCK IN YOUR CUPBOARD

Want to have the right tea on hand for any occasion? Our tea experts recommend the following teas. "If you had a tea lover come over, you could hit just about any food pairing need with this list," promises Canada's first tea sommelier Michael Obnowlenny. "Just remember to make your purchases from a premium tea shop."

Your starter stash of a half-dozen teas:

1. BREAKFAST BLEND OR BLACK TEA, *with or without milk, to accompany everything from breakfast to pastries and desserts, to heavier meats and even spicier foods. "A bold, in-your-face black tea like Darjeeling, Ceylon, and Kenyan will give you a lot of different properties," says Michael Obnowlenny.*

2. ASSAM TEA, *which is a robust black tea that can be drunk with milk. "It's a great morning tea, and also goes especially well with creamy desserts," says Kai Andersen. New York's Tamarind Tea Room turned the authors on to salmon and lamb sandwiches with Assam tea.*

3. OOLONG TEA, *which can accompany lighter to heavier foods, depending on the specific tea. Andersen recommends it as a generally fuller, rounder tea that pairs well with everything from fish and meat to dessert.*

4. CHINESE GREEN TEA, *which can accompany seafood and shellfish.* "More refined green teas should be drunk by themselves, but other Chinese green teas are wonderful with fish or other lighter dishes," says Andersen.

5. JAPANESE SENCHA GREEN TEA, *which pairs as beautifully with seafood as it can with chocolate.* "Rich, sweet, and bitter, a really strong Japanese green tea is the perfect match for chocolate," says James Labe. Andersen also likes it with any Japanese or Korean fare.

6. HERBAL TEAS, *such as chamomile and mint, which make nice digestives when sipped after meals.*

"Chamomile pairs well with food that has a roasted quality — anything from nuts to meats," says Labe. "Dark chamomile is also good with mint, such as mint ice cream. And peppermint tea is an easy match with chocolate, and equally fine with vanilla."

As a bonus, consider having FRUIT TISANES *on hand as well.* "These are blends of different fruits and flowers, and not actual teas," explains Obnowlenny. "You might want to have dark berries (blue and black), raspberries, and saskatoon. You'd also want citrus (orange, pineapple, lemon) as well as a side stock of rose hip and hibiscus to add color."

If you are a novice still discovering your tea preferences, consider *hojicha*, a roasted Japanese green tea. Kai Andersen says, "*Hojicha* is a good tea to start with because it is very flexible with food and works with almost everything. It is so smooth that it can be paired with anything from main courses to desserts to just strawberries. It also happens to be very forgiving in its preparation, so it's hard to ruin."

COFFEE

Most of the time, enjoying coffee is a morning, afternoon, or post-meal/dessert occasion. It is not typically the first drink most people reach for when eating a salad or steak. That doesn't minimize its importance, however.

Coffee can add a lot to a meal, especially if you think regionally. An Italian roast coffee or an espresso pairs beautifully with tiramisu or biscotti. A *café con leche* [coffee with steamed milk] is great with *tres leches* cake for dessert at the end of a Mexican meal. With a Vietnamese meal, enjoying Vietnamese coffee [coffee with condensed milk] with crème caramel is like having *two* desserts!

Coffee's country of origin can provide a clue as to the coffee's likely characteristics. Dub Hay, senior vice president of Starbucks, shares an overview of what to expect from coffees from these major growing regions:

EAST AFRICA: *These coffees have floral and berry notes, and are light-bodied to mild.*

CENTRAL AND LATIN AMERICA: *These coffees have notes of nuts like almonds and nut breads, and are crisp and clean with subtle flavors.*

ASIA: *This style is typically full-bodied and darker-roasted. These coffees have notes of sweetness and caramel.*

The degree to which the coffee beans have been roasted can also provide an indication of the coffee's flavor, body, and suitability for pairing. While different companies have different names for their roasts, the most common categories are light-, medium-, and dark-roasted coffees, which are best paired with light, medium, and heavy dishes, respectively.

OTHER BEVERAGES

When people aren't drinking wine, they are often thrilled when you offer them something besides water, such as an unusual iced tea or other nonalcoholic beverage.
— PATRICK O'CONNELL, chef-owner, the Inn at Little Washington (Virginia)

We hope that soon behind us are the days when nondrinkers are made to feel like second-class citizens. There are many signs that this change is well underway.

At the French Laundry in Napa Valley and Per Se in New York City, master sommelier Paul Roberts has famously paired nonalcoholic juices and infusions with the restaurant's tasting menu for both children and nondrinking adults. At The Modern in New York City, sommelier Stephane Colling changes his water offering monthly, while Joe Catterson in Chicago has featured a food and water pairing on Alinea's tasting menu. The Blue Hill Café at Stone Barns proudly serves Fizzy Lizzy sparkling fruit juices.

When it comes to what to drink with a meal, we are in a new era of beverage abundance. BevNet.com, which covers the bottled and canned drink industry, has reviewed more than two thousand different beverages on its web site. Posted reviews cover beverages ranging from America's first mass-marketed soft drink, Moxie cherry cola, which originated in 1884 in New England as a health drink, to Fizzy Lizzy, the New York newcomer that produces award-winning beverages superior to other sparkling juices or "adult sodas" that contain more filler juice (e.g., white grape, apple, pear) than that of the advertised flavor. FineWaters.com reviews hundreds of bottled waters, with more than a hundred from the United States alone. Starbucks.com offers more than twenty styles of beans and blends, not counting decaffeinated coffees, while independents like New York's Ito En and Seattle's TeahouseChoice.com offer dozens of different kinds of tea.

The quality of soda has changed dramatically with the advent of entrepreneurs entering the market and creating a whole new segment of "grown-up sodas" with better ingredients that are less sweet and more sophisticated in flavor.

Years after tasting them while traveling on a book tour, we still recall the fabulous pairings of freshly made ginger-lemon soda with an Indian curry at Vij's restaurant in Vancouver — as well as of refreshing *agua fresca* (crushed fresh fruit, such as watermelon or strawberries, lime or lemon juice, sugar, and water, served ice-cold) with our Mexican food at Pancho Villa in San Francisco. Chef Traci Des Jardins takes the latter pairing upscale by making her *agua frescas* with fruit purchased at the San Francisco farmers' market, and serving them with fresh tacos at her restaurant Mijita.

The next beverage frontier? There's no telling. At Blue Hill at Stone Barns in Pocantico Hills, New York, chefs Dan Barber and Michael Anthony have even ended dinners with a tiny glass of artisanally made vinegar served as a digestif. Anthony says, "The vinegar is made by Erwin Gegenbauer, and has residual sugar from the Traminer grapes used to make it." Barber adds, "Here is a man who is a real artisan, who believes so much in his product that he wants you to drink it!"

PART II:
Beverages: Serving Them Up Right

TEMPERATURE

Many experts stressed the importance of serving beverages at their proper temperature so they're best able to show their flavors.

With wine, the most common mistake is serving red wines too warm. Steven Jenkins of New York City's Fairway Market comments, "It is a crime! Room temperature, being seventy-two degrees, is ten to fifteen degrees too high for a big red wine [given that cellar temperature is fifty-five degrees]. You are sure as hell not going to taste the wine, much less the food."

A red wine that is too warm tastes hot and harsh. Alpana Singh of Everest explains, "If your wine is too warm, the first thing you taste is the alcohol and not the fruit. If it is chilled, it will bring out the fruit and bring down the alcohol. A lighter red wine brought down a couple of degrees really brings out that fruit." On the other hand, a white wine that is served too cold tastes boring and lean because its flavors are not able to open up.

Most of us don't have our own temperature-controlled wine cellars at home. We simply pull wine from the wine rack or the bag we brought it home in — or straight from the fridge. What's the easiest way to make sure you're serving it at the right temperature? Veritas's Tim Kopec gave us a very simple rule: "Put your red wine *in* the refrigerator for fifteen minutes before serving — and pull your white wine *out* of the refrigerator fifteen minutes before serving."

Wines can be served at the wrong temperature just as easily in restaurants as at home. We'll cup our hands around too-cold glasses of white wine to warm them enough to release their aromas and flavors. If we find our red wine has been stored on a too-warm shelf, we'll ask our server for a chilled glass to pour it into to cool it slightly.

Water has its own ideal temperature, and Michael Mascha of FineWaters.com cautions us not to drink it too cold. "If you have a nice bottle of water and add ice cubes, you are cooling down the water too much to enjoy it," he advises. "You want to drink your water at cellar temperature. By the way, you should at least think about the source and age of your ice if you choose to use it. Old ice cubes not only dilute the water you just poured, but can also add odors from the freezer."

Like red wine and water, beer is best served close to cellar temperature. "Temperature is important because if beer is served too cold, it hides the taste," says chef and food and beverage director Carlos Solis of Sheraton Four Points/LAX. "Good quality beer should be served at fifty to fifty-five degrees. I serve most [mass-marketed beers] at just above freezing, and the people who drink them like them that cold."

Iced tea has been called "the house wine of the South" — and if you need any further convincing that temperature makes a world of difference to the beverages you serve, just imagine drinking barbecue with *hot* tea instead of *iced tea*. "Barbecue would not work with hot tea, but it works great with iced tea," says Ito En's Kai Andersen. "Iced tea also works with strong Korean or Indian food. Black tea with chilled milk would be like drinking a *lassi* [a yogurt drink] with an Indian dish."

GLASSWARE

Once you've got it to the perfect temperature, you'll want to serve a beverage in the ideal glassware.

Does your choice of glass make a difference to what you are drinking? "The choice of glassware is instrumental in the perception of wine on all levels: sight, smell, and taste," explains Maximilian Riedel, chief executive officer of Riedel Glassware and an eleventh generation glassmaker. He continues:

The clarity of the glass — very thin and free of color and design — enables the wine drinker to see the color and texture of the wine even before experiencing it on a more visceral level.

The size of the bowl has a pronounced effect on the aroma a person will get from the wine. The bowl must be large enough for air to swish through the wine when it is vigorously swirled, opening up the bouquet. As the nose can recognize hundreds of times more smells than the tongue can perceive tastes, much of how someone experiences wine is through their sense of smell. The thinness of the lip and shape of the bowl help guide the wine as it enters the mouth.

What are the best glasses for various wines? In Riedel's opinion:

Red wine, which generally needs more air to open up, requires a larger bowl than most white wines require.

White wine needs a bowl generous enough to allow it to open, whereas water requires nothing more than a vessel that is comfortable to the user and aesthetically pleasing to the eye.

The long, thin line of the Champagne flute allows the wine to preserve its effervescence where a flatter glass would increase the rate of dissipation.

While in the old black-and-white films stars always seemed to be looking fabulous sipping out of wide-mouthed flat glasses, unfortunately, looking that good was killing their Champagne because it dissipated the bubbles so quickly. Today, the glass of choice is a flute.

For best enjoyment, Tim Kopec recommends investing in your glassware before you invest in your wine cellar. "You are better off spending a hundred dollars on glasses from Riedel or Spiegelau than on spending a hundred dollars on the wine and serving it out of crappy glasses [that are the wrong size for the wine or that have a very thick lip]," he says. "This investment will also last a lot longer than the wine for one party."

Every high-quality beverage deserves to be treated with the same respect as wine — so pull out your best stemware for them, too. Riedel makes not only glassware for wine, but also glasses specifically designed for water, sake, beer, and other beverages. Happily for price-conscious consumers, they've introduced lower-priced glassware lines that are still of excellent quality.

No matter what your choice of glassware, it's vital that you make sure it's been recently and thoroughly cleaned before filling it with a beverage you want to enjoy. Tim Kopec of Veritas warns, "If you go to your relatives' house and they are so excited that they break out their best glasses that have not been used in seven months, no matter what you put in that glass, it will smell like the cupboard."

Now, what to pour into that perfectly selected, perfectly clean glass? Turn to Chapter 5 . . .

Chef Colin Alevras on the Tasting Room's All-American Wine List

We have an all-American wine list in deference to the European model — meaning that if we were in France, we would drink French wine, and if we were in Italy, we would drink Italian wine. In order to respect that tradition [of local ingredients paired with local wines] and to put it into a context for our restaurant, which is based on all local products, we thought we should serve only American wines. Certainly, these days, there is no lack of great American wines.

When I'm deciding what to pair with a wine, it all comes down to the wine's acid, oak, and tannin. Is the wine rich and unctuous, or palate cleansing? **With a white wine, you want to pair it with food that's the opposite [Chapter 3's concept of "contrast"], and a red wine with food that is more complementary ["compare"].** For example, if you have an oaky, rich white, you need a dish with more acid to cut through it and to create a more balanced mouthfeel. With red wine, it is the opposite: the bigger the wine, the bigger the food.

American wine is democracy in action: You can plant [any grape] you want anywhere you want, and if it is good, people will drink it. If it doesn't work, you are always allowed to change your mind and to plant something else. By contrast, in France, it is against the law to plant certain [varietals] in certain places. There is a legal body that regulates vineyards and wine production — and you can't simply plant things because you want to. In the United States, you see winemakers are still experimenting and discovering what works. No one thought in the 1960s that you could grow grapes in places like Santa Barbara or the Sonoma Coast.

In Burgundy, they have evolved their grapes and their soil over a thousand years to get to where they are. In the United States we are still experimenting. I would hope that in the next thousand years, we'll figure it out, too.

What are some quintessential American wine varietals?

RIESLING FROM THE FINGER LAKES: *I like to pair these Rieslings with fresher, even raw (as opposed to cooked) dishes that feature ingredients like trout and nettles that give a sense of the region [which is heavily forested].*

PETITE SIRAH: *This is a monster wine for serious braised meats (beef, lamb) and other big food, such as game (duck, squab, venison), wild mushrooms, and strong cheeses (e.g., hard, blue).*

ZINFANDEL: *This is a versatile grape that reflects where it's grown. I'd pair it with similar dishes as with Petite Sirah (red meats, mushrooms, cheeses). I like its consistent juiciness that pairs well with heavier meats, and find that the ripest Zinfandels (with a hint of residual sugar) stand up to spicy foods (such as those with chiles). Late Harvest Zinfandel makes a natural pairing for dark chocolate — more so than even vintage port — as well as for most kinds of cheeses.*

RHÔNE WHITES, SUCH AS VIOGNIER AND ROUSSANNE: *These do very well in California and Virginia.*

I like to pair fragrant, peachy and honeyed Viognier with fresh vegetables lightly dressed with lemon and olive oil, or fresh fruits. (The Tasting Room has carried Viogniers from California's Calera, Gregory Graham, Jaffurs, Jeanne Marie, Miner Family Vineyards, and Spencer Roloson.)

Roussanne is my "go-to wine" for balancing structure with acidity. Roussanne can do it all! It's the perfect white wine for red wine drinkers because, with eyes closed, it would be hard to tell this rich, full-bodied, earthy wine apart from a red. While I can pair brighter Roussannes with fish and shellfish, I can pair other Roussannes with Asian or Southwest-style red meats served with lime or other citrus. (The Tasting Room has carried Roussannes from California's Alban Vineyards, Copain, Sine Qua Non, and Tablas Creek.)

PINOT NOIR: *I also admire and have carried Pinot Noirs coming out of both Oregon (e.g., Ken Wright Cellars, St. Innocent) and Sonoma (e.g., Littorai, Lookout Ridge, Peay Vineyards, Radio Coteau). I find Oregon Pinots earthier, with more mushroomy and funky flavors, and find that they pair well with simple sautéed mushroom dishes. Sonoma Pinots have more structure and better backbone, and pair better with white game birds (such as pheasant), terrines, and preserved meats. Central Coast Pinots are right in between — not as big as Sonoma Pinots, but with great structure, making them more versatile for pairing with everything from fish to lighter meats.*

Some of Alevras's favorite American wines on the . . .

. . . *East Coast?*

In New York's Finger Lakes region, HERMANN J. WIEMER makes beautiful *Riesling* (which pairs well with seafood, light meats, fruit, and cheese), including *Late Harvest Riesling* (which pairs well with lobster, cream sauces, fresh fruit, and cheese) and *Gewürztraminer* (which pairs well with spicy foods, rich sauces, and/or fruit desserts).

On New York's Long Island, CHANNING DAUGHTERS (BRIDGEHAMPTON) does a great job with northern Italian varietals such as *Vino Bianco*. SCHNEIDER VINEYARDS (NORTH FORK) started from scratch and is mastering *Cabernet Franc* (which pairs well with duck, game, and other grilled dishes). And PAUMANOK (NORTH FORK) is a second generation family and is making some great Bordeaux blend reserve wines (with *Cabernet Franc* and *Merlot*).

. . . *West Coast?*

LITTORAI (SONOMA COAST): *Chardonnay* and *Pinot Noir*

PEAY VINEYARDS (SONOMA COAST): *Pinot Noir, Syrah, Chardonnay, Viognier,* and *Roussanne/Marsanne*

BREWER-CLIFTON (SANTA BARBARA): *Chardonnay* and *Pinot Noir*

(ERIC) HAMACHER CELLARS (OREGON): *Chardonnay* and *Pinot Noir*

KEN WRIGHT CELLARS (WILLAMETTE VALLEY, OREGON): Their *Pinot Noir* is a great wine.

TONY SOTER (OREGON): The Tasting Room has offered *Soter Firefly Rosé* (of *Pinot Noir*) by the glass.

BOB FOLEY (NAPA): *Petite Sirah* from Switchback Ridge is handsdown the biggest and most fun wine; I've been known to describe it as a cross between cold espresso and blood.

CHAPTER FIVE

What *to* Drink *with* What *you* Eat

Matching Beverages to Foods

As I ate the oysters with their strong taste of the sea and their faint metallic taste that the cold white wine washed away, leaving only the sea taste and the succulent texture, and as I drank their liquid from each shell and washed it down with the crisp taste of the wine, I lost the empty feeling and began to be happy and to make plans.

— ERNEST HEMINGWAY, *A Moveable Feast*

People get stuck in the idea that there is only one wine for every dish. I like to pour two and let people taste how each affects the dish differently.

— BELINDA CHANG, wine director, Osteria Via Stato (Chicago)

When pairing foods and beverages, there are two fundamental ways to start: matching beverages to the food (that is, starting with the food to be eaten, and selecting the best beverage to accompany it), or matching food to the beverage (beginning with a bottle of wine, beer, sake, etc., and finding its best food complements). We use food as the starting point in this chapter, while the second approach will be covered in the next.

The tables that follow echo the groundbreaking charts in our book *Culinary Artistry*, which presented the opinions of top culinary minds on the subject of "what goes with what." Here, we've used the same approach: We traveled North America, spending thousands of hours interviewing the world's foremost sommeliers and other beverage experts on their most recommended food and drink pairings, and scouring their memories along with their menus, Web sites, and/or cookbooks for pairing insights. Then, we compiled their advice into the comprehensive, easy-to-use listings that follow.

The rest of this chapter comprises an alphabetical list of foods — from aïoli to zucchini blossoms — as well as of cuisines (from Asian to Vietnamese), courses (from appetizers to desserts), and even occasions (from a summer picnic to Thanksgiving dinner). We include countless specific dishes, helping you distinguish between a choice for salmon when it's say, with a citrus sauce instead of a red wine sauce. There are also headings for different spices, herbs, sauces, and other flavorings. Now, you'll be able to find the right beverage to accompany any one of almost a dozen kinds of chile peppers, and to discover which wines best complement Domino's pizza and Popeye's fried chicken.

A few tips to help you get started: Pay attention to the specific caveats after many of the recommendations, which will help guide you to the ultimate, not just OK, choice (e.g., in some cases, a less sweet Riesling may work fine with an apple tart, while a sweeter one would be *divine*). Also, some listings have notes at the end of beverages to AVOID, which will help you steer clear of choosing a drink that would bring out the worst, instead of the best, in your meal. Dishes that are based around a meat protein, such as fried chicken or beef stew, are listed under that protein — except for fish which, because of the great variety of flavors and textures, are listed separately (i.e., salmon, sole). Other general headings range from pastas to sandwiches to soups.

Finally, we've devised a basic ranking system to let you know which pairings are truly stellar. Those beverages that appear in **BOLD CAPS** with an asterisk (*) are ethereal, time-honored classics; these "marriages made in heaven" comprise the top 1 or 2 percent of pairings. Next, we have very highly recommended pairings in **BOLD CAPS**. **Bold,** noncapitalized listings are frequently recommended pairings; and plain text listings are recommended pairings. But remember: even when just a single top-notch sommelier recommends a wine with a certain dish, it's very high praise indeed.

Armed with the expert information that follows, you'll learn how to better show off that recipe for your mom's meat loaf, or better match your favorite Chinese take-out meal, by pairing it with the best choice of beverage. From here on out, you have some of America's top sommeliers at your disposal to provide their personal recommendations as to what to drink.

MATCHING BEVERAGES *to* FOODS

```
KEY: Beverages mentioned in regular type are pairings suggested by one or more experts.

Those in **bold** were frequently recommended by a number of experts.

Those in **BOLD CAPS** were very highly recommended.

Those in *BOLD CAPS** with an asterisk (*) are "Holy Grail" classic pairings that all
gourmands will want to experience once (or more!) in their lifetimes.
```

ACIDIC (OR TART) FOODS OR DISHES
(E.G., GOAT CHEESE, TOMATOES)

ACIDIC WINE (E.G., ACIDIC WHITES: PINOT GRIGIO/PINOT GRIS, SAUVIGNON BLANC; ACIDIC REDS: PINOT NOIR, YOUNG ZINFANDEL; SEE ALSO CHAPTER 6, PAGE 200)

Acid likes acid! Acidic foods will help heighten the fruit in wine.

— MADELINE TRIFFON, MS, director of wine, Matt Prentice Restaurant Group (Detroit)

ADVENTURE

any wine you've never tasted before! (E.G., HAVE YOU TRIED GRÜNER VELTLINER? SAVENNIERES? SPARKLING SHIRAZ?)

AFTER DINNER

liqueurs, esp. nut-flavored (e.g., with almonds [amaretto], hazelnuts [Frangelico], walnuts [Nocello])

spirits (e.g., Armagnac, brandy, Calvados, Cognac, Madeira, port, sherry)

Brandy cocktails are excellent after dinner — especially a Sidecar: Cognac, Cointreau, fresh lemon, and our signature touch of fresh orange or, better yet, tangerine. Nut liqueurs are not to be missed.

— RYAN MAGARIAN, mixologist, Kathy Casey Food Studios (Seattle)

AFTERNOON

coffee and coffee drinks (e.g., cappuccino, latte)

tea, esp. green or herbal

tisane, fruit

AÏOLI

Albarino

Grüner Veltliner

ROSÉ, DRY

Savennieres

Soave

Verdelho

ALMONDS (ESP. ROASTED)

IN GENERAL

beer

Chablis

Chardonnay

Côte-Rôtie, esp. with smoked almonds

fruit juices, esp. apple, apricot, or strawberry, and esp. sparkling (e.g., Fizzy Lizzy)

Madeira, Bual or Malmsey

Moscatel

Pinot Noir, esp. in Asian dishes

port, vintage or tawny

Prosecco

Sauternes

Sauvignon Blanc

*SHERRY, ESP. FINO OR MANZANILLA

DESSERTS

Barsac

Champagne, esp. rosé

ice wine

Late Harvest Riesling

Madeira

Muscat

port

Sauternes

sherry, sweet (e.g., cream or oloroso)

Tokaji

Vin Santo

ANCHOVIES

Frascati

Greco di Tufo

lemon-based beverages (e.g., sparkling lemon juice)

Muscadet

Orvieto

red wine, fruity

Riesling

I am an anchovy freak! With a few fillets of artisanal anchovies, a handful of Marcona almonds, and some really cold fino sherry, I am in heaven for hours. Just take little tastes over and over and experience the waves of flavors. Indeed, an anchovy will marry to a dry middle-aged goat cheese. This is a great combination, and most people haven't had it.

— STEVEN JENKINS, *cheesemonger, Fairway Market (NYC)*

ROSÉ, ESP. DRY (e.g., Bandol) AND/OR SPANISH ROSADO
Sauvignon Blanc
SHERRY, ESP. FINO OR MANZANILLA
Trebbiano
Txakoli
Verdicchio
Vernaccia

ANISE (SEE ALSO FENNEL)
Pinot Noir
Viognier

ANTIPASTO (ITALIAN HORS D'OEUVRES)
beer, esp. lager or pilsner
Chianti
Dolcetto d'Alba
Frascati
Greco di Tufo
Montepulciano
Orvieto
Pinot Grigio
rosé, dry
Soave
Trebbiano
Valpolicella
Verdicchio
Vernaccia

APERITIF (PRE-MEAL DRINKS, ESP. WITH CANAPÉS)
Albarino
Arneis
beer, esp. fruity and/or wheat
CHAMPAGNE, ESP. DRY (e.g., Blanc de Blancs or Brut)

Chenin Blanc
Condrieu
Dolcetto
Lillet
Pinot Blanc, Alsatian
Pinot Grigio / Pinot Gris
RIESLING, ESP. GERMAN
Sauvignon Blanc
SHERRY, ESP. FINO OR MANZANILLA
sparkling wine, esp. dry (e.g., Asti, Cava, Prosecco)
Sylvaner, Alsatian
vermouth
Vouvray, dry

APPETIZERS (SEE APERITIF)

APPLES

IN GENERAL
Calvados
Chardonnay
Chenin Blanc
cider, esp. dry or hard
cocktails, esp. made with applejack, brandy, Cognac, Cointreau, Grand Marnier, Kirsch, Madeira, rum
eau-de-vie, apple
Gewürztraminer
ginger ale
lemon-based drinks (e.g., lemonade, sparkling lemon juice)
Pinot Gris
red wine
RIESLING, ESP. GERMAN (OFF-DRY TO SWEET)
rum

Sauvignon Blanc
sparkling wine
tea, Darjeeling or Ali Shan Oolong
vermouth
Viognier

DESSERTS
Bonnezeaux, esp. with tarte Tatin
Calvados
Chenin Blanc, sweet
cider, sweet, esp. with tarte Tatin
coffee, esp. with milk (e.g., café au lait, caffe latte), and esp. with apple pie
Gewürztraminer
ice wine
Late Harvest white wine (e.g., Gewürztraminer, Riesling)
Madeira, esp. with Tarte Tatin
Moscato d' Asti
MUSCAT, ESP. WITH TARTE TATIN
Muscat de Beaumes-de-Venise
Quarts de Chaume
RIESLING, ESP. GERMAN (FROM OFF-DRY TO VERY SWEET)
RIESLING, LATE HARVEST
SAUTERNES
Sćmillon, Late Harvest
sherry, esp. oloroso
sparkling wine, esp. demi-sec
Tokaji, Hungarian
Vin Santo, esp. with nutty desserts
Vouvray, sweet

With a simple apple dessert like apple pie, Sauternes is a soft and sweet accompaniment. But if you serve that same apple pie with caramel sauce, it makes the wine taste flat.
— MADELINE TRIFFON, MS, director of wine, Matt Prentice Restaurant Group (Detroit)

APRICOTS

IN GENERAL
Chenin Blanc, esp. Loire
cocktails, esp. made with brandy, Cognac, Cointreau, Grand Marnier, Kirsch
Condrieu
fruit-based (esp. lemon or raspberry) drinks (e.g., Fizzy Lizzy)
ginger ale
Riesling, German, esp. Auslese or Late Harvest
Verduzzo, Italian
Viognier

DESSERTS
apricot ale
ice wine
Madeira
Moscato d'Asti
Muscat de Beaumes-de-Venise
Muscat, esp. orange
Muscatel
port, tawny
Riesling, Late Harvest
Sauternes
Semillon, sweet

tea, Bai Hao oolong
Tokaji, sweet Hungarian

ARTICHOKES
Arneis
Brouilly, esp. with artichoke hearts
Chablis
Champagne, esp. Blanc de Blancs or brut (i.e., dry), and esp. with marinated artichokes
Chardonnay, esp. no oak, and esp. with artichokes with hollandaise
Chenin Blanc, California
dry wine
Frascati, esp. with fried artichokes
Greco di Tufo
Grüner Veltliner
higher-acid wine
lemon-based drinks (e.g., lemonade, sparkling water with lemon, etc.)
Mâcon, white
Muscadet
Orvieto
Pinot Gris, esp. Alsatian
Pouilly-Fumé

Everyone says artichokes don't work with wine because there is the chemical in them that makes everything else taste sweeter. If that is the case, then just expect what you are drinking to have its balance shifted. If you have a wine that is so dry and hard to drink on its own, with artichokes it will taste better and come into a nice range.
— DAVID ROSENGARTEN, editor in chief, DavidRosengarten.com

There are ways of helping a dish marry well with wine. I was at Alain Chapel and the restaurant served artichoke hearts with veal and sweetbreads. We were drinking "fancy" wine, and I thought, "This is going to be a huge faux pas." However, they cooked the artichoke hearts in jasmine tea, which made them less stemmy-tasting. If you are going to serve artichoke hearts, manzanilla or fino sherry is the magical pairing. That is a great party right there: Get a few people together cook and stuff some artichokes any way you want, and serve a fresh chilled manzanilla. It will be a great way to start your dinner!
— TIM KOPEC, wine director, Veritas (NYC)

Riesling, esp. Alsatian

Rioja, white

ROSÉ, ESP. DRY FRENCH (e.g., Bandol or Tavel) OR ITALIAN

Sancerre

SAUVIGNON BLANC, DRY, ESP. NEW ZEALAND

Sémillon, dry

sherry, fino or manzanilla, esp. with artichoke hearts

Soave

Verdicchio, esp. with lemon vinaigrette

Vermentino, esp. with Parmesan cheese

Vernaccia

Vinho Verde, esp. with fried artichokes

Viognier

white wine, dry and light-bodied

AVOID

red wine, esp. high in tannin

sweet wine (esp. since artichokes bring out sweetness)

Artichokes make your wine taste a little sweeter. So if you paired Riesling Kabinett with it, it would taste more like a Spätlese.

— BERNARD SUN, beverage director, Jean-Georges Management (NYC)

ARUGULA

Arneis, Italian

Chablis

Chardonnay

lemon-based drinks (e.g., lemonade, sparkling water with lemon, etc.)

Pinot Blanc

Sauvignon Blanc

ASIAN (ESP. PACIFIC RIM) CUISINE

beer, esp. a light ale, lager, or pilsner

Champagne, including rosé

Chardonnay, dry to semidry

Chenin Blanc, esp. with citrus-flavored dishes

cocktails, sweet and/or made with light white spirits (e.g., gin, vodka)

Côtes du Rhône

GEWÜRZTRAMINER

Muscadet, esp. with spicier dishes

Nero d'Avola, Italian

Pinot Blanc, esp. with spicier dishes

Pinot Grigio/Pinot Gris (no oak), esp. with citrus-flavored dishes

Pinot Noir

plum wine, at the end of the meal

rice wine (e.g., Japanese sake, Chinese Shaoxing, etc.)

Riesling, Alsatian or Australian

RIESLING, GERMAN (from Kabinett to Spätlese in sweetness), ESP. WITH SPICIER DISHES

rosé

Sauvignon Blanc, dry to semidry, and/or New Zealand

sparkling wine, including rosé

Syrah/Shiraz, esp. spicy

TEA

Tokay

Viognier

Vouvray, esp. with citrus-flavored dishes

water

Zinfandel, esp. with spicier dishes

AVOID

big, bold wine

Chardonnay, oaky

Asian foods are so complex in flavor (sweet, spicy, sour, bitter, salty) that it is always best to pair them with green tea, which should be drunk at the end of the meal to aid digestion. This practice is traditional in most Asian cultures. That said, most people like beer or a glass of wine. If choosing wine, a light to medium-bodied white wine that is dry to semidry is best, such as dry to semidry Sauvignon Blanc, Gewürztraminer, Tokay, and Chardonnay. I have even tried Pinot Gris and Viognier, which also do well. Rice alcohol comes in several forms: distilled hard spirits (some are over 100 proof and should be used for cooking only, as in drunken shrimp), liqueurs, or wine. Generally I like hard spirits at the end of a meal, if at all, to help digestion and cleanse the palate. Rice wine can be had throughout the meal. Liqueurs that are sweet are not my favorite. Instead, at the end of the meal I would rather have plum wine, which has a bold, fruity note without the intense alcohol content. Beer seems to be a favorite with many people when it comes to Asian foods. I would say this: Choose a fairly light blond beer (lager, pilsner, or ale). Most people tend to go with the popular Sapporo, 33, Saigon, Taj Mahal, Bintang, OB, Kingfisher, and Singha, for example. Those do the trick.

— CORINNE TRANG, author, *Essentials of Asian Cooking*

Asian cuisine pairs well with light white spirits (i.e., gin, vodka) cocktails.

— RYAN MAGARIAN, mixologist, Kathy Casey Food Studios (Seattle)

Vong has the funnest wine list: Because the food is South Asian with Thai, Vietnamese, and Chinese influences, it lends itself to a lot of wines. The list features a lot of Alsatian and [German] Kabinett Riesling, Gewürztraminer, and other wine people can't pronounce that are all great food wines. We sell some reds, because there is a portion of the population that drinks red wine no matter what. Red wines that work with the food are Pinot Noir, spicy Syrah, and Nero d'Alba from Sicily. At 66, our Chinese restaurant, wine is traditionally a tough match, so we offer lots of aromatic whites.
— BERNARD SUN, beverage director, Jean-Georges Management (NYC)

With Asian dishes, you have to look at their sweet and sour or tangy factor. In Vietnamese, Chinese, or Thai dishes, you are looking to balance between the sweetness and the acid — not necessarily the heat. You are working with soy or fish sauce and chili paste, and all the flavors are mixed together. That is why people go with Kabinett or Spätlese Riesling; it is a less complex wine that is balanced with fruit and acid.
— ALPANA SINGH, MS, Everest (Chicago)

ASPARAGUS

IN GENERAL
Beaujolais, esp. with grilled asparagus
beer, esp. wheat
Bordeaux, white, dry
Burdundy, white, esp. when served with butter or hollandaise
CHABLIS, ESP. WHEN SERVED WITH BUTTER OR HOLLANDAISE
Champagne
CHARDONNAY, ESP. UNOAKED AND ESP. WHEN SERVED WITH BUTTER OR HOLLANDAISE
Chenin Blanc, esp. Loire Valley
Fumé Blanc
Gewürztraminer
Graves, white
GRÜNER VELTLINER
lemon-based drinks (e.g., lemonade, sparkling water with lemon, etc.)
Muscadet

MUSCAT, DRY, ESP. ALSATIAN
Pinot Blanc, esp. with butter or hollandaise
Pinot Grigio / Pinot Gris
POUILLY-FUMÉ, ESP. WHEN SERVED CHILLED
Prosecco
RIESLING, ALSATIAN AND/OR DRY, ESP. WHEN SERVED CHILLED AND/OR WITH LEMON BUTTER
Riesling, German, esp. dry
rosé, esp. Old World, and esp. with grilled asparagus and/or with vinaigrette
sake
Sancerre
*****SAUVIGNON BLANC, DRY, ESP. NEW ZEALAND**
Savennieres, esp. when asparagus is served hot
Sémillon
Soave
sparkling wine
Verdicchio
Vermentino

Vouvray
white wine, off-dry

WHITE
Champagne
Muscat
Pinot Bianco
Riesling, Alsatian Grand Cru

AVOID
red wine, esp. high in tannin
white-wine, oaked

TIP: You can make asparagus or artichokes more amenable to pairing with wine by serving them with a cheese sauce.

Very thin, fingerlike asparagus spears don't have that chemical component that clashes with wine that the thicker-ones have. If you're going to serve asparagus with Champagne, make sure you select pencil-thin asparagus.
— LISANE LAPOINTE, ambassador, Dom Pérignon

Asparagus, which is almost impossible to match in terms of food, would work with New Zealand Sauvignon Blanc especially well, because of the acid. Most of the time I would ask the chef to blanch his asparagus a little more to cut the aggressiveness of the flavor.
— BERNARD SUN, beverage director, Jean-Georges Management (NYC)

I have served asparagus often with a Chablis Premier Cru Montee de Tonnerre 1984 and been ravished by the marriage.
— RICHARD OLNEY

AUTUMN
apple cider
Bordeaux, red
Burgundy, red
Cabernet Sauvignon
Champagne
Hermitage
red wine, esp. fuller-bodied
Rhône red wine
Rioja
Sauternes and other sweet dessert
   wine
tea, esp. maple

*Every season, we change the tea
selection and food pairings.
Last fall, we offered a butternut
squash cranberry compote with
a warm chocolate torte and
paired it with maple tea.*
— MICHAEL OBNOWLENNY,
   Canada's first tea sommelier

AVOCADOS (SEE ALSO
GUACAMOLE)
Beaujolais
Champagne, esp. brut
CHABLIS
**Chardonnay, esp.
   California/New World**
Gewürztraminer
grapefruit juice, sparkling (e.g.,
   Fizzy Lizzy)
Grüner Veltliner
Lambrusco
lime-based drinks (e.g., limeade,
   sparkling water with lime, etc.)
Pinot Blanc
Pinot Gris
rosé, esp. dry
Sancerre
**SAUVIGNON BLANC, ESP.
   NEW ZEALAND**
tomato-based drinks (e.g., Bloody
   Mary, Virgin Mary)
Torrontés, Argentinian

*Once I opened a bottle of
Ravenau Chablis at home. I
happened to have a grapefruit
and avocado and pumpkin seeds
on hand, and ended up making
a salad with those things. I just
threw it together, and wasn't
thinking about pairing. When I
tasted it with the Chablis, I
found it was really, really good
together. Those components —
the fattiness of the avocado, the
sharp citrus of grapefruit —
together with the Chablis just
really worked well. It's fun
when that happens.*
— TRACI DES JARDINS, chef,
   Jardiniere (San Francisco)

BABA GANOUSH (SEE
EGGPLANT)

BACON
Beaujolais
**beer, esp. smoked or stout with
   heartier dishes**
Burgundy, red
Chablis
**Chardonnay, dry and/or
   unoaked, esp. with a BLT
   sandwich**
Grenache
Malbec
Merlot
Lambrusco
Pinot Gris, Alsatian
**PINOT NOIR, ESP.
   CALIFORNIA, OREGON,
   OR OTHER NEW WORLD**
Riesling, esp. Spätlese
Rioja
rosé
sherry, oloroso
Shiraz

sparkling wine
Syrah
Tempranillo (no oak)
Zinfandel

*With bacon, I like New World
Pinot Noir, which tends to be
more bold and oaky with more
of those bacony flavors.*
— DANIEL JOHNNES,
   beverage director, Daniel (NYC)

BAGEL, WITH
SMOKED SALMON
AND CREAM CHEESE
Champagne
citrus spritzer (e.g., grapefruit or
   orange juice)
sparkling wine

*As I usually eat bagels, cream
cheese, and lox for breakfast —
or as a first meal of the day at
any rate — I usually drink coffee (milk, no sugar).
   Salty as real lox is, and
because I would be eating it in
the morning, I might also have
a glass of orange or grapefruit
juice, which helps cut through
the salt and fat of the cream
cheese. My sister swears by a
Mimosa, and there are times I'd
love a screwdriver. (With
smoked salmon alone, I'd think
of Champagne or Prosecco,
although chilled vodka is
great.)
   I have recently gotten into
the habit of making grapefruit
or orange juice spritzers (to cut
the calories of the juice, and
add some flavor to my seltzer).*

One of those would be terrific with bagels, lox, and cream cheese.

— ARTHUR SCHWARTZ, author, *New York City Food*

BAGNA CAUDA
(ITALIAN GARLIC AÏOLI WITH VEGETABLES)
Barbera
Dolcetto
Gavi
Sauvignon Blanc

BAKED ALASKA
Asti
cocktail, sweet
sparkling wine, sweet

A dessert like Baked Alaska is a bit easier than others to select a cocktail to accompany: all you have to do is make sure it is slightly sweet, but not such that it would compete.

— ROBERT HESS, founder, DrinkBoy.com

SOUTHERN BEAUTY

HERE IS ROBERT HESS'S RECIPE FOR A COCKTAIL TO ACCOMPANY BAKED ALASKA

1 1/4 ounces brandy

1 1/4 ounces Southern Comfort

Stir with ice. Strain into a cocktail glass. Garnish with lightly beaten cream, spooned onto the top as a layer.

BAKLAVA
Muscat, esp. Beaumes-de-Venise

Riesling, sweet
Sauternes
tea
Tokaji, Hungarian

BANANAS (INCLUDING DESSERTS)
Australian stickies
Banyuls
beer, esp. chocolate or wheat
brandy
Champagne
cocktails, esp. made with Armagnac, brandy, Calvados, Cognac, Kirsch, or rum
coconut-based drinks
Gewürztraminer
Late Harvest wine, esp. Riesling
Madeira, esp. Malmsey
Muscat or Muscat de Beaumes-de-Venise
port, esp. tawny
Quarts de Chaume
rosé
rum
Sauternes
sherry, esp. PX
sparkling wine, esp. rosé

Our banana cheese pie goes beautifully with Quarts de Chaume.

— ERIC RENAUD, sommelier, Bern's Steak House (Tampa)

BARBECUE (BARBECUED MEATS WITH SMOKY AND/OR SWEET SAUCE)

IN GENERAL
ale, very hoppy
Barbera, esp. with vinegar-based sauce
Beaujolais, esp. cru
BEER, ESP. *SMOKED, AMBER, LAGER, OR WHEAT

Cabernet Sauvignon, esp. Chilean or Napa, and esp. with beef brisket
Champagne rosé
cherry cola (e.g., Cherry Coke, Dr. Pepper)
Chianti
cocktail with brown spirit (e.g., **Bourbon,** brandy, aged rum, whiskey), esp. citrus- or iced tea–based
cola (e.g., Coca-Cola)
Côtes du Rhône
cream soda
Gewürztraminer
Grenache
ICED TEA
lemonade, with or without Bourbon or brandy and/or a few dashes of Angostura bitters
Malbec
Merlot, esp. California or South American
mint julep
oaked wine
pale ale
Petite Sirah
Pinotage, South African
Pinot Noir
Rhône red wine, esp. with dry-rubbed barbecue
Rioja
rosé/Rosado, dry
SHIRAZ, AUSTRALIAN
Syrah
Valpolicella, esp. with beef
***ZINFANDEL, CALIFORNIA, ESP. WITH BEEF AND/OR SPARERIBS**
Zinfandel, white

RIBS
Barbera
beer, esp. lager or wheat
Cabernet Franc
Cabernet Sauvignon
Châteauneuf-du-Pape
cocktail with brown spirit

Côtes du Rhône Villages

Pinot Noir

Rhône red wine, esp. young

rosé / Rosado, Spanish

SHIRAZ, ESP. YOUNG

Syrah

tannic wine

ZINFANDEL, CALIFORNIA, ESP. YOUNG

Zinfandel, white

When you barbecue, you often have many different dishes — from chicken to beef. Also, barbecuing often happens in summer outside when it is hot, so be aware that Shiraz and Zinfandel can be a little heavy at this time of year. You need a wine that will go with a lot of different foods, so I like country wines — and particularly rosé, because it goes with everything.

— JEAN-LUC LE DÛ,
Le Dû's Wines (NYC)

With hot, sweet foods — like barbecue and certain Asian dishes — I like sweet, low-alcohol wines, specially with bubbles.

— MADELINE TRIFFON, MS,
director of wine, Matt Prentice
Restaurant Group (Detroit)

With barbecue, you definitely want a brown spirit (i.e., Bourbon, brandy, aged rum)–based citrus cocktail. A Whiskey Daisy (whiskey, orange curaçao, fresh lemon, and soda over crushed ice) or a classic Mint Julep both work — as would a simple Bourbon or brandy lemonade with a few dashes of Angostura bitters. The brown spirit and the richness of the barbecue complement each other, while the acid cleanses and refreshes the palate.

— RYAN MAGARIAN,
mixologist, Kathy Casey Food
Studios (Seattle)

Tannin goes with barbecue, whether in the form of iced tea or red wine . . . Wine is essentially barbecue sauce with alcohol in it.

— DANNY MEYER, leading a
"Wine for Swine" seminar
at Blue Smoke (NYC)

BARBECUE SAUCE

IN GENERAL

Cabernet Sauvignon

Merlot

Riesling, German, esp. Spätlese

Shiraz, esp. fruity

slightly sweet wine

Zinfandel, esp. fruity

WITH CHICKEN

Chenin Blanc

Zinfandel, esp. fruity

WITH FISH

Sauvignon Blanc, esp. New World

Sémillon

BASIL (SEE ALSO PESTO)

Cabernet Sauvignon

Champagne, rosé

Chardonnay (no oak)

Châteauneuf-du-Pape, white

Chianti

Gavi

Merlot

Nebbiolo

Orvicto

Pinot Grigio

rosé

SANGLOVESE, ESP. WITH HEARTIER DISHES

SAUVIGNON BLANC

Shiraz / Syrah

Soave

Zinfandel, red and white

BASS (SEE ALSO STRIPED BASS AND OTHER MILD FISH, E.G., FLOUNDER, SEA BASS, SOLE)

Barbera d'Alba, esp. with grilled bass

Burgundy, white, esp. with baked or broiled bass and/or in a white wine sauce

Chablis

Champagne

Chardonnay (no oak), esp. with grilled bass

Muscadet

Pinot Bianco

Pouilly-Fumé

Pouilly-Fuissé, esp. with grilled bass

Riesling

Sancerre

Sauvignon Blanc

Soave

BAY LEAF

Barbera

Cabernet Sauvignon

Chianti

Pinotage

Sangiovese

Sauvignon Blanc

Zinfandel

BEANS

BAKED

beer

Cabernet Franc

Grenache

Nebbiolo

Primitivo

Shiraz

Zinfandel

BLACK

beer

cocktails, esp. made with Madeira

orange juice, sparkling (e.g., Fizzy Lizzy)

Rhône red wine

RED (TYPICALLY SERVED WITH RICE)

Chianti

Shiraz

Zinfandel

WHITE

Burgundy, white

Chablis

red wine

sparkling wine

BEANS, GREEN (SEE ALSO HARICOT VERTS)

Riesling

Sancerre

Sauvignon Blanc, esp. California

BEEF (SEE ALSO HAMBURGERS, STEAK)

IN GENERAL

Barbaresco

Barolo

beer, esp. dry porter or pale ale

Bordeaux, red

Brunello

Burgundy, red

CABERNET SAUVIGNON

Châteauneuf-du-Pape

Chianti

cocktails, esp. made with Madeira

Merlot, California

Pinot Noir

Rhône red wine

Rioja

sherry, oloroso

SHIRAZ/SYRAH

tea, esp. black and oolong

Zinfandel

BARBECUED BRISKET

Chianti

Shiraz

Zinfandel

BARBECUED RIBS (SEE BARBECUE)

BEEF BOURGUIGNON

Barolo

Beaujolais

beer, esp. Belgian ale

Bordeaux, red

***BURGUNDY, RED**

Cabernet Sauvignon

Châteauneuf-du-Pape

Côtes du Rhône, esp. young

Dolcetto

PINOT NOIR

Rioja

Shiraz/Syrah

Zinfandel

BOILED

Beaujolais

BORDEAUX WINE SAUCE

Bordeaux, red (e.g., Margaux or Médoc)

BRAISED

Aglianico

Barbaresco

Barbera

BAROLO

Beaujolais

beer, Chimay

Burgundy, red

Chianti, esp. Classico

CÔTES DU RHÔNE

Rhône red wine

rosé

Zinfandel

BRAISED IN BEER

beer

CARNE ASADA

Malbec

CARPACCIO

Arneis

Barbaresco

Barbera

Barolo

Champagne, rosé

Pinot Noir

rosé, esp. dry

Sangiovese

CASSEROLE

Cabernet Sauvignon

Syrah / Shiraz

Zinfandel

Beef tacos are easy with wine. You can go dry or fruity. I like a Syrah from Argentina. — JILL GUBESCH, sommelier, Frontera Grill and Topolobampo (Chicago)

Shabu Shabu Beef with Sesame Sauce, paired with High Mountain oolong tea. — KAI ANDERSEN, Kai Restaurant (NYC)

Beef Bourguignonne is simmered so long, it can overwhelm a red Burgundy. You really need something with a little more body, like a Châteauneuf-du-Pape. — JEAN-LUC LE DÛ, Le Dû's Wines (NYC)

The fat and protein in beef softens tannic wines, like a Brunello or Cabernet Sauvignon. — MADELINE TRIFFON, MS, director of wine, Matt Prentice Restaurant Group (Detroit)

With beef dishes, Cabernet Sauvignons and Bordeaux blends are generally good choices. We serve a dish with beef tenderloin which we pan-sear and serve with a gratin of Peruvian potatoes, chili-infused Hollandaise sauce, spicy red-wine essence, that cries out for a big California Cabernet. Something old from Heitz or Phelps or Beringer or even the newer cult wines from Maya, Harlan Estates, or Araujo would be terrific. For the drier Cabernets or the sophisticated wines from Mondavi or blends like Dominus, or the great Bordeaux, beef prepared in a little plainer style is excellent. — JANOS WILDER, chef-owner, Restaurant Janos (Tucson)

COLD
Beaujolais
Cabernet Sauvignon
Champagne
Merlot
rosé

CORNED (SEE CORNED BEEF)

WITH GINGER
Brunello
Burgundy, red

WITH GRAVY
beer

GRILLED (ASIAN-STYLE)
sake
Shiraz

POT ROAST
Cabernet Sauvignon
Merlot, esp. Chilean
Zinfandel

PRIME RIB
Burgundy, red, esp. young
Cabernet Sauvignon
Chianti Classico Riserva
Gamay
Merlot
Pinot Noir
Shiraz
Zinfandel

RIB ROAST
Bordeaux, red
Burgundy, red
Cabernet Sauvignon, esp. Napa
Malbec

Merlot
Pinot Noir, esp. California or Oregon

ROAST
ale, British and/or pale
Barbaresco
Barbera
Barolo
BORDEAUX, RED
Burgundy, red
Cabernet Sauvignon, California
Châteauneuf-du-Pape
Malbec
Merlot
PINOT NOIR
Priorato
Ribera del Duero
Rioja
Shiraz / Syrah
Taurasi
Zinfandel

SHORT RIBS
Cabernet Sauvignon
Petite Sirah
Ribera del Duero
Rioja
Shiraz / Syrah
ZINFANDEL

Certified Angus Beef Short Ribs with Shiraz Pan Reduction, with Clos de los Siete (Malbec, Merlot, Cabernet, Syrah) — MADELINE TRIFFON, MS, director of wine, Matt Prentice Restaurant Group (Detroit)

STEAK (SEE STEAK)

STEWED (E.G., BEEF BOURGUIGNON)
ale or beer
Barolo
Bordeaux, red
Cabernet Sauvignon, esp. French
Châteauneuf-du-Pape
Côtes du Rhône, red
Crozes-Hermitage
Malbec
Nebbiolo

Pinot Noir
Rhône red wine
Rioja
SHIRAZ/SYRAH
Zinfandel

STIR-FRIED (ASIAN-STYLE)
Cabernet Sauvignon
Merlot, fruity, esp. with soy sauce
Pinot Noir, California or Oregon, esp. with orange
Syrah/Shiraz, esp. with teriyaki-style beef
Zinfandel, fruity, esp. with soy sauce

STROGANOFF
Barbera
Bordeaux, red
Brunello
Cabernet Sauvignon
Côtes du Rhône
Hermitage
Merlot
Rhône red wine
Zinfandel, lighter-bodied

TACOS
agua fresca
Cabernet Sauvignon
Merlot
Syrah, esp. Argentinian or French
Tempranillo, Spanish

TARTARE (SEE STEAK TARTARE)

TENDERLOIN, ROASTED
Burgundy, red
India pale ale
Merlot

WELLINGTON
Bordeaux, red
Burgundy, red
Pinot Noir
Rioja

BEETS
Cabernet Sauvignon
Gewürztraminer

lemon-based drinks (e.g., lemon-ade, sparkling water with lemon, etc.)
Merlot
Pinot Gris, Alsatian
Pinot Noir, esp. fruity
RIESLING, ESP. GERMAN, ESP. WITH ROASTED BEETS
rosé
Sancerre
Sauvignon Blanc, esp. New Zealand

Roasted beets and Riesling are great together.
— ALAN MURRAY, MS, wine director, Masa's (San Francisco)

BÉARNAISE (SEE SAUCE, BÉARNAISE)

BERRIES

IN GENERAL
Asti
Beaujolais
Brachetto d'Acqui
Cabernet Franc
Cabernet Sauvignon
Cahors
Champagne, rosé
cocktails, esp. made with Framboise
Muscat, esp. off-dry to sweet
Pinot Noir
port
Riesling, Late Harvest
Riesling, off-dry to sweet
rosé
sparkling wine, from dry to sweet
Zinfandel, light-bodied

DESSERTS
ice wine
Late Harvest wines, esp. Riesling
Muscat, esp. black
port, ruby or vintage
Vouvray, sweet

BIRYANI (INDIAN RICE-BASED DISH)
Pinot Noir, fruity, oaked, esp. from Santa Barbara or New Zealand
white wine, esp. with saffron-flavored rice

With biryani, I'd want Pinot Noir — particularly a fruity one with more oak to it, like a Russian River style. Also, a Pinot Noir from New Zealand or Santa Barbara has baking spice flavors or spice notes like cumin and coriander notes to it.
— ALPANA SINGH, MS, Everest (Chicago)

BISCOTTI
Asti
espresso
ice wine
Late Harvest white wine
Marsala
Muscat, esp. orange
port, tawny, esp. with nutty biscotti
Rhône wine, red
sherry, sweet (e.g., cream or PX)
***VIN SANTO**
Zinfandel

BISTECCA ALLA FIORENTINA
(FLORENTINE BEEFSTEAK)
Brunello di Montalcino
Chianti
Rosso di Montalcino

BITTER FOODS AND DISHES (ANYTHING FROM ARUGULA TO GRILLED FOODS)
Cabernet Sauvignon
Pinot Noir

Sauvignon Blanc
wine with moderate tannin

AVOID
overly tannic wines

BLACKBERRIES
Brachetto
coffee, esp. Kenyan
Maury
Muscat de Beaumes-de-Venise
MUSCAT, BLACK
port, esp. ruby
**Riesling, German, esp. off-dry to
sweet**
Riesling, Late Harvest
tea, Bai Hao oolong

BLINI, WITH CAVIAR OR SMOKED SALMON (SEE ALSO CAVIAR AND SMOKED SALMON)
Champagne, esp. Blanc de Blancs
vodka

BLT (SEE SANDWICHES, BLT)

BLUEBERRIES
(INCLUDING DESSERTS)
Asti
Brachetto
Champagne
cocktails, esp. made with
    Bourbon, Cognac, Cointreau,
    Grand Marnier
coffee, esp. Ethiopian Harrar
ice wine
Late Harvest wine
lemon- or lime-based drinks (e.g.,
    lemonade, sparkling water with
    lime, etc.)
**Muscat, off-dry to sweet (e.g.,
    Beaumes-de-Venise, orange)**
peach-based drinks (e.g.,
    sparkling peach juice)
port
RIESLING, LATE HARVEST

Riesling, off-dry to sweet
sparkling wine, sweet
Vouvray, sweet

*People drink Ethiopian coffee
for its intense flavor of blueberries. I'd want to drink this coffee
with a plate of blueberry pancakes.*

— DUB HAY, senior vice
president, Starbucks

BLUEFISH
Bordeaux, white
Burgundy, white
**Chardonnay, esp. California
    and/or oaked**
Gewürztraminer
Hermitage, white
Italian white wine
**Sauvignon Blanc, California,
    esp. with grilled fish**
Volnay

BOAR, WILD (SEE ALSO RECOMMENDATIONS FOR GAME AND PORK)
Barbaresco
Barbera
Barolo
Cabernet Sauvignon
**CHIANTI CLASSICO, ESP.
    RISERVA**
Mourvèdre
Rhône red wine
Ribera del Duero
Rioja
SHIRAZ / SYRAH
Super Tuscan
Syrah
Zinfandel, California

AVOID
white wine

BOILED DISHES
light-bodied wine

BOUILLABAISSE (SEE SOUP, BOUILLABAISSE)

BRAISED DISHES (ESP. RED MEATS)
beer
Cabernet Sauvignon
Champagne, rosé
red wine, full-bodied
Shiraz / Syrah
Zinfandel

BRANDADE (MASHED POTATOES AND SALT COD)
Albarino
Chablis, cru
Pinot Grigio / Pinot Gris
rosé
Sancerre
Sauvignon Blanc
Verdicchio

BRATWURST (SEE SAUSAGE, BRATWURST)

BREAD
IN GENERAL
ale and beer
Chardonnay, buttery California

TOASTED, AS FOR BREAK-
FAST
tea, esp. oolong

*Sourdough bread and wine
don't work. We have a tasting
group that gets together to taste
all these old red wines, and
someone once brought sourdough bread. The sourness
changes the pH balance on your
palate, so your gauge is off and
low-acid wines taste flabby. In
fact, one guy in our group who's*

BREAD PUDDING
ice wine
Late Harvest wine (e.g., Chenin Blanc, Muscat, Riesling)
Madeira
Muscat, esp. orange
port
Riesling, esp. Late Harvest
Sauternes
sherry, esp. sweet
Tokaji
Vin Santo

BREAKFAST / BRUNCH
apple juice or sparkling apple cider, esp. with French toast or pancakes
Beaujolais
beer, wheat
Bloody Mary
Brachetto d'Acqui
Burgundy, red, with steak and eggs
Burgundy, white, with lobster omelet
Champagne
Champagne, rosé, esp. with French toast or pancakes
Chardonnay, California, creamy (no oak), with lobster omelet
Clamato (clam-tomato) juice, esp. with vegetable omelet
coffee, esp. before the food
fruit juice
grapefruit juice
iced tea
lemonade
mimosa-style cocktail made with Champagne mixed with lychee or pear juice, esp. with French toast or pancakes
Moscato d'Asti

The universal antidote to breakfast is sparkling Shiraz, which has low alcohol and a fair amount of acidity. I served it as one of a dozen different wines at an event where people went to the buffet and piled their plates. The number one wine that went with everything from Fruit Loops to pancakes with or without fruit was the sparkling Shiraz, followed by Brachetto d'Acqui and Moscato d'Asti.

— JOSHUA WESSON, wine director, Best Cellars

Coffee has far too much tannin for most of the dishes usually served at breakfast. So, the coffee comes first (i.e., before food).

Then, with pancakes and French toast, I usually like a nice glass of pear juice — or more correctly in my house, sparkling pear cider. With two kids, I'm frequently at IKEA and usually come home with a case of theirs; it's not too sweet and the sparkle offsets the richness of the usual accompaniments to these dishes. Apple cider would make a suitable substitute, though the softness of the pear is just about perfect.

Savory egg dishes need something drier. I like to have a bit of tomato juice, plain for plain eggs and V8 or Clamato for veggie omelets. Meat omelets get a bit of beef broth mixed into the tomato juice (Bloody Bull–style) for a little extra body.

"Brunch" is usually more of an event and the alcohol is almost always flowing, but the same principles apply. Coffee is never served with food. I usually serve French toast or pancakes first with a nice rosé Champagne or a mimosa made with pear nectar or lychee juice.

[With egg dishes], I like to serve wine — and almost always white. Eggs Benedict or a ham/sausage omelet gets a nice Alsatian Pinot Gris (e.g., the drier styles from Zind-Humbrecht or Josmeyer). Veggie omelets get a nice Sauvignon Blanc from the Loire Valley for grassier, more vegetal flavors, like Alphonse Mellot or Henri Bourgeois Sancerre. A lobster omelet gets a nice white Burgundy or suitably rich California Chardonnay. (For the latter, I prefer the creamy, spicy styles from Russian River and Criots Bâtard-Montrachet.)

Dishes with more spice like huevos rancheros *get something a bit sweeter, like a great German Riesling. (I highly recommend a Spätlese from the Pfalz for a fatter version, or one from J.J. Prum for more power).*

A red wine only hits the table if I've decided to make everyone take a long nap by setting out steak and eggs. Here, the juice of choice is a nice, meaty red Burgundy.

— SCOTT CALVERT, sommelier, the Inn at Little Washington (Virginia)

orange juice

pear juice or sparkling pear cider, esp. with French toast or pancakes

Pinot Gris, Alsatian, esp. with eggs Benedict or smoked meat (e.g., ham, sausage) omelet

Riesling, German, with Mexican-style eggs such as *huevos rancheros*

Sauvignon Blanc, esp. Loire Valley, and esp. with vegetable omelet

Shiraz, sparkling, esp. with French toast or pancakes with berries

sparkling wine

tea, esp. Assam, black, Ceylon, Darjeeling, Lapsang Souchong, smoked black, or Yunnan

tomato juice, esp. with eggs and omelets, or tomato juice with beef broth with meat omelet

vegetable juice (e.g., V8), esp. with vegetable omelet

BROCCOLI

Chardonnay, esp. New World

lemon-based drinks (e.g., lemonade, sparkling water with lemon, etc.)

Sauvignon Blanc

BROCCOLI RABE

Italian white wine, esp. Locorotondo

Riesling, off-dry

Sauvignon Blanc

AVOID

red wine

Locorotondo is an Italian white wine, and if you taste it on its own, it's a little hard to take. It's a heavy, old-style wine that's a little oily. With broccoli

rabe, however, it becomes a wonderful combination. I served this pairing to a food society. When its members tasted the wine, they looked at me like I was crazy. But after they tasted it with the broccoli rabe, I heard a big "WOW!"

— CHARLES SCICOLONE, wine director, I Trulli and Enoteca (NYC)

BROWNIES (SEE ALSO CHOCOLATE)

Banyuls

beer, stout, esp. imperial

Bourbon

coffee, esp. medium- to dark-roasted and/or Guatamalan Antigua

espresso-based beverages

Muscat

port

sherry, PX

BROWN SUGAR

Riesling, sweet

Sauternes

BRUNCH (SEE BREAKFAST/BRUNCH)

BRUSSELS SPROUTS

Sauvignon Blanc

BUFFALO CHICKEN WINGS (OFTEN SERVED WITH BLUE CHEESE DIP)

ale, highly hopped

BEER

Champagne, rosé

rosé, off-dry

Zinfandel

At the end of a long day, I like a beer. It is low-acid, which is why it goes so well with a lot of spicy food. In fact, that is why beer and spicy chicken wings go together: the hops, low acidity, and bubbles coat the tongue and fight off the heat.

— BERNARD SUN, beverage director, Jean-Georges Management (NYC)

BUTTER AND BUTTER SAUCE (E.G., BEURRE BLANC)

Burgundy, white

Champagne

CHARDONNAY, ESP. BUTTERY CALIFORNIA

Viognier

BUTTERSCOTCH (INCLUDING DESSERTS)

coffee, dark-roasted

CABBAGE AND CABBAGE-BASED DISHES (E.G., CHOUCROUTE)

IN GENERAL

beer, esp. light and/or wheat

Cabernet Franc

cocktails, esp. made with Madeira

Gewürztraminer, esp. Alsatian

Hermitage, red, esp. aged, and esp. with green cabbage

RIESLING, ESP. DRY

wine, esp. white

RED

apple-based drinks (e.g., sparkling apple juice)

Dolcetto

Merlot

red wine

CAESAR SALAD (SEE SALAD, CAESAR)

CAJUN CUISINE

beer, esp. lager, pilsner, or wheat
Chardonnay, esp. with spicy fish
Gewürztraminer, Alsatian
Riesling, off-dry
Sauvignon Blanc
Zinfandel, esp. with meats

CAKE (INCLUDING CUPCAKES)

IN GENERAL
Asti
Champagne, esp. extra dry (except with very sweet cake)
coffee
ice wine
Madeira (e.g., Bual or Malmsey)
Marsala
milk
Moscato d'Asti
Muscat, sweet
Muscatel
port, tawny
Riesling, German (esp. sweet)
Riesling, Late Harvest
Sauternes
sherry, cream
sparkling wine, esp. demi-sec
tea
Tokay
Vin Santo
Vouvray, sparkling

ALMOND
Coteaux du Layon
Moscato d'Asti
Vin Santo

ANGEL FOOD
Champagne
Madeira
port
Riesling, sweet
sparkling wine

CITRUS-FLAVORED
coffee, esp. light-roasted
Muscat
tea

COFFEE
coffee
ice wine
Muscat
tea, esp. black
Vin Santo

POUND
coffee, esp. light-roasted
Late Harvest white wine (e.g., Riesling)
Muscat, esp. orange
port
sherry, sweet (e.g., cream)
tea

SPICE
beer, esp. Belgian-style ale (e.g., Unibroue)
Muscat
port, tawny
Vin Santo

AVOID
wine and Champagnes less sweet than the cake

Having birthday cake or wedding cake with a brut Champagne toast is horrifying! If the dessert is sweeter than the wine, it makes the wine taste drier. My favorite all-purpose sweet wine is Moscato d'Asti.
— MADELINE TRIFFON, MS, director of wine, Matt Prentice Restaurant Group (Detroit)

CALAMARI (SEE SQUID)

Pair fried calamari with sweet-spicy Thai sauce with wheat beer. The sauce has heat, acidity, and sweetness, just like the beer. Pilsner would not work as well. If you wanted wine, you'd have Gewürztraminer — but the beer also has carbonation that cleanses the palate.
— GARRETT OLIVER, brewmaster, Brooklyn Brewery

CALZONE (SEE ALSO PIZZA)
Lambrusco
Syrah / Shiraz

CANAPÉS (SEE APERITIF)

CANNELLONI (SEE ALSO PASTA FOR SPECIFIC SAUCES)
Chianti
Dolcetto
Frascati
Montepulciano
Sangiovese

CANNOLI (ITALIAN RICOTTA CHEESE DESSERT)
coffee, esp. medium-roasted
Moscato d'Asti

CANTALOUPE (SEE ALSO MELON)
Asti
Banyuls
Champagne, dry
Chenin Blanc, sweet
Riesling, sweet

CAPERS
Beaujolais, high-acid
beer
Muscadet
Pinot Grigio / Pinot Gris, esp. dry
Pinot Noir, esp. from Russian River Valley

rosé, dry
Sancerre
Sauvignon Blanc
white wine, dry

CARAMEL, INCLUDING SAUCES AND DESSERTS

Champagne, esp. demi-sec
coffee, dark-roasted and/or
    Guatamalan Antigua
Madeira, esp. Malmsey
Muscat, esp. Beaumes-de-Venise
PORT, TAWNY
Riesling, sweet (e.g.,
    Trockenbeerenauslese)
Sauternes
sherry, sweet (e.g., PX)

CARAWAY SEEDS

Gewürztraminer
Merlot
Pinot Noir
Riesling
Sauvignon Blanc
Shiraz / Syrah

CARIBBEAN CUISINE

**BEER, ESP. LAGER OR RED
STRIPE**
Cabernet Sauvignon, esp. with
    meat dishes
**cocktails, esp., made with rum
(e.g., Mojitos)**
fruit juice (e.g., sparkling pine-
    apple)
ginger beer
Gewürztraminer
Riesling, esp. off-dry, and esp.
    with spicy dishes
Rioja, esp. with meat dishes
Sauvignon Blanc, esp. with
    seafood
sparkling wines, esp. with fried
    dishes

sweet beverages, esp. with spicier
    dishes
Zinfandel, esp. with jerked dishes

CARPACCIO (THINLY SLICED RAW BEEF)

Barbera
CHAMPAGNE, ROSÉ
Chianti Classico
Dolcetto
Merlot
Prosecco
rosé, dry
Sangiovese
Valpolicella

CARROTS

beer, esp. wheat beer
Chablis
Chardonnay, New World
cider
cocktails, esp. made with brandy,
    Madeira, or Marsala
Dolcetto
ginger ale
Grüner Veltliner
lemon-based drinks (e.g., lemon-
    ade, sparkling water with
    lemon, etc.)
Muscat, esp. with desserts (e.g.,
    carrot cake)
orange-based drinks (e.g., Fizzy
    Lizzy sparkling orange juice)
Riesling, esp. drier
Sauvignon Blanc, New Zealand
Sémillon
Tokaji, esp. with desserts (e.g.,
    carrot cake)
Soave
Viognier

CASHEWS

Pinot Noir
Prosecco
tea, spiced (e.g., Yerba Chai),
    with cashew desserts

CASSEROLES (SEE BEEF, CASSEROLE)

CASSOULET (CASSEROLE OF WHITE BEANS AND MEATS)

Armagnac (after dinner)
Barbera
beer, esp. French
***CAHORS, FRENCH**
Rhône red wine
rosé, dry
SYRAH / SHIRAZ
Zinfandel

*Cahors is thought to be the ideal
accompaniment to cassoulet.*

— RICHARD OLNEY

*In the Languedoc region of
France, cassoulet is held together
with fat upon fat upon fat:
goose, foie gras, and sausage.
After one spoonful, you love it.
After two, it's still wonderful.
But after three, you've had quite
enough. Meanwhile, the wine of
the region [Cahors] is so tannic
it tastes like the tannin is ripping away the inside of your
mouth. Both the dish and the
wine are very flawed. But a miracle occurs when you combine
the two: If you have a spoonful
of the cassoulet followed by a sip
of the wine, the fat of the dish
tames the tannin in the wine,
while the tannin cuts the fat in
the dish. Together, they become
a revelation.*

— CRAIG SHELTON,
chef/owner, the Ryland Inn
(New Jersey)

An Armagnac is a fine digestive dessert after a cassoulet.

— LINDSEY SHERE, long-time pastry chef, Chez Panisse (Berkeley, California)

CATFISH (SEE ALSO OTHER MILD FISH, E.G., FLOUNDER, SEA BASS, SOLE)

Beaujolais

beer

Chablis

Chardonnay, esp. French with fried or sautéed catfish

Gewürztraminer, esp. with blackened catfish

iced tea ("The house wine of the South"!)

Lambrusco

Muscadet

Pinot Blanc, Alsatian

Pinot Gris

Pouilly-Fumé

Riesling, esp. dry

Sancerre

sparkling wine

CAULIFLOWER

Cabernet Sauvignon, young

Gewürztraminer, esp. Alsatian

Italian white wine

lemon-based drinks (e.g., lemonade, sparkling water with lemon, etc.)

Pinot Gris, esp. Oregon

Riesling, esp. German and/or off-dry

Sauvignon Blanc

sparkling wine

CAVIAR

aquavit

beer, esp. light-bodied e.g., (dry pilsner or Tecate with lemon)

*CHAMPAGNE, DRY, ESP. BLANC DE BLANCS

Chardonnay, California

cocktails, esp. made with vodka

gin martini, esp. with a softer gin (e.g., Bombay Sapphire or Hendricks)

lemon-based drinks (e.g., sparkling water with lemon, etc.)

Pinot Gris, esp. Alsatian

sake

sparkling wine, dry

Tokay, esp. Alsatian

Txakoli

vermouth

*VODKA, ESP. WITH STRONG CAVIAR AND/OR WITH BLINI AND SOUR CREAM

Caviar and Champagne? Forget about it! Champagne is too sweet with caviar. I once did a huge tasting and 99 percent of the Champagnes I tried were unsatisfying because they clashed with the caviar. I prefer vodka: it is dry, without a lot of taste, so you can concentrate on the flavor of the caviar.

— JEAN-LUC LE DU, Le Dû's Wines (NYC)

I think Champagne and caviar can be a great match. I just think you have to be careful what Champagne you serve. The Champagne should be really vibrant and crisp, and Blanc de Blancs is a great Champagne with it. Whereas if you're going to serve a barrel-fermented or wood-aged Champagne with body, I think caviar can really destroy the flavors. Also, regarding the age of the

Champagne: I think it should be young and crisp and fresh.

— DANIEL JOHNNES, beverage director, Daniel (NYC)

CELERY

Sauvignon Blanc

CELERY ROOT

Riesling, dry

Sancerre

CEVICHE

Albarino

beer, esp. lighter lagers

Chablis

Champagne

Chenin Blanc

Gewürztraminer

Grüner Veltliner

Muscadet (no oak)

Pinot Gris

Riesling, esp. Alsatian and German

sake

SANCERRE

*SAUVIGNON BLANC, ESP. NEW ZEALAND

sherry, manzanilla

sparkling wine

Verdicchio

VINHO VERDE, ESP. YOUNG AND DRY

A Riesling Trocken from Germany is one of my favorite matches for ceviche. Our ceviche can be made with lime or sour orange and they have so much acid [ceviche is raw fish marinated in the juice to cook it]. These wines are outstanding because they have tangerine,

RICK BAYLESS'S CEVICHE CLÁSICO Classic Ceviche

Serves 8 as an appetizer, 12 as a nibble

1 pound fresh skinless snapper, bass, halibut, or other ocean fish fillets (the fish I listed I like because they have a large flake or meaty texture), cut into 1/2-inch cubes or slightly smaller

About 1 1/2 cups fresh lime juice

1 medium white onion, chopped into 1/4-inch pieces

2 medium to large (1 pound) tomatoes, chopped into 1/4-inch pieces

Fresh hot green chiles to taste (roughly 2 to 3 serranos or 1 to 2 jalapeños), stemmed, seeded, and finely chopped

1/3 cup chopped fresh cilantro, plus a few leaves for garnish

1/3 cup chopped pitted green olives (choose manzanillos for a typical Mexican flavor)

1 to 2 tablespoons olive oil, preferably extra-virgin (optional but recommended to give a glistening appearance)

salt

3 tablespoons fresh orange juice OR 1/2 teaspoon sugar

1 large or 2 small ripe avocados, peeled, pitted, and diced

Tostadas, tortilla chips, or saltine crackers for serving

1. MARINATING THE FISH: In a 1 1/2-quart glass or stainless steel bowl, combine the fish, lime juice, and onion. You'll need enough juice to cover the fish and allow it to float somewhat freely; too little juice means unevenly "cooked" fish. Cover and refrigerate for about 4 hours, until a cube of fish no longer looks raw when broken open. Pour into a colander and drain off the lime juice.

2. THE FLAVORINGS: In a large bowl, mix together the tomatoes, green chiles, cilantro, olives, and optional olive oil. Stir in the fish, then taste and season with salt, usually about 3/4 teaspoon, and orange juice or sugar (the sweetness of the orange juice or sugar helps balance some of the typical tanginess of the ceviche). Cover and refrigerate if not serving immediately.

3. SERVING THE CEVICHE. Just before serving, stir in the diced avocado, being careful not to break up the pieces. For serving, you have several options: Set out your ceviche in a large bowl and let people spoon it onto individual plates to eat with chips or saltines; serve small bowls of ceviche (I like to lay a bed of frisée lettuce in each bowl before spooning in the ceviche and serve tostadas, chips, or saltines alongside; or pile the ceviche onto chips or tostadas and pass around for guests to consume on these edible little plates. Whichever direction you choose, garnish the ceviche with leaves of cilantro before setting it center stage.

WORKING AHEAD: The fish may be marinated a day in advance; after about 4 hours, when the fish is "cooked," drain it so that it won't become too limey. For the freshest flavor, add the flavorings to the fish no more than a couple of hours before serving.

Sommelier Jill Gubesch's Wine Recommendations: With the ceviche, I like 2003 Dr. von Basserman-Jordan, Trocken, Pfalz, Germany, or 1999 Argyle Brut from Willamette Valley, Oregon; a nice crisp Champagne is also great with ceviche, such as the NV L. Aubry Fils, Brut, Premier Cru, Jouy-les-Reims, France.

which brings out the lime flavor and has enough acidity that it won't finish sweet. Ceviche has so much acid that with the wrong wine it can make a wine finish sweet. Even a dry wine can finish sweet against ceviche. Champagne also works well with ceviche because of the acidity and citrus quality.

— JILL GUBESCH, sommelier, Frontera Grill and Topolobampo (Chicago)

Ceviches work well with crisp white wines with good floral qualities, balanced acid, and in some cases a hint of residual sugar. That leads us to German Riesling and its counterparts in Alsace as well as Pinot Gris, Gewürztraminer, Grüner Veltliner, Albarino, Verdicchio, Sauvignon Blanc from New Zealand, and Sancerre, among others.

— Janos Wilder, chef-owner, Restaurant Janos (Tucson)

CHARCUTERIE (COLD SLICED MEATS)
Aligoté
Barbera
*BEAUJOLAIS CRU
beer
Burgundy, white
Chenin Blanc
Côtes du Rhône
Dolcetto
Gewürztraminer
Merlot
Muscadet
Pinot Gris
red wine, fruity
Riesling, Alsatian

rosé
Sancerre
Sauvignon Blanc
Vouvray, esp. sec
white wine, dry

With charcuterie, I like Vouvray and Chenin Blanc–based wines because I like a mellow white wine. Their lower acidity and a little mineral element make them work great. I also love Gewürztraminer.

— JEAN-LUC LE DÛ, Le Dû's Wines (NYC)

CHEESE
ASSORTED CHEESES IN GENERAL
beer, esp. amber, fruit or lager
CIDER, HARD, ESP. APPLE OR PEAR
fortified wine, lightly sweet
*GEWÜRZTRAMINER, ALSATIAN

MOSCATO D'ASTI
port, esp. tawny, and esp. with blue and other strong cheeses
Riesling, esp. off-dry to sweet, and esp. with milder cheeses
Sauvignon Blanc, esp. New Zealand and/or dry, acidic, fruity
sherry, sweet
SWEETER WINES
water, with very fine bubbles and high TDS (e.g., Borsec from Romania)
WHITE WINE, ESP. FULL-BODIED AND/OR OFF-DRY
or, serve two wines: a drier, acidic, fruity Sauvignon Blanc, and a big, fruity Cabernet Sauvignon or Zinfandel

ALT URGELL Y LA CERDANYA (SPANISH COW'S MILK CHEESE)
beer
white wines, esp. oaked

AMERICAN (PROCESSED WHITE OR YELLOW SOFT COW'S MILK CHEESE)
beer, esp. pilsner

ASIAGO (ITALIAN HARD
COW'S MILK CHEESE)
Barbaresco, esp. with aged cheese
Barbera
Barolo

Chardonnay, esp. oaky New
    World
Nebbiolo
sherry, esp. fino

BABY BEL (FRENCH SOFT
COW'S MILK CHEESE
SIMILAR TO DUTCH EDAM)
Beaujolais

BABY SWISS
Asti

What Is the Most Cheese-Friendly Beverage in the World?

Alsatian Gewürztraminer is the most cheese-friendly wine in the world.
— JEAN-LUC LE DÛ, owner, Le Dû's Wines (NYC)

I agree about Gewürztraminer. If I had to name another beverage that is perfect, I would be leaving out numerous others: any quality Sauvignon Blanc or Pinot Noir, or a Normandy or Brittany hard pear cider or hard apple cider . . .
— STEVEN JENKINS, cheesemonger, Fairway Market (NYC)

In general, wines that are meant for sipping and not quaffing make for better marriages with cheese. A sweet wine or a fruity wine will offer more opportunity for success with pairing of a wide range of cheeses. Tannins often clash with cheeses, so red wines are less successful in general. A cheese with a higher butter-fat content tends to dilute the harsh tannins [in red wines] better. Cow's milk cheeses tend to work best with reds . . . I've found more marriages made in heaven with white wines . . . Gewürztraminer is fairly versatile across a broad range of cheese types. However, I think I would go with a superior and sparkling Moscato d'Asti. That is not a beverage of choice for me but it's almost impossible to go wrong with it if I'm pairing with cheeses . . . By the way, beer is also good with cheese because of its texture. It has effervescence, which helps dilute acidities and lift the heaviness of so many cheeses off the palate so they don't lay down flat. Beer also soothes the extremes in flavor profiles with its texture. India pale ale works well with a wide range of cheeses, from an aged Gouda to a Stilton.
— MAX MCCALMAN, maître fromager, Picholine and Artisanal Cheese Center (NYC)

What Are the Most Beverage-Friendly Cheeses in the World?

Hard cheeses are most reliable as cheese partners for any beverage, whether wine, beer, or sake. It is not always the very best match, but it's certainly the most reliable. A hard cheese is set and knows what it is. A good farmhouse Cheddar from England can go with a broad spectrum of wines. And I've never found a beverage that didn't pair with Sprinz from Switzerland, which I consider the great, great grandfather of Parmesan. Beyos from Spain made from cow's milk has done very well in tastings; it has a long finish, and if you leave it on your tongue, it dissolves into butter. It stands up very well to alcohol, too. Mahon from Majorca also works well. The cows eat salty vegetation and it gets a brine bath when it is made. It's not disagreeable; it just has a salt note that you notice. Sheep's milk cheese also work well with a wide variety of wine, beer, and spirits because they are nutty and buttery.
— MAX MCCALMAN, maître fromager, Picholine and Artisanal Cheese Center (NYC)

BANON (FRENCH SOFT
CHEESE, USUALLY GOAT'S
MILK)
Burgundy, white
Crozes-Hermitage
rosé

BEAUFORT (SWISS
UNPASTEURIZED COW'S
MILK CHEESE)
Bordeaux
Burgundy, white
Champagne, Blanc de Noirs
Châteauneuf-du-Pape
Côtes du Rhône
Hermitage, white
Pinot Noir, esp. California
Rhône red wine
Sauternes

BEL PAESE (ITALIAN
CREAMY COW'S MILK
CHEESE)
Barbera
Chardonnay, esp. light

BEYOS (SPANISH CHEESE)
most wine

BLEU D'AUVERGNE
(FRENCH CREAMY COW'S
MILK BLUE)
Bordeaux, red
Monbazillac
Sauternes/Barsac
sweet wine

BLUE (SEE ALSO CHEESE,
GORGONZOLA,
ROQUEFORT, AND STILTON)
Banyuls
Cabernet Sauvignon
ice wine
Madeira
Merlot
Muscat
**port, esp. tawny and vintage,
and esp. with semi-hard
cheese**
sake, aged
Sauternes
sherry, esp. dry (e.g., fino or
sweet, oloroso)

sparkling wine
SWEET WINE
Zinfandel

*If you are having a blue cheese
such as Fourme d'Ambert or
Roquefort, I think a sweet wine
is so much more interesting than
any other wine.*
—JEAN-LUC LE DÛ,
Le Dû's Wines (NYC)

BOERENKAAS (DUTCH
FARMER'S CHEESE)
Bourbon (e.g., Kentucky)
Calvados
gin
spirits
whiskey

BOURSIN (FRENCH
SPREADABLE TRIPLE-
CREAM CHEESE, OFTEN
FLAVORED WITH GARLIC

AND HERBS OR PEPPER)
Gewürztraminer
Sancerre

BRICK (AMERICAN COW'S
MILK CHEESE)
Chardonnay
Pinot Grigio
Riesling
Sauvignon Blanc

BRIE (FRENCH BLOOMY-
RIND COW'S MILK CHEESE)
**Beaujolais, esp. with young
cheese**
beer, esp. dry stout or framboise
**Bordeaux, red, aged, esp. with
aged cheese**
**Cabernet Sauvignon, esp. with
American brie**
**CHAMPAGNE, BLANC DE
BLANCS OR ROSÉ**
Chardonnay
Pinot Noir
Riesling, esp. dry

Sauvignon Blanc
sherry, esp. sweet
SPARKLING WINE

BRIE DE MEAUX (FRENCH
A.O.C. BLOOMY-RIND COW'S
MILK CHEESE)
beer, stout
Burgundy, esp. aged red or white
Champagne

BRILLAT SAVARIN (FRENCH
TRIPLE-CREAM CHEESE)
Bordeaux, red, esp. Margaux
Champagne

BRIN D'AMOUR (CORSICAN
SHEEP'S MILK CHEESE)
Burgundy, white
Champagne, rosé
Riesling, Alsatian

BRITISH CHEESE, IN
GENERAL
beer and ale

BÛCHERON (FRENCH FRESH
GOAT CHEESE)
Chardonnay
Sauvignon Blanc

BURRATA (ITALIAN COW'S
MILK CHEESE)
beer, esp. fruit
Champagne, rosé

CABRALES (SPANISH COW'S
MILK BLUE CHEESE)
Bordeaux, red, esp. Pauillac
Rioja
**SHERRY, DRY (e.g., manza-
nilla) OR SWEET (e.g.,
oloroso, PX)**
sparkling wine, esp. Cava
sweet wine

CAMEMBERT (FRENCH RAW
BLOOMY-RIND COW'S MILK
CHEESE)
Beaujolais
beer, esp. pilsner
BORDEAUX, RED, ESP. AGED
Burgundy, red, esp. light
Cabernet Franc
Cabernet Sauvignon
Calvados

CHAMPAGNE, ESP. BRUT
Chardonnay
Châteauneuf-du-Pape
Chenin Blanc
**cider, hard (dry or sweet) and/or
Normandy**
Médoc
Merlot
Pinot Noir
Riesling, dry
sake, aged
Sauvignon Blanc
**SPARKLING WINE, DRY (e.g.,
Cava) TO SWEET (e.g.,
Moscato d'Asti)**

CANTABRIA (SPANISH
COW'S MILK CHEESE)
young, fruity red wine

CANTAL (FRENCH COW'S
MILK CHEESE, EARLY
CHEDDAR-STYLE)
Beaujolais
Burgundy, red
Champagne
Chardonnay
Côte d'Auvergne
Pomerol
Pouilly-Fuissé

CASTELMAGNO (ITALIAN
RAW COW'S MILK CHEESE)
Barbaresco
BAROLO

*I had a food and wine revela-
tion that changed my life when
I was twenty years old. It was
1988, and I was living in
Piedmont. I was in the garage
of a famous winemaker,
Luciano Sangrone. He opened
up a bottle of 1985 Barolo
Cannubi Boschis and served it
to me with Castelmagno cheese.
I saw the light.*
— JOSEPH BASTIANICH,
restaurateur and owner, Italian
Wine Merchants (NYC)

CHAROLAIS (FRENCH GOAT
CHEESE FROM BURGUNDY)
Mâcon, white

CHAOURCE (FRENCH
BLOOMY-RIND DOUBLE-
CREAM COW'S MILK
CHEESE)
Chablis
Champagne, esp. Blanc de Noirs

CHAUMES (FRENCH COW'S
MILK CHEESE)
Burgundy, white
Pinot Noir, esp. California

CHAVIGNOL (FRENCH GOAT
CHEESE FROM THE LOIRE
REGION)
Mâcon, white
Sancerre

CHEDDAR (BRITISH DRY
SEMI-HARD COW'S MILK
CHEESE)
Amarone
barley wine
**BEER, ESP. BROWN ALE OR
INDIA PALE ALE**
Beaujolais, esp. with aged cheese
**Bordeaux, red, esp. with aged
cheese**
**CABERNET SAUVIGNON,
ESP. CALIFORNIA, WITH
STRONG CHEDDAR**
Champagne, esp. with mild
Cheddar
**CHARDONNAY OAKY, ESP.
WITH MILD CHEDDAR**
Claret
Gewürztraminer
Merlot
**Pinot Noir, esp. Oregon or
Sonoma**
port, ruby or vintage
red wine, esp. dry and light-
bodied
Rhône red wine
Rioja, esp. with strong Cheddar
sherry, esp. dry (e.g., amontillado
or oloroso)
Shiraz/Syrah
Zinfandel, esp. fruity

CHESHIRE (BRITISH HARD
COW'S MILK CHEESE)
beer and ale
Burgundy, red
Chardonnay
cider
Côtes du Rhône
Pouilly-Fumé

CHÈVRE (FRENCH GOAT
CHEESE)
Beaujolais, cru
beer, fruit or wheat
Chenin Blanc, dry
Moscadello di Montalcino
Pineau des Charentes
Pinot Gris
Pouilly-Fumé
rosé
rose tea
***SANCERRE**
**SAUVIGNON BLANC, ESP.
   CALIFORNIA AND/OR DRY**
Savennieres
Vouvray, dry
white wine, high-acid
AVOID
oaked wine

CHIMAY (BELGIAN
TRAPPIST-STYLE COW'S
MILK CHEESE)
beer
CHIMAY BEER

COLBY (AMERICAN COW'S
MILK CHEESE)
beer, esp. brown ale
Bordeaux, red
Champagne
Chardonnay
Dolcetto
Pinot Noir
port
Riesling
sherry, esp. dry
Zinfandel

COMTE (FRENCH COW'S
MILK CHEESE)
beer, esp. porter or stout
Champagne

Grüner Veltliner
Pinot Noir

COTIJA (MEXICAN AGED
COW'S MILK CHEESE)
Chardonnay
Riesling

CREAM CHEESE (AMERICAN
COW'S MILK CHEESE
SPREAD)
Champagne
Chardonnay
ice wine
Pinot Noir, New World
Zinfandel, white

>   DESSERTS (SEE ALSO
>   CHEESECAKE)
>   ice wine
>   Late Harvest wine
>   Sémillon, sweet

CROTTIN (FRENCH GOAT
CHEESE)
Arneis
Champagne
Chenin Blanc
Pouilly-Fumé
SANCERRE
Sauvignon Blanc

DANISH BLUE (SEE ALSO
OTHER BLUE CHEESES)
beer, esp. dry stout
Cabernet Sauvignon
port
Sauternes

DERBY (BRITISH COW'S
MILK CHEESE)
Chenin Blanc
Sauvignon Blanc

DOUBLE GLOUCESTER
(BRITISH COW'S MILK
CHEESE SIMILAR TO VERY
MILD CHEDDAR)
beer, esp. brown ale
Riesling
Rioja
Sancerre

DRY JACK (CALIFORNIA
DRY COW'S MILK CHEESE)
(SEE CHEESE, MONTEREY
JACK)

EDAM (DUTCH OR
AMERICAN FIRM COW'S
MILK CHEESE)
beer, esp. wheat ale
Champagne, esp. dry

Pinot Noir
red wine, medium-bodied
RIESLING
Shiraz / Syrah
Zinfandel

EMMENTAL (FRENCH OR
SWISS COW'S MILK CHEESE)
Beaujolais
beer, esp. dark
Burgundy, white
Côtes du Rhône
Merlot
Riesling, esp. Alsatian
Shiraz / Syrah
Zinfandel

EPOISSES (FRENCH
WASHED-RIND COW'S MILK
CHEESE FROM BURGUNDY)
**Burgundy, red, esp. with an aged
cheese**
**Burgundy, white, esp. with a
young cheese**
**Champagne, esp. Blanc de Noirs
or rosé**
Châteauneuf-du-Pape
**Gewürztraminer, esp. full-
bodied, low-acid, fruity**
MARC DE BOURGOGNE
(MADE FROM THE LEFT-
OVER PRESSINGS OF
BURGUNDY WINE
GRAPES)
Sauternes

*Epoisses, which I brought to
America [as its first importer]
defines my phrase "excruciat-
ingly delicious." It is so good,
it hurts. This cheese is beautifully married to Marc. The
recipe for the cheese is that it is
washed by hand with the Marc.*
— STEVEN JENKINS, cheese-
monger, Fairway Market (NYC)

EXPLORATEUR (FRENCH
TRIPLE-CREAM COW'S MILK
CHEESE)
Burgundy, red
**Champagne, esp. Blanc de
Blancs**

FETA (GREEK SHEEP'S MILK
CHEESE)
Assyrtiko, Greek
Beaujolais
beer, esp. wheat
Chardonnay, esp. unoaked
Merlot
Ouzo
Pinot Blanc
Pinot Gris
Pinot Noir
RETSINA
Riesling
Sauvignon Blanc

FONTINA (SWEDISH COW'S
MILK CHEESE WITH BRIGHT
RED RIND)
BARBARESCO
Barbera
BAROLO
Chenin Blanc
Chianti
Dolcetto
Gewürztraminer
Late Harvest wine
Nebbiolo
Pinot Grigio
Riesling
Soave
Verdicchio

FOURME D'AMBERT
(FRENCH CREAMY BLUE
CHEESE)
BANYULS
Beaujolais
Bordeaux, red
Burgundy, red
Crianza
Gewürztraminer, Alsatian
PORT, VINTAGE

GAMONEDO (SPANISH
LIGHTER BLUE CHEESE)
sherry, amontillado

GARROTXA (SPANISH GOAT
CHEESE WITH GREY RIND)
beer, stout
Chardonnay, esp. Premier and
    Grand Cru
Priorat
Ribera del Duero
Riesling, Alsatian

GLOUCESTER (BRITISH
COW'S MILK CHEESE)
beer, esp. brown ale
Pinot Noir
Zinfandel

GOAT (A WIDE RANGE OF
CHEESES ALL MADE FROM
GOAT'S MILK, FROM FRESH
AND CREAMY TO AGED AND
CRUMBLY)
**beer, esp. Belgian, Saison, or
    wheat, esp. with aged goat
    cheese**
Bordeaux, white
Cabernet Franc
Chablis
**Champagne, regular or rosé with
    fresh goat cheese**
Chardonnay, New World
Late Harvest wines, esp. with
    aged goat cheese
Pinot Noir
Pouilly-Fumé
***SANCERRE, with fresh goat
    cheese**
**SAUVIGNON BLANC, ESP.
    NEW ZEALAND OR
    CALIFORNIA, WITH
    FRESH GOAT CHEESE**

sparkling cider (apple or pear), esp.
    with desserts or sweet dishes
sparkling wine
Syrah, aged, esp. with aged goat
    cheese

*Goat cheese in a dish will help
to heighten the fruit in a wine.*
— MADELINE TRIFFON, MS,
    director of wine, Matt Prentice
    Restaurant Group (Detroit)

*Aged goat cheese totally breaks
the structure of a red wine . . . If
you serve a fresh or slightly
aged goat cheese with a
Sauvignon Blanc, you can have
a lot of pleasure.*
— JEAN-LUC LE DÛ,
    Le Dû's Wines (NYC)

*Pineau des Charentes, which is
half-way between a wine and a
Cognac, is a magnificent
accompaniment to goat cheese
from that area [of France]. If
you taste it once, you will keep
it in the house all the time! It is
delicious in the summertime.*
— STEVEN JENKINS, cheese-
    monger, Fairway Market (NYC)

GORGONZOLA (ITALIAN
COW'S MILK BLUE CHEESE)
Amarone
Barbaresco
Barbera
barley wine
BAROLO
Brunello di Montalcino
Chianti Riserva
eau-de-vie, pear (e.g., Poire
    William)
Gewürztraminer
Gigondas
Late Harvest wines (e.g.,
    Riesling)
port, vintage and/or tawny

Sauternes
sherry, esp. drier
sparkling cider e.g., apple or pear
sparkling wine, off-dry to sweet
    (e.g., Moscato d'Asti)
sweet wine, esp. Italian
Zinfandel

GOUDA, AGED (DUTCH
AMBER-COLORED AGED
COW'S MILK CHEESE)
**ale, amber, brown, or India
    pale**
Barbaresco
Barolo
**BEER, ESP. BELGIAN SAISON
    OR PORTER**
Bordeaux, red
Brunello di Montalcino
Burgundy, white
Cabernet Sauvignon
Champagne
Chardonnay
Chenin Blanc
Côte-Rôtie
Dolcetto
Merlot
Pinot Blanc
**RIESLING, ESP. GERMAN
    AND/OR SPÄTLESE**
sherry

GRANA (ITALIAN AGED
COW'S MILK CHEESE FOR
GRATING)
Amarone
Barolo
Barbaresco
Brunello di Montalcino
Prosecco

GRUYÈRE (SWISS COW'S
MILK CHEESE)
**BEER, ESP. DOPPELBOCK,
    DARK LAGER,
    OKTOBERFEST OR
    PORTER**
Burgundy, red
Burgundy, white
**CHAMPAGNE, ESP. DRY,
    BLANC DE BLANCS,
    AND/OR VINTAGE**

Chardonnay, esp. Old World
Gewürztraminer
Pinot Noir
Riesling, off-dry to Late Harvest
Sauvignon Blanc
sherry, fino
sparkling wine, off-dry
**white wine, esp. dry and
    medium-bodied**
Zinfandel

HAVARTI (DANISH COW'S
MILK CHEESE, SOMETIMES
WITH EITHER DILL OR
PEPPER ADDED)
beer, esp. lager or pilsner
Cabernet Sauvignon, esp.
    California
CHARDONNAY
Chenin Blanc
Muscadet
Riesling
Rioja
Sauvignon Blanc

JARLSBERG (NORWEGIAN
COW'S MILK CHEESE IN
"SWISS" STYLE)
Chablis
Pinot Noir

LANCASHIRE (BRITISH
CHEDDAR-STYLE COW'S
MILK CHEESE)
Chardonnay
Grüner Veltliner
Muscadet
Pinot Noir
port, tawny

LIVAROT
beer, French [blonde] biere de
    garde, (e.g., Castelain)
cider, Normandy
Gewürztraminer, Alsatian
sherry, esp. oloroso

MAHON (SPANISH COW'S
MILK CHEESE)
beer
fruity wine
port, tawny
red wine, with aged Mahon
Rioja

MAJORERO (SPANISH HARD
GOAT CHEESE)
dry, fruity red and white wine
sherry, esp. manzanilla and
    oloroso

MANCHEGO (SPANISH
SHEEP'S MILK CHEESE)
Cava, with young cheese
Muscat, sweet Spanish
Priorat
Ribera del Duero
**RIOJA, ESP. RISERVA, WITH
    AGED MANCHEGO**
**SHERRY, ESP. AMONTIL-
    LADO, OR FINO WITH
    YOUNG CHEESE**
Syrah/Shiraz, esp. aged
AVOID
tannic red wine

MAROILLES (FRENCH
WASHED-RIND COW'S MILK
CHEESE)
beer, esp. Belgian
Burgundy, red
Champagne
Châteauneuf-du-Pape
Côtes du Rhône
gin, esp. Genever
Tokay Pinot Gris, Alsatian

*People in the Netherlands and
northern France have been
drinking cold gin with stinky
cow's milk cheese like Maroilles
from time immortal. It is a
classic.*
    — STEVEN JENKINS, cheese-
    monger, Fairway Market (NYC)

MASCARPONE (SEE
MASCARPONE)

MIMOLETTE (FRENCH HARD
ORANGE, CHEDDAR-STYLE
CHEESE)
barley wine
Cahors
Champagne, rosé, with aged
    cheese
Saint-Émilion
tea, oolong

MONTENEBRO (SPANISH
GOAT CHEESE WITH
STRONG FLAVOR)
Moscato d'Asti
Muscat
Riesling
rosé
Sauternes
sherry sweet
white wine, Alsatian

MONTEREY JACK
(AMERICAN MILD COW'S
MILK CHEESE)
beer, esp. pilsner
Bordeaux, red
**Cabernet Sauvignon, esp. with
    dry Jack**
Chardonnay, esp. California
Chenin Blanc
Merlot, esp. with dry Jack
port, tawny
Riesling
sherry, dry, esp. with dry Jack
Shiraz/Syrah, esp. with dry Jack
ZINFANDEL

MORBIER (FRENCH
UNPASTEURIZED TWO-
LAYER COW'S MILK CHEESE
SEPARATED BY ASH)
ARBOIS, WHITE OR RED
Barbera d'Alba
Beaujolais, cru
Burgundy, white
Côtes du Rhône
Riesling, Alsatian

MOZZARELLA (ITALIAN
FRESH COW'S MILK CHEESE)
Aglianico
beer, wheat
Chablis
Chianti
Dolcetto
Fiano
Greco di Tufo
Orvieto
Pinot Grigio
Pinot Noir
Prosecco
Sangiovese
Soave

MUENSTER (ALSATIAN OR GERMAN PUNGENT WASHED-RIND COW'S MILK CHEESE)

Barbera

Beaujolais

beer (e.g., Belgian, Chimay, brown ale, or amber lager)

Bordeaux, red

Burgundy, red

Dolcetto

*GEWÜRZTRAMINER, ALSATIAN, ESP. LOW-ACID, FRUITY

Gewürztraminer, Late Harvest Alsatian

Madeira

Muscadet

port, tawny

Riesling, Alsatian

sherry, fino or oloroso

Syrah / Shiraz

Tokay Pinot Gris

Zinfandel

PARMESAN (ITALIAN HARD COW'S MILK CHEESE)

AMARONE

Barbaresco

Barbera

BAROLO

beer, amber or pale ale, or lager

Brunello di Montalcino

Cabernet Sauvignon, esp. young California

Calvados

Champagne, esp. dry

Chardonnay

Chianti, esp. aged

Marc (French grappa)

Prosecco

red wine, full-bodied

Sangiovese

Scotch, double-blended

sherry, esp. cream or fino

Super Tuscans

Valpolicella

Zinfandel

Six-year-old Parmesan — that you have somehow gotten your hands onto and broken up into little pieces on the plate for snacking on as if they were almonds — it's cheese that is not just strong, but also complex. It will require a strong, complex Super Tuscan or Barolo or a really old Chianti to do it justice. I would even consider passing on wine altogether and having a double-blended Scotch or Marc and even Calvados.

— STEVEN JENKINS, cheese-monger, Fairway Market (NYC)

PAVE AFFINOIS (FRENCH SOFT WHITE COW'S MILK CHEESE MADE WITHOUT ANIMAL RENNET)

Sancerre

Sauvignon Blanc

PECORINO (ITALIAN SHEEP'S MILK CHEESE)

Amarone

Barolo

beer, esp. brown ale

BRUNELLO DI MONTALCINO

CHIANTI CLASSICO AND/OR RISERVA

Lungarotti, esp. with cheese from Umbria

Merlot

port, esp. tawny

red wine, esp. full-bodied Italian

Sancerre, dry red or rosé, esp. with Corsican Pecorino

Sangiovese

Valpolicella

Zinfandel

PIAVE (ITALIAN COW'S MILK CHEESE)

Champagne, rosé

Grenache

sherry, fino

PIERRE ROBERT (FRENCH TRIPLE-CREAM CHEESE)

beer, fruit or Saison

BORDEAUX, RED, ESP. MARGAUX

PONT-L'EVEQUE (FRENCH WASHED-RIND COW'S MILK CHEESE)

beer or ale (e.g., Chimay)

Bordeaux, red

BURGUNDY, RED

Cabernet Sauvignon

cider, hard

Meursault

Pinot Noir

port, tawny

Rhône red wine

white wine, Alsatian (e.g., Gewürztraminer, Muscat, Riesling, Tokay Pinot Gris)

PORT SALUT (FRENCH COW'S MILK CHEESE)

Beaujolais

Bordeaux, red, lighter-bodied

Burgundy, red

Cabernet Sauvignon

Champagne, dry, esp. with younger cheese

Côtes du Rhône

Pinot Noir

red wine, light-bodied with younger cheese to full-bodied with aged cheese

Riesling

PROVOLONE (ITALIAN COW'S MILK CHEESE, MILD OR PUNGENT DEPENDING ON AGE)

Bardolino, esp. with young Provolone

Barolo

beer, esp. pale ale

Cabernet Sauvignon

Chardonnay

Chenin Blanc

Chianti Classico or Riserva

Dolcetto

Merlot

red wine, full-bodied Italian

Riesling
Syrah / Shiraz
Vin Santo

RACLETTE (FRENCH OR SWISS COW'S MILK CHEESE)
Barbera
Beaujolais
Chablis
Gewürztraminer
Pinot Noir
Riesling, esp. dry
Sancerre
Sangiovese
Sauvignon Blanc
Syrah

REBLOCHON (FRENCH UNPASTEURIZED COW'S MILK CHEESE)
Burgundy, red, esp. young
Burgundy, white, esp. Aligoté
fruity wine, red or white
Hermitage
PINOT NOIR, ESP. LIGHT-BODIED
port, vintage
Riesling, German Kabinett
Sancerre
Sauvignon Blanc
Saint-Émilion

RICOTTA (ITALIAN MILD YOUNG COW'S MILK CHEESE)
Brachetto
Chardonnay
Chenin Blanc
Lambrusco
Marsala, dry
Pinot Grigio
port, aged
Sauvignon Blanc

ROBIOLA (ITALIAN WASHED-RIND COW'S MILK CHEESE)
Amarone
Barbaresco
Barolo
Prosecco
red wine, full-bodied Italian

ROMANO (ITALIAN HARD COW'S MILK CHEESE)
Barbaresco
Barbera
Barolo
Brunello
Chianti
Merlot
Nebbiolo
red wine, Italian
Sangiovese

RONCAL (SPANISH SHEEP'S MILK CHEESE)
Albarino
Burgundy, white
Merlot
red wine, Spanish, esp. Navarra
Rioja
rosé, esp. Spanish
sparkling wine, esp. Cava
Zinfandel, esp. fruity

ROQUEFORT (FRENCH SHEEP'S MILK BLUE CHEESE)
Banyuls
Barsac
beer, esp. Belgian ale or Chimay
Burgundy, red
Burgundy, white
Cabernet Sauvignon, fruity
Châteauneuf-du-Pape
Crianza
ice wine
Late Harvest wine, esp. Zinfandel
Madeira
Meursault
Muscat, esp. Beaumes-de-Venise or Rivesaltes
PORT, ESP. RUBY, TAWNY AND/OR VINTAGE
red wine, full-bodied
Rhône red wine
Riesling, Alsatian and/or Late Harvest
***SAUTERNES**
sherry, sweet, esp. oloroso, or PX
SWEET WINES, ESP. FULL-BODIED
Zinfandel

SAINT-FELICIEN (FRENCH COW'S MILK CHEESE)
Chardonnay, esp. dry
Sauvignon Blanc, esp. dry

SAINT-MARCELLIN (FRENCH SOFT COW'S MILK CHEESE)
Côte-Rôtie
Hermitage, white or red
Muscat de Beaumes-de-Venise
Rhône red wine

SAINT-NECTAIRE (FRENCH SEMI-SOFT COW'S MILK CHEESE)
Beaujolais
Bordeaux, red, esp. Graves, Margaux, or Saint-Émilion
Burgundy, white
Châteauneuf-du-Pape
Côtes du Rhône
Languedoc, red
Pinot Noir
Rhône red wine
Riesling, esp. Alsatian
Vouvray, esp. demi sec

SBRINZ (SWISS HARD COW'S MILK CHEESE)
anything
Beaujolais
Champagne
port, vintage
white wine, Alsatian

SELLES-SUR-CHER (FRENCH GOAT CHEESE, USUALLY SOLD AS ASH-COVERED DISKS)
Bordeaux, white
Burgundy, white
Sancerre
Sauvignon Blanc

SERENA (SPANISH EWE'S MILK CHEESE COAGULATED WITH CARDOON RENNET)
port, tawny
red wine, full-bodied Spanish
Ribera del Duero

SHEEP'S MILK CHEESE (SEE ALSO SPECIFIC CHEESES)
ale, amber

Cahors

Riesling, off-dry or Late Harvest, esp. with aged cheese

sherry, esp. with aged cheese

SMOKED CHEESE

beer, esp. ale, lager, or smoked

Gewürztraminer, Alsatian

Muscat

Shiraz

whiskey

STILTON (BRITISH COW'S MILK BLUE CHEESE)

Barbaresco

*BARLEY WINE

Barolo

beer, esp. Belgian ale or India pale ale

Bordeaux, red

ice wine

Madeira

*PORT, ESP. TAWNY OR VINTAGE

red wine, full-bodied

Rhône red wine

Riesling, Late Harvest

Rioja

SAUTERNES

sherry

sweet wine

tea, Lapsang Souchong

Zinfandel

It's traditional in England to have Stilton with port. I don't think there's a better match in the world between cheese and wine than that.

— Jean-Luc Le Dû,
Le Dû's Wines (NYC)

SWISS (AMERICAN COW'S MILK CHEESE, IMITATION OF EMMENTAL)

beer, esp. Octoberfest

Gewürztraminer

Pinot Noir

Rhône red wine

white wine, Alsatian

TALEGGIO (ITALIAN SOFT COW'S MILK CHEESE)

Barbaresco

Barolo

Brunello di Montalcino

Chianti Riserva

Muscat de Rivesaltes

Nebbiolo

TELEME (CALIFORNIA COW'S MILK CHEESE)

beer, fruit

Cabernet Sauvignon, California

Chardonnay, esp. unoaked California

Merlot, California

Sancerre

Sauvignon Blanc, California

TETE DE MOINE (SWISS SHAVED PUNGENT COW'S MILK CHEESE)

BEER, ESP. ALE, PORTER, AND STOUT

Châteauneuf-du-Pape

Late Harvest wine

Hermitage

port, vintage

red wine, full-bodied

TETILLA (SPANISH PEAR-SHAPED COW'S MILK CHEESE)

Albarino

sherry, dry and/or fino

Spanish white wine

sparkling wine, esp. Cava

TORTA DEL CASAR (SPANISH SHEEP'S MILK CHEESE)

Albarino

Burgundy, red

red wine, full-bodied (e.g. Syrah)

sherry, fino, manzanilla, oloroso, or PX

sweet wine

TRIPLE CRÈME (FRENCH CHEESE WITH 60 TO 75 PERCENT OR MORE BUTTERFAT)

beer, esp. fruit

CHAMPAGNE, ESP. BLANC DE BLANCS

Madeira

sparkling wine

white wine, dry

VACHERIN (FRENCH OR SWISS RAW COW'S MILK CHEESE)

Beaujolais

Bordeaux, red

Burgundy, red and white

Chablis

Champagne, Blanc de Blancs

Chardonnay

fruity wine

Pinot Gris

Pinot Noir

Puligny-Montrachet

Riesling, Alsatian

Tokay Pinot Gris

VIN JAUNE, WITH VACHERIN MONT D'OR

Zinfandel

A Vacherin Mont d'Or is the second greatest cheese in the world [after Pecorino]. I thought this cheese with all its power would demand a Cabernet or Shiraz or something big — but it doesn't. Vin Jaune is a gentle wine, and turned out to be the perfect pairing because the cheese is complex, but not strong. People often mistake strength for complexity.

— Steven Jenkins, cheesemonger, Fairway Market (NYC)

VALDEON (SPANISH COW'S MILK BLUE CHEESE, SOMETIMES MAY INCLUDE GOAT'S MILK)

Beaujolais cru

Gamay

Jumilla, Spanish

Muscat

sherry, sweet, esp. Pedro Ximenez

sweet wines (e.g., Late Harvest wines, Sauternes)

A LAST WORD *on* CHEESE & BEVERAGE PAIRING

I don't want just one cheese, I'm happy to have two, very very happy to have three, but I get edgy at four. At four, your taste buds can't process all the information. It is also an insult to the other three cheeses you have, because you don't want them to have to compete. I am happy with three cheeses and two beverage choices. Have a red and white wine — or if you are a freak for one or the other, have two very different reds or very different whites. That is the best way to make subjective choices about what goes with what, for yourself. After you taste, reflect. Did the flavors meld? Overwhelm each other? Come from the same area? Share the same historical traditions? All those things make it more fun.

— STEVEN JENKINS, cheesemonger, Fairway Market (NYC)

It's very hard to create a cheese plate and then select a good wine to match with three or four cheeses — unless they're all from the same region, such as a selection of chèvres from the Loire Valley or something like that. Pairing wine with cheese is extremely specific. On our tasting menu, we pair a single wine to a single cheese.

— TRACI DES JARDINS, chef, Jardiniere (San Francisco)

At Everest in Chicago, we offer a cheese course with cow, sheep, and goat's milk cheeses. A Bordeaux will go with the cow but not the goat. Port will work with many cheeses, but not with the goat. The best wine to serve would be a white, like a Gewürztraminer, but people want their red wine! A lighter-style Zinfandel like Kunin from Paso Robles has the candy-fruit quality of a port, maintains its acidity, and yet is not too heavy to go with the goat cheese. However, there is no single wine that will go perfectly with all three cheeses. The key elements when pairing wine to cheese is the latter's acidity, texture, and stinkiness. If it is a high-acid cheese, you need a high-acid white wine. Goat cheese tends to be very high-acid, and for this you need Sancerre. With fat, buttery cheeses like Camembert, Robiola, and Explorator, it becomes a textural pairing: you need a wine with as much texture as the cheese itself. That is where you get into your golden, syrupy dessert wines like Sauternes, Tokay, and port. With hard-skinned cheese such as Parmesan or Manchego, you can get into robust red wine territory with some tannin, fruit, and high acid. With Parmesan, go with Barbaresco or Barolo to contrast with the crumbliness and sharpness of the Parmesan. With the Manchego, go with Rioja. With stinky cheeses, a low-acid, fruity Gewürztraminer can help mask the funkiness of cheeses like Epoisses or Muenster and add balance.

— ALPANA SINGH, MS, Everest (Chicago)

When it comes to food and beverage pairings, there is what's "acceptable," which is what's OK for most people. Then there is the "revelation," which is the next level. A good example of the latter would be Humboldt Fog cheese [a California goat cheese] paired with Hennepin, which is a Belgian-style Saison beer that is bright with some funkiness in the background, orangey, peppery, and relatively dry. The acidities grab each other, but the beer has a very fine bead which scrubs the palate. The flavors dance, with one spiraling into the other. Another "revelation" pairing would be English barley wine like J.W. Lees Harvest Ale with Colston-Basset Stilton. You can't find where the beer ends and the cheese begins — the beer is the drinkable version of the cheese, and the cheese is the edible version of the beer.

— GARRETT OLIVER, brewmaster, Brooklyn Brewery

VERMONT SHEPHERD
(AMERICAN SHEEP'S MILK
CHEESE)
Chardonnay
fruity wine
Pinot Noir
port, tawny and/or vintage
Syrah
Riesling, off-dry

ZAMARANO (SPANISH
SHEEP'S MILK CHEESE)
Albarino
red wines, esp. young and fruity
Rioja
sherry, esp. aged
sparkling wine, dry, esp. Cava
white wine, esp. dry
Zinfandel

*Brie and Camembert work great
with a Cabernet-based red
Bordeaux.*

— JEAN-LUC LE DÛ,
Le Dû's Wines (NYC)

CHEESEBURGERS (SEE
HAMBURGERS, WITH CHEESE)

CHEESECAKE
Asti
beer, fruit-flavored
Champagne, esp. demi-sec
**Chardonnay, California, esp. big
and buttery**
Chenin Blanc
coffee, esp. medium-roasted
espresso, esp. with Italian-style
cheesecake
ice wine
**Late Harvest white wines, esp.
Riesling**
Madeira, Malmsey
Moscato d'Asti
**MUSCAT, BLACK OR
ORANGE, ESP. CALIFOR-
NIA (e.g., Quady Essencia)**
**MUSCAT DE BEAUMES-DE-
VENISE**

port, esp. tawny, and esp. with
chocolate cheesecake
Quarts de Chaume
**RIESLING, ESP. SWEET (e.g.,
Beerenauslese, Trockenbeerenauslese, Late Harvest)**
**Sauternes, esp. with fruit-topped
cheesecake**
Sémillon, sweet
sherry, sweet cream
sparkling wines
tea, Darjeeling
Vouvray, sweet

*I'd pair cheesecake with a light,
floral, peachy Moscato d'Asti.*

— SCOTT TYREE, sommelier,
Tru (Chicago)

*With cheesecake, you want a
big, buttery California
Chardonnay — one with
Kendall-Jackson sweetness with
vanilla.*

— DAVID ROSENGARTEN,
editor in chief,
www.DavidRosengarten.com

CHEESE PUFFS OR
CHEESE STRAWS
acidic wines
Barbara d'Asti, with prosciutto
and Parmesan gougères
beer, esp. lager
Burgundy, red and white
Chablis
**Champagne, esp. Blanc de
Blancs or brut**
Chardonnay
Mâcon-Villages
Pinot Noir
sparkling wine

CHEESE SAUCE AND
CHEESY DISHES
acidic wines
**Chardonnay, esp. with little to
no oak**
Pinot Noir

*With rich, cheesy food, you want
wines with cleansing acidity.*

— MADELINE TRIFFON, MS,
director of wine, Matt Prentice
Restaurant Group (Detroit)

CHEESESTEAK, PHILADELPHIA (SEE SANDWICHES, CHEESESTEAK, PHILADELPHIA)

CHERRIES

IN GENERAL

Beaujolais
beer, esp. cherry-flavored
Cabernet Sauvignon
cocktails, esp. made with Armagnac, brandy, Cognac, Grand Marnier, Kirsch
lemon-based drinks (e.g., lemonade, sparkling water with lemon, etc.)
PINOT NOIR
tea, Keemun Black

DESSERTS

Banyuls
beer, esp. cherry-flavored
Champagne, rosé
cherry wine
ice wine
Kirsch
Muscat, black, esp. California or Beaumes-de-Venise
PORT, ESP. RUBY OR VINTAGE
red wine, sweet (e.g., Late Harvest Zinfandel)
Riesling, esp. sweet or Late Harvest
Sauternes

CHERVIL

Champagne, rosé
Chardonnay
Gewürztraminer
Riesling
Sancerre
Sauvignon Blanc
Syrah (e.g., Côte-Rôtie, Hermitage)

An herb can change the taste of a wine. If you taste a Northern Rhône Syrah like a Côte-Rôtie or Hermitage and bite into a piece of chervil, it lengthens the feeling of the wine on the palate. It gives the wine an extra dimension on the palate.
— JEAN-LUC LE DÛ, Le Dû's Wines (NYC)

CHESTNUTS
(INCLUDING DESSERTS)

Asti, esp. with desserts
cocktails, esp. made with brandy, Chartreuse, Cognac, Marsala
Muscat, black or orange
port
Sauternes
Shiraz / Syrah
Viognier, Late Harvest

CHICKEN

IN GENERAL

Beaujolais
Cabernet Sauvignon, esp. aged
CHARDONNAY
cocktails, esp. made with Armagnac, brandy, Calvados, Cognac, Madeira, or vodka
Dolcetto
lemon-based drinks (e.g., lemonade, sparkling water with lemon, etc.)
Merlot
PINOT NOIR, ESP. OREGON OR OTHER NEW WORLD
Riesling, esp. with lighter dishes
sherry, amontillado

WITH ARTICHOKES

Sauvignon Blanc

BAKED, WITH CREAM SAUCE

CHARDONNAY, ESP. FULL-BODIED CALIFORNIA

BAKED, WITH TOMATO SAUCE

Barbera

BARBECUED (WITH BARBECUE SAUCE)

Chenin Blanc
Chardonnay, New World
Riesling, esp. German
Syrah / Shiraz
ZINFANDEL

CACCIATORE

Chianti Classico

COLD

Beaujolais
Riesling, German
rosé

COQ AU VIN (CHICKEN, WITH RED WINE SAUCE)

Beaujolais
BURGUNDY, RED
Mercurey, red
Pinot Noir, esp. California, and esp. with mushrooms
Rhone red wine
Saint-Émilion

TIP: Serve the same wine used to make the dish.

WITH CREAM SÁUCE

Chardonnay (no or light oak)
Pinot Blanc, esp. Alsatian
Pinot Gris, esp. Oregon or New Zealand
Viognier

WITH CURRY SAUCE

beer, esp. lager or pale ale
Champagne, Blanc de Noirs
Chardonnay
Gewürztraminer

FRIED

beer, esp. lager
bubbly beverages, (e.g., beer, sparkling wine)
Champagne
Chardonnay, esp. California (no oak)
Chianti, esp. light-bodied
Pinot Gris, esp. Oregon

Pinot Noir, esp. Russian River
  Valley
rosé, esp. dry
**SAUVIGNON BLANC, ESP.
  WITH NO OR LIGHT OAK**
**SPARKLING WINE, E.G.,
  CAVA OR PROSECCO,
  WITH HOT OR COLD
  CHICKEN**
Vermentino

  KFC
  Gewürztraminer, Alsatian
  Pinot Noir
  sherry, dry Spanish

  POPEYE'S
  sherry, dry Spanish

WITH FRUIT SAUCE
Riesling

WITH GARLIC
Pinot Noir
Sauvignon Blanc, California

GRILLED
Beaujolais
beer
**Chardonnay, esp. big, oaky
  California**
Côtes du Rhône
Pinot Grigio / Pinot Gris
Riesling, esp. off-dry
Sauvignon Blanc, esp. California
Shiraz / Syrah
Zinfandel

HASH
Champagne
Riesling, dry Alsatian
sparkling wine

HERBED
Bandol, esp. with Provençal-style
  herbs
Beaujolais
rosé
Sauvignon Blanc

JERKED (I.E., JAMAICAN-
STYLE)
beer, esp. light and Red Stripe
Gewürztraminer

rosé
sparkling wine
KIEV (STUFFED WITH
BUTTER)
beer
Burgundy, white

**Chardonnay, esp. buttery
  California**
WITH LEMON OR LIME
beer, esp. lager or pilsner
Champagne, esp. rosé

Chardonnay, California and/or
  unoaked
Riesling
Sauvignon Blanc, California

LIVER (SEE LIVER, CHICKEN)

WITH MISO
Riesling, German Kabinett

WITH MUSHROOM SAUCE
Chianti Classico
Pinot Noir

WITH MUSTARD
**Chardonnay, esp. with Dijon
  mustard**

PAPRIKA
Cabernet Sauvignon

POACHED
Burgundy, white
Pinot Noir, esp. Russian River
Riesling

POT PIE
Beaujolais or Beaujolais Villages
sparkling wine, esp. California

ROASTED
Barbera
Beaujolais
Bordeaux, red
BURGUNDY, RED
Burgundy, white
**CHARDONNAY, ESP.
  CALIFORNIA OR OTHER
  NEW WORLD**
Chianti, esp. Classico
Côtes du Rhône
Crozes-Hermitage
Dolcetto
Dolcetto d'Alba
Merlot
Pinot Gris, esp. Oregon
PINOT NOIR, ESP. OREGON
Rioja, esp. Reserva
Syrah / Shiraz

ROASTED, WITH GARLIC
AND/OR HERBS
Sauvignon Blanc

SAUTÉED, WITH TOMATO
SAUCE
Chianti
Montepulciano
Shiraz / Syrah

SOUP (SEE SOUP, CHICKEN)

STEWED
white wine, full-bodied

STIR-FRIED
beer, esp. lager and pilsner
Gewürztraminer
Riesling

SWEET-AND-SOUR
Gewürztraminer, Alsatian
Riesling, off-dry

TAGINE (MOROCCAN-
STYLE)
Pinot Gris
rosé

TANDOORI
Beaujolais
beer, esp. lager
Shiraz
Zinfaudel

WITH TARRAGON
Bordeaux, white
Burgundy, white
Chardonnay

THAI-STYLE CURRY
Riesling
white wine, Alsatian (e.g.,
  Gewürztraminer, Pinot Blanc)

TIKKA MASALA (INDIAN-
STYLE BUTTER CHICKEN)
Beaujolais Villages
beer, esp. wheat
Cabernet Sauvignon, Indian
Chenin Blanc
cider, mulled
Côtes du Rhône
Gewürztraminer
Riesling
Sauvignon Blanc, New Zealand
Shiraz, Australian
sparkling wine

Viognier
Zinfandel

*Grilled Lemon Herb Chicken
Breast, with Logan Chardonnay*
  — MADELINE TRIFFON, MS,
  director of wine, Matt Prentice
  Restaurant Group (Detroit)

CHICKPEAS
rosé, dry
Sauvignon Blanc

CHILE RELLENOS
Gavi
Gewürztraminer, Alsatian
Sauvignon Blanc, New Zealand
white wine, off-dry

CHILES (SEE ALSO SALSA)

IN GENERAL
acidic wines
Beaujolais
BEER
Cabernet Sauvignon
Chenin Blanc, off-dry
Dolcetto
fruitier wine
Fumé Blanc
Gewürztraminer
less tannic wine
light-bodied wine
low-alcohol wine
Merlot
off-dry to sweet wine
Pinot Gris / Pinot Grigio
Pinot Noir, esp. fruity California
**RIESLING, GERMAN, ESP.
  AUSLESE AND/OR OFF-
  DRY**
RIOJA
**SAUVIGNON BLANC, ESP.
  NEW ZEALAND**
sherry
Shiraz
sweet wine

Tempranillo
unoaked wine
ZINFANDEL, RED OR WHITE

AVOID
full-bodied wine
high-alcohol wine
oaked wine
tannic wine

ANAHEIM
Riesling, German

ANCHO
Sauvignon Blanc, esp. full-bodied
Shiraz
Syrah, northern Rhône
Tempranillo

CASCABEL
Pinot Noir, California

CHIPOTLE
Malbec, Argentian
Tempranillo

GUAJILLO
Syrah, California or Languedoc

HABANERO
Chardonnay, New World
Viognier

JALAPEÑO
Pinot Gris, Oregon
Sauvignon Blanc, New Zealand

PASILLA
Barbera, esp. with a roasted tomato and pasilla sauce
Cabernet, Chilean
Chianti, esp. with a roasted tomato and pasilla sauce
Zinfandel

POBLANO
Riesling, dry

SERRANO
Pinot Gris, Oregon
Riesling, German Kabinett
Sauvignon Blanc, Loire Valley

THAI
Riesling, esp. Spätlese

With chiles, I like German Riesling — and with Shiraz or Zinfandel, they're no problem!
— JEAN-LUC LE DÛ, Le Dû's Wines (NYC)

Green chiles tend to work best with white wines, while dried chiles work best with reds. When pairing wine to Mexican dishes, you start with the sauce first, and then its chile base. A lot of chiles have the same flavor profiles that you find in wine. With a guajillo, you get bright, aggressive spice — so you think of varietals that show bright fruit, like raspberry or other red ripe fruit. With a sauce made with pasilla, you have chocolatey undertones and coffee flavors. How many wines have that black fruit, leathery cocoa finish? When pairing wine, I may or may not mirror the flavors of a chile. Sometimes mirroring is the best way to go, especially if it is a straight pasilla chile sauce where the chile is the main flavor. However, I will contrast as well, depending on the sauce. If I am working with a roasted tomato and pasilla sauce, that changes the match because of the impact of the vine-ripe tomatoes. So with a sauce like that, I will go to the flavor of the tomato and look at an Italian varietal like Chianti or Barbera.
— JILL GUBESCH, SOMMELIER, Frontera Grill and Topolobampo (Chicago)

CHILI
Beaujolais
BEER, ESP. LAGER, PILSNER, OR WHEAT
Cabernet Sauvignon
Côtes du Rhône
Malbec
red wine, full-bodied
Riesling
rosé, esp. dry
Shiraz / Syrah
sparkling wine
ZINFANDEL, ESP. FRUITY AND/OR LIGHT-BODIED

CHINESE CUISINE
(SEE ALSO HUNAN CUISINE AND SZECHUAN CUISINE)
Beaujolais, esp. with spicier meat dishes

BEER, ESP. PILSNER OR WHEAT, AND ESP. WITH SPICIER DISHES
Champagne, esp. with dim sum or fish dishes
Champagne, rosé
Chardonnay, esp. Australia or California, lighter-bodied, no oak or light oak
Chenin Blanc, esp. off-dry
fruity wine
GEWÜRZTRAMINER, ALSATIAN, ESP. WITH SPICIER DISHES
Grüner Veltliner
Pinot Noir, esp. with duck and meat dishes
RIESLING, ESP. DRY TO OFF-DRY (e.g., German Kabinett), AND ESP. WITH CANTONESE FOOD
rosé, esp. fruity and esp. with spicier dishes

liqueur, fruit-flavored
MADEIRA, BUAL OR MALMSEY
Marsala
MAURY, ESP. WITH BERRIES OR CHERRIES
milk, esp. with chocolate chip cookies
Moscatel
Moscato d'Asti, esp. with lighter desserts
MUSCAT, ESP. CALIFORNIA BLACK OR ORANGE
Muscat de Beaumes-de-Venise
plum wine, sweet Japanese
*PORT, RUBY, TAWNY, OR VINTAGE, ESP. WITH RICHER DESSERTS
raspberry wine
red wine, esp. sweet
Riesling, Late Harvest
rum
sake, sweet
Sauternes
Scotch, single-malt (served very cold)
SHERRY, PX
sherry, sweet
sparkling wine, sweet, esp. with lighter desserts
tea, esp. Kenyan or African black or Japanese green
Tokaji, sweet
Vin Santo, esp. with lighter desserts
Vouvray
water (e.g., Fiji)
whiskey
Zinfandel

DARK (I.E., BITTERSWEET OR SEMISWEET)
Asti
Banyuls
beer, Doppelbock, malty and/or Imperial stout
Cabernet Sauvignon
Cognac
Framboise
Madeira, Malmsey
Malaga, aged
Maury

Sauvignon Blanc, esp. New Zealand, and esp. with fried appetizers and/or seafood
7-Up, esp. blended with spirits (e.g., Cognac)
sparkling wine, esp. with dim sum
tea, esp. Chinese
Viognier
Vouvray
white wine, aromatic and/or off-dry
Zinfandel, white

AVOID
tannic wine

CHIVES
Chardonnay
Pinot Grigio/Pinot Gris
Pinot Noir
Sancerre
Sauvignon Blanc
Zinfandel

CHOCOLATE

IN GENERAL
Asti, esp. with lighter desserts
*BANYULS, ESP. VINTAGE, AND ESP. WITH CREAMIER, RICHER DESSERTS
BEER, ESP. FRUIT-FLAVORED BEER WITH FRUITY DESSERTS; MALTY AND/OR BROWN ALE; PORTER OR STOUT, ESP. CHOCOLATE, IMPERIAL, OR OATMEAL STOUT
Cabernet Sauvignon, dry, with bittersweet chocolate
Champagne, esp. dry or rosé
cocktails, esp. made with rum
COFFEE, ESP. MEDIUM- TO DARK-ROASTED OR ESPRESSO OR GUATAMALAN ANTIGUA
Cognac
fortified wine
FRAMBOISE
ice wine
Late Harvest wine

With our chocolate soufflé, the classic pairing is Banyuls, which is an exquisite match. However, for those who are looking for some excitement in their pairings, we also have a chocolate stout that is a wonderful match. — RICHARD BREITKREUTZ, general manager, Eleven Madison Park (NYC)

Chocolate desserts can be a big problem, as they can overpower many wines. Here I look for something sweet, like a sweet fortified wine such as Sherry, Madeira, or Marsala. — PIERO SELVAGGIO, owner, Valentino (Los Angeles)

The idea that red wine and chocolate go together disturbs me. I don't think it works. Port or Banyuls or another fortified wine, yes; Cabernet Sauvignon, no. Banyuls is magical, because very few wines work with chocolate desserts. — JOSEPH SPELLMAN, MS, Joseph Phelps Vineyards

African tea is great with desserts, because its natural berry aromas work so well with chocolate. — MICHAEL OBNOWLENNY, Canada's first tea sommelier

Bourbon and aged rum Manhattans (bourbon, sweet vermouth, and angostura bitters) are splendid with chocolate, which can't be said of most wines. — RYAN MAGARIAN, mixologist, Kathy Casey Food Studios (Seattle)

Muscat, black
PORT, ESP. VINTAGE OR TAWNY
red wine, esp. sweet
sake
Scotch, single-malt (chilled)
sherry, PX
Zinfandel, esp. very ripe and/or Late Harvest

MILK (I.E., SWEET)
Gewürztraminer
Madeira, esp. amber
Moscato d'Asti
MUSCAT, ESP. BEAUMES-DE-VENISE OR ORANGE
port, tawny
sherry, PX
Tokaji, sweet

WHITE
berry-flavored drinks

Late Harvest wine
Moscato d'Asti
Muscat, esp. Beaumes-de-Venise
MUSCAT, ORANGE
orange-flavored drinks (e.g., Fizzy Lizzy sparkling orange juice)

CHOUCROUTE (SEE ALSO SAUERKRAUT)
beer, esp. lager or wheat
Chablis, no oak
Gewürztraminer, Alsatian
kirsch after choucroute garnie
Pinot Blanc, esp. Alsatian
Pinot Gris, Alsatian
***RIESLING, ALSATIAN OR GERMAN KABINETT**
white wine, Alsatian

Have a tiny glass of kirsch and a handful of perfect fresh cherries after choucroute garnie. — LINDSEY SHERE, long-time pastry chef, Chez Panisse (Berkeley, California)

CHRISTMAS
Douglas Fir Sparkle cocktail
egg nog

We created a sparkling cocktail called the Douglas Fir Sparkle: I infused a bottle of gin with a tender piece of Douglas Fir overnight. I shook the gin with lemon and simple syrup, and topped the drink with a splash of Champagne. It was fantastic! People freaked out — it said "holidays!" We served it with roasted potatoes and caviar, and Brie with apple chutney. — KATHY CASEY, chef/owner, Kathy Casey Food Studios (Seattle)

CHURCH'S FRIED CHICKEN
sparkling wine, e.g., Italian Prosecco or German sekt

I'm a Church's man when it comes to chicken. I like sparkling wine, but not Champagne — because all the nuance and subtlety gets washed away. My favorite combination is a well-made sekt. — JOSHUA WESSON, wine director, Best Cellars

------

CHURROS (SPANISH FRIED-DOUGH DESSERT)
Champagne, esp. demi-sec

Moscato d'Asti
sparkling wine, esp. Cava

CILANTRO
Barbera
beer, esp. American ale
Chenin Blanc, esp. Loire Valley
Gewürztraminer
Pinot Grigio/Pinot Gris
Riesling, esp. German Kabinett
Sémillon
SAUVIGNON BLANC, ESP. LOIRE VALLEY OR NEW ZEALAND

CINNAMON
Champagne or other sparkling wine
Chenin Blanc, esp. Loire Valley
Gewürztraminer
Merlot
Pinot Noir
Shiraz / Syrah
Zinfandel

CITRUS (SEE ALSO LEMON, LIME, ORANGE, ETC.)
beer
Chardonnay
Riesling, esp. German Beerenauslese with citrus desserts
Sauvignon Blanc, esp. New Zealand
tea, esp. Darjeeling or Lapsang Souchong

CLAMS
IN GENERAL (I.E., RAW, STEAMED, OR BAKED)
Albarino
Aligoté
Beaujolais or Beaujolais Villages
beer, esp. lighter lagers, pilsners, and dry or oyster stout
CHABLIS
Champagne, esp. Blanc de Blancs

Chardonnay
Chassagne-Montrachet
cocktails, esp. made with Pernod
Gewürztraminer, esp. German or Long Island
*MUSCADET
PINOT GRIGIO, ESP. ITALIAN, OR PINOT GRIS, ESP. OREGON
Pouilly-Fumé, esp. with rich preparations
Riesling
rosé, esp. dry, and esp. with baked clams or spicier preparations
sake
Sancerre
SAUVIGNON BLANC, ESP. NEW ZEALAND
Savennieres
sherry, fino
sparkling wine, esp. Cava or Prosecco
tomato-based drinks (e.g., Bloody Mary or Virgin Mary)
Vinho Verde
Vouvray, esp. with spicy preparations
white wine, no oak

AVOID
oaked wines

CHOWDER (SEE SOUP, CLAM CHOWDER)

With clams, the preparation means so much. I love steamed clams — but always with a little spice, some pepper flakes, cayenne, or even some chorizo. For dishes like that, I think of rosé.

—DANIEL JOHNNES,
beverage director, Daniel (NYC)

CLOVES
Chardonnay, esp. oaked
Chenin Blanc
Gewürztraminer

Pinot Noir
Riesling
Syrah
Viognier
Zinfandel

COCONUT AND COCONUT MILK
Chardonnay, esp. buttery and/or oaked
ice wine, esp. with coconut desserts
pineapple juice
Pinot Gris, slightly sweet
Riesling, esp. German
sparkling wine
tropical fruit drinks, sparkling, esp. mango, passion fruit or pineapple
Viognier
white wine, Late Harvest, esp. with coconut desserts

COD (SEE ALSO SALT COD, HADDOCK)
IN GENERAL
Ansonica
Beaujolais
beer, esp. ale, lager, or pilsner, and esp. with fried cod
Burgundy, red, esp. with cod wrapped in bacon or pancetta
Burgundy, white, esp. with baked, broiled, or sautéed cod
Champagne
CHARDONNAY, ESP. BIG, BUTTERY CALIFORNIA
Chenin Blanc, esp. dry
Chianti, light-bodied
cider, dry
Meursault
Pinot Noir, esp. with cod wrapped in bacon or pancetta
Riesling, esp. dry German
Rosado, dry Spanish, esp. with romesco sauce
rosé, dry French, esp. with brandade
sake

Sancerre
Sauvignon Blanc
Sylvaner, Alsatian
Viognier
Vouvray

BLACK
Chardonnay, esp. California
white wine, full-bodied

COFFEE-FLAVORED DESSERTS
Banyuls
Champagne, esp. brut
coffee
coffee-flavored stout (e.g., espresso stout)
cocktails, esp. made with Cognac or hazelnut liqueur (e.g., Frangelico)
Madeira, esp. Malmsey
Maury
Muscat, Beaumes-de-Venise or black
port, tawny and vintage
sherry, sweet, esp. oloroso

COLD SAVORY FOODS AND DISHES
Beaujolais
Chenin Blanc
chilled beverages
Gewürztraminer, esp. Alsatian
lighter-bodied wine
off-dry wine
Riesling, dry
rosé

COLLARD GREENS
Sauvignon Blanc
white wine

CONSOMMÉ
Madeira
sherry, esp. amontillado or fino

COOKIES (SEE ALSO BISCOTTI)
Asti
Champagne, esp. demi-sec
coffee
ice wine
Madeira, esp. with chocolate chip cookies
milk
Moscato d'Asti
MUSCAT
Muscat, esp. black or orange, and esp. with chocolate cookies
Muscat de Beaumes-de-Venise
port, esp. vintage
Riesling, Late Harvest
Sauternes
sherry, sweet (e.g., cream or PX), esp. with almond or other nut cookies
sparkling wine
tea
Vin Santo, esp. with nut cookies

CORIANDER
Beaujolais
beer, wheat
Champagne, rosé
Chardonnay
earthy, mineral wine
Gewürztraminer
lemon- and lime-flavored drinks (e.g. lemonade, sparkling water with lime)
Pinot Noir
Riesling
Rioja
Sauvignon Blanc
Shiraz/Syrah
Viognier

CORN (SEE ALSO SOUP, CORN)
Champagne
*CHARDONNAY, BUTTERY, OAKY CALIFORNIA
Chenin Blanc
Pinot Gris, esp. Alsatian

Riesling, dry
Sauvignon Blanc, New Zealand
sparkling wine

BREAD
Chardonnay, esp. buttery California

CORN CHIPS (SEE ALSO DORITOS)
cola, e.g., Coca-Cola

CORNED BEEF
IN GENERAL
Beaujolais or Beaujolais Villages
beer, esp. dark lager or Irish ale
Champagne
cider
Merlot
milk
Pinot Blanc, Alsatian
Pinot Gris, Alsatian
Riesling, off-dry
soda, Dr. Brown's Cel-Ray, esp. with a corned beef sandwich
Zinfandel

HASH
beer, esp. ale or lager
Champagne

CORNISH GAME HENS
Beaujolais
Bordeaux, red
Chardonnay
Chianti Classico
Dolcetto
Gewürztraminer
Grenache
Merlot
Navarra
Pinot Grigio/Pinot Gris
Pinot Noir

COUSCOUS
beer, esp. dark with darker meats
Cabernet Franc

Chardonnay
Côtes du Rhône
fruit juices
Grenache
Merlot
Petite Sirah
Pinot Grigio / Pinot Gris, esp.
    with seafood
ROSÉ, ESP. DRY
Shiraz
Vin Gris
Viognier
Zinfandel

CRAB

IN GENERAL
beer, esp. lighter lagers, pilsners,
    and wheat beers
Burgundy, white
Chablis, French
Champagne
Chardonnay, esp. California or
    French (no oak) and esp. with
    richer dishes
Chenin Blanc
cocktails made with Cognac or
    Madeira
high-acid wines
lemon-based drinks (e.g., lemon-
    ade, sparkling water with
    lemon, etc.)
Meursault
Pinot Bianco / Pinot Blanc
Pinot Grigio / Pinot Gris
***RIESLING, ESP. GERMAN,**
    KABINETT AND/OR
    SPÄTLESE
rosé, dry
Sauvignon Blanc, esp. California
Savennieres
sparkling wine
Vinho Verde
Viognier

AVOID
oaked wines

BOIL (WITH SPICES)
beer, esp. pilsner and esp.
    Pilsner Urquell

WITH BLACK BEAN SAUCE
Cognac mixed with 7-Up or water
Gewürztraminer, Alsatian
Rosé

CRAB CAKES
beer, esp. India pale ale
Burgundy, white
CHARDONNAY, ESP.
    CALIFORNIA
Riesling, dry Alsatian or German
SAUVIGNON BLANC, ESP.
    CALIFORNIA
sparkling wine (e.g., Cava,
    Champagne, Prosecco)
Viognier

WITH CORIANDER AND/OR
OTHER SPICES
Gewürztraminer

DUNGENESS
BURGUNDY, WHITE (e.g.,
    Meursault, Puligny-
    Montrachet)
Chardonnay, California or Italy
Riesling, esp. dry
Sauvignon Blanc, California
Sémillon

WITH GRAPEFRUIT
Sauvignon Blanc, esp. New
    Zealand

SOFT-SHELL
Bordeaux, white, esp. dry
Champagne, esp. with deep-fried
    crabs
Chardonnay, esp. buttery
Chenin Blanc
cocktails made with Pernod
ginger ale
lemon- or lime-based drinks (e.g.,
    lemonade, sparkling water with
    lime, etc.)
RIESLING, ESP. GERMAN
    DRY TO OFF-DRY
Sancerre
Sauvignon Blanc
Savennieres
Viognier

STONE CRAB CLAWS
Chablis, esp. French

Chardonnay, esp. rich and buttery
rosé

Riesling is the best wine for
crab.
    — SANDY D'AMATO, chef-
        owner, Sanford Restaurant
        (Milwaukee)

At the Slanted Door [a
Vietnamese restaurant in San
Francisco], I had a whole
Dungeness crab with white
Burgundy Meursault to go with
the butter sauces.
    — JILL GUBESCH, sommelier,
        Frontera Grill and Topolobampo
        (Chicago)

Cold crab salads, like the one I
have on the menu now with
Dungeness crab, fingerling
potatoes, mushroom chips, fresh
artichoke bottoms (often consid-
ered the scourge of wine pair-
ings), herbs and a golden raisin
sherry vinaigrette, can pair
equally well with a Grand Cru
White Burgundy, a floral and
somewhat fruity Chardonnay
from the Central Coast of
California, some of the Italian
Chardonnays, or something
more steely like Sémillon.
    — JANOS WILDER, chef-
        owner, Restaurant Janos (Tucson)

CRANBERRIES AND
CRANBERRY SAUCE
Beaujolais
Merlot
orange-based drinks (e.g., Fizzy
    Lizzy sparkling orange juice)
Pinot Gris, Alsatian

Riesling, German, esp. Kabinett or Spätlese
Shiraz
Zinfandel

CRAYFISH (AKA CRAWFISH)

beer, esp. wheat
Burgundy, white, esp. with sautéed crayfish and/or cream sauce
Chablis, esp. with cream sauce and/or morels
Champagne, rosé
CHARDONNAY, ESP. NEW WORLD
Chenin Blanc
cocktails made with Cognac
Montrachet
Pinot Blanc
Pinot Grigio
Riesling, esp. with grilled crayfish
rosé
Sancerre
white wine, dry

CREAM

SAVORY DISHES AND SAUCES
Burgundy, white
Champagne
CHARDONNAY, BUTTERY
Pinot Gris
Riesling, Alsatian
Sauvignon Blanc
sparkling wine
tea, green
Viognier

AVOID
red wine

DESSERTS (E.G., CUSTARDS, PUDDINGS, ETC.)
beer, oatmeal stout
ice wine
Late Harvest wine
Madeira
Muscat
port, tawny
Riesling, sweet

Sauternes
Vouvray, sweet

CREAM CHEESE (SEE CHEESE, CREAM)

CRÈME BRÛLÉE/CRÈME CARAMEL (CARAMELIZED CUSTARD)

Barsac
Champagne, esp. demi-sec
ice wine
Late Harvest wine, esp. Riesling
Madeira, esp. Malmsey
Mostcato d'Asti
MUSCAT, ESP. BEAUMES-DE-VENISE OR RIVESALTES
port, esp. tawny
Riesling, esp. sweet (e.g., German Auslese or Beerenauslese)
SAUTERNES
SHERRY, SWEET, ESP. CREAM OR SWEET OLOROSO
sparkling wine
tea, esp. Earl Grey
Tokaji, Hungarian

CREOLE CUISINE

Beaujolais
beer
Chardonnay
cocktails, citrus-based
Gewürztraminer, esp. Alsatian
lower-alcohol wine
off-dry to sweet wine
Riesling, German off-dry
Sauvignon Blanc, New Zealand
sparkling wine
white wine, esp. Alsatian

AVOID
high-alcohol wine
tannic wine

One of the ways I deal with pairing wine with our hotter dishes is by keeping the alcohol low and by sometimes having a little bit of residual sugar in the white wines. I find that both alcohol and tannin will amplify the heat in a dish, while even a small amount of residual sugar — say, three grams — will ameliorate that heat.
— MATT LIRETTE, sommelier, Emeril's New Orleans

CRÊPES

FRUIT OR SWEET
Asti
Calvados, with apple crêpes
Champagne, esp. sweet (i.e., demi-sec or doux)
Gewürztraminer, Alsatian
Late Harvest wine
Muscat, esp. orange
Riesling, Late Harvest
Sauternes
sherry, sweet
sparkling wine, esp. off-dry to sweet
Vouvray, esp. sparkling

SAVORY
Champagne, esp. Blanc de Blancs, with seafood crêpes
Chardonnay
cider, dry and/or sparkling
Pinot Blanc, Alsatian
Pinot Noir, esp. with mushrooms

CRUDITÉS (RAW VEGETABLES)

Beaujolais
beer, esp. lager
Chardonnay, esp. Italian
Chenin Blanc, dry
Chianti
PINOT BIANCO / PINOT BLANC
Pinot Grigio
rosé
Sauvignon Blanc

sparkling wine (e.g., Cava or
Prosecco)
Vouvray

CUCUMBERS
cocktails made with Hendricks
gin, which has cucumber notes
to it
Riesling, esp. German Kabinett
rosé
Sauvignon Blanc
Soave

CUMIN
Champagne, rosé
Chardonnay
Pinot Noir, esp. with red meat
Riesling, esp. dry
Rioja
**Sauvignon Blanc, esp. New
Zealand**
Shiraz / Syrah, esp. with red meat
Tempranillo
Viognier
Zinfandel

CURRANTS
Banyuls, esp. with currant desserts
Beaujolais, esp. with red currants
Crème de Cassis, with black cur-
rants
Grenache, esp. with red currants
port, esp. with currant desserts

CURRIES (SEE ALSO
INDIAN CUISINE AND THAI
CUISINE)

IN GENERAL
Beaujolais, esp. with beef or lamb
beer, esp. India pale ale
Chardonnay, esp. New World
cider, mulled
**GEWÜRZTRAMINER, ESP.
ALSATIAN**
Merlot, esp. with spicier curries
Pinot Gris

RIESLING, ESP. SPÄTLESE,
AND ESP. WITH CHICKEN
OR FISH
rosé
sake, aged
**Sauvignon Blanc, esp. New
Zealand**
sherry, drier, esp. amontillado
Shiraz / Syrah
tea, Assam
Viognier
Vouvray, esp. with sweeter curries
**ZINFANDEL, ESP. WITH
BEEF OR LAMB**
Zinfandel, white

COCONUT-BASED (INDIAN
OR THAI)
Chardonnay, esp. California
**RIESLING, OFF-DRY GER-
MAN**
Viognier

WITH FISH, SEAFOOD, OR
POULTRY
Condrieu
Tokay

WITH VEGETABLES
sparkling wine

CUSTARD (SEE ALSO
CRÈME BRÛLÉE / CRÈME
CARAMEL, QUICHE)

SAVORY
Chardonnay, esp. with roasted
garlic
Chenin Blanc
Chinon, esp. with roasted peppers
Côtes du Rhône
Gewürztraminer
Lambrusco, esp. with Parmesan
Riesling, aged, esp. with butternut
squash
rosé, esp. with red peppers
Sauvignon Blanc, esp. with
asparagus
Viognier, esp. with peas
Vouvray, esp. with peas

SWEET (INCLUDING
CUSTARDY DESSERTS)
Asti
Banyuls
cocktails, esp. made with Cognac,
Cointreau, or Marsala
**ice wine, esp. with citrus-
flavored custard**
Late Harvest wine, esp. Riesling
**Muscat, esp. Late Harvest or
orange with orange-flavored
custard**
Muscat de Beaumes-de-Venise
**PORT, TAWNY OR VINTAGE
SAUTERNES**
sherry, sweet (e.g., cream)
**sparkling wine, demi-sec, esp.
with citrus-flavored custard**
Vouvray, sweet

*With a custard dessert, I prefer
a Late Harvest Riesling.*
— JEAN-LUC LE DÙ,
Le Dû's Wines (NYC)

DATES
cocktails, esp. with brandy or rum
Madeira, Malmsey
Muscat
PORT, TAWNY or ruby
**SHERRY, ESP. SWEET (e.g.,
cream, oloroso, PX)**
Tokaji, Hungarian

DEEP-FRIED DISHES
(SEE FRIED FOODS)

DESSERTS (SEE ALSO
SPECIFIC DESSERTS AND KEY
INGREDIENTS)
beer, brown ale, imperial stout, or
Lambic fruit beer
Champagne, demi-sec, doux, or
sweet, esp. with airy desserts
(e.g., mousse, soufflé)
coffee
Moscato d'Asti, esp. with airy
and / or fruit desserts

When pairing with desserts, the sweetness of the wine needs to be at least equal to the dish, or else the wine will taste sour. That is key. — BERNARD SUN, beverage director, Jean-Georges Management (NYC)

Fruit Lambic beers work with panna cotta, cheesecake, and fruit desserts. They are very pretty served in Champagne glasses. — GARRETT OLIVER, brewmaster, Brooklyn Brewery

With dessert, I like a lighter, sweet wine that is not too syrupy. One of my favorites is from South Africa: Vin de Constance from the Paarl region near Capetown is not heavy or cloying and has a wonderful freshness on the finish. — STEPHANE COLLING, wine director, The Modern at the MoMA (NYC)

Tung Ting, an oolong tea, is brilliant after a dessert wine.
— JAMES LABE, tea sommelier and owner, Teahouse Kuan Yin (Seattle)

Dessert and Wine Pairing with Don Tillman of ChikaLicious

ChikaLicious is a unique twenty-seat dessert bar in New York City owned by husband-and-wife team Don and Chika Tillman that serves a twelve-dollar prix fixe three-course dessert menu, with a paired wine for an additional seven dollars. With their dessert and food pairings (which have included a Dios Baco cream sherry to accompany an Apple Pudding Cake with Granny Smith Sorbet and Crème Fraîche Sauce, and Quady Essensia Orange Muscat with Poached Pear with Asian Pear Salad and Lemon-Verbena Ice Cream) described as "perfect" in a recent *Zagat Survey*, who better to ask about how to pair desserts with wine? Don reports:

> *Because our menu changes almost daily, I rely on particular varietals, then enact tastings to find what works best with a particular dessert concept. Were I able to afford it, I might pair five-sixths of our desserts with a '67 Chateau d'Yquem, or an '85 Salon Blanc de Blancs, and call it a day.*
>
> *We have two staple desserts. This first is a Fromage Blanc Island Cheesecake, which we pair with a Jurancon Uronlat for its exotic fruits and honey aromas, which highlight the complex simplicity of the fromage blanc. The other is a Chocolate Tart, which we pair with Mas Amiel 10 Ans d'Age Cuvée Speciale [a Grenache-based fortified wine]. Its deep mahogany color, along with chocolate and coffee aromas, allow one to appreciate the wonder that is Valrhona.*
>
> *We offer two pairings with our cheese plate: a Vinum Petite Sirah, which explodes across the palate with blackberry, blueberry, and chocolate, thereby precluding me from the need to plate fruit; and Graham's Six Grape Port, whose bright plum and fig richness are a wonderful match with our date puree.*

Tillman observes that the pairing process is more art than science. "At times, what I believe will be a wonderful pairing does not always end up being so," he admits before adding, "but then again, half the fun is in all that sipping to get it right prior to menu placement!"

Muscat, black or orange, esp. with berry or other fruit, nut, and/or rum desserts

Muscat de Beaumes-de-Venise

port, ruby or vintage, esp. with berry or other fruit desserts

Riesling, sweet, esp. with fruit and/or nut desserts

Sauternes, esp. with creamy and/or fruit desserts

sherry, sweet, esp. with fruit desserts

sparkling wine, sweet

tea, esp. African, black, Darjeeling, yunnan

Vin Santo, esp. with almond, hazelnut, nut, and/or fruit desserts

----

DILL
beer, esp. lager
Chardonnay
Chenin Blanc
Pinot Grigio/Pinot Gris
Retsina
Riesling, esp. German
SAUVIGNON BLANC
Sémillon
Viognier
white wine

DIM SUM
CHAMPAGNE
Riesling, esp. German
Sauvignon Blanc, esp. New Zealand
SPARKLING WINE
TEA, CHINESE
white wine, lighter-bodied

DOMINO'S PIZZA (SEE PIZZA, DOMINO'S)

DORITOS (TORTILLA CHIPS)

PLAIN
sparkling wine

SPICY
Zinfandel, esp. Dry Creek Valley or Sonoma County

Don't laugh, but spicy Doritos go great with a Dry Creek Valley or Sonoma County Zinfandel!

— SCOTT TYREE, sommelier, Tru (Chicago)

DOUGHNUTS (AND OTHER SWEET FRIED DOUGH)
Asti
Champagne
cider
coffee
milk
Moscato d'Asti
sparkling wine
Vin Santo

At the end of the first season of the hit TV show Desperate Housewives, *after expressing her need to run across the street to her home to get some milk, Teri Hatcher's character Susan Mayer explained to her boyfriend Mike Delfino, "I can't have doughnuts and juice — it's unnatural!"*

DUCK

IN GENERAL

Aglianico

Barbaresco

Barolo

beer, esp. fruit, pale ale, or Trappist ale

Bordeaux, red

Burgundy, red

Cabernet Sauvignon, esp. California

Châteauneuf-du-Pape

cocktails made with Armagnac, Bourbon, brandy, Calvados, Cognac, Cointreau, or Grand Marnier

Côtes du Rhône, red

cranberry juice, sparkling, (e.g., Fizzy Lizzy)

fruit-based, drinks esp. apple, cherry, or black currant (e.g., Fizzy Lizzy)

sparkling apple juice

Gewürztraminer, esp. Alsatian

ginger ale

Grenache

MERLOT

orange juice, sparkling (e.g., Fizzy Lizzy)

PINOT NOIR, ESP. CALIFORNIA

red wine, medium to full-bodied

Rhône red wine

Riesling, esp. German Spätlese

sake, esp. aged

sherry, amontillado

Shiraz / Syrah

tea, esp. black or Darjeeling

Zinfandel

WITH BLACK PEPPER

Champagne, rosé

Châteauneuf-du-Pape

cocktails made with Cognac

Pinot Noir, esp. California

Shiraz / Syrah

Zinfandel

BRAISED

Barbera

Syrah

CONFIT

Bandol, red

Bordeaux

Cabernet Sauvignon

CAHORS

Merlot

Pinot Noir

Saint-Émilion

WITH CORIANDER

Gewürztraminer

tea, Assam

WITH CURRY SAUCE

Gewürztraminer

Rhone reds, e.g., Côte-Rôtie, Hermitage

WITH FRUIT SAUCE

Cabernet Sauvignon

cider, hard, esp. with apples

Gewürztraminer, esp. with apples, figs, or oranges

Grenache, spicy, esp. with cherries

Muscat

Pinot Noir

Riesling

Sauternes

Viognier

Zinfandel, esp. with berries

GRILLED

Beaujolais

Bordeaux, red

Cabernet Franc

Cabernet Sauvignon, esp. California

Merlot, California

Pinot Noir

Rioja

Syrah

Zinfandel

WITH MUSHROOMS

Burgundy, red

Pinot Noir

WITH ORANGE SAUCE (À L'ORANGE)

GEWÜRZTRAMINER

Pinot Noir

RIESLING, ESP. GERMAN AUSLESE

PEKING

Burgundy, red

Gewürztraminer

Merlot

Pinot Noir

Riesling, off-dry German, esp. Auslese

Shiraz / Syrah

Zinfandel

ROASTED

Barbera

Bordeaux, red

Burgundy, red

Cabernet Sauvignon

Châteauneuf-du-Pape

PINOT NOIR

Rhône, red wine, esp. Côte-Rôtie

Rioja

Saint-Émilion

Shiraz / Syrah

Viognier

Zinfandel

SMOKED

Burgundy, red

Burgundy, white

WITH SOY SAUCE

Champagne, rosé

Cognac mixed with 7-Up

Gewürztraminer, dry

DUMPLINGS, ASIAN

(SEE ALSO DIM SUM)

Champagne

sparkling wine

ÉCLAIR, CHOCOLATE

coffee, medium to dark-roasted

EEL

Amarone, esp. with eel sushi

aquavit, esp. with smoked eel

Champagne, esp. with grilled eel

lemon-based drinks (e.g., lemonade, sparkling water with lemon, etc.)

Pinot Noir
Riesling, esp. with smoked eel
rosé, esp. with grilled eel
sake, esp. aged
Sancerre
Savennieres, esp. with smoked eel
sherry, fino, esp. with smoked eel
Zinfandel, esp. with eel sushi

EGGPLANT

IN GENERAL
Bandol
Barbera
Chianti
lemon-based drinks (e.g., lemon-
   ade, sparkling water with
   lemon, etc.)
Pinot Noir
red wine, full-bodied
rosé
Syrah
tannic wines
Tempranillo
Zinfandel

BABA GANOUSH
Champagne, rosé
Pinot Grigio
Rosé
Vernaccia

DEEP-FRIED
sparkling wine

GRILLED
Aglianico
Cabernet Sauvignon, young
Rhône red wine
Shiraz / Syrah
tannic red wine

PARMESAN
Aglianico
Barbera
Chianti
Sangiovese
Syrah / Shiraz

*The miracle tannin-fighter of
all time is eggplant, which has
a inherent bitterness to it.
Grilled eggplant will totally
smooth out a young, tannic
Cabernet Sauvignon.*

— DAVID ROSENGARTEN,
editor in chief,
www.DavidRosengarten.com

EGG FOO YUNG

Pinot Grigio / Pinot Gris
Viognier

EGG ROLLS (SEE SPRING ROLLS)

EGGS AND EGG-BASED DISHES (E.G., FRITTATAS, QUICHES, SPANISH TORTILLAS; SEE ALSO BREAKFAST/BRUNCH)

IN GENERAL
Beaujolais
beer, wheat
Burgundy, white
**CHAMPAGNE, ESP. BLANC
   DE BLANCS AND/OR DRY**
**CHARDONNAY, FRUITY
   WITH LITTLE OR NO OAK**
Gewürztraminer
Muscadet, dry
Pinot Blanc, Alsatian
Pinot Gris / Pinot Grigio
Riesling, esp. Alsatian
rosé, esp. New World
Sancerre
Sauvignon Blanc or Fumé Blanc
Soave
SPARKLING WINE, DRY
tea, esp. Darjeeling
tomato juice
AVOID
oaked wine

DEVILED
Champagne
Sauvignon Blanc
sparkling wine (e.g., Prosecco)

BENEDICT
Champagne
Chardonnay, no oak
Pinot Blanc, esp. Alsatian

FRITTATAS (ITALIAN
OMELETS)

   IN GENERAL
   Champagne
   sparkling wine (e.g., Prosecco)

   POTATO AND EGG
   Sangiovese

   RICOTTA
   Chardonnay, Italian

HUEVOS RANCHEROS (AND
OTHER SPICY EGG DISHES)
Champagne
Riesling, German, esp. Spätlese
Sauvignon Blanc, New Zealand
sparkling wine

OMELETS
CHAMPAGNE
Beaujolais
beer, wheat, esp. with goat cheese
**Burgundy, white, esp. with
   lobster**
Champagne
**Chardonnay, unoaked, and esp.
   with cheese, herbs, lobster,
   and/or smoked salmon**
Chenin Blanc, esp. dry, and esp.
   with cheese
**Côtes du Rhône, esp. with ham
   and/or mushrooms**
**Pinot Blanc, Alsatian, esp. with
   cheese and/or herbs**
**Pinot Gris, esp. with bacon,
   ham, and/or mushrooms**
Pinot Noir, esp. with ham and/or
   mushrooms
**Riesling, esp. with bacon, ham,
   and sausage, and esp. with
   Gruyère cheese**
rosé, dry, esp. with herbs and/or
   vegetables

**Sauvignon Blanc, esp. with herbs
and/or vegetables**

sherry, esp. when served cold,
Spanish-style

Soave

sparkling wine

tomato juice

vegetable juice, esp. with vegetables

white wine, Alsatian, esp. with
Gruyère cheese

QUAIL

Champagne

Chardonnay

sparkling wine

QUICHES

Beaujolais

beer, esp. wheat ale or beer

Burgundy, white

Champagne

**Chardonnay (no oak), esp. with
Quiche Lorraine**

Côtes du Rhône, esp. with Quiche
Lorraine

Pinot Blanc, esp. Alsatian

**Pinot Gris, esp. dry and/or
Oregon**

Riesling, Alsatian and/or dry

rosé

Sauvignon Blanc, esp. California
and esp. with asparagus quiche

sparkling wine, esp. dry

Sylvaner, Alsatian

**white wine, Alsatian (e.g.,
Riesling), esp. with Quiche
Lorraine**

WITH STEAK

Burgundy, red

*With eggs, stay away from
wine with wood (i.e., oaked
wines). Wood and eggs are an
awful combination. If you want
to make someone suffer, serve
them barrel-aged Chardonnay
with an egg salad sandwich.*

— JOSHUA WESSON,
wine director, Best Cellars

*Eggs with white Burgundy is a
magical combination.*

— DEREK TODD, sommelier.
Blue Hill at Stone Barns
(New York)

EMPANADAS (MEAT-
FILLED PASTRIES)

Malbec, Argentinian

Merlot, esp. Chilean

red wine, Spanish

rosé

Shiraz / Syrah

Zinfandel

ENCHILADAS

Beaujolais

beer

Dolcetto

Gewürztraminer

Grüner Veltliner

Petite Sirah

Riesling

**Sauvignon Blanc, New Zealand,
drier**

ENDIVE

apple-based drinks (e.g., Fizzy
Lizzy sparkling apple juice)

lemon-based drinks (e.g., lemonade, sparkling water with
lemon, etc.)

EPAZOTE

Chianti Classico

Pinot Noir, esp. New Zealand

Torrontés, Argentinian

ESCABECHE

Pouilly-Fumé

Sauvignon Blanc, New Zealand

Verdicchio

ESCARGOTS (SEE SNAILS)

ETHIOPIAN CUISINE
(SEE RECOMMENDATIONS FOR
INDIAN CUISINE)

*Ethiopian cuisine is difficult.
Like Indian cuisine, its curries
and also its tangy injera bread
are tough matches. However,
whatever you drink with Indian
food will work with Ethiopian.*

— ALPANA SINGH, MS,
Everest (Chicago)

FAJITAS

Beaujolais

Cabernet Sauvignon, esp. with
steak

Chardonnay, esp. with chicken

Malbec, esp. with beef

Merlot, esp. with beef

Pinot Noir

**Sauvignon Blanc, New Zealand,
esp. with peppers**

Shiraz, esp. with beef

Valpolicella, esp. with beef

Zinfandel, esp. with beef

FALL (SEE AUTUMN)

FENNEL

Barbera

Chardonnay, esp. buttery

Chenin Blanc

cocktails made with Pernod

Grüner Veltliner, Austrian

lemon-based drinks (e.g., lemonade, sparkling water with
lemon, etc.)

Pinot Blanc, Alsatian or New
World

Pinot Grigio / Pinot Gris

Pinot Noir

Pouilly-Fumé

Riesling

Sancerre

SAUVIGNON BLANC
Soave
vermouth
Viognier

FETTUCINE (SEE PASTA)

FIGS (INCLUDING DESSERTS)
Champagne, rosé
Chenin Blanc, esp. Loire Valley
cocktails made with Cointreau,
   Curaçao, or Marsala
fruit-based drinks, esp. orange or
   raspberry (e.g., Fizzy Lizzy
   sparkling orange juice)
Madeira, esp. Malmsey
Moscato
Muscat, esp. black
PORT, ESP. TAWNY
red wine from Provence
Riesling, esp. off-dry to sweet
rosé, esp. with prosciutto and figs
sherry, esp. sweet
sparkling wine, esp. Cava or
   Prosecco
Vin Santo
Zinfandel

FISH (SEE ALSO SEAFOOD,
SHELLFISH, AND SPECIFIC
SEAFOOD)

IN GENERAL
Bardolino
Beaujolais
beer, esp. ale, pilsner, or wheat
Burgundy, red
Burgundy, white
Chablis
Champagne
Chardonnay
Chenin Blanc
cider, esp. hard and/or sparkling
cocktails made with gin, ver-
   mouth, or vodka
Gavi
Gewürztraminer
lemon-based drinks (e.g., lemon-
   ade, sparkling water with
   lemon, etc.)

Muscadet
Orvieto
Pinot Bianco
**PINOT GRIGIO / PINOT
   GRIS**
Pinot Noir
Rhine white wine
**Riesling, esp. with lighter dishes,
   and esp. Spätlese**
Rioja
rosé
Sancerre, esp. with lighter dishes
**SAUVIGNON BLANC, ESP.
   WITH OILIER FISH**
Sémillon
Soave, esp. with lighter dishes
tea, esp. green and oolong
Viognier
wine, esp. white

AVOID
oaked white wine (except with
   butter or cream sauces)
tannic wines

BAKED
Chardonnay
Riesling

BAKED IN SALT
Burgundy, white

BARBECUED
Sauvignon Blanc, esp. New
   Zealand

BLACKENED
beer
Chardonnay
Chenin Blanc
Pinot Blanc
Pinot Noir, esp. Oregon
Sauvignon Blanc

BROILED
Muscadet
Riesling, Alsatian
Sancerre

WITH BUTTER SAUCE
Chardonnay, oaky

AND CHIPS (FRIED FISH
AND THIN-SLICED
POTATOES)
beer or ale
Champagne
Chardonnay, esp. unoaked
Pinot Blanc

Pinot Grigio
Riesling
rosé, dry (e.g., Bandol)
Sauvignon Blanc (no oak)
Soave
sparkling wine

WITH CREAM SAUCE
beer, esp. porter or dry stout
Chardonnay (no oak)

WITH CURRY SAUCE
Gewürztraminer, German
Riesling, German Spätlese

WITH GARLIC
Old World wine (i.e., from
    France and Italy)
Sauvignon Blanc
Viognier

WITH GINGER
Chardonnay, California
Riesling, off-dry
Sauvignon Blanc

GRILLED
Albarino
**Chardonnay, esp. California or
    Chilean**
Navarra
Pouilly-Fumé
rosé
Sancerre
Sauvignon Blanc
Sémillon
Vinho Verde

WITH HERBS
Sauvignon Blanc
Sémillon

WITH LEMON
Chardonnay, esp. California
Sauvignon Blanc

MCDONALD'S FILET-O-FISH
Sauvignon Blanc, esp. New
    Zealand

WITH MUSHROOMS
Pinot Noir

PAN-FRIED
Sauvignon Blanc

POACHED
Burgundy, white

water, still or with very small
    bubbles (e.g., Badoit or Spa)
SMOKED (SEE SMOKED FISH,
SMOKED HADDOCK,
SMOKED SALMON, AND
SMOKED TROUT)

STEAMED
Champagne, dry
Sauvignon Blanc
sparkling wine, dry
white wine, dry (e.g., Muscadet)

STEWED
rosé, esp. dry French or Spanish
Sauvignon Blanc
white wine, dry

*When in doubt, just grab a
Gewürztraminer. It will work
with any kind of fish or shellfish.* — SANDY D'AMATO,
chef-owner, Sanford Restaurant
(Milwaukee)

FLAN (SEE ALSO CRÈME
CARAMEL AND CUSTARD)
port, tawny
sherry, oloroso

FLOATING ISLAND
(DESSERT OF EGG-WHITE
CLOUDS ON VANILLA CUSTARD
SAUCE)
Champagne
Late Harvest white wine
sparkling wine

FLOUNDER (SEE ALSO
OTHER MILD FISH, E.G.,
HALIBUT, SEA BASS, SOLE)
**Burgundy, white, esp. with
    baked or broiled flounder**
Chablis
Chardonnay, esp. California
Chenin Blanc
cocktails made with Cognac
Muscadet
Pinot Blanc, Alsatian, esp. with

sautéed flounder
Pinot Grigio
Pinot Noir, esp. California or
    Oregon
Pouilly-Fumé
Riesling, German
Sancerre
Sauvignon Blanc
Valpolicella

FLUKE (SEE ALSO OTHER
MILD FISH, E.G., HALIBUT, SEA
BASS, SOLE)
Chablis
Champagne
Muscadet
Riesling
Sancerre

FOIE GRAS
IN GENERAL
Armagnac
Banyuls
Barsac
beer, Belgian (e.g., Duchesse de
    Bourgogne)
Burgundy, red
**CHAMPAGNE, DRY, ROSÉ,
    DEMI-SEC, OR SEC**
cocktails made with brandy,
    Cognac, or Madeira
Condrieu
fruit-based drinks, esp. apple or
    grape (e.g., sparkling apple
    juice)
**Gewürztraminer, esp. Late
    Harvest**
**GEWÜRZTRAMINER, ESP.
    OFF-DRY TO SWEET**
ice wine
Late Harvest wine, Alsatian
Muscat
**PINOT GRIS, ESP. FRUIT-
    FORWARD ALSATIAN
    AND/OR LATE HARVEST**
Pinot Noir
port, ruby or tawny
Puligny-Montrachet, esp. with
    duck foie gras
Quartes de Chaume

I pair foie gras terrine near the beginning of a meal with drier wines, and sautéed foie gras near the end of a meal with sweeter wines.
— DANIEL BOULUD, chef-owner, Daniel (NYC)

A winemaker from Alsace once told me, "Just remember to drink Pinot Gris with duck foie gras, and Gewürztraminer with goose foie gras."
— JOSEPH SPELLMAN, MS, Joseph Phelps Vineyards

Be brave enough to say you don't like something even if it is considered a classic pairing. I brought home some foie gras and served it not with Sauternes or Banyuls, but with a big red wine because I don't happen to like sweet wine. While it doesn't appeal to me, having a split for guests is OK because they might like it. With foie gras, I also like to drink a chilled Armagnac.
— STEVEN JENKINS, cheesemonger, Fairway Market (NYC)

Riesling, esp. Auslese, off-dry, and/or Late Harvest
root beer
sake, esp. aged
***SAUTERNES**
sherry, esp. PX
Tokaji, Hungarian
Vouvray, demi-sec

ROASTED OR SEARED
Bordeaux, red, esp. Pomerol
ice wine
Pinot Gris, dry Alsatian

TERRINE, TORCHON, OR PÂTÉ
Gewürztraminer, esp. Alsatian and/or dry
Gewürztraminer, esp. Late Harvest
Late Harvest wine
Pinot Gris, esp. Alsatian
Riesling, esp. Alsatian and/or dry
RIESLING, LATE HARVEST
SAUTERNES
sweet wine
Tokay Pinot Gris, Alsatian

FONDUE

CHEESE
Burgundy, white

Champagne, esp. with Gruyère cheese
Chardonnay, California, esp. with little to no oak
Chenin Blanc, dry
Côtes du Rhône, red
Dolcetto
Muscat
Pinot Noir, esp. with smoked meats
Riesling, Alsatian
Sauvignon Blanc, New Zealand
sparkling wine

TIP: Drink the same wine you used to make the fondue.

MEAT
Bordeaux, red
Cabernet Sauvignon, esp. California
Shiraz/Syrah

FRENCH FRIES

beer
Burgundy, white (esp. Mâcon)
Champagne

FRENCH TOAST (SEE BREAKFAST/BRUNCH)

FRIED FOODS
beer
CHAMPAGNE
fruity wine
high-acid wine
light-bodied wine
Sauvignon Blanc
sherry, fino and manzanilla
SPARKLING WINE, DRY
white wine

FRITTATAS (SEE EGGS, FRITTATAS)

FRITTO MISTO (FRIED FISH AND VEGETABLES)
Chardonnay, esp. Italian
Frascati
Gavi
Nebbiolo
Orvieto
Pinot Grigio
Sangiovese
Soave
sparkling wine, e.g., Prosecco
Tocai
Vermentino

FRUIT, DRIED
Asti
Champagne, dry or sec
Gamay
Grenache
Late Harvest wine (e.g., Zinfandel)
PORT, TAWNY
sherry, sweet
Vin Santo

FRUIT, FRESH

IN GENERAL (INCLUDING FRUIT SALAD)
Asti
CHAMPAGNE, ESP. ROSÉ AND/OR SWEET
Chenin Blanc, off-dry

Gewürztraminer, off-dry

Late Harvest wine (e.g., Gewürztraminer)

Madeira, esp. Bual or Malmsey

MOSCATO D'ASTI

Muscat, esp. Beaumes-de-Venise

RIESLING, OFF-DRY TO SWEET

Sauternes

sparkling wine, esp. semisweet and sweet

tea, esp. Keemun or white Silver Needle

DESSERTS (E.G., TARTS)

Asti

Barsac

beer, Belgian Lambic and/or other fruit beers, or stout

Champagne, esp. Blanc de Blancs or demi-sec (sweet)

Gewürztraminer, sweet

ICE WINE

Late Harvest wine

Moscato d'Asti

Muscat, esp. Beaumes-de-Venise

RIESLING, ESP. GERMAN AUSLESE OR LATE HARVEST

SAUTERNES

Tokaji

Vin de Glaciere

Vin Santo

Unique to Australia are the "stickies" of Rutherglen, especially the Muscat. These unctuous, sweet wines are the right match for a special fruit-based dessert that you spent a lot of time making — or picking out of the pastry shop display.

— JAN STUEBING,
United States regional manager,
Wine Australia

SALSAS AND SAUCES (I.E., WITH SAVORY FOOD)

Chardonnay, esp. California

Merlot

Pinot Gris

Riesling

Sauvignon Blanc, esp. California or New Zealand

Viognier

TROPICAL

Asti

beer, Belgian Lambic raspberry-flavored

Champagne, semi-sweet

cocktails made with Cointreau, Kirsch, or rum

Gewürztraminer

ice wine, esp. with desserts

Late Harvest white wine

lemon- and lime-flavored drinks (e.g., lemonade, sparkling water with lime)

Muscat

rum, esp. dark

Sauvignon Blanc, New Zealand

GAME (SEE ALSO RECOMMENDATIONS FOR RABBIT, VENISON, BOAR, ETC.)

Aglianico

Amarone

Bandol, esp. with stewed game

Barbaresco

BAROLO

beer, dark ale, **DOPPELBOCK**, porter, or stout

Bordeaux, red

Brunello di Montalcino

Burgundy, red

Cabernet Sauvignon, California

Châteauneuf-du-Pape, esp. with roasted game

cherry-based drinks, e.g., sparkling cherry juice

cocktails made with gin or Madeira

Côte-Rôtie

Côtes du Rhône

Hermitage

Pinot Noir

Rhone red wine, esp. northern

Rioja

SHIRAZ / SYRAH, ESP. WITH GRILLED, ROASTED, AND/OR FRUIT PREPARATIONS

Zinfandel, esp. with grilled and/or fruit preparations

AVOID

highly tannic wine

GAME BIRDS (SEE ALSO PHEASANT AND SQUAB)

Barbaresco

Barolo

Bordeaux, red, esp. with unhung birds

Brunello di Montalcino

Burgundy, red, esp. lighter-bodied, and esp. with birds that have been hung

Cabernet Sauvignon, New World

Châteauneuf-du-Pape

Claret, esp. aged

Côte-Rôtie

Musigny, red

Pinot Gris

Pinot Noir, esp. Oregon

Priorat

red wine

Rioja

Shiraz / Syrah

GARLIC (SEE ALSO AÏOLI AND ONIONS)

Barbera

beer, esp. Belgian

Burgundy, esp. with roasted garlic

Cabernet Sauvignon, esp. with roasted garlic

Chardonnay, esp. with roasted garlic

fruity wine

Gewürztraminer

Pinot Noir

Riesling, esp. German and/or off-dry

rosé, esp. Bandol and/or dry

Sauvignon Blanc

sherry, dry (e.g., fino)

Shiraz / Syrah

sparkling wine

Viognier

white wine, dry, esp. with raw garlic
Zinfandel

GAZPACHO
Italian white wine from Lugana
Pouilly-Fumé
Riesling, German Kabinett
Sauvignon Blanc
SHERRY, DRY, ESP. FINO OR MANZANILLA
Soave
Viognier

Gazpacho is a very high-acid dish that can kill so many wines. I like it with a Lugana from Veneto, which has a bright minerality and is a clone of Trebbiano.
— DEREK TODD, sommelier, Blue Hill at Stone Barns (New York)

GEFILTE FISH
Pinot Blanc, esp. Alsatian
Sauvignon Blanc

GERMAN CUISINE
(SEE ALSO SPECIFIC DISHES AND INGREDIENTS)
beer, esp. German
wine, esp. German, and esp. Riesling from dry (e.g., Kabinett) to very sweet, (e.g., Trockenbeerenauslese)

GINGER
IN GENERAL (SAVORY DISHES)
Champagne
Chardonnay, esp. California and/or oaked
GEWÜRZTRAMINER, ESP. ALSATIAN
Muscat
Pinot Grigio

Pinot Noir
RIESLING, ESP. OFF-DRY TO SWEET
sake
Sauvignon Blanc
Shiraz/Syrah
sparkling wine
Viognier
white wine, esp. fruity and/or off-dry
Zinfandel

DESSERTS (E.G., GINGERBREAD)
Champagne, off-dry to sweet
Gewürztraminer, Late Harvest
Moscato d'Asti
MUSCAT, SWEET, ESP. BEAUMES-DE-VENISE OR ORANGE
Riesling, sweet
Sauternes/Barsac
Sémillon, sweet
Tokaji, Hungarian
Vin Santo

There has always been a synergy between ginger and Gewürztraminer, and wasabi and Riesling.
— BRIAN DUNCAN, wine director, Bin 36 (Chicago)

GNOCCHI (SEE ALSO PASTA TO SEARCH BY SAUCE)
Merlot
Pinot Grigio
Valpolicella

Gnocchi with a simple ragout is great with Valpolicella.
— JEAN-LUC LE DÛ, Le Dû's Wines (NYC)

GOAT
Cabernet Sauvignon, esp. with barbecued goat
Malbec, esp. Argentinian, and esp. with barbecued goat

Ribera del Duero, Spanish, esp. with barbecued goat
Syrah, esp. with stewed goat

GOUGÈRES
(SEE CHEESE PUFFS)

GRAPEFRUIT
Champagne
cocktails made with Campari, Cointreau, Curaçao, Grand Marnier, rum, or vodka
ice wine, esp. with grapefruit desserts
Muscat, orange, esp. with grape-fruit desserts
Pouilly-Fumé
Riesling, esp. with grapefruit desserts
Sauvignon Blanc, esp. New Zealand
sparkling wine
Vinho Verde

GRAVLAX
aquavit
beer
CHAMPAGNE, ESP. BLANC DE BLANCS OR BRUT
Chardonnay
Gewürztraminer
Pinot Gris, Alsatian
Rhône white wine
Riesling, esp. German Kabinett or Spätiese
Vouvray, dry

GREEK CUISINE
Beaujolais
beer, esp. lager
Bordeaux, white
cocktails made with Greek brandy
Greek wine
Pinot Grigio
Retsina
Rioja, esp. with meat dishes
Roditys, Greek
rosé, dry

Sauvignon Blanc
Shiraz, esp. with meat dishes
Valpolicella
white wine, dry
Zinfandel, esp. with meat dishes

GREEN BEANS (SEE BEANS, GREEN AND HARICOT VERTS)

GRILLED DISHES (SEE ALSO SPECIFIC FISH, MEAT, POULTRY, AND VEGETABLES)

Beaujolais
Cabernet Sauvignon, esp. California
CHARDONNAY, ESP. CALIFORNIA OR CHILEAN
cocktails made with brown spirits (e.g., Bourbon, brandy, rum), served with grilled red meats
Crianza
fruity wine
Fumé Blanc
Gewürztraminer
medium- to full-bodied wine
Merlot

Navarra
OAKED WINE
Petite Sirah
Pinot Noir
red, tannic wine
Riesling
rosé, esp. dry
Rhone red wine
Sangiovese
Sauvignon Blanc
SHIRAZ / SYRAH
sparkling wine
Super Tuscan
Vin Gris
*ZINFANDEL, RED

GROUPER

Arneis
Burgundy, white, esp. with sautéed fish
Chardonnay, esp. with sautéed fish
rosé, esp. with grilled fish
Sauvignon Blanc
Sémillon

The cooking technique will in part dictate the wine. If a dish is grilled and has a smoky flavor, then you look to Zinfandel, Rhône wines, and spicy Italian wines from Southern Italy made from Syrah or Cabernet clone. These wines pick up a peppery flavor from their terroir *that goes well with grilled foods.*

— PIERO SELVAGGIO, owner, Valentino (Los Angeles)

Brown spirit cocktails with Bourbon, brandy, or aged rum can stand up well to many grilled meats. My favorite cocktail/meat pairing is a horseradish-infused vodka shaken with a rinse of Grand Marnier — giving it just enough orangey sweetness to balance out the heat. The garnish is the meat itself, a grilled beef tenderloin tip seasoned only with salt and pepper and served instead of an olive.

— RYAN MAGARIAN, mixologist, Kathy Casey Food Studios (Seattle)

GUACAMOLE (MEXICAN AVOCADO DIP)

beer
Champagne
Chardonnay, esp. unoaked New World
Grüner Veltliner
margarita
Pinot Grigio
Riesling, German Kabinett
Sancerre
SAUVIGNON BLANC, ESP. CHILEAN OR NEW ZEALAND
Torrontés

I like guacamole and chips with a margarita — or with a crisp white like Sancerre, Torrontés or Grüner Veltliner, which is peppery and brings out the chile flavor. Trevor Jones's unoaked Chardonnay from Australia is amazing — he calls it the "Virgin Chardonnay" because it has not seen wood.

— JILL GUBESCH, sommelier, Frontera Grill and Topolobampo (Chicago)

GUAVAS

Riesling, German Kabinett
tropical fruit drinks, esp. banana, pineapple, e.g., Fizzy Lizzy sparkling pineapple juice
white wine, off-dry

GULAB JAMUN (INDIAN DEEP-FRIED MILK BALLS)

Gewürztraminer, off-dry to sweet
Muscat, orange

Gulab jamun is syrupy, so you need to find a wine that is just as syrupy. Go with an orange Muscat or Gewürztraminer. You want to look for a wine with some floral notes to it and that will go with the rose water that is often served with gulab jamun.

— ALPANA SINGH, MS, Everest (Chicago)

HADDOCK (SEE ALSO RECOMMENDATIONS FOR COD AND SMOKED HADDOCK)
Burgundy, white
Chablis
Chardonnay
lemon-based drinks (e.g., lemonade, sparkling water with lemon, etc.)
Pouilly-Fumé
Riesling, esp. Alsatian
Sauvignon Blanc

HALIBUT (SEE ALSO OTHER MILD FISH, E.G., FLOUNDER, SEA BASS, SOLE)
IN GENERAL
Bordeaux, white
BURGUNDY, WHITE
CHABLIS
CHARDONNAY, NO OR LIGHT OAK
Grüner Veltliner
Muscadet
Pinot Grigio / Pinot Gris, esp. with braised halibut
Pinot Noir, esp. American
Pouilly-Fumé
Riesling, esp. German Kabinett
Sancerre, esp. with creamy sauce
Sauvignon Blanc, esp. with creamy sauce
Savennieres
Viognier, esp. drier

Vouvray, dry
white wine
BAKED OR ROASTED
Burgundy, white
Pinot Blanc
Pinot Noir, esp. Oregon
GRILLED
Chardonnay, esp. Napa Valley
Gewürztraminer
Pinot Noir
Sauvignon Blanc
Viognier
POACHED
Burgundy, white
Chablis, esp. French
SAUTÉED
Chardonnay, California
Riesling, Alsatian

HAM
IN GENERAL
BEAUJOLAIS, ESP. CRU
beer, esp. ale, lager, or smoked lager
Burgundy, red
Chablis
Champagne
Chardonnay, no or light oak
Chinon, red
cider
cocktails made with Bourbon, Madeira, or vermouth
cola (e.g., Coca-Cola)
Gewürztraminer
ginger ale
Lambrusco
Mâcon, red
Malbec
Merlot
pineapple juice, sparkling (e.g., Fizzy Lizzy)
Pinot Grigio
PINOT NOIR, ESP. CALIFORNIA AND/OR LIGHTER-BODIED, AND ESP. WITH MUSTARD SAUCE

RIESLING, ESP. DRY
ROSÉ, ESP. DRY, OFF-DRY, AND/OR SPARKLING
sherry, fino, esp. with Spanish ham
sherry, oloroso
Tempranillo, no oak
Valpolicella
Vin Gris
Zinfandel, esp. young
IBÉRICO (SPANISH ACORN-FED CURED HAM)
Champagne
Ribero del Duero
rosé, Spanish
sherry, manzanilla
sparkling wine, esp. Cava
ITALIAN (E.G., PARMA; SEE PROSCIUTTO)
WITH PINEAPPLE
Chardonnay, New World, esp. oaked
rosé
SERRANO (SPANISH-STYLE THINLY SLICED HAM)
Rioja, white (no oaked)
sherry, dry, esp. fino or manzanilla
sparkling wine, esp. Cava
Tempranillo

The single greatest edible thing on the planet has got to be Ibérico ham. There is nothing more amazing on earth. It is as important as cheese.

— STEVEN JENKINS, cheesemonger, Fairway Market (NYC)

The wine consumed with Ibérico ham in Spain varies depending on the region: Sherry (manzanilla) in Andalucía, Ribera del Duero red wine in Castille, and Cava in Catalonia. In 2002 in Germany, we conducted a tasting of Ibérico ham with ten selected Spanish wines. The best matches were a 1997 Conde de Siruela, Crianza, Bodega Santa Eulalia, DOP: Rivera del Duero (red wine), and 2001 De Casta, Bodega Miguel Torres, DOP: Penedés (rosé).

In 2004, we conducted a tasting during the Salone del Gusto exhibition in Torino, including various selected wines from Spain, Italy, France, and Argentina. The best match for Ibérico ham, according to the participants, was a Champagne. In fact, Real Ibérico is now conducting cross-promotional activities together with Dom Pérignon in Italy.

— MIGUEL ULLIBARRI,
Real Ibérico of Spain

HAMBURGERS

IN GENERAL
BEAUJOLAIS, ESP. WITH KETCHUP
beer, esp. amber ale, Bass ale, or pilsner
Bordeaux, red
Burgundy, red
CABERNET SAUVIGNON, ESP. CHILEAN OR OTHER INEXPENSIVE
Chianti
Côtes du Rhône, red
Dolcetto d'Alba
lemonade
Malbec
Merlot
milkshake
Pinot Noir
red wine, light- to medium-bodied

rosé / Rosado, Spanish
SHIRAZ / SYRAH, ESP. LIGHTER-BODIED
Valpolicella
*ZINFANDEL

WITH CHEESE
Cabernet Sauvignon
Merlot
Pinot Noir
rosé
Syrah
water with bubbles (e.g., Apollinaris or San Pellegrino)
Zinfandel, red or white

WITH CHEESE AND BACON
beer, esp. Schlitz
Rioja

WITH EVERYTHING
beer, esp. Belgian

GRILLED
beer, esp. brown ale, American or English
Cabernet Sauvignon
Côtes du Rhône
Merlot
Monastrell
Shiraz
*ZINFANDEL

WITH MUSTARD
beer
sparkling wine

WITH SWEET PICKLE RELISH
Gewürztraminer
Zinfandel, white

MCDONALD'S (SEE MCDONALD'S BIG MAC)

RARE
red wine, aged

WELL-DONE
red wine, young and fruity

I think a bacon Cheddar hamburger goes well with a Rioja, which has its own smoky flavor

that goes with the bacon — or even a frosty mug of Schlitz.

— SCOTT TYREE, sommelier,
Tru (Chicago)

HARICOT VERTS
(FRENCH GREEN BEANS)
Sancerre
Sauvignon Blanc

HAZELNUTS AND HAZELNUT OIL

IN GENERAL
Burgundy, white
Chardonnay, oaky New World
port, vintage

DESSERTS
Madeira, Malmsey
Quarts de Chaume
Riesling, Auslese
Sauternes
sherry, esp. sweet oloroso
Vin Santo

HERBS (INCLUDING HERBED DISHES AND SAUCES; SEE ALSO SPECIFIC HERBS)
Beaujolais
Cabernet Franc
Cabernet Sauvignon
Chianti
Gewürztraminer
Grüner Veltliner
Merlot
Pouilly-Fumé
Rhône red wine, esp. with dried herbs
Riesling, esp. Alsatian
Rioja
Sancerre
SAUVIGNON BLANC
Sémillon, esp. with dried herbs
Shiraz
Viognier, esp. with dried herbs
Zinfandel

AVOID
aged, complex wines

HERRING (SEE ALSO SMOKED FISH)
aquavit
beer
Champagne
Muscadet
Riesling, esp. dry
Sancerre
Sauvignon Blanc
sherry, esp. fino

HOJA SANTA (RICH, AROMATIC HERB COMMONLY USED IN MEXICAN COOKING)
Riesling, dry, esp. Alsatian or
    Australian

Hoja Santa, also known as the holy leaf *is sweet and anise-like in its flavor. It pairs well with dry Riesling from Alsace or Australia, which provides a beautiful flavor match.*

— JILL GUBESCH, sommelier, Frontera Grill and Topolobampo (Chicago)

HOLLANDAISE (SEE SAUCE, HOLLANDAISE)

HONEY
IN GENERAL
Chenin Blanc, esp. Loire
Pinot Gris, Alsatian
Riesling, esp. off-dry to sweet
DESSERTS
ice wine
Late Harvest white wine, esp.
    Riesling
Muscat, esp. orange

Syrah
Vin Santo

HORS D'OEUVRES (SEE APERITIF)

HORSERADISH
Beaujolais
BEER, ESP. ALE
Champagne, esp. brut rosé
Gewürztraminer
off-dry to slightly sweet wine
Pinot Grigio
Pinot Noir
Riesling, Alsatian
Rioja
rosé
Sauvignon Blanc
Shiraz
sparkling wine
tomato-based beverages (e.g.,
    Bloody Mary or Virgin Mary)
Viognier, California
Zinfandel

TIP: To make horseradish (a known wine-killer) more wine-friendly, add cream.

HOSTESS TWINKIE
Asti

HOT DOGS
IN GENERAL
Barbera
Beaujolais
BEER, ESP. LAGER
Champagne
Gamay
Merlot
Muscat, dry
Pinot Gris / Pinot Grigio
Pinot Noir, esp. Oregon
red wine, Spanish Crianza
**RIESLING, ESP. GERMAN
    KABINETT**
ROSÉ / ROSADO, SPANISH

soda
Syrah
Zinfandel, red or white
CHICAGO-STYLE (WITH RELISH, PICKLE AND ALL THE TRIMMINGS)
Vouvray, demi-sec
Zinfandel

HOT DISHES (SEE SPICY DISHES)

HUITLACOCHE (CORN SMUT; USED LIKE MUSHROOMS IN MEXICAN COOKING)
Burgundy, red
Pinot Noir, esp. French or
    California
Tempranillo

Huitlacoche goes great with red Burgundy. All the earthiness of the huitlacoche is just gorgeous with the wine. Tempranillo also works great because of its mushroomy/earthy "forest floor" element.

— JILL GUBESCH, sommelier, Frontera Grill and Topolobampo (Chicago)

HUMMUS
Burgundy, white
Champagne, rosé
Chardonnay, California (buttery)
Chianti
Greek white wine
Pinot Grigio, Italian
Pinot Noir
rosé
**Sauvignon Blanc, esp. New
    Zealand**
Vernaccia
white wine, dry

HUNAN CUISINE (SEE ALSO ASIAN CUISINE AND SPICY DISHES)

Beaujolais, esp. with spicier meat dishes

beer

Gewürztraminer, Alsatian

Riesling, esp. off-dry (e.g., Spätlese or Auslese)

sparkling wine, esp. off-dry

ICE CREAM

beer, fruit

Champagne

ice wine

Late Harvest wine

liqueur, fruit

Madeira

Moscato d'Asti

MUSCAT, ESP. BLACK OR ORANGE

MUSCAT DE BEAUMES-DE-VENISE

port, esp. tawny, and esp. with chocolate ice cream

root beer

Sauternes

Scotch, single malt, esp. with vanilla ice cream

sherry, sweet (e.g., cream, PX, or oloroso), esp. with vanilla ice cream

Vin Santo

water

AVOID
high-alcohol wine

INDIAN CUISINE

Beaujolais or Beaujolais-Villages

BEER, ESP. LAGER, PALE ALE, INDIA PALE ALE, PILSNER, OR WHEAT BEER, AND ESP. WITH CURRIES AND OTHER SPICY-HOT DISHES

Bordeaux, esp. white

Cabernet Sauvignon

Chablis

chai tea, esp. for breakfast

Champagne, esp. rosé

Chardonnay, esp. aged California or other New World and esp. with tandoori chicken

Chenin Blanc, esp. with chicken tikka masala

chilled, off-dry wine

cider, mulled, esp. with chicken tikka masala

cocktails made with citrus, honey, mango, papaya, saffron, vodka, and/or yogurt

Côtes du Rhône, esp. with chicken tikka masala or braised meat dishes

Fanta orange soda

fruit drinks or punch, esp. with creamy dishes

fruity wine

Gamay

GEWÜRZTRAMINER, ESP. ALSATIAN OR GERMAN

Hungarian wine

lassi (Indian yogurt drink), esp. with the hottest dishes and/or halibut or salmon

lemonade or limeade

Malbec, esp. with chicken and lamb dishes

MERLOT, ESP. WITH CHICKEN, LAMB, OTHER MEAT, AND/OR SWEET CURRIES

Petite Sirah, esp. with meat dishes

Pinot Grigio / Pinot Gris, esp. aged

Pinot Noir, esp. with tandoori dishes

Rhône red wine, esp. with braised meat dishes

RIESLING, ESP. SPÄTLESE WITH SPICY KEBAB AND FISH DISHES

Rioja, esp. with duck dishes

rosé, esp. with spicier dishes

SAUVIGNON BLANC, NEW ZEALAND, ESP. WITH SALADS, SPICY APPETIZERS, CUMIN, CURRY, OR STAR ANISE

7-Up

shandy, esp. with halibut, lamb, kebabs, salmon

Shiraz / Syrah

sparkling wine, esp. with fried and/or milder dishes

tea

Torrontés, esp. with radish paratha

Viognier

Vouvray, aged and/or demi-sec

water, sparkling

white wine, off-dry, esp. Alsatian

Zinfandel, light-bodied, esp. with red meat dishes

AVOID

fine wine

high-alcohol wine (e.g., Shiraz)

highly tannic wine (e.g., Cabernet Sauvignon)

oaked wine

Brooklyn India pale ale (IPA) can stand up to heat. It has enough presence. There are many spicy dishes that off-dry whites can't even stand up to — but IPA can.

— GARRETT OLIVER, brewmaster, Brooklyn Brewery

INDONESIAN CUISINE

beer, esp. lager or pilsner

Chardonnay

Riesling, German

Shiraz

tea, Chinese and/or ginger

ITALIAN CUISINE (SEE SPECIFIC INGREDIENTS AND DISHES)

When it comes to pairings, the first and most fundamental question is, Do you want to create harmony or dissonance?

Pairing Beverages with Indian Cuisine

White wheat beers are very good with Indian food because they have notes of coriander and orange zest. Classics like Hoegaarden have a crispness that cuts through the food rosé also works great with Indian food that has a little heat to it.

— RICHARD BREITKREUTZ, general manager, Eleven Madison Park (NYC)

I love to go out for Indian food, which has a lot of spice and complexity. I was surprised to find that the same wines that work with our [Mexican] food work with Indian food. New Zealand Sauvignon Blanc works well with starters like samosas or matar paneer (green peas and cheese). Côtes du Rhône works great with "butter chicken" (also known as chicken tikka masala), which is really spicy. I also order radish paratha, which works with Argentina Torrontés, which brings out the sweet radish flavor.

— JILL GUBESCH, sommelier, Frontera Grill and Topolobampo (Chicago)

With Indian food, you have your traditional cliché pairings of Gewürztraminer and Riesling, which are fine. If you are looking at the brown spices like cumin, star anise, and coriander, what works well is an oxidized white wine with a little age to it that will accentuate the spices used in Indian food — like a Chenin Blanc or an old Vouvray or Pinot Gris, or even older California Chardonnay with a ripeness of fruit to it. Something with a little fruit to it will help tone down the heat. With red wines, you want to get something that is not too high in tannins or alcohol because it will magnify the heat of a dish — and not in a good way. A fruit forward, light- to medium-bodied, slightly chilled red wine is great. Beaujolais, Gamay, Pinot Noir, and lighter Zinfandel all work well.

— ALPANA SINGH, MS, Everest (Chicago)

I'm Indian, and love Indian food. With north Indian foods like spicy kebabs or fish dishes, I love Riesling Spätlese or demi-sec Vouvray. Sauvignon Blanc can work very well with appetizers, lighter dishes, and salads, like a chickpea and mint salad. With hearty braised lamb and other meat dishes, my favorite wines are Clos Hermitage, Saint-Estephe, and Côtes du Rhône.

— RAJAT PARR, MS, wine director, Mina Group

Shiraz, almost across the board, goes well with Indian food. Among Old World wines, Alsatian whites are generally good. We also have good results with Hungarian wines, which can be difficult to find but work well because they have a lot of fennel and cumin notes to them. I must warn you that they are not inexpensive, unfortunately. As for nonalcoholic drinks, I love a Devi lemonade, which has elderberry and lychee in it. In India, we often drink Fanta Orange or 7-Up, which are both great because of their citrus notes. In India, a very popular drink served in restaurants is made with 7-Up, lime juice cordial, and beer, and is refreshing and delicious. Another popular drink is a shandy, which is beer with lemonade and a splash of soda. All complement the food beautifully.

— SUVIR SARAN, chef, Dévi (NYC)

With Indian food, try saffron in a vodka infusion, which is great — as are the flavors of citrus, honey, mango, papapa, and yogurt.

— RYAN MAGARIAN, mixologist, Kathy Casey Food Studios (Seattle)

CESARE CASELLA

There is such a synergy of products of the same terroir — and that is very Italian. "If it grows together, it goes together" really prevails at the Italian table.

— JOSEPH BASTIANICH, restaurateur and owner, Italian Wine Merchants (NYC)

We love Campari, and the Negroni, with its mysterious intermingled notes of bitter and sweet, stands up to many Italian red meat preparations. As an aperitif, I favor the use of gin with an Italian flavoring component — namely, vermouth.

— RYAN MAGARIAN, mixologist, Kathy Casey Food Studios (Seattle)

JAMAICAN CUISINE
(SEE CARIBBEAN CUISINE)

JAMBALAYA
beer, esp. lager
Chardonnay, Calfornia, esp. with chicken and/or seafood
Chenin Blanc, dry, esp. with seafood
Pinot Noir
Sancerre
Sauvignon Blanc, California or New Zealand
Syrah
Tempranillo
Zinfandel

JAPANESE CUISINE
(SEE ALSO SASHIMI, SUSHI, AND TERIYAKI)
Beaujolais
beer, esp. Japanese and/or lager
Burgundy, red and white
Chablis, esp. with raw fish dishes
Champagne, esp. Blanc de Blancs and esp. with raw fish dishes or tempura
Chenin Blanc
cocktails made with cucumber, lime, sake, and/or vodka, esp. with fish, sushi, or tempura
drier wine
fruity wine
Gewürztraminer
Merlot, esp. with grilled or teriyaki dishes
miso soup
Muscadet, esp. with raw fish dishes
Pinot Grigio
Riesling, esp. with sushi
*SAKE
Sancerre, esp. with fried or grilled foods
Sauvignon Blanc, esp. with sushi
sparkling wine, red or white, esp. with sashimi and sushi
TEA, ESP. GREEN (ESP. HOJICHA) OR BARLEY
Vouvray, sparkling
whiskey, on ice
white wine, light-bodied
Zinfandel, red or white

The use of sake and fresh cucumber proofed with a neutral spirit (vodka) and balanced with a touch of sugar and lime will line up great with most sushi, tempura, and Japanese fish preparations.

— RYAN MAGARIAN, mixologist, Kathy Casey Food Studios (Seattle)

KATHY CASEY'S CUCUMBER SAKE COCKTAIL

Serves 1

IF YOU ARE A SUSHI LOVER, THEN YOU HAVE TO TRY THIS ASIAN-INFLUENCED MARTINI. IT IS PERFECT SERVED WITH SUSHI OR OTHER ASIAN AND PACIFIC RIM DISHES OR APPETIZERS. THE CUCUMBER FLAVOR COMES THROUGH CRISP AND CLEAN. USE A LARGE REGULAR MARKET CUCUMBER (WHICH HAS MORE FLAVOR RATHER THAN THE MILDER ENGLISH VARIETY) FOR THIS RECIPE.

3 slices cucumber, each torn in half

1 1/2 ounces vodka

1/2 ounce premium sake

3/4 ounce fresh lime juice

3/4 ounce simple syrup

Thin slice cucumber, for garnish

Drop the torn cucumber slices into a cocktail shaker. Fill shaker with ice, then add vodka, sake, lime juice, and simple syrup. Cap and shake vigorously until very cold. Strain into a chilled martini glass. Garnish with floating cucumber slice.

JICAMA
citrus-based drinks, esp. lime
  (e.g., limeade, sparkling water
  with lime, etc.)
Pinot Gris

JUNIPER BERRIES
cocktails, esp. made with gin
white wine, Alsatian
Zinfandel

KALE
white wine

AVOID
red wine

KFC FRIED CHICKEN
Gewürztraminer, Alsatian
Pinot Noir
sherry, dry Spanish

KETCHUP
slightly sweet wine

KIDNEYS
Barbera

Beaujolais

Bordeaux, red, esp. lighter-bodied

BURGUNDY, RED

Cabernet Sauvignon

Chianti

cocktails made with brandy,
  Cognac, gin, Madeira, Marsala,
  or vermouth

lemon-based drinks (e.g., lemonade, sparkling water with
  lemon, etc.)

Pinot Noir

Rioja

Shiraz/Syrah

Zinfandel, esp. fruity

KIT KAT CANDY BAR
tea, African

Kit Kats come in lots of flavors now, like vanilla, orange, raspberry, and strawberry. You would serve the latter with a blended African tea comprised of 75 percent Kenyan [to pair with the chocolate] and 25 percent berry berry.
— MICHAEL OBNOWLENNY,
  Canada's first tea sommelier

KIWI FRUIT
cocktails made with Kirsch
Late Harvest wine
lime-based drinks (e.g., limeade,
  sparkling water with lime, etc.)

KOREAN CUISINE

Furmint, dry Hungarian
Grenache Blanc from Priorat
Hermitage Blanc
high-acid wine
Pouilly-Fumé
Riesling, Kabinett
Syrah, Qupé, esp. with grilled sweet and spicy beef
tea, esp. barley or green
Txakoli
Vinho Verde

AVOID
Burgundy, white
Chardonnay

I love Korean food, but it's hard to have any kind of wine with it unless you have a Vinho Verde or something that's really high in acid — like a Kabinett Riesling from a really lean vintage, or Txakoli or high-acid Pouilly-Fumé. The acidity in kimchee just kills wine, and it's all over.
— RAJAT PARR, MS, wine director, Mina Group

I love kimchee so much! It is kind of funky so I have found what works is a dry Hungarian wine made from the Fermint grape that is used to produce their famous sweet dessert wines. The dry version has an oxidated edge to it which works with the kimchee. If you can find a Grenache Blanc from Priorat which also has an oxidated edge that will work as well, or Hermitage Blanc also works great with those flavors. With the grilled sweet and spicy beef that you cook yourself, I like Qupé Syrah Bienesseto from the Santa Maria Valley because it is not too heavy. [Qupé winemaker] Bob Lindquist–style of wines are typically lower alcohol for New World wines; they are very much in a French style and not heavy on their feet, with elegance but still some fruit to them. I like his wines as food wines because of that.
— JILL GUBESCH, sommelier, Frontera Grill and Topolobampo (Chicago)

KUMQUATS

cocktail with aquavit, gin, rum, or vodka
green apple juice, sparkling (e.g., Fizzy Lizzy)
pineapple juice, sparkling (e.g., Fizzy Lizzy)

KUNG PAO CHICKEN

beer
fruity wine
Gewürztraminer
Riesling, off-dry to sweeter

LAMB

IN GENERAL
Amarone
Barbaresco
Barbera
Barolo
beer, American or British brown, pale, or dark ale, or porter or stout
*BORDEAUX, RED
Burgundy, red
CABERNET SAUVIGNON, ESP. CALIFORNIAN OR CHILEAN

Champagne, rosé
Châteauneuf-du-Pape
Chianti
Claret
cocktails made with Madeira or rum
Côtes du Rhône
Crozes-Hermitage
lemon-based drinks (e.g., lemon-ade, sparkling water with lemon, etc.)
Malbec
Merlot
Pinot Noir, esp. California or Oregon
Rhône red wine, northern (e.g., Côte-Rôtie, Hermitage)
Ribera del Duero, esp. Reserva
RIOJA
sherry, oloroso
SHIRAZ, AUSTRALIAN OR SYRAH
tea, Darjeeling

pranillo
ANDEL, ESP. FRUITY

BABY (DELICATELY FLA-VORED LA...)
Bordeaux, re... ...odied
Ribera del Duero
Rioja
rosé
Zinfandel

BARBECUED
Cabernet Sauvignon
Malbec, esp. Argentinian
Ribera del Duero

BRAISED
Gigondas
Hermitage
Malbec
Rioja
Shiraz/Syrah

Pairing with Lamb

We've found that some of the dishes we make that show off the flavors of the [Southwestern] region pair well with Syrahs. We offer a dish called Lamb Four Ways from the Heart of Mexico that consists of a Lamb's Tongue Tostada, Barbacoa Lamb Leg Tamale, Double Chop of Lamb Rack with a Chipotle and Pepita Recado and a Native Seeds Mole served with a soup made from the juices from the Barbacoa. As you can imagine, there are a lot of big flavors rolling around in this dish with notes that range from fruity to spicy to earthy to gamey. Some of the Châteauneuf-du-Papes work well here, as they are blended with a variety of grapes from the Rhône and seem to complement the flavors of the dish well. Wines made with just Syrah work well, too. They can come from the Rhône or Australia or California. If they are well-made, have plump fruit, decent tannins, and a long finish, they'll be a great match.
— JANOS WILDER, chef-owner, Restaurant Janos (Tucson)

Even though I'm a vegetarian, I once lived in Greece — so lamb is the one meat I'll eat from time to time. The gaminess of lamb matches well with Old World–style reds with animale character — that is, sweat, barnyard, sausagey, or brett — a leathery flavor and fragrance. Lamb with a northern Rhône red or Syrah is like cousins meeting — the flavors will melt into each other!
— MADELINE TRIFFON, MS, director of wine, Matt Prentice Restaurant Group (Detroit)

For lamb dishes, I like American or British brown ale.
— GARRETT OLIVER, brewmaster, Brooklyn Brewery

BURGERS
Shiraz

CHOPS
Aglianico
Bordeaux, re   young
CABERNET SAUVIGNON
Malbec, esp. with grilled chops
Merlot
Rioja, esp. with grilled chops
Syrah/Shiraz
Tempranillo, esp. with grilled chops

CURRY
Gewürztraminer
Merlot, California
Rhône, white
Riesling, esp. German Kabinett
ROSÉ, BANDOL
Shiraz

GRILLED
Aglianico

Bordeaux, red, esp. with grilled lamb leg
Cabernet Sauvignon
Rhône or Rhône blend
Rioja, esp. Reserva
Shiraz/Syrah
ZINFANDEL, ESP. FRUITY

WITH HORSERADISH
Rioja

KEBABS OR SOUVLAKI
Cabernet Sauvignon
Pinot Gris
rosé, dry, fruity
Zinfandel

MOROCCAN-SPICED TAGINE
Petite Sirah
rosé
Viognier
Zinfandel

WITH MUSHROOMS AND HERBS
Bordeaux, red, esp. Pauillac
Crozes-Hermitage

ROASTED
Barolo
BORDEAUX, RED
CABERNET SAUVIGNON
Chianti, esp. Classico
Médoc
Merlot, California
Pinot Noir, California or Oregon
Rioja, esp. Reserva
Shiraz

ROASTED LEG OF
BORDEAUX, RED
Cabernet Sauvignon, esp. Napa Valley
Médoc
Rioja

ROASTED WITH GARLIC
Zinfandel

ROASTED WITH MUSTARD
Burgundy, red
Côtes du Rhône

ROASTED RACK OF
Bandol
BORDEAUX, RED
Brunello di Montalcino
Cabernet Sauvignon, California
Merlot
Syrah
Zinfandel

ROASTED WITH ROSEMARY
Cabernet Sauvignon

SHANKS
CABERNET SAUVIGNON
Merlot
Rioja
Zinfandel

SHOULDER
Bordeaux, red
Shiraz

SPICED
Bandol
Châteauneuf-du-Pape
Chianti
Pommard
Shiraz / Syrah

STEW
beer, esp. ale or stout
Bordeaux, red or white
Cabernet Sauvignon, esp.
  Chilean
Chianti
Côtes du Rhône
Merlot
Pinot Noir, esp. New World
RIOJA
Syrah / Shiraz

LANGOUSTINES (SEE
ALSO PRAWNS AND SHRIMP)
Albarino
Burgundy, white
Chablis
Chardonnay, California (no oak)

Chenin Blanc, lightly oaked, esp.
  with langoustines wrapped in
  bacon

LASAGNA (SEE ALSO
PASTA)
Barbera
Cabernet Sauvignon, esp. Old
  World
CHIANTI, ESP. CLASSICO
Pinot Noir, esp. with mushroom
  lasagna
Sangiovese
Vino da Tavola, red

LATIN AMERICAN CUISINE

You must *drink cocktails with Latin food! It not only goes with the festive vibe that is Latin cooking, but so many of the key herbs, spices, vegetables, and chiles used in the cooking mesh perfectly in cocktails. A fresh Sage Margarita with its extraordinary balance of earthy dryness, acidity, and light sweetness works with Latin food across the board. By simply changing the tequila that you are using, you can accompany different dishes at different points in the meal. A Sage Margarita with a spicy silver tequila runs amok with glee during the first course, while with a reposado or anejo tequila it can make a good playmate for Churrasco and rich mole preparations.*

— RYAN MAGARIAN,
mixologist, Kathy Casey
Food Studios (Seattle)

LEEKS (SEE ALSO ONIONS)
Chardonnay
cider
Muscadet
Riesling

LEMON

IN GENERAL
Burgundy, white
Chablis
Muscadet
Pinot Grigio
Riesling
Sancerre
SAUVIGNON BLANC

SAUCES (E.G., WITH SAVORY
FOOD)
Pinot Noir
Sauvignon Blanc
Verdicchio

SWEET DESSERTS
Asti, esp. with lighter desserts
beer, esp. wheat ale
coffee, esp. light-roasted
Gewürztraminer, Alsatian and/or
  Late Harvest
ice wine
Madeira
Moscato d'Asti
Muscat, esp. California and/or
  white or orange
Muscat de Beaumes-de-Venise
RIESLING, LATE HARVEST
  AND/OR SWEET (e.g.,
  Beerenauslese or Trocken-
  beerenauslese)
SAUTERNES, ESP. WITH
  CREAMY AND/OR HOT
  DESSERTS
Sauvignon, Late Harvest
Sémillon, sweet (esp. with creamy
  desserts)
Tokaji, sweet
Vouvray, sweet

LEMONGRASS
Chardonnay
Chenin Blanc

Pinot Grigio/Pinot Gris
Riesling
Sancerre
SAUVIGNON BLANC
Scheurebe, German
Vouvray

LIME

IN GENERAL
beer, esp. American ale or lager
Champagne
Furmint, Hungarian
high-acid wine
Pinot Gris, Oregon
Riesling
**SAUVIGNON BLANC, ESP.
  HIGH-ACID**
Verdelho, Australian

WITH SEAFOOD
Chenin Blanc, esp. California
Pinot Gris, Oregon
Riesling
Sauvignon Blanc, New Zealand
Vouvray

SWEET DESSERTS (E.G., KEY
LIME PIE, TARTS)
Champagne, demi-sec
coffee, esp. light-roasted
ice wine
Muscat, orange
**Riesling, esp. Late Harvest or
  other sweet**
Sauternes

*Lime in a dish will help to calm
the acidity in wine.*
— MADELINE TRIFFON, MS,
director of wine, Matt Prentice
Restaurant Group (Detroit)

LINGUINE (SEE ALSO
PASTA TO SEARCH BY SAUCE)

LINZER TORTE
(RASPBERRY-FLAVORED
DESSERT)
beer, Lambic Framboise

coffee
ice wine

LIVER

CALF'S
Beaujolais, esp. with grilled liver
beer, esp. ale or porter
Bordeaux, red
Burgundy, red, esp. lighter-bodied
Châteauneuf-du-Pape
Chianti Classico
Côtes du Rhône, red
lemon-based drinks (e.g., lemon-
  ade, sparkling water with
  lemon, etc.)
Merlot
Pinot Noir
red wine, lighter-bodied
Rioja, esp. Crianza
rosé
Sangiovese
Syrah / Shiraz

CHICKEN (SEE ALSO PÂTÉ)
Barbera
Burgundy, red, esp. with bacon
Chardonnay, Italian
Chianti, esp. with grilled liver
cocktails, esp. made with brandy,
  Cognac, or Madeira
Côtes du Rhône, red
Gewürztraminer, dry Alsatian
Madeira
Merlot
Muscadet, dry
Pinot Noir, esp. with bacon
Riesling, dry Alsatian
Sangiovese, esp. with grilled
Sauvignon Blanc
sherry, esp. amontillado
Vernaccia
**white wine, dry Alsatian (e.g.,
  Gewürztraminer, Riesling)**

LOBSTER

IN GENERAL
Arneis
beer

***BURGUNDY, WHITE, ESP.
  FULL-BODIED (e.g.,
  Chassagne-Montrachet,
  Corton-Charlemagne,
  Mersault, Montrachet)**
**CHAMPAGNE, ESP. BLANC
  DE BLANCS OR ROSÉ**
***CHARDONNAY, ESP.
  CALIFORNIA (I.E., BUT-
  TERY, OAKY)**
cocktails made with Bourbon,
  brandy, Cognac, or Madeira
Condrieu
**Gewürztraminer, Alsatian, esp.
  with broiled lobster**
lemon-based drinks (e.g., lemon-
  ade, sparkling water with
  lemon, etc.)
Orvieto
Pinot Blanc
Pinot Grigio/Pinot Gris
Pinot Noir, esp. Russian River or
  Oregon
**Riesling, esp. Alsatian or
  German Kabinett**
Rioja, white
rosé
**Sauvignon Blanc, esp. New
  Zealand**
Savennieres
Soave
sparkling wine
Trebbiano
Verdicchio
Vermentino
Vernaccia
Viognier
Vouvray

COLD
Champagne, Blanc de Blancs
Chenin Blanc
Riesling, dry

WITH A CREAM SAUCE (E.G.,
LOBSTER NEWBURG)
Chablis, Grand Cru
Champagne
Chardonnay, buttery

WITH CURRY
Tokay
Viognier, esp. Condrieu

FRICASSEE
Meyer lemon soda / sparkling
    juice

WITH GINGER
Burgundy, white
Champagne, esp. dry

GRILLED OR BROILED
Burgundy, white, esp. Mersault
Champagne
Chardonnay, California
Gewürztraminer
Sancerre
Savennieres

MOUSSE
Burgundy, white
Champagne

ROASTED
Burgundy, white (e.g., Puligny-
    Montrachet)

ROLL (SEE SANDWICHES,
LOBSTER ROLL)

SOUFFLÉ
Burgundy, white
Chardonnay
Graves, white

STEAMED WITH BUTTER
Burgundy, white
Chardonnay
Marsanne
Mercurey Blanc
Pinot Gris / Pinot Grigio
sparkling wine
Vouvray, dry

STEAMED WITH LEMON
Chablis, esp. Grand Cru
Chardonnay, esp. French
Vouvray, dry

WITH THAI SPICES
Burgundy, white, esp. Meursault
Champagne
Chardonnay
Sauvignon Blanc, New Zealand
sparkling wine
Viognier

WITH VANILLA
Burgundy, white, esp. Meursault

AVOID
red wine

LYCHEES
Champagne, rosé
Gewürztraminer, esp. Alsatian
    and/or Late Harvest
ice wine
Late Harvest white wine
Muscat
sake, esp. sweeter

MACADAMIA NUTS,
ESP. IN DESSERTS
Australian stickies (rich, complex,
    over-the-top dessert wines)
Madeira, esp. Malmsey
Muscat
port, tawny
Sauternes
sherry, sweet (e.g., PX)
Tokaji, Hungarian
Vin Santo

Our macadamia nut ice cream
goes great with a dark, rich
tawny port, a heavier Muscat,
or Australian stickies.
— ERIC RENAUD, sommelier,
    Bern's Steak House (Tampa)

MACARONI AND
CHEESE (WITH
TRADITIONAL CHEDDAR
CHEESE)
Beaujolais
beer or ale
Burgundy, white
CHARDONNAY, ESP. WITH
    LITTLE TO NO OAK
Chenin Blanc, dry
Merlot
Pinot Grigio
Pinot Noir
sparkling wine

Macaroni and cheese has a
creamy, palate-coating sauce.
Chardonnay is a fat and sassy
pairing — they meld together
— while white Burgundy pro-
vides firmer acidity and more
contrast.
— MADELINE TRIFFON, MS,
    director of wine, Matt Prentice
    Restaurant Group (Detroit)

MACKEREL
Beaujolais-Villages
beer, esp. pilsner or wheat beer
Chardonnay, Italian
cider, dry
Graves, white
lemon-based drinks (e.g., lemon-
    ade, sparkling water with
    lemon, etc.)
MUSCADET, ESP. DRY
Pinot Grigio
Rhône wine, low-acid (e.g.,
    Marsanne, Viognier)
Riesling, Alsatian
sake, esp. dai ginjo
Sancerre
SAUVIGNON BLANC, ESP.
    NEW WORLD
Sémillon
Vinho Verde
white wine, dry

Mackerel is often served in
vinegar with onion, so you need
a low-acid wine from the
Rhone.
— JEAN-LUC LE DÙ,
    Le Dû's Wines (NYC)

MAHI-MAHI
Barbera d'Alba, esp. with grilled
    mahi-mahi
Burgundy, red, esp. with grilled
    mahi-mahi
Pinot Grigio / Pinot Gris
Pinot Noir

Pouilly-Fumé
tropical fruit drinks esp. papaya,
pineapple (e.g., Fizzy Lizzy
sparkling pineapple juice)

MALT
port, tawny
sake, sweet

*I'll pair a 10-year-old tawny
port with our malted pudding.*
— PAUL GRIECO, general
manager, Hearth (NYC)

MANGOES
IN GENERAL
Chardonnay
cocktails made with Kirsch or
rum
Condrieu
Gewürztraminer
ice wine
lime-based drinks (e.g., limeade,
sparkling water with lime, etc.)
raspberry-based drinks (e.g.,
Fizzy Lizzy sparkling
raspberry-lemon juice)
**RIESLING, ESP. SWEETER OR
LATE HARVEST**
rum, white
Sauvignon Blanc, esp. New World
Viognier

DESSERTS
Champagne, demi-sec
ice wine
Late Harvest white wine
Muscat (e.g., de Rivesaltes)
Sauternes

MAPLE SYRUP
Burgundy, white
Chardonnay, buttery
Riesling, German
Shiraz, sparkling
Viognier

MARJORAM
Merlot
Pinot Noir
Retsina
Sauvignon Blanc
Sémillon

MASCARPONE (ITALIAN
FRESH TRIPLE-CREAM
"CHEESE")
beer, fruit
Champagne, esp. dry
limoncello, Italian liqueur
Marsala
Moscato d'Asti
Muscat
Riesling, Late Harvest
sweet wine

MAYONNAISE
Chablis, unoaked
Champagne
**CHARDONNAY, UNOAKED
TO LIGHTLY OAKED**
martini, gin
slightly sweet wine
sparkling wine

MCDONALD'S BIG
MAC
Beaujolais-Villages
Cabernet Sauvignon
Cabernet / Shiraz blend
Chenin Blanc
Gewürztraminer
Riesling, off-dry
rosé, off-dry
Zinfandel, white

McDONALD'S
FILET-O-FISH
SANDWICH
Sauvignon Blanc, esp. New
Zealand

MEAT LOAF
Beaujolais
Bordeaux, red
CABERNET SAUVIGNON
Dolcetto
Malbec
MERLOT
Pinot Noir
Zinfandel

MEDITERRANEAN
CUISINE (E.G., ANCHOVIES,
OLIVES, PEPPERS, ETC.)
Champagne, rosé
Châteauneuf-du-Pape, white
Pinot Blanc
red wine, esp. tart Old World
rosé
Verdicchio, esp. with onion-based
dishes

*With Mediterranean cuisine,
you want to drink tart, drying
Old World red wines.*
— MADELINE TRIFFON, MS,
director of wine, Matt Prentice
Restaurant Group (Detroit)

MELON
IN GENERAL
Banyuls
berry-flavored drinks (e.g., Fizzy
Lizzy sparkling raspberry-
lemon juice)
Champagne, esp. demi-sec
cocktails made with Cognac,
Cointreau, Curaçao, Grand
Marnier, Kirsch, or Madeira
Gewürztraminer
ginger ale
ice wine
Late Harvest wine
lemon- or lime-based drinks (e.g.,
lemonade, sparkling water with
lime, etc.)
Moscato d'Asti

Muscat, esp. Beaumes-de-Venise
or orange

Pinot Blanc

PORT

Riesling, esp. off-dry to sweet

rosé

sherry, esp. cream

**tea, fine Keemun black, esp.
with honeydew melon**

Vouvray, demi-sec

WITH PROSCIUTTO

lemon-based drinks (e.g., lemonade, sparkling water with
lemon, etc.)

Madeira

Muscat, dry

Pinot Grigio/Pinot Gris

port

rosé, esp. California

sherry, oloroso

**sparkling wine, dry, esp.
Prosecco**

Vernaccia

MERINGUES

Asti

**Champagne, esp. sweet
MOSCATO D'ASTI**

Muscat, esp. Beaumes-de-Venise
or orange

Sauternes, esp. with creamy
desserts

sparkling wine, esp. sweet

MEXICAN CUISINE

(SEE ALSO CHILES BECAUSE
MEXICAN DISHES SHOULD BE
PAIRED TO THEIR SAUCES AND
NOT THEIR MEATS)

IN GENERAL

agua fresca **(nonalcoholic
Mexican fruit drink)**

Albarino, esp. with fish and
seafood

**Barbera, esp. with tomato-based
sauces**

Beaujolais Cru

**BEER, ESP. LAGER, DOUBLE
BOCK (ESP. WITH BEANS,
MUSHROOMS),** Mexican,
pilsner, porter (esp. with mole),
or wheat

Cabernet Sauvignon, esp.
Chilean, and esp. with meat
dishes

Champagne, dry

**Chenin Blanc esp. with salty
and/or spicy appetizers**

Chianti

Gewürztraminer

Grenache

Grüner Veltliner

horchata (dairy-free beverage
made from rice and almonds),
esp. with spicy dishes

**Malbec, esp. with beef, lamb, or
pork**

MARGARITAS

**Merlot, light and/or New World,
esp. with meat**

Mexican wine (e.g., Château
Camou) and beer

off-dry to sweeter wine

Petite Sirah

Pinot Grigio/Pinot Gris, esp.
with spicier dishes

Pinot Noir

**RIESLING, ESP. OFF-DRY
GERMAN**

rosé, esp. with spicier dishes

Sangiovese, esp. with tomato-
based sauces

**SAUVIGNON BLANC, ESP.
NEW ZEALAND** AND ESP.
WITH SEAFOOD, VEG-
ETABLE, AND HERBED
DISHES

Shiraz/Syrah, esp. with meat

**SPARKLING WINE, DRY (e.g.,
Cava, sparkling Vinho Verde,
and New Mexican Gruet)**

tamarindo (Mexican "lemonade"
made with tamarind)

tequila

Valpolicella

Viognier

**ZINFANDEL, ESP. WITH
MEAT**

APPETIZERS, ESP. FRIED

Albarino

Champagne

sparkling wine, dry

AVOID

highly tannic wine

At Mexican restaurants, I'll drink margaritas and beer. When it comes to beer, beer snobs look at Mexican beer and ask, "What do those exist for? It is piss water!" I contend they are fundamentally different from American piss-water beers. Bad American beer smells like a frat house floor to me. It is brewed from rice and corn, not even barley, for God's sake. Tecate and Corona beers are clean and light and don't have a lot of character, but they cleanse that chile oil from your palate. There are some better beers, like Pacifico and Negro Modello, which have more character. If the Mexican food is lower on the lower heat scale and in the spectrum of flavors of tomatillos, epazote, cilantro and green chiles, it seems to blend well with New Zealand Sauvignon Blanc. For red wine with Mexican food, I find a well-behaved Zinfandel works, especially with meat dishes, as long as the dish is not on the spicy side. For spice, I like bubbles. I would never drink a delicate Champagne with spicy Mexican, because the Champagne would be lost. Other bubblies work great, however, such as Cava, sparkling Vinho Verde, and New Mexican Gruet.
— DAVID ROSENGARTEN, editor in chief, www.DavidRosengarten.com

Wine offers more thrilling complexity than any other beverage — more intricate layerings of aroma, more diversity of flavor, more spirit — which means wine is absolutely the most perfect match for the complex, varied dishes Mexico's classic cooks have turned out for centuries.
— JILL GUBESCH, sommelier, Frontera Grill and Topolobampo (Chicago)

With Mexican food you want to drink a lager like Pilsner Urquell. Corona and Heineken will work as well.
— CARLOS SOLIS, food and beverage director/chef, Sheraton Four Points LAX

I had an editor of Gourmet *with me at La Palapa restaurant and we had a smoked beer with a mushroom quesadilla. Though he wasn't into smoked beers, with this combination, he said, "Hey!" When smoked beer is paired with a pork chop or pork tenderloin in a pipian [Mexican green pumpkin-seed sauce] sauce, it is great! Mexican food is extremely earthy. Everything from the beans to the smoked chiles gives a lot of earthiness that is counterpointed by lime juice to create tension. So earthy, malty beers work. Double bocks that smell and taste like dark bread out of the oven with toffee notes play into beans and mushrooms.*
— GARRETT OLIVER, brewmaster, Brooklyn Brewcry

TIP: Chef Zarela Martinez of Zarela in New York first told us of the resurgence in Mexican wine-making, and introduced us to the Mexican wine **Château Camou,** which is similar to a French Viognier and a delicious accompaniment to Mexican food.

MIDDLE EASTERN CUISINE
Beaujolais or Beaujolais-Villages
Chianti Classico
fruity wine
Pinot Grigio

Pinot Noir, New World
Riesling
rosé, dry
Sauvignon Blanc
Shiraz/Syrah
Valpolicella
Vernaccia
Viognier

AVOID
highly tannic wine

MINESTRONE (SEE SOUP, MINESTRONE)

MINT
IN GENERAL
Cabernet Franc
CABERNET SAUVIGNON, CALIFORNIA
Gewürztraminer
Merlot
Pinot Noir
Riesling
Sauvignon Blanc
Shiraz/Syrah

DESSERTS
Asti
Moscato d'Asti
Muscat de Beaumes-de-Venise
tea, green and/or vanilla

MISO AND MISO SOUP

Champagne
Chardonnay
Pinot Noir, California
sake
sparkling wine

MOLE (MEXICAN SAUCE)

IN GENERAL
beer, esp. brown ale or porter
Riesling, German Auslese
Zinfandel, esp. with fruity mole

No wine can come close to a match like porter with mole sauce. It is the bomb!
— GARRETT OLIVER, brewmaster, Brooklyn Brewery

MONKFISH

Burgundy, white, esp. Condrieu or Puligny-Montrachet
CHARDONNAY, ESP. CALIFORNIA
Châteauneuf-du-Pape, white
cider
Gewürztraminer, Alsatian, esp. with Asian spices or curry sauce
Hermitage, white
lemon-based drinks (e.g., lemonade, sparkling water with lemon, etc.)
Pinot Bianco
Pinot Gris, esp. Alsatian
Pinot Noir, esp. Californian
red wine, young and tannic
Rhône white wine
Riesling, esp. Alsatian and/or dry, esp. with roasted monkfish

rosé
Tokay

MORELS (SEE MUSHROOMS, MORELS)

MORNING (SEE ALSO BREAKFAST/BRUNCH)

coffee
tea, black, esp. Assam, Ceylon, late Darjeeling, and Yunnan

MOROCCAN CUISINE

Cabernet Sauvignon
Riesling, off-dry
Rioja
rosé, esp. with salad
Sauvignon Blanc, esp. with chicken and fish
TEA, MINT, AFTER THE MEAL
Vin Gris
Viognier

MOUSSAKA (GREEK EGGPLANT AND LAMB CASSEROLE)

Cabernet Sauvignon
Chianti
Côtes du Rhône
GREEK WINES (e.g., Nemea, Retsina, Roditys)
Ribera del Duero
Rioja

MOUSSE (AIRY DESSERTS)

Champagne, esp. sweet
Moscato d'Asti
sparkling wine, esp. semisweet

MUFFINS, FRUIT

coffee, light-roasted

MUSHROOMS AND MUSHROOM SAUCES

IN GENERAL
aged wines
Barbaresco
Barbera
Barolo
Bordeaux, red, esp. Pomerol
BURGUNDY, RED
Cabernet Sauvignon, esp. with portobellos
Champagne, esp. French
Chardonnay (no oak), esp. with mushrooms in cream sauce
Châteauneuf-du-Pape, White
Chenin Blanc
cocktails made with Madeira
lemon-based drinks (e.g., lemonade, sparkling water with lemon, etc.)
Madeira
Malbec
Merlot
Pinot Blanc
*PINOT NOIR, ESP. OREGON
red wine
Rioja
Sauvignon Blanc
sherry
sparkling wine
Zinfandel

CHANTERELLES
Arneis, Italian
Riesling
Tokay Pinot Gris, Alsatian
white wine, off-dry

MORELS
Burgundy, red
Burgundy, white (e.g., Meursault)
Cabernet Sauvignon
Champagne
Chardonnay, California
lemon-based drinks (e.g., lemonade, sparkling water with lemon, etc.)
Merlot
PINOT NOIR

Mushrooms are magical when it comes to wine. It is the one ingredient that can create a platform for wine to show well. Mushrooms are spectacular with red wines with an earthy aroma, or white wines with some age. — TIM KOPEC, wine director, Veritas (NYC)

Pinot Noir and mushrooms are a slam dunk.
— TRACI DES JARDINS, chef, Jardiniere (San Francisco)

Mushrooms are delicious with wine as long as the characteristics of the mushrooms and the wine are compatible. In general, I prefer chanterelles with slightly off-dry white wines, such as dry German, Alsatian, or Austrian Rieslings. Morels are usually better when paired with creamier and milder meats like veal and they then are wonderful with Burgundy, Bordeaux, Napa Valley and Washington State Cabernets. Spanish Tempranillo, Barolo and big Tuscan wines can go with the meatier mushrooms, like shiitake, hedgehogs, and porcini. — LARRY STONE, MS, Rubicon (San Francisco)

We do a lot of dishes with both foraged and cultivated varieties of mushrooms. Some of those dishes — like the Mushroom Baklava — are terrific with earthy Pinot Noirs. Not every Pinot Noir will work with this: Some, while excellent, are crafted to show off their fruit. For this dish, I'm looking for a wine that is a little more austere, where I can taste the soil and the sun. That might take me to the Côtes Nuit, or to some of the vineyards in Oregon or Josh Jensen's Calera single vineyard Pinot Noirs that he makes in a very Burgundian style. — JANOS WILDER, chef-owner, Janos (Tucson)

rosé
Sancerre
Sauternes
Vouvray

OYSTER
Arneis, Italian
Sauvignon Blanc
Sémillon

PORCINI (CÈPES)
Barolo
Bordeaux, red, esp. dry (e.g., Pomerol)
cocktails made with Marsala
Merlot
Pinot Noir
Tempranillo

PORTOBELLO
Cabernet Sauvignon
Pinot Noir

SHIITAKE
Barolo
beer, esp. Sapporo or other Japanese beer
Bordeaux
Brunello di Montalcino
Burgundy, red
Cabernet Sauvignon
Chablis Grand Cru
Grüner Veltliner
Merlot
Pinot Gris / Pinot Grigio
red wine, dry, esp. Italian, Portuguese, or Spanish

sake
Tempranillo

WILD
Barbaresco
Barbera
Barolo
Beaujolais
Chardonnay
Châteauneuf-du-Pape
Chianti Classico Riserva
Condrieu
Merlot
PINOT NOIR
Rioja, red
Sangiovese
sparkling wine
Super Tuscan
Viognier

MUSSELS

IN GENERAL
Albarino
BEER, ESP. BELGIAN OR GERMAN WEISS OR WHEAT, OR PILSNER
Burgundy, white
Chablis
Champagne, esp. with steamed mussels
Chardonnay, esp. California (esp. with a butter, cream, and/or garlic sauce)
cocktails made with Cognac or Pernod
Graves, dry white
lemon-based drinks (e.g., lemonade, sparkling water with lemon, etc.)
*MUSCADET
Pinot Grigio / Pinot Gris
Riesling, esp. dry
rosé
Sancerre
SAUVIGNON BLANC, ESP. CALIFORNIA OR NEW ZEALAND, AND ESP. WITH GARLICKY, HERBY, AND/OR SPICY MUSSELS
Savennieres

Sémillon, esp. aged
sherry, esp. amontillado or fino
sparkling wine
Traminer/Riesling
Verdicchio
Viognier
Vouvray

WITH COCONUT MILK
AND/OR SPICINESS
Chardonnay
Grüner Veltliner
Riesling, off-dry
Sauvignon Blanc
Sylvaner, off-dry
Viognier

*Australia's Rosemount
Vineyards makes a Traminer/
Riesling that is Gewürztraminer
and Riesling blended together. I
had it with mussels in a cream,
butter, and white wine reduction. The mussels were sweet,
and the cream sweetened up as
it reduced — and with the
wine, it was great.*

— JOSHUA WESSON,
wine director, Best Cellars

MUSTARD AND MUSTARD SAUCE
Burgundy, white
Chablis
CHARDONNAY (NO OAK)
cider
Côtes du Rhône
Merlot
Pinot Grigio/Pinot Gris
Pinot Noir
Riesling, esp. German Kabinett
Sancerre
**Sauvignon Blanc, New Zealand,
esp. with Dijon or sweet mus-
tard**
Shiraz/Syrah

Zinfandel
TIP: Dijon mustard is the most
wine-friendly mustard.

NACHOS (SEE ALSO MEXICAN CUISINE)
beer, esp. lager
margaritas
sparkling wine
Zinfandel

NECTARINES (SEE ALSO PEACHES)
CHAMPAGNE, DEMI-SEC
ice wine
Moscato d'Asti
Muscat, esp. Beaumes-de-Venises
**RIESLING, SWEET (e.g.,
Beerenauslese, Late Harvest)**
Sauternes or Barsac
sparkling wine, esp. sweet
Vouvray, demi-sec

NUTMEG
Burgundy, white
Cabernet Sauvignon
Chardonnay, esp. oaked
Merlot
Pinot Blanc
Pinot Noir, esp. New World
Syrah
Viognier
Zinfandel

NUTS (SEE ALSO SPECIFIC NUTS)
IN GENERAL (INCLUDING
SAVORY DISHES)
Beaujolais
beer, esp. ale
Chardonnay
Chianti
Madeira, esp. dry
Merlot
Pinot Noir

port, tawny or vintage
red wine
Sangiovese
**SHERRY, DRY, ESP. AMON-
TILLADO AND FINO**
**SHERRY, SWEET, ESP.
OLOROSO**
sparkling wine, esp. off-dry
tannic red wines
Zinfandel

*Nuts are an underappreciated
accompaniment to wine. You
want them with the skin on, so
the flavor harkens to the tannins
of the red wine.*

— STEVEN JENKINS, cheese-
monger, Fairway Market (NYC)

DESSERTS
Amaretto
Angelica
Asti
Banyuls
Champagne, demi-sec
Chardonnay
Late Harvest wine
MADEIRA
Marsala
Muscat
**PORT, ESP. TAWNY OR
VINTAGE**
**SHERRY, ESP. SWEET (e.g.,
cream, oloroso, or PX)**
sparkling wine, esp. brut
Vin Santo

OLIVE OIL AND OLIVES
Albarino
Bandol wines
beer
Gewürztraminer
red wine, esp. Old World
Riesling
Rioja
**ROSÉ, ESP. DRY, ESP. WITH
SALAD**

Sauvignon Blanc
*SHERRY, DRY, ESP. FINO, MANZANILLA OR AMONTILLADO, AND ESP. WITH GREEN OLIVES
sparkling wine
vermouth / vermouth spritzer

OMELET (SEE EGGS, OMELETS)

ONIONS

COOKED (SEE ALSO SOUP, ONION)
Beaujolais
beer
Burgundy, white
Champagne
Chardonnay, esp. buttery
Côtes du Rhône
Gewürztraminer, esp. Alsatian
Grüner Veltliner
Merlot
Pinot Blanc, Alsatian, esp. with onion tart
Pinot Gris, Alsatian, esp. with onion tart
Riesling, Alsatian and/or Late Harvest, esp. with onion tart
rosé
Shiraz / Syrah
sparkling wine
Tempranillo
Verdicchio
WHITE WINE, ALSATIAN

RAW (AS IN A SALAD OR AS A GARNISH)
beer or ale
rosé
white wine, dry

When pairing wine to food, I watch out for onions, chives, and leeks because they are so strong and pungent. If they are roasted or sautéed, they are much milder and more wine friendly. — TIM KOPEC, wine director, Veritas (NYC)

ORANGES

DESSERTS
Asti
Champagne
coffee, esp. light-roasted
ice wine
Moscato d'Asti
MUSCAT, ESP. ORANGE, OR BEAUMES-DE-VENISE
plum wine, Japanese
Riesling, Late Harvest
Riesling, sweet
Sauternes
sparkling wine
tea, Assam or sweet Yunnan
Tokaji, Hungarian

SAVORY DISHES
cocktails made with Armagac, brandy, Cointreau, Grand Marnier, or Kirsch
Gewürztraminer
RIESLING, GERMAN
Sauvignon Blanc, New World
Sémillon
sherry
sparkling wine
tea

TIP: With his dish of Shrimp with Blood Orange and Fennel Salad, chef Cesare Casella of New York City's Maremma restaurant serves a glass of sparkling wine to which a spoonful of blood orange juice has been added.

OREGANO
beer
Cabernet Sauvignon
Châteauneuf-du-Pape
Dolcetto
Gigondas
Merlot
Nebbiolo
Sangiovese, including Chianti
SAUVIGNON BLANC
Shiraz / Syrah
Zinfandel

OREO COOKIES
Banyuls
milk
port

Milk's Favorite Cookie. — OREO'S ADVERTISING CAMPAIGN SLOGAN

OSSO BUCO (AND OTHER RICH, MEATY DISHES)
Barbaresco
Barbera
BAROLO
Brunello di Montalcino
Cabernet Sauvignon
Dolcetto d'Alba
Merlot
Pinot Noir
red wine full-bodied
Shiraz / Syrah
Super Tuscans
Valpolicella
Zinfandel

OXTAILS
Barbaresco
Barolo
Beaujolais Cru
beer, esp. brown ale
Brunello di Montalcino
Burgundy, red
Châteauneuf-du-Pape
cocktails made with Madeira
Madeira, esp. aged
Merlot
Ribera del Duero
sherry, amontillado
Syrah / Shiraz
Zinfandel

OYSTERS

IN GENERAL (I.E., RAW OR STEAMED)

Albarino

Aligoté

beer, esp. stout (e.g., dry or oyster) and esp.*GUINNESS, lager, pilsner, or porter, esp. when oysters are dressed (e.g., with oyster sauce or mignonette)

Bordeaux, white

Burgundy, white

Cava

***CHABLIS, DRY FRENCH (*NOT* CALIFORNIA)**

CHAMPAGNE, ESP. BLANC DE BLANCS AND/OR DRY

Chardonnay (no oak)

Chenin Blanc, dry

cider, draft

cocktails made with Pernod

high-acid wine

lemon-based drinks (e.g., lemonade, sparkling water with lemon, etc.)

Loire Valley white wine

low-alcohol wine

***MUSCADET, ESP. WITH FRESH, BRINY OYSTERS**

Pinot Blanc

Pinot Grigio

Riesling, very dry (e.g., Trocken-style)

Chef Rebecca Charles's "Pearls" of Pairing Oysters

Raw Oysters

I love Champagne so much I drink it with raw oysters, simply because I love Champagne! It is my drink. The primary flavor of an oyster is its brininess and minerality, so you want a high-acid wine that is dry and minerally with a really crisp, clean finish. You don't want a fat and flabby wine — and oak is the biggest no-no when it comes to oysters and wine. You won't go wrong with **Chablis, Sauvignon Blanc,** or **unoaked Chardonnay.** If you want an inexpensive wine, **Muscadet** and **Pinot Blanc** are great choices. A Pinot Blanc is light with a green apple flavor that goes great with oysters. Muscadet is a legendary combination, and it is noted as *the* oyster wine. If you have a wine with a little fizz and apple, it is great. Another wine not to overlook is **rosé.** A rosé with a little fruit is great with a fat rich oyster like Kumamoto from California. For a still wine (if I am not drinking Champagne), **Sancerre** is the perfect oyster wine because it can be green-apple-y; it is fresh with good fruit but not too much. For my money, this is it. My favorite Sancerre is Crochet — and Croix du Bois is also terrific. However, if I am sitting by the water, I want a pint of beer! The beer needs to be a simple beer that is not too colorful. Go for something that is more golden in color, like a **lager** or **pilsner.** I would choose a German or Czech beer because they are slightly bitter and light in flavor. **Vodka** is a good combination with oysters — the only problem is that after a couple of vodkas, you aren't tasting the oysters. I like **hard cider** (such as Maeve's Draft Cider) with oysters because it has enough sweetness and backbone to stand up to oysters. Neither will overpower the other.

Cooked Oysters

When you are pairing a drink to a cooked oyster, you need to look at the other ingredients and not just the oyster. What is your sauce? A grilled oyster topped with a flavored beurre blanc is wonderful. I like to add tarragon or even some diced beet to the beurre blanc. With a butter sauce, you want something to cut it — so **Chablis, Sauvignon Blanc,** or **Muscadet** would all work. If you have a sweeter butter sauce, you can also pair a fruitier wine with a hint of sweetness like **dry Riesling** or **Grüner Veltliner.** In the south, they grill oysters and top them with a sweet barbecue sauce — again, look to Germany and Austrian varietals. Oyster Pan Roast is made with sherry and cream, and would be good with a **dry sherry.** In the case of Oysters Rockefeller, you would have **Champagne,** because that is the traditional pairing. However, I find a cold **vodka** to be an even better pairing.

sake, esp. ginjo

Sancerre

SAUVIGNON BLANC, DRY, ESP. CALIFORNIA OR NEW ZEALAND

Savennieres

sherry, dry, esp. fino or manzanilla

SPARKLING WINE

Tocai Friulano, dry

Txakoli

Vinho Verde

vodka

Vouvray, dry

white wine (no oak)

WHITE WINE, VERY DRY AND TART

AVOID

fruity wine

high-alcohol wine

low-acid wine

OAKED WINES (WITH RAW OYSTERS)

red wine

Riesling, other than the driest of dry

sweet wine

tannic wine

WITH BUTTER OR CREAM SAUCE

Burgundy, white

Champagne

Chardonnay, esp. buttery

Châteauneuf-du-Pape, white

WITH CIDER VINEGAR MIGNONETTE SAUCE

cider

Muscadet, esp. apple-y

Sauvignon Blanc, esp. apple-y

FRIED

Chardonnay, California

SPARKLING WINE

water with big bubbles (e.g., Apollinaris)

PAN-ROAST

Chablis

sherry, dry

When it comes to very briny seafood and oysters, it is very hard to find a satisfactory wine. I encourage people to try sake with oysters. Oysters are also really good with dry manzanilla sherry — however, it is even harder to get people to try sherry than it is to get them to try sake. Some people have an aversion to sherry; they think it is for old ladies, or they think I mean cream sherry, which would be God-awful with oysters. Kumumato oysters, which are very delicate, work well with wine. Belon or Speciales work best with sake.

— LARRY STONE, MS, Rubicon (San Francisco)

An oyster is either a salty ball of fat, or it is a salty creamy ball of fat — so you need something with acidity. A wine with oak is not going to work, and you want to keep the alcohol down, so you need a razor-sharp bottle of wine. The classic pairing would be Chablis or Muscadet, which is what all the Brits drink. Try Tocai Friulano from Northern Italy or German Riesling in the Trocken style, because they can both be very dry. — GREG HARRINGTON, MS

Chablis with oysters is a classic pairing — but not with every oyster, because oysters have different structures. A good Olympia, Malpeque, or Belon is where you need Chablis. But with some of the monstrous Gulf oysters, Chablis is not the right match. A Kumumoto has an intense flavor, so a more intense wine like Sancerre can hang with it. I personally don't think Riesling and oysters ever cut it. Even a very dry Riesling has a particular fruitiness that does not harmonize well with the minerality and saltiness of the oyster. Riesling does not do so well in salty soil, the way Chardonnay and Sauvignon Blanc or Muscadet can. I don't think Champagne works so well with oysters, either. The texture of bubbles doesn't work well. You get a very metallic experience when you join the briny characteristic of the oyster with the slightly sweet character of the Champagne. A humble wine like Muscadet, from the mouth of the Loire River, is made out of the same stuff as the oyster is — and pairs perfectly.

— JOSEPH SPELLMAN, MS, Joseph Phelps Vineyards

Rinse your glass with a little sake to get just the essence of it, and pour it out. Fill the glass with ice, add cucumber, vodka, and lime sour, and shake. This cocktail is crisp and beautiful with oysters, mussels, or sashimi.

— KATHY CASEY, chef/owner, Kathy Casey Food Studios (Seattle)

PO' BOY (FRIED OYSTER
SANDWICH)
beer, esp. lager or pilsner

ROCKEFELLER
Champagne
vodka

STEW
Albarino
Chardonnay, esp. big and buttery
Riesling, Alsatian and/or dry
Sémillon, California
sherry, fino

BELON
Chablis
Muscadet

sake
sherry, dry, esp. manzanilla

EAST COAST (E.G., BLUE
POINTS OR MALPEQUES,
WHICH TEND TO HAVE
SMOOTH SHELLS AND TO BE
LARGER, THINNER, LEANER,
MILDER, AND SALTIER)
beer, esp. stout
Champagne
Pinot Gris
Sauvignon Blanc
sherry, esp. dry

JAPANESE (WHICH TEND TO
BE FATTER AND RICHER)
rosé
sake

KUMAMOTO
Chenin Blanc
Pinot Gris
rosé
sake
Sancerre
Sauvignon Blanc, esp. New
    Zealand
Vinho Verde

LOUISIANA (WHICH TEND
TO BE LARGER, MUDDIER
OYSTERS)
Chablis
fuller-bodied wine
Muscadet

MALPECQUE
Chablis

OLYMPIA
Chablis

SPECIALES
sake

WELLFLEET
Champagne

WEST COAST (E.G.,
OLYMPIA, WHICH TEND TO
HAVE ROUGH TEXTURED
SHELLS, AND TO BE SMALL-
ER, MEATIER, RICHER,
CREAMIER, AND SWEETER
WITH MORE MINERALITY)
Chablis
Chardonnay, dry
Pinot Blanc, dry
Sauvignon Blanc, California

PAD THAI (THAI RICE-
NOODLE DISH)
beer, esp. Singha or wheat
Gewürztraminer, Alsatian
low-alcohol wine
off-dry to sweeter white wine
**Riesling, German, esp. Kabinett
    or Spätlese**
Sauvignon Blanc, New Zealand
sparkling wine
white wine, Alsatian or off-dry
    German

AVOID
high-alcohol wine
tannic wine

With Pad Thai, I'll drink German Spätlese or Kabinett. If it is Kabinett, it will be from the Rheingau; if Spätlese, from the Mosel. If I have Gewürztraminer, it will be from Alsace. You want slightly off-dry German whites or full-flavored Alsatian wines. You need low-alcohol, sweetness, and/or a highly perfumed wine, which is what marries best.

— TIM KOPEC, wine director, Veritas (NYC)

PAELLA

Albarino
Beaujolais, esp. young
red wine, young Spanish
Ribera del Duero, esp. with chicken and sausage paella
RIOJA, ESP. WITH MEATY PAELLA
Rioja, white, esp. with shellfish paella
ROSÉ, DRY SPANISH OR CÔTES DE PROVENCE
sherry, fino or manzanilla
Shiraz, young
Tempranillo
Txakoli
Viognier, Spanish, esp. with seafood paella
Viura

PANCAKES (SEE BREAKFAST/BRUNCH)

PANNA COTTA
(ITALIAN CUSTARD-LIKE DESSERT)
Asti
Late Harvest Riesling
Moscato d'Asti
Muscat, esp. orange

PAPAYAS

Chardonnay
Gewürztraminer
ginger ale
Late Harvest wine
lemon- or lime-based drinks (e.g., lemonade, sparkling water with lime, etc.)
port
Riesling
tropical fruit (esp., passion fruit, pineapple) juice, sparkling (e.g. Fizzy Lizzy)
Viognier

PAPRIKA

beer, esp. lager
Blaufränkisch
Bordeaux, red, esp. aged
Cabernet Sauvignon, young
Hungarian wine
Merlot
Zinfandel, fruity

PARSLEY
SAUVIGNON BLANC

PASSION FRUIT

Champagne
Late Harvest wine
Moscatel
Moscato d'Asti
Muscat
Riesling, sweet, esp. Auslese, Late Harvest, or Trockenbeerenauslese
Sauternes

PASTA (NOTE: MATCH THE WINE TO THE SAUCE)

IN GENERAL (IN CASE YOU'RE ASKED TO BRING THE WINE FOR "PASTA" — AND DON'T KNOW THE SAUCE!)
Barbera
beer, esp. amber or lager
Chianti
Italian wine, esp. red
Primativo
Sangiovese

WITH ARTICHOKES
Sauvignon Blanc
Vermentino

With paella, I prefer a white Albarino or Txakoli wine, because they have clean, fresh acidity — although I also really enjoy a red wine. Paella is a family dish that is often cooked outside in the orange groves over vine or tree trimmings. The dish has a smokiness from being cooked outside. Also, it is not made with stock, but with spring water. If meat is used, it is often sautéed in the pan before the rice is put in, so you have an element of smoke. You have that pinch of saffron that is a note you have to look for. All this leads me to Riojas, because they have a smoky quality to them.

— RON MILLER, maître d'hôtel, Solera (NYC)

I prefer rosé with paella, as sometimes Rioja can be a little too earthy with it.
— JEAN-LUC LE DÛ, Le Dû's Wines (NYC)

BAKED (E.G., LASAGNA)
CHIANTI
Merlot

WITH BEETS
Sangiovese

BOLOGNESE
Cabernet Sauvignon, esp. New World
Chianti
Merlot, New World
Sangiovese
Zinfandel

WITH BUTTER SAUCE
Chardonnay, esp. buttery
Pinot Grigio / Pinot Gris
Vernaccia

ALLA CARBONARA
Amarone
Barbera d'Alba
Chardonnay, esp. lighter-bodied Italian
Chianti Classico
Orvieto Classico
Pinot Bianco
Pinot Grigio

WITH CHEESE SAUCE
Barbera
Chardonnay, esp. lighter-bodied Italian
Chianti
Dolcetto
Pinot Grigio / Pinot Gris
Riesling, esp. German Kabinett

WITH CHICKEN STOCK
Barbaresco

WITH CLAM SAUCE
Arneis
Burgundy, white
Chardonnay, New World (no oak)
Prosecco, dry
Soave

WITH CREAM SAUCE
CHARDONNAY, ITALIAN
Gavi
Pinot Bianco
Pinot Grigio
Prosecco
Riesling, esp. German Kabinett
Soave

WITH CREAMY SEAFOOD SAUCE
Chardonnay
Vernaccia
Viognier

AL FREDO
CHARDONNAY, ESP. BUTTERY

WITH LOBSTER
Burgundy, white, esp. Mersault
Champagne
Chardonnay, New World
Riesling

WITH MEATBALLS AND/OR MEAT SAUCE
Barbera d'Alba or d'Asti
Chianti, esp. Classico (or Rufina)
Dolcetto d'Alba
Merlot, esp. Italian
Montepulçiano d'Abruzzo
Nebbiolo
Sangiovese
Valpolicella
Zinfandel

WITH MUSHROOMS
Barbera
Chardonnay, Italian
Dolcetto
Merlot
PINOT NOIR, ESP. NEW WORLD
rosé, esp. fruity

WITH MUSSELS
Chenin Blanc
Pinot Grigio
Riesling
Rosé
Sauvignon Blanc
sparkling wine, dry
Vino Nobile di Montepulciano

WITH OLIVE OIL
Barbera, esp. with garlic and/or herbs
Chianti, esp. with garlic
Dolcetto, esp. with dried chili flakes
Galestro
Sauvignon Blanc
Soave, esp. with dried chili flakes
Valpolicella
Vermentino, esp. with garlic

WITH PESTO (SEE PESTO)

PRIMAVERA (LIGHT CREAM SAUCE WITH VEGETABLES)
Arneis
Chardonnay
Pinot Grigio
Prosecco
Sauvignon Blanc, New World

WITH RED SAUCE (SEE PASTA, WITH TOMATO SAUCE)

WITH RICOTTA CHEESE (E.G., LASAGNA, MANICOTTI, RAVIOLI)
CHIANTI CLASSICO OR RISERVA, ESP. WITH TOMATO SAUCE
Montepulciano
Zinfandel

WITH SARDINES
Chardonnay, Italian

Verdicchio
Vinho Verde
white wine, esp. Sicilian

WITH SAUSAGE
Barbera
Syrah
Zinfandel

WITH SEAFOOD
Albarino
Chardonnay, light-bodied Italian
Frascati
Muscadet
Orvieto
Pinot Grigio
Sauvignon Blanc
Soave
VERDICCHIO
Vermentino
Vernaccia

WITH SHELLFISH
Chardonnay, Italian
Gavi
Pinot Grigio
Verdicchio

WITH SHRIMP
Chardonnay, California or Italian
Orvieto
Soave

WITH TOMATOES, FRESH CRUSHED
Dolcetto
Pinot Grigio
Sauvignon Blanc

WITH TOMATO SAUCE
BARBERA
beer, esp. amber or lager
CHIANTI
Montepulciano
Pinot Grigio
Sangiovese
Sauvignon Blanc, New World
Verdicchio
Zinfandel, esp. fruity
AVOID
tannic red wine

WITH VEGETABLES
Barbera
Chardonnay, Italian (no oak)
Chianti, esp. young
Dolcetto
Pinot Grigio
Sauvignon Blanc
Soave

PASTRAMI (SEE SANDWICHES, PASTRAMI)

PASTRIES
Champagne, esp. sweet
coffee
Madeira
Muscat de Beaumes-de-Venise
port, tawny
sparkling wine, esp. off-dry to sweet
tea, esp. Assam, black, or English breakfast

PÂTÉ
BEAUJOLAIS (OR OTHER LIGHT REDS), ESP. WITH COUNTRY-STYLE PÂTÉ
beer, esp. stronger lagers
Burgundy, white
Chardonnay, esp. with seafood or vegetable pâté
Riesling, dry, esp. with seafood pâté
Riesling, German, esp. Spätlese, and esp. with liver pâté
rosé
SAUTERNES, ESP. WITH CHICKEN OR GOOSE LIVER PÂTÉ
Sémillon

PEACHES (INCLUDING DESSERTS)
Amaretto
Asti
berry-flavored drinks, esp. raspberry or strawberry (e.g., Fizzy Lizzy sparkling raspberry juice)

Champagne, demi-sec and/or
   rosé
cocktails made with Bourbon,
   brandy, Calvados, Cassis,
   Cognac, Cointreau, framboise,
   Grand Marnier, **Kirsch**,
   Madeira, Marsala, or rum
ice wine
liqueur, raspberry
Madeira
Marsala
Moscato d'Asti
Muscat, orange
**MUSCAT DE BEAUMES-DE-
   VENISE**
orange-based drinks (e.g.,
   orangeade, sparkling water
   with orange, etc.)
port, tawny
raspberry lemon juice, sparkling
   (e.g., Fizzy Lizzy)
**RIESLING, SWEET, ESP.
   GERMAN AUSLESE OR
   LATE HARVEST**
SAUTERNES
sherry, sweet
sparkling wines, esp. demi-sec
tea, oolong, esp. Bai Hao
Vin Santo
Viognier, off-dry to Late Harvest
Vouvray, sparkling and/or sweet
white wine, Late Harvest

PEANUTS AND
PEANUT SAUCE
beer, esp. lager
Chardonnay, oaked
Gewürztraminer
gin and tonic
Riesling

AVOID
red wine

*Blue Smoke restaurant [in New
York City] has an appetizer on
the menu called Blue Smoke
Peanuts. They bring a jar on a
tray with an unbroken cap and
screw-off top and put it on the*

*table. That's the appetizer —
and they are really good. To
drink? A gin and tonic. When I
became of drinking age, I
would sit down with my dad
and have one with a big jar of
Planters peanuts.*

— DAVID ROSENGARTEN,
editor in chief,
www.DavidRosengarten.com

PEARS (SEE ALSO
RECOMMENDATIONS FOR
APPLES)
Asti
**BANYULS, ESP. WITH PEARS
   POACHED IN RED WINE**
Cassis
**Champagne, esp. demi-sec, esp.
   with pear soufflé**
Chardonnay, esp. with savory
   courses (e.g., salad)
cocktails made with Armagac,
   Bourbon, brandy, Calvados,
   Cognac, Curaçao, Grand
   Marnier, Kirsch, Marsala, or
   Muscat
coffee, esp. light-roasted and/or
   with milk
**Gewürztraminer, sweet, esp. Late
   Harvest**
ginger ale
ice wine
**LATE HARVEST WINES, ESP.
   RIESLING, SÉMILLON,
   AND ESP. WITH PEAR
   TART**
lemon-based drinks (e.g., lemon-
   ade, sparkling water with
   lemon, etc.)
Moscato d'Asti
Muscat, black or orange
Muscat de Beaumes-de-Venise
orange-based drinks (e.g., Fizzy
   Lizzy sparkling orange juice)
**RIESLING, ESP. GERMAN
   OFF-DRY TO SWEET, AND
   ESP. BEERENAUSLESE OR
   LATE HARVEST**

Sauvignon Blanc, esp. with savory
   courses (e.g., salad)
Sauternes
sparkling wine, sweet
tea, black, esp. Assam or Yunnan

PEAS
Burgundy, white
Chardonnay, buttery
Chenin Blanc
Grüner Veltliner, dry
**SAUVIGNON BLANC, NEW
   ZEALAND**
Viognier
Vouvray, esp. dry

PECANS (ESP. PECAN PIE
AND OTHER DESSERTS)
Champagne
cocktails made with Bourbon or
   rum
ice wine
**MADEIRA, ESP. BUAL OR
   MALMSEY**
Muscat de Beaumes-de-Venise
Moscato d'Asti
Muscat
PORT, ESP. TAWNY
sherry, oloroso or PX
tea, spiced (e.g., Yerba Chai)
Tokaji

PEPPER, BLACK
beer
CABERNET SAUVIGNON
Champagne, rosé
Gewürztraminer
Sangiovese
Shiraz/Syrah
Zinfandel

*Black pepper in dishes such as
steak au poivre does great
things to wine. An aged ten- to
fifteen-year-old Cabernet
Sauvignon is great. I love old*

American Cabernets — they are better than people give them credit for.
— JEAN-LUC LE DÛ,
Le Dû's Wines (NYC)

PEPPERS, BELL

Beaujolais
Cabernet Franc
Cabernet Sauvignon
Côtes du Rhône
Merlot
Riesling, esp. with red and green peppers
Rioja
rosé, esp. Spanish Rosado, and esp. with red peppers
SAUVIGNON BLANC
Sémillon, esp. with red peppers
Syrah, esp. with green peppers stuffed with beef
Tempranillo
Viognier, esp. with red peppers
Zinfandel, esp. with red and green peppers

PEPPERS, CHILE (SEE CHILES)

PEPPERS, PIQUILLO

sherry, dry, esp. fino

PERCH

Chenin Blanc
rosé
Sauvignon Blanc, California
Vouvray

PERSIMMONS

brandy, esp. pear
cocktails made with brandy or Kirsch
Muscat de Beaumes-de-Venise, esp. with persimmon dessert

PESTO

Albenga
Barbera
Burgundy, white
Chablis
CHARDONNAY (NO OAK) ESP. ITALIAN
Châteauneuf-du-Pape, white
Cinque Terre
Dolcetto
Gavi
Greco di Tufo
Meursault
Pinot Grigio/Pinot Gris
SAUVIGNON BLANC
Soave
sparkling wine, dry
Vermentino
Vernaccia
white wine, esp. Italian

Pesto is from Liguria, and should be matched with a wine from the region like Albenga, Cinque Terre, or Vermentino.
— PIERO SELVAGGIO, owner, Valentino (Los Angeles)

When you have cheese and pine nuts, you need a little body, so I would go with a Chardonnay-based wine from the Old World [e.g., white Burgundy, Chablis, Meursault, etc.].
— JEAN-LUC LE DÛ,
Le Dû's Wines (New York)

PHEASANT

apple-based drinks (e.g., sparkling apple juice, etc.)
Barolo
beer, esp. pale ale
BORDEAUX, RED, ESP. POMEROL OR SAINT-EMILION, AND ESP. WITH ROASTED PHEASANT

BURGUNDY, RED, ESP. WITH ROASTED PHEASANT
Cabernet Sauvigon
Champagne, rosé
Chardonnay, big and oaky California
cocktails made with brandy, Calvados, Madeira, Masala, or whiskey
lemon-based drinks (e.g., lemonade, sparkling water with lemon, etc.)
Merlot
orange-based drinks (e.g., sparkling water with orange)
Pinot Noir, esp. full-bodied, California, and/or Oregon
Riesling, esp. when served with apples
Rioja
Shiraz/Syrah

PICKLES

beer, esp. lighter ale and lager

PICNICS

BEAUJOLAIS
chilled wine (red and white)
inexpensive wine
lemonade
Pinot Noir
raspberry lemon sparkling juice (e.g., Fizzy Lizzy)
Riesling, dry to off-dry
ROSÉ/ROSADO, SPANISH, ESP. DRY
soda
sparkling wine
tea, iced
Zinfandel, light-bodied
Zinfandel, white

PIE

coffee, medium-roasted, esp. with cream-based pie
coffee, light-roasted, esp. with fruit-based pie

PIKE

Riesling, esp. dry Alsatian
Sauvignon Blanc
sparkling wine
Vouvray

PINEAPPLE

IN GENERAL
beer, esp. Blanche
berry-flavored drinks, esp. raspberry or strawberry (e.g., sparkling raspberry juice)
cocktails made with brandy, Cognac, **Cointreau,** Grand Marnier, **Kirsch,** or **rum**
coconut-flavored drinks
Riesling, off-dry, esp. German
rum, esp. dark
Viognier

DESSERTS
Champagne, esp. demi-sec
coffee, esp. medium-to-dark-roasted
Gewürztraminer, sweet, esp. Late Harvest
ice wine
LATE HARVEST WINE, ESP. RIESLING AND SAUVIGNON BLANC
Moscato d'Asti
MUSCAT, SWEET, ESP. BEAUMES-DE-VENISE OR ORANGE
Riesling, sweet, esp. Auslese or Late Harvest
rum, esp. dark
Sauternes
Vin Santo

TIP: We love **Quady Electra** (a 4-percent-alcohol orange Muscat), especially with pineapple desserts.

PISTACHIOS

Asti
Chardonnay, esp. Italian
red wine, esp. fruity Italian
tea, Darjeeling or fired oolong
white wine, Italian

PIZZA

IN GENERAL (I.E., TOMATO AND CHEESE)
BARBERA, ESP. CALIFORNIA OR ITALIAN
BEER, ESP. AMBER ALE, ITALIAN, LAGER, PILSNER, AND/OR OTHER LIGHT-BODIED BEER
Blaufränkisch, Austrian
Cabernet Sauvignon, esp. aged
Champagne
CHIANTI, ESP. CLASSICO
cola, e.g., Coca-Cola
Côtes du Rhône
Dolcetto d'Alba
Lambrusco
Malbec
Merlot
Montalpulciano, esp. d'Abruzzo
Morellino di Scansano
Picon Biere, Alsatian
Pinot Grigio
Pinot Noir
Prosecco, esp. with white pizza
red wine
rosé, dry, esp. California, Spanish and/or dry, and esp. with anchovies
SANGIOVESE
sparkling wine (e.g., Prosecco) and other bubbly beverages
Syrah / Shiraz, red or rosé
Tuscan red wine
Valpolicella

water, sparkling, esp. with medium to large bubbles (e.g., Ramlosa)

ZINFANDEL, ESP. LIGHTER-BODIED

WITH MUSHROOMS
Châteauneuf-du-Pape
Pinot Noir

WITH PEPPERONI
Barbera
beer, esp. American lager
Chianti
Montepulciano d'Abruzzo

WITH PEPPERS AND ONIONS
Cabernet Franc
Chianti
Sauvignon Blanc

WITH SAUSAGE
Barbera
Primitivo
Syrah
Zinfandel

PIZZA, DOMINO'S

(I.E., SWEETER-THAN-AVERAGE PIZZA)
Barbera
Malbec, Argentinian
Merlot
Sangiovese, esp. with pepperoni

AVOID
Cabernet Sauvignon
Syrah
Zinfandel

If you watch people in a Neapolitan restaurant, they're drinking sparkling water, Coke, and beer with their pizza, or they'll serve Prosecco with white pizza — all things with bubbles.
— CHARLES SCICOLONE, wine director, I Trulli and Enoteca (NYC)

Everything goes with pizza. I especially love fruity Tuscan wines like Morellino di Scansano or Montepulciano d'Abruzzo.
— JOSEPH BASTIANICH, restaurateur and owner, Italian Wine Merchants (NYC)

Pizza is tough. Everyone says Chianti goes with pizza, but I think it is the worst pairing — because the average American pizza is sweet, and Chianti is anything but sweet. Chianti is acidic and tannic with dried fruit flavor. Sweetness needs sweetness, and you get that from fruit or sugar. I recommend California Barbera, which is a little more fruity than Italian Barbera. If you want to get esoteric, you can drink Blaufränkisch from Austria.
— GREG HARRINGTON, MS

I'm a pepperoni and mushroom guy myself. Given my choice, I'd drink something Italian. I always like Sangiovese and Chianti. But Montepulciano d'Abruzzo could work very well, as could a Barbera or Dolcetto. If I have a pizza, I don't like to have anything too fancy or complicated with it. I like to have something that fits the level of the occasion — which is not to say that if someone poured a big, fancy bottle that I would never drink it!
— GEORGE COSSETTE, co-owner, Silverlake Wine (Los Angeles)

Pizza and red sauce are notoriously difficult to pair with wine. This is a perfect time to drink inexpensive Chianti or Sangiovese because they go well. I have learned this the hard way, because I have opened up fancy Bordeaux or California cult wines since I have access to such great wine — but this food kills those wines and it is not a pleasure. So, find the most delicious, inexpensive, palatable Chianti that you take pleasure from and have it in your cellar for this reason alone!
— TIM KOPEC, wine director, Veritas (NYC)

PLANTAINS
Chardonnay, buttery
cocktails made with rum
sparkling wine, esp. with fried plantains

PLUMS (INCLUDING DESSERTS)
Asti
Banyuls
cocktails made with brandy or Muscat
eau-de-vie, plum
ginger ale
ice wine
lemon-flavored drinks (e.g., lemonade, sparkling water with lemon, etc.)
Moscato d'Asti
Muscat, black
Muscat de Beaumes-de-Venise
orange-flavored drinks (e.g., Fizzy Lizzy sparkling orange juice)
PORT, ESP. RUBY OR VINTAGE

red wine, sweet (e.g., Late
  Harvest Zinfandel)
**RIESLING, SWEET OR LATE
  HARVEST**
tea, oolong, esp. Bai Hao
Zinfandel, Late Harvest

POACHED DISHES
acidic wine
light-bodied wine
Pinot Gris/Pinot Grigio
Riesling
white wine, esp. fruity

AVOID
intensely flavored wine
tannic wine

PO' BOY (SEE SANDWICHES, PO' BOY, AND OYSTERS, PO' BOY)

POLENTA (SEE ALSO KEY INGREDIENTS)
beer, esp. sweeter
**CHARDONNAY, BUTTERY,
  ESP. WITH CHEESE
  AND/OR MUSHROOMS**
Dolcetto
Italian wine
**Merlot, esp. New World, and
  esp. with cheese and/or mush-
  rooms**
**Pinot Noir, esp. Oregon, and
  esp. with mushrooms**
rosé, esp. Côtes de Provence
Soave, esp. with Gorgonzola
sparkling wine, dry, esp. Prosecco

POLISH CUISINE
(ALSO APPLIES TO RUSSIAN AND
OTHER EASTERN EUROPEAN
CUISINES)
beer, esp. Polish
Cabernet Franc, esp. with cabbage
  dishes
Chinon or other Loire Valley red
  wine

Gewürztraminer
milder wine
Riesling, off-dry

AVOID
big-flavored wine
Cabernet Sauvignon
Shiraz

*Polish food is mild, so you want
mild wines — not California
Cabernet or Australian Shiraz.
A Loire Valley red like Chinon
works well. These foods have a
lot of cabbage in them that goes
well with Cabernet Franc. As
Cabernet Franc ages, it takes on
a vegetal character like bell
pepper, green peppercorn, or
eggplant.*

— TIM KOPEC, wine director,
Veritas (NYC)

POMEGRANATES
(INCLUDING DESSERTS)
citrus juice beverages (e.g.,
  sparkling lemon or orange
  juice)
ice wine, esp. with desserts
red wine, fruity, esp. with savory
  dishes (e.g., Pinot Noir,
  Zinfandel)
Riesling, Late Harvest, esp. with
  desserts
Sauternes, esp. with desserts
Sauvignon Blanc, esp. with savory
  dishes

POPCORN
Champagne
Chardonnay, esp. buttery
Scotch, esp. a smoky, peaty one
  (e.g., Laphroaig)
sparkling wine

*The infamous cheese/caramel
mix at Garrett's Popcorn [a
Chicago landmark] would be
great with Champagne!
Garrett's is one my favorite
things. I'd recommend Bruno
Paillard Premier Cuvée, which
has a nice richness to it.*

— JILL GUBESCH, sommelier,
Frontera Grill and
Topolobampo (Chicago)

POPEYE'S FRIED CHICKEN
sherry, dry Spanish

*Popeye's should offer sherry at
all its locations! It helps cleanse
the palate, and that salty tang
to it mirrors the saltiness of the
fried food. It's a staggering
match.*

— PAUL GRIECO, general
manager, Hearth (NYC)

PORK (SEE ALSO RECOMMENDATIONS FOR BACON, HAM, SAUSAGE, ETC.)
apple-flavored drinks (e.g.,
  sparkling apple juice)
BEAUJOLAIS, ESP. CRU
**beer, esp. amber ale, lager, or
  Oktoberfest**
Champagne
**CHARDONNAY, ESP. CALI-
  FORNIA**
cocktails made with brandy,
  Calvados, Cognac, Marsala, or
  whiskey
fruit-flavored drinks
**GEWÜRZTRAMINER, ESP.
  ALSATIAN**
ginger ale
Merlot, esp. fruity, esp. with pork
  chops

orange-flavored drinks (e.g., sparkling water with orange)

Pinot Blanc, esp. Alsatian

Pinot Gris, esp. Alsatian

PINOT NOIR, ESP. LIGHTER-BODIED

Ribera del Duero

RIESLING, ESP. ALSATIAN AND/OR DRY, AND ESP. WITH RICHER DISHES

rosé, dry

sake, esp. koshu

Shiraz / Syrah

tea, esp. oolong

Tempranillo

Viognier

white wine

ZINFANDEL, ESP. LIGHTER-BODIED

CHOPS, ESP. GRILLED OR ROASTED

beer, esp. double bock

Merlot

Pinot Gris / Pinot Grigio

Pinot Noir, esp. California

Riesling, esp. Alsatian or German Kabinett

Zinfandel, esp. with fruit sauce

WITH CREAMY SAUCE

Chardonnay (light oak)

WITH FRUIT OR FRUIT SAUCE (E.G., APPLES)

Chardonnay

GEWÜRZTRAMINER

Riesling

Viognier

Vouvray

GRILLED

Chardonnay, New World (light oak)

Chianti

Merlot

Pinot Noir

rosé

Zinfandel

LOIN, ESP. ROASTED

Burgundy, red, esp. young and fruity

PINOT NOIR

Riesling, esp. American or Spätlese

WITH MUSHROOMS

Chardonnay (light oak)

Pinot Noir

WITH MUSTARD SAUCE

Chardonnay (light if any oak)

ROASTED

Beaujolais

Chardonnay, New World, full-bodied, light oak

Chianti

Gewürztraminer, esp. Alsatian

Pinot Gris, esp. Alsatian

RIESLING, ESP. KABINETT OR SPÄTLESE

Rioja

rosé, dry

Tokay Pinot Gris

Zinfandel

SPICE-RUBBED OR OTHER SPICY

Gewürztraminer

When Wednesday night comes around and you are having pork chops, it's a wonderful thing to remember that a double bock beer is great with pork chops — and only costs two dollars!

— GARRETT OLIVER, brewmaster, Brooklyn Brewery

PORK RINDS, FRIED

beer

sherry, fino

sparkling wine

PORTUGUESE CUISINE

Portuguese red wine (e.g., Alentejo and Douro), esp. with red meat

Vinho Verde, esp. with seafood

POSOLE (MEXICAN HOMINY STEW)

beer, esp. Mexican (e.g., Corona or Pacifico)

Sauvignon Blanc, New Zealand

POTATO CHIPS

IN GENERAL

beer

Champagne

sparkling wine

BARBECUE

Zinfandel

SALT-AND-VINEGAR

cola, esp. Coca-Cola

POT AU FEU (FRENCH MEAT AND VEGETABLE STEW)

Beaujolais

Côtes du Rhône, esp. young

Greco di Tufo

POT ROAST (SEE BEEF, POT ROAST)

POULTRY (SEE ALSO CHICKEN, CORNISH GAME HENS, GUINEA HENS, AND TURKEY)

Chardonnay

Pinot Gris

Sauvignon Blanc

sparkling juice, esp. cranberry or orange

POUND CAKE (SEE CAKE, POUND)

PRETZELS

BEER, ESP. BOCK, GERMAN LAGER, OR OKTOBERFEST

Picon Biere, Alsatian

Zinfandel, white

A Picon Biere is an orange-flavored brown liqueur from Alsace to which you add about an ounce of beer. It is considered an Alsace aperitif, which you could compare to a Kir. People drink it on the coldest day of winter or the hottest day of summer — and with an Alsatian pretzel, it is to die for.
— STEPHANE COLLING, wine director, The Modern at the Museum of Modern Art (NYC)

PRIME RIB (SEE BEEF, PRIME RIB)

PROFITEROLES

(DESSERT CREAM PUFFS)

Madeira

Muscat, esp. Beaumes-de-Venise or orange

port, vintage

PROSCIUTTO

BARBERA, ESP. D'ALBA

beer, esp. lager

CHAMPAGNE, ROSÉ

Chardonnay, Italian

Chianti

Dolcetto

Lambrusco

melon-flavored drinks (e.g., sparkling water with melon puree)

Orvieto

PINOT GRIGIO

Prosecco, esp. when served with figs or melon

rosé, dry

Sangiovese

sherry, fino

Soave

TOCAI FRIULANO

Trebbiano

Valpolicella, esp. Classico

Verdicchio

Vernaccia

PRUNES

Armagnac

Banyuls

Burgundy, red

cocktails made with Armagnac, brandy, Kirsch, or rum

lemon-flavored drinks (e.g., lemonade, sparkling water with lemon, etc.)

Madeira, esp. Bual

Moscatel

port, tawny

Sauternes

sherry, oloroso

PUMPKIN

IN GENERAL

Chardonnay, buttery California

cocktails made with Bourbon, Cognac, or rum

Gamay

Gewürztraminer, esp. off-dry

ginger ale

Riesling, esp. off-dry

Shiraz

Valpolicella

Viognier

white wine, off-dry

DESSERTS (E.G., PIE OR PUDDING)

coffee, esp. with cinnamon

Late Harvest wine (e.g., Riesling)

MADEIRA, ESP. MALMSEY

Muscat, esp. Beaumes-de-Venise

PORT, TAWNY

Sauternes

Sémillon, sweet

SHERRY, SWEET, (e.g., cream or oloroso)
Tokaji, Hungarian

QUAIL, ESP. GRILLED OR ROASTED
BORDEAUX, RED
BURGUNDY, RED
Cabernet Sauvignon
Champagne, esp. rosé
Chardonnay, big and oaky New World
cider
cocktails made with Cognac or gin
Côtes du Rhône, red
lemon-based drinks (e.g., lemonade, sparkling water with lemon, etc.)
PINOT NOIR, ESP. NEW WORLD OR OREGON
RIOJA, ESP. RESERVA
Shiraz / Syrah

QUAIL EGGS
Champagne
Chardonnay
sparkling wine

QUESADILLAS
(MEXICAN TORTILLAS WITH MELTED CHEESE)
beer
Cava
Chardonnay, esp. with chicken
margaritas
Merlot
rosé
Sauvignon Blanc
sparkling wine

QUINCES
IN GENERAL
cocktails made with Cognac

DESSERTS
Gewürztraminer, esp. Alsatian

ice wine
Madeira
Muscat de Beaumes-de-Venise
Riesling, Late Harvest

PASTE (E.G., SERVED WITH CHEESE)
Late Harvest wine

RABBIT
IN GENERAL
Bandol, esp. aged, and esp. with stewed rabbit
Barbaresco, esp. with stewed rabbit
Barolo, esp. with stewed rabbit

Beaujolais
beer, esp. ale
Bordeaux, red
Burgundy, red
Champagne, French
Chardonnay, California oaky,
esp. with grilled rabbit
Chateauneuf-du-Pape, white, esp.
with stewed rabbit
Chianti, esp. Classico
Chinon, aged
cider
cocktails made with brandy or
Marsala
Côte-Rôtie
Hermitage
Merlot
Pinot Gris, Alsatian, esp. with
stewed rabbit
Pinot Noir, esp. lighter and/or
Oregon
Pomerol
Ribera del Duero
Rioja
sherry, amontillado
Shiraz / Syrah
Volnay
wine, red
Zinfandel

WITH CHANTERELLES AND
CREAM SAUCE
Burgundy, white, esp. Corton-
Charlemagne
Chardonnay

WITH MUSTARD
Beaujolais
Burgundy, red
Chardonnay
Gewürztraminer
Merlot
Pinot Noir
Syrah

WITH RED WINE SAUCE
Barolo
red wine used in the sauce

RADISHES
Sauvignon Blanc

RAISINS
Beaujolais
Grenache
Madeira, Malmsey
port, tawny
sherry, sweet

RASPBERRIES

IN GENERAL
Beaujolais, esp. Villages
Champagne, esp. rosé
cocktails made with brandy (esp.
raspberry), Cassis, Cognac,
Grand Marnier, or Kirsch
eau-de-vie
lemon-flavored drinks (e.g.,
lemonade, sparkling water with
lemon, etc.)
Moscato d'Asti
Muscat, esp. black or Muscat de
Rivesaltes
RIESLING, ESP. OFF-DRY TO
SWEET (e.g., German
Spätlese, Auslese,
Beerenauslese, or Late
Harvest)
Sauternes
Shiraz, sparkling
Zinfandel, esp. lighter-bodied

DESSERTS
Banyuls
beer, raspberry-flavored Lambic
or wheat
CHAMPAGNE, ESP. DEMI-
SEC OR ROSÉ
Framboise
ice wine
Moscato d'Asti
port, esp. ruby or tawny
RIESLING, LATE HARVEST,
ESP. WITH CREAMY
DESSERTS
Sauternes
sparkling wine, esp. semisweet

RATATOUILLE
(PROVENÇAL DISH OF
EGGPLANT, TOMATOES,
ZUCCHINI, ETC.)
Cabernet Sauvignon
Merlot, esp. light
ROSÉ, DRY
Zinfandel

REDFISH,
BLACKENED
Chardonnay
Gewürztraminer, Alsatian
Pinot Blanc
Riesling, Alsatian
Sauvignon Blanc, California

RED SNAPPER
beer, esp. lager
Burgundy, white
Cabernet Franc
Chardonnay, California
Chenin Blanc
Pinot Noir, esp. American or
New Zealand, with grilled
snapper
Riesling, German
Rioja, white, oaked
Rosado, Spanish
rosé, esp. Bandol and/or dry,
and esp. with grilled snapper
sake, esp. daiginjo
SAUVIGNON BLANC, ESP.
NEW WORLD, AND ESP.
BAKED, ROASTED,
AND/OR WITH GARLIC
Sémillon, esp. with grilled
snapper
Vinho Verde, esp. with grilled
snapper
Vouvray

RELISH, PICKLE
slightly sweet wine

RHUBARB (INCLUDING DESSERTS, E.G., TARTS)
Champagne
cocktails made with brandy
Gewürztraminer
MUSCAT, ESP. ORANGE
**Riesling, German Beerenauslese
or Late Harvest**
Riesling, off-dry
Sauternes
sweet wine

RICE PUDDING
Banyuls
beer, esp. imperial stout
Madeira
Muscat, esp. Black
port, esp. tawny
Riesling, esp. sweet
Sauternes
sherry, sweet
sparkling wine, esp. sweet

RICH DISHES (I.E., CREAMY, FATTY, AND/OR OILY)
Champagne
acidic beverages
sparkling wine
tea, esp. pu-erh, after a rich dish
vermouth spritzer

Cut richness with a little acid. With a creamy dish, have something kind of sprite and lively — or with a steak, have something with some acidity and tannin. Like you use a knife to cut through the steak, that acidity and precision will also cut through the flavor and lift the palate a little bit.
— GEORGE COSSETTE,
co-owner, Silverlake Wine
(Los Angeles)

RILLETTES (PÂTÉ-LIKE MEAT SPREAD)
VOUVRAY

RISOTTO
IN GENERAL
Barbaresco
Barbera
Bardolino
Brunello
Champagne, esp. aged
**Chardonnay, esp. lighter-bodied
and/or Italian**
Dolcetto
Pinot Bianco
Pinot Grigio
Soave Classico, esp. young
sparkling wine, esp. Prosecco
Valpolicella

AVOID
too-fruity wine
too-tannic wine

WITH ASPARAGUS
Italian white wine
Sauvignon Blanc

WITH GAME
Brunello di Montalcino

WITH GORGONZOLA
Valpolicella

WITH HERBS
Sauvignon Blanc

WITH MUSHROOMS
Barbaresco
Barbera
Burgundy, white
**PINOT NOIR, ESP.
CALIFORNIA**
red wine, light-bodied
white wine, earthy

WITH ONIONS
rosé, esp. Bandol

WITH PUMPKIN (OR
BUTTERNUT SQUASH)
Riesling, dry

Viognier
white wine, off-dry

WITH SEAFOOD
Chardonnay (no oak)
Sauvignon Blanc

WITH SHRIMP OR SQUID
Soave

WITH VEGETABLES
**Chardonnay, esp. Italian (no
oak)**
Pinot Bianco / Pinot Blanc
Pinot Grigio
Tocai

WITH WHITE TRUFFLES
Barbaresco
Burgundy, white
Champagne, aged

With risotto, a red wine with too much fruit comes off as brash and gets in the way of the silken creaminess. And you don't want a red wine with too much tannin, because it can end up tasting harsh against the soft, oozy richness of the risotto. Aged Champagne that has gone nutty, earthy, and rich and lost some of its bubbles retains its acidity and is a stunning and remarkable combination with risotto. — JOSHUA WESSON,
wine director, Best Cellars

ROASTED DISHES (SEE ALSO SPECIFIC FOODS)
Champagne, rosé
medium- to full-bodied wines
red, aged wine

ROSEMARY
CABERNET SAUVIGNON
Champagne, rosé
Châteauneuf-du-Pape

Gigondas
Merlot
Pinot Noir
red wine
Riesling
Sangiovese
Sauvignon Blanc
Shiraz / Syrah
Zinfandel

*The thought of rosemary leads
me to red wine like Cabernet
Sauvignon.*

— JEAN-LUC LE DÛ,
Le Dû's Wines (NYC)

RUSSIAN CUISINE (SEE ALSO POLISH CUISINE)
vodka

SAFFRON
Albarino
Cabernet Franc
Chardonnay
Merlot
Rioja
rosé, dry
sherry, dry
Viognier
white wine, dry

SAGE
Merlot, esp. New World
Pinot Noir
red wine
Riesling
Sauvignon Blanc
Shiraz / Syrah

TIP: Adding the herb sage to a
dish can make it more red
wine–friendly.

SAG PANEER (INDIAN-STYLE CREAMED SPINACH)
Pinot Gris

*Sag paneer is great with Pinot
Gris. The dish has earthiness as
well as silkiness to it, and so
does Pinot Gris.*

— ALPANA SINGH, MS,
Everest (Chicago)

SALAD
IN GENERAL
BEAUJOLAIS
**beer, esp. lager or wheat beer
and ale (esp. dry brown)**
Champagne
Chardonnay, esp. unoaked and/or
Australian
Chenin Blanc
cocktails, esp. made with lemon,
lime, or grapefruit
Fiano, Italian
Gamay
Pinot Blanc, Alsatian
Pinot Grigio / Pinot Gris
Riesling, dry
Rioja, white
ROSÉ, esp. dry
Sancerre
**SAUVIGNON BLANC, NEW
WORLD**
sherry, dry, esp. with cheese
and/or nuts
sparkling wine, esp. dry
Tocai, Italian
vermouth spritzers
Vinho Verde
Viognier
white wine, esp. dry

ANTIPASTI
Italian white wine (e.g., Orvieto,
Pinot Grigio, Soave,
Verdicchio)

ASIAN (SEE ALSO SALAD, CHICKEN, ASIAN-STYLE)
Riesling, esp. off-dry

ASPARAGUS
beer, wheat
Chardonnay (no oak)
Sauvignon Blanc

BEEF, COLD SLICED
Beaujolais

BEET, WITH GOAT CHEESE
beer, esp. lighter ale and lager
Pinot Blanc
Sauvignon Blanc

CAESAR
Arneis
Beaujolais
beer, esp. wheat
Chablis
**CHARDONNAY, esp. New
World and/or lightly to mod-
erately oaked**
Riesling, off-dry
rosé, dry
Sancerre
Sauvignon Blanc
sparkling wine, esp. Prosecco
water, still, with moderate TDS
(e.g., Wattwiller)

*Caesar salad has lots of
Parmesan cheese and a vinegar-
based dressing, so Arneis — a
nutty white wine with good
acidity from Piedmont —
works great.*

— SCOTT TYREE, sommelier,
Tru (Chicago)

CALAMARI
rosé
Savennieres

CHEF'S
Chardonnay, New World
Riesling, dry
Soave
Viognier
Zinfandel, white

CHICKEN
Beaujolais
beer, esp. ale or wheat
**CHARDONNAY, French or New
World**
Chenin Blanc, dry
Pinot Grigio
Riesling, esp. German
rosé

Sancerre
SAUVIGNON BLANC, New Zealand
Valpolicella
Vouvray

CHICKEN, ASIAN-STYLE
Chardonnay
Chenin Blanc
Riesling
Viognier
Vouvray

CHICKPEA
rosé
Vin Gris

CITRUS-BASED (E.G., WITH GRAPEFRUIT, ETC.)
Rioja, white

COBB (GREENS WITH ROQUEFORT, AVOCADO, CHICKEN, ETC.)
Beaujolais
Chardonnay
Gewürztraminer
Pinot Noir, esp. when heavy on the bacon
Sauvignon Blanc
Zinfandel

CRAB
Champagne, esp. Blanc de Blancs
Pinot Blanc
Riesling, dry
Sauvignon Blanc
Soave
sparkling wine
Viognier
Vouvray

WITH CREAMY DRESSING
Chardonnay, California

DUCK
Beaujolais
Pinot Noir

FIG, GORGONZOLA, AND WALNUT
Gewürztraminer, Alsatian
Sauternes, drier

FISH, MARINATED
beer

FRUIT
Asti
beer, esp. fruit and/or wheat
Gewürztraminer, off-dry
Moscato d'Asti
Riesling, off-dry to sweet
sparkling wine
Vinho Verde

GREEK (I.E., WITH FETA CHEESE)
Greek white wine (e.g., Assyrtiko or Robolo)
Rosado, Spanish or rosé, dry
Sauvignon Blanc

GREEN (I.E., PRIMARILY LETTUCE, HERBS)
beer, esp. wheat
Chardonnay
Pinot Blanc, esp. Alsatian
rosé
Sauvignon Blanc

GREEN, WITH GOAT CHEESE
Pouilly-Fumé
Sancerre
Sauvignon Blanc

HEARTS OF PALM
grapefruit juice, sparkling
Meyer lemon soda, dry
Riesling, dry

LOBSTER
Burgundy, white
Champagne, esp. Blanc de Blancs
Pouilly-Fumé
sparkling wine, esp. dry

MAYONNAISE-BASED
Riesling, dry

MUSHROOM
Beaujolais
beer, esp. ale
Pinot Blanc
rosé
Sancerre
Vernaccia

NIÇOISE
Côtes du Rhône, esp. white

Riesling, dry
Rosado, Spanish
ROSÉ, DRY, esp. Bandol
Sauvignon Blanc
Viognier
Zinfandel

OCTOPUS
Albarino
Italian white wine (e.g., Gavi, Verdicchio)

PASTA
Chardonnay, Italian or New World

POTATO
rosé, dry
white wine, Alsatian

SEAFOOD
Albarino
Champagne, esp. Blanc de Blancs
Chardonnay, esp. with mayonnaise-based seafood salad
PINOT GRIGIO / PINOT GRIS
Riesling, esp. dry
Sauvignon Blanc
Soave
sparkling wine
Verdicchio

SHRIMP
Chardonnay
Soave

SPINACH
Beaujolais
Chardonnay, esp. lighter-bodied and unoaked
Merlot, esp. with bacon
Orvieto
Pinot Noir, esp. with bacon
Sauvignon Blanc
Soave
Vernaccia

TOMATO
Barbera
rosé, dry
Sancerre

**SAUVIGNON BLANC, NEW
    WORLD**
Verdicchio

TUNA
Frascati
Riesling, dry German (e.g.,
    Kabinett)
rosé, dry
Vernaccia

VEGETABLE, GRILLED
Merlot
Sauvignon Blanc

VINAIGRETTE-BASED
Chablis
Champagne
Riesling, dry German

WALDORF
Pinot Gris
Riesling
rosé
sparkling wine
Viognier

WHITE BEAN
Chardonnay

*Acidic fresh fruit cocktails —
especially those with lemon,
lime, or grapefruit — are an
awesome complement to salads.
Not only does the freshness of
the cocktail complement a salad*
*of fresh, local vegetables, but
the acid in the cocktail and the
acid found in a lot of salad
dressings work as a favorable
link between the two — just as
you would serve a higher-acid
wine to negate the sourness in
the salad dressing.*

— RYAN MAGARIAN, mixolo-
    gist, Kathy Casey Food Studios
        (Seattle)

TIP: Add other components such
as meats, cheeses, and nuts to
make a salad more wine-friendly.

SALAMI (AND SIMILAR COLD SLICED MEATS)

Barbera
Bardolino
Beaujolais
beer, esp. lager
Chianti
Merlot
Montepulciano
Pinot Noir, esp. California
Rhône red wine
Riesling, esp. dry or off-dry
rosé, dry
Verdicchio
Zinfandel, California

SALMON

IN GENERAL
Beaujolais
beer, esp. Belgian ale, pale ale, or Saison, with grilled salmon
Burgundy, red
Burgundy, white, esp. with poached or steamed salmon
Chablis
Champagne, esp. rosé
CHARDONNAY, ESP. BUTTERY CALIFORNIA WITH GRILLED OR POACHED SALMON
Chardonnay, esp. no or light oak
cocktails made with Cognac, Madeira, vermouth, or vodka
lemon- or lime-flavored drinks (e.g., lemonade, sparkling water with lime, etc.)
Pinot Gris, esp. Alsatian or Oregon
***PINOT NOIR, ESP. YOUNG OREGON WITH GRILLED OR PAN-ROASTED SALMON**
Riesling, esp. with poached or steamed salmon
rosé
sake, esp. aged or honjozo or junmai
Sauvignon Blanc
Savennieres

WITH BUTTER SAUCE
Sancerre

WITH CHILE RUB
Champagne, rosé

WITH CITRUS OR TROPICAL FRUIT SAUCE
Burgundy, white
Chardonnay, California

WITH COCONUT MILK
Chardonnay, buttery California

WITH CREAM SAUCE
Burgundy, white
Chardonnay, California

CURED (SEE GRAVLAX)

WITH DILL
Sauvignon Blanc

WITH FENNEL
rosé, esp. dry

WITH GRILLED RED ONIONS
Beaujolais

WITH HOLLANDAISE
Burgundy, white, esp. Meursault
Chardonnay

WITH LEMON SAUCE (ESP. POACHED SALMON)
Chardonnay, esp. California and esp. with dill
Sauvignon Blanc
sparkling wine

WITH MISO
Chardonnay (no oak)

RAW OR TARTARE
Champagne
Sauvignon Blanc, California
sparkling wine

ROE
Champagne
sake
sparkling wine

SMOKED (SEE SMOKED SALMON)

I don't think there's a much better pairing with salmon than Pinot Noir. I'm almost embarrassed to say it because it's so stereotypical and so obvious. But that's okay — so is Roquefort cheese and Sauternes. But the fact of the matter is that they're both perfect pairings. I think some sommeliers will sometimes recommend wild pairings just to get away from what's obvious, maybe to justify their position, or to assert their knowledge. I think it's good to push the envelope sometimes and to encourage people to try other things. But when you have something that's really a perfect match, why? Why serve anything else?
— DANIEL JOHNNES, beverage director, Daniel (NYC)

Instead of pouring a glass of Pinot Noir with grilled salmon, pour a glass of Saison Dupont. People will see fireworks! If the salmon has a crack of black pepper on it, it will be an even better match because it will pick up on the pepper of the beer.
— GARRETT OLIVER, brewmaster, Brooklyn Brewery

With salmon, you want a drink that will talk back to all the fat — one made with a heavier spirit like a vodka, or something like a mojito infused with cherries. Cherries are great with salmon because they cut the fat and add tang. A Manhattan or an Old Fashioned made with amber rum would also work great.
— KATHY CASEY, chef/owner, Kathy Casey Food Studio (Seattle)

SALSA (SEE ALSO CHILES)
beer, esp. lager
margaritas
Riesling, off-dry
Sauvignon Blanc, New Zealand
Syrah / Shiraz
Zinfandel

SALT COD
Albarino
Chablis
Champagne
Frascati
Grüner Veltliner
Pinot Bianco
Pinot Grigio
Rioja
rosé, esp. dry
Sauvignon Blanc, New Zealand
**sherry, dry, esp. fino or man-
    zanilla**
Soave
sparkling wine, esp. Cava

SALTY FOODS AND DISHES
acidic wine
beer
CHAMPAGNE
cocktails, esp. made with fresh cit-
    rus (e.g., Cosmopolitan, Tom
    Collins) and / or slightly sweet
cold wine
fruity wine
Gewürztraminer
Muscadet
Pinot Grigio / Pinot Gris
Pinot Noir
Riesling
rosé, dry
Sauvignon Blanc
Sémillon
sherry
soda
SPARKLING WINE
sweet (or at least off-dry) wine

tea, esp. black or Lapsang sou-
    chong
white wine, esp. dry
Zinfandel
AVOID
high-alcohol wine (i.e., over
    12–13 percent)
oaked wine
tannic wine

*With salty foods, you want
fresh, fruity wines — even
wines with a kiss of sweetness to
them.*

— MADELINE TRIFFON, MS.,
director of wine, Matt Prentice
Restaurant Group (Detroit)

*Salty dishes and acid work
great as opposites. Salt is
refreshed by acidic wines,
whereas if you serve something
salty with a white wine from
California with 14 percent alcohol, the wine will taste hotter
and harsher.*

— DAVID ROSENGARTEN,
editor in chief,
www.DavidRosengarten.com

*The acidity of fresh citrus can
easily balance a salty dish. A
Tom Collins with Plymouth
gin, fresh lemon, sugar, and
soda is a perfect complement to
most salty fish dishes. The sim-
plicity of a vodka cocktail such
as a Cosmopolitan shouldn't
miss, either. Slightly sweeter
fruit cocktails work nicely in a
contrasting fashion to salty
foods.*

— RYAN MAGARIAN,
mixologist, Kathy Casey Food
Studios (Seattle)

SALUMI (SEE ALSO CHARCUTERIE AND PROSCIUTTO)
Brunello
Dolcetto
Lambrusco, red
Taurasi
Valpolicella

SAMOSAS (INDIAN FRIED DUMPLINGS)
Champagne, demi-sec or rosé
rosé
Sauvignon Blanc, New Zealand
Shiraz, sparkling, with meat
    samosas
sparkling wine, esp. fruity
    California

*What I like with samosas is
demi-sec Champagne or
California sparkling wine,
something with a little fruit to
it. A rosé Champagne or a
Schramsberg or Pacific Echo
Brut sparkling wine would also
work well. The reason I want
something with some sweetness
is that I want to contrast the
heat and tanginess of the
tamarind dip that is served with
the samosas. Sparkling Shiraz
works well if there is meat
inside the samosa; it contrasts
with the dark spices of the
tamarind dip. In general, I like
fried foods with Champagne.
The fatty richness of the fried
dough gets cut by the bubbly
richness of the wine. It is nice
contrast to the texture.*

— ALPANA SINGH,
MS, Everest (Chicago)

SANDWICHES (SEE ALSO HAMBURGERS)

IN GENERAL
Beaujolais
beer
iced tea
lemonade
Riesling, dry

BLT (BACON, LETTUCE, TOMATO)
Beaujolais
beer, esp. dark lager
Chardonnay
Chianti
Pinot Grigio
Pinot Noir, esp. if the sandwich is heavy on the "B"
rosé, dry
sparkling wine

CHEESESTEAK, PHILADELPHIA
beer
Cabernet Sauvignon
Merlot
Syrah / Shiraz
Zinfandel

CHICKEN
Chardonnay, New World
Riesling, esp. Spätlese
rosé
tea, esp. Lapsang Souchong

CORNED BEEF
beer, esp. lager
Dr. Brown's Cel-Ray soda

CREAM CHEESE
tea, Darjeeling

CROQUE MONSIEUR (GRILLED HAM AND CHEESE)
Beaujolais
Chardonnay

CUCUMBER
tea, Ceylon black
tea, iced

EGG SALAD
Pinot Bianco
Pinot Grigio / Pinot Gris
Sylvaner
tea, Darjeeling
Traminer
AVOID
oaked wine

GYRO
beer, esp. amber

HAM
Beaujolais
pineapple juice, sparkling (e.g., Fizzy Lizzy)
rosé, dry
tea, Earl Grey

HAM AND CHEESE (E.G., GRUYÈRE)
Beaujolais
beer
Côtes du Rhône
Merlot
Pinot Gris, Alsatian
rosé, dry

ITALIAN BEEF (CHICAGO-STYLE SLICED BEEF SUBMARINE)
beer, esp. pilsner
Sancerre
soda

I love Mr. Beef (which specializes in Italian beef sandwiches) and it is one of the top places I recommend to people visiting Chicago. I usually just have a soda, but I would like something crisp like a Sancerre to go with the spiciness.
— JILL GUBESCH, sommelier, Frontera Grill and Topolobampo (Chicago)

LOBSTER ROLL
beer, esp. Czech Pilsner
Champagne

Riesling, esp. German
rosé
Semillon, Australian
Verdelho, Australian
white wine, unoaked
AVOID
Sauvignon Blanc, herbaceous

PASTRAMI
Beaujolais
beer, esp. darker lager
Champagne
Dr. Brown's Cel-Ray soda
sparkling wine
Zinfandel

PO' BOY (SEE ALSO OYSTERS, PO' BOY)
beer
root beer, esp. Barq's

REUBEN
beer, esp. dark lager
Dr. Brown's Cel-Ray soda

ROAST BEEF
Beaujolais
Merlot
Riesling, esp. German Spätlese
tea, Kenyan black
Valpolicella

SALAMI
Merlot
rosé
Sangiovese
Zinfandel

SMOKED SALMON
sparkling wine
tea, Lapsang Souchong

SOFT-SHELL CRAB
beer

STEAK, SLICED
Syrah

TEA
tea

TOMATO AND MOZZARELLA
Vinho Verde

TUNA SALAD
rosé

Sauvignon Blanc, esp. with tuna salad without sweet relish

white wine, dry young, esp. with tuna salad with sweet relish

TURKEY
Beaujolais-Villages, esp. chilled
Chardonnay, esp. New World
Riesling, dry
rosé, esp. French
Zinfandel, red or white

TURKEY CLUB
Champagne
rosé

With a corned beef sandwich, I don't care for wine. I especially like [Dr. Brown's] Diet Cel-Ray soda because it is not as sweet as regular Cel-Ray. A hoppy, light, crisp, clean lager beer also works well.

— JOSHUA WESSON,
wine director, Best Cellars

SARDINES
Albarino
Beaujolais-Villages
Gavi, esp. with grilled sardines
lemon-based drinks (e.g., lemonade, sparkling water with lemon, etc.)

MUSCADET, ESP. WITH GRILLED SARDINES
Pinot Gris, esp. with grilled sardines
rosé
Sancerre, esp. with grilled sardines
SAUVIGNON BLANC, ESP. NEW WORLD
sherry, dry
Soave Classico
Txakoli
Vermentino
Vernaccia
*VINHO VERDE, ESP. WITH GRILLED SARDINES
white wine dry

SASHIMI (SEE ALSO SUSHI)
CHAMPAGNE
Chardonnay, more minerally
Muscadet
Pinot Grigio
Riesling, dry (e.g., German Kabinett)
SAKE
Sancerre, esp. dry
Sauvignon Blanc, New World
Savennieres
SPARKLING WINE
tea, Chinese green
Vouvray

SATAY (ASIAN-STYLE SKEWERED MEAT, FISH, OR POULTRY, SERVED WITH PEANUT SAUCE)
Chardonnay
Gewürztraminer, Alsatian
sparkling wine

SAUCE (SEE ALSO PASTA FOR PASTA SAUCES)

BÉARNAISE
Beaujolais
Champagne
Chardonnay, esp. California and/or oaky
Pinot Gris, Alsatian
Riesling, esp. German
sparkling wine
Vouvray

BLACK BEAN, ASIAN-STYLE
Gewürztraminer
Riesling, dry
Vouvray

BUTTER (E.G., BEURRE BLANC, SEE ALSO BUTTER AND BUTTER SAUCE)
Chardonnay, buttery
white wine, acidic

CHEESE
beer, esp. porter or dry stout
Dolcetto
Pinot Grigio

CLAM
Arneis
Gavi
Pinot Grigio
Sauvignon Blanc
Soave
Vernaccia

CREAM
Chardonnay
white wine, Alsatian

HOISIN
Chardonnay, big and oaky

HOLLANDAISE
Bordeaux, white
Burgundy, white, esp. Meursault
CHAMPAGNE, DRY
CHARDONNAY, OAKED
Pinot Gris, Alsatian
Sancerre
sparkling wine
Vouvray
white wine

MARINARA (ITALIAN
MEATLESS TOMATO SAUCE)
Barbera
Chianti
Orvieto
Sangiovese

MAYONNAISE
Champagne
Chardonnay
sparkling wine
white wine

PONZU
Riesling
Sauvignon Blanc
Shiraz / Syrah
sparkling wine, dry
Zinfandel

PUTTANESCA
Pinot Noir
Sangiovese
Vernaccia
Zinfandel

RED WINE REDUCTION
Cabernet Sauvignon
RED WINE
Syrah

ROMESCO
Albarino
Priorato
Ribera del Duero
Rioja
rose or Spanish Rosado

SEAFOOD

IN GENERAL (SEE PASTA,
WITH SEAFOOD)

CREAM-BASED
white wine

TOMATO-BASED
red and rosé wine

TOMATO
acidic wine
Barbera
Chianti
Sangiovese
Sauvignon Blanc

VINEGAR-BASED
acidic wine

WHITE WINE
white wine
TIP: Adding a splash of the wine
you're drinking to the sauce can
build a bridge between the food
and the wine.

*What I'll do is taste and adjust
the sauce once I can actually
taste the wine, so I'll refine as I
go. It's nice sometimes to finish
a red wine sauce with some of
the wine you're drinking, so it's
not boiled or with the alcohol
blown off, but literally just a
little to finish the sauce.*
— Traci Des Jardins, chef,
Jardiniere (San Francisco)

*Champagne is a great match
with hollandaise sauce. The
sauce helps the wine express
itself a little more because even
a dry Champagne has a little
sugar to it.*
— Jean-Luc Le Dû,
Le Dû's Wines (NYC)

SAUERKRAUT (SEE ALSO
CHOUCROUTE)
apple-flavored drinks (e.g.,
sparkling apple juice)
**beer, esp. darker German and/or
lager**
Gewürztraminer, esp. Alsatian
**Riesling, esp. dry (e.g., German
Kabinett)**

SAUSAGE

IN GENERAL
apple-flavored drinks (e.g.,
sparkling apple juice)
**BEAUJOLAIS, ESP. WITH
GARLIC AND/OR GRILLED
SAUSAGE**
**beer, esp. pale ale, or amber and
dark lager, and esp. with
bratwurst**
Champagne, esp. with chorizo
cider
Côtes du Rhône
Gewürztraminer
Italian red wine, esp. with Italian
sausage
Malbec
Merlot
Pinot Gris
RIESLING, DRY OR OFF-DRY,
ESP. WITH HOT, SPICY, OR
WHITE SAUSAGE
**Shiraz / Syrah, esp. with grilled
sausage**
sparkling wine, esp. with spicy
sausage
Valpollicella
white wine, Alsatian, esp. with
andouille sausage
**ZINFANDEL, ESP. WITH
GRILLED SAUSAGE**

BRATWURST
BEER, esp. lighter-style pilsner
Zinfandel

CHICKEN OR TURKEY
red wine, light-bodied (e.g.,
Beaujolais, Pinot Noir)
white wine (e.g., Chardonnay,
Gewürztraminer, dry Riesling)

CHORIZO (SPICY SPANISH SAUSAGE)
Albarino
beer
Champagne
Chardonnay
Navarra
Pinotage
Rioja
Rosado
sherry, esp. fino or manzanilla
Shiraz / Syrah
Tempranillo, Spanish
Toro, Spanish

ITALIAN
Barbera
Chianti
Dolcetto
Montepulciano
Rosso di Montalcino

KIELBASA (I.E., HIGHLY SEASONED)
beer, esp. ale or lager
sparkling wine

SAUCISSON (FRENCH GARLICKY SAUSAGE)
BEAUJOLAIS
Burgundy, white
Côtes du Rhône

SEAFOOD
Burgundy, white
Chardonnay (no oak)
Sylvaner

SMOKED
Riesling, dry (e.g., German Kabinett)

SPICY
Bandol, red
Beaujolais
Chablis
Chianti
Dolcetto
Montepulciano
Pinot Gris
Riesling
Rioja
Shiraz
Zinfandel

WHITE (E.G., BOCKWURST, BOUDIN BLANC, ETC.)
beer, esp. lager or pale ale
Chenin Blanc
Pinot Gris, Alsatian
Riesling, Alsatian

The bubbles in Champagne will distract from the heat of spicy chorizo as it cools and clears the palate. The low alcohol in Riesling or Chardonnay will cool the heat, while any sweetness will neutralize the heat.

— MADELINE TRIFFON, MS, director of wine, Matt Prentice Restaurant Group (Detroit)

SCALLOPS

IN GENERAL
beer
Bordeaux, white
BURGUNDY, WHITE, ESP. WITH RICHER (e.g., braised) PREPARATIONS
Chablis Grand Cru, esp. with bay scallops
CHAMPAGNE, ESP. BLANC DE BLANCS, AND ESP. WITH STEAMED SCALLOPS
CHARDONNAY, ESP. WITH GRILLED OR SAUTÉED SCALLOPS
Châteauneuf-du-Pape, white
Chenin Blanc
cocktails made with brandy, gin, Pernod, or vermouth
Grüner Veltliner
lemon- or lime-flavored drinks (e.g., lemonade, sparkling water with lime)
Pinot Blanc
Pinot Grigio / Pinot Gris
Pouilly-Fuissé
RIESLING, DRY OR MEDIUM-DRY, ESP. WITH SAUTÉED SCALLOPS
SAUVIGNON BLANC, ESP. WITH BAKED OR ROASTED SCALLOPS

slightly sweet wine
Soave, esp. Classico
sparkling wine
tea, Bao Jong oolong
Viognier
Vouvray, esp. demi-sec, esp. with baked or roasted scallops

AVOID
red wine

WITH BROWN BUTTER
beer, dark (e.g., Taddy Porter), with caramelized scallops

WITH CAVIAR
Burgundy, white
Champagne, esp. Blanc de Blancs

CEVICHE
Grüner Veltliner
Sancerre

WITH CHINESE SPICES
Riesling, off-dry
white wine, Alsatian, off-dry

WITH CITRUS SAUCE (GRAPEFRUIT, LEMON, LIME, AND/OR ORANGE)
Chardonnay, esp. lighter-bodied
Riesling
Sauvignon Blanc, New Zealand

COQUILLES ST. JACQUES (SCALLOPS IN WHITE WINE SAUCE)
beer, esp. Blanche
Chablis, French
Champagne, esp. brut
Pouilly-Fumé
Sauvignon Blanc

IN CREAM SAUCE
BURGUNDY, WHITE, ESP. MEURSAULT
Champagne
Chardonnay, esp. New World
Riesling, esp. German and/or semidry

WITH GINGER
Pinot Blanc, Alsatian
Rhône, white
Riesling

GRILLED
CHARDONNAY, BUTTERY
Riesling, Alsatian and/or dry

SAUTÉED
Burgundy, white
Champagne, esp. brut
Chardonnay
RIESLING, DRY

WITH SOY SAUCE
Pinot Noir
sake

THAI-STYLE
Chardonnay, California, esp. with
  coconut milk
Sauvignon Blanc, esp. with
  lemongrass and chiles

*One of the funnest dinners I
have ever done was with the
Westchester [New York] association of country club chefs. I
paired seared diver sea scallops
with brown butter sauce with a
Taddy Porter from Samuel
Smith, which is a dark beer
with a buttery, residual sugar
and caramel taste to it, and a
slightly chocolatey aroma. They
were surprised to see a light dish
with a dark beer. We decon-
structed the scallop, which is
sweet, with a caramel sear, and
the butter in the brown butter
sauce. With the beer, I am
delivering a round, soft buttery
flavor with caramel. You have
carbonation that scrubs the
palate and removes fat and oil.
This audience of chefs was
shocked, and said it was one of
the best food and beverage combinations they have ever had.*
— GARRETT OLIVER,
brewmaster, Brooklyn Brewery

SCANDINAVIAN
CUISINE
aquavit
beer, lager
schnapps

SCHNITZEL (SEE VEAL,
WIENER SCHNITZEL)

SCONES
tea, esp. English Breakfast or
  Nilgiri

SCROD (SEE ALSO COD)
Chardonnay

SEA BASS (SEE ALSO OTHER
MILD FISH SUCH AS HALIBUT,
TROUT, ETC.)
Burgundy, white, esp. with
  baked/roasted sea bass
**Chablis, esp. Grand Cru, and
  esp. with baked/roasted sea
  bass**
Champagne, esp. with sautéed sea
  bass
**CHARDONNAY, ESP. WITH
  NO OR LIGHT OAK, AND
  ESP. WITH BAKED OR
  ROASTED SEA BASS**
Châteauneuf-du-Pape, white
cocktails made with Madeira
Bordeaux, white
lemon-flavored drinks (e.g.,
  lemonade, sparkling water with
  lemon)
**Pinot Grigio, Italian, or Pinot
  Gris, esp. California or
  Oregon**
Pinot Noir
Pouilly-Fumé
Sancerre
Sauvignon Blanc, esp. with garlic
Verdejo, esp. with baked/roasted
  sea bass
Verdicchio
Vermentino

SEAFOOD (SEE ALSO FISH,
SHELLFISH, AND SPECIFIC
SEAFOOD)

IN GENERAL
Albarino
**beer, esp. wheat, and with sim-
  ple and/or fried dishes**
Champagne
**CHARDONNAY, ESP. WITH
  BOILED, GRILLED, OR
  STEAMED SEAFOOD**
cider, Spanish
citrus-flavored soda or sparkling
  juices (e.g., grapefruit, lime,
  orange)
cocktails, esp. made with vodka
  (e.g., vodka martini)
lemon-flavored drinks (e.g.,
  lemonade, sparkling water with
  lemon)
Martini circa 1900 (i.e., 50/50
  gin/dry vermouth, with a few
  dashes of orange bitters)
**Pinot Grigio / Pinot Gris, esp.
  with poached seafood**
**RIESLING, ESP. DRY WITH
  LIGHTER AND/OR
  POACHED DISHES**
sake
SAUVIGNON BLANC
**SHERRY, DRY, ESP. FINO OR
  MANZANILLA**
Soave
sparkling wine, esp. with fried
  seafood
Txakoli
**VIOGNIER, ESP. WITH
  BOILED OR STEAMED
  SEAFOOD**
vodka martini

AVOID
oaked wine, esp. with delicate
  seafood or oily fish
tannic wine (e.g., Cabernet
  Sauvignon, Chianti, Merlot,
  Syrah), esp. with delicate
  seafood

COCKTAIL OR PLATEAU
(I.E., PLATE OF COLD
SEAFOOD)
Chablis
Champagne
Muscadet
Sancerre
Sauvignon Blanc
sparkling wine

IN CREAM SAUCE (E.G.,
SEAFOOD MORNAY)
CHARDONNAY
Chenin Blanc, esp. dry
Gavi
**PINOT GRIGIO / PINOT
GRIS**
white wine

IN CURRY SAUCE
Gewürztraminer, German
Riesling, German

IN GARLIC SAUCE
Sauvignon Blanc
Viognier

IN MUSHROOM SAUCE
Pinot Noir

SAUSAGE
Pinot Gris
Viognier

IN TOMATO SAUCE
red and rosé wine

SEA URCHIN
Burgundy, white
Chablis, esp. Grand Cru
Champagne, esp. Blanc de Blancs
lemon- or lime-flavored drinks
   (e.g., lemonade, sparkling
   water with lime)
Riesling, esp. Alsatian and/or dry
rosé
Sancerre
sparkling wine

SESAME (INCLUDING
SESAME OIL AND SAUCE)
Chardonnay, oaked
Riesling, esp. German

sake
Viognier

SHARK (SEE SWORDFISH)

SHELLFISH (SEE ALSO
SEAFOOD AND SPECIFIC
SHELLFISH)

IN GENERAL (I.E., RAW OR
STEAMED)
ALBARINO
**BEER, esp. lager, pale ale, pil-
sner, porter, dry or oyster
stout, or wheat, and esp. with
fried or sautéed shellfish**
Bordeaux, white
Burgundy, white
**CHABLIS, ESP. WITH RAW
OR WITHOUT CREAM
SAUCE**
**CHAMPAGNE, ESP. DRY OR
SEC, AND ESP. WITH
FRIED OR SAUTÉED
SHELLFISH**
**CHARDONNAY, NO OR
LIGHT OAK, ESP. WITH
BUTTER SAUCE**
Chenin Blanc
cocktails made with gin, ver-
   mouth, or vodka
Gavi
lemon-flavored drinks (e.g.,
   lemonade, sparkling water
   with lemon)
***MUSCADET, ESP. WITH
RAW SHELLFISH**
Pinot Blanc
Pinot Gris / Pinot Grigio
POUILLY-FUMÉ
**RIESLING, ESP. DRY AND/OR
ALSATIAN**
rosé, esp. dry
sake
*SANCERRE
**SAUVIGNON BLANC, esp. New
Zealand or other New World,
and esp. with garlicky shell-
fish**
Sémillon

sherry, esp. dry (e.g., fino and
   manzanilla)
Soave
**SPARKLING WINE, ESP.
WITH FRIED OR SAUTÉED
SHELLFISH**
tea, Darjeeling or Japanese green
Txakoli
Vinho Verde
Viognier, esp. with herbed shell-
   fish
Vouvray
white wine, dry

AVOID
red, tannic wines with delicate
   seafood, esp. Cabernet
   Sauvignon, Chianti, big
   Merlot, Syrah

GRILLED
Chardonnay
Pouilly-Fumé
Sancerre
Sauvignon Blanc
Sémillon

WITH MANGO SALSA
Chardonnay, California

WITH MAYONNAISE-BASED
SAUCE
Chardonnay
Pinot Blanc
Riesling
Sauvignon Blanc

*Like Sancerre and Pouilly-
Fumé, Muscadet washes down
raw shellfish to perfection.*
— RICHARD OLNEY

SHEPHERD'S PIE
Beaujolais
Cabernet Sauvignon
Syrah
Zinfandel

SHISH KEBABS
beer, esp. lager or pilsner

SHORT RIBS (SEE BEEF, SHORT RIBS)

SHRIMP

IN GENERAL
Aligoté, esp. with chilled shrimp
BEER, ESP. AMBER ALE, PIL-SNER, PORTER, STOUT, OR WHEAT, AND ESP. WITH BARBECUED OR SPICY BOILED SHRIMP
Bordeaux, white
Burgundy, white, esp. Meursault, and esp. with baked shrimp
Chablis
Chardonnay, esp. California
citrus-flavored drinks, esp. lemon, lime, orange (e.g., sparkling water with lemon)
cocktails made with brandy, Cognac, Madeira, Pernod, or vodka
Grüner Veltliner
high-acid wine
Muscadet, esp. with chilled shrimp
Pinot Gris/Pinot Grigio
Riesling, esp. dry or off-dry Alsatian and esp. with barbe-cued shrimp
SAUVIGNON BLANC, ESP. NEW ZEALAND, AND ESP. WITH BARBECUED SHRIMP
sparkling wine

AVOID
oaked wine
red wine

BOILED (WITH SPICES)
beer, pilsner (e.g., Pilsner Urquell or Stella Artois)

COCKTAIL
Aligoté
Champagne
Chardonnay
Chenin Blanc
Muscadet
Pinot Blanc
Riesling

Sauvignon Blanc
sparkling wine (e.g., Cava or Prosecco)

CURRIED
Gewürztraminer, esp. Alsatian

WITH GARLIC
beer, esp. Pilsner

GRILLED
Albarino
beer, esp. Tecate
Burgundy, white, esp. Meursault
CHARDONNAY, ESP. BUT-TERY, OAKY CALIFORNIA
Grüner Veltliner
margarita
Riesling

WITH LEMON
Burgundy, white
Chardonnay, California

"PEEL AND EAT"
Chardonnay
Riesling
Sauvignon Blanc, New Zealand

WITH PESTO
Pouilly-Fumé

RÉMOULADE
martini, gin

WITH ROMESCO SAUCE
rosé or Spanish rosado

SAUTÉED
Burgundy, white
Chablis
Muscadet
Pinot Bianco

SCAMPI
Chablis
Chardonnay, Italian

SPICY OR WITH SAUSAGE
beer
Gewürztraminer
Riesling, Alsatian

WITH SWEET-AND-SOUR SAUCE
Chenin Blanc

I've always tended to pair martinis with mayonnaise-based sauces, as the gin just seems to go so nicely. When coming up with a cocktail to pair with Shrimp Rémoulade, I designed a martini in the classic proportions, substituting Peychaud's bitters for orange bitters.
— ROBERT HESS, founder, DrinkBoy.com

TILLICUM

THIS BRACING COCKTAIL FROM ROBERT HESS PAIRS NICELY WITH SHRIMP RÉMOULADE

2 1/4 ounces gin (esp. Plymouth)

3/4 ounces dry vermouth

2 dashes Peychaud's bitters

Stir the gin, vermouth, and bitters with ice. Strain into a cocktail glass. Garnish with a slice of smoked salmon skewered flat on a pick.

Robert Hess notes, "In taste-testing this drink with the Shrimp Rémoulade, I tried the drink with several different gins — with rather surprising results. There was a clear difference among the gins I tried (Boodles, Hendrick's, and Plymouth, the three I had on hand), with Plymouth the one that stood out as pairing the best."

SKATE
Albarino
Burgundy, white, esp. with sautéed skate
Chardonnay, no or light oak, esp. with sautéed skate
Pouilly-Fumé, esp. with sautéed skate

Riesling, dry, (e.g., Alsatian or German Kabinett)

Sancerre

Sauvignon Blanc, light oak, esp. with sautéed skate

SMOKED OR SMOKY-FLAVORED FOODS AND DISHES

beer

Champagne, esp. with smoked sturgeon

Champagne, rosé

fruity wine

Gewürztraminer

Pinot Grigio / Pinot Gris

Pinot Noir

Riesling

rosé, dry

Sauvignon Blanc (no oak)

Sémillon (no oak)

Shiraz

sparkling wine

Viognier

whiskey, neat

Zinfandel

AVOID

high-alcohol wine

oaked wine

tannic wine

SMOKED FISH

aquavit

beer, esp. ale or lager

Burgundy, white

Champagne, esp. Blanc de Blancs

Chardonnay, esp. New World

RIESLING, DRY, ESP. ALSATIAN, GERMAN KABINETT, OR MOSEL

Sancerre

Sauvignon Blanc, esp. California or New Zealand

SHERRY, DRY, ESP. FINO OR MANZANILLA

sparkling wine

vodka

AVOID

steely white wine

SMOKED HADDOCK

Gewürztraminer, Alsatian

rosé

sherry

Vouvray

white wine, dry or off-dry

SMOKED SALMON

aquavit

BEER, esp. ale, lager, pale pilsner, smoked beer, dry stout, or wheat

Chablis, esp. Premier Cru

CHAMPAGNE, ESP. BRUT, DRY ROSÉ, OR BLANC DE BLANCS

CHARDONNAY, NEW WORLD

Gewürztraminer, Alsatian, dry

lemon-flavored drinks (e.g., lemonade, sparkling water with lemon, etc.)

Pinot Grigio / Pinot Gris

Pinot Noir

RIESLING, esp. dry to off-dry

Sancerre

Sauvignon Blanc, esp. New Zealand

Savennieres

Scotch, single-malt

sherry, dry (e.g., fino or manzanilla)

sparkling wine

Tokay, Alsatian

vodka

Vouvray

water, minerally (e.g., Vichy)

whiskey

SMOKED TROUT

beer, esp. pale ale, lager, or pilsner

Champagne

Chardonnay, esp. oaky

Gewürztraminer

RIESLING, DRY

SANCERRE

SAUVIGNON BLANC, CALIFORNIA

---

sherry, dry, esp. fino or manzanilla

sparkling wine

SNAILS

Burgundy, white, esp. with garlic butter sauce

Chablis, dry

Champagne, esp. with Champagne butter sauce

Pouilly-Fumé

Riesling, dry

rosé, dry

Sauvignon Blanc

sherry, amontillado

sparkling wine (e.g., Prosecco)

Sylvaner, Alsatian

white wine

AVOID

red wine

SNAPPER (SEE RED SNAPPER)

SOBA NOODLES

Gewürztraminer

Riesling

sake

tea

Viognier

SOLE (SEE ALSO OTHER MILD FISH SUCH AS HALIBUT, TROUT, ETC.)

IN GENERAL

***BURGUNDY, WHITE,** ESP. WITH FRIED OR GRILLED SOLE

CHABLIS, ESP. WITH SOLE WITH A BUTTER SAUCE

Champagne, esp. with poached sole

CHARDONNAY, ESP. LIGHT-BODIED OR NO OAK, AND ESP. WITH FRIED OR SAUTÉED SOLE AND/OR WITH CREAM SAUCE

cocktails made with Marsala or
vermouth

lemon-flavored drinks (e.g.,
lemonade, sparkling water with
lemon)

Pinot Bianco

Pinot Grigio

Pouilly-Fumé

**Riesling, esp. Alsatian or
Kabinett, and esp. with grilled
sole and/or sole with white**

wine sauce

Sancerre

Sauvignon Blanc, esp. with
sautéed sole

Soave, esp. with a lemon sauce

Viognier, esp. with sautéed sole

**white wine, light-bodied and/or
from Northern France**

DOVER

**BURGUNDY, WHITE, ESP.
AGED**

Chablis, aged French

Chardonnay

Chassagne-Montrachet, aged

Gavi

Meursault, esp. with grilled sole

Sauvignon Blanc

Sémillon

*Dover sole with a simple beurre
blanc and served with white
Burgundy is ethereal.*

— ALAN MURRAY, MS, wine
director, Masa's (San Francisco)

SORBET

Asti

Champagne

eau de vie, compared or contrasted to the sorbet flavor

grappa

liqueur, fruit

Moscato d'Asti

sparkling wine, sweet

AVOID

high-alcohol wine

SORREL

Champagne, rosé

Chardonnay (no oak)

Grüner Veltliner

Riesling, dry Alsatian

**Sauvignon Blanc, esp. New
Zealand**

vermouth, dry

SOUFFLÉ

IN GENERAL

**Champagne, esp. Blanc de
Blancs**

sparkling wine

CHEESE

Champagne

Pinot Noir

Sancerre (with goat cheese)

Sauvignon Blanc (with goat
cheese)

sparkling wine

SWEET

Asti

Banyuls, with chocolate soufflé

Champagne, esp. demi sec

Crème de Framboise, esp. with
chocolate soufflé

Late Harvest wine (e.g., Riesling)

Madeira, esp. Bual or Malmsey

Moscato d'Asti

Muscat

port, esp. tawny or vintage, with
chocolate soufflé

Riesling, esp. off-dry to sweet

Sauternes

sparkling wine

SOUP

IN GENERAL

***SHERRY, ESP. DRY (SERVE
IN A SMALL GLASS AFTER
ADDING A SPLASH OF
SHERRY TO THE SOUP)**

BEAN WITH BACON

Chianti

Pinot Noir

Shiraz / Syrah, esp. with spicier
soup

Zinfandel

BLACK BEAN

Cahors

Côtes du Rhône

sherry, oloroso

BORSCHT (BEET SOUP)

beer, esp. pilsner

Merlot

Sauvignon Blanc

vodka

Zinfandel, white

BOUILLABAISSE

Bandol, white

Bordeaux, white

Burgundy, white

CASSIS, WHITE

Champagne, rosé

Chardonnay, esp. California

**PROVENCAL WHITE WINE
(e.g., Cassis or Chateau-
Simone-Blanc)**

Riesling

**ROSÉ, ESP. DRY (e.g.,
Provencal or Tavel)**

Sauvignon Blanc

Sémillon, esp. older

sherry

BROTH (SEE SOUP,
CONSOMME)

BUTTERNUT SQUASH (SEE
SOUP, PUMPKIN)

CAULIFLOWER

Chenin Blanc

CHEESE

beer, esp. ale

CHICKEN

Chardonnay

Chenin Blanc

Pinot Noir

CLAM CHOWDER

MANHATTAN (TOMATO-
BASED)

Beaujolais

Merlot

Rioja

NEW ENGLAND (CREAM-BASED)

Burgundy, white

Chablis

CHARDONNAY, ESP. BUTTERY, OAKY CALIFORNIA

Pinot Grigio/Pinot Gris

Tocai Friulano

COLD

Madeira

sherry

sparkling wine

CONSOMMÉ

Bordeaux, white

Madeira

Pinot Noir

sherry, esp. amontillado or fino

CORN

Burgundy, white, esp. Mersault

Chardonnay, buttery California

Madeira, dry and aged, with corn chowder

Riesling, dry, esp. German Kabinett

Verdelho

Viognier

CRAB BISQUE

Chardonnay, big and buttery

SHERRY, ESP. AMONTILLADO OR FINO

CREAM (E.G., CHICKEN, MUSHROOM, SEAFOOD)

beer, esp. lager or pilsner

Bordeaux, white

Chardonnay

Sauvignon Blanc

Soave

Viognier

CUCUMBER (COLD, WITH MINT OR OTHER HERBS)

Frascati

Pinot Gris

Sauvignon Blanc

sparkling wine

Verdicchio

FISH

Pinot Blanc

rosé, dry

Sauvignon Blanc

FISH CHOWDER

beer

Chardonnay

cider

white wine, dry

FRUIT

beer, fruit

Champagne

Moscato d'Asti

Riesling, esp. German Kabinett

sparkling wine

GARLIC

Crozes-Hermitage, white

Pinot Gris

GAZPACHO

Albarino

Cava

Rioja, white

Sauvignon Blanc

Spanish white or red wine

Txakoli

GUMBO

BEER, ESP. PALE ALE OR LAGER

Pinot Noir, esp. Oregon or other New World

Zinfandel, white

LOBSTER BISQUE

Champagne

Chardonnay, esp. big and buttery

MISO (SEE MISO AND MISO SOUP)

MINESTRONE

Barbera

beer, esp. lager

CHIANTI

SANGIOVESE

Sauvignon Blanc

MUSHROOM

Pinot Noir

Prosecco

CREAM OF

Burgundy, white

Chardonnay, esp. California

Merlot

rosé

ONION OR FRENCH ONION (E.G., TOPPED WITH MELTED CHEESE)

Beaujolais or Beaujolais Nouveau

beer

Burgundy, red or white

Chardonnay, esp. California

Côtes du Rhône, red

Grüner Veltliner

sherry, dry, esp. manzanilla

white wine, Alsatian (e.g., Pinot Blanc or Pinot Gris)

PEA

Beaujolais

Chardonnay, buttery

Gewürztraminer, dry

Grüner Veltliner, dry

Sauvignon Blanc

PEPPER, BELL

Gewürztraminer, Alsatian

Sauvignon Blanc, California

Vouvray

POTATO (SEE ALSO SOUP, VICHYSSOISE)

Chardonnay

Chianti

PUMPKIN, SWEET POTATO, AND WINTER SQUASH (E.G., BUTTERNUT)

Chardonnay

Gewürztraminer

Riesling, dry to off-dry

sparkling wine

Viognier

RIBOLITA (ITALIAN BEAN SOUP)

Chianti

Super Tuscan (i.e.,
 Merlot/Sangiovese blend)

ROOT VEGETABLE
Champagne, rosé

SEAFOOD
Albarino
Sauvignon Blanc
Vinho Verde

SEAFOOD BISQUE OR
CHOWDER (SEE ALSO SOUP,
CLAM CHOWDER, SOUP,
FISH CHOWDER, AND SOUP,
LOBSTER BISQUE)
Burgundy, white
Chardonnay, esp. California or
 other New World
Sauvignon Blanc

SEAFOOD STEW
rosé, dry
Sauvignon Blanc

SQUASH, WINTER (SEE
SOUP, PUMPKIN)

STRAWBERRY
Moscato d'Asti
Pinot Noir, fruity

SWEET POTATO (SEE SOUP,
PUMPKIN)

TOMATO
Chianti
Gewürztraminer, dry
rosé, esp. with chilled soup
Sauvignon Blanc

TORTILLA (MEXICAN)
Rioja
Sauvignon Blanc, New Zealand

VEGETABLE
Sauvignon Blanc
Soave, esp. with green vegetables

VEGETABLE, CREAM OF
Chardonnay

VICHYSSOISE (COLD
POTATO-LEEK SOUP)
Bordeaux, white, esp. dry
Sauvignon Blanc
sherry, fino, or manzanilla

WINTER SQUASH (SEE SOUP,
PUMPKIN)

*A drier Madeira with corn
chowder is brilliant.*
— ALAN MURRAY, MS, wine
director, Masa's (San Francisco)

SOUR DISHES (E.G.,
FEATURING CITRUS, VINEGAR,
ETC.)
acidic wine (see p. 200)
dry wine

SOUTHWESTERN
CUISINE (E.G., CAYENNE-
AND CHILI-SPICED; SEE ALSO
TEX-MEX CUISINE)
beer
Bordeaux, red, esp. with beef
**Cabernet Sauvignon, California,
 esp. with beef**
Gewürztraminer
Pinot Noir, esp. with mushrooms
**Riesling, esp. German, and esp.
 with ceviche and spicy dishes**
Rioja
Sauvignon Blanc, esp. New
 Zealand
Shiraz/Syrah, esp. with lamb
**Zinfandel, California, esp. with
 chile-flavored dishes**

SOY SAUCE (SEE ALSO
CHINESE CUISINE AND
JAPANESE CUISINE)
Beaujolais
beer
Chablis
Champagne, esp. rosé
Chardonnay, esp. with little to no
 oak
cocktails (e.g., Cognac and 7-Up)
fruity wine
GEWÜRZTRAMINER
high-acid wine

low-tannin wine
Merlot
**PINOT NOIR, ESP.
CALIFORNIA**
**RIESLING, ESP. GERMAN OR
AUSTRIAN, AND/OR OFF-
DRY**
rosé, dry
sake
Sauvignon Blanc, esp. New
 Zealand or unoaked
sparkling wine, dry
Zinfandel

AVOID
tannic wine

SPAGHETTI (SEE PASTA)

SPANISH CUISINE (SEE
ALSO SPECIFIC INGREDIENTS
AND DISHES)
Fried foods (South Central): crisp,
 clean white wine
Rice dishes (Mediterranean):
 Viognier, Spanish, esp. with
 seafood
Roasted dishes (Central): sherry,
 esp. amontillado or oloroso
Stewed dishes (North and
 Atlantic): sherry, esp. amontil-
 lado, fino, or oloroso

SPICY FOODS AND
DISHES (E.G., ETHIOPIAN,
HUNAN, INDIAN, MEXICAN, AND
SZECHUAN CUISINES)
acidic wine
Beaujolais
**BEER, ESP. LAGER, PILSNER,
WHEAT, AND/OR MALTY**
Champagne
Chenin Blanc, esp. off-dry
chilled beverages
cocktails (e.g., mojitos)
fruity off-dry red and white wine
GEWÜRZTRAMINER
Grüner Veltliner

lighter-bodied wine
lower-alcohol wine
mojitos
Moscato d'Asti
Muscadet
off-dry to sweeter wine
Pinot Grigio / Pinot Gris
Pinot Noir, esp. California
Rhône red wine
**RIESLING, ESP. GERMAN
(e.g., Spätlese) AND/OR
OFF-DRY**
Rioja
rosé, dry
Sauvignon Blanc, esp. California
Shiraz / Syrah
sparkling wine, esp. inexpensive
sweet wine, esp. when there's a
     sweet element to the dish
tea
Vinho Verde
Viognier
Vouvray, esp. sec or demi sec
**ZINFANDEL, CALIFORNIA,
ESP. YOUNG**

AVOID
high-alcohol wine
oaked wine
tannic wine

*I learned while working at
Chicago's Frontera Grill that
when pairing chiles, you need to
be very careful of the tannins in
red wine. It reminds me of a
cartoon where you see a person
with fire coming out of his
mouth — because if you make
that mistake, it just gets hotter
and hotter! I once tried to con-
vince a table to not order a tannic Cabernet Sauvignon with a
dish featuring pastilla chiles. I
gave my warning, then poured
the wine they chose — and soon
saw a woman standing up*
*because her mouth was on fire!
At another restaurant, I once
had some gentlemen who insist-
ed on ordering Sangiovese with
their blackened catfish — a bad
idea. I stayed in proximity and
checked back in to see if everything was OK. One looked up
and choked out — because he
could barely speak! — that the
fish was good but so hot. I
brought a bottle of Gewürztraminer for them to taste — a
good idea. With one taste, they
said, "Now we get it!"*
— BRIAN DUNCAN,
wine director, Bin 36 (Chicago)

*A mojito made with rum, lime
juice, sugar, and mint is a great
cleansing cocktail with spicy
food.* — RYAN MAGARIAN,
mixologist, Kathy Casey Food
Studio (Seattle)

*Spicy heat is calmed by sweet-
ness, low alcohol, and bubbles.*
— MADELINE TRIFFON, MS,
director of wine, Matt Prentice
Restaurant Group (Detroit)

SPINACH (AND OTHER GREENS)
Beaujolais
CHARDONNAY (NO OAK)
lemon-flavored drinks (e.g.,
     lemonade, sparkling water with
     lemon)
Pinot Grigio
Pinot Noir, New Zealand
Sauvignon Blanc, esp. California
Sémillon
Soave
white wine, dry

AVOID
red wine

SPINACH PIE (SPINACH AND FETA CHEESE PASTRY)
Grüner Veltliner
Retsina
Sauvignon Blanc (no oak)

SPRING
Beaujolais
Cabernet Franc
Chardonnay, lighter-bodied with
     little to no oak
Gewürztraminer
Greek white wine
margarita, sorrel
Muscadet
red wine, lighter-bodied
Riesling
rosé
Sauvignon Blanc
Vouvray
white wine

*In spring and summer, it is hard
to work red wine onto our menu,
versus in the fall and winter
when it is much easier. During
the spring and summer, we will
incorporate mushrooms into
dishes because they are so red
wine–friendly.*
— DAN BARBER, Chef, Blue
Hill at Stone Barns (New York)

SPRING ROLLS (ASIAN FRIED EGG ROLLS)
beer, esp. Bass ale
Chablis
Champagne
Riesling
sake
sparkling wine

SQUAB (PIGEON; SEE ALSO RECOMMENDATIONS FOR PHEASANT)

Barbaresco
Beaujolais
BORDEAUX, RED
Burgundy, red, esp. with squab with foie gras
CABERNET SAUVIGNON, ESP. CALIFORNIA, AND ESP. WITH GRILLED OR ROASTED SQUAB
Champagne, rosé
cocktails made with brandy or Cognac
Crozes-Hermitage
Pinot Noir, esp. with roasted squab
Riesling, Alsatian, esp. with squab with foie gras
Rioja
Sangiovese
Shiraz / Syrah, esp. with roasted squab
Zinfandel, esp. aged

The gaminess of roasted squab with Syrah or Shiraz is a great match.
— ALAN MURRAY, MS, wine director, Masa's (San Francisco)

SQUASH

ACORN OR BUTTERNUT
Chardonnay, California buttery
Gewürztraminer, dry to off-dry
Riesling, dry to off-dry
tea, maple or Indian
Viognier
white wine, off-dry

SPAGHETTI
Gewürztraminer, off-dry
Riesling, esp. off-dry

SQUID (AKA CALAMARI)

IN GENERAL
Beaujolais-Villages
Gavi
lemon-flavored drinks (e.g., lemonade, sparkling water with lemon)
Mâcon
Pinot Bianco, esp. with grilled squid
Navarra
Orvieto
rosé, esp. dry
Sauvignon Blanc, esp. with grilled squid
Soave
Verdicchio
wine white, esp. dry
Zinfandel

FRIED
beer, wheat, esp. when served with a spicy sauce
Champagne
Gewürztraminer, esp. California or German
Pinot Grigio
rosé, dry
Sancerre, esp. with aïoli
Sauvignon Blanc, esp. with aïoli
sparkling wine (e.g., Cava or Prosecco)
Trebbiano
Vermentino
Vinho Verde

STAR ANISE

Pinot Noir
Sauvignon Blanc, esp. New Zealand

STEAK (SEE ALSO BEEF)

IN GENERAL
ale, dark, esp. highly hopped
Barbaresco
Barolo
Beaujolais
beer, esp. porter and stout
Bordeaux, red
Brunello di Montalcino
Burgundy, red
*CABERNET SAUVIGNON, ESP. CALIFORNIA
Chianti, esp. Riserva
cocktails made with Bourbon, brandy, Cognac, Madeira, or whiskey
Côtes du Rhône
Malbec
Merlot
Rhone red wine, esp. spicy
Shiraz / Syrah, esp. with grilled steak
ZINFANDEL, ESP. CALIFORNIA, ESP. WITH GRILLED STEAK

WITH ANCHOVIES
Côtes du Rhône
sherry, oloroso

WITH BERNAISE
Barolo
Beaujolais
Chardonnay

BISTECCA ALLA FIORENTINA (FLORENTINE-STYLE T-BONE STEAK)
Brunello di Montalcino
Chianti, esp. Classico Riserva
Montepulciano
Sangiovese

WITH BLACK PEPPER (STEAK AU POIVRE)
Barolo
CABERNET SAUVIGNON, ESP. AGED AMERICAN
Châteauneuf-du-Pape
Côte-Rôtie
Grenache
Hermitage
oaked red wine
Merlot
Petite Sirah
Pinot Noir
Rhone red wine
Saint-Émilion
Shiraz / Syrah
Zinfandel, esp. peppery

WITH BLUE CHEESE
Cabernet Sauvignon, esp. with Roquefort
Sangiovese, esp. with Gorgonzola

CHÂTEAUBRIAND
Bordeaux, red, esp. aged
Burgundy, red, aged, esp. with
    sautéed mushrooms

CHICKEN-FRIED (I.E., WITH
CREAM GRAVY)
beer
Cabernet Sauvignon
Champagne, rosé
Merlot
Zinfandel, white

WITH CHILES
Rhône red wine
Syrah
Zinfandel

CHUCK
Barolo
Zinfandel

COLD OR ROOM
    TEMPERATURE (SLICED)
beer
Beaujolais
Pinot Noir, esp. California

DELMONICO
Côte-Rôtie
Hermitage
Rhône red wine

FILET MIGNON
Bordeaux, red
Burgundy, red
Cabernet Franc
CABERNET SAUVIGNON
Chianti, esp. aged
MERLOT
Pinot Noir
RED WINE, OLDER
sherry, oloroso, esp. with grilled
    filet
Shiraz
Super Tuscan
Zinfandel, esp. with grilled filet

FRITES (WITH FRIES)
Beaujolais
Cabernet Sauvignon

FLANK
Beaujolais

Chianti
Côtes du Rhône
Dolcetto
Merlot
Nebbiolo
Shiraz / Syrah

GRILLED
beer, esp. brown ale
Brunello di Montalcino
CABERNET SAUVIGNON
Chianti
Crianza
Merlot
Monastrell
Petite Sirah
red wine, Spanish Reserva
Rhône red wine
Sangiovese
SYRAH / SHIRAZ
ZINFANDEL

GROUND
Merlot

HANGER
Beaujolais-Villages
Côtes du Rhône
Merlot, esp. Napa Valley

MEDIUM-WELL TO WELL-
DONE
aged wine
Beaujolais
beer, brown ale, esp. with charred
    steak
Gamay
Merlot
fruity wine
AVOID
tannic wine (e.g., Cabernet
    Sauvignon)

WITH MEXICAN-STYLE
SALSA
Maipo, Chilean

WITH MISO
Shiraz

WITH MUSHROOMS OR
MUSHROOM SAUCE
Barbaresco
Barolo

Bordeaux, red
Burgundy, red
Cabernet Sauvignon, New World
Shiraz

WITH MUSTARD
Côtes du Rhône
Grenache
Shiraz

PORTERHOUSE
Barbera
Cabernet Sauvignon, American
Chianti
Saint-Émilion

RARE TO MEDIUM-RARE
Bordeaux, red, esp. young
Burgundy, red, esp. young
Cabernet Sauvignon, esp. young
    New World
Grenache
tannic wine
young wine

RIB EYE
CABERNET SAUVIGNON,
    ESP. CALIFORNIA
Merlot
Rioja
Sangiovese
Spanish red wine
Syrah
Zinfandel

SHELL
Beaujolais
Cabernet Sauvignon, esp. Napa
    Valley

SIRLOIN
Barolo
Bordeaux, red
Cabernet Sauvignon, esp. with
    cheese (e.g., blue, Cantal)
Chianti Classico
Hermitage, red
Merlot
Rhône red wine
Rioja
Shiraz
Zinfandel

SKIRT
Beaujolais
Côtes du Rhône
**Shiraz / Syrah, esp. with strong
spices**
Zinfandel

STRIP (NEW YORK)
Bordeaux, red
Burgundy, red, aged, esp. with
sautéed mushrooms
**CABERNET SAUVIGNON,
ESP. YOUNG NAPA VALLEY**
Côte-Rôtie
Hermitage
Merlot
Petite Sirah
Rhone red wine
Shiraz

WITH TAMARI SAUCE
Merlot, esp. California

T-BONE
Bordeaux, red
Cabernet Sauvignon
Chianti Classico
Merlot
Sangiovese
Shiraz, esp. with grilled T-bone

WITH TOMATO SAUCE
Chianti

TIP: Consider choosing a wine
according to how you like your
steak cooked. If you like your
meat well-done, you should know
that all that cooking removes the
fat which will heighten the perception of the tannin in the
wine — which is why you'll want
to avoid tannic Cabernet
Sauvignons with well-done steaks.
If you're a Cabernet Sauvignon
loyalist, you might want to consider ordering your steaks rare or
medium-rare.

*Big, bad red steakhouse wines
pair perfectly with steaks: The
salt smoothes the "edge," the
protein softens the "bite," and
the fat erases the "bark." Filet*

*mignon doesn't have a lot of
fat, so I'd pair one with older
red wines like Bordeaux,
Cabernet Sauvignon, or
Chianti. A porterhouse has more
fat, so it's more about how it's
butchered and prepared. A rib
eye is fat and tough, but tasty,
so I'd pair it with a chunky,
rustic, complex Spanish red or
Zinfandel. And I'd pair a New
York strip steak with a young,
spunky concentrated red, like a
young Napa Cabernet
Sauvignon. Pepper-crusted
steak goes with New World
wines with an illusion of sweetness from oak.*
— MADELEINE TRIFFON, MS,
director of wine, Matt Prentice
Restaurant Group (Detroit)

*While Bern's offers several
sauces to accompany our dry-
aged steaks — including
Béarnaise, Gorgonzola, porcini
port, and wild mushroom and
truffle jus — serious wine
drinkers won't order a sauce,
which can be so flavorful as to
overpower the wine.*
— ERIC RENAUD, sommelier,
Bern's Steak House (Tampa)

*If one were to ever want to drink
white wine with steak — not
that I'd recommend it — a
white Burgundy is one of the
better choices. It is richer and
fattier with a nice clean acidity.*
— ERIC RENAUD, sommelier,
Bern's Steak House (Tampa)

STEAK TARTARE
Beaujolais
Bordeaux, red
Brunello
Burgundy, red, esp. young
Cabernet Sauvignon
Chablis
Champagne, rosé
Chianti Classico
Dolcetto
Gewürztraminer, spicy
martini, esp. vodka
Merlot
Pinot Noir, esp. Russian River
red wine, dry
rosé
Sangiovese
sparkling wine, esp. brut and/or
rosé
vodka

*I love Pinot Noir from the
Russian River Valley with
steak tartare. These Pinots are
richer, and have the power to
combat wine killers [e.g.,
capers, Tabasco, etc.].*
— ERIC RENAUD, sommelier,
Bern's Steak House (Tampa)

STEAMED DISHES
acidic wine
light-bodied wine
Pinot Grigio/Pinot Gris
Riesling
white wine, light-bodied
AVOID
intensely-flavored wine
tannic wine

STEWS AND
STEWED DISHES (SEE
ALSO KEY INGREDIENTS)
ale, esp. full-bodied
Barolo, esp. with meat or game

Beaujolais
Cabernet Sauvignon
Châteauneuf-du-Pape
Gewürztraminer, Alsatian
Gigondas
Rhone red wine
sherry, amontillado
Shiraz / Syrah

STIR-FRIED DISHES
beer, esp. lager or Tsingtao
Gewürztraminer
lighter-bodied wine
Pinot Grigio
Riesling, esp. off-dry
rosé
Sauvignon Blame
sparkling wine
white wine
Zinfandel, white

STRAWBERRIES
(INCLUDING DESSERTS)
Asti
Banyuls
Beaujolais
Brachetto d'Acqui
**CHAMPAGNE, ESP. DEMI-
SEC OR ROSÉ**
cocktails made with Cassis,
Cognac, Cointreau, Curaçao,
Grand Marnier, Kirsch, or
Sambuca
fruit-flavored drinks, esp. banana,
orange, or pineapple (e.g.,
Fizzy Lizzy sparkling pineapple
juice)
ice wine
lemon-flavored drinks (e.g.,
lemonade, sparkling water with
lemon)
Moscato d'Asti
Muscat, esp. black
Muscat de Beaumes-de-Venise
Pinot Noir, esp. Alsatian
port, ruby or tawny
Riesling, off-dry to sweet
**SAUTERNES, ESP. WITH
CREAMY DESSERTS**

**Sémillon, Late Harvest, esp.
when served with heavy or
whipped cream**
Shiraz, sparkling
**sparkling wine, esp. semisweet
tea, Kukicha or Kyoto Cherry
Rose**
Viognier
**Vouvray, sweet, esp. with straw-
berry shortcake**

*I remember a wild strawberry and
fresh mint soup that had been
made with Brut Imperial Rosé
and served with Dom Pérignon
Rosé 1990 that was amazing.*
— LISANE LAPOINTE,
ambassador, Dom Pérignon

*One of the best pairings we've
ever done was of Champagne-
marinated strawberries with
Kyoto Cherry Rose tea. This is
traditional Japanese sencha tea
blended with cherry blossoms.
This tea has been around for
centuries and it is almost sacri-
legious to blend it, but we did
and it tasted great.*
— MICHAEL OBNOWLENNY,
Canada's first tea sommelier

STRIPED BASS
(DELICATE, FLAKEY FISH AKA
ROCKFISH)
BURGUNDY, WHITE, ESP.
WITH GRILLED BASS
CHARDONNAY, ESP.
CALIFORNIA, AND ESP.
WITH GRILLED BASS
delicate white wine with little oak
(with grilled bass) or no oak
(with bass that is not grilled)
Pinot Blanc, Alsatian, esp. with
grilled bass
Pinot Gris/Pinot Grigio
Sauvignon Blanc
Viognier

SUKIYAKI (SEE ALSO
JAPANESE CUISINE)
Champagne
sparkling wine
Zinfandel

SUMMER
agua fresca (Mexican fruit drink)
Albarino
Arneis
batidas, Brazilian tropical fruit
cocktails
Beaujolais
beer, esp. Lambic (e.g., Framboise)
Bellinis (white peach juice and
Prosecco)
Caipirinhas
Campari spritzer
Cava
Chablis
Chenin Blanc
Cosmopolitans
Cuba Libra cocktail
Daiquiris
Dolcetto
fruit-based drinks
fruit-"tinis" and other fruit cocktails
Gewürztraminer
gin and tonic
Greek white wine
Grüner Veltliner
ice-based drinks
ice cream shakes, sodas, and other
drinks
iced coffee, iced tea, and other
iced drinks
lemonade, limeade, and other
fruit ades
lighter-bodied wine
lime rickey, cherry or raspberry
Long Island Iced Tea (citrusy cola
cocktail)
mango lassi (yogurt drink)
margaritas
martini, esp. cucumber
milkshakes
mojitos
Pimm's Cup

pina coladas
Pinotage, South African
Pinot Grigio / Pinot Gris
Planter's rum punch
Prosecco
punch
red wines, light-bodied
Riesling
rosé
Sancerre
sangria
Sauvignon Blanc
slightly chilled red wine (e.g.,
   Beaujolais, lighter Zinfandel)
sparkling wines
tea, esp. green and/or iced (esp.
   black)
tea, Thai iced
Txakoli
Viognier
Vouvray
water, flat and sparkling
white wine, esp. chilled
Zinfandel, white

*Wine has seasons. Summer is
not for big tannic red wine —
they don't feel good any more
than a big, heavy meat dish
does at that time of year.
Winter is for fuller, richer wine.
Summer is for white wines and
lighter red wines.*
   — BRIAN DUNCAN, wine
      director, Bin 36 (Chicago)

SUMMER ROLLS, VIETNAMESE
Champagne
Riesling, off-dry
Sauvignon Blanc, New Zealand
sparkling wine

SURF AND TURF (I.E., LOBSTER AND STEAK)
Pinot Noir, Oregon, with both
Riesling, Alsatian, with the lobster
Syrah / Shiraz, with the steak

SUSHI (SEE ALSO SASHIMI)

IN GENERAL
ale
Amarone, with eel
BEER, ESP. JAPANESE, LAGER,
   OR SUMMER ALE
Burgundy, red
Burgundy, white
Chablis, esp. aged
CHAMPAGNE, ESP. BLANC
   DE BLANCS, AGED, OR
   BRUT ROSÉ
Chardonnay (no oak)
cocktails esp. made cucumber,
   sake, or vodka
miso soup
Muscadet
Pinot Grigio
Riesling, esp. dry to off-dry,
   (e.g., German Kabinett), and
   esp. with spicy sushi
SAKE, ESP. DAI GINJO AND
   JUNMAI DAI GINJO
Sauvignon Blanc, esp. California
sherry, esp. chilled fino and man-
   zanilla
SPARKLING WINE
tea, green or oolong
Vouvray, aged and/or dry
Vouvray, sparkling, demi-sec
water, still or with very small
   bubbles and low TDS
white wine, dry, acidic, light-
   bodied, low-alcohol
Zinfandel, esp. with eel, plum
   sauce, or tuna

AVOID
high-alcohol wine
oaked wine

CRAB
Chenin Blanc

EEL
Amarone
Gewürztraminer, off-dry
Riesling, off-dry
Zinfandel

MACKEREL
Sauvignon Blanc, New Zealand

SALMON
Chenin Blanc, dry
Pinot Noir
Riesling, dry and/or German
   Kabinett

SCALLOPS
Chenin Blanc

SEA URCHIN
Vouvray

SQUID
Muscadet

SWEET SHRIMP
Champagne

TUNA OR YELLOWTAIL
Champagne, esp. with ahi tuna
Chardonnay
sparkling wine
Zinfandel

*With sushi, I drink a dry
oolong tea or sake or ale. Wine
doesn't work for me.*
   — JEAN-LUC LE DÛ,
      Le Dû's Wines (NYC)

*With sushi, you want sake,
because you are working with
something rice-based and you
need something pure to match
the fish. Great sushi is so pure
that a glass of wine may mask
the flavor of the dish. If you do
drink wine, you'll want a neutral wine like a Chablis, which
works because it has no oak.*
   — BERNARD SUN, beverage
      director, Jean-Georges
      Management (NYC)

*I absolutely love sushi and
Japanese food, and have it at
least once a week. You want to
pair it with acidity, low alcohol,
and no wood at all. The greatest thing with sushi is old, dry*

Vouvray or old Chablis, or old Champagne — as age gives you the aroma of soy.

— RAJAT PARR, MS, wine director, the Mina Group

Personally, I find wine far better and more flexible to pair with sushi than sake. Sparkling Vouvray Demi-Sec is great with sushi across the board. At Nobu, I ordered Champagne, Gewürztraminer, Riesling, and Ridge Lytton Springs Zinfandel. Everyone I was with said I was crazy [to order Zinfandel], but it was the only bottle we reordered throughout the night. This Zinfandel with tuna was like tasting tuna for the very first time! It's also wonderful with eel or plum sauce. You need to break every dish down: Amarone is incredible with eel because of the darker barbecue flavors. Chenin Blanc has a great affinity to the natural sweetness of crab and scallop flavors, and draws them out. White Burgundy and less oaky Chardonnay also work with sushi. A more minerally style of Chardonnay works well with sashimi, especially shellfish. And the spicier you like your offering, the better the match will be with Riesling!

— BRIAN DUNCAN, wine director, Bin 36 (Chicago)

SWEET-AND-SOUR, DISHES AND SAUCES
Chenin Blanc, off-dry
fruity wine

GEWÜRZTRAMINER, OFF-DRY
high-acid wine
Pinot Gris
Riesling
Sauvignon Blanc, New Zealand
slightly sweet wine
Zinfandel

Southeast Asian food is usually sweet and sour, with a decent amount of acidity. There are two ways to look at pairings: Do you want something tart, to go with the acid — or something sweet, to balance it out? If the dish is spicy, you might want a sweet and lower-acid wine. Acid pushes the acid up, so an acidic wine makes an acidic dish twice as acidic. If you like spicy food, a high-acid wine is OK. If you like only a little heat, then go with a low-acid wine like Gewürztraminer or Pinot Gris.

— BERNARD SUN, beverage director, Jean-Georges Management (New York)

SWEETBREADS
Beaujolais
Bordeaux, red, esp. lighter-bodied
Burgundy, red, esp. lighter-bodied
BURGUNDY, WHITE
Champagne, esp. French, and esp. with sautéed sweetbreads
Chardonnay, California buttery, esp. with mustard suace
Chianti
cocktails made with brandy, Madeira, or Marsala
Gewürztraminer, Alsatian
lemon-flavored drinks (e.g., lemonade, sparkling water with lemon)

Pinot Noir, esp. Oregon
Riesling, esp. German, off-dry, and/or Spätlese
rosé, dry
Sauvignon Blanc, California
sherry, oloroso

SWEET FOODS AND DISHES (SEE ALSO DESSERT)
Champagne, esp. demi-sec
Chenin Blanc
cocktails, sweet
dessert wine, with desserts
fruity wine
Gewürztraminer
ice wine
Late Harvest wine
Madeira
port
RIESLING, GERMAN AND/OR OFF-DRY TO SWEET
sparkling wine, semisweet or sweet
sweeter wine
tea, esp. black
Viognier
Vouvray, demi-sec

AVOID
dry wine

Sweetness in food likes sweetness in wine.

— MADELINE TRIFFON, MS, director of wine, Matt Prentice Restaurant Group (Detroit)

SWEET POTATOES
Chardonnay, California
fruit-flavored drinks, esp. apple or orange (e.g., sparkling apple juice)
Gewürztraminer, esp. off-dry
ginger ale
Riesling, off-dry to sweet
sparkling wines with at least a bit of sweetness
Viognier

SWISS CHARD
Sauvignon Blanc

SWORDFISH

IN GENERAL

Burgundy, red, esp. with grilled swordfish

Burgundy, white, esp. with baked or broiled swordfish

Cabernet Sauvignon, esp. with black pepper

Champagne

CHARDONNAY, ESP. CALIFORNIA, AND ESP. WITH BAKED, BROILED, OR GRILLED SWORDFISH

lemon-flavored drinks (e.g., lemonade, sparkling water with lemon)

PINOT NOIR, ESP. OREGON

Riesling, dry Alsatian

Sancerre

Sauvignon Blanc

Sémillon, esp. with grilled swordfish

sparkling wine

WITH BACON

Sauvignon Blanc

Zinfandel, esp. lighter-bodied

WITH LEMON BUTTER SAUCE

Chablis, esp. Premier Cru

Sancerre

Sauvignon Blanc, esp. California

WITH PEPPERCORN CRUST

Cabernet Sauvignon

Grüner Veltliner

Shiraz / Syrah

ROASTED

Chardonnay, esp. California

Sauvignon Blanc

One of our signature dishes is a take on steak au poivre, which is swordfish in a peppercorn crust. This is a dish that can be paired with red or white wine. We have great success with Grüner Veltliner, which has a little white pepper hint in its background and enough acid to refresh your mouth. The dish also works with Australian Shiraz, which can be rich and plummy. Syrah and Cabernet Sauvignon work, too.

— BRIAN DUNCAN,
wine director, Bin 36 (Chicago)

SZECHUAN FOOD
(SEE ALSO ASIAN CUISINE AND SPICY FOODS)

Beaujolais, esp. with spicier meat dishes

beer

Gewürztraminer, Alsatian, esp. with spicier dishes

Riesling, off-dry (e.g., Spätlese or Auslese)

rosé, esp. with spicier dishes

sparkling wine

TABASCO

beer

low-alcohol wine

Pinot Noir, esp. Russian River

sparkling wine

Vinho Verde

AVOID

high-alcohol wine

most red wine

When you have hot spice, it exaggerates the alcohol in the wine, so look for low-alcohol wines that are refreshing. If a dish has too much Tabasco, then grab a beer.

— JOSHUA WESSON,
wine director, Best Cellars

TABBOULEH (SEE ALSO MIDDLE EASTERN CUISINE)

Pinot Noir

rosé, dry

Sauvignon Blanc

tea, mint, esp. spearmint

TACO BELL GORDITAS

rosé

Sauvignon Blanc, esp. New Zealand

sparkling wine

TACOS

IN GENERAL

beer, esp. pilsner or Tecate

BEEF

beer, esp. Tecate

Cabernet Sauvignon

Côtes du Rhône

Merlot

Syrah

Tempranillo

Zinfandel

TAMARIND

Pinot Noir

Riesling

TANDOORI DISHES
(SEE ALSO INDIAN CUISINE)

beer

Gewürztraminer

tea, Assam

Zinfandel, esp. with tandoori chicken

With tandoori chicken, I want Zinfandel!

— ALPANA SINGH, MS,
Everest (Chicago)

TAPAS

IN GENERAL
Albarino
beer, esp. lager
Cava
Priorat, esp. with grilled or
 stewed tapas
Rioja, white
rosé, dry
***SHERRY, DRY, ESP. FINO OR
 MANZANILLA**
Txakoli
Vinho Verde

AVOID
red wine

*Sherry pairs so well with tapas
because the high alcohol goes
with the big flavors and cuts
through all the richness while
providing a contrasting texture.*
 — STEVE BECKTA, owner,
 Beckta Dining & Wine (Ottawa)

*With tapas, I start with rosé or
Rioja, then move into Priorat
with stewed and grilled tapas.*
 — JEAN-LUC LE DÛ,
 Le Dû's Wines (NYC)

TAPENADE (PROVENÇAL
PASTE OF OLIVES, CAPERS, AND
ANCHOVIES)
Champagne, esp. Blanc de Blancs
ROSÉ, DRY
Sauvignon Blanc
sherry
Zinfandel

TARRAGON
Arneis
Burgundy, white
Chardonnay (no oak)
Merlot

Pinot Noir
Sauvignon Blanc
Viognier

TART FOODS
fruity wine
tart-crisp wine

*Tart likes tart. Tartness in foods
softens the tartness in wines, so
tart foods pair well with fruity
and/or tart-crisp wine.*
 — MADELINE TRIFFON, MS,
 director of wine, Matt Prentice
 Restaurant Group (Detroit)

TEMPURA (JAPANESE
BATTERED AND FRIED
VEGETABLES AND/OR
SEAFOOD)

IN GENERAL
beer, esp. lager or wheat beer
Chablis

Champagne, esp. dry
cocktails, esp. made with cucumber, sake, and vodka
sake, esp. honjozo or junmai
Sancerre
Sauvignon Blanc
**sparkling wine, esp. brut or
 extra dry**

SEAFOOD
Gewürztraminer, dry
Muscadet
Sauvignon Blanc
sherry, dry, esp. fino

TERIYAKI (JAPANESE
SWEET-SAUCED MEAT)
Bandol, red, with beef
**Beaujolais or Beaujolais-Villages,
 with beef**
Merlot
Pinot Noir, with salmon
Riesling, esp. off-dry, with
 chicken, pork, or seafood
rosé
Zinfandel, with beef

TEX-MEX CUISINE

(SEE ALSO MEXICAN CUISINE AND SOUTHWESTERN CUISINE)

Beaujolais
beer
Sauvignon Blanc, New Zealand

THAI BASIL

Sauvignon Blanc

THAI CUISINE

IN GENERAL
Beaujolais, esp. with curries and other spicy dishes
BEER (E.G., ALE, PILSNER, SINGHA, OR WEISS), ESP. WITH CURRIES AND OTHER SPICY DISHES
Chablis
Champagne, esp. brut
Chardonnay, oaked, esp. with curries
Chenin Blanc, esp. with fish
cocktails made with coconut, cilantro, curry paste, ginger, lime, sugar, and/or vodka
GEWÜRZTRAMINER
Grüner Veltliner, Austrian
low-alcohol wine
Nero d'Avola, Italian
off-dry wine to sweeter wine
Pinot Bianco/Pinot Blanc
Pinot Gris (esp. Alsatian)/Pinot Grigio
Pinot Noir
***RIESLING, ESP. GERMAN, OFF-DRY, AND/OR SPÄTLESE, AND ESP. WITH DISHES WITH COCONUT MILK AND/OR EXTRA SPICINESS**
rosé, esp. with spicier dishes
SAUVIGNON BLANC, NEW ZEALAND, ESP. WITH LEMONGRASS AND/OR VEGETABLE DISHES
Shiraz, fruity, with beef dishes

sparkling wine
Syrah, spicy, esp. with meat
Thai iced coffee or tea
Vouvray, esp. with sweeter dishes

AVOID
high-alcohol wine, esp. with spicier dishes
tannic wine

I live near Chinatown, where there's also a lot of Thai food. Its classic pairing is Gewürztraminer, but sometimes that can overwhelm. I find Alsatian Riesling or Tokay Pinot Gris more versatile.

— RICHARD BREITKREUTZ, general manager, Eleven Madison Park (New York)

With the sweeter curries that have coconut milk, I love German Riesling. They go well with the ginger. With the lemongrass dishes, I tend to go more toward Sauvignon Blanc in the Sancerre style that is leaner. Vouvray also works well with something that has a sweeter note. With Vouvray, you get a richness of fruit more towards the pear style and still some minerality and acidity, which gives you balance.

— JILL GUBESCH, sommelier, Frontera Grill and Topolobampo (Chicago)

On Sunday nights, my wife Maureen and I always have Thai food, and always order the same dishes, from hot and sour shrimp and pineapple soup

to potsticker dumplings with chili soy sauce. Everything goes great with an off-dry Riesling — either a German Riesling, or a Niagara Riesling — or a Gewürztraminer or an Alsatian Tokay Pinot Gris. You want something "pretty" and off-dry after all that savory heat.

— STEVE BECKTA, owner, Beckta Dining & Wine (Ottawa)

With Thai food, try a cocktail with the fresh flavors of coconut, cilantro, yellow curry paste, lime, sugar, and vodka — also known as the Ultimate Thai Cocktail. It may be a little over the top, but it's a truly wonderful combination with a Chicken Larb Gai Salad. We have also had success with something as simple as a fresh Ginger Cosmopolitan, made by hand-pressing fresh ginger into a classic Cosmopolitan, and garnishing it with orange zest to draw out the sensory experience into one more dimension: smell.

— RYAN MAGARIAN, mixologist, Kathy Casey Food Studios (Seattle)

THAI FISH SAUCE (SEE ANCHOVIES)

THYME

beer
Cabernet Sauvignon
Champagne, rosé
Chardonnay
Châteauneuf-du-Pape

Gigondas
Merlot
Pinot Grigio / Pinot Gris
Pinot Noir
red wine
SAUVIGNON BLANC
Syrah
Zinfandel

TIRAMISU
Asti
Madeira, esp. Malmsey
Marsala
Moscato d'Asti
**MUSCAT, SWEET AND/OR
BLANC**
port, esp. tawny
Sauternes
sherry, sweet
Vin Santo

TOFU
SAKE, ESP. DAIGINJO
tea, oolong, esp. with fried tofu

TOMATILLOS
Burgundy, red
Côtes du Rhône
Riesling, esp. Alsatian
**Sauvignon Blanc, esp. New
Zealand**
Syrah, esp. New World

*If I'm pairing wine to a sauce
using tomatillos, I have to look
at what time of year it is: If it is
summer, tomatillos can come in
so sweet and with such low acid
that they can handle a richer
wine like a New World Syrah.
A Syrah has rich, spicy fruit, so
it is bright enough to hold up to
the sweet caramelized sugar of
tomatillos.*
— JILL GUBESCH, sommelier,
Frontera Grill and Topolobampo
(Chicago)

TOMATOES
IN GENERAL
**Albarino, esp. with tomato con-
fit**
**BARBERA, ESP. WITH
COOKED TOMATOES**
**CHIANTI, ESP. WITH
COOKED TOMATOES**
Gewürztraminer, dry, esp.
German from Pfalz, and esp.
with raw tomatoes
Italian white wine
Pinot Grigio, esp. with raw toma-
toes
**Pinot Noir, esp. with cooked
tomatoes**
Riesling, dry, esp. with raw toma-
toes
**rosé, e.g., Bandol, esp. with raw
tomatoes**
**SANGIOVESE, ESP. WITH
COOKED TOMATOES**
**SAUVIGNON BLANC, ESP.
NEW ZEALAND, AND ESP.
WITH RAW TOMATOES**

FRIED GREEN
Pinot Grigio
Sauvignon Blanc

*With tomato sauce, I like reds
with equal parts acidity and
tannin, like Chianti and
Sangiovese.*
— MADELINE TRIFFON, MS,
director of wine, Matt Prentice
Restaurant Group (Detroit)

*There is no better wine for raw
tomatoes than Gewürztraminer.
People forget that a tomato is a
fruit and high in acid. So, if
you pair it with a fruity high-
acid wine, it is like tasting a
tomato for the very first time. If
you want to show off and can't
really cook, get a platter of a
bunch of different colored tomatoes, drizzle a nice olive oil,
sprinkle with sea salt and fresh
basil — then serve it with your
Gewürztraminer. People will
think you are a rock star! I
would recommend a German
Gewürztraminer from the Pfalz
region because it is higher in
acid and doesn't have the over-
ripeness that the Alsatian ones
do.* — BRIAN DUNCAN,
wine director, Bin 36 (Chicago)

TORO (JAPANESE TUNA)
sake, esp. honjozo or junmai

TORTILLA CHIPS
Champagne
Sauvignon Blanc, New Zealand,
esp. with chips and salsa
sparkling wine

TORTILLAS
Chardonnay, esp. New Zealand

TROUT (SEE ALSO OTHER
MILD FISH SUCH AS BASS,
HALIBUT, ETC., AND SMOKED
TROUT)
Bordeaux, white, esp. sautéed
trout with butter and/or lemon
Burgundy, white, esp. Meursault,
and esp. with butter sauce
Chablis
**Champagne, esp. Blanc de
Blancs and/or vintage, and
esp. with trout with soy sauce**
**Chardonnay, esp. lighter-bodied,
and esp. with lemon sauce**
**Chenin Blanc, esp. with grilled
trout and/or trout with
almonds**
cocktails made with brandy or
Pernod
Gewürztraminer

lemon-flavored drinks (e.g., lemonade, sparkling water with lemon)

Pinot Bianco / Pinot Blanc, esp. with trout with almonds

Pinot Gris, Alsatian, esp. with trout with almonds

Pinot Noir, with grilled trout

Pouilly-Fumé

RIESLING, ESP. ALSATIAN AND/OR DRY, AND ESP. WITH GRILLED OR SAUTEÉD TROUT

Riesling, German, esp. Kabinett, and esp. grilled and/or with butter or cream sauce

Sancerre

Sauvignon Blanc

sparkling wine, esp. Prosecco

Vouvray, dry

FRENCH QUARTER

ROBERT HESS OF DRINKBOY.COM CREATED THIS COCKTAIL TO ACCOMPANY A DISH OF TROUT ALMONDINE AT ANTOINE'S IN NEW ORLEANS.

2 1/2 ounces brandy

3/4 ounce Lillet

Stir brandy and Lillet with ice. Strain into a cocktail glass. Garnish with a thin "quarter" wheel of lemon.

TRUFFLES

aged wine

***BARBARESCO, BEST-QUALITY, WITH WHITE TRUFFLES**

Barbera

***BAROLO, BEST-QUALITY, WITH WHITE TRUFFLES**

Bordeaux, red, esp. Pauillac

Burgundy, red, esp. aged

Burgundy, white

Champagne, esp. brut

Chardonnay, oaked

cocktails made with Cognac or Madeira

Côtes du Rhône

Dolcetto

Pinot Noir

Pomerol

Ribera del Duero

You can't not talk about truffles with Barolo and Barbaresco. When fall truffle season hits, this is a pairing I can't wait for.

— BERNARD SUN, beverage director, Jean-Georges Management (New York)

TUNA

IN GENERAL

Beaujolais

Burgundy, white

Cabernet Franc

Cabernet Sauvignon, esp. with tuna with black pepper

Champagne, rosé

CHARDONNAY, esp. no oak and/or Italian or California

Châteauneuf-du-Pape

Gigondas

ginger ale

lemon- or lime-flavored drinks (e.g., lemonade, sparkling water with lime)

Merlot, esp. New World and/or light oak

Pinot Grigio

***PINOT NOIR, ESP. CALIFORNIA OR OREGON**

Rhône red wine

Riesling

rosé

sake, esp. honjozo or junmai

Sauvignon Blanc, esp. California or New Zealand

Shiraz

Viognier

Zinfandel

CASSEROLE

Beaujolais

Chardonnay, esp. unoaked

CEVICHE

Chenin Blanc

Muscadet

Riesling, dry to off-dry

GRILLED

beer, esp. lager with spicy dishes

Cabernet Sauvignon

Chardonnay, California

Côtes du Rhône, red

Merlot

PINOT NOIR, ESP. CALIFORNIA

Sauvignon Blanc

tea, green

NIÇOISE (SEE SALAD, NIÇOISE)

WITH PESTO

Chardonnay

Chianti

RAW (E.G., CARPACCIO OR TARTARE)

Champagne, esp. brut or rosé

Pinot Gris

Riesling, dry (e.g., German Kabinett)

Sauvignon Blanc, esp. New Zealand

sparkling wine, dry

Viognier

TURBOT

BURGUNDY, WHITE

Chablis

Champagne, esp. with poached turbot

CHARDONNAY, ESP. LIGHT OAK, AND ESP. WITH GRILLED TURBOT

lemon-flavored drinks (e.g., lemonade, sparkling water with lemon)

Pouilly-Fumé

GREGORY SHORT'S AHI TUNA TARTARE WITH AVOCADO, MANGO, AND MANGO VINAIGRETTE

Serves 4

2 ripe Hayden mangos

About 2 tablespoons lemon juice

About 1 tablespoon low-sodium soy sauce

3 pounds sashimi-grade Yellowfin tuna, cut into 1/4-inch dice

1 tablespoon extra-virgin olive oil

Salt

Black pepper

1 ripe avocado, peeled and cut into 1/4-inch dice

Toast points and lightly dressed baby lettuce, for serving (optional)

1. Peel and cut 1 mango into 1/4-inch dice; reserve cold. Peel and cut the fruit away from the pit of the remaining mango.

2. To make the vinaigrette: Place the large mango pieces in a blender and puree until smooth. (Use a little water to help puree the fruit if necessary.) Season with the lemon juice and soy sauce to taste. Reserve the vinaigrette cold.

3. In a large bowl, combine the tuna, olive oil, and diced mango; season with salt and black pepper. Gently stir in the avocado. Check seasoning and reserve cold.

4. To serve: Divide the tuna mixture among 4 plates using a round cookie cutter or other circular mold. Garnish with a few small pools of the mango vinaigrette at the base of the tuna. Serve with toast points and lightly dressed baby lettuces if you like.

SOMMELIER ALAN MURRAY'S WINE PAIRING: *Willakenzie Estate Pinot Gris Oregon 2003*

TURKEY (SEE ALSO RECOMMENDATIONS FOR CHICKEN)

IN GENERAL (I.E., ROASTED)

Beaujolais, esp. Nouveau
Burgundy, white
Cabernet Sauvignon
CHARDONNAY, ESP. CALIFORNIA OR OTHER NEW WORLD WITH LITTLE TO NO OAK
cocktails made with Madeira or Marsala
cranberry juice, sparkling (e.g., Fizzy Lizzy)
Gewürztraminer
Merlot
PINOT NOIR
Riesling
Rioja Reserva
Sauvignon Blanc
Shiraz / Syrah
Vouvray
Zinfandel

HASH

Riesling, dry and/or Alsatian
rosé

LEFTOVERS (SERVED COLD)

Beaujolais
Pinot Noir
Riesling, German

SMOKED

rosé, dry

THANKSGIVING DINNER (WITH STUFFING, CRANBERRY SAUCE, ETC.)

Amarone
Beaujolais
Burgundy, white
Cabernet Sauvignon
Chablis
Chardonnay, California
fruity wine
Gewürztraminer
Merlot
off-dry wine
Pinot Gris
Pinot Noir, esp. New World
Riesling, dry and/or Kabinett
Shiraz, still or sparkling
sparkling wine, esp. brut and/or rosé
Syrah
ZINFANDEL, ESP. FRUITY

Thanksgiving is the most problematic holiday for a sommelier because no two tables are the same and no two bites are the same. The best you can hope for is a choice that will please most of the people most of the time. Dry sparkling Shiraz is breathtakingly spectacular with Thanksgiving dinner. It hits every note and has something for everyone. It is the ultimate "Zelig" wine — it chameleons right into the perfect match.

— JOSHUA WESSON, *wine director, Best Cellars*

VANILLA

Asti, esp. with desserts
Banyuls, esp. with desserts
Burgundy, white
Champagne
Chardonnay, esp. big and buttery California
coffee
ice wine, esp. with desserts
Moscato d'Asti, esp. with desserts
port, esp. tawny, and esp. with desserts
Riesling, sweet or Late Harvest
sherry, PX, esp. with desserts
sparkling wine

VEAL

IN GENERAL

Beaujolais
beer, esp. with simple and/or fried dishes
BORDEAUX, RED
Brunello
Burgundy, red
Burgundy, white
Cabernet Franc
Cabernet Sauvignon
Champagne, rosé
Chardonnay
Chianti, esp. Classico
cider
cocktails made with Madeira, Marsala, or vermouth
Dolcetto
Gamay
lemon-flavored drinks (e.g., lemonade, sparkling water with lemon)
Merlot, esp. dry and/or Chilean
Pinot Gris
Pinot Noir
Riesling
Sangiovese
Soave
Vouvray
white wine, or lighter-bodied red wine
Zinfandel, esp. lighter-bodied

BRAISED SHANKS OR SHOULDER

Bordeaux, red, esp. young
Pinot Noir, California, esp. with rosemary
Rhône red wine
Super Tuscan
Syrah

CHOPS

Barolo
Bordeaux, red
Burgundy, red
Cabernet Sauvignon
cocktails made with Cognac or Madeira
Pinot Noir, esp. California
Rioja

WITH CREAM SAUCE

Burgundy, white
CHARDONNAY, ESP. LIGHTER-BODIED

Pinot Gris
Riesling, dry

GRILLED
Burgundy, red
Malbec
Rioja
Syrah

LOIN, ROASTED
Bordeaux, red
Burgundy, white

WITH CITRUS SAUCE
Chablis
Chardonnay, esp. New World

MARSALA
Arneis
Chardonnay
Chianti
Merlot

WITH MORELS
Burgundy, red
Chardonnay (with oak)
Pinot Gris
Vouvray

OSSO BUCO (SEE OSSO BUCO)

PARMESAN
Brunello
Chianti

ROASTED
Bordeaux, red
Brunello de Montalcino
Burgundy, red
Burgundy, white
Cabernet Sauvignon
Chardonnay
Chianti, esp. Classico
Grenache, old-vine
Merlot
Pinot Gris, esp. Alsatian or German
Pinot Noir
Valpolicella

SCALLOPINE
Pinot Grigio
Rioja
Soave

sparkling wine, esp. California and/or brut

WIENER SCHNITZEL
beer, pilsner
Grüner Veltliner
Riesling, German
Sancerre
Sauvignon Blanc
Zinfandel

VEGETABLES AND VEGETARIAN DISHES (SEE ALSO TOFU AND SPECIFIC VEGETABLES)

IN GENERAL
Beaujolais
Bordeaux, red
Champagne, esp. rosé
Chardonnay, (no oak)
Grüner Veltliner, esp. lighter-bodied
Merlot
Pinot Gris
Riesling, dry
rosé, esp. dry
SAUVIGNON BLANC, ESP. NEW ZEALAND
sparkling wine
Viognier
white wine, esp. drier and unoaked

WITH BEANS (AND OTHER EARTHY FLAVORS)
Merlot
red wine

WITH CREAM OR CHEESE SAUCE
beer
Chardonnay
cider, sparkling

WITH GOAT CHEESE
Sancerre
Sauvignon Blanc

GRILLED
Beaujolais
Chardonnay, esp. oaky California
Merlot
ROSÉ / ROSADO, ESP. DRY AND/OR NEW WORLD
Zinfandel

MOUSSE
Champagne
Riesling
sake, esp. daiginjo

STEAMED
sake, esp. daiginjo
white wine, esp. lighter-bodied

STIR-FRIED
Sauvignon Blanc

TART OR PIE
Pinot Blanc, Alsatian

VEGGIE BURGER
beer, esp. lager or pilsner
cider, hard and/or sparkling
rosé, off-dry

AVOID
tannic red wine

Veggie burgers tend to be bland, blank canvases, so it becomes more about the condiment you are slapping on. With ketchup, go with an off-dry rosé. — JOSHUA WESSON, wine director, Best Cellars

Vegetables are trickier than meat or fish. Often, it's about the sauce. The key is minerality, which is what both vegetables and grapes are sucking up out of the earth.
— DEREK TODD, sommelier, Blue Hill at Stone Barns (New York)

Alan Murray's Pairing Tips for Vegetarian Menus

I have been pairing wines for vegetarian tasting menus at Masa's for over five years. It produces some challenges and it leads you to **unoaked white wines,** wines that are not **bone dry.** It is a good place to drink **rosé.** The menu doesn't rely on cream and richness, and you are really trying to highlight the freshness of the ingredients, so oaked and low-acid wines don't play into the equation.

We are serving a summer bean salad of three different beans dressed with a vinaigrette as the first course on the menu. It was a struggle to find a wine that would work. For this dish, I serve a **Champagne.**

With a winter soup, I like to pair **Madeira.** A corn chowder works great with a dry Madeira like Verdelho. Most people would serve a Chardonnay or Viognier, but they become alcoholic and flat. Madeira really lifts this dish. An older vintage works better than a young vintage because it is a little mellower. It is an ethereal combination.

I work hard on this. If I ordered a vegetarian menu and the sommelier served me four white wines, I would not be talking to them! Most people are looking forward to their glass of red wine and that can be the biggest challenge to the menu.

If we finish with pasta or risotto, it is easy. We are currently finishing with a roasted squash, and for that I cheat a little by serving a **rosé Champagne.** Rosé works well when we serve a variety of things on the plate like chickpea hummus, eggplant caviar, and some other subtle flavors. However, it is just too much for one red wine to handle. I could serve a powerful red wine like a Grenache or a Châteauneuf-du-Pape if a guest wanted it, but it would dominate the pairing. So the wine would work; it just wouldn't be a finessed pairing.

VENISON

Amarone

Barbaresco

BAROLO

beer, esp. ale or brown ale or *DOPPELBOCK

Bordeaux, red

Cabernet Sauvignon, esp. California

Champagne, rosé

Châteauneuf-du-Pape

cocktails made with brandy, gin, or Madeira

Côte-Rôtie

fruit-flavored drinks, esp. apple or cherry (e.g., sparkling apple juice)

Gigondas

Hermitage

Merlot

Petite Sirah

Pinot Noir, New World

RHONE RED WINE

sherry, oloroso

***SHIRAZ / SYRAH,** ESP. NEW WORLD, AND ESP. WITH GRILLED VENISON

tea, Darjeeling

ZINFANDEL, ESP. CALIFORNIA, AND ESP. WITH STEWED VENISON

AVOID

white wine

Coming up with blended pairings for complex dishes can be very logical. Our chef at The Fairmont in Toronto created a dish of venison with chocolate sauce. We found an ideal pairing with a Darjeeling and Kenyan tea blend in the ratio of 70 to 30, with the proportions being in essentially the same ratio as the venison to the sauce. The Darjeeling worked with the venison and the Kenyan worked with the chocolate sauce.

— MICHAEL OBNOWLENNY, Canada's first tea sommelier

VIETNAMESE CUISINE

Barbaresco with lower-acid dishes, and esp. with beef

Barolo with lower-acid dishes and esp. with beef

beer, esp. Chimay (esp. with pork) or Weissbier

Burgundy, red

Chardonnay, light (no oak)

Chenin Blanc

Côtes de Beaunes

GEWÜRZTRAMINER

ginger ale

Grüner Veltliner

lime-flavored drinks, (e.g. limeade, sparkling water with lime)

Pinot Gris, esp. Alsatian or Oregon

red wine, light-bodied

RIESLING, ESP. GERMAN

Sauvignon Blanc, esp. New Zealand, and esp. with seafood and/or vegetable dishes

tea

Viognier

Zinfandel, California

AVOID
high-alcohol wine
very tannic wine

VINAIGRETTE

beer

Chablis

Champagne

Chardonnay

high-acid wine

Marsala

Pinot Grigio

Riesling, off-dry, esp. with a ginger vinaigrette

Sauvignon Blanc

Verdicchio

Vinho Verde

AVOID
low-acid wine
red wine

In San Francisco, we have two Vietnamese restaurants that have two totally different kinds of wines that go with their food — because their dishes have different structures. Every chef cooks differently, Vietnamese chefs included, so every Vietnamese restaurant is different. You have to taste the food, and then choose the wine. At Ana Mandara, the chef's food went with great with white Burgundies, red Rhône, and California Meritage wines because his food was more influenced by French cuisine. His family enjoyed French cuisine and he studied at Cordon Bleu, so his range, balance, and harmony of dishes were geared toward a classic European balance. Charles Phan is the very talented chef at the Vietnamese restaurant The Slanted Door, and his food is more assertive, aggressively acidic with a brighter profile. It is has a narrower range in the balance of the dishes. As he says, "It's more like Vietnamese street food" — and those dishes lend themselves to more acidic bright wines like Sauvignon Blanc from the Loire Valley or Grüner Veltliner from Austria — and his wine list reflects that.

— LARRY STONE, MS, Rubicon (San Francisco)

Vietnamese food has a lot of spicy flavors, which call for aromatic whites that are off-dry with a little residual sugar and a floral element. I associate Pinot Blanc with melon, Gewürztraminer with lychee, and Viognier with mango and papaya. We also brought in a lot of beer for our Vietnamese Le Voyage menu. We featured Chimay which is a very rich red beer from Belgium that goes great with caramel pork with ginger.

— STEVE BECKTA, owner, Beckta Dining & Wine (Ottawa)

With Vietnamese food, I like a Weissbier because it is a beer with some character and it is not too light. For wine, I like a Gewürztraminer. Sometimes [e.g., with beef dishes], I will drink red wine like an Italian Barolo or Barbaresco from Piedmont. When you pair red wine, you have to be careful by choosing a dish with less acid.

— STEPHANE COLLING, wine director, The Modern at the MoMA (NYC)

People always say that you can't drink wine with salad because "the vinaigrette will kill the wine." Yet if you serve it with a high-acid wine, they will neutralize each other, and it becomes a wonderful thing.

— DAVID ROSENGARTEN,
editor in chief,
www.DavidRosengarten.com

A salad with a vinaigrette is about the biggest anti-wine dish you can come up with. The acid level in a vinaigrette is so high it makes a wine taste sour. To counteract that, you need something with that kind of acid level. As silly as it might sound, Champagne or Chablis are great because of their high acid levels.

— BERNARD SUN, beverage
director, Jean-Georges
Management (NYC)

TIP: Vinegar's high acidity will make it tough to pair with any wine. In general, use white wine vinegar in salads to be served with white wines, and red wine vinegar when serving red wines (such as Marsala, which is one of the rare wines that can stand up to vinegar). To make any salad more wine friendly:

• Use a higher proportion of olive oil to vinegar when making the dressing.

• Change the balance of flavors by adding other flavorful ingredients such as anchovies, bacon, cheese, or nuts.

• Substitute balsamic vinegar (which is sweeter) for a more acidic vinegar — or consider substituting lemon juice, mustard, or *verjus* for the vinegar altogether.

VINEGAR

BALSAMIC
Cabernet Sauvignon
Lambrusco
Merlot
Ribera del Duero
Riesling, esp. with aged balsamic
Valpolicella

CIDER
beer
Bordeaux, white
cider
Muscadet, apple-y
Sauvignon Blanc, apple-y

MALT
beer

When you're pairing food to fine, aged wines, don't use any vinegar at all. I stay away from vinegar completely. There are other acids you can use — such as verjus, *lemon juice, white wine, red wine, and any kind of citrus juice — so the first thing to do is to figure out how to balance your acids in your food.*

— TRACI DES JARDINS, chef,
Jardiniere (San Francisco)

If you make your mignonette [to serve with raw oysters] with cider vinegar, it is fabulous with Muscadet or a Sauvignon Blanc with a lot of apple flavor to it. This way, you are pairing the mignonette to the wine.

— REBECCA CHARLES, chef-
owner, Pearl Oyster Bar (NYC)

WALNUTS AND WALNUT OIL

IN GENERAL
Cabernet Sauvignon
Chardonnay, oaky California
Madeira
Merlot
Pinot Noir
PORT, ESP. TAWNY OR VINTAGE
Riesling
sherry, esp. fino, manzanilla, or oloroso

DESSERTS
Amaretto
coffee
Madeira, Malmsey
Muscat
PORT, TAWNY OR RUBY
sherry, esp. oloroso
tea, Lapsang Souchong

WASABI

Champagne
Gewürztraminer
RIESLING, OFF-DRY
sake
Sauvignon Blanc, New World
sparkling wine, esp. Cava
Zinfandel

AVOID
Cabernet Sauvignon
red wine, tannic

I've served wasabi peas [Japanese snack foods] in my tastings to get people over thinking that they didn't like Riesling. Put some wasabi in someone's mouth who doesn't know what it is; it is such a prominent, intense flavor that it needs immediate correction. I'll have people taste the wine, then the wasabi peas and the wine together — and finally, they get it. After the tasting, guess which wine they want to buy? Knowing what doesn't work is just as important: If you had those peas with a Cabernet Sauvignon, it would be a fight. People need Riesling on the table to save their lives and palates!

— Brian Duncan, wine director, Bin 36 (Chicago)

WATERMELON
Champagne, brut rosé or demi-sec
Riesling, esp. Kabinett
Sambuca

"WHEN IN DOUBT"
Beaujolais, young
Champagne
cider, hard or sparkling
Pinot Noir, young California
red wine, young, fruity, low-alcohol, and unoaked
Riesling
rosé
sparkling wine

WHITE CASTLE HAMBURGERS
Riesling, off-dry
rosé
Zinfandel, white

WIENER SCHNITZEL
(SEE VEAL, WIENER SCHNITZEL)

WINE-BASED FOODS
(E.G., FONDUE AND SAUCES)
wine used in making the dish or sauce

WINTER
barley wine
Beaujolais Nouveau
Bloody Mary
Bordeaux, aged red and white
Brunello
Burgundy, esp. aged red
Cabernet Sauvignon
CHAMPAGNE, ESP. AT HOLIDAY TIME
Champagne punch
Chardonnay, full-bodied, moderately to very oaky
consommé
egg nog
full-bodied wine
HOT BEVERAGES (e.g., chocolate, cider, cocoa, tea, toddies, etc.)
martini, apple
mulled beverages (e.g., cider and wine)
Pinot Noir
port
red wine, esp. fullest-bodied
rich wine
Rioja
rum, hot buttered
Sangiovese
Sauternes and other full-bodied sweet dessert wines
tannic wine
Zinfandel

I change my wine list with the season. In winter, you want richer and warmer wines, while summer calls for light and crisp wines.

— Stephane Colling, wine director, The Modern at the MoMA (NYC)

In the winter, Indians like to drink warm mulled cider with a little splash of Cognac and it is superb. It works because you have spiciness from the cider and a little kick from the Cognac, which is fun. For my mulled cider I use star anise, tons of orange rind, clove, cardamom, ginger, red chile, black pepper, and very little cinnamon. If you use too much cinnamon, the cider will taste too sweet and "American." This drink is very balanced for Indian food because Indian food has a lot of citrus, freshness, and warm spices. Drinking mulled cider, your mouth will have the same balance. This would be good with what we call "dishes with sauces" — especially a tomato-based curry or other curries. Chicken tikka massala would be a perfect pairing.

— Suvir Saran, chef, Dévi (NYC)

YAMS (SEE SWEET POTATOES)

YELLOWTAIL (SEE SUSHI)

YOGURT AND YOGURT SAUCES
Burgundy, white
Chardonnay, New World
fruit-flavored drinks
Retsina
Riesling, off-dry to sweeter
rosé, dry
Sauvignon Blanc
sparkling wine
white wine, dry

ZABAGLIONE (ITALIAN FROTHY CUSTARD MADE WITH MARSALA)

Asti

Champagne, dry to sweet

coffee, esp. Italian

Madeira, Malmsey

MARSALA, SWEET

Moscato d'Asti

Muscat, esp. Beaumes-de-Venise

port

Prosecco

Recioto di Soave

Riesling, German, esp.
  Trockenbeerenauslese

Sauternes

sparkling wine

Vin Santo

ZUCCHINI

Barbera, esp. with tomato sauce

Beaujolais

Dolcetto

Montepulciano

Sancerre

Sauvignon Blanc

VALPOLICELLA, ESP. WITH TOMATO SAUCE

white wine, dry

ZUCCHINI BLOSSOMS (ESP. FRIED)

Arneis

Burgundy, white, esp. Chassagne-
  Montrachet

Chardonnay

Gewürztraminer, dry

Pinot Blanc

Pinot Grigio

Riesling

Sauvignon Blanc

Soave

**white wine, lighter-bodied, esp.
  Italian**

CHAPTER SIX

What *to* Eat *with* What *you* Drink

Matching Foods to Beverages

You need to pay attention to the reaction between wine and food, because a great wine can be spoiled by a mismatched flavor.

— TRACI DES JARDINS, chef, Jardiniere (San Francisco)

When it comes to love, we've always heard that there are always "lots of other fish in the sea." Likewise, there is always more than one fish (or other food) to match any particular wine or beverage. Just as in love, however, there is a much smaller number of matches that are truly made in heaven. In this chapter, we'll present some of the best possible food mates for your drink of choice. You may have received an unfamiliar bottle of wine as a gift, or you might have sampled and purchased an interesting new wine at a wine store tasting and wonder what to serve to accompany it that will showcase its best qualities. Or you may have learned that your favorite dessert wine can be overpowered by a too-strong dessert, and you'd like to make sure you serve it alongside one that complements it best.

Often the occasion of having a special beverage on hand — whether wine or sake or beer — will dictate the pairing process, demanding that one "work backwards" from the process described in the previous chapter to come up with foods that suggest a good match. Here's where to turn! In the rest of this chapter, you'll find an extensive alphabetical list of beverages, including wine, beer, sake, tea, coffee, and water. Each beverage is followed by a list of foods, ingredients, and even cooking techniques that can provide a good match for the drink.

As in the previous chapter, we've marked "ethereal" pairings with ***BOLD CAPS** and an **asterisk(*).** Very highly recommended matches are in **BOLD CAPS,** while highly recommended pairings are in **bold,** and recommended complements appear in plain text.

If you've read our experts' recommendations and want to take the next step in making an even better pairing, it's helpful to do a bit of homework. For example, search the Internet for information on the beverage you're matching to see if you can find information on how it was made (e.g., if the wine was barrel-fermented, you can expect at least some oakiness), tasting notes (e.g., perceived acidity, sweetness, and/or tarmin), or other useful information.

Christopher Tracy, winemaker at Channing Daughters Winery in Bridgehampton, New York, points out that knowing the wine varietal can be just the starting point:

> If you're looking for a match for Sauvignon Blanc, the classic pairings will come to mind such as oysters, fresh goat cheese, asparagus, and those sorts of things. But say you learn that this particular Sauvignon Blanc has barrel-fermented notes and that when it was made, it had some Chardonnay added for roundness, and part of it had barrel-fermented notes. Then, you'll have a sense that you're going to get some spice or richer notes, maybe some vanilla [from the oak] — and you know you could add a meat component or an egg or something else to play off the Chardonnay in the wine.

As you expand your knowledge of wine, you'll be able to take into consideration ever-greater distinctions among various wines. It's a wonderful exercise to taste the same varietal from different regions, so you can get a sense of the often substantial differences. Taste, for example, a California Sauvignon Blanc (which is often grassy and herbaceous) next to a New Zealand Sauvignon Blanc (which is often characterized by a citrus-like fruitiness). Or host a side-by-side tasting of Alsatian versus Austrian versus German Rieslings, so you can appreciate their differences in flavor.

For those times when you get ready to throw your hands up, that this is all too difficult and/or time-consuming, we've got a solution for that, too: Reach for a bottle of either Riesling or Pinot Noir, which our wine experts told us to be two of the most versatile wines for food and wine pairing. Having a bottle of each on hand, or bringing either one to a friend's dinner party, is a good bet no matter what's on the menu. Or, when in doubt, serve bubbly (i.e., Champagne or another sparkling wine) — which can turn any meal into a memorable occasion!

As you look through the following pages, we hope you'll come to think of different beverages as your friends. "Just as in your circle of friends, there are those with whom you go to the movies, and others whom you consult for serious life advice," muses sommelier Brian Duncan of Bin 36 in Chicago. Expand your circle of friends through embracing a wider range of wines and other beverages — for every day, for special occasions, for picnics, and for comfort-seeking nights and adventurous days (or vice versa!). There's a world of pleasure just waiting for you to explore.

MATCHING FOODS *to* BEVERAGES

KEY: Beverages mentioned in regular type are pairings suggested by one or more experts.

Those in **bold** were frequently recommended by a number of experts.

Those in **BOLD CAPS** were very highly recommended pairings.

Those in ***BOLD CAPS** with an asterisk (*) are "Holy Grail" classic pairings that all gourmands will want to experience once (or more!) in their lifetimes.

NOTE: For newcomers to the world of wine, deciphering references to wines can often be confusing. The same wine can be referred to by its grape (Pinot Noir) or its region of origin (Burgundy). The confusion has become so heatedly debated in global circles that it's led to trade embargos and legislation to allow clearer labeling for consumers. In the charts below, you can find wines referred to in different manners, so that a variety of key words you might find on a label that intrigues you will offer you a point of entry. We'll encourage you to persevere through the maze that is the language of wine, and to emerge with new insights into some new, great food pairings.

By Type of Wine

ACIDIC WINE (E.G., WHITES SUCH AS WHITE BORDEAUX, CHAMPAGNE, CHENIN BLANC, ITALIAN WHITE WINE, MUSCADET, PINOT GRIGIO / PINOT GRIS, RIESLING, SANCERRE, SAUVIGNON BLANC, VINHO VERDE, VOUVRAY; REDS SUCH AS BEAUJOLAIS, RED BURGUNDY, CHIANTI, GAMAY, PINOT NOIR, SANGIOVESE)

acidic food and dishes
charcuterie (e.g., prosciutto, sausage)
cream sauces
fatty food and dishes (e.g., pâté)
salty food and dishes
rich food and dishes
salad
tomatoes
vinegar, vinaigrette

Acid likes acid.
— MADELINE TRIFFON, MS, director of wine, Matt Prentice Restaurant Group (Detroit)

AGED WINE
filet mignon
fish, mild (e.g., swordfish, tuna, turbot)
jus, with meat dishes
meat, red
pork
simple dishes
veal

AVOID
garlic
mint
onions
sauce, esp. cream, fruit, sweet, and/or sour
strong herbs or other flavorings

At Rubicon, we had wines going back one hundred years that were very delicate. As soon as you open those wines, a lot of them start to dissipate. So, you don't want food to be the starring player in those kinds of scenarios. Instead, you want to make sure the food is there to support and play a secondary role to the wine. As a chef, I have no problem with that. In fact, I take great relish in that kind of task, to just be the supporting player rather than having to create my own show. I think that's hard for some chefs because you really have to be careful about what you use and the range of flavors, so you don't knock the wine out.
— TRACI DES JARDINS, chef, Jardiniere (San Francisco)

CHILLED WINE
cold dishes

EARTHY, FLINTY, MINERALLY WINE
coriander
dried spices

FRUITY WINE
cranberry
fruity sauces

FULL-BODIED WINE

RED
beef
braised dishes
game (e.g., venison)
red meat
stewed dishes
stronger-flavored food

WHITE
lobster, esp. with butter or cream sauce

HERBACEOUS WINE
(E.G., GRASSY SAUVIGNON BLANC)
herbs, esp. green
parsley

HIGH-ALCOHOL WINE (I.E., WINES WITH MORE THAN 12 PERCENT ALCOHOL; E.G., BARBARESCO, BAROLO, MANY CALIFORNIA WINES)
somewhat sweet dishes
richer dishes

AVOID
delicate dishes
salty dishes, which can make such wines taste bitter
spicy dishes

If you are drinking Austrian wine with spicy food, you need be careful because some wine-makers vinify all the sugar out of the must, thereby making higher-alcohol wines — and high-alcohol wine does not *make for a good pairing with spice.*

— TIM KOPEC, wine director, Veritas (NYC)

HIGH-TANNIN WINE
(I.E., YOUNG RED WINES; E.G., BAROLO, BARBARESCO, RED BORDEAUX, CABERNET SAUVIGNON, MERLOT, SYRAH, ZINFANDEL)

bitter dishes, or dishes with bitter notes

black pepper

broccoli rabe

cheese

creamy dishes

duck

eggplant, grilled

FATTY DISHES

greens, bitter

grilled meat and/or vegetables

lamb

meat, red, esp. served rare

olives, black

rich dishes

salty dishes

steak, esp. served rare

walnuts

AVOID

creamy cheese

fish

spicy food, (e.g., chile peppers)

When you want to pair a dish to a big red monster of a wine, you'll want to match the tannins in the wine by bringing out tannic aspects in the food. I once

---

paired a tannic red wine with a dish of squab with a walnut red wine sauce, for which I infused the sauce with walnuts, so the tannin from the skins of the walnuts was picked up in the sauce, sort of mirroring the flavors of the tannic red wine served with it.

— TRACI DES JARDINS, chef, Jardiniere (San Francisco)

LIGHT-BODIED WINE

RED (E.G., PINOT NOIR)

fish

salmon

WHITE (E.G., LIGHT RIESLING AND SAUVIGNON BLANC)

boiled dishes

chicken

lighter dishes

lighter sauces that are not concentrated

poached dishes

seafood

shellfish, esp. boiled or poached

steamed dishes

vegetables, esp. lighter

LOW-ACID WINE (E.G., GEWÜRZTRAMINER, PINOT GRIS, MANY ITALIAN WINES)

garlic

olive oil

spicy food

LOW-ALCOHOL WINE (I.E., WINES WITH LESS THAN 12 PERCENT ALCOHOL; E.G., GERMAN RIESLING, SPANISH TXAKOLI)

light food and dishes

salty food and dishes

LOW-TANNIN WINE
(E.G., BARBERA, BEAUJOLAIS, DOLCETTO, LOIRE VALLEY WHITE, PINOT GRIGIO, PINOT NOIR, RIESLING, VALPOLICELLA)

chicken

fish

simple food

spicy (mildly) food

turkey

AVOID

intensely flavored food (e.g., braised meat dishes)

NEW WORLD WINE
(E.G., BEYOND EUROPE)

bolder-flavored cuisine

OAKY WINE (E.G., CALIFORNIA CHARDONNAY)

barbecue

butter sauce

chicken, grilled

creamy food and sauces

fatty food

fish

grilled meat and other foods

meat served rare or medium-rare

roasted food (e.g., meat, etc.)

seafood

vanilla

AVOID

lighter food and dishes

raw/uncooked food

salty food and dishes

sushi and sashimi

too-sweet dishes

You cannot have raw food with wooded white wine — it's offensive on the palate.

— RAJAT PARR, MS, wine director, the Mina Group

Wines with little to no oak tend to be better at food pairing. Oak that is good for the wine may not be good for the food. The exception is if you are having a barbecue — in that case, the more oak, the better. If you are grilling chicken, pop open that big oaky California Chardonnay!

— BERNARD SUN, beverage director, Jean-Georges Management (NYC)

I'm not going to name any names, because a lot of collectors with cellars really like those big, buttery California Chardonnays, and they pay a lot of money for them. But if someone brings one in and they want to pair it with food, I do find it a bit challenging. However, there are tricks you can remember for pairing with these wines. I'll serve fish or other seafood with big butter sauces, often with just a hint of vanilla bean — because you've got to make sure it doesn't get too sweet. But the vanilla accent can help balance those flavors in the wine. I actually once prepared a foie gras dish with a vanilla bean sauce for a big, fat white wine with a fair amount of acidity that also had quite a bit of wood on it, and it worked pretty well.

— TRACI DES JARDINS, chef, Jardiniere (San Francisco)

OLD WORLD WINE
(ESP. BORDEAUX, CHARDONNAY, PINOT NOIR)
classic French food
simply prepared meat

AVOID
fusion food
garlic, raw
high-acid food
spiciness
sweetness
vinegar

SWEET WINE (E.G., ASTI,
SOME CALIFORNIA CHARDONNAYS, CHENIN BLANC, GERMAN WINE, LAMBRUSCO, LATE HARVEST WINE, PORT, RIESLING, SAUTERNES, SHERRY, VOUVRAY)
cheese
duck
desserts
fruit, esp. tropical
game

I think the single style of wine that is the most under-appreciated in the American market is sweet wine. Not dessert wine, with its residual sugar of more than one hundred grams per liter, but wine with some residual sugar in the range of ten to forty grams per liter. Too many people have been turned off to sweet wine somehow. It's a shame, because they work unbelievably well at the table with savory food. I think the Loire Valley is home to some of the greatest wines with residual sugar levels and the accompanying acid levels needed to balance them out. Vendanges Tardives wines from Alsace work wonders with duck, rabbit, game, geese, or veal. The majority of sweet wines should be consumed with cheese, from a Late Harvest Riesling with Muenster, to a sweet Muscat from Spain with Manchego.

— PAUL GRIECO, general manager, Hearth (NYC)

I try to encourage people to not be afraid of sweet wines. I have made it my personal mission to allay the fear of sweet wine, because they are perfect food wines. You can find all levels of sweetness and flavor profiles, from citrus to exotic tropical. They are packed with flavor and work anywhere in the meal. As Americans, we have all probably cut our teeth on super-sweet, cloying, flabby, badly made sweet wine. Many people have memories of bad experiences with overly sweet wines — however, many have not had the opportunity to taste a well-made exquisitely-balanced wine with some sweetness and great acidity. Or they might not have had a sweet wine that has been paired properly with the right dish. It's a shame, because Riesling is also an inexpensive wine that is not hard to find.

— SCOTT TYREE, sommelier, Tru (Chicago)

goose

nut dishes

rabbit

richer dishes

salty food

savory dishes with sweet notes (e.g., fish with fruit salsa)

spicier food

sweet dishes

veal

TIP: Desserts should never be sweeter than the wine served to accompany them — and nor should savory dishes. With the latter, it's possible to balance flavors by adding a final note of acid to the dish in the form of a dash of vinegar or a squeeze of lemon or lime or other citrus.

By Name of Beverage

AGLIANICO (ITALIAN FULL-BODIED RED WINE FROM BASILICATA)

beef, esp. braised, grilled or stewed

cheese, esp. savory and/or strongly-flavored (e.g., Gouda, Provolone)

cheese, Pecorino

duck

game and game birds, esp. roasted

lamb, esp. grilled

meatballs

meat, esp. roasted or stewed

osso buco

pasta, esp. baked (e.g., lasagna)

pizza

pork

sausage

spicy dishes

squab

steak

stew, esp. rich

TIP: Aglianico goes perfectly with a spicy sausage pizza.

AGUA FRESCA (MEXICAN FRUIT ADE WITH LIME OR LEMON)

beef taco, esp. with hibiscus *agua fresca*

fish taco, esp. with cucumber *agua fresca*

Mexican food

tacos

ALBARINO (SPANISH MEDIUM-BODIED WHITE WINE FROM GALACIA)

appetizers

bacalao (dried salt cod)

brandade

Cajun seafood

ceviche

chorizo

crab

FISH, ESP. GRILLED AND/OR SPICY PREPARATIONS

lobster

mussels, steamed

octopus

oysters

paella

pasta

pil pil sauce

pizza, esp. pepperoni

poultry

rice-based dishes

salad, esp. seafood salad

sardines

scallops

seafood, esp. spicy dishes

SHELLFISH DISHES, ESP. SPICY

shrimp, esp. grilled

spicy dishes

vegetable dishes and vegetables, roasted

Albarino is often compared to Riesling in its style. There are many price ranges and styles, so try a few and find one you like. Any kind of shellfish is a great pairing with Albarino. If you can get mussels from the Mediterranean, serve them out of the shell with pimenton oil or simply steamed. The classic pairing is pulpo ala Gallego *which is octopus boiled with sea water and potatoes, sprinkled with pimenton and coarse salt.*

— RON MILLER, maître d'hotel, Solera (NYC)

ALE (TOP-FERMENTED, MADE FROM MALT AND HOPS; SEE ALSO BEER, PORTER, STOUT)

IN GENERAL

meat, red

robust dishes

stew

AMBER (TOP-FERMENTED, AMBER TO DEEP RED IN COLOR)

Asian food

barbecue

Caribbean food

cheese

chicken, esp. roasted

fish, esp. fried

Indian food, esp. curries

meat, esp. cold

Mexican cuisine

pasta

pizza

pork

robust dishes

salad, esp. lettuce-based

sandwiches

soup

spicy dishes

tomato-based dishes and sauce

AVOID

sweet dishes

Amber ale: This style has nice caramel to it. It goes well with the light taste of lettuce. We make a salad with blue cheese, caramelized walnuts, bacon, and coriander vinaigrette, and it goes great with an amber ale. This beer works with Asian, Indian, and Caribbean food, because it has notes of orange peel, banana, and coriander.

— CARLOS SOLIS, food and beverage director/chef, Sheraton Four Points/LAX (Los Angeles)

BROWN (AMERICAN OR EN-GLISH, FULL-BODIED, LOW IN HOPS)
almonds
burritos
Cajun food
chicken, fried
game, esp. with American brown ale
hamburgers
lamb, grilled
sausage
smoked fish, esp. with English brown ale
steak

NUT BROWN (DRY, CARAMELIZED MALT ALE)
beef, esp. grilled (steaks) or roasted
cheese, from Gouda to sheep's milk to Stilton
chicken, esp. fried or roasted
Chinese food
sausage
spicy food

Nut brown ale is a beer version of a good Madeira: It's a nutty, brown, and toasty winter-style ale, and made for sipping, not quaffing. — MAX MCCALMAN, maître fromager, Picholine and Artisanal Cheese Center (NYC)

INDIA PALE (DRY, STRONG, HIGHLY HOPPED)
barbecue
CHEESE AND CHEESE DISHES
chicken
crab cakes
curry, mild
empanadas
enchiladas
fish
guacamole
hamburgers
Indian food
mackerel
meat, red, esp. served cold
Mexican food
pizza
pork
SALMON
salmon, smoked
salsa
sandwiches
sausage, spicy
seafood
shrimp, esp. grilled
Tex-Mex food
Vietnamese food
tapas
Thai food

India pale ale is good with seafood, especially salmon. If you wanted to compare it to a wine, it would be like Sauvignon Blanc. It is the dryness and hoppiness of the beer that cuts down the strong flavor of the fish. If you like spicy food to taste even hotter, this is what a lot of people drink to achieve that.

— CARLOS SOLIS, food and beverage director/chef, Sheraton Four Points/LAX (Los Angeles)

PALE (TOP-FERMENTED, FULL-BODIED, VERY HIGH IN HOPS)
barbecue
beef
burritos
Cajun food
cheese, esp. Cheddar, Cheshire, Gruyère
chicken, esp. roasted or tandoori
chili
duck
fish
fried food
guacamole
gumbo
hamburgers
lamb
lighter dishes
lobster
meat, esp. rich
Mexican and Tex-Mex food (e.g., enchiladas, empanadas, fajitas, tacos)
pizza
salmon, esp. grilled
salsa
sausage, esp. spicy
seafood, esp. fried and/or spicy
SPICY DISHES
Thai food
Vietnamese food
vinegar-based dishes

SCOTTISH (TOP-FERMENTED, CARAMELIZED WORT)
beef, roasted
ham
lamb, roasted
sandwiches
sausage

SPICED (I.E., FLAVORED WITH SPICES, E.G., CINNAMON)
carrot cake
desserts, spiced
pumkin pie

ALIGOTÉ (FRENCH LIGHT-BODIED WHITE WINE FROM BURGUNDY)

clams
oysters
seafood
shellfish, esp. served chilled
shrimp

ALSATIAN WINE (SEE ALSO GEWÜRZTRAMINER, MUSCAT, PINOT BLANC, PINOT GRIS, RIESLING, SYLVANER, ETC.)

cheese
fish
meat white
spicy dishes

Alsatian wines are more food-friendly than the wines of any other region or country I know.
— DANIEL JOHNNES, beverage director, Restaurant Daniel (NYC)

ALVARINHO (SEE VINHO VERDE; ALBARINO)

AMARONE (ITALIAN DRY, FULL-FLAVORED, FULL-BODIED RED WINE FROM THE VENETO REGION)

beef, esp. grilled
CHEESE, esp. aged, creamy, and/or strongly flavored, and esp. Gorgonzola, Gouda, Grana Padano, Parmesan, Robiola
game and game birds
LAMB, ESP. BRAISED, GRILLED, STEWED, AND/OR WITH SPICES
MEAT, ESP. RED, AND ESP. BRAISED, ROASTED, OR STEWED

mushrooms and mushroom sauce
nuts
osso buco
pasta
pesto
risotto, esp. with Parmesan
short ribs, esp. braised
steak
turkey
venison

Amarone is a great wine. It has a very earthy quality, and high alcohol which people like. With Amarone, I want a meat dish that has been braised, or something with a mushroom sauce. Amarone also has a touch of sweetness, so it is versatile. The good thing about Amarone: it is great with meat. The bad thing about Amarone: it is expensive and you rarely see it by the glass.
— BERNARD SUN, beverage director, Jean-Georges Management (New York)

AQUAVIT (FLAVORED VODKA)

cheese, creamy
fish, oily and/or smoked

ARMAGNAC (DEEP-COLORED BRANDY FROM SOUTHWEST FRANCE)

apples
duck
figs
foie gras
fruit
prunes

ARNEIS (ITALIAN LIGHT- TO MEDIUM-BODIED WHITE WINE FROM THE PIEDMONT REGION)

antipasto
aperitif
beef, esp. raw (e.g., carpaccio)
Caesar salad
cheese, goat
chicken
fish, esp. light and/or poached dishes
fruit
lobster
PASTA, ESP. WITH HERBED AND OTHER LIGHT SAUCES, INCLUDING PESTO
prosciutto, esp. with melon
salad
SEAFOOD, ESP. LIGHT, GRILLED, AND/OR ROASTED
shrimp
veal
vegetables

ASTI (ITALIAN LIGHT DRY TO SEMISWEET SPARKLING WINE — FORMERLY KNOWN AS ASTI SPUMANTE — FROM THE PIEDMONT REGION)

almonds and almond desserts
aperitif, esp. drier Asti
berries
biscotti
cake
cheese, esp. mild
COOKIES, ESP. LIGHT
DESSERTS, ESP. FRUIT AND/OR SIMPLE
FRUIT, ESP. FRESH AND/OR SALAD
lemon desserts
meringues
mousses, esp. chocolate
peaches and peach desserts
pears and pear desserts
raspberries and raspberry desserts,
soufflés, esp. lemon

AUSTRALIAN WINE

Asian food, esp. with Australian Riesling

beef, esp. with Shiraz

chicken, barbecued, esp. with Sauvignon Blanc

desserts, esp. fruit, and esp. with Australian stickies

fish, barbecued, esp. with Australian Sauvignon Blanc

fish dishes, simple (e.g., with vinaigrette), esp. with Australian dry Riesling or Chardonnay

full-flavored dishes, esp. with Australian red wine

hamburgers, esp. with Shiraz

Indian food, esp. with Australian red wine

lamb, esp. with Shiraz

picnics, esp. with sparkling Shiraz

salad, esp. with Australian Chardonnay

sandwiches, esp. chicken or fish, and esp. with Australian Chardonnay

shellfish dishes, simple (e.g., with vinaigrette), esp. with Australian dry Riesling

shrimp, barbecued, esp. with Australian Sauvignon Blanc

spicy dishes, esp. with Australian red wine

Thai food, esp. with Australian Riesling

Thanksgiving dinner, esp. with sparkling Shiraz

trout, esp. with Australian Chardonnay

vegetarian dishes, esp. with Australian Chardonnay

BANDOL (FRENCH PROVENÇAL WINE)

IN GENERAL

charcuterie

game

garlic

meat, esp. barbecued or grilled

olives

Provençal dishes

rosemary

tomato

vegetables, esp. barbecued or grilled

wild boar

RED (FULL-BODIED)

beef

charcuterie

fish, esp. grilled

lamb, esp. roasted

meat, barbecued

meat, red

pasta

pizza

pork, esp. roasted

sausage

vegetables, esp. roasted

venison

wild boar

ROSÉ (MEDIUM-BODIED)

anchovies

brandade

fish

peppers, roasted

Provençal dishes

seafood

tapas

tuna

The fresh, crisp flavors of Australia's dry Rieslings are ideal with Asian-influenced foods — Thai especially. The wines have hints of lime and mineral notes that work beautifully with this sort of food. Unwooded Chardonnay is also a trendy wine in Australia: The freshness of the fruit — without any oak influence — works beautifully with vegetarian meals, salad courses, and chicken or fish sandwiches. Sauvignon Blanc or the Semillon-Sauvignon Blanc blends are perfect when you're throwing shrimp on the barbie . . . or chicken or fish. The earthy flavors of the Australian Sauvignon Blanc with its lemon/citrus edge complement the charcoal grill technique and fleshy character of the meat. And Shiraz, of course, is the wine of choice for lamb or beef. But Shiraz (like Zinfandel) comes in many styles — from light and fruity to big and rich. So, it could be hamburgers with a light (inexpensive) Shiraz — and it can be slightly chilled in the summertime! Then work on up to the Barossa or McLaren Vale Shiraz for the ribs and racks. Chilled sparkling Shiraz — a uniquely Australian fizz — works for summer picnics. But it is ideal for that all-American Thanksgiving dinner. Dark in color and dry, the bubbles bring out the fruit and spice in Shiraz, so the match with turkey, dressing, and cranberry sauce is better than anything else you can find. Also unique to Australia are the "stickies" of Ruthergien, especially the Muscat. These unctuous, sweet wines are the right match for a special fruit-based dessert that you spent a lot of time making (or picking out of the pastry shop display).

— JAN STUEBING, United States regional manager, Wine Australia

WHITE (LIGHT-BODIED, DRY)
bouillabaisse
fish, esp. grilled
lobster

Bandol is austere, rough stuff. I wouldn't have it with a seafood terrine, but it's great with charcuterie or wild boar.
— TIM KOPEC, wine director, Veritas (NYC)

BANYULS (FRENCH FULL-BODIED SWEET RED WINE FROM THE ROUSSILLON REGION)
berries and berry desserts
cheese, blue, (e.g., Roquefort), esp. strong
CHOCOLATE AND CHOCOLATE DESSERTS, ESP. CREAMY
dark chocolate desserts
coffee-flavored desserts
duck
foie gras terrine
fruit, dried
hot fudge
ice cream
nuts
strawberries and strawberry desserts
tiramisu

Banyuls is magical, because very few wines work with chocolate desserts.
— JOSEPH SPELLMAN, MS, Joseph Phelps Vineyards

BARBARESCO (ITALIAN DRY, FULL-FLAVORED RED WINE FROM THE PIEDMONT REGION; SEE ALSO RECOMMENDATIONS FOR LIGHTER BAROLO)
BEEF, ESP. BRAISED, GRILLED, ROASTED, OR STEWED
cassoulet

CHEESE, ESP. FULL-FLAVORED AND/OR HARD (e.g., FONTINA, Gouda)
chicken, esp. braised or stewed
duck and duck confit
eggplant, esp. Parmesan
fish in red wine sauce
GAME AND GAME BIRDS, ESP. BRAISED OR ROASTED
garlic
lamb, esp. grilled or roasted
liver
meat, esp. red, and esp. roasted or stewed
mushrooms
offal
osso buco
oxtails, esp. braised or stewed
pasta, esp. tomato-sauced
pheasant
pork, esp. roasted
pot roast
rabbit
risotto
steak
stew
TRUFFLES, WHITE, AND TRUFFLE OIL
veal, roasted
vegetables, roasted
vegetarian dishes
venison
wild boar

BARBERA (ITALIAN MEDIUM-BODIED, HIGH-ACID, FRUITY RED WINE FROM THE PIEDMONT REGION)
aïoli
anchovies
antipasti
barbecue, esp. ribs
basil
bass, esp. grilled
beans
beef
cheese, esp. soft or semi-soft (e.g., fontina)
cheese, esp. full-flavored (e.g., Pecorino)

chicken, esp. grilled or roasted
chicken liver
chili
Chinese food
duck, braised
fish, esp. grilled
game birds
garlic
ham
hamburgers, esp. with bacon and cheese
herb-based sauce
Italian tomato-based dishes
lamb, esp. grilled, roasted, or stewed
lasagna
liver, esp. chicken
mahimahi, esp. grilled
MEAT, RED, ESP. GRILLED OR ROASTED
mushrooms, esp. grilled and/or wild
osso bucco
PASTA, ESP. WITH TOMATO, RICH CREAM, MEAT, OR PESTO SAUCE
PIZZA, ESP. PEPPERONI
pork, esp. grilled or roasted chops
poultry
prosciutto
rich dishes
risotto, esp. mushroom
robust dishes
salami
salmon, esp. grilled
sausage, esp. grilled
seafood, esp. sauced
soup, esp. hearty
spicy dishes
squab, esp. braised
steak
stew, esp. beef and lamb
swordfish, esp. grilled
TOMATOES AND TOMATO SAUCE
veal chops, esp. grilled or roasted
vegetables, esp. root, and esp. grilled or roasted

AVOID
fish, delicate and/or white
shellfish

To me, one of the best food wines is Barbera, because it's a red grape with good acidity. It can carry everything from meat dishes to certain seafood, especially sauced. It's a really versatile wine. — CHARLES SCICOLONE, wine director, I Trulli and Enoteca (NYC)

A pepperoni pizza pairs perfectly with Barbera d'Alba, which is fruity, fat, juicy, and delicately spicy with great acidity.
— SCOTT TYREE, sommelier, Tru (Chicago)

For all that red sauce [in Italian pasta and pizza], the answer is Barbera. It has the highest acidity, lots of fruit, and no tannin. You need to find the old-style Barbera that has not been aged in new oak, which is a dream wine for Italian food. The way you can spot an old-style wine is by price: If it is under twelve dollars, it is old style; if it is over twenty dollars, it is new style. Here is a wine where you want to spend less! Look for an old-fashioned Barbera from the cheapest area. In descending order of cost and famousness:
— Alba is the most famous (and expensive) for Barbera d'Alba.
— Asti is a little less famous (and expensive) for Barbera d'Asti.
— You'll spend the least for a wine that is just as good as the others from Monferrato: Barbera del Monferrato.
— DAVID ROSENGARTEN, editor in chief, www.DavidRosengarten.com

BARDOLINO (ITALIAN, LIGHT-BODIED, DRY RED WINE FROM THE SOUTHEAST AREA OF LAKE GARDA IN VERONA)

antipasti
chicken, esp. roasted or in a salad
fish, esp. fattier fish
liver, calf's
pasta, esp. with fish or tomato sauce
pizza
prosciutto with melon
quail
risotto
salami
salmon, grilled

BARLEY WINE (TOP-FERMENTED, EXTRA-STRONG, DARK, RICH ALE)

cheese, esp. blue (e.g., *STILTON), goat, and/or strong
cheese, Cheddar
cheese, Gruyère
chocolate, dark, and dark chocolate desserts

TIP: Think of barley wine as less of a beer (or wine), and more akin to a port or sweet sherry.

BAROLO (ITALIAN DRY, BITTER, TANNIC, FULL-FLAVORED RED WINE FROM THE PIEDMONT REGION)

BEEF, ESP. BRAISED, GRILLED, OR STEWED
CHEESE, ESP. BLUE, HARD (e.g., Parmesan, Pecorino) SHARP, AND/OR STINKY
cheese, fontina
cheese, Gouda
chestnuts
chicken, esp. braised or stewed
duck
eggplant, esp. Parmesan
GAME, ESP. BRAISED OR STEWED
lamb, esp. grilled, roasted, stewed, and/or shanks

MEAT, ESP. RED, AND ESP. RICH, BRAISED, ROASTED (ESP. SERVED RARE), AND/OR STEWED
mushrooms
oily food and dishes
osso buco
oxtails, esp. braised or stewed
pasta, esp. with rich meat sauce
pheasant
pork, esp. roasted
pot roast
rabbit, esp. braised
rich food and dishes
risotto
short ribs
steak, esp. sirloin and with rich sauces
stew, esp. beef or lamb
*TRUFFLES, WHITE
turkey
venison, esp. with chestnuts
wild boar

At Campanile [restaurant, where Cossette was formerly the sommelier], some people would come in without a lot of wine knowledge who might have read an article about Barolo and thought it sounded good to them. They'd drink a Barolo that was really a wonderful Barolo — then they'd comment, "It's kind of light." Barolo, until ten or fifteen years ago, was considered to be a big wine. Well, now many wines have got 15 percent alcohol. The wine world has changed so much that when you taste something that has a big flavor but still has balance and elegance, it seems light.
— GEORGE COSSETTE, co-owner, Silverlake Wine (Los Angeles)

meat loaf

mushrooms

offal (e.g., ears, feet, tails, testi-
cles, tripe, etc.)

omelets

pasta, with vegetables

pepper, black

picnics

pizza

poached dishes

**PORK, ESP. CHOPS, ROAST,
OR SAUSAGE**

pot au feu

prosciutto

Provençal dishes (e.g., featuring
capers, olives)

quiche

**raspberries and raspberry
desserts**

risotto, esp. mushroom and/or
vegetable

roasted dishes

**SALADS, e.g., frisée with
lardons, Greek, grilled
vegetables, pasta, etc.**

salami

**sandwiches, e.g., BLT, grilled
cheese**

**SAUSAGE, ESP. *EN CROÛTE*
OR GRILLED**

sautéed dishes

spicy dishes

**steak, esp. as steak frites (i.e.,
with French fries)**

stew

strawberries and strawberry
desserts

summertime

Thai curry

Thanksgiving dinner

tuna, esp. grilled

turkey, roasted

vegetables, esp. grilled, raw, or
roasted

*Beaujolais — a wonderful day-
off wine, for the beach.*
— DANIEL JOHNNES,
beverage director, Daniel

BARSAC (FRENCH WHITE
DESSERT WINE; SEE ALSO
SAUTERNES)

bananas and banana desserts

biscotti

cheese, esp. blue

cookies

desserts

fruits

ice cream

nuts

tarte Tatin (caramelized apple tart)

BEAUJOLAIS (FRENCH
DRY, LIGHT-BODIED, RED WINE
MADE FROM GAMAY GRAPES; SEE
ALSO BEAUJOLAIS NOUVEAU
AND BEAUJOLAIS-VILLAGES)

Asian dishes, esp. salty

bacon

barbecue

beef stew, esp. with fuller-bodied
wine

bistro dishes

brunch

***CHARCUTERIE OR COLD
CUTS, ESP. WITH
BEAUJOLAIS CRU**

cheese, Cheddar

**cheese, esp. mild, soft, and/or
goat (e.g., chèvre)**

cherries and cherry desserts

**CHICKEN, ESP. GRILLED OR
ROASTED**

chicken salad and other cold
chicken dishes

coq au vin

curries

**fish, esp. halibut, and esp. in red
wine sauce**

grilled meat and other foods

ham

hamburgers

Italian dishes

lamb, esp. stewed

liver, calf's, esp. grilled

lunch

macaroni and cheese

**meat, esp. roasted, stewed,
and/or served cold**

To pair fish with red wine, cook the fish with things that go with red wine — like bacon. Gamays have a real bacon fat to them, which comes from the toastiness of the oak. You have acidity in goat cheese that will work with the acidity in Gamay. And Gamay, like Pinot Noir — they're cousins — has a natural earthiness that plays well off many mushrooms.

— STEVE BECKTA, owner, Beckta Dining & Wine (Ottawa)

BEAUJOLAIS NOUVEAU (TWO-MONTH-OLD FRENCH LIGHT-BODIED RED WINE, OUT IN NOVEMBER)

cheese, esp. goat
chicken
meat, esp. grilled or roasted
pasta, esp. with lighter sauce:
pork
salmon
turkey
veal

BEAUJOLAIS-VILLAGES (FRENCH LIGHT-BODIED RED WINE THAT IS CONSIDERED A NOTCH ABOVE REGULAR BEAUJOLAIS)

cheese, esp. Brie and Cheddar
meat, grilled
salmon, esp. grilled
sausage, esp. poached
tuna, esp. grilled
turkey, esp. served cold

BEER (ALCOHOLIC BEVERAGE MADE FROM FERMENTABLE SUGARS, HOPS, WATER, AND YEAST; SEE ALSO ALE, LAGER, PILSNER, PORTER, STOUT)

IN GENERAL
almonds
Asian food
barbecue
burritos
Cajun food
Caribbean food
cheese, esp. sheep's milk
chicken, esp. barbecued
chiles
Chinese food, esp. spicy
Creole food
cured meat
curries
fried food
garlic
hamburgers
hot dogs
Indian food
Mexican food
nuts
olives
peanuts
peppers, esp. sweet
picnics
pizza
potato chips
PRETZELS
salsa
sandwiches
***SAUSAGE**

shellfish, esp. fried
smoked food
Southwestern food
soy sauce
spareribs, esp. barbecued
spicy food
strongly flavored food
tapas
Tex-Mex food
Thai food

Beer is seasonal. Restaurants sell much more in the spring and summer, especially if there is outdoor seating.

— GREG HARRINGTON, MS

BLANCHE (LIGHT-BODIED TOP-FERMENTED WHITE BEER)

apples
barbecue
brunch
cheese, goat, fresh
citrus
eggs Benedict
fish, white
omelets
orange or other citrus
pineapple
pork

rabbit
salad
salmon, esp. grilled or smoked
scallops
seafood
shellfish
veal

*With our Blanche de Brooklyn,
I will make an omelet with
sautéed Granny Smith apples
and goat cheese. This beer has
notes of curaçao, orange peel,
and coriander. It shows how a
beer can be light and still have a
lot of flavor. It is very delicate
and starts out lighter than some
white wines will. It works with
John Dory or shellfish and the
gentle notes of fish because it has
only a little acidity.*

—GARRETT OLIVER,
brewmaster, Brooklyn Brewery

BOCK (GERMAN MALTY,
FULL-BODIED, BOTTOM-
FERMENTING)
chicken
duck
HAM
lamb
mole sauce
pork
sausage
short ribs
venison

BOCK, DOUBLE (DOPPEL-
BOCK, GERMAN VERY
MALTY, FULL-BODIED,
BOTTOM-FERMENTING)
cheese
chiles rellenos
desserts
DUCK
GAME
ham, esp. prosciutto
Mexican food
nuts

peppers
PORK
pumpkin (e.g., pumpkin pie)
sausage
spiced desserts (e.g., spice cake)
squash, winter
VENISON

*Venison meets its closest [bever-
age] partner in Doppelbock.*

— GARRETT OLIVER,
brewmaster, Brooklyn Brewery

FRUIT (FRUIT LAMBIC BEER,
TYPICALLY LOW IN ALCO-
HOL WITH INTENSE FRUIT
CHARACTERISTICS)
after dinner
brunch
cheese, esp. fresh goat and creamy
cheesecake
chocolate, esp. dark, and chocolate desserts
creamy desserts
custard and custard-like desserts
duck and duck confit
egg dishes
foie gras
fruit desserts, salad, or sauce, esp.
lighter
ice cream
mascarpone
mole (Mexican sauce)
salad, esp. with cheese and/or
fruit soufflés
venison

HEFE WEIZEN (SUMMER-
BREWED WHEAT BEER
WITH A SWEET-AND-SOUR
QUALITY)
cheese
fruit
lemon
pork, esp. sweet-and-sour
shellfish

OKTOBERFEST (GERMAN
LAGER WITH A BREAD
AROMA AND GOLDEN
COLOR)
barbecue, dry-rubbed
chicken
choucroute

fish
hamburgers
meat, esp. grilled
pork
pretzels
sausage
AVOID
seafood, delicate preparations
tomatoes

SAISON (MEDIUM-BODIED,
HIGHLY-HOPPED SPICY
BEER WITH CITRUS NOTES)
aperitif
cheese
chicken
crab cakes
curry
fish, esp. heavier fish (e.g.,
salmon, tuna)
jambalaya
spicy dishes
Mexican food (e.g., chiles, salsa)
salad
sausage
seafood and shellfish, esp. boiled,
raw, or steamed
spicy dishes
steaks
summertime
Thai food
Vietnamese food

*If I had to choose a single style
of beer to have with every meal
for the rest of my life, it would
be Saison.*

— GARRETT OLIVER,
brewmaster, Brooklyn Brewery

SMOKED (BEER WITH
SMOKY FLAVORS AND
AROMAS; E.G., GERMAN
RAUCHBIER)
bacon
*BARBECUE
cheese, esp. smoked
fish, esp. smoked
grilled food
ham
hamburgers

Indian food, esp. meat-based
Mexican food, esp. meat-based
PORK
roasted food
sausage
seafood, grilled
smoked meat and fish
spicy food and dishes
steak

WHEAT (PRIMARILY GERMAN
AND BELGIAN; LIGHT IN
COLOR AND FLAVOR; AKA
WEIZEN BIER)
Asian food
barbecued meat
calamari
cheese, goat
**CHICKEN, ESP. LIGHT AND
SPICY**
Chinese food
CRAB AND CRAB CAKES
egg dishes (e.g., omelet, quiche)
FISH, ESP. FRIED
fried food
grilled cheese sandwich
ham
Indian food
jerked chicken
lighter dishes
lobster
meat
Mexican food
oysters
Pad Thai with shrimp
pasta
pork
rich dishes
SALAD
sauerkraut
sausage
scallops
SEAFOOD
shellfish
shrimp, esp. grilled
soup
spicy dishes
sushi
Tex-Mex food
Thai food
vegetable dishes

*We pour Hoegaarden, a
Belgian wheat beer, with jerk
chicken and spicy Asian dishes.
It is very refreshing and cooling
with spicy food.*

— CARLOS SOLIS, food and
beverage director/chef, Sheraton
Four Points/LAX

BLAUFRÄNKISCH
(AUSTRIAN RED WINE)
cheese, hard
chicken
creamy sauce
duck
game and game birds
lamb
ostrich
oxtails
pastrami
pork
salmon
steak
veal
vegetables, esp. grilled
venison
wild boar

BLOODY MARY (SPICED
TOMATO JUICE AND VODKA
COCKTAIL)
brunch
corned beef hash
eggs
Mexican food
oysters
shellfish
smoked fish

BONNEZEAUX (FRENCH
DESSERT WINE FROM COTEAUX
DE LAYON)
apples and apple desserts
cheese, blue (e.g., Roquefort)
desserts
foie gras, esp. terrine

pear and pear desserts
tarte Tatin (caramelized apple
tart)

BORDEAUX, RED
(FRENCH MEDIUM-BODIED
WINE; SEE ALSO CABERNET
SAUVIGNON, GRAVES,
MÉDOC, POMEROL, SAINT-
ÉMILION, ETC.)
barbecued meat
**BEEF, ESP. BRAISED,
GRILLED, OR ROASTED**
cheese, aged (e.g., cheddar,
Colby)
**cheese, esp. hard and/or stinky
(e.g. blue [Roquefort], Brie,
Camembert), esp. with young
Bordeaux**
cheese, Gouda
chicken, esp. fried or roasted
**duck, esp. confit, grilled, or
roasted**
filet mignon
foie gras
fondue, meat
**game and game birds, esp.
roasted**
goose, roasted
ham
***LAMB, ESP. ROASTED**
liver
**MEAT, RED, ESP. ROASTED
OR GRILLED**
osso buco
pheasant, esp. roasted
picnics (with young Bordeaux)
pork, esp. roasted
poultry
prime rib
quail
**roast beef, esp. cold in a sand-
wich**
roasted meat, esp. with aged
Bordeaux
squab
**steak, esp. grilled and esp. with
young Bordeaux**
stew, beef
sweetbreads
tofu, esp. grilled or smoked

veal, esp. roasted

venison

wild boar

AVOID

poultry, plain white meat (which may taste metallic in this pairing)

TIDBIT: While on tour with our book *Chef's Night Out*, we shot a television segment in the home of rock star Sammy Hagar, who showed us his private wine cellars with wines he accumulated in part after having requested first-growth Bordeaux in his contract while on tour as the lead singer for Van Halen. A couple of nights later, we ended up sharing a great bottle of red wine after bumping into each other at the restaurant Bizou in San Francisco.

BORDEAUX, WHITE

(FRENCH DRY, LIGHT-BODIED WINE; SEE ALSO SAUVIGNON BLANC)

cheese, goat

chicken, roasted

Dover sole

FISH, ESP. BARBECUED OR GRILLED

game birds, roasted, esp. quail

LOBSTER

meat, white

mussels

oysters

poultry

rabbit

salmon, esp. with hollandaise

scallops

SEAFOOD

SHELLFISH

shrimp

soft-shell crabs

trout, esp. sautéed

vegetables

BRACHETTO D'ACQUI (ITALIAN SWEET RED SPARKLING WINE)

berries, esp. red

brunch

CHOCOLATE, ESP. DARK

desserts, esp. caramel, cream, and/or fruit-based

French toast

fruit and fruit salad

mascarpone

pancakes

pastries

peaches

raspberries

ricotta cheese

strawberries

waffles

BRUNELLO (ITALIAN DRY, MEDIUM-BODIED RED WINE FROM TUSCANY AKA BRUNELLO DI MONTALCINO)

bean dishes

beef, esp. roasted

CHEESE, ESP. AGED ASIAGO, GOUDA, PARMESAN, PECORINO

chicken, grilled

duck, esp. roasted

eggplant, esp. Parmesan

GAME (e.g., venison, wild boar), ESP. STEWED

GAME BIRDS (e.g., pheasant, quail), ESP. ROASTED

grilled meat

LAMB AND LAMB CHOPS, ESP. ROASTED

liver, chicken

MEAT, ESP. RED, AND ESP. BRAISED, ROASTED, OR STEWED

MEAT SAUCE

mushrooms, esp. grilled or stewed

oxtails

pasta with meat sauce (e.g., beef, duck, rabbit)

rabbit

risotto, esp. with game and meat

soup, esp. hearty meat and/or vegetable

STEAK, AGED AND/OR GRILLED

stew, esp. hearty meat and/or vegetable

vegetables, esp. grilled

venison

BURGUNDY, RED

(SEE ALSO PINOT NOIR)

BEEF, ESP. BRAISED, ROASTED, OR STEWED, WITH FULLER-BODIED WINES

BEEF BOURGUIGNON

cheese, esp. Brie, Camembert, and other mild cheeses

cherries

chicken, esp. coq au vin or roasted

duck, esp. grilled or roasted, and esp. with fuller-bodied wine

earthy-flavored food

fish, esp. roasted

foie gras

GAME, ESP. GRILLED OR ROASTED

game birds

goose, esp. grilled or roasted

ham

hamburgers

kidneys

lamb, esp. roasted or stewed

liver, chicken

mahimahi, grilled

MEAT, RED, ESP. LIGHTER AND/OR ROASTED

MUSHROOMS, e.g., porcini, portobello

offal

pheasant, esp. roasted

pork, roasted

poultry

prime rib, esp. served rare

quail, esp. roasted

rabbit

rare-cooked beef and other red meat

roasted dishes

salmon, esp. baked, grilled, or roasted

seafood

squab

stew, esp. beef

swordfish, grilled

truffles and truffle oil

turkey, roasted

veal, esp. roasted, with mush-rooms, and/or red wine sauce

vegetable dishes

venison, esp. with fuller-bodied wine

BURGUNDY, WHITE

(MEDIUM TO FULL-BODIED; SEE ALSO CHARDONNAY, CHASSAGNE-MONTRACHET, MEURSAULT, POUILLY-FUISSÉ, PULIGNY-MONTRACHET, ETC.)

bass, esp. baked or broiled

butter and butter sauce

cheese, esp. Brie, Chaumes, Saint-Andre, Saint-Nectaire, etc.

CHICKEN, ESP. POACHED OR ROASTED

clams

cod, esp. baked or broiled

corn

crab

crab claws, stone

crayfish, esp. sautéed

cream sauce

Dover sole, esp. with a beurre blanc (butter sauce)

FISH, ESP. WHITE, AND ESP. GRILLED, POACHED, ROASTED, AND/OR WITH RICH SAUCE

flounder, esp. baked or broiled

garlic, esp. roasted

halibut

John Dory, esp. seared and/or with cream sauce

lemon

LOBSTER, ESP. BOILED, POACHED, OR STEAMED

mushrooms

mussels, esp. steamed

oysters

pastas or gnocchi, esp. with butter sauce

pork, esp. loin

risotto, esp. mushroom

salmon, esp. grilled

salmon, smoked

scallops

sea bass

seafood, esp. with rich sauce

shellfish

shrimp, esp. baked or sautéed

SOLE

sweetbreads

swordfish, esp. baked or broiled

trout

truffles, white, and truffle oil

turbot, esp. baked, broiled, or roasted

turkey

vanilla

veal, esp. in cream sauce and/or roasted

"Burgundy 101" with Daniel Johnnes, Beverage Director of Daniel

In Burgundy, there are only two grapes you have to know: **Chardonnay** for the white, and **Pinot Noir** for the red. A classic-style white Burgundy is more minerally, a little leaner, and not as full-bodied as an American or Australian Chardonnay. Red Burgundy is a little more lean and focused than Pinot Noirs from California, Oregon, New Zealand, or any other New World country that makes more deeply colored, robust, full-bodied Pinot Noir. Burgundy is more floral, and delicate on the palate — you taste the fruit, and then the aftertaste is a little more mineral and higher acid and restrained than a New World Pinot Noir.

The other thing you need to know is that when you climb the ladder of Burgundy, going from a generic wine to a Grand Cru, you'll see an increase in nuance, complexity, and intensity.

The best advice I can give people when they buy Burgundy, which is a bit of a roulette game, is to look for producers who are tried and true. They may be wines you may have previously tasted and enjoyed, or you can ask sommeliers and wine merchants, or read reviews in various publications. Equate a Burgundy to another crafted product like a handmade pair of shoes. Look for the name of the producer, whether Michel Lafarge, Domaine Leflaivre, Dominique Lafont, or another. When they put their name on the bottle, they're very proud.

I love making scallops, shrimp, or steelhead trout in a croûte de sel *(salt-baked crust), and having it with white Burgundy.*

— ALAN MURRAY, MS, wine director, Masa's (San Francisco)

In the top 1 or 2 percent of perfect pairings for me would be a classic like Bresse chicken with mushroom sauce and truffles paired with Burgundy. One taste of that, and you immediately think, "This wine was made for this dish!"

— BERNARD SUN, beverage director, Jean Georges Management (NYC)

CABERNET FRANC
(FRENCH MEDIUM-BODIED RED WINE FROM BORDEAUX AND THE LOIRE VALLEY)

BEEF, ESP. LEAN, AND ESP. ROASTED

cabbage

charcuterie

cheeses, esp. strong-flavored (e.g., goat)

chicken, barbecued

DUCK

earthy dishes

EGGPLANT

fish, esp. grilled

GAME, ESP. WITH FULLER-BODIED WINE

grilled dishes, esp. meat

ham, baked

hamburgers

LAMB, ESP. CHOPS, LOIN, AND/OR ROASTED

liver, esp. calf's

MEAT, RED, ESP. GRILLED AND/OR ROASTED

mushrooms

pasta, esp. hearty, with red sauce and/or spicy

pâté

peppers, bell

pheasant

pizza

PORK, ESP. WITH FRUIT SAUCE AND/OR ROASTED

poultry, esp. grilled

rabbit

roasted meat and other food

salad

salmon, grilled

sausage

sautéed dishes

smoked meat

spicy food

steak, esp. with pepper

stew

sweetbreads

Thanksgiving dinner

tomato

tuna

turkey

vegetables, esp. roasted and vegetarian dishes

venison, esp. with fuller-bodied wine

zucchini

As Cabernet Franc ages, it takes on a vegetal quality reminiscent of peppers or eggplant — and marries well with vegetables.

— TIM KOPEC, wine director, Veritas (NYC)

CABERNET SAUVIGNON (FULL-BODIED RED WINE)

basil

bay leaf

BEEF, ESP. BRAISED, GRILLED, ROASTED, OR STEWED

braised dishes

broiled dishes

CHEESE, ESP. AGED, BLUE, AND/OR STINKY (e.g., Brie, Camembert)

cheese, Gorgonzola

cheese, Gouda, esp. aged

cheese, Parmesan

chicken, roasted

chocolate, esp. dark bittersweet

currants, black

duck, esp. roasted

egg dishes, stronger

eggplant

filet mignon

GAME AND GAME BIRDS

garlic, esp. light

goose

grilled meat

hamburgers, esp. grilled, and esp. with California Cabs

heavier dishes

*LAMB, ESP. BRAISED, GRILLED, OR ROASTED, OR RACK OF

lentils

liver, calf's

MEAT, RED, ESP. BRAISED, CURED, GRILLED, ROASTED, SMOKED, AND/OR RICH (FATTY)

meat-flavored sauce

meat loaf

mint

Moroccan cuisine, esp. dishes with lamb

mushrooms

mustard, esp. Dijon

nuts

onions

oregano

osso buco

pasta, esp. with Italian Cabs

pepper, black

peppers, bell

pork

pot roast

potatoes

poultry

prime rib

rabbit

red wine sauce

rib-eye steak

rich dishes and/or sauce

risotto, esp. mushroom

roast beef

roasts

rosemary

sausage, esp. with Argentinian Cabs

sauces, esp. rich and/or robust

sautéed dishes

short ribs

smoked meats

squab, esp. grilled

STEAK (e.g., rib-eye), ESP. GRILLED) AND/OR SERVED RARE WITH YOUNGER CABS OR AU POIVRE WITH CALIFORNIA CABS

stew, meat

thyme

veal

vegetables, grilled

venison, esp. grilled or roasted

walnuts

AVOID

delicate dishes

fish, esp. smoked

fruit

oysters

seafood and shellfish

spicy dishes

Where to find great Cabernet Sauvignon: This would be a toss-up between hillside vine-yards in California and Pomerol in France. There are also wonderful Cabernets made in Spain and Italy.

— JEAN-LUC LE DÙ, Le Dù's Wines (NYC)

If you want to drink that big cult Cabernet Sauvignon that was just released, pair it with food that is slightly bitter. A grilled steak picks up a little bitterness from the charring, so the combination works.

— DAVID ROSENGARTEN, editor in chief, www.DavidRosengarten.com

TIDBIT: At dinner with one of his daughters while researching this book, we learned that Bruce Willis drinks "nothing but Opus One," a Cabernet Sauvignon-based Bordeaux-style blend from Napa Valley.

CAHORS (FRENCH FULL-BODIED RED WINE FROM THE SOUTHWEST)

beef, esp. roasted

***CASSOULET**

charcuterie

cheese, strongly-flavored (e.g., blue)

duck and duck confit

lamb, esp. stewed

meat, red

mushrooms

pork, esp. roasted

rabbit, esp. braised or stewed

squab

CALVADOS (APPLE BRANDY FROM NORMANDY)

apples and apple desserts

bread pudding

CHEESE, ESP. WITH RINDS THAT HAVE BEEN WASHED WITH CALVADOS OR CIDER (e.g., *CAMEMBERT, Livarot, Pavadoche, or Pont-l'Eveque)

cream sauce

desserts

Calvados is from a region that is arguably the most prolific cheese-producing region in the world. It is a joy to be confronted with washed-rind cheeses that have been rubbed with Calvados or cider — like Pavadoche, Pont-l'Eveque, or

CANNONAU (ITALIAN FULL-BODIED, GRENACHE-BASED, RED WINE FROM SARDINIA)

bacon
lamb
meats, esp. grilled or roasted
pasta with meat sauce
pork
tuna

CASSIS (FRENCH WHITE WINE FROM PROVENCE)

BOUILLABAISSE
cheese, goat
chicken, esp. stewed
fish
seafood
shrimp

CAVA (SPANISH MEDIUM-BODIED SPARKLING WINE FROM CATALONIA)

WHITE
barbecue
cheese (esp. cabrales) and cheese-based dishes

Chinese food, esp. dim sum
desserts
eggs
figs, fresh
FISH, ESP. FRIED
fried food, esp. appetizers
ginger
ham, Serrano
hors d'oeuvres
Japanese food
pasta, esp. with seafood sauce
quiche
roasted dishes
salad
salmon
salmon, smoked
sashimi
sautéed dishes
soup
SUSHI
TAPAS

ROSÉ
Chinese food
egg dishes (e.g., omelet, Spanish tortilla)
salmon, esp. grilled

CHABLIS (FRENCH MEDIUM-BODIED CHARDONNAY-BASED WINE FROM BURGUNDY)

avocado
butter sauces, light
cheese, esp. goat cheese
chicken, esp. grilled or roasted
clams
cream sauce
FISH, ESP. WHITE (e.g., Dover sole)
fried food
fruit salsa and sauce, very light (e.g., passion fruit)
halibut, esp. poached
lobster, esp. boiled or grilled, with Grand Cru
mussels
oysters, cooked (e.g., Oysters Bienvenue or Rockefeller)

*OYSTERS, ESP. RAW, AND ESP. WEST COAST, BELON, MALPECQUE, OLYMPIA
pork, esp. loin
risotto, seafood
salmon, esp. poached or sautéed
salmon roe
scallops
seafood
SHELLFISH, ESP. RAW
SHRIMP, ESP. GRILLED
snails
sole
spicy dishes
striped bass
swordfish
trout, esp. sautéed
tuna
vegetables and vegetarian dishes

Chablis has a seaweed quality to it that makes it especially good with West Coast oysters.

— PAUL ROBERTS, MS, the French Laundry (Napa) and Per Se (NYC)

CHAMPAGNE (CARBONATED WINE FROM SECONDARY FERMENTATION, USUALLY MEDIUM-BODIED; SEE ALSO CAVA, PROSECCO, AND SPARKLING WINE)

IN GENERAL
appetizers
apricots
Asian food, esp. moderately spicy
asparagus
bacon, esp. with eggs
braised dishes
brunch
butter and butter sauce
calamari, fried
canapés
caramel
caramelized foods
*CAVIAR

cheese, esp. salty and/or
  Beaufort, Brie, Camembert,
  Cantal, Comte, Gouda,
  Gruyère, Manchego, Parmesan
chicken
Chinese food, esp. seafood
cinnamon
clams
cod
coriander
crab, esp. salad and light dishes
crawfish
**cream sauce and other creamy
  dishes**
crêpes, esp. savory
cumin
curries, esp. vegetarian
EGGS AND EGG DISHES
fish, esp. with cream sauce, and
  esp. oily
foie gras
French fries
FRIED FOOD
fruit desserts (e.g., tarts)
ginger and gingerbread
gravlax
grilled food
ham
hollandaise sauce
honey
Indian food
Japanese food
lemongrass
licorice

LOBSTER
mascarpone
monkfish
mushrooms
nutmeg
nuts, esp. roasted and/or salty
omelets
onions, sautéed sweet
OYSTERS, ESP. KUMAMOTO
peaches
peppers
plums
POPCORN
pork
quail
quiche
rabbit, esp. stewed
roasted dishes
saffron
salad
salmon
SALMON, SMOKED
salmon roe
salt cod
salty food
sashimi
scallops, esp. sautéed or seared
scampi
sea bass
seafood
sea urchin
shellfish
shrimp and langoustines
skate

smoked food
snails
sole, esp. poached
soufflés
soup
soy sauce
spicy food
steamed dishes
sturgeon
sturgeon, smoked
SUSHI
sweetbreads, esp. sautéed
trout
truffles
tuna, esp. tartare
turbot, esp. poached
turkey
vanilla
veal
vegetable dishes, lighter

*Champagne is incredibly versa-
tile with food — so when in
doubt, drink bubbly!*
— BELINDA CHANG, wine
director, Osteria via Stato
(Chicago)

*We host a big Champagne event
every year, and this year, we
rented a popcorn popper and
served popcorn with truffle butter, which put out this amazing*

aroma and was gorgeous paired with Champagne. One year we ran out of popcorn, so I had the chef start sending out plates of French fries and it also worked great. Champagne works with anything fried!

— BRIAN DUNCAN, wine director, Bin 36 (Chicago)

BLANC DE BLANCS (FRENCH CARBONATED WINE MADE WITH 100 PERCENT CHARDONNAY GRAPES)
*CAVIAR
cheese, esp. Parmesan
fish, esp. smoked
fried foods
OYSTERS
sea bass
sea urchin
truffles, white

I think Champagne and caviar can be a great match. But the Champagne should be really young, vibrant, and crisp. Blanc de Blancs is a great Champagne to pair with caviar. However, if you're serving a barrel-fermented or wood-aged Champagne with body, I think caviar can destroy the flavors.

— DANIEL JOHNNES, beverage director, Daniel (NYC)

There are some rules I still believe in — such as, "You can't start a meal better than with Champagne." I used to think that cold vodka went best with caviar, but then found that vodka tends to deaden your palate and keeps you from tasting the incredibly briny and oily character

of the caviar. Now, I prefer Blanc de Blancs Champagne.

— JOSEPH SPELLMAN, MS, Joseph Phelps Vineyards

BLANC DE NOIRS (FRENCH CARBONATED WINE MADE WITH 100 PERCENT PINOT NOIR GRAPES)
canapés
eggs and egg dishes (e.g., omelets)
salmon
shellfish
smoked fish
sushi

BRUT (DRY)
aperitif
chicken, esp. roasted
Chinese food
oysters
shellfish
smoked fish
sushi

DEMI-SEC (SWEET)
desserts
fresh fruit

DOUX (SWEETEST)
desserts
pastries

ROSÉ (FRENCH CARBONATED WINE MADE WITH PINOT NOIR AND/OR PINOT MEUNIER GRAPES)
appetizers
barbecue
beef (served the color of the Champagne, i.e., rare)
beets
berries
bouillabaisse
braised dishes
carpaccio, beef
carrots
celebrations
cheese (e.g., Brie, Epoisses, fresh goat cheese)
CHERRIES
chocolate

crawfish
duck
figs
fish
game birds, roasted
grilled food
ham
LAMB (SERVED THE COLOR OF THE CHAMPAGNE, I.E., RARE)
lobster
meat, red
offal
peaches
pepper, black
plums
PORK
poultry
prosciutto
quail
RASPBERRIES
roasted dishes
salad
SALMON, ESP. GRILLED OR SMOKED

seafood
shellfish
smoked food
STRAWBERRIES
Thanksgiving dinner
tomatoes
tuna
Valentine's Day
veal

SEC (SLIGHTLY SWEET)
aperitif
foie gras
fruit, dried
nuts
shellfish
AVOID
red meat
sweet dishes with dry Champagne

I hosted some events a few years ago where we "went around the world" with different Champagnes. Brut Imperial was paired with Japanese-Asian food and sushi. Brut Rosé was paired with Mediterranean dishes featuring olive oil and tomatoes. White Star was paired with American food, where it shined with everything from twice-baked potatoes to chili. There was even a mini-hamburger with a pickle on it, which I thought would never work — but the combination was so good, it blew people's minds. After this event, no one was thinking of bringing beer to their next summer barbecue! To me, it's no surprise that White Star is the bestselling Champagne in America, because it goes so well with American food.

— LISANE LAPOINTE,
Dom Pérignon ambassador

One's choice of Champagne is very personal. Some people like the yeastiness of Krug, while others prefer the delicateness of Pol Roger. I always ask people's preferences. Those who like Krug might also enjoy an exceptional bottle of Delamotte's "Clos des Mesnil" Brut non vintage, which is the second label of the Champagne house Salon — or of Egly-Ouriet, Ambonnay, Grand Cru Brut nonvintage. Each sells for about one-quarter to one-third of the price of Krug.

— ERIC RENAUD, sommelier,
Bern's Steak House (Tampa)

TIDBIT: We interviewed so many Chicago sommeliers that we had occasion to learn that Oprah Winfrey's favorite Champagne is Cristal.

CHARBONO (ITALIAN FULL-BODIED, RICH, RED WINE FROM THE PIEDMONT REGION)

cheese
game birds
meat, red, esp. grilled or roasted
pasta

AVOID
seafood

CHARDONNAY
(MEDIUM- TO FULL-BODIED, RICH, COMPLEX WHITE WINE PRODUCED IN MANY PARTS OF THE WORLD)

IN GENERAL
almonds
avocado
bacon
basil

bluefish, esp. with a full-bodied, buttery Chardonnay
braised dishes, esp. made with white Chardonnay
BUTTER AND BUTTER SAUCE (including brown butter sauce)
catfish, esp. fried or sautéed
cheese, esp. creamy, goat, and/or sheep's milk (e.g., Brie, Camembert, Gouda, Jack, Parmesan)
***CHICKEN, ESP. BAKED, FRIED, GRILLED, ROASTED, OR IN CREAM SAUCE**
clams, esp. baked or fried
coconut
cod, esp. baked
corn
CRAB, INCLUDING DUNGENESS AND SOFT-SHELL, AND CRAB CAKES
crayfish
CREAM AND CREAM SAUCE
curries, with unoaked Chardonnay
eggs and egg dishes (e.g., omelet, quiche)
FISH, WHITE, ESP. GRILLED, SAUTÉED, IN CREAM SAUCE, OR COOKED IN A SALT CRUST
flounder
fritto misto (fried vegetables and fish)
fruit- and tropical fruit–based chutneys, salsa, and sauce
game hens
garlic, esp. roasted, and esp. with unoaked Chardonnay
ginger
goose
grilled dishes
guacamole, with unoaked Chardonnay
halibut, esp. grilled and/or with lighter-bodied Chardonnay
ham
lemon and lemon-based sauce
LOBSTER, ESP. GRILLED, AND ESP. WITH A CALIFORNIA AND/OR

FULL-BODIED BUTTERY CHARDONNAY

mango and other tropical fruits

mayonnaise

meat, esp. lighter meat, and esp. grilled or smoked

monkfish, esp. baked, broiled, or sautéed

mushrooms and wild mushrooms

mustard, esp. Dijon

nutmeg

orange

oysters, esp. cooked (e.g., fried or sautéed)

pasta and pasta salad, esp. with creamy sauce

peanuts

pears

peppers, bell

pesto

pheasant

polenta

pork, esp. grilled, roasted, and/or with a full-bodied, unoaked Chardonnay

poultry

rabbit

risotto

roasted dishes

saffron

sage, fresh

salad, with unoaked Chardonnay

salad, Caesar

SALMON, ESP. GRILLED, ROASTED, AND/OR WITH LEMON SAUCE, AND ESP. WITH A FULL-BODIED, UNOAKED CHARDONNAY

sandwiches, esp. chicken or turkey

sautéed dishes

SCALLOPS, ESP. SAUTÉED

scrod, esp. sautéed

sea bass, esp. roasted or sautéed

SEAFOOD, ESP. GRILLED, SAUTÉED, AND/OR WITH RICH (e.g., butter or cream) SAUCE

seafood salad

shellfish, with unoaked Chardonnay

shrimp and prawns, esp. boiled or grilled with an unoaked Chardonnay

smoked fish (e.g., salmon)

snapper, esp. grilled and/or with a light-bodied Chardonnay

sole, esp. fried or sautéed with an unoaked Chardonnay

soup, esp. creamy

sour cream

squash

swordfish, esp. baked, broiled, grilled, or roasted

tarragon

thyme

trout, esp. with an unoaked Chardonnay

tuna, esp. grilled

turbot, esp. sautéed

turkey, esp. roasted and/or served cold

VEAL, ESP. GRILLED OR ROASTED, AND ESP. WITH A FULL-BODIED CHARDONNAY

vegetables and vegetable dishes

AVOID

chiles and chile-based salsa

cilantro

dill

fish, oily

red meat

Chardonnay never shows as well as when there's butter or dairy in a dish. — CRAIG SHELTON, chef-owner, the Ryland Inn (New Jersey)

I am not a big fan of California Chardonnay because to me it is so sweet, it's like drinking pineapple juice. But if you take that wine and pair it with grilled swordfish with a mango salsa, the dish knocks the sweetness out of the Chardonnay — it becomes a dry white wine, and other flavors of the wine emerge.

— DAVID ROSENGARTEN, editor in chief, www.DavidRosengarten.com

Where can you find great Chardonnay? Number one would be White Burgundy from France. Number two would be Italy — and California is coming on because it is becoming more balanced and less oaky.

— JEAN-LUC LE DÙ, owner, Le Dù's Wines (NYC)

TIDBIT: We interviewed so many Chicago sommeliers that we had occasion to learn of Oprah Winfrey's favorite Chardonnay: a Peter Michael Chardonnay from Sonoma that she is said to enjoy *very* well chilled.

AUSTRALIAN
cheese (e.g., blue, Brie, Gouda)
chicken
duck
fish
grilled dishes
meat, light and/or white
pasta, with cream sauce
soup, cream-based
sweet-and-sour dishes
swordfish
turkey
vegetables, esp. grilled

CALIFORNIA

LIGHT-BODIED (AND MOST MINERALLY)
cheese
Chinese food
fish
halibut
meat, white and light
Philippine food
snapper
Vietnamese food

MEDIUM-BODIED
cheese (e.g., Camembert)
chicken, esp. roasted
turkey, esp. roasted

FULL-BODIED (AND OAKI-EST)
duck
hoisin sauce
oyster sauce
pork
quail
salmon, esp. grilled
salmon, smoked
veal

ITALIAN (FULL-BODIED)
chicken
fritto misto (fried fish and vegetables)
pasta, esp. with cream sauce
risotto, esp. with cheese
salmon, poached or grilled
seafood, esp. soup and stews

CHASSAGNE-MONTRACHET
(FRENCH FULL-BODIED WHITE WINE FROM BURGUNDY; SEE ALSO BURGUNDY, WHITE)
chicken, esp. with lemon
clams
crab, esp. steamed
Dover sole
duck
LOBSTER, ESP. STEAMED
pumpkin
scallops, esp. sautéed

CHÂTEAUNEUF-DU-PAPE (FRENCH FULL-BODIED WINE FROM THE RHONE VALLEY)
RED (SPICY, DENSE, EARTHY, RICH)
beef
cheese
duck, esp. roasted or as confit
eggplant, esp. baked or grilled
fish
game, esp. roasted
game birds, esp. roasted
goose, esp. roasted

LAMB, ESP. ROASTED OR STEWED
meat, esp. barbecued, braised, or roasted
mushrooms
pot au feu
poultry
quail, esp. roasted
RABBIT, ESP. BRAISED
short ribs, esp. braised
steak, esp. strip
stew

WHITE
cheese, esp. pungent (e.g., Roquefort)
chicken
fish
foie gras
hazelnuts
lobster
nuts
pasta, esp. with white truffles
pork
scallops
shellfish
tuna
veal

CHENIN BLANC
(FRENCH LIGHT TO MEDIUM-BODIED CRISP, ACIDIC WHITE WINE FROM THE LOIRE VALLEY)
apples and apple desserts, esp. with sweeter Chenin Blanc
Asian food, esp. citrus-flavored and esp. with off-dry Chenin Blanc
barbecue
Boudin blanc (white sausage)
calamari
charcuterie
cheese, esp. goat (e.g., Selles-sur-Cher) with drier Chenin Blanc
chicken, esp. barbecued or with creamy sauce
Chinese food, esp. with off-dry Chenin Blanc
citrus
clams
corn

crab

dill

FISH, ESP. SAUTÉED AND/OR WITH LEMON

flounder, esp. grilled

foie gras, esp. seared, and esp. with sweeter Chenin Blanc

fried food

halibut

herbs

Japanese food

langoustines

Mexican food

poached dishes

pork, esp. roasted

poultry

SALAD

sautéed dishes

scallops

SEAFOOD

shellfish

smoked fish (e.g., salmon)

spicy food

steamed dishes

striped bass

trout, esp. grilled

vegetables

Vietnamese food

At The Modern, my favorite dish on the menu is langoustine wrapped in bacon with Greek yogurt cream that I serve with a Chenin Blanc from De Trafford. The softness of the langoustine, the smokiness of the bacon, and the pungent yogurt contrast with the slight oak of the Chenin Blanc. It's an explosion of flavors! — STEPHANE COLLING, wine director, The Modern at the MoMA (NYC)

CHIANTI (ITALIAN MEDIUM-BODIED RED WINE)

acidic food

baked pasta, esp. with tomato sauce (e.g., cannelloni, lasagna)

basil

beans and bean-based dishes

beef, esp. braised or stewed

calf's liver with onions

carpaccio

cheese, esp. Italian (e.g., mozzarella, Parmesan, Pecorino, Provolone)

CHICKEN, ESP. BRAISED (ESP. IN TOMATO SAUCE), GRILLED, OR ROASTED

game, esp. with Chianti Riserva

grilled meat and other food

herbs, Italian

lamb, esp. grilled, roasted, and/or spiced, and esp. with Chianti Classico or Riserva

liver, esp. calf's or chicken

meat, red, esp. simply grilled or roasted

mushrooms, esp. grilled

olive oil

osso buco

pancetta

*PASTA, ESP. CHIANTI CLASSICO WITH MEAT AND/OR TOMATO SAUCE (e.g., Bolognese)

PIZZA, ESP. WITH CHIANTI CLASSICO

pork, esp. grilled, roasted, and/or chops

pot roast

poultry

prime rib, esp. with aged and/or Chianti Riserva

prosciutto

quail, esp. grilled

rabbit

ravioli

risotto, esp. mushroom

soup, esp. minestrone

STEAK, ESP. GRILLED WITH AGED AND/OR CHIANTI RISERVA

stew, esp. tomato-based

TOMATO-BASED SAUCE

veal, grilled or roasted

vegetables, grilled

wild boar

AVOID

shellfish

spicy dishes, esp. with finer Chiantis

strongly flavored dishes

sweet dishes

CHILEAN WINES (WHICH HAVE A MEATY SMOKINESS TO THEM)

barbecue

beef

casseroles

cheese

game

meat, red

sausage

stew

South America must export its wine with the local decline of wine consumption. They have cheap land, cheap labor, and the technical capacity to make good wine and beat the classic regions at their own game at half-price or less. You can buy a Chilean Cabernet under eight dollars that may well be a much better wine than a Bordeaux or Napa Valley Merlot at twenty dollars.

— JOSEPH SPELLMAN, MS, Joseph Phelps Vineyards

CHIMAY (UNPASTEURIZED, FULL-BODIED BELGIAN ALE MADE BY TRAPPIST MONKS)

beef, esp. stewed, and esp. Flemish-style

cheese, esp. **CHIMAY**

desserts, esp. with chocolate and/or custard, and esp. with Chimay Blue

fish, esp. with Chimay Blue or Triple

game, esp. with Chimay Blue or Red

poultry, esp. with Chimay Red or Triple

meat, red, esp. barbecued or grilled, and esp. with Chimay Blue

meat, white, esp. with Chimay Red

shellfish, esp. with Chimay Blue or Triple

stew, meat

Chimay makes three ales: The Blue label is dark and like a Merlot wine. I would pair it with a beef stew made in the Flemish style — and even with desserts like chocolate-dipped strawberries or a light chocolate cake. Chimay also makes a Triple White that is closer to Champagne.

— CARLOS SOLIS, food and beverage director/chef, Sheraton Four Points (Los Angeles)

CHINON (FRENCH MEDIUM-BODIED RED WINE FROM THE LOIRE VALLEY, MADE WITH CABERNET FRANC; SEE ALSO CABERNET FRANC)

cheese goat, esp. aged

chicken

duck

game birds, esp. roasted

goose

grilled dishes

ham

hamburgers

hot dogs

lamb

lobster

Polish food

pork

rabbit

salami

SALMON, ESP. GRILLED

shrimp, esp. grilled

sushi, esp. richer fish

turbot

veal

vegetables (e.g., roasted peppers, spinach)

Chinon is a wine I like that I think has a Pinot Noir personality. Its tannins are modest, and there's emphasis on ripe fruit flavors, so there's enough good acidity. I think it can be really nice with salmon — especially grilled, because of the tannin in the Cabernet Franc [grapes], as well as with grilled shrimp and turbot.

— DANIEL JOHNNES, beverage director, Daniel (NYC)

CIDER

HARD (ALCOHOLIC FERMENTED APPLE JUICE)

apples and apple desserts, esp. with French (wine-like) cider

chicken

cheese, esp. Brie, Cheddar, Colby, Livarot, Muenster, Pont L'Eveque, etc.

cream sauce, esp. with French (wine-like) cider

crêpes, savory and sweet, esp. with dry French (wine-like) cider

duck, fish, esp. salmon, trout

fruit

oysters, esp. with English (beer-like) cider and/or hard cider

pork

rabbit, esp. cooked in cider

seafood, esp. with French (wine-like) cider or Spanish cider

shellfish, esp. with French (wine-like) cider

spicy dishes, esp. with French (wine-like) cider

turkey

SWEET (NON-ALCOHOLIC FRESH-PRESSED APPLE JUICE)

apple desserts

doughnuts, esp. fried

CIRO ROSSO (ITALIAN MEDIUM-BODIED RED WINE FROM CALABRIA)

beans, white

eggplant Parmesan

lamb, esp. braised or stewed

lasagna

pasta, esp. with mushrooms

peperoncini

pizza

spicy dishes

CLARET (FRENCH MEDIUM-BODIED RED WINE FROM BORDEAUX, MADE MAINLY FROM CABERNET SAUVIGNON, MERLOT, AND CABERNET FRANC; SMALL AMOUNTS OF MALBEC AND PETIT VERDOT ARE ALSO USED)

cheese (e.g., Cheddar)

game and game birds

lamb

meat

pork

poultry

COCKTAILS (DRINKS MADE WITH HARD LIQUOR)

Japanese snacks are great with cocktails — especially wasabi peas. They are sweet and savory, and great with Cosmopolitans or apple martinis. I think the wasabi pea obliterates what was on your palate and the cocktail obliterates the wasabi pea.

— ROCCO DISPIRITO, chef

Cocktails at Blue Hill at Stone Barns

PHILIPPE GOUZE

Chefs Dan Barber and Mike Anthony are proud of the innovative way their general manager Philippe Gouze has worked with them to infuse the spirit of the farm at Blue Hill at Stone Barns into the restaurant's cocktail offerings. "Philippe grew up in the south of France, and he has created a variety of drinks drawing from the land — from berry-infused Sangria to honey oat–infused vodka to bloody sorrel margarita," Anthony told us. Barber added, "When you come here [to Blue Hill at Stone Barns], you are coming to a place that is created in a barn and is about agriculture. When you walk into the bar, you see people drinking these drinks; it also lets you know that this is a serious of-the-moment and provocative place. By matching these cocktails to the season, we are linking the whole thing together. We have the opportunity to link a drink to the season and local produce."

Gouze himself explained to us, "I wanted to find a way to link the farm to the cocktails. The first thing a server does in most restaurants is take a cocktail order. Here, they start by introducing our seasonal cocktail, and mention what kind of seasonal fruit or vegetable is in the drink."

—*Spring: "In spring, the first thing out of the ground was sorrel. It is lemony and tangy, so I thought of a margarita, which also has a sour, lemony flavor. I replaced the lime juice in a margarita with sorrel, and it was winner. We also had rhubarb in the spring. We juiced the rhubarb raw, and used it to replace the cranberry juice in a Cosmopolitan — and it was a huge winner."*

—*Summer: "We had some purple basil come in, so we did our own version of a Mojito, replacing the mint with the purple basil. It's incredibly refreshing. During the summer, we also serve a martini made with cucumber juice with Hendricks gin, which has cucumber notes to it."*

—*Fall: "We use carnival squash in the fall. When you process it, the juice comes out a florescent orange color. It then gets mixed with dark rum and a drop of Campari."*

—*Winter: "It is hard to find ingredients to work with during the winter. Apples are in, so we made apple martinis with Calvados."*

Gouze continued, "The thing about seasonal cocktails is that once the season is over, it's over. People will come back for a rhubarb cocktail, and we will tell them, 'It is too late — come back next year!'" Gouze finds that inspiration can strike anywhere: "I wanted to do something with vodka, so I went into the kitchen and stared at the shelves. I saw some oats and thought, 'Well, vodka is a grain.' So I infused the vodka with the oats and added honey at the end. It took a few tries, but it is really amazing."

How do cocktails pair with food? Says Gouze, "We serve a house-made charcuterie plate and other small snacks in the bar. However, cocktails are mostly served before dinner or after the meal, not with it. A cocktail with cucumber is light and refreshing for before the meal. I like wine with my dinner — maybe because I am French? If you're not careful, cocktails can be too harsh and flavorful during the meal. I think beet vodka makes a good intermezzo, providing a burst of flavor. I will ideally serve this between two courses where the first one had beet in it, so the beet vodka provides a reminder of what just happened. Our fig and fennel vodka is a great after dinner, and is more of a digestif."

Chef Kathy Casey and Mixologist Ryan Magarian on General Guidelines for Potentially Agreeable Marriages of Food and Cocktails

RYAN MAGARIAN: Too many people think of cocktails as only alcohol delivery vehicles. Instead, we take the approach that creating a cocktail is like building your own wine.

KATHY CASEY: A good cocktail has a lot of structure. Use only the best ingredients, including premium spirits and fresh juices. When you use the best ingredients, you make them shine.

RYAN MAGARIAN: We see cocktails as enhancing the experience of a dish when they are designed to bring out flavors. Too many cocktails are poured with a very heavy hand — and the extra booze destroys the cocktail. To us, a great cocktail is all about balance. Our guideline is one-and-a-half to two ounces of spirits per cocktail — tops. A glass of wine has about the same amount of alcohol, although the cocktail has a little more heat from the spirit.

Aside from the alcohol, cocktails have three basic elements: the sweet, the acid, and what we call the third dimension, which is something fresh added to provide a dry note — which is what makes the cocktail go from "good" to "Oh-my-God-what-is-this?" For example, Kathy makes a drink known as the Lemon Drop, which is vodka, lemon, and sugar — but adding some crushed verbena to it sends it over the top.

The source of alcohol in cocktails can be categorized as light, medium, heavy, and super heavy:

LIGHT: *vodka, gin, rum, light aperitifs (such as Lillet, sake, Champagne)*
MEDIUM: *lighter brandies, light amber rum, reposado tequila, lighter scotch*
HEAVY: *Bourbon, brandy, heavier scotch, dark rum*
SUPER-HEAVY: *80-plus proof spirits like Bourbon or rum*

Sweet and/or acid can come from fruit, such as apple, pear, peach, or apricot.
Dry components could be grapefruit, lemon, or lime.

KATHY CASEY: When creating a cocktail, we look at the menu first. At the restaurant Thai Ginger, we looked in the kitchen and saw galangal, lime, Thai basil, cucumber, and curry, among other things.

RYAN MAGARIAN: This led us to create a spin on the Mojito, by adding fresh cilantro. The simple addition of an herb or spice can change the whole effect of a cocktail.
Other guidelines from Casey and Magarian:

- *Don't serve large cocktails with food. Keep the total volume of alcohol to less than two ounces per drink. In this case, too much is definitely a bad thing.*
- *Spirits work better in a well-balanced cocktail than all by themselves.*
- *Experiment with gin and vodka before a meal, and rum, whiskey, and brandy during and after a meal.*
- *White spirits (i.e., vodka, gin) are a good place to start, as they can act as a canvas for painting flavors to your exact specifications.*
- *Aromatic garnishes (e.g., orange zest) are especially important when it comes to cocktails with food. They add another dimension to the flavor experience.*
- *You'll know you have a winner when both the flavors of the dish and those of the cocktail are equally enhanced.*

I personally find cocktail pairings to be more exciting from a culinary standpoint. Not only is wine a "been there, done that," but if you are trying to do a wine pairing and a particular wine doesn't quite work, you have to pick a different wine. However, with a cocktail, if a pairing doesn't quite work, you can identify what the issues are and actually change the cocktail to make the pairing work better.
— ROBERT HESS, founder, DrinkBoy.com

COFFEE

IN GENERAL
apple pies and tarts
breakfast dishes, esp. wheat-based
brunch, esp. wheat-based
chocolate and chocolate desserts
pancakes
waffles

AFRICAN (E.G., ETHIOPIAN, WHICH PRODUCES LIGHTER-BODIED, MILDER COFFEES WITH FLORAL AND BERRY NOTES)
chocolate and chocolate desserts
lemon desserts

AVOID
savory food

AGED (WHICH IMPARTS SPICY COMPONENTS TO ITS FLAVOR)
bread pudding
pumpkin pie
spiced desserts

ASIAN PACIFIC (E.G., FROM INDONESIA, JAVA, SUMATRA; BIG, BOLD COFFEE WITH LOWER ACIDITY)
savory food

CENTRAL AND LATIN AMERICAN (I.E., MORE SUBTLE, ROUNDED COFFEE WITH CRISP, CLEAN ACIDITY)
berries
biscotti
breakfast
carrot cake
cookies
doughnuts
lunch
muffins, lightly flavored
nuts and nut breads
scones, esp. light

DARK-ROASTED (E.G., ITALIAN, FRENCH, VIENNA ROAST; GREEN COFFEE BEANS ARE ROASTED, PRODUCING A "SECOND CRACK" IN THE BEAN AND RELEASING SUGARS THAT CARAMELIZE; VERY LITTLE ACIDITY AND BITTERSWEET)
cake, full-flavored
chocolate, esp. dark, and esp. chocolate desserts
desserts, rich and creamy
ice cream

ESPRESSO
biscotti
cookies
tiramisu

FRENCH ROAST
peppers, roasted red and yellow, esp. with olive oil

ICED (MADE WITH EAST AFRICAN COFFEE)

ITALIAN ROAST
antipasto
biscotti

KENYAN
fruit desserts
lemon desserts
scones, esp. with fruit

LIGHT-ROASTED (E.G., KENYAN, MOCHA JAVA; BRIGHT, ACIDIC, TOASTED GRAIN TASTE)
berry desserts
fruit and fruit desserts

MEDIUM-ROASTED (E.G., COSTA RICAN, GUATEMALAN, VIENNESE; ACIDIC AND BRIGHT, BUT LACKS GRAIN TASTE)
cheesecake
custard desserts
lemon desserts
tiramisu

COGNAC OR COGNAC-BASED COCKTAILS
Asian food
duck, roasted
foie gras
pork
rich dishes
squab, roasted

CONDRIEU (FRENCH FULL-BODIED WHITE WINE FROM THE RHÔNE VALLEY, MADE WITH VIOGNIER GRAPES; FRUITY AND FLORAL PERFUME)
apricots
chicken
crab
curries
filet mignon, esp. with citrus hollandaise (a rare recommendation of white wine with red meat!)
fish
foie gras
fruit
lobster

mango
monkfish
mushrooms, wild
osso buco
pork, esp. roasted, and esp. with fruit
rice and risotto
salmon
seafood, esp. rich preparations

I have a sentimental attachment to Condrieu: It was the house wine of [Fernand Point's legendary restaurant in France] La Pyramide.
— DAVID WALTUCK, chef-owner, Chanterelle (NYC)

CORTON-CHARLEMAGNE
(FRENCH FULL-BODIED WHITE WINE FROM BURGUNDY)
chicken, esp. roasted
fish, white, esp. Dover sole, halibut, sole, turbot
lobster
rabbit
shellfish, esp. lobster, shrimp
veal, esp. with lemon sauce

COTEAUX DU LAYON (FRENCH SEMISWEET OR SWEET WHITE WINE MADE FROM CHENIN BLANC GRAPES)
cheese, blue (e.g., Roquefort)
chocolate, dark, esp. creamy dessert with sweet Coteaux du Layon
fish
foie gras, esp. sautéed
pâté
pears and pear desserts, esp. with sweet Coteaux du Layon
rillettes

CÔTE-RÔTIE (FRENCH FULL-BODIED RED WINE FROM THE RHÔNE VALLEY)
BEEF, ESP. BRAISED, GRILLED, OR STEWED
cheese, esp. strongly flavored (e.g., Brie, Camembert, Epoisses, Reblochon)
duck
game, esp. roasted
ham
lamb, esp. roasted
meat, red
mushrooms
mustard
pork or pork belly
rabbit
steak, esp. rib-eye, and/or with pepper
veal
venison

I think there's an image of Côte-Rôtie as being very full-bodied and heavy. But because it's very far north for a Syrah, it shouldn't be thought of in the same category as Hermitage. Côte-Rôtie lends itself to more refined cuisine, a little more delicate nuance. An old Côte-Rôtie can taste very much like an old Burgundy, with beautiful perfume of dried flowers and spice, very soft tannins, and very fresh flavors. It's made from the same grape as Hermitage, but a totally different expression of it.
— DANIEL JOHNNES, beverage director, Daniel (NYC)

CÔTES DU RHÔNE
(FRENCH MEDIUM-BODIED RED WINE FROM THE RHÔNE VALLEY; DARK FRUIT AND LICORICE WITH MODERATE TANNINS)

barbecue, esp. ribs
beef, esp. braised or stewed
charcuterie
cheese, esp. Port Salut, Saint-Nectaire
chicken, esp. roasted
chicken tikka masala
chili
egg dishes (e.g., omelets)
fish, esp. stew
hamburgers
meat, esp. with herbs
Mexican food, esp. spicy
mushrooms
onions, cooked (e.g., onion soup)
oxtails, esp. braised or stewed
pizza
quail
salad, Niçoise
sandwiches, esp. ham and cheese
sausage
steak, esp. grilled
stew
truffles
tuna, grilled
vegetables, esp. grilled and/or root
wild boar

CROZES-HERMITAGE
(FRENCH FULL-BODIED RED FROM THE RHÔNE VALLEY)
beef, esp. braised or stewed
braised dishes
duck
game
lamb
meat, esp. roasted
pork, esp. roasted
stew, esp. beef
venison

DESSERT WINE (E.G., MOSCATO D'ASTI, VIN DE GLACIERE, ETC.)
desserts
on their own — with nothing

DOLCETTO (ITALIAN LIGHT- TO MEDIUM-BODIED RED WINE FROM THE PIEDMONT REGION)

CHICKEN, ESP. GRILLED, ROASTED, AND/OR WITH TOMATO SAUCE

chili

game birds, esp. roasted

garlic

hamburgers

MEAT, RED, ESP. GRILLED, ROASTED, AND/OR SERVED COLD

meat loaf

mushrooms

onions

PASTA, ESP. WITH CHEESE AND/OR VEGETABLES

PASTA, ESP. WITH SIMPLE (e.g., tomato) SAUCE

pesto sauce

pizza

pork, esp. chops

prosciutto

risotto

salad, (e.g., salad Niçoise)

salami

salmon, grilled

sausage, esp. grilled

seafood

steak tartare

tomatoes and tomato-based dishes

tuna

veal, esp. chops

DOURO (PORTUGUESE MEDIUM-BODIED RED WINE; RUBY RED HUE, AND TOBACCO, CEDAR, AND CHERRY AROMAS)

game

lamb

meat, red

vegetables, braised and stewed

EAU DE VIE (ALCOHOL FLAVORED WITH FRUIT, E.G., PEAR, RASPBERRY)

sorbet, esp. fruit

ENTRE-DEUX-MERS (FRENCH MEDIUM-BODIED WHITE WINE FROM THE BORDEAUX REGION; FRESH AND FRUITY DRY WINE WITH GRAPEFRUIT, LYCHEE, AND PEACH AROMAS)

cheese, (e.g., Boursin, goat, Saint-Andre)

fish, esp. lean

oysters

salad

SEAFOOD

shellfish, esp. raw

ESPRESSO

biscotti

FALANGHINA (ITALIAN MEDIUM-BODIED ACIDIC WHITE WINE FROM CAMPAGNA)

Caprese salad

fish, lightly prepared

FIANO (ITALIAN MEDIUM-BODIED, DRY, AROMATIC WHITE WINE FROM CAMPAGNA)

Asian food, esp. spicy but not too hot

Central American food, esp. spicy but not too hot

fish, esp. lighter dishes

herbs, fresh

prawns, grilled

salad (e.g., Caprese)

seafood, esp. lighter dishes

shrimp, grilled

spicy dishes

vegetables, esp. summer

FRAMBOISE LAMBIC BEER (RASPBERRY-FLAVORED BEER FROM BELGIUM)

after dinner

brunch

cheese, esp. fresh goat

cheesecake

chocolate

custard and custard-like desserts

duck

egg dishes

Linzer torte

mascarpone

mole (Mexican sauce)

venison

and effervescence make it like drinking a Mimosa! I don't think they work with dessert, because they can overpower it. They do make a wonderful after-dinner drink, however.

— CARLOS SOLIS, food and beverage director/chef, Sheraton Four Points LAX (Los Angeles)

In the summer, I like Lambic beers like Framboise. It is a little sweet in general, but during the summer it is great. It is a sipping beer for dessert. It has a raspberry sweetness to it and hits the spot.

— BERNARD SUN, beverage director, Jean-Georges Management (New York)

FRASCATI (ITALIAN LIGHT-BODIED WHITE WINE FROM THE ROME REGION)
calamari, fried
fish, esp. fried and/or spicy preparations
light dishes
octopus
pasta, esp. al fredo and other creamy
salad, seafood
SEAFOOD
spaghetti alla carbonara
spicy Italian dishes

FRENCH WINE

The French have been brilliant at promoting place as the primary reason to value a wine. To the French, it is not about flavor, or alcohol, or intensity, or color, but about the sense of truth that comes through wine because of its sense of place . . . The distinctions that uniquely make Champagne or Chablis or Puligny-Montrachet different from its neighbor Meursault can only be found in the soil differences. Once you understand that, they are the most intellectually delicious wines. A great Côte-Rôtie or a great Burgundy is to me the most exciting thing you can drink. There is a lot of French wine that does not have the benefit of being from a primary site nor of a great tradition or historical importance. A lot of it! But that is also true of Australia, Chile, and many other places around the world.

— JOSEPH SPELLMAN, MS, Joseph Phelps Vineyards

FRUIT JUICE, SPARKLING (NON-ALCOHOLIC FRUIT JUICE MIXED WITH SPARKLING WATER)

As upscale restaurants seek non-alcoholic pairings, they're having great success with upscale beverages such as Fizzy Lizzy (which is carried at Blue Hill at Stone Barns). Here are a sampling of Fizzy Lizzy flavors, and a few of the foods they complement:

apple: cheese, (esp. goat cheese) duck, game birds, foie gras, pork
cranberry: cheese, chicken, duck, game, turkey
grapefruit: fish, shellfish
orange: chicken, chocolate, duck, cranberries
passion fruit: spicy cuisines (e.g., Caribbean, Latino, Southwestern)

pineapple: ham, mahimahi; spicy cuisines (e.g., Caribbean, Latino, Southwestern)

raspberry lemon: melon, peaches, picnics

FUMÉ BLANC (SEE SAUVIGNON BLANC)

GALESTRO (ITALIAN LIGHT-BODIED, FRUITY WHITE WINE FROM TUSCANY)

antipasto and appetizers

casual food and dishes

cheese

FISH

meat, white

PASTA, ESP. WITH CHEESE OR CREAM SAUCE

prosciutto

risotto

salty food and dishes

seafood

veal

GAMAY (SEE BEAUJOLAIS)

GAVI (ITALIAN FULL-BODIED WHITE WINE FROM THE PIEDMONT REGION, MADE WITH CORTESE; NOTES OF CITRUS, GRASS, NUTS)

almonds

anchovies, grilled

chicken

FISH, ESP. FRIED AND/OR WHITE

meat, white

mussels

octopus, esp. grilled

PASTA, ESP. WITH CREAM OR PESTO SAUCE

risotto, esp. cheese

salad

salmon

sea bass

SEAFOOD, ESP. IN SOUP OR STEWS

tomatoes, raw

tuna

veal

vegetables, esp. fried or roasted

GEWÜRZTRAMINER (MEDIUM-BODIED WHITE WINE; VERY AROMATIC WITH TROPICAL FRUITS OF LYCHEE AND PASSION FRUIT AND PERFUMED FLOWERS)

ASIAN FOOD, ESP. SPICY (e.g., Hunan, Szechuan), AND ESP. WITH ALSATIAN GEWÜRZTRAMINER

Caribbean food

CHEESE, ESP. SOFT AND/OR STRONG/AGED (e.g., Camembert, Epoisses), *MUENSTER, ROQUEFORT

chicken, esp. stronger-flavored

CHINESE FOOD, ESP. WITH GERMAN AND/OR SWEET- ER GEWÜRZTRAMINER

choucroute garni, esp. with Alsatian Gewürztraminer

cilantro

cinnamon

clams, esp. fried

clove

coconut

Cornish game hen

Creole food

CURRIES

duck, esp. Peking or roasted

fish (e.g., monkfish, red snapper), esp. spicy preparations

foie gras, esp. with drier Gewürztraminer

fruit, esp. tropical (e.g., guava, mango, papaya, passion fruit, pineapple, etc.), and fruit chutney and salsa

garlic

GINGER

gravlax and other cured foods

HAM

honey

Hunan food

INDIAN FOOD, ESP. WITH GERMAN GEWÜRZTRAMINER

lobster, esp. broiled or grilled

meat, white

onions, esp. sweet (e.g., onion tart)

pasta, esp. with garlic and olive oil

pâté, esp. duck liver

pepper, black or white

PORK, ESP. ROASTED

prosciutto, esp. with melon

rich-flavored dishes and sauces

roasted dishes

salad

salsa

salmon

sauerkraut

SAUSAGE

scallops

seafood, esp. stronger-flavored and/or fried

shellfish (e.g., crab, shrimp), esp. spicy preparations

SMOKED FOOD, ESP. CHEESE (e.g., Gouda, moz-zarella), FISH (e.g. salmon), MEAT, AND OTHER DISHES

soy sauce

SPICY FOOD (delicately to moderately spicy)

squash, winter

stir-fried dishes

sweet (slightly) dishes

sweet potatoes

Szechuan food

THAI FOOD (e.g., curries, Pad Thai), ESP. WITH GERMAN GEWÜRZTRAMINER

TURKEY

veal, esp. roasted

vegetarian dishes and vegetables, esp. grilled

Muenster cheese with Gewürz-traminer is a classic pairing — but it's even better if you put caraway seeds with the cheese. It just takes it to another level.

— DANIEL JOHNNES, beverage director, Daniel (NYC)

LATE HARVEST (WHITE DESSERT WINE; GOLDEN AMBER COLOR, APRICOT AND HONEY AROMAS, SWEET WITH A BALANCE OF ACIDITY)

cheese, esp. blue or Muenster

coconut desserts (e.g., macaroons)

foie gras

fruits, esp. tropical, and esp. fruity desserts

lychees

mango

papaya

I really like a Late Harvest Gewürztraminer with Muenster cheese. They are from the same area and are a perfect regional pairing.

— STEPHANE COLLING, wine director, The Modern at the MoMA (NYC)

GIGONDAS (FRENCH MEDIUM-BODIED RED WINE FROM THE RHÔNE VALLEY; BLACK CHERRY, PLUM, SWEET HERB, AND MUSHROOM AROMAS)

beef, stewed

cheese, esp. soft

game, esp. roasted

meat, esp. roasted

steak

stew

GIN AND GIN COCKTAILS

Asian crispy spring rolls

clams

crabs

oysters

pork

salmon

seafood

shellfish

GINGER ALE (GINGER-FLAVORED SOFT DRINK)

carrots

crab

duck

fish, esp. red snapper, salmon, tuna

ham

melon

pears

pork, esp. pork chops

pumpkin

stir-fried dishes

sweet potatoes

GRAVES (AN APPELLATION IN BORDEAUX, FRENCH MEDIUM-BODIED RED WINE; CURRANT, RIPE BLACK FRUIT, AND TOBACCO CHARACTER-ISTICS AND A BLACKISH PURPLE HUE; MOST FAMOUS WINERY IS CHÂTEAU HAUT-BRION)

duck

fish (e.g., mackerel, monkfish, salmon, tuna)

goose

lobster

scallops

GRECO DI TUFO

(ITALIAN FULL-BODIED WHITE WINE FROM AVELLINO; CLEAN, PLEASANT, DRY)

anchovies

CHICKEN

couscous

fish

fritto misto (fried vegetables and seafood)

monkfish

pasta, esp. with cream sauce

poultry

risotto, esp. with cheese

salmon

SEAFOOD, ESP. IN SALAD, SOUP, AND STEW

spicy (moderately) dishes

squid

veal

GRENACHE (RED GRAPE GROWN IN FRANCE AND SPAIN; VERY FRUITY WITH BLACKBERRY SWEETNESS AND HINTS OF PEPPER; THE KEY GRAPE IN CHÂTEAUNEUF-DU-PAPE, IT IS OFTEN USED TO MAKE ROSÉ AND VEGA SICILIA; SEE ALSO CHÂTEAUNEUF-DU-PAPE)

barbecue

beans

beef

braised dishes

cheese

chicken

duck, esp. roasted

eggplant

foie gras

grilled dishes

hamburgers

LAMB, ESP. GRILLED

MEAT, ESP. RED, AND ESP. BARBECUED OR ROASTED

mushrooms, esp. wild

osso buco

pasta

pizza

pork

poultry, roasted

red snapper

roasts and other roasted dishes

sausage

shellfish

smoked meat

spicy dishes, esp. Asian

steak, esp. barbecued or grilled

stew and other stewed dishes, esp. Moroccan

turkey

veal

I love Grenache, which is Pinot Noir but kicked up a notch!
— ALPANA SINGH, MS, Everest (Chicago)

GRÜNER VELTLINER

(AUSTRIAN MEDIUM-BODIED WHITE WINE; VERY FRUITY WITH LYCHEE, CELERY, AND WHITE PEPPER CHARACTERISTICS)

abalone
artichokes
ASPARAGUS
bacon
ceviche
cheese, esp. stinky, fatty, rich, and/or blue
chicken, esp. fried
duck, esp. breast
fish
fried food
greens
herbs
Indian food
Japanese food
lobster
meat, white
mushrooms
oysters
pasta
PORK
poultry
salad
sausage
SCALLOPS
seafood
shellfish
shrimp
snails
soy
SUSHI
sweetbreads, esp. roasted
swordfish
Thai food and spices
uni
VEAL, ESP. ROASTED

vegetables
wasabi
Wiener Schnitzel

Austrian Grüner Veltliner is very Sauvignon Blanc–like, so once you get people to taste it, they find they love it.
— KAREN KING, beverage director, The Modern at the MoMA (NYC)

I'm a huge fan of Austrian wines — particularly Grüner Veltliner. I tell people, "When in doubt, get Grüner Veltliner and you'll be OK." In Austria — or Germany or Alsace, for that matter — it's not uncommon to serve white wine with sausage and pork. Grüner Veltliner also has a richness and power that can stand up to even more flavorful dishes. — GEORGE COSSETTE, co-owner, Silverlake Wine (Los Angeles)

HERMITAGE (FRENCH MEDIUM- TO FULL-BODIED WINE FROM THE NORTHERN RHÔNE VALLEY)

RED (SPICY, FRUITY, TANNIC)
BEEF, ESP. AU POIVRE, AND ESP. BRAISED, GRILLED, ROASTED, OR STEWED
braised dishes
cheese, esp. blue or hard
duck
GAME, ESP. BRAISED, ROASTED, OR STEWED
garlic
LAMB, ESP. BRAISED
meat, esp. red, and esp. roasted
mushrooms

mustard
pork
squab
steak, esp. grilled Porterhouse
STEWED DISHES
truffles
VENISON, ESP. BRAISED OR STEWED

I think Hermitage is great with really robust dishes, such as game and stews.
— DANIEL JOHNNES, beverage director, Daniel (NYC)

WHITE
cheese, esp. pungent
chicken
crab
fish
LOBSTER
meat, white
pork
shellfish
shrimp
veal

ICE WINE (SWEET WHITE WINE MADE FROM GRAPES THAT HAVE BEEN NATURALLY FROZEN ON THE VINE THEN PICKED; PEAR, APRICOT, APPLE FLAVORS; VERY RICH; MADE IN AUSTRIA, GERMANY, CANADA, AND NEW YORK'S FINGER LAKES REGION; AKA EISWEIN)

apples and apple desserts
blueberries and blueberry desserts
cake
CHEESE, ESP. SOFT AND/OR BLUE (e.g., Stilton)
cheesecake
COOKIES (e.g., SHORT-BREAD)
CUSTARD-STYLE DESSERTS (e.g., crème brûlée)
DESSERTS, ESP. CREAMY AND/OR FRUITY

duck
foie gras
FRUIT, ESP. POACHED
FRUIT DESSERTS
LEMON DESSERTS
lime desserts
macadamia nuts
nuts and nut desserts
PEACHES AND PEACH DESSERTS
pork
pound cake
shortbread

AVOID
cheese, goat
chocolate desserts

JURANÇON (FRENCH WHITE WINE FROM THE SOUTH-WEST REGION, CAN BE DRY OR SWEET IN STYLE; VERY FRESH AND AROMATIC WHEN DRY, EXOTIC FRUIT AND HONEY AROMAS WHEN SWEET AND AGED)
cheese (e.g., Fourme d'Ambert, Roquefort), with sweet Jurançon
chicken, esp. roasted
fish, esp. salmon or trout, with dry Jurançon
foie gras, esp. duck, with sweet Jurançon
ham, esp. with melon
meat, with dry Jurançon

LAGER (TOP-FERMENTING BEER BREWED PRIMARILY FROM MALTED BARLEY, HOPS, AND WATER; LIGHT IN COLOR, HIGH IN CARBONATION WITH A MILD HOP FLAVOR)

IN GENERAL
Asian food
barbecue
Caribbean food

cheese, esp. Gouda and Jarlsberg
chicken
fish
French fries
fried food
Indian food
lighter dishes
meat, white
pizza
poached dishes, esp. with lighter-bodied lager
pork
poultry
salad
SPICY FOOD
steamed dishes, esp. with lighter-bodied lager
Thai food
turkey
veal

Lager, which has notes of orange peel, banana, and coriander, works well with spicy food — especially Thai. I recommend Spaaten from Germany, which is one of the lightest lagers I've ever tried. Lager does not work with Mexican food. It is much better with Asian, Indian, and Caribbean food.
  — CARLOS SOLIS, food and beverage director/chef, Sheraton Four Points/LAX (Los Angeles)

AMBER (TOP-FERMENTING, WITH MORE MALT THAN A LAGER; LIGHT TOASTED MALT WITH A GENTLE CREAMINESS)
beef
cheese
chicken, esp. fried, grilled, or roasted
ham
hamburgers
hot dogs

meat, esp. red
PIZZA
pork and pork chops
poultry, esp. roasted
sausage, esp. grilled
SPICY FOOD

AVOID
seafood, esp. delicate dishes

DARK (TOP-FERMENTING, WITH SWEETISH NOTES AND HINTS OF CHOCOLATE; MALT ACCENTS WITH LOW HOP BITTERNESS)
bacon
cheese
chicken, esp. roasted
Chinese food
corned beef
duck
fish, stronger
ham
meat, esp. red, roasted, and/or stewed
mushrooms
pastrami
pork
risotto, esp. mushroom
robust dishes
sandwiches
sauerkraut
sausage
spicy dishes
stews
sweet-and-sour dishes
venison

VIENNA (AUSTRIAN AMBER LAGER WITH A YEASTY AROMA)
chicken dishes, heavier (e.g., goulash, paprikash)
Mexican food
onions
pork dishes, esp. ribs
pretzels, esp. with mustard

AVOID
red meat

LAMBRUSCO (ITALIAN LIGHT-BODIED RED WINE FROM THE EMILIA-ROMAGNA REGION; STRAWBERRY, RASPBERRY, AND CHERRY FLAVORS WITH LIGHT SPARKLE AND CLEAN FINISH)

bacon
calzone
CHEESE, ESP. RICOTTA
ham
meat
pasta
pizza, esp. pepperoni
prosciutto
rabbit
SALUMI
sausage, esp. grilled
vinegar, balsamic

Lambrusco is a sommelier favorite. It is great at midnight, and it is refreshing during the summer. It's like red wine with panties!

— JOSEPH BASTIANICH, restaurateur and owner, Italian Wine Merchants (NYC)

LASSI (INDIAN SALTY OR SWEET YOGURT-BASED DRINK)

Indians do not know what a mango lassi is — it is a concoction of the West! I do love a mango lassi, though. In India, a lassi is plain yogurt with only a pinch of sugar, so that it is not cloying. I also love a salty lassi, which I find has more bounce to it. A South Indian lassi is made with chilled yogurt and a bloomed oil of curry leaves, mustard seed, red chile, cumin seed, and coconut. This goes perfectly with salmon or halibut with a South Indian coconut mint chutney. It gives you a spicy flavor with cooling yogurt, which provides great balance in the stomach for digestion. In India, we use no emulsifiers, corn syrup, pectin, or gelatin for our yogurt, so it is runnier. Here in the United States, I recommend using Greek yogurt or Ronnybrook Farms yogurt, because it is great and has nothing added. In India, lassi is drunk with street food like chat, poori, or okra, which is a perfect match.

— SUVIR SARAN, chef, Dévi (NYC)

LATE HARVEST WINE (MADE FROM GRAPES LEFT ON THE VINE LONGER THAN USUAL; VERY RIPE, SUGAR-FILLED GRAPES PRODUCE SWEET DESSERT WINES)

bread pudding
CHEESE, ESP. BLUE (e.g., Roquefort), GOAT, AND/OR SALTY
custard desserts (e.g., crème brûlée)
desserts
foie gras
FRUIT AND FRUIT DESSERTS
NUTS AND NUT DESSERTS
pound cake
shortbread

AVOID
chocolate and chocolate desserts, except with Late Harvest Zinfandel

I love Late Harvest German and Austrian wines with any kind of blue cheese.

— TRACI DES JARDINS, chef, Jardiniere (San Francisco)

LEMONADE

barbecue
Indian food
salads

LEMONADE

HERE IS CHEF CHARLEEN BADMAN'S POPULAR RECIPE FOR LEMONADE FROM ANNE ROSENZWEIG'S GREENWICH VILLAGE RESTAURANT INSIDE IN NEW YORK CITY

Serves 12

2 cups sugar

9 cups water

2 cups fresh-squeezed lemon juice

1/2 cup puree of strawberries, watermelon, or other favorite fruit (optional)

In a saucepan, heat sugar with two cups of water. Bring to a simmer for two minutes. Remove from heat and cool this simple syrup.

In large pitcher, mix lemon juice with remaining water. Add half of the simple syrup and taste.

If desired, add optional fruit puree at this time. Adjust the sweetness of the lemonade to your liking with the remaining simple syrup.

Pour over ice and garnish with a slice of lemon.

I love lemonade with rum and ginger syrup! For ginger syrup, I soak ginger in water, boil it until the ginger softens, puree it, and strain it. Then I add some sugar and cook it. You add that to fresh lemonade with rum. It is superb, and goes with most Indian food. Strawberry lemonade also works well with Indian street food. — SUVIR SARAN, chef, Dévi (NYC)

LILLET (FRENCH SWEET APERITIF WINE FROM BORDEAUX)
hors d'oeuvres
shellfish

People forget about aperitivos. *Lillet is a wine with orange and botanicals. It has a great color, and I like the way the slice of orange drapes over the ice cubes. It tastes great, it's inexpensive, and people are impressed when you order one. People think, "Lillet . . . I should know about that. I'll have one, too!"* — ROCCO DISPIRITO, chef

------

LOCOROTONDO
(ITALIAN WHITE WINE)
broccoli rabe

MÂCON, WHITE
(FRENCH WINE FROM BURGUNDY)
artichokes
calamari
charcuterie
cheese, esp. French goat cheese (chèvre)
French fries
gougères
ham
sausage
seafood, esp. stewed

MADEIRA (FORTIFIED WHITE WINE FROM THE ISLAND OF MADEIRA, SOUTHWEST OF PORTUGAL; FLAVORS OF CARAMEL WITH A WALNUT FINISH)
after dinner
almonds and almond desserts
apricots and apricot desserts
bananas and banana desserts
bread pudding
cake
caramel and caramel desserts
charcuterie, esp. smoked meats and, esp. with drier Madeira
CHEESE, ESP. BLUE (e.g., Roquefort) OR MILD (e.g., Taleggio)
CHOCOLATE, ESP. MILK, AND ESP. CHOCOLATE DESSERTS
coffee and coffee desserts
consommé
cookies
cream and creamy desserts
custards and custardy desserts (e.g., crème caramel, flan)
dates and date desserts
desserts
figs and fig desserts
fruitcake
hazelnuts and hazelnut desserts
marzipan
meat, served cold
mushrooms, esp. with drier Madeira
NUTS AND NUT DESSERTS
oxtails, esp. with drier Madeira
peaches and peach desserts
PECANS AND PECAN DESSERTS (e.g., pecan pie)
peppers, roasted red
praline
PUMPKIN AND PUMPKIN DESSERTS (e.g., pumpkin pie)
rich dishes
SOUP AND BROTH, ESP. WITH DRIER MADEIRA
tarte Tatin (caramelized apple tart)
walnuts and walnut desserts

Types of Madeira

Madeira's four styles, from lightest and driest, to darkest and sweetest:

1) Sercial, a light and dry aperitif

2) Verdelho, an aperitif

3) Bual, a dessert wine

4) Malmsey, the darkest, richest, and sweetest Madeira, and a dessert wine

*Madeira will last almost for-
ever, even after it is opened.
You can put a bottle of Madeira
on top of your refrigerator in
July and spend August in the
Hamptons, and it will still be
great when you get home. If you
splurged and spent two hundred
dollars on a really great bottle,
it's something you could go back
to ten or fifteen times — so if
you average that out, it is not a
lot of money to invest in your
own pleasure. Besides, who is
worth it more than you?*

— TIM KOPEC, wine director,
Veritas (NYC)

*Madeira is by far the best value
in the wine world, except for
sherry.*

— GREG HARRINGTON, MS

MADIRAN (FRENCH FULL-
BODIED RED WINE FROM THE
SOUTHWEST BLACK FRUIT,
SPICE, AND GRILLED BREAD
CHARACTERISTICS)

cassoulet
cheese, esp. blue
duck and duck confit
game, esp. roasted
lamb, esp. stewed
meat, esp. braised or stewed
short ribs, esp. braised
steak
stew

MALAGA (FORTIFIED WINE
FROM THE SPANISH REGION IN
ANDALUCIA, VERY SMALL
PRODUCTION; NUTTY AND
MEDIUM-DRY TO SMOKY AND
RAISINY SWEET)

milk chocolate and milk chocolate
   desserts

MALBEC (ARGENTINIAN
FULL-BODIED RED WINE; RICH
IN TANNINS WITH DRIED FRUIT,
BLACK CURRANTS, AND PLUM;
ALSO GROWN IN BORDEAUX
AND CAHORS)

bacon
barbecue
**BEEF, ESP. ROASTED OR
   STEWED**
cassoulet
chili
chipotles
empanadas
fajitas, esp. beef
ham
hamburgers
Indian food, esp. chicken, lamb
**LAMB, ESP. BARBECUED,
   BRAISED, OR ROASTED**
**MEAT, ESP. BARBECUED,
   BRAISED, OR GRILLED**
meat loaf
Mexican beef, lamb, or pork dishes
mushrooms
**pizza, esp. with mushrooms
   and/or sausage**
pork, esp. barbecued
prime rib
sausage
spicy dishes
STEAK, GRILLED
stew
veal

MARGARITA (COCKTAIL
OF TEQUILA, TRIPLE SEC OR
COINTREAU, AND FRESH LIME
JUICE OVER ICE; NAMED AFTER
THE WOMAN WHO CREATED
THE COCKTAIL)

MEXICAN FOOD
spicy food
tacos

*When I drink margaritas with
Mexican food, I will specifically ask the bartender to not*

---

*make them so sweet. It is better
for the food to have the higher
acid.*

— DAVID ROSENGARTEN,
editor in chief,
www.DavidRosengarten.com

MARGAUX (SEE MÉDOC)

MARSALA (ITALIAN
FORTIFIED DESSERT WINE;
DARK AMBER IN COLOR, WITH A
RICH, SMOKY FLAVOR; VARIES
FROM DRY TO SWEET)

anchovies, esp. with dry Marsala
biscotti, esp. with sweet Marsala
cake
**CHEESE, ESP. GOAT,
   PECORINO, OR RICOTTA,
   AND ESP. WITH DRY
   MARSALA**
chocolate
desserts
meat, smoked
nuts
olives, esp. with dry Marsala
seafood stew, tomato-based
zabaglione

*The year I lived in Sicily, I drank
Marsala with everything from
savory foods to chocolate. It
changed my perspective. I had a
tomato-based seafood stew with
capers and pine nuts that was
amazing with it. It is funny because
in Italy, this so normal. The revelation was how natural it was. It's
not jarring — there is power in the
harmony and seamlessness of com-
bining these seemingly odd flavors.
That is what wins you over. It is
not the sledgehammer on the head;
it is the normality of it.*

— JOSEPH BASTIANICH,
restaurateur and owner,
Italian Wine Merchants (NYC)

MARSANNE (FRENCH WHITE GRAPE PRODUCING WINE WITH VERY STRONG ALCOHOL CONTENT; FLAVORS OF PLUM, CARAMEL, AND PINEAPPLE)
cheese
chicken
curries
ham
lobster, esp. boiled or steamed
pâté
pork
risotto, esp. sweeter (e.g., pumpkin, squash)
seafood
smoked fish
vegetable dishes

MAURY (FRENCH FORTIFIED RED WINE FROM THE LANGUEDOC-ROUSSILLON REGION; FRUITY, WITH BLACK PLUM, BLACK TRUFFLE AND BLACKBERRY CHARACTERISTICS; SEE ALSO RECOMMENDATIONS FOR BANYULS)
berries
cheese, blue (e.g., Roquefort)
cherries
chocolate and chocolate desserts
coffee and coffee-flavored desserts
fruit, dried
nuts

MÉDOC (AREA IN BORDEAUX PRODUCING MEDIUM- TO FULL-BODIED RED WINE OF BLACK PURPLE HUE, BIG CHEWY TANNINS, AND RICH PLUMMY AROMAS)
duck
game, esp. roasted
lamb, esp. grilled or roasted
liver

meat, red, esp. roasted
steak
stew

MERCUREY BLANC (FRENCH FULL-BODIED WHITE WINE FROM BURGUNDY; DRY AND REFRESHING, CLEAN AND BRIGHT WITH CITRUS AND CREAM)
lobster, esp. boiled or steamed
salmon, esp. served cold
swordfish, esp. baked or roasted

MERITAGE (AMERICAN RED WINE MADE IN THE STYLE OF BORDEAUX; BLENDING OF CABERNET SAUVIGNON, MERLOT, CABERNET FRANC, MALBEC, AND PETIT VERDOT)
beef
duck
lamb
salmon, esp. grilled
steak

MERLOT (MEDIUM-BODIED RED WINE WITH HINTS OF BERRY, PLUM, AND CURRANT; FULL-FLAVORED)
BEEF, ESP. GRILLED OR ROASTED (e.g., pot roast, prime rib)
braised dishes
casseroles, esp. with vegetables
charcuterie
CHEESE, ESP. BLUE AND OTHER FULL-FLAVORED CHEESE (e.g., Camembert, Cheddar, dry Jack, Gorgonzola, Gouda, Jarlsberg, Parmesan)
CHICKEN, ESP. BRAISED, GRILLED, OR ROASTED
chili
cranberries
currants

DUCK, ESP. GRILLED OR ROASTED
eggplant
fish, esp. fatty
fruit and fruit sauces
game
game birds, with lighter-bodied Merlots
garlic
goose, esp. roasted
grilled food
hamburgers
herbs
LAMB AND LAMB CHOPS, ESP. GRILLED, ROASTED, OR STEWED
liver, calf's, with onions
MEAT, RED, ESP. GRILLED
meat loaf
MUSHROOMS, ESP. GRILLED
mustard, esp. Dijon
onions and onion soup
oregano
pasta, esp. with meat and/or tomato sauce
pepper, black
peppers, bell
pizza
PORK, ESP. LOIN, AND ESP. GRILLED OR ROASTED
poultry
quail
rabbit
rich dishes
risotto, esp. with mushrooms
rosemary
salmon
sandwiches
sausage
sautéed dishes
squab
STEAK, ESP. FILET MIGNON AND/OR GRILLED
stew, esp. with beef and/or vegetables
swordfish
tarragon
thyme
tomatoes and tomato sauce
tuna

TURKEY, ESP. ROASTED
VEAL AND VEAL CHOPS
venison
walnuts

Where to find great Merlot:
The two best Merlots are from
France and Italy. The Italian
ones are tremendous! When
Merlot is planted in the right
area of Napa, it makes wonder-
ful wines. You want some that
are from hillside plantings like
Howell Mountain Vineyards.
— JEAN-LUC LE DÛ,
Le Dû's Wines (NYC)

California Merlot is great with
lamb chops and chicken.
— SUVIR SARAN, chef, Dévi
(NYC)

Merlot is a simple wine, so it
should be paired with simple
food — like a simple pasta or
pizza.
— STEVE BECKTA, owner,
Beckta Dining & Wine (Ottawa)

MEURSAULT (FRENCH
MEDIUM- TO FULL-BODIED
WHITE WINE FROM BURGUNDY)
cheese, esp. Roquefort
fish, esp. cod, turbot
lobster
mushrooms
risotto, esp. with seafood
seafood
shrimp
veal

MOJITOS (COCKTAIL MADE
FROM RUM, LIME JUICE, SUGAR,
AND MINT)
Caribbean food

fish, esp. spicy
spicy food

MONASTRELL (THICK-
SKINNED GRAPE THAT MAKES
SPANISH MEDIUM- TO FULL-
BODIED RED WINE; LOTS OF
TANNIN, BLACKBERRY, SPICE,
PEPPER, AND LEATHER
NUANCES; SEE ALSO
MOURVÈDRE)
cheese, esp. Manchego
fish, esp. grilled
frog legs
game
hamburgers, esp. grilled
lamb, esp. grilled or roasted
MEAT, ESP. RED AND ESP.
    GRILLED OR STEWED
mushrooms
olives
oxtails
pâté
pork
poultry, esp. grilled
smoked or cured meat
steak, esp. grilled
STEW, ESP. WITH MEAT
    AND/OR VEGETABLES
venison

MONTEPULCIANO
D'ABRUZZO (ITALIAN
MEDIUM- TO FULL-BODIED RED
WINE; RUBY-RED VIOLET HUE,
BLACK CHERRY AND LICORICE
AROMAS, CHEWY TANNINS, AND
BALANCED ACIDITY)
chicken, esp. grilled or roasted
LAMB, ESP. BRAISED,
    GRILLED, ROASTED, OR
    STEWED
MEAT, ESP. GRILLED OR
    ROASTED
mushrooms, esp. grilled
octopus, esp. stewed with toma-
    toes

PASTA, ESP. WITH MEAT,
    MUSHROOM, AND/OR
    TOMATO SAUCE
peperoncino
pizza, esp. with mushrooms
pork, esp. grilled or roasted
poultry
risotto, esp. mushroom
sausage
soup, esp. full-bodied
spiced dishes
steak, esp. grilled
stews
veal chops, esp. grilled or roasted

MONTRACHET (SEE
BURGUNDY, WHITE)

MOSCATO D'ASTI
(ITALIAN SWEET SEMI-
SPARKLING WHITE WINE FROM
THE PIEDMONT REGION)
apples and apple desserts
berries and berry desserts
biscotti
brunch
cake
citrus-flavored desserts (e.g.,
    lemon, orange)
cookies
DESSERTS, ESP. FRUIT
FRUIT, ESP. FRESH, SUM-
    MER, AND/OR SALAD
ginger and ginger-flavored
    desserts
ice cream
light, airy desserts (e.g., mousses,
    soufflés)
mascarpone and mascarpone
    desserts
meringues
panettone
peaches and peach desserts
raspberries and raspberry desserts
sorbet, esp. fruit

Moscato d'Asti is my favorite all-purpose sweet wine. It's overtly sweet — sweeter than Asti [Spumante] — and low in alcohol. It will even coexist with chocolate. It's irresistible!

— MADELINE TRIFFON, MS, director of wine, Matt Prentice Restaurant Group (Detroit)

MOSCHOFILERO

(GREEK WHITE WINE; DRY, CITRUSY)

artichokes

cheese, goat

chicken

fish (e.g., halibut, swordfish, tuna)

mussels

peppers, roasted

sardines

seafood

MOURVÈDRE (PRIMARY

GRAPE IN BANDOL RED AND ROSÉ WINES; FRENCH GRAPE PRODUCES MEDIUM- TO FULL-BODIED RED WINE; SEE ALSO BANDOL AND MONASTRELL)

liver, calf's

meat, red

sausage

wild boar

MÜLLER-THURGAU

(GERMAN LIGHT-BODIED WHITE WINE; DESCRIBED AS A CROSS BETWEEN RIESLING AND SYLVANER)

asparagus

fish, e.g., salmon, trout

light dishes

meat

pork

salad

salty dishes

scallops

seafood

shrimp

smoked food

spicy dishes

MUSCADET (FRENCH

LIGHT-BODIED WHITE WINE FROM THE LOIRE VALLEY; ITS WHITE GRAPE HAS CITRUS, GREEN APPLE, AND SALT CHARACTERISTICS; AKA MELON DE BOURGOGNE)

aperitif

clams

fish (e.g., bass)

***MUSSELS**

***OYSTERS**

salad

sardines

seafood, esp. raw

SHELLFISH, ESP. RAW

shrimp

A Muscadet by itself has hardly any flavor; it is just crisp and lemony. With a salad, the acid in the vinaigrette cancels the acid in the wine, and all the fruit flavors come out. It is a beautiful thing!

— DAVID ROSENGARTEN, editor in chief, www.DavidRosengarten.com

MUSCADINE (NATIVE

AMERICAN GRAPE GROWN IN THE SOUTHERN UNITED STATES)

cheese, goat

wreckfish

MUSCAT (FRAGRANT

DESSERT WINE OF SPICE AND PEACH; SLIGHTLY UNCTUOUS, COMPLEX, AND LIQUEUR-LIKE WITH HINTS OF CANDIED ORANGE PEEL)

IN GENERAL

berries, esp. with lighter-bodied
Muscat
biscotti
cake
caramel and caramel desserts
**cheese, esp. blue, aged Cheddar,
Muenster, and/or soft-ripened**
**chocolate, esp. dark, and choco-
late desserts**
cream and creamy desserts
custards
desserts, esp. light and/or mild
**FRUIT, FRESH OR DRIED,
AND FRUIT DESSERTS**
gingerbread
honey
ice cream
melon, esp. with lighter-bodied
Muscat
nut desserts
panna cotta
pears, esp. poached and/or ripe
pecan pie
soufflés
very creamy desserts

DE BEAUMES DE VENISE
(FRENCH FULL-BODIED
FORTIFIED WHITE DESSERT
WINE FROM THE RHÔNE
REGION)
**CARAMEL AND CARAMEL
DESSERTS**
cheese, blue
**CHOCOLATE AND CHOCO-
LATE DESSERTS**
cookies
crème brûlée
desserts
fruit and fruit desserts
ice cream, esp. vanilla
lemon and lemon desserts
orange and orange desserts
pastries
rhubarb and rhubarb desserts
toffee and toffee desserts

BLACK (RED GRAPE WITH
CHOCOLATE, ROSE, AND
ORANGE
CHARACTERISTICS; AKA
MUSCAT HAMBURG)

**BERRIES AND BERRY
DESSERTS**
cheese, esp. blue
cherries and cherry desserts
CHOCOLATE, ESP. DARK
cream
foie gras
fruit
ice cream, vanilla
orange and orange desserts
peaches and pears, esp. poached
vanilla
LATE HARVEST (SWEET
DESSERT WINE WITH
CARAMEL, DRIED PEAR,
AND APPLE AROMAS,
BALANCED WITH ACIDITY)
cheese
foie gras
LIQUEUR (AUSTRALIAN
LIQUEUR WITH PERFUME
OF ORANGE, RAISINS, AND
HONEY)
chocolate and chocolate desserts
cream and cream desserts
desserts
figs and fig desserts
ice cream
mocha and mocha desserts
nuts and nut desserts
ORANGE (WHITE GRAPE
ORIGINATING IN ITALY;
CONCENTRATED HONEY,
ORANGE BLOSSOM NOSE,
CRISP ACIDITY)
caramel and caramel desserts
cheese, blue
chocolate and chocolate desserts
orange and other citrus desserts
AVOID
certain milk chocolate desserts, as
muscat may overwhelm them

MUSIGNY (FRENCH
MEDIUM- TO FULL-BODIED RED
WINE)
game birds, roasted
wild mushrooms (e.g., cepes or
morels)

NAVARRA (AREA IN
NORTHERN SPAIN PRODUCING
MEDIUM-BODIED RED WINE
WITH CHERRY, CEDAR, AND
CIGAR AROMAS AND SPICY
TANNINS)
cheese, esp. soft
Cornish game hens
fish, esp. grilled
lamb
meat, esp. grilled
pork

NEBBIOLO (ITALIAN
MEDIUM-BODIED WINE FROM
GRAPES GROWN IN THE
PIEDMONT AREA; DOMINANT
GRAPE IN BARBARESCO AND
BAROLO; WITH MUSHROOM,
VIOLET, AND BLACK CURRANT
CHARACTERISTICS; SEE ALSO
BARBARESCO AND BAROLO)
beef, esp. unsalted tenderloin
**CHEESE AND CHEESE FON-
DUTA**
chicken
game
lamb
**MEAT, ESP. RED AND
ROASTED**
mushrooms
offal
pasta, esp. with meat sauce
pork
veal

*Nebbiolo is the most tannic
grape in the world! Try it by
itself, and a young, tannic red
wine is just mean. But take a
bite of unsalted beef tenderloin,
then go back to the wine.
Trumpets will blare!*
— MADELINE TRIFFON, MS,
director of wine, Matt Prentice
Restaurant Group (Detroit)

NEGROAMARO
(ITALIAN MEDIUM-BODIED RED WINE FROM PUGLIA)

cheese, esp. aged
game
liver
MEAT, RED, ESP. ROASTED
pasta

NERO D'AVOLA
(ITALIAN LOW-ACID MEDIUM-TO FULL-BODIED RED WINE FROM SICILY)

arancini (rice croquettes)
beef, esp. roasted
lamb, esp. roasted
liver
meat, red, and meatballs
pasta, esp. baked
pork ribs, esp. barbecued
swordfish, esp. with capers

ORVIETO (ITALIAN LIGHT-TO MEDIUM-BODIED WHITE WINE FROM THE UMBRIA REGION)

antipasto
calamari, esp. fried
cheese, goat
fish, esp. light or poached dishes
lobster
pasta, esp. lighter ones (e.g., with butter, tomatoes, and/or truffles)
pizza, esp. lighter ones
prosciutto, esp. with melon
risotto
salad
seafood
sole, esp. poached

PAUILLAC (FRENCH FULL-BODIED RED WINE FROM BORDEAUX)
beef
cheese

game, esp. roasted
lamb, esp. roasted
meat, esp. roasted
mushrooms

PETITE SIRAH
(NEW WORLD FULL-BODIED RED WINE)

barbecue
beef
charcuterie
CHEESE
chicken
GAME
grilled dishes
hamburgers
lamb, esp. braised
meat, red
Mexican food
oxtails
pork
sauce, rich and/or robust
sausage
steak, esp. grilled
stew

PICOLIT (ITALIAN DESSERT WINE MADE FROM DRIED GRAPES, FROM THE FRIULI REGION)
berries
biscotti
cake, esp. with nuts
cheese, esp. strongly flavored (e.g., Brie, gorgonzola)
desserts, simple and/or creamy
foie gras
fruit
pâté

PILSNER (DRY BEER WITH PRONOUNCED HOPPY TASTE, FROM THE CZECH REPUBLIC)
Asian food, esp. spicier
caviar
cheese, esp. lighter
chicken

chiles
clams
corned beef
duck
fatty food and dishes
FISH, ESP. FRIED
fried food
fruit
ham and cheese sandwich, esp. grilled
hamburgers
Indian food
lighter dishes
meat, grilled
Mexican and Tex-Mex food
MUSSELS
pastrami
PIZZA
pork
poultry
prosciutto
salads
salmon, esp. smoked
salsa
SAUSAGE
seafood
shellfish (e.g., crab, lobster, shrimp)
SPICY DISHES
tacos
Thai food
trout, esp. smoked
veal
Vietnamese food

AVOID
delicate fish dishes
very hearty dishes

Real German or Czech pilsners work well with so many different foods because they are dry, bitter, and cut right through to let the food do the talking.
— GARRETT OLIVER, brewmaster, Brooklyn Brewery

PINOTAGE (SOUTH AFRICAN FULL-BODIED RED WINE)

barbecued ribs
cheese, Cheddar
cheese, goat
game (e.g., venison) and game birds (e.g., duck, quail), esp. roasted
hamburgers
liver
pizza
stew

PINOT BIANCO (ITALIAN LIGHT- TO MEDIUM-BODIED WHITE WINE)

almonds
crab
fish
shrimp, esp. sautéed
sole
squid, esp. grilled

PINOT BLANC (FRENCH MEDIUM-BODIED WHITE WINE, ESP. ALSATIAN AND CALIFORNIA; SIMILAR TO CHARDONNAY)

Asian food
baked foods
butter sauces
catfish, esp. sautéed
cheese
CHICKEN, ESP. ROASTED OR AS A SALAD
chives
clams
crab
egg dishes, (e.g., omelets, quiche)
fish, esp. white, and esp. light baked or grilled dishes
flounder, esp. sautéed
garlic
grilled food
halibut, esp. baked
ham
leeks
lemon
mushrooms
onions
oysters
parsley
pasta, esp. simple
pâté
pork

poultry
rabbit
salad, esp. green or chicken
SALMON
sausage
sautéed food
SCALLOPS
seafood
shellfish
shrimp and prawns
smoked fish
sole
spicy food
swordfish, esp. grilled
Thai food, esp. curries
trout
tuna, esp. grilled
TURKEY, ESP. ROASTED
veal
VEGETABLE DISHE

PINOT GRIGIO / PINOT GRIS (NORTHERN ITALIAN LIGHT- TO MEDIUM-BODIED WHITE WINE BEST DRUNK YOUNG; PINOT GRIS, FROM THE WESTERN UNITED STATES, IS SIMILAR BUT FULLER-BODIED; ALSATIAN PINOT GRIS IS THE FULLEST-BODIED OF ALL AND ALSO KNOWN AS TOKAY D'ALSACE)

acidic food
ANTIPASTO
appetizers
apples, esp. tart
arctic char
Asian-spiced food
bacon
basil
calamari, fried
charcuterie (e.g., bresaola, speck)
CHEESE, ESP. GOAT, SHEEP'S MILK, OR SMOKED
cheese, mild (e.g., fontina, mozzarella, Muenster, ricotta)
CHICKEN, ESP. FRIED, GRILLED, POACHED, ROASTED, OR SAUTÉED
chives

choucroute

clams

crab

cream sauce, light

duck

fennel

FISH, ESP. WHITE, AND ESP. BAKED, GRILLED, OR POACHED

fritto misto (fried vegetables and fish)

fruits, fresh, and fruit salsa and sauce

game and game birds

garlic

ginger

gnocchi

grilled food

halibut

ham

herbs

lemon, esp. as a sauce

lettuce

light dishes

lobster

meat, white

melon

MUSSELS

mustard

nuts, esp. roasted hazelnuts

olive oil

omeletes, esp. vegetable

onions, esp. cooked (e.g., onion tart)

oranges

oysters

PASTA, ESP. WITH SEAFOOD OR SHELLFISH

pâté

pears

peas

pesto

picnics

poached dishes

PORK, ESP. ROASTED

poultry

prosciutto

quail

rabbit

richer, fattier dishes

SALAD

salami

SALMON

sandwiches

sardines, esp. grilled

sausage

sautéed dishes

SCALLOPS

sea bass

SEAFOOD DISHES, ESP. VERY LIGHT

SHELLFISH

shrimp

smoked cheese, fish (e.g., salmon, trout), and meat

sole

spicy food, mildly

steamed dishes

swordfish, esp. grilled

tarragon

thyme

tomatoes and tomato sauces

trout

tuna, esp. grilled

turkey

veal, esp. lighter dishes

vegetables

LATE HARVEST (FRENCH FULL-BODIED DESSERT WINE FROM ALSACE)

desserts with fruit and/or nuts

PINOT NOIR (FRENCH, CALIFORNIAN, AND OREGONIAN LIGHT- TO FULL-BODIED FRUITY RED WINE)

bacon

basil

BEEF, ESP. LEAN AND/OR ROASTED, AND ESP. WITH FULL-BODIED PINOT NOIR

beets

charcuterie

cheeses, esp. goat (aged), mild, and/or soft (e.g., Brie, Camembert, Chaumes, feta, Gruyère, Swiss, Vacherin)

cherries, esp. tart

CHICKEN, ESP. BRAISED, POACHED, OR ROASTED

cinnamon

cloves

*DUCK, ESP. ROASTED**

earthy flavored food and dishes

eggplant

enchiladas

fennel and fennel seed

fish

foie gras

French food

game, esp. roasted esp. with full-bodied Pinot Noir

game birds, esp. roasted

ginger

greens, esp. braised or sautéed, and esp. with bacon

grilled meat and other food

ham, esp. baked

herbs and herb-based sauces

jambalaya

kidneys

LAMB

lasagna

liver

meat, esp. lighter, red, grilled, roasted, and/or served cold

MUSHROOMS AND MUSH-ROOM SAUCE

onions

oregano

partridge, esp. roasted

pasta, esp. heartier pasta and/or with tomato and/or vegetable sauce

pepper, black

pesto

pheasant, esp. roasted

PORK, ESP. LOIN

prunes

poultry, esp. roasted

quail, esp. grilled or roasted

rabbit

risotto, esp. with mushrooms

roasts, esp. beef, and esp. with full-bodied Pinot Noir

*SALMON, ESP. BROILED, PAN-ROASTED, POACHED, OR GRILLED**

sausages, esp. grilled

sautéed dishes

scallops

seafood
**smoked meat and other food
(but not fish)**
soy sauce
spinach pie
squab, esp. grilled or roasted
stew, esp. beef
swordfish
tarragon
thyme
tomatoes and tomato sauces
truffles, white, and truffle oil
**TUNA, ESP. AHI AND/OR
GRILLED**
turkey, esp. roasted
VEAL, ESP. CHOPS
vegetables, in general, but esp.
  root
vegetarian dishes
venison, esp. with full-bodied
  Pinot Noir

AVOID
fruit and fruit-based dishes or
  sauces

smoked fish
spicy dishes
strongly flavored dishes
sweet dishes

TIP: How can you tell whether a
Pinot Noir is light- or full-
bodied? Don't just check out the
alcohol level — check out the
price. Less expensive American
Pinots tend to be lighter-bodied,
while more expensive Pinots tend
to be fuller-bodied.

*Where to find great Pinot Noir:
The best Pinot Noir is still
made in Burgundy. Its finesse
among alcohol, fruit, and minerality is amazing. It is the
standard to which Pinot is
measured. Number two would
be from the Sonoma Coast in
California, followed by Central
New Zealand (Otago). I would
also note the Pinots coming*

*from Italy, Oregon and the
Central Coast of California.*
— JEAN-LUC LE DÛ,
Le Dû's Wines (NYC)

*I love goat's milk cheeses with
Pinot Noir. They are great com-
panions. The young fresh goat
milk cheese is great for younger,
tangier wines, while aged goat
cheese goes with richer, layered
wine. Anything with mush-
rooms, including mushroom
pizza, works with Pinot Noir.*
— BRIAN DUNCAN,
wine director, Bin 36 (Chicago)

POMMARD (FRENCH RED
WINE FROM BURGUNDY)
beef, esp. grilled
charcuterie
lamb
pork
veal

PORT (PORTUGUESE
FORTIFIED SWEET WINE FROM
OPORTO, USUALLY RED)

IN GENERAL
apples
caramel
**CHEESE, BLUE (e.g.,
  Gorgonzola, Roquefort,
  *STILTON)**
cherry desserts
***CHOCOLATE, ESP. BITTER-
  SWEET, DARK, AND/OR
  CHOCOLATE DESSERTS**
coffee and coffee-flavored
  desserts
desserts
meat, esp. red and/or smoked
nuts and nut desserts
peaches, poached
pears, esp. poached
raspberries and raspberry desserts
walnuts

RUBY (PORTUGUESE YOUNG, RED, NONVINTAGE PORT)

berries and berry desserts

cheese, blue

cherries and cherry desserts

TAWNY (NONVINTAGE RED PORT AGED IN WOOD)

almonds and almond desserts

apples and apple desserts

cake

caramel and caramel desserts

cheese, esp. aged (e.g., Cheddar, Pecorino) with aged port

*CHOCOLATE, ESP. DARK, BITTERSWEET, AND CHOCOLATE DESSERTS

dates

foie gras

FRUIT, DRIED, AND DRIED FRUIT DESSERTS

ice cream, esp. vanilla

NUTS AND NUT DESSERTS

pear and pear desserts

pumpkin pie

walnuts and walnut desserts

VINTAGE (A BLEND OF RED PORT GRAPES FROM A YEAR DECLARED A VINTAGE YEAR)

almonds

cheese, esp. blue, Cheddar, Forme d'Ambert, Roquefort, ***STILTON**

CHOCOLATE AND CHOCOLATE DESSERTS

walnuts and walnut bread

PORTER (BRITISH DARK, SWEET ALE; SEE ALSO RECOMMENDATIONS FOR STOUT)

barbecue

braised dishes

Cajun food

cheese, esp. blue and Cheddar

chocolate

fish, fried

ham

hamburgers

meat

mushrooms

OYSTERS

rosemary

salmon

shrimp, grilled

steak

stew

Tex-Mex food (e.g., burritos)

POUILLY-FUISSÉ
(FRENCH FULL-BODIED WHITE WINE FROM BURGUNDY)

cheese, esp. fresh goat or Pecorino

chicken

fish, esp. with butter or cream sauce

ham, esp. baked

pasta

prosciutto

quiche

salmon

scallops

shellfish

smoked fish

veal

vegetables

POUILLY-FUMÉ
(FRENCH DRY MEDIUM-BODIED WHITE WINE FROM THE LOIRE VALLEY)

appetizers

asparagus

CHEESE, GOAT

CHICKEN, ESP. CREAMY DISHES

crab

crayfish

fish

ham

lobster, esp. grilled

mussels

salmon

SALMON, SMOKED

seafood

shellfish

shrimp, grilled

trout

turbot

veal, esp. with cream sauce

PRIMITIVO (ITALIAN FULL-BODIED RED WINE FROM PUGLIA; SIMILAR TO AMERICAN ZINFANDEL)

cheese, esp. strong

meat, esp. grilled

PASTA, ESP. WITH MEAT AND/OR SPICY SAUCE

poultry, esp. grilled

sausage

vegetable dishes, esp. spicy

PRIORAT (SPANISH FULL-BODIED RED WINE FROM CATALONIA)

beef, esp. braised

cassoulet

cheese, Manchego

duck and duck confit

game and game birds

lamb

meat

paella, esp. made with fideo noodles instead of rice

rabbit

stew

swordfish, esp. grilled

Priorato is very hot right now, with lots of people coming in and planting new vineyards. However, its older winemakers are still the best — their vines go down thirty feet through rocky soil to find nourishment. These are intense, not bashful, wines. Paella made with fideo noodles instead of rice is what they make in this region. You could make the dish with game, duck, quail, or rabbit. At Solera [in New York City], we serve cazuelas of duck confit, snails, and aïoli, which would be fantastic with this wine. — RON MILLER, maître d'hotel, Solera (NYC)

PROSECCO (ITALIAN LIGHT-BODIED SPARKLING WINE FROM VENETO)

WHITE
almonds
appetizers
asparagus
Chinese food
nuts
prosciutto
salad
salmon, smoked
shrimp, esp. chilled
sushi

ROSÉ
barbecue
charcuterie
picnics
salad
sandwiches

PULIGNY-MONTRACHET (FRENCH FULL-BODIED DRY WHITE WINE FROM BURGUNDY; SEE ALSO BURGUNDY, WHITE)

almonds
cheese, esp. Epoisses, goat, Vacherin
chicken, esp. roasted
cod, esp. sautéed
crab
cream sauce
ham
LOBSTER
monkfish
risotto, esp. with truffles
scallops
SHRIMP, PRAWNS, AND LANGOUSTINES
sole
turbot
veal, esp. in a cream sauce

QUARTS DE CHAUME (FRENCH SWEET WHITE DESSERT WINE MADE WITH DRIED GRAPES FROM THE LOIRE VALLEY)

apple desserts, esp. tarte Tatin
banana desserts
fruit desserts

Quarts de Chaume is not as sweet or as syrupy as Sauternes, and very elegant. — ERIC RENAUD, sommelier, Bern's Steak House (Tampa)

RECIOTO (ITALIAN SWEET RED WINE MADE WITH DRIED GRAPES FROM THE VENETO REGION)

cake
CHEESE, ESP. BLUE (e.g., Roquefort, Stilton), CREAMY (e.g., Epoisses), OR SALTY (e.g., Parmesan, Pecorino)
chocolate, esp. dark, and chocolate desserts
cookies
creamy desserts
fruit and fruit desserts
nuts, esp. pecans, and nut desserts

RETSINA (GREEK STRONG RED OR WHITE WINE, WITH PINE RESIN ADDED DURING FERMENTATION)

Greek food
dill
eggplant
cheese, feta
hummus
olives, esp. Greek
pungent food
spinach and spinach pie
taramasalata

RHÔNE

RED (FRENCH, MEDIUM- TO FULL-BODIED)
beef, esp. stewed
beef cheeks
cassoulet
chicken, esp. barbecued
DUCK, ESP. ROASTED
game and game birds
goose
kidneys
LAMB, ROASTED
liver, esp. calf's
MEAT, ESP. ROASTED, SMOKED, OR STEWED
Mexican food, esp. meaty and/or spicy
mushrooms
short ribs, braised
squab
steak
STEW, ESP. BEEF AND/OR VEGETABLE
tuna, esp. grilled
vegetables, esp. root
venison

The meatiness in Rhône reds likes lamb. — MADELINE TRIFFON, MS, director of wine, Matt Prentice Restaurant Group (Detroit)

WHITE (FRENCH, FULL-BODIED WINE FROM THE NORTHERN RHÔNE; E.G., VIOGNIER)

beans, white
bouillabaisse
cheese, esp. Gruyère or Port Salut
Cornish game hens, esp. roasted
crab
curries
custards, savory, esp. with nutmeg
fish, esp. white
pork
poultry
seafood

RIBEIRO (SPANISH LIGHT-BODIED WHITE WINE)
ceviche
fish, grilled
lobster
shellfish

The wines here show a little more minerality and are dry. Despite the fact that this area is away from the coast, shellfish is still the pairing. Any simple grilled fish works, especially lobster. The other dish that is beautiful with this wine is ceviche. The less adornment on the fish preparation, the better.

— RON MILLER, maître d'hotel, Solera (NYC)

RIBERA DEL DUERO (SPANISH FULL-BODED RED WINE)
beef, esp. grilled or roasted
cheese esp. aged or creamy
game, esp. grilled or roasted
LAMB AND LAMB CHOPS, ESP. ROASTED
meat, esp. grilled or roasted
pork
sausage
short ribs
spicy food
steak
stews
vegetables, root, esp. roasted

Ribera del Duero is a big, extracted, intense style of wine. You will find traditional styles that are lean and hard, as well as newer styles with more fruit in the international style. Game is very popular in this region, but lamb chops are best for this wine. One of the best food experiences in my life was having baby lamb chops grilled over vine trimmings with olive oil and salt in this region.

— RON MILLER, maître d'hotel, Solera (New York City)

RIESLING (GERMAN AND ALSATIAN LIGHT-BODIED WHITE WINE WITH VARYING DEGREES OF SWEETNESS; SLIGHTLY SWEET WITH FRUIT)

IN GENERAL
appetizers
APPLES AND APPLE DESSERTS
ASIAN FOOD
asparagus, served cold, esp. with Alsatian Riesling
bacon
beets, roasted
Cajun food
ceviche
charcuterie, esp. with Alsatian Riesling
CHEESE, ESP. BLUE, SOFT, AND/OR TRIPLE CRÈME (e.g., Brie)
CHICKEN, ESP. POACHED OR LIGHTLY SAUTÉED
Chinese food, esp. spicier dishes with German Riesling
choucroute, esp. with Alsatian Riesling
cilantro
coconut
corn

crabs, including soft-shell crabs

Creole food

CURRIES, MILDER

delicate dishes

DUCK, ESP. ROASTED, AND ESP. WITH OFF-DRY TO SWEET RIESLING (ESP. AUSTRIAN)

FISH, ESP. POACHED, LIGHTLY SAUTÉED, OR WITH CREAM SAUCE

foie gras, esp. with sweeter Riesling

FRUIT, ESP. SUMMER (e.g., cherries, melon, peaches), AND FRUIT SALAD, SALSA, AND SAUCE

ginger

goose, esp. with off-dry to sweet Riesling

halibut, esp. sautéed

HAM, ESP. BAKED

hamachi, esp. light preparation (e.g., as carpaccio)

honey

Indian food

lemongrass

lighter dishes

lime, esp. with drier Riesling

lobster, esp. poached

mango and mango chutney/salsa

meat

mussels

nutmeg

onions, esp. sweet (e.g., in soups or tarts)

orange

oysters, esp. baked

pâté, esp. with sweeter Riesling

peaches and peach desserts

peanuts

peppers, bell or chile

picnics, esp. with dry German Riesling

poached dishes

PORK, ESP. ROASTED, SMOKED, STEWED, AND/OR WITH FRUITY SAUCE

poultry, esp. with off-dry Riesling

prosciutto

rabbit

Riesling is the greatest wine varietal.

— ALAN MURRAY, MS, wine director, Masa's (San Francisco)

Where to find great Riesling: Number one would be Germany followed by Alsace and Australia.

— JEAN-LUC LE DÛ, Le Dû's Wines (NYC)

Spätlese and Auslese Rieslings go with light crab dishes, shrimp, and many Asian dishes. Goat cheeses are wonderful with them, too, because of the mineral element.

— JEAN-LUC DÛ, Le Dû's Wines (New York)

German Rieslings are generally lighter and lower in alcohol, with more floral citrus notes about them. Alsatian wines are generally bigger, richer, and driven by much more fruit as well as minerality. Then I think straddling right between them are the Austrian Rieslings, which have mind-blowing acidity. The great Austrian Rieslings are grown on primary rock, and that stuff just shines through the wines. Because these are vital differences, I'd want to know what someone was having for dinner to be able to recommend one. Do they just want to have an aperitif at five o'clock? German Mosel Riesling, with its low 8-percent alcohol, is perfect — like soda pop. If they want something more substantial to go with a first course dish, I'd probably recommend an Austrian Riesling. Then with a game entrée, I'd probably recommend an Alsatian Riesling with a little bit of age on it.

— PAUL GRIECO, general manager, Hearth (NYC)

Riesling doesn't have to just be served with light dishes and seafood. The sweeter they are, the more they can handle caramelization [often a result of roasting] and sweet dishes.

— TIM KOPEC, wine director, Veritas (NYC)

Riesling is the only grape worth talking about in Germany. German wines tend to be lighter (i.e., with lower alcohol), but with more residual sugar than Alsatian wines.

— DANIEL JOHNNES, beverage director, Daniel (NYC)

raw dishes

red snapper, esp. grilled

SALAD, ESP. GREEN, FRUIT, AND/OR SEAFOOD

SALMON, ESP. POACHED, AND ESP. WITH DRY RIESLING

SALMON, SMOKED

sausage

sautéed dishes

SCALLOPS, ESP. AS TARTARE, SAUTÉED, OR SEARED

SEAFOOD DISHES, LIGHT

SHELLFISH, ESP. WITH DRY RIESLING

shrimp

smoked and cured food (e.g., fish and meat) esp. with dry German Kabinett

sole

SPICY (MODERATELY) DISHES

steamed dishes

stir-fried dishes

sushi, esp. with off-dry German Riesling

THAI FOOD, ESP. WITH GERMAN RIESLING

TROUT, ESP. SAUTÉED

trout, smoked

tuna, esp. as tartare

turkey, esp. roasted

vegetables, esp. grilled or roasted

Vietnamese food

TIP: The sweetness levels of Riesling grapes, in ascending order from driest to sweetest, are Kabinett, Spätlese, Auslese, Beerenauslese (BA), Trockenbeerenauslese (TBA), and Eiswein.

TIP: Kabinett and Spätlese Rieslings range in sweetness from dry (*trocken*), to half-dry, which is also referred to as off-dry (*halbtrocken*), to sweet.

AUSLESE (GERMAN WHITE SWEET DESSERT WINE)

Asian dishes featuring coconut milk

avocado

black bass

bread pudding

cheese, esp. rich

DESSERTS

foie gras, esp. sautéed

fruit, esp. tropical

ham

hamachi

honey-mustard sauce

lobster

pâté

richer dishes

savory dishes with a touch of sweetness

strawberries

sweet dishes

venison, esp. with aged Riesling

BEERENAUSLESE (GERMAN WHITE SWEET DESSERT WINE MADE FROM GRAPES SHRIVELED ON THE VINE)

caramel and caramel desserts

cheese, salty

desserts

FOIE GRAS

fruit, esp. apricots and peaches

sweet food

EISWEIN (GERMAN OR CANADIAN WHITE SWEET DESSERT WINE MADE FROM GRAPES FROZEN ON THE VINE; AKA ICE WINE)

avocado

cheese, rich

desserts

foie gras

pâté

sweet food

KABINETT (DRIEST GERMAN RIESLING)

Asian food

beets, roasted

chicken

garlic and garlicy dishes

hazelnuts

lighter dishes

pork

poultry

raw dishes

seafood

shellfish

spicy dishes

Thai food

trout

tuna tartare

vegetables

vinaigrette sauce

AVOID

butter sauce

LATE HARVEST (GERMAN SWEET WHITE WINE)

APPLES AND APPLE DESSERTS

apricot desserts

bread pudding

cheese, blue

citrus desserts

cookies, esp. nut

crème brûlée and other custard desserts

crêpes fruit

desserts, esp. lighter

foie gras

FRUIT AND FRUIT DESSERTS

ham

honey

PEACHES AND PEACH DESSERTS

pears and pear desserts

plums and plum desserts

pork

pecan pie

SPÄTLESE (GERMAN MEDIUM-BODIED, OFF-DRY TO SWEET, WHITE WINE)

Asian food

bacon

black bass

cheese

chicken

cold dishes

crab

cream sauce

duck, roasted

fish, esp. richer dishes

fried dishes

fruit and fruit sauces

ham

lobster

PORK

risotto

salad, esp. spicy Asian

salty dishes

sandwiches

SCALLOPS

smoked food

spicy dishes

sweetbreads

Thai food

tuna, esp. as tartare

veal

TROCKENBEERENAUSLESE (GERMAN SWEET DESSERT WHITE WINE MADE FROM LATEST POSSIBLE HARVEST)

cheese, salty (e.g., blue)

desserts, esp. apple (esp. tarts), caramel, cherry, creamy, and/or custards

DESSERTS, FRUIT

foie gras

fruit, fresh, esp. tropical

sweet food

AVOID

heavier dishes

RIOJA

RED (SPANISH, MEDIUM TO FULL BODIED)

beef

cheese, Cabrales

cheese, esp. hard and esp. with fruity Rioja

CHEESE, MANCHEGO

chicken, esp. roasted, and esp. with aged and/or lighter Rioja

chorizo, esp. with fruity and/or young Rioja

duck, esp. grilled or roasted

fish dishes, spicy, esp. with fruity and/or young Rioja

game and game birds, esp. roasted or stewed

goat

herbs, dried, esp. rosemary and thyme

*LAMB, ESP. BRAISED, GRILLED, ROASTED, SAUTÉED, OR STEWED

liver

meat, red, esp. roasted

mushrooms

offal, esp. with lighter and/or aged Rioja

olive oil

paella

peppers, sweet

pheasant

pizza

PORK, ESP. BARBECUED OR ROASTED

poultry, esp. roasted or stewed

prime rib, esp. with aged Rioja

ratatouille

ribs

roast beef

salmon

sausage

squab

steak, grilled

STEW

turkey, esp. dark meat

veal, esp. scallopine

VEGETABLES, ESP. SAUTÉED OR STEWED

WHITE (SPANISH, LIGHT TO MEDIUM-BODIED)

cheese, Manchego

chicken, esp. barbecued or grilled

clams, esp. steamed

crab

cream sauce

fish, esp. grilled

ham, Serrano

mussels, esp. steamed

olives

onion tart

Ron Miller on Rioja: Great Standards at a Great Price

Tempranillo is the main grape of Rioja. It is the equivalent of Pinot Noir in France. The region has three classifications of its wine, which helps you understand the quality of the wine:

1. *Crianza*, loosely translated, means *nursery*. Before it is released, the wine must spend one year in French or American oak in the bordelaise-size barrel, which is 225 liters.

2. *Reserva* must spend one year in the barrel and two years in the bottle before it is released.

3. *Gran Reserva* is made only in the best years and must spend two years in the barrel and two years in the bottle before release.

Because of these classifications, the wine in the Crianza stage would really be reserve wine for the rest of the world. This commitment gives you a pretty amazing young wine with structure, sophistication, and nuance that wines in other parts of the world released after their first birthday would never have. So, if you want to try something new with your **roast** or **stew**, you will get a certain sophistication with Rioja that you are not going to get from wines at a similar price point from anywhere else in the world.

paella
poultry
pork
salmon
sardines
sausage, esp. spicy
seafood
shrimp, esp. sautéed
tapas
zarzuela

The one white wine I am very fond of that does age well is old white Rioja. There are only two houses that do them any more, Murrietta and Lopez de Heredia.
— DAVID ROSENGARTEN,
editor in chief,
www.DavidRosengarten.com

RODITIS (GREEK LIGHT-BODIED WHITE WINE)
cheese, esp. mild
chicken
fish, esp. grilled
lemon
olive oil
seafood

ROOT BEER
(NONALCOHOLIC CARBONATED BEVERAGE)
foie gras
hamburgers, esp. grilled
vanilla ice cream

ROSADO (SPANISH LIGHT-TO MEDIUM-BODIED ROSÉ WINE)
anchovies
meat, cured
olives
paella
peppers, red
rice dishes

salad
sausage
seafood
tapas, esp. cold
vegetable dishes

Navarra and Rioja are two regions that have produced great Rosado wines for years. This is a springtime wine, and should be drunk soon after release. This wine is great with simple cold tapas like seafood salad, pepper and eggplant salad, and white beans with chorizo.
— RON MILLER,
maître d'hotel, Solera (NYC)

ROSÉ (LIGHT- TO MEDIUM-BODIED PINK WINE TYPICALLY MADE FROM RED GRAPES; LIGHT-COLORED BECAUSE OF MINIMAL CONTACT WITH GRAPE SKINS; SEE ALSO ROSADO)
anchovies, esp. grilled
aperitif and/or with canapés, esp. dry rosé
baba gannoush
barbecue and barbecue sauce
beef, esp. spicier dishes
bouillabaisse
brandade
CHARCUTERIE, ESP. WITH DRY ROSÉ
cheese, esp. mild
cheese, Parmesan
chicken
chiles
cold dishes, esp. meat
couscous
crab, esp. boiled or steamed
cranberries
duck
eggs and egg dishes
FISH, ESP. FRIED, GRILLED, OR STEWED

ham, esp. Serrano
hamburgers
herbs
hot dogs
hummus
Indian food
lobster
meat, esp. white
melon
Mexican food
olive oil
olives
paella
pâté, esp. with dry rosé
peanuts and peanut sauce
peppers, bell, esp. red
picnics
pizza
PORK, ESP. GRILLED OR ROASTED
poultry
prosciutto and melon
quiche, esp. with dry rosé
raspberries
ratatouille
red snapper, grilled
saffron
SALAD, ESP. GREEN AND COMPOSED, AND ESP. WITH DRIER ROSÉ
salad Niçoise
salmon
sandwiches, esp. beef or pork
sardines
sausage, esp. grilled
seafood
sea urchins
shellfish
SHRIMP, ESP. GRILLED
smoked poultry and fish
soup
spicy food, esp. with fuller-bodied rosé
stew
strawberries
summertime
Szechuan food
tarragon
Thai food

tomatoes, raw
tomato sauce
tuna
turkey, esp. roasted
veal
vegetables, esp. with drier rosé
vegetarian dishes

AVOID
cream sauce
oysters, raw

Rosé has one foot in the red world and one foot in the white world. The fact that it is a red that wants to be a white, or white that wants to be a red, means that it will try twice as hard to please you. Rosés can be off-dry to bone dry. Those with just the smallest touch of sweetness — so little that you can

barely pick it up — are natural with food. For so much of the food that we eat — from mayonnaise to scallops to ketchup on a hamburger — you need a wine with some level of sweetness. Otherwise, you will detonate a dry wine. There are some people who drink only red or only white wine. Rosé is a wine that can make peace with mooks like that.

— JOSHUA WESSON,
wine director, Best Cellars

TIDBIT: While we enjoy a rustic rosé as much as the next rosé lover, we had occasion to try Uma Thurman's favorite rosé (from a case she'd given as a gift to a friend of ours), and loved the delicate structure and silky elegance of the 2004 Domaines Ott

Chateau de Selle Côtes de Provence Rosé, which has been cited as "the finest rosé in the world."

ROUSSANNE (FRENCH FULL-BODIED WHITE WINE FROM THE RHÔNE VALLEY)
cheese
ham
pasta
pâté
pork
poultry
risotto
smoked fish and meat
vegetable dishes

SAGRANTINO (ITALIAN FULL-BODIED RED WINE FROM UMBRIA)
pasta
truffles, black

SAINT-ÉMILION (FRENCH MEDIUM-BODIED RED WINE FROM BORDEAUX)
beef
cheese, esp. Saint-Nectaire, Reblochon
chicken, esp. coq au vin
duck, esp. confit or grilled
lamb
squab

SAKE (JAPANESE RICE WINE)
IN GENERAL
canapés
caviar
ceviche
chervil
chicken
crab
fennel
FISH, ESP. LIGHT, WHITE, OR RAW

Rosés can be served with anything.
— JULIA CHILD

I think rosé is a vastly overlooked category. So much of it's just the image — people are afraid of the image of white Zinfandel, or not being thought to be sophisticated. With rosé, I love grilled sausages, hamburgers, and fish. I think that's one you can serve with even a fairly delicate white-fleshed fish that's been grilled, when the preparations could lean more toward red wine. A wine like rosé has the body of a red wine, but it's chilled and refreshing.
— DANIEL JOHNNES, beverage director, Daniel (NYC)

Techniques open the door to different wines, and rosé is often a very good bridge. Does it have a place on a tasting menu? Will people feel disappointed if they get one? Some are really fantastic and can be a perfect pairing. We are serving a dish with saffron and tarragon and can pair it with a light red, but it works better with a rosé. I would personally never look down on a pairing just because it is paired with rosé — however, I think people have a negative feeling toward rosé.
— MICHAEL ANTHONY, chef, Blue Hill at Stone Barns (New York)

KEISHI RIKIMARU

ginger	
lemongrass	
lobster	
lychees	
meat, raw (e.g., carpaccio, tartare)	

**OYSTERS, ESP. CREAMY
  (VERSUS BRINY)**

pork belly
prosciutto
salmon
SASHIMI
seafood, esp. mild and raw
shellfish
shrimp
smoked meat
sushi
tofu
tomato
veal loin

AVOID

beef, esp. heavier preparations
creamy dishes, esp. heavier preparations
game, esp. heavier preparations
meat, red, esp. heavier preparations
very spicy food

AGED (FULL-BODIED, RICH;
SOME ARE ALSO KNOWN AS
KOSHU)

cheese, esp. blue and Camembert
curries
desserts
duck
fish, esp. fattier (e.g., eel, salmon)
foie gras
meat, esp. rich, strongly flavored
pork and pork belly
salmon
sweet dishes

Sake does not have a lot of acidity, which makes it tough to pair with food. It is a misconception about how well sake and sushi go together. Once you put wasabi and the rice with it, it will flatten most sake. It's great with sashimi, though. As for oysters, you would want it with creamy oysters rather than real briny oysters.
— GREG HARRINGTON, MS

I think sake is a great aperitif. If you're taking it out of the context of Japanese food, and you're going to have a backyard barbecue, I think sake might be a nice thing to serve. The danger is that it's a little higher in alcohol. I think it makes a nice complement to a lot of dishes that use fish or that have maybe a little smoky flavor. I think with the right sake, you could pair something like prosciutto or another kind of smoked meat.
— GEORGE COSSETTE,
co-owner, Silverlake Wine (Los Angeles)

Sake ranges from light- to full-bodied: nama ʒake is the lightest, followed by ginjo, daiginjo, junmai, and then aged sake. But the range in body for sake is smaller than for wine — say, only from a light white wine to Merlot. So with heavier preparations of beef in rich sauces, you might want to drink wine.
— HIROMI IUCHI, vice president, Jizake

The Japanese don't pair sushi with sake because it is rice on rice. They will, however, pair sashimi with sake. That being said, if you were to have sake with sushi, a junmai daiginjjo, ginjo, or daiginjo would work. You'd want to avoid junmai because it has a rice-y quality to it, which would be too much.
— PAUL TANGUAY, beverage director, Sushi Samba (NYC)

Aged sake is the richest type of sake. It's almost sherry-like, and can be served in a brandy-style glass.
— HIROMI IUCHI,
vice president, Jizake

Koshu (aged) sake is a darker golden or brown hue, and can pair with red meat and pork.

— ROGER DAGORN, maître d'hotel, Chanterelle (NYC)

DAIGINJO (MEDIUM-BODIED, AROMATIC, DELICATE, SMOOTH, YET RICH)
aperitif
asparagus
caviar
fish, lighter (e.g., snapper)
fluke
fruit
grapefruit
lighter dishes
oysters, esp. light and creamy style
poached dishes
ponzu sauce
salad
shrimp, sweet
squid
tofu
vegetables, esp. light preparations (e.g., mousses or steamed)
yuzu dressing

DRY
fish, white
herbs
meat, white
mushrooms
oysters, raw
seafood
shellfish
truffles

GINJO (AROMATIC, SMOOTH, LIGHT-BODIED)
artichokes
asparagus
fish, raw and/or marinated
fluke
poached dishes
ponzu sauce
salsa
shrimp, sweet
squid
yuzu dressing

The test of a great [sake] brewer is its ginjo. Dewazakura Oka ginjo is my all-time favorite sake. It has a lot of structure and aromatics, from melon to white pepper. This one stands up to food and is my go-to sake. My other favorite sake is Ginjo Okunomatsu, which has won gold medals in the United States National Sake Appraisal in multiple categories. It has nice structure, is a little fruity and round with a licorice finish — and calls for food.

— PAUL TANGUAY, beverage director, Sushi Samba (NYC)

HONJOZO (LIGHTER, RICHER STYLE)
buttery dishes
creamy dishes
fish, oily and/or stronger-flavored
fried food
mackerel
meat
oysters
pork, esp. fried
salmon
tempura
toro

tuna, esp. fatty

JUNMAI (RICH, MEDIUM-BODIED)
buttery dishes
cod, grilled
creamy dishes
fish, stronger-flavored, esp. grilled
fried food
mackerel
meat
oysters, esp. heavier, minerally style
pork, esp. fried
salmon
sautéed dishes
tempura
teriyaki
toro
tuna, fatty

Junmai is the best style of sake for food pairing because it has higher acidity than other sake. It works with meat, fried foods like tempura, and richer sauces — even cream sauces. You do need to be aware that its sweetness varies, and to select a sake of appropriate sweetness or dryness.

— PAUL TANGUAY, beverage director, Sushi Samba (NYC)

On our menu, I have a chilled tomato consommé that has a salad of crab, tomato concassé drops of chervil coulis, and black caviar floating in it. I also serve another dish of raw oyster in tomato aspic with chervil and black pepper that works beautifully with sake. There are no Asian ingredients in either of these dishes, but they both go very well with sake. — DAVID WALTUCK, chef-owner, Chanterelle (NYC)

Daiginjo is the great communicator that will bring Americans to sake. It is cold and fruity and people just love it! People taste it, and want a second glass. Remember that when the food comes, you probably want to switch to junmai and honjozo and finish with an aged sake. — PAUL TANGUAY, beverage director, Sushi Samba (NYC)

JUNMAI GINJO
fruit, esp. fresh (e.g., apples)
salad
seafood
vegetables, esp. fresh

We only serve junmai and jun-mai ginjo sake, which are in another class of sake and which make for better pairing with food.

— ROGER DAGORN, maître
d'hotel, Chanterelle (NYC)

KIJOSHU (SWEET, PORT-LIKE)
cheese
chocolate
desserts with cheese or fruit
eel
foie gras
malt
pork, esp. caramelized and/or
   served with apple sauce

Kijoshu is a sweet sake that works really well with chocolate or malt.

— ROGER DAGORN, maître
d'hotel, Chanterelle (NYC)

NAMA ZAKE (LIGHTEST-BODIED, VERY SOFT, UNPASTEURIZED)
fish, white meat
salad

SPARKLING
aperitif
desserts, esp. light and/or creamy
fruit, esp. fresh
salmon roe
AVOID
fried food, as it doesn't have the
   bubbles to stand up to it

Sparkling sake can be served in Champagne flutes to enjoy the bubbles. Lighter sakes should be served in thin-rimmed glasses,

while more full-bodied sakes can be served in round glasses.

— HIROMI IUCHI,
vice president, Jizake

Sparkling sake can range from dry to super-sweet. It is not Champagne, and it does not have large bubbles like Champagne. Most of the sparkling sakes in the United States are very sweet and high in acid, so they would work well with fruits, and light or creamy desserts.

— PAUL TANGUAY, beverage
director, Sushi Samba (NYC)

SWEET
ceviche
daikon
desserts, esp. creamy and/or
   cakes
fish, oily
fried food (e.g., tempura)
fruit, dried, esp. apples and apricots
ginger
lime
rice
seaweed
sesame
shellfish, esp. sweet
soba
spicy food

With desserts, I like to serve a mystery wine where the guests have to guess what it is. My favorite will have them guess-ing, "Sherry? Port?" — and it will be sweet sake!

— ROGER DAGORN, maître
d'hotel, Chanterelle (NYC)

UNFILTERED (SOMETIMES HAS THE APPEARANCE OF MILKY WATER)
coconut
desserts
fruit, esp. fresh
game birds
offal
tapioca
AVOID
rice dishes
serving this sake hot

TIP: Sake labels feature an **SMV**, which stands for *sake meter value*. This is an indicator of its relative sweetness (a number preceded by a -) or dryness (which is preceded by a +), and ranges from -15 (very sweet) to +15 (very dry). Sake is often categorized as *very dry, dry, sweet,* or *very sweet.* Paul Tanguay of Sushi Samba provided us with these pairing tips:

VERY SWEET *(e.g., Late Harvest wine sweetness): Higher-alcohol sakes in this category work with desserts, while lower alcohol sakes work with some spicy foods.*

SWEET *(e.g., California Chardonnay sweetness): Sweet sakes would work with sweet dishes like teriyaki or desserts.*

DRY *(e.g., French Chardonnay dryness): Dry sakes work well with shellfish, especially oysters.*

VERY DRY *(e.g., Sancerre dry-ness): Very dry sakes work well with high-acid dishes like ceviche.*

TIP: Sake labels also list alcohol content. A low-alcohol sake is 8 to 10 percent, and an undiluted sake is 17 to 20 percent, with 15 to 16 percent being about average. As with wine, the percentage of alco-hol has some correlation with the sake's body (i.e., the higher the alcohol, the fuller-bodied the sake).

SANCERRE (FRENCH MEDIUM-BODIED ACIDIC WHITE WINE MADE FROM SAUVIGNON BLANC GRAPES FROM THE LOIRE VALLEY; SEE ALSO SAUVIGNON BLANC)

acidic food and sauces

appetizers

asparagus

ceviche

*CHEESE GOAT, ESP. FRESH CHÉVRE

FISH, ESP. LIGHTER DISHES

lemon and lemon sauce

OYSTERS, ESP. BLUE POINT, KUMAMOTO, OR MALPEQUE

salad

salmon

salmon, smoked

SHELLFISH

tomatoes

trout

vegetables, esp. raw

AVOID

sweet dishes

SANGIOVESE (ITALIAN MEDIUM-BODIED RED WINE, PRIMARILY FROM TUSCANY; SEE ALSO CHIANTI, BRUNELLO DI MONTALCINO, ETC.)

beef, esp. braised or stewed

charcuterie

CHEESE

cheese, fontina

cheese, Parmesan

chicken, esp. braised or stewed

chili

eggplant

fennel

game hens

grilled dishes

ham

hamburger

herbs, esp. fresh

lamb

liver, calf's

meat, red

meat loaf

mushrooms and mushroom dishes

oregano

pancetta

pan-fried dishes

PASTA, ESP. WITH SIMPLE (I.E., TOMATO AND/OR MEAT) SAUCE

peppers, bell, roasted

pizza

polenta

pork

poultry

prosciutto

quail

rabbit

risotto

roasted dishes

rosemary

salami

SAUSAGE

sautéed dishes

seafood

smoked meat

sour cream or crème fraîche

squab

STEAK, ESP. GRILLED

thyme

TOMATO-BASED SAUCE

tomatoes

turkey

VEAL, ESP. CHOPS

vegetable dishes

zucchini

SAUTERNES (FRENCH WHITE DESSERT WINE FROM BORDEAUX)

ALMONDS AND ALMOND DESSERTS

APPLES AND APPLE DESSERTS

apricots and apricot desserts

berries and berry desserts

biscotti

cake, esp. almond-, butter-, or citrus-flavored

caramel and caramel desserts

cheese, esp. BLUE (e.g., *ROQUEFORT) and/or soft (e.g., Fontainebleau)

coconut

cookies

CUSTARD AND CUSTARD DESSERTS (e.g., crème brûlée)

desserts, esp. rich

duck

fish

floating island

*FOIE GRAS

FRUIT AND FRUIT DESSERTS, ESP. TROPICAL

ham

hazelnuts

lemon desserts

mango and mango desserts

nuts

pâté, esp. chicken liver

PEACHES AND PEACH DESSERTS

PEARS AND PEAR DESSERTS

pecan pie

pineapple desserts

poultry

quince

raspberries, esp. in a tart or sauce

soufflés

strawberries and strawberry desserts

sweetbreads

walnuts

AVOID

chocolate desserts

too-sweet desserts

Sauternes and foie gras can be a remarkable pairing. However, if you start a menu with Châteaux d'Yquem and foie gras, which is an extraordinary combination, it will end up rolling over everything else. There are generally only three producers of Sauternes that we'll pour by the glass: Climens, Coutet, and Raymond-Lafon. In all my years of tasting, these are the three that I think are a little more of that classic style, in that they're not quite as sweet and not quite as unctuous [and will lead better into the next course].

— Paul Roberts, MS,
the French Laundry (Napa)
and Per Se (NYC)

Sauternes and Roquefort is a symbiotic relationship. I can remember over twenty years ago having that for the first time in France, at Georges Blanc.

— Traci Des Jardins,
chef, Jardiniere (San Francisco)

Many vintages of Sauternes are not that sweet. I tasted five different vintages of Château d'Yquem and they were very different. The 1970 is really better as a table wine; have it with lobster. Sweet wine with savory food is something of a declining fashion these last thirty years. It killed the German wine business and is killing the Sauternes business by marginalizing it to dessert or foie gras — which is unfortunate and unfair. I visited a Sauternes producer and they served their wines with a vegetable course, a very light liver course, and meat course. All wines were different vintages and made perfect sense. That to

me is much more enlightening than the tried and true.

— Joseph Spellman, MS,
Joseph Phelps Vineyards

Almonds and peaches, separate or in combination, are perhaps two of the most successful accompanying flavors to a Sauternes. — Richard Olney

------

SAUVIGNON BLANC
(NEW WORLD LIGHT- TO MEDIUM-BODIED ACIDIC WHITE WINE; SOMETIMES GRASSY, CITRUSY, AND/OR WITH SLIGHT OAK)

IN GENERAL
acidic food
appetizers
artichokes
Asian food, esp. spicy dishes
ASPARAGUS
basil
calamari
celery
cheese, esp. tart, and esp. Brie, Camembert, feta, GOAT, and Parmesan
CHICKEN, ESP. FRIED, POACHED, ROASTED, OR SAUTÉED
chiles
chives

CILANTRO

citrus

clams

cod

Cornish game hens

crab

crudités

cucumber

cumin

curry

dill

Dover sole

fennel

FISH, ESP. WHITE, POACHED, SAUTÉED, LIGHTLY GRILLED, AND/OR WITH MEUNIERE

sauce

fried food

fruit salsa and sauce

GARLIC

greens

grilled food

ham

HERBS (ESP. FRESH), HERBAL DISHES, AND SAUCE

Indian food, esp. lighter dishes with coriander or mint

lemon (e.g., sauced) and lemon-flavored dishes

lemongrass

mango

Mexican food, esp. with cilantro

mussels

mustard, esp. Dijon

octopus, esp. grilled

oily food

onions, esp. spring

oregano

OYSTERS, ESP. RAW

parsley

pasta, esp. light and/or with cream or seafood sauce

peas

pepper, black

PEPPERS

pesto

PORK, ESP. GRILLED

poultry

quiche, esp. vegetable

red snapper

rich food

risotto, esp. herbed

SALAD, ESP. COMPOSED, LIGHT, AND/OR WITH GOAT CHEESE

salmon, esp. grilled or poached

salsa (e.g., salsa verde)

sautéed dishes

scallops

sea bass

SEAFOOD, ESP. POACHED OR LIGHTLY GRILLED

seafood salad

shallots

SHELLFISH, ESP. POACHED, SAUTÉED, OR LIGHTLY GRILLED

shrimp

smoked fish (e.g., salmon)

snapper, esp. baked

sole

soup, esp. light or creamy

spicy (moderately) dishes

spring rolls, esp. vegetable

steamed dishes

sweet sauce

swordfish, esp. grilled

tarragon

Tex-Mex food

Thai food

thyme

tomato sauce salsa

TOMATOES, ESP. RAW

trout

tuna (e.g., tuna tartare)

TURKEY

veal

VEGETABLES AND VEGETARIAN DISHES, ESP. GREEN AND/OR GRILLED, AND ESP. WITH NEW ZEALAND SAUVIGNON BLANC

vinaigrette

yogurt

zucchini

AVOID

meat, red

salty food and dishes, with New Zealand Sauvignon Blanc

seafood dishes, with New Zealand Sauvignon Blanc

Where to find great Sauvignon Blanc: For a sense of terroir *it is hard to beat the wines from the Northern Loire Valley like Pouilly-Fumé and Sancerre. Number two would be Italy and then New Zealand, where you find ones with character.*

— Jean-Luc Le Dû, Le Dû's Wines (NYC)

LATE HARVEST (FROM THE NEW WORLD, SWEET, PRIMARILY FROM CALIFORNIA AND CHILE)

apples and apple desserts

cheese

foie gras

fruit desserts

pears and pear desserts

SAVENNIERES (FRENCH MEDIUM-BODIED DRY WHITE WINE FROM THE LOIRE VALLEY)

apples and apple desserts

asparagus

cheese, goat

clams, steamed

crab, esp. baked

crab, soft shell, esp. sautéed

FISH, ESP. MILD WHITE

halibut, esp. poached

lobster, esp. steamed

mussels, steamed

pear and pear desserts

pork, esp. roasted

poultry, esp. roasted or in a cream sauce

salad, seafood

salmon

shellfish

smoked fish

squid

sushi

turkey

SCHEUREBE (GERMAN MEDIUM- TO FULL-BODIED WHITE WINE)

butter sauce

desserts, esp. custard and fruit desserts

fruit and fruit desserts, salsa, and sauce

rich dishes

scallops, esp. with a beurre blanc

shellfish

spicy dishes

sweet dishes

vanilla

SCOTCH, SINGLE-MALT (E.G., DALWHINNIE); SINGLE-MALT SCOTCH IS MADE AT A SINGLE DISTILLERY, AND USES MALT BARLEY AS ITS ONLY GRAIN)

dark chocolate

game

meat, esp. braised, smoked, or stewed

oysters, esp. rich

smoked fish

SÉMILLON (FRENCH MEDIUM-BODIED WHITE WINE, USUALLY FROM GRAVES IN BORDEAUX; SEE ALSO RECOMMENDATIONS FOR BORDEAUX, WHITE, AND SAUVIGNON BLANC)

asparagus

bouillabaisse

celery

CHICKEN, ESP. ROASTED

chiles

chives

clam chowder

cod, esp. roasted

Cornish game hens

cream sauce

dill

FISH, ESP. GRILLED OR STEWED

foie gras

grilled dishes

halibut

herbs

lemongrass

mackerel, esp. grilled

MEAT, LIGHT AND/OR WHITE

monkfish

mullet, esp. grilled

mussels

oysters

PORK, ESP. CHOPS, AND ESP. WITH APPLES OR OTHER FRUIT

poultry

quail

rich dishes

risotto

salad

salmon, smoked

sautéed dishes

scallops, esp. seared

sea bass

seafood and seafood soup

shellfish

smoked fish

spicy dishes

stew and other stewed dishes

sweetbreads

swordfish

tomatoes, raw

turkey, esp. grilled

vegetables

vegetarian dishes

zucchini

LATE HARVEST (NEW WORLD SWEET DESSERT WINE, MADE IN STYLE OF SAUTERNES)

cheese, esp. Roquefort

fruity desserts

nuts and nut desserts

SHANDY (BEER MIXED WITH LEMONADE AND A SPLASH OF SODA)

halibut, esp. with coconut and mint

Indian food

kebabs

lamb chops

salmon tikka

tandoori-cooked dishes

SHERRY (SPANISH FORTIFIED WHITE WINE FROM JEREZ DE LA FRONTERA; MUST BE CONSUMED SOON AFTER BOTTLE IS OPENED)

ALMONDS

anchovies

artichoke hearts

calamari, esp. fried

charcuterie

cheese (e.g., Gouda)

chiles

chocolates and chocolate desserts, esp. creamy

chorizo

consommé

fish, esp. fried, grilled, or smoked

fried food

gazpacho

HAM, CURED, ESP. SPANISH

Solera's Ron Miller on Where to Start with Sherry

Sherry is a wine that is not well understood, yet it goes well with so many dishes — not just as an aperitif, but throughout a meal. The wines have been aged from anywhere from three to five years and are still very delicate — and they sell for ridiculously low prices.

For some, sherry is an acquired taste, as a dry, almost austere-tasting wine. Sherry has many different expressions, from mineral to quasi-sweet, even with no residual sugar. The sweetness comes from the quality of the grape and how it is enhanced by the wood.

Sherry is released four times a year and they are now being dated on the back. You want to look for a release date of something less than six to eight months prior. After that, they tend to start to oxidize.

Once sherry is opened, it should be refrigerated and consumed within a couple of days maximum. Because of this, I recommend buying sherry in small bottles [for home consumption].

At Solera, we have about thirty sherries, which is more than you will find in most bars in Spain. We give many away, so people can see how well they go with food.

Sherry needs food because of its alcohol content, which can range from 15 to 22 percent. In Spain, sherry is never consumed without food. I will drink sherry at ten in the morning, but it will be with some tortilla [Spanish potato omelet] or almonds or another bite of food.

Amontillado and oloroso might be the easiest place to start, since both have elements of nuts and caramel and those are flavors most people are familiar with. They also have notes of sweetness and are both pretty accessible.

Amontillado works well with cheese as well as heartier food, like chicken or game.

Oloroso works with beef in a Cabrales cheese sauce. This would not be considered an alternative to red wine, but a parallel.

Fino sherry is the perfect match for tapas because it is so versatile. On our tapas menu are vegetables, seafood, cheese, and charcuterie, just to name a few — and fino goes well with just about everything. It's also a perfect pairing with almonds and olives — and great with sliced ham like Serrano or an Italian prosciutto. America loves fried food — and sherry is perfect with everything from fried fish to fried calamari. Sherry is also great with tempura, which originated in Portugal and Spain, by the way — not Japan.

From the lightest and driest to the heaviest and sweetest:
DRY: *fino and manzanilla*
OFF-DRY: *amontillado*
MODERATELY SWEET: *oloroso*
SWEET: *cream*
VERY SWEET: *PX*

Other pairings to try with sherry:

Fino or amontillado, which is the lighter style of fino, is the perfect foil for steamed mussels.

With ham, instead of a fruity red wine like Merlot, try fino or montilla or a young amontillado.

Grilled or sautéed shrimp is perfect with manzanilla, which is made by the seaside with the vineyards at sea level. Some people say the waves crash onto the vines, which is not true, but you get the idea. Manzanilla has a crispness and minerality, and is the only wine that tastes salty. So, with these flavors of sandy clay and chalky soil with almond notes, these flavors pair so well.

With tortilla, because it is rich and has potato and egg, take your pick of any sherry.

Manchego cheese goes well with a complex sherry like Pedro Ximenez or an Amontillado.

meat, smoked

nuts, esp. almonds, and esp. roasted and/or salted

OLIVES, ESP. GREEN

oysters

salad, esp. with fruit and nuts

salty snacks

sardines, esp. grilled or fried

sausage, esp. chorizo

seafood

shrimp

SOUP

TAPAS (SPANISH APPETIZERS, E.G., NUTS, OLIVES, SERRANO HAM)

tapenade

tortilla (potato omelette)

vegetables, esp. grilled, marinated, and/or roasted

AMONTILLADO (AGED FINO FROM ANDALUCIA; SERVE COOLER THAN ROOM TEMPERATURE; CONSUME SOON AFTER OPENING)

ALMONDS

caramel

CHEESE, ESP. DRY/HARD (e.g., from aged Cheddar to young Manchego to smoked sheep's milk)

chicken

chorizo

consommé

desserts

duck

game, esp. braised

ham

NUTS

olives

rabbit

sausage

snails

soup

spicy food

stew

TAPAS, ESP. RICHER DISHES

walnuts

CREAM (BLEND OF SWEET AND DRY SHERRIES)

apples and apple-flavored desserts

cake

caramel and caramel desserts

CHEESE, ESP. BLUE (e.g., Cabrales) AND/OR FIRM

dates

desserts

figs

nuts and nut desserts

pears and pear desserts

pies

FINO (VERY DRY; AGED BETWEEN SIX AND NINE YEARS; SERVE VERY WELL CHILLED)

ALMONDS

antipasto

cheese

chorizo

FRIED FOOD

ham, esp. prosciutto, Iberian, Serrano

nuts

OLIVES, ESP. GREEN

oysters

sashimi

SEAFOOD

shellfish

shrimp

soup

sushi

***TAPAS**

tempura

tortilla

turkey, roasted

vegetables, esp. roasted

MANZANILLA (VERY DRY; MADE ONLY IN SANLUCAR DE BARRAMEDA)

ALMONDS

aperitif

cheese, Cabrales

FRIED FOOD

HAM, ESP. IBERIAN OR SERRANO

NUTS, ESP. ALMONDS

OLIVES, ESP. GREEN

OYSTERS, ESP. BELON

poultry

scallops

SEAFOOD

shad roe

shellfish

shrimp

sushi

***TAPAS**

OLOROSO (FULLER-BODIED)

beef, esp. with drier sherry

cake

CHEESE, ESP. BLUE AND/OR HARD

cheese, Manchego

desserts, esp. with sweeter sherry

flan

lamb

mushrooms

NUTS

olives

ostrich

pâté

pie

soup, esp. cream-based and/or pureed

venison

PX (SWEET, DARK, UNCTUOUS; FROM JEREZ; AKA PEDRO XIMINEZ)

banana desserts

cheese, esp. blue (e.g., Roquefort)

CHOCOLATE AND CHOCOLATE DESSERTS, ESP. DARK CHOCOLATE

cookies, (e.g., biscotti)

crème brûlée

desserts

figs

flan

fruit, dried

ICE CREAM, INCLUDING PX POURED OVER VANILLA ICE CREAM

NUTS (ESP. PECANS) AND NUT DESSERTS

pecan pie

prunes

pumpkin pie

rice pudding

SWEET (FULL-BODIED, SWEET, MADE BY BLENDING A SWEET GRAPE INTO OLOROSO)

after dinner
almonds
chocolate and chocolate desserts
desserts

SHIRAZ/SYRAH (FULL-BODIED RED WINE MADE FROM THE SYRAH GRAPE; SHIRAZ IS MADE EXCLUSIVELY IN AUSTRALIA)

BARBECUE AND BARBECUE SAUCE, ESP. SPARERIBS

beef, esp. grilled, roasted, or stewed

braised dishes

casseroles (e.g., cassoulet)

CHEESE, ESP. AGED AND/OR HARD (e.g., Gouda, Parmesan, Pecorino)

chicken, esp. barbecued, braised, roasted, and/or with spices

chili

curries

DUCK, ESP. GRILLED, PEKING (WITH HOISIN SAUCE), OR ROASTED, AND ESP. WITH BIGGER RHÔNE SYRAH

eggplant, esp. grilled

game and game birds, esp. with Rhône Syrah

goose, esp. with bigger Rhône Syrah

GRILLED MEAT AND OTHER FOOD

hamburgers, esp. with ketchup

hearty dishes

LAMB, ESP. GRILLED, ROASTED, OR STEWED

MEAT, ESP. RED AND ESP. BARBECUED, BRAISED, GRILLED, ROASTED, OR STEWED

MUSHROOMS AND WILD MUSHROOMS

osso buco

pasta, esp. rich

pepper, black

pizza

pork

poultry, esp. grilled or roasted

rabbit

ratatouille

ribs, esp. with barbecue sauce

rich food

salmon

sauce, esp. hearty

SAUSAGE, ESP. GRILLED

smoked meat

spicy meat

squab, esp. roasted

STEAK, ESP. GRILLED WITH PEPPER OR STEAK SAUCE

stew, esp. meat

TUNA, ESP. GRILLED OR STEWED

turkey, roasted

veal and veal chops

VENISON, ESP. GRILLED OR ROASTED

wild boar, esp. with Rhône Syrah

AVOID
fish, delicate
seafood, lighter
shellfish

On a large-scale basis, Australia makes the best Shiraz in the world. On a vintage-to-vintage basis from a small estate, you must look at the Syrah of northern Rhône of France and Côte-Rôtie and Hermitage. I also see wonderful Syrahs from Italy in Piedmont and Sicily as well.

— JEAN-LUC LE DÙ, Le Dû's Wines (NYC)

TIP: Australian Shiraz is fruitier and more delicate than Syrah made elsewhere in the world.

SHIRAZ, SPARKLING (AUSTRALIAN SPARKLING WINE, WHICH RANGES FROM DRY TO SWEET)

aperitif

barbecued food

berries

breakfast / brunch

cereal, sweet

cheese, esp. blue

chocolate

desserts, esp. chocolate

duck

French toast, esp. served with red fruit

fruit, fresh, esp. red

ham

maple syrup

meat, esp. grilled

pancakes, esp. served with red fruit

pastries

pork

raspberries

strawberries

tuna, esp. grilled

turkey, roasted, as for Thanksgiving dinner

waffles, esp. served with red fruit

Sparkling Shiraz picks up anything with red fruit like strawberries or raspberries. It is sweet enough to handle the sweetness of Fruit Loops. It can also hold its own with maple syrup, where you want something sweet that can also cut through the intensity.

— JOSHUA WESSON, wine director, Best Cellars

SILVANER (SEE SYLVANER/SILVANER)

SOAVE (ITALIAN LIGHT-BODIED WHITE WINE FROM THE VENETO REGION; SOAVE CLASSICO IS MORE MEDIUM-BODIED)

antipasto

cheese, goat

CHICKEN, ESP. AS A SALAD

clams

crab

FISH, ESP. BAKED, FRIED, POACHED, OR OTHER LIGHT PREPARATION

lobster

PASTA, ESP. WITH SEAFOOD

pesto

pizza, esp. lighter

polenta, esp. with Gorgonzola cheese

prosciutto

risotto

salad

salt cod

scampi, esp. with Soave Classico

sea bass

SEAFOOD

shellfish, esp. light

shrimp

skate

sole

soup

swordfish

trout

vegetables

Spirits and Cocktail Expert Gary Regan on Pairing Food with Spirits

I've attended more than a few whiskey dinners, with a different single malt of Bourbon being paired with each course, and in my opinion these rarely work well. Why? Because even though there are vast differences between specific whiskeys, the chef is given one basic flavor profile to work with, and this results in a sometimes monotonous meal. Whiskey is whiskey, when all's said and done.

Cocktails work much better than straight spirits when pairing with food. There are so many flavors from which to choose.

Best, I find, is to allow the chef to prepare a menu, then let the cocktail expert figure out drinks to go with each course.

One must be very careful not to over-serve people. Cocktails can be dangerous. Plus, there's the gulping factor: We like to gulp drinks while we're eating, and gulping a drink such as, say, a Manhattan, can be very hazardous. Thus, long drinks should come into play, too.

I find that vermouth, both dry and sweet, is a very useful ingredient for this. Dry vermouth spritzers, for instance, can be very refreshing alongside **salads** or any **oily foods.** And adding very small quantities of limoncello, or Cointreau, or Chambord, can add nuances to complement all sorts of specific foods within the salad.

Margarita and tonic is another great drink — this one served alongside **Mexican** or other **spicy foods.** Divide one margarita between three or four tall, ice-filled glasses, top them off with tonic water, and add a squeezed wedge of lime. Works really well. Mojitos work well here, too.

Also try Champagne cocktails using small amounts of, say, a Manhattan cocktail, as a base: Divide one Manhattan among four flutes, top with Champagne, and perhaps add a lemon-twist garnish. This goes very well alongside **red meat.**

One must be careful not to serve too many sweet drinks alongside food — and many cocktails can be overly sweet.

Another great drink alongside food, especially **seafood,** is a Martini, circa 1900, which is fifty-fifty gin and dry vermouth, and a few dashes of orange bitters.

It's also possible to slip in just one neat whiskey in a cocktail dinner, such as a very smoky bottling like Ardbeg or Laphroaig, for instance, with **smoked foods.** True, this doesn't balance out the food, but sometimes smoke with smoke works very well indeed.

So, a spirits-only beverage menu might feature a dry cocktail aperitif (gin/vodka Martini), vermouth spritzer with salad, wine with entrée, and either a straight spirit or a sweetish cocktail with dessert.

SPARKLING WINE
(SPARKLING WINE NOT MADE IN THE CHAMPAGNE REGION OF FRANCE; E.G., SPANISH CAVA, ITALIAN PROSECCO, GERMAN SEKT, ETC.; SEE ALSO CHAMPAGNE, CAVA, PROSECCO, VOUVRAY, SPARKLING, ETC.)

APPETIZERS
Asian food, esp. spicy dishes
berries
brunch
CAVIAR
charcuterie
cheese, esp. Parmesan
chicken
CHINESE FOOD, ESP. SPICY DISHES
chips
crab cakes
desserts
dim sum
EGGS AND EGG DISHES
ethnic food
fish
fried food
gougères (cheese puffs)
hors d'oeuvres
Indian food, esp. spicy dishes
macaroni and cheese
meat, white
oysters
pasta
pizza
popcorn
pork
potato chips
prosciutto
salad
salmon, smoked
SALTY FOOD
sautéed dishes
seafood
shellfish
snails
soufflés
soup
spicy food

strawberries
SUSHI
tapas
tempura
Thai food
turkey
veal, esp. scallopine
vegetables
vegetarian dishes

STOUT (IRISH BLACK, FULL-BODIED, DARK BEER WITH DARK BROWN HEAD)
barbecued meat, esp. ribs
braised dishes
Cajun food
cheese, Stilton
cheese and cheese-sauced dishes
chicken, esp. roasted
chocolate and chocolate desserts (e.g., mousse)
desserts, esp. fruit and/or mildly sweet
fish, esp. in cream sauce
fruit desserts
grilled dishes
ham
hamburgers
meat, esp. roasted
Mexican food, esp. with black beans or chiles
*OYSTERS, ESP. WITH GUINNESS STOUT
poultry, esp. roasted
salmon, esp. grilled
sausage
shellfish
steak
stew
swordfish, esp. grilled
tuna, esp. grilled

Guinness is deceiving: You'd think it would go with dessert, but it is actually very light. It is just dark colored. American stouts are much more dessert-friendly. Beer has more flavors than wine and makes the dessert a little less sweet because the beer compensates.
— CARLOS SOLIS, food and beverage director/chef, Sheraton Four Points/LAX

IMPERIAL STYLE (WITH A PRONOUNCED CHOCOLATE FLAVOR)
cheesecake
chocolate desserts
game, esp. grilled
ice cream
meat, esp. grilled or smoked
panna cotta

AVOID
light desserts

When pairing, be sure to consider the relative weight of the dish. I tried pairing a chocolate stout with a dessert, and the beer by itself was amazing — but with the dessert, it was too light. Unfortunately, it left you with the aftertaste of beer.
— PHILIPPE MARCHAL, sommelier, Daniel (NYC)

CREAM (OFF-DRY)
caramel desserts
cheesecake
chocolate desserts, esp. creamy
fruit desserts
nut desserts

DRY
barbecue
cheese, strong
hearty food
meat dishes
oysters
stew

IMPERIAL (BRITISH, ORIGINALLY BREWED FOR ST. PETERSBURG COURT; BLACK TO TAR-COLORED, THICK ROASTED FLAVOR)
brownies

cheese, blue, esp. Stilton

cheesecake, esp. with fruit

CHOCOLATE, ESP. DARK DESSERTS

coffee/espresso

steak, esp. with black pepper sauce

walnuts

We serve an imperial stout with cheesecake with raspberry sauce reduction.

— CARLOS SOLIS, food and beverage director/chef, Sheraton Four Points/LAX

OATMEAL (BRITISH, DARK, MEDIUM TO FULL-BODIED, MADE WITH OATMEAL; RANGING FROM MORE ROASTED TO SWEET)

barbecue

bread, dark

cheese, strong (e.g., aged Stilton)

chocolate desserts, esp. with sweet stout

crab cakes

eggs

fruit desserts

ham

hearty food

ice cream

meat dishes

mole sauce

oysters

steak

stew

OYSTER (BRITISH, SWEET)

ham

oysters

roast beef

SWEET (BRITISH, MEDIUM TO FULL-BODIED, ALMOST CREAMY AND MILD)

caramel and caramel desserts

chocolate and chocolate desserts

fruit and fruit desserts

nuts and nut desserts

pancakes

SUPER TUSCAN

(ITALIAN MEDIUM TO FULL-BODIED BLENDED RED WINE)

beef, esp. roasted

chops

game

garlic

grilled dishes

herbs, esp. rosemary, thyme

lamb, esp. braised or chops

meat

mushrooms, esp. grilled

olive oil

pasta with meat sauce (e.g., pappardelle with wild boar)

pork

rosemary

salumi

sausage

steak, esp. grilled

venison

wild boar

If I was drinking a Super Tuscan, I would want a meat dish like venison or game, depending on the vintner.

— BERNARD SUN, beverage director, Jean-Georges Management (NYC)

SYLVANER/ SILVANER (MEDIUM-BODIED, ACIDIC WHITE WINE FROM ALSACE [SYLVANER] AND GERMANY [SILVANER])

appetizers

chicken, esp. creamy or grilled preparations

choucroute

fish, esp. creamy or grilled preparations

onion tart

oysters

pork, esp. braised or stewed

quiche

shellfish

In Alsace, Riesling is king — but I love Sylvaner, which is a forgotten grape and considered a very basic wine from Alsace. It is my favorite wine. It is dry, but you can also find a Late Harvest Sylvaner that is very, very intriguing.

— STEPHANE COLLING, wine director, The Modern at the MoMA (NYC)

SYRAH (SEE SHIRAZ/SYRAH)

TAURASI (ITALIAN FULL-BODIED SPICY RED WINE FROM CAMPANIA)

cheese, esp. aged

game

gnocchi

lamb

meat, esp. roasted

monkfish, esp. in spicy sauce

salumi

spicy dishes

steak, grilled

TEA

IN GENERAL

afternoon tea

breakfast/brunch

Chinese food

dim sum

Tea is a green plant with leaves that are glossy and stiff. When the leaf is picked, it withers. After picking, the leaves get heated and manipulated into a style. When it comes to the three main styles of tea, they are differentiated by how and when their level of oxidation is stopped. For instance, a green tea that is dried over a quick fire would be Darjeeling. Japanese tea is steamed to halt the oxidation, then dried. Green is stopped earliest, oolong is medium, and black is stopped last. Green and black teas are the best made from the youngest, smallest leaves. Oolong is made from big souchong leaves that are great for it, but not for black or green tea. Though oolong is in the middle, it is significantly different from the other two.

— JAMES LABE, tea sommelier/owner, Teahouse Kuan Yin (Seattle)

TIP: While it's an oversimplification to say that **"green and oolong teas go with white meats, while black teas and darker oolong teas go with red meats,"** it can be a useful starting point.

TIP: Have proper respect for beverage accompaniments, including the quality of the sweeteners offered with teas and coffees (as our experts are quick to point out that brown or crystal sugar brings out the flavor better than pulverized, bleached sugar does).

My favorite tea is Taiwan Oolong/Bao Jong. This is the greenest of the oolongs, and it has a finish that lingers with a lilac or orchid aftertaste. It is smooth, sweet, and ethereal. Unfortunately, it does not keep well, so if you get some, enjoy it soon thereafter.

— JAMES LABE, tea sommelier/owner, Teahouse Kuan Yin (Seattle)

AFRICAN (SOUTH AFRICAN PLANT IN THE LEGUME FAMILY USED TO MAKE A RED TEA-LIKE DRINK)
chocolate
curries

tandoori food

ASSAM (INDIAN, FULL-BODIED)
bacon
beef
breakfast/brunch
desserts, esp. with chocolate, custard, fruit, and/or lemon
duck
game
lamb
meat, red
Mexican food
mushrooms
orange
pastries
pears, raw
salmon
spicy food
steak

Assam tea goes very well after white wine.

— MICHAEL OBNOWLENNY, Canada's first tea sommelier

BAO JONG
scallops

BLACK (DARK, FULLY FERMENTED)
beef
cheesecake
cherries, esp. with Keemun black tea
chocolate, esp. dark with Kenyan, or milk with Yunnan black tea
cream sauce
curry
dessert, esp. custard, fruit, and/or raspberry
fruit salad made with melon, esp. with Keemun black tea
game
Indian food (e.g., potato dosa), with hot or iced tea
meat, esp. red, and esp. with Keemun black tea
melon, esp. honeydew, and esp. with Keemun black tea
pasta with tomato sauce, esp. with Keemun black tea

pastries
pears, raw, esp. with Yunnan black tea
spicy food
steak
strongly flavored food, esp. with Keemun black tea
sweet food, esp. with Yunnan black tea

CEYLON (SRI LANKAN FULL-BODIED BLACK TEA)
breakfast
cucumber
desserts, fruit, esp. with bananas, citrus, cream cheese, fruit, and/or vanilla
dill
pasta
pecan pie
sandwiches
spicy foods

CHAMOMILE (HERBAL TEA OF DRIED CHAMOMILE FLOWERS)
meat
mint or peppermint, esp. with dark chamomile tea
nuts
turkey, roast, esp. dark meat

CHRYSANTHEMUM (CHINESE HERBAL TEA OF DRIED CHRYSANTHEMUM FLOWERS)
chicken
shellfish
swordfish

Chrysanthemum is a good, all-purpose herbal tea to drink with savory food.

— JAMES LABE, tea sommelier/owner, Teahouse, Kuan Yin (Seattle)

DARJEELING (INDIAN FULL-BODIED BLACK TEA)
acidic food
afternoon tea
carrot cake
cheese
cheesecake

chicken, esp. with pistachios

chocolate

citrus and citrus dishes

cream cheese

curries, esp. tomato-based

desserts, esp. rich and/or with
  apples, apricots, cream, custard,
  raspberries, strawberries, or
  vanilla

duck

egg dishes (e.g., quiche)

fruit, fresh

game

ginger

lamb

lemon

lunch

meat, esp. red

orange

pasta, esp. with cream sauce

pecan pie

pumpkin pie

sausage

shellfish

spicy food

veal

venison

TIP: As one of the lighter black
teas, Darjeeling is incredibly
versatile.

*With duck or lamb, you'd want
to serve Darjeeling fairly hot, to
cut the fat on your palate.
Essentially, that's what a
Cabernet Sauvignon or Shiraz
would do. Darjeeling, by the
way, goes very well when served
after Cabernet Sauvignon and
Shiraz.*

— MICHAEL OBNOWLENNY,
Canada's first tea sommelier

EARL GREY (BLACK TEA
FLAVORED WITH OIL OF
BERGAMOT)

cheese, strong

chicken

chocolate

custard desserts (e.g., crème brûlée)

game

ham

meat

pork

ENGLISH BREAKFAST
(BLEND OF BLACK TEA
VARIETIES, USUALLY ASSAM
AND CEYLON)

chicken

heavier dishes

meat

pastries

pork

scones, esp. with clotted cream

GOLDEN MONKEY
(CHINESE, FULL-BODIED,
BLACK TEA FROM THE
FUJIAN PROVINCE)

desserts, esp. chocolate and/or
  berry

GREEN (CHINESE, LIGHT-
BODIED; MADE FROM
GREEN, NON-FERMENTED
LEAVES)

Asian food

cheese, creamy, goat, and/or
  strong

chicken

chocolate, esp. with Japanese
  green tea

creamy dishes

FISH

fruit, fresh, esp. with sweeter teas
  melon

pears, cooked (e.g., poached)

poultry

rice

salad

sashimi, esp. with Chinese green
  tea

SEAFOOD

**SHELLFISH, ESP. WITH
JAPANESE GREEN TEA**

spicy dishes

sushi

sweets, Japanese-style (e.g., dried
  candies, red bean cakes)

tuna, esp. grilled or sautéed

*Asian foods are so complex in
flavor (sweet, spicy, sour, bitter, salty) that it is always best
to pair them with green tea,
which should be drunk at the
end of the meal to aid digestion.*

This practice is traditional in most Asian cultures.

— CORINNE TRANG, author, *Essentials of Asian Cooking*

GREEN OOLONG (LIGHT-BODIED, WITH FLORAL PERFUME)

lobster

pears, cooked (e.g., poached)

scallops

TIP: In Japan, green tea is steeped for one to two minutes, while in China it is steeped for three to five minutes.

HIBISCUS

chocolate and chocolate desserts

fruit salad, esp. with pears

ice cream, esp. vanilla

ICED (BREWED HOT AND SERVED COLD; FLAVOR AND BODY VARIES DEPENDING ON TEA USED)

barbecue

catfish

cole slaw

hush puppies

Southern food

TIDBIT: Iced tea is so ubiquitous that it has been called the "house wine" of the South!

To make iced tea, you want to start with a good quality black tea from Ceylon or Kenya in the loose leaf form. Steep the tea leaves properly in hot water. You'll want to brew your tea double to triple strength, so it stands up to the ice. Lemon and mint are optional — but ideally no sugar. If you do use citrus, you want to use no more than 5 to 10 percent, tops, in your tea.

— MICHAEL OBNOWLENNY, Canada's first tea sommelier

My three top choices for iced tea would be hibiscus, Assam, and then Japanese green with lemon because it is so refreshing. When I was the tea sommelier at Heartbeat in the W Hotel in New York, [restaurateur] Drew Nieporent would drink three pitchers of this a day!

— JAMES LABE, tea sommelier/owner, Teahouse Kuan Yin (Seattle)

INDIAN

butternut squash

JASMINE (FULL-BODIED; LEAVES ARE MIXED WITH JASMINE PETALS BEFORE FERMENTING)

lemongrass

lobster

poultry

salad

seafood

KENYAN (FULL-BODIED BLACK TEA)

chocolate

KYOTO CHERRY ROSE (JAPANESE, MEDIUM-BODIED, GREEN TEA WITH CHERRY AND ROSE FLAVORS)

strawberries

LEMON GINGER

poultry

seafood

MAPLE

butternut squash

cranberry

pumpkin

MINT

chocolate and chocolate desserts

mint-flavored dishes

Moroccan food, after dinner

North African food, after dinner

vanilla and vanilla desserts

OOLONG (CHINESE, PARTIALLY FERMENTED; SOMEWHERE BETWEEN GREEN AND BLACK TEA; USUALLY FROM TAIWAN [FORMOSA] AND FUCHIEN AND CHIANGSI PROVINCES)

apples, esp. with Ali Shan oolong

apricots and apricot desserts

beef

blackberries

chicken

chocolate

dessert, esp. with Ti Kuan Yin oolong

digestif

duck, esp. with darker oolong

fish, esp. with greenish oolong

fruit, fresh

ginger

grilled food

lobster, esp. with greenish oolong

meats, grilled, esp. with darker oolong

peaches

pecan pie

plums

scallops, esp. with greenish oolong

seafood, esp. with greenish oolong

shellfish, esp. with greenish oolong

spicy food

PLUM OOLONG (CHINESE, MEDIUM-BODIED; SOUR PLUM ADDED BEFORE DRYING)

meat

pork

poultry

seafood

PU-ERH (CHINESE; OFTEN BLENDED WITH CHRYSANTHEMUM, FROM THE YUNNAN PROVINCE)

chicken

chocolate

cinnamon

digestif

dim sum

duck

fatty or oily food

fried food

meat

stir-fried dishes

strawberries

ROOIBOS (E.G., YERBA CHAI)
cashew bars
nuts and nut-based desserts
pecan pie

TANGERINE
breakfast
omelet, (e.g., Indian spiced or
   vegetable)

VIOLET MINT
apple, baked
caramel
coconut
cream
strawberries

In India, we like to drink tanger-
ine tea. It is made of water with
tangerine peel, spices, and honey
and it is believed to keep you
young and healthy. My mother
has one every morning, and it is
said to keep her complexion
peaches and cream. In India, you
would have this tea at breakfast.
A typical breakfast might be a
masala omelet which has red
onion, freshly chopped cilantro,
green chile, and black pepper.
With that you would have toast
with salted butter.

— SUVIR SARAN,
chef, Dévi (NYC)

TEMPRANILLO
(SPANISH FRUITY FULL-BODIED
RED WINE)
beans
beef, esp. braised or stewed
braised dishes
charcuterie
cheese
duck
fish, esp. grilled
game and game birds, esp.
   served with fruit
garlic

grilled dishes
lamb, esp. chops and/or grilled
lentils
meat, esp. red and/or roasted
mushrooms
paella
pork, esp. grilled
poultry, esp. roasted
rice dishes
roasted dishes
sautéed dishes
steak
stew
veal
vegetables, esp. root, and esp.
   roasted
venison

Tempranillo is an underrated
varietal for food and wine pair-
ing. I find it very versatile.
There are many examples that
don't have a lot of oak and sub-
stantial acidity. There are many
Tempranillos that you would
mistake for Pinot Noir, except
they don't have the lusciousness
of Pinot. There is a triangle
between Sangiovese,
Tempranillo, and Pinot Noir.
They are very close to each
other in flavor, tannin, and
acid. The difference comes in
the elegance of the fruit and
richness of the grape.

— GREG HARRINGTON, MS

TEQUILA (MEXICAN
ALCOHOLIC SPIRIT MADE FROM
THE AGAVE CACTUS)
chiles
guacamole
Latin American food
Mexican food
salty dishes
spicy dishes

Tequila is fine, but you don't
get the flavor match up that you
do with wine. In Mexico, they
have a blanca tequila before
dinner, and after dinner they
will have a reposado or an
anejo. They don't typically
match tequila with food
because, flavor-wise, you are
not going to get a great match.
There are three categories of
tequila: 1) blanca, *which is*
aged no more than two months;
2) reposado, *which has rested*
and spent anywhere from two
months to up to one year in oak;
and 3) anejo, *which has spent*
at least one year in oak. It will
have vanilla tones or, if it was
aged in an old Bourbon barrel,
it will pick up those tones as
well. That is why this one is
particularly good after dinner.

— JILL GUBESCH, sommelier,
Frontera Grill and Topolobampo
(Chicago)

TOCAI FRIULANO
(ITALIAN MEDIUM-BODIED
WHITE WINE)
chicken
fritto misto (fried vegetables and
   seafood)
pasta, esp. with cream sauce
pork
prosciutto
risotto, esp. with cheese
salad
salmon, poached or grilled
salumi
scallops
seafood, esp. in soup or stews
shrimp, esp. grilled
veal
vegetables, summer

Tocai has a great minerality with pepper on the finish, which is wonderful with pork.

— DEREK TODD, sommelier, Blue Hill at Stone Barns (New York)

TOKAJI, SWEET
(HUNGARIAN SWEET WHITE DESSERT WINE)

cheese, blue
chocolate desserts
crème brûlée
custard
desserts
foie gras
fruit desserts, esp. rich and sweet
nuts

TOKAY, AUSTRALIAN
(AUSTRALIAN SWEET WHITE LIQUEUR WINE)

caramel and caramel desserts
chocolate and chocolate desserts
cream-based desserts

TOKAY PINOT GRIS
(FRENCH FULL-BODIED PINOT GRIS FROM ALSACE; AKA TOKAY D'ALSACE, BUT NO RELATION TO HUNGARIAN TOKAY; SEE ALSO PINOT GRIS, ALSATIAN)

cheese
fish, e.g. monkfish
foie gras
game
goose
lobster
meat, esp. white, and esp. roasted
mussels
spicy dishes
turkey
venison

TORRONTÉS
(SPANISH LEMONY MEDIUM-BODIED WHITE WINE FROM RIBEIRO)

Asian food, esp. Thai and Vietnamese

chicken
citrus fruit (e.g., lemon)
fish
guacamole
Mexican food
seafood and shellfish
sushi

TREBBIANO (ITALIAN LIGHT-BODIED WHITE WINE)

antipasto
fish, esp. fried or poached
lobster
prosciutto
risotto
salad
seafood
soup, seafood

TRINCADEIRA
(PORTUGUESE MEDIUM-BODIED RED WINE)

ham
lamb
pork, esp. roasted
swordfish, esp. grilled
tuna, esp. grilled

TXAKOLI (SPANISH LIGHT-BODIED, HIGH-ACID, SEMI-SPARKLING, WHITE WINE FROM THE BASQUE REGION; AKA TXACOLI AND CHACOLI)

anchovies, esp. marinated
bacalao (salt cod)
cheese
crab
fish, esp. grilled
garlic
oysters
pil pil sauce
pork
sardines, esp. marinated
seafood
shellfish
shrimp
sushi
Thai food
vinegar

Txacoli is a difficult wine to spell and pronounce [CHOC-o-lee] but it is great for summer-time and shellfish. It matches with lots of different fish preparations, from boquerones to tuna belly. A classic pairing from the Basque country would be shrimp sautéed in very hot olive oil with garlic and guindilla pepper.

— RON MILLER, maître d'hotel, Solera (NYC)

VALPOLICELLA
(ITALIAN LIGHT-BODIED DRY RED WINE FROM THE VENETO REGION)

barbecued dishes
braised dishes
cheese (e.g., Fontina, Pecorino, ricotta)
CHICKEN, ESP. GRILLED OR ROASTED
curries
eggplant
fish, esp. grilled
ham
hamburgers
lasagna
liver, calf's and chicken
meat, esp. grilled or roasted
Mexican food
mushrooms, esp. fried
PASTA, ESP. WITH LIGHTER, AND/OR TOMATO SAUCE, AND/OR BAKED
PIZZA
polenta, esp. with meat sauce
pork
prosciutto
quail
quiche
RISOTTO, ESP. WITH GORGONZOLA, MUSH-ROOM, SAUSAGE, AND/OR VEGETABLES
salmon, grilled
salumi
SAUSAGE, ESP. PORK AND/OR GRILLED

stew
tomato sauce
tuna
turkey, esp. roasted
veal, esp. roasted
vegetables and vegetable dishes,
  esp. richer

VERDELHO/
VERDEJO (PORTUGUESE
DRY MEDIUM-BODIED WHITE
WINE [VERDELHO] AND SPANISH
MEDIUM-BODIED WHITE WINE
FROM RUEDA [VERDEJO])
appetizers
ceviche
crab cakes
fish, white, esp. grilled
Indian food
pasta, esp. with pesto
salad
sea bass, esp. baked
seafood
shellfish
spicy dishes
vegetables, esp. roasted

VERDICCHIO (ITALIAN
DRY LIGHT-BODIED WHITE
WINE)
antipasti
artichokes, esp. with lemon
asparagus
calamari
crab, soft-shell
fish, cured or smoked
**FISH, ESP. WHITE, AND ESP.
  GRILLED, POACHED, OR
  ROASTED**
lobster
meat, white
mussels and *frites* (French fries)
onions
orange
**PASTA, ESP. CREAMY
  AND/OR WITH SEAFOOD**
prosciutto
risotto, esp. with asparagus
  and/or seafood

salad
scallops
sea bass, esp. roasted
SEAFOOD, ESP. GRILLED
seafood salad
shrimp, esp. grilled
stew, seafood
tomatoes
vegetable dishes

VERMENTINO (ITALIAN
AROMATIC MEDIUM-BODIED
WHITE WINE FROM SARDINIA
AND LIGURIA, ALSO GROWN IN
CORSICA)
anchovies
calamari, esp. fried
**FISH, ESP. SIMPLE (e.g.,
  GRILLED SEA BASS)**
fritto misto (fried fish and vegetables)
olive oil
pasta, esp. with pesto
pesto
pizza
poultry, esp. simple
SALAD
seafood
shellfish
vegetables, esp. roasted

VERNACCIA (ITALIAN
CRISP MEDIUM-BODIED WHITE
WINE FROM SIENA)
antipasto
artichokes
asparagus
bean dishes, esp. stewed
chicken, esp. grilled or roasted
**FISH, ESP. FRIED, GRILLED,
  OR POACHED**
lobster
meat, white
**PASTA, esp. butter, cheese, or
  cream sauce and/or with
  seafood**
prosciutto with melon
risotto, esp. with asparagus
  and/or seafood
salad

SEAFOOD
soup, esp. bean or seafood
veal

VIENNA LAGER (SEE
LAGER, VIENNA)

VINHO VERDE
(PORTUGESE, HIGH-ACID,
LIGHT-BODIED, VERY DRY, SEMI-
SPARKLING WHITE WINE)
Asian food
calamari, fried
ceviche
chicken
clams, esp. steamed
cold cuts
crab and crab cakes
fish, esp. fried or grilled
fruit and fruit salad
garlic
lemon
light dishes
lobster
mussels
picnics
prosciutto
red snapper, esp. grilled
salad
salsa
salt cod
*****SARDINES, ESP. GRILLED**
sausage
SEAFOOD
scallops
shrimp
spicy dishes
squid, esp. fried
stew, esp. seafood
tomatoes, esp. raw
vegetables, esp. green
vinaigrette

VIN JAUNE (FRENCH DRY
MEDIUM-BODIED WHITE WINE,
YELLOW IN COLOR; FROM THE
JURA REGION)
asparagus, white

cheese, Reblochon
duck
fish, fried
foie gras
game birds
ham, Serrano
lobster
morels
salmon
seafood
shellfish, fried
turbot

VINO NOBILE (ITALIAN MEDIUM- TO FULL-BODIED RED WINE MADE FROM SANGIOVESE; AKA VINO NOBILE DI MONTEPULCIANO)

cheese
chicken, esp. braised or stewed
game and game birds
meat, esp. braised and stewed
pasta
pizza
steak
veal, esp. osso buco
wild boar

VINO NOVELLO (ITALIAN YOUNG, FRUITY RED WINE)

cheese
CHESTNUTS, ROASTED
fruit, dried
game
meat, esp. grilled
mushrooms, porcini
pasta
pizza
salad
salami
truffles
walnuts

Vino Novello is like the Beaujolais Nouveau of Italy. With roasted chestnuts, it is ethereal!
— ROCCO DiSPIRITO, chef

VIN SANTO (ITALIAN BLENDED SWEET DESSERT WINE FROM TUSCANY)

apple desserts
***BISCOTTI, ESP. HAZELNUT**
cake
cheese
cookies
crème brûlée
fruit and fruit desserts
hazelnuts
NUTS, NUT BREADS, AND NUT DESSERTS
pear desserts
pecans
sorbets, esp. tropical fruit
walnuts

Vin Santo and hazelnut biscotti are one of the best matches in heaven!
— PIERO SELVAGGIO, owner, Valentino (Los Angeles)

VIOGNIER (FRENCH DRY, FLORAL, FULL-BODIED WHITE WINE FROM THE RHÔNE VALLEY)

appetizers
apricots
artichokes
Asian food
braised dishes
BUTTER AND BUTTER SAUCE
carrots
CHEESE
chestnuts
CHICKEN, ESP. ROASTED AND/OR WITH CREAM SAUCE
Chinese food
citrusy dishes, esp. with lemon
coconut
crab and soft-shell crab
CREAM AND CREAM-BASED SAUCE
cumin
CURRIES

duck, esp. roasted
fennel
FISH, ESP. WHITE AND/OR STEWED
foie gras
grilled dishes
hazelnuts
Indian food
LOBSTER
mushrooms
NUTS, ESP. ROASTED
olives
orange
peaches
peppers, red bell, esp. roasted
PORK, ESP. ROASTED
poultry
pralines
rich food
rosemary
salad, esp. pasta
salmon, cured
sautéed dishes
scallops
sea bass
scallops
seafood
shellfish
shrimp
skate
smoked fish and other foods
sole
spiced (slightly) dishes, esp. with cinnamon, cumin, curry, or nutmeg
squash
stewed dishes
Thai food
tomatoes
veal
vegetables and vegetable dishes

AVOID
very earthy dishes
very salty dishes

I love Viognier. At its best, it has an amazing peaches-and-cream–like aroma, and great body and balance. I find an aromatic, acidic Viognier works best

*with food, especially rich dishes
with butter or cream and some
kind of nut. My favorite producers are Peay and Cold Heaven.*

— RAJAT PARR, MS,
wine director, the Mina Group

*Viognier is beautiful with
Indian food, because of its lovely balance of fruit.*

— SUVIR SARAN,
chef, Dévi (NYC)

VODKA AND VODKA-BASED COCKTAILS (COLORLESS LIQUOR DISTILLED FROM GRAINS OR POTATOES; ORIGINALLY RUSSIAN OR POLISH)

CAVIAR
cheese, creamy
fish, oily and/or smoked
oysters
pickled vegetables

VOLNAY (FRENCH MEDIUM-BODIED RED WINE FROM BURGUNDY; SEE ALSO RECOMMENDATIONS FOR BURGUNDY, RED)

cheese, Epoisses
chicken, esp. roasted
duck
game and game birds
lamb
meat
mushrooms
rabbit
salmon, esp. grilled
sweetbreads

VOUVRAY (FRENCH DRY, MEDIUM-BODIED, WHITE WINE FROM THE LOIRE VALLEY)

almonds
appetizers

asparagus
cheese, esp. **goat**
chicken, esp. with cream sauce
clams, steamed
fried food
fruit and fruit desserts
gravlax
lobster, esp. steamed
mussels, steamed
oysters
pasta
pork, esp. with dried fruit
poultry, esp. in a cream sauce
quiche
RILLETTES
salad, seafood
salmon
SCALLOPS, ESP. BAKED
shrimp
soufflés
sushi
TROUT, ESP. BAKED AND/OR WITH CREAM SAUCE
veal, esp. with cream sauce

*Vouvray is one of the most
food-friendly wines. When there
are eight people at a table and
they have ordered eight different appetizers, I prefer to serve
Chenin Blanc or Vouvray.
These wines will hit more points
on the table than others because
of their acidity and fruit. They
are also great with fried foods.*

— BRIAN DUNCAN, wine
director, Bin 36 (Chicago)

SPARKLING
brunch
cheese, goat
desserts, esp. caramel, cream,
   and/or fruit-based
Japanese food
oysters
poultry, esp. with cream sauce
salad
scallops
shellfish

shrimp
soup
sushi
trout

*If you want to make a friend,
give them a taste of sparkling
Vouvray, with its combination
of green apple, honeysuckle,
white peach, and juicy acidity.
It's a wine that makes your
taste buds stand up and salute!
It is a great starter for parties.*

— BRIAN DUNCAN, wine
director, Bin 36 (Chicago)

SWEET
apple desserts
apricot desserts
cheese, creamier and/or lighter
   (e.g., goat, Gorgonzola)
foie gras
fruit desserts
lemon desserts
nut desserts
peach desserts
pear desserts
strawberry desserts, esp. creamy

WATER, MINERAL
THE CATEGORIES ARE FROM
FINEWATERS.COM'S SCALE
(FROM BOLDLY SPARKLING TO
STILL): BOLD, CLASSIC, LIGHT,
EFFERVESCENT, AND STILL.

BOLD (WITH BIG BUBBLES;
E.G., PERRIER, SARATOGA
SPRINGS)
appetizers, crispy
chips
fried food
hamburgers, esp. with cheese
hors d'oeuvres
nuts
oysters, fried
pizza

CLASSIC (E.G., APOLLINARIS,
SAN PELLEGRINO)
calamari, fried
chocolate desserts with nuts

hors d'oeuvres

main courses

meat, red

steak

LIGHT (WITH SMALL BUBBLES, E.G., RAMLOSA, SOLE)

cheese

chocolate desserts

entrées

fish, sautéed or poached

meat, red

poultry

second courses

sushi

turkey

EFFERVESCENT (E.G., BADOIT, BORSEC, VOSS)

caviar

chocolate desserts

desserts

pie, pumpkin

poultry

salad

second courses

STILL (E.G., EVIAN, FIJI, VOLVIC)

caviar

desserts

first courses

fish, poached

salad, Caesar

seafood, esp. light

sushi

tea

WEIZEN, HEFE (SEE BEER, HEFE WEIZEN)

WHISKEY (LIQUOR MADE FROM FERMENTED GRAIN MASH AGED IN WOOD; FROM THE UNITED STATES, CANADA, SCOTLAND, IRELAND)

apples

bacon

beef

cheese, esp. blue

chicken, esp. fried or grilled

chocolate and chocolate desserts

cinnamon

duck

figs

foie gras

fruit, dried

game

Irish food

Japanese food

mushrooms, esp. wild (e.g., morels)

oysters

pickled foods (e.g., ginger)

pork, esp. roasted

sauerkraut

seafood, esp. grilled

shellfish

smoked fish, esp. salmon

smoky-flavored dishes

spicy-dishes

steak

stew

sukiyaki

sushi

tempura

teriyaki

venison

wasabi

yakitori

ZINFANDEL

RED (CALIFORNIA MEDIUM- TO FULL-BODIED RED WINE; SPICY BERRY AND PEPPER FLAVORS)

Asian food, esp. spicy meat dishes

bacon

*BARBECUED MEAT, ESP. CHICKEN OR PORK (ESP. RIBS)

*BARBECUE SAUCE, SWEET (NOT SPICY)

basil

beans, esp. black

BEEF, ESP. GRILLED, STEWED, OR ROASTED WITH FULL-BODIED ZINFANDEL

berries and berry sauces

braised dishes

casseroles, esp. beef

cassoulet

cheese, dry Jack

cheese, goat, esp. aged

cheese, Parmesan

CHEESE, ESP. RICH AND/OR STRONG (e.g., blue, feta, Stilton)

chicken, esp. barbecued or grilled

cinnamon

clove

dessert

DUCK

eggplant (e.g., eggplant Parmesan)

fennel seed

figs

game, esp. stewed

game birds

garlic

GRILLED MEAT AND OTHER FOOD

HAMBURGERS, ESP. GRILLED, AND ESP. WITH CHEESE

hearty dishes

hot dogs

Japanese food, spicier

LAMB, ESP. LEG OR RACK OF LAMB, AND ESP. BRAISED OR ROASTED

MEAT, ESP. RED, AND ESP. BARBECUED, GRILLED, OR ROASTED

meat-flavored dishes and sauces

Mexican food, esp. spicy meat dishes

mint

mushrooms

olives

onions and onion soup

oregano

osso buco

pasta, esp. baked and/or heartier (e.g., lasagna, spaghetti and meatballs)

pepper, black

peppers, bell

PIZZA

ponzu sauce

PORK, ESP. CHOPS AND/OR ROASTED

rabbit

roasted meat (e.g., beef) and other dishes

rosemary

sage

salt and saltier dishes

SAUSAGE, ESP. SPICY AND/OR GRILLED

smoked food (e.g., cheese, meat, etc.)

soy sauce

spaghetti and meatballs

spareribs

SPICY DISHES, ESP. MEAT

STEAK, ESP. GRILLED AND/OR AU POIVRE

stew, esp. beef or game

sweet-and-sour dishes (e.g., Asian dishes)

tomatoes and tomato sauce

TURKEY, ESP. ROASTED

veal, esp. shanks and/or braised

vegetables, esp. grilled and/or root

vegetarian dishes, esp. with light- to medium-bodied Zinfandel

venison

wasabi

AVOID

cream sauce

fish

oysters

seafood

shellfish

WHITE (CALIFORNIA SWEET BLUSH WINE MADE FROM RED ZINFANDEL GRAPES)

appetizers

Asian food, (e.g., Chinese, Thai)

barbecue sauce, tomato-based

barbecued meat, esp. lighter

berries

charcuterie

cheese, mild (e.g., Cheddar, Jack), esp. served with fruit

CHICKEN, ESP. BARBECUED, FRIED, OR GRILLED, AND ESP. WITH SWEET BARBE-CUE SAUCE

cold cuts

crab

curries

fish, esp. grilled

fruit and fruit salsa/sauce

ginger

grilled food

HAM

hamburgers, esp. with ketchup

hot dogs, esp. with ketchup

ketchup

meat, white, esp. barbecued, grilled, or roasted

Mexican food

mustard

onions

pasta, esp. lighter

picnics

pizza, pepperoni

pork

ribs, esp. with sweet barbecue sauce

salad

salmon, esp. barbecued or grilled

sautéed dishes

scallops

seafood

shrimp

spicy food

TURKEY, ROASTED OR SMOKED

vegetables, esp. grilled or roasted

When people ask me if I like white Zinfandel, the geeky side of me says, "It is the cheese-burger of the culinary world" . . . but I love cheeseburgers!

— GREG HARRINGTON, MS

We find lots of room for Zinfandels. I am particularly fond of many of Paul Draper's selections from Ridge Vineyards — and Helen Turley's Zinfandels are always tasty. When you get away from those big names, there are many smaller vineyards that also do a wonder-ful job. Zinfandels have tended to be good values as well and pair equally well with quail stuffed with chili spoonbread and wrapped in mesquite-smoked bacon on a bean cake with coffee-tinged BBQ sauce and pearl onions, or with flank steak rubbed with pureed dried chiles, pecans, orange juice, and garlic, grilled and served with sim-ple oven-roasted potatoes and mushroom escabeche.

— JANOS WILDER, chef-owner, Janos (Tucson)

Sometimes you find combinations by accident. When I was starting out, I would try to taste as often as I could, so I would go to "BYOB" restaurants. I once went to a sushi bar with a bottle of Zinfandel because that is what I happened to have with me. Talk about a lesson! A light bulb went off when I tasted how the ripeness of Zinfandel is a great foil to edgier flavors like soy, sweet and sour, ponzu, and even wasabi, where it will temper the heat.

— BRIAN DUNCAN, wine director, Bin 36 (Chicago)

CHAPTER SEVEN

At *the* Table *with the* Experts

Pairing Menus from Some of America's Best Restaurants

DANNY MEYER

Normally, in any well-thought-out dinner, you start with something simple, and then move into something more intense and complex as you go along. If you go the other way, then it's either disappointing or you can't even taste the wine . . . What you want to do is have a progression. You have to pace it, such as by starting out with a delicate Riesling, then perhaps a Loire Valley Chenin Blanc, followed by a Chardonnay, and winding up with an older Pinot Noir.

— LARRY STONE, MS, Rubicon (San Francisco)

Pairing a single dish with a beverage versus composing an entire menu is akin to listening to a single movement instead of an entire symphony.

There is an art to composing a menu so that it moves along an arc, building to a crescendo, with a peaceful resolution in the end. While we explored the edible aspect of this art in our book *Culinary Artistry*, potables such as wine and other beverages play an equally critical role.

In this chapter, you'll find special menus pairing food with wine and other beverages that represent some of the best efforts of leading experts at some of America's very best restaurants. They exemplify some of the general rules, or "grading principles," that allow a meal to unfold with grace. When referring to food, *grading* implies an ascension of flavors and textures, from milder and lighter to heavier and stronger. With regard to wine, grading suggests a progression of increasing "weight" (body) and "volume" (flavor intensity), such as in the following principles:

- *White wine before red wine*
- *Lighter-bodied wine before fuller-bodied wine*
- *Lower-alcohol wine before higher-alcohol wine*
- *Drier wine before sweeter wine*
- *Younger wine before aged wine*
- *Simple wine before complex wine*
- *Humble wine before grand wine*

Applying these principles to beverages served over the course of a single menu results in the following diverse examples:

OLD WORLD PROGRESSION: *Riesling → Loire Valley Chenin Blanc → white Burgundy → aged red Burgundy*

NEW WORLD PROGRESSION: *sparkling wine → light, crisp white (e.g., Sauvignon Blanc) → fruity red (e.g., Pinot Noir) → tannic red (e.g., Cabernet Sauvignon)*

GLOBAL ECLECTIC PROGRESSION: *light Nigori sake → heavier sake → Alsatian Gewürztraminer → Rhône red*

To this end, beverage director Daniel Johnnes of Daniel observes, "I am a strong proponent of white wine with a cheese plate. But at the end of a fine meal, after the entrée, you have to follow the previous wine with something equally good in breeding or better. It has to be something like a Batard-Montrachet, or a really good Premier Cru white Burgundy, or perhaps a white Hermitage — something with stature and breeding and class."

THE ORDER OF A MENU

If I'm creating a tasting menu with five different wines, I generally like to start with Champagne. Then I'll serve a crisp white, either Riesling or something light from the Loire Valley, before segueing into heavier white Burgundy. Then, it will be on to Pinot Noir and probably ending with Rhône [red].

— TRACI DES JARDINS, chef, Jardiniere (San Francisco)

Some experts suggest that when pairing a beverage, it's as important to consider the order of the dish on the menu as it is the dish's component ingredients. In general, a dish served as an appetizer should be paired with a lighter wine than a dish served as an entrée — even if both the appetizer and the entrée feature the same ingredients.

Master sommelier Joseph Spellman recalls that when he worked with foodstuffs not classically thought to be wine-friendly at Charlie Trotter's in Chicago, it opened up a new way of thinking about food and wine pairing over the course of a menu. "What do you do with a ginger-infused sauce the first time you see it?" he muses. "My answer? It depends as much on its position — that is, which course it is in the meal — as its flavor. The wine needs to be related to the [progression] of wine flavors as much as to the individual dish's flavor."

In a restaurant setting, the chefs and sommeliers who apply grading principles when designing their food and beverage menus, respectively, will find themselves simpatico when it comes time to pairing the two. "At the inn, chef [Patrick O'Connell]'s approach is purely about progression, which plays into the hands of wine pairing," says Scott Calvert, sommelier at the Inn at Little Washington. "Patrick's dishes start delicate, and move on from there."

Chef David Waltuck takes a classic French-inspired approach to his tasting menu at New York's Chanterelle. "We serve a cold appetizer, a hot appetizer, a fish course, a meat course, cheese, and then dessert," he says, "This classic format lends itself to a wine progression."

Chanterelle's master sommelier Roger Dagorn describes how he matches wines from the Old World and New World to Waltuck's menu:

1. TO START: *Champagne*

2. FIRST COURSE: *I'll pair it with sake, sherry, or a fruity white wine (e.g., Riesling).*

3. SECOND COURSE: *For David's signature seafood sausage, I tend to like a fuller-bodied white wine like Viognier or Pinot Gris. I have gone to a red wine like Pinot Noir, or Uva Rara ("rare grape") from Lombardy, which is great with seafood and truffles.*

4. MEAT COURSE: *We like to serve wines from France, Spain, Italy, and Hungary.*

5. CHEESE COURSE: *We serve several different cheeses which change every month. We may serve full-bodied red, an aromatic fruity white (e.g., Gewürztraminer), or a fortified wine like sherry, port, Madeira, or Commandaria St. John from Crete.*

6. DESSERT COURSE: *I have fun with dessert. Sauternes is obvious, so I try not to use that. I like Muscatel from Spain, or Tokai from Australia, or a Late Harvest wine from the Loire Valley. An Austrian Auslese is off the beaten track here, but the most popular wine of the region there. I have also served Framboise Lambic beer or rum, which are both great with chocolate.*

FUN WITH BEVERAGES: BREAKING THE RULES

On tasting menus, I have served sake followed by Madeira and then Champagne.
People are surprised not that *I'm serving Champagne, but* when.

— ALAN MURRAY, MS, Masa's (San Francisco)

In this day and age, pushing the envelope can involve featuring different beverages in the same meal. Our experts have found their own ways of finessing this.

"The name of this restaurant is 'The Modern,' so without going too crazy, I like to shock and have fun with some of my wine choices," admits wine director Stephane Colling. "For example, I like to reverse the usual order of white wine before red. After starting with a light red like Gamay or Pinot Noir, I'll move into a very dry or off-dry white like a Montlouis from the Loire Valley. This works very well with cheese, as I find a white is more refreshing to finish a meal."

Offering a flight — that is, the sommelier's choice of beverages — with its tasting menu allows Chanterelle the opportunity to introduce nontraditional beverages such as sake rather easily. Says master sommelier Roger Dagorn:

> In fact, the reception has been so strong that I have people coming back and asking for the sake they had last year or even an all-sake pairing. I now have anywhere from fifteen to thirty sakes on hand.
>
> We're traditional in that we start with simpler-flavored sakes and work our way up into heavier and more complex styles, but this [grading] approach is unique to Western cuisine. In Japan, they don't follow grading like we do here. There, sake is not taken as seriously when it comes to formal pairings with food. It is more based on the moment.

Waltuck most often sees sake make an appearance in any of the first three courses on a menu, especially the first course. "What that has, in addition to being a good pairing, is 'entertainment value' or theater," he says. "It is the opportunity to serve guests something they may not have had before."

Experiencing the seamless integration of another beverage into a wine flight can be an inspiration. Joseph Spellman remembers a coup of fellow sommelier Scott Tyree at an event: "The chef was from Cleveland, and served foie gras and veal bratwurst with mustard as a 'wink-wink cutesy' dish — and Scott paired a Great Lakes stout from Cleveland with it," Spellman recalls. "It was a rich, beautiful, fun pairing, and the beer did not interrupt the pleasures of the wines that were served either before and after."

PAIRING MENUS FROM SOME OF AMERICA'S BEST RESTAURANTS

We hope you'll be inspired to come up with new pairing and menu ideas for yourself through these ten menus, which represent proud achievements of some of America's best restaurants. You'll find everything from a menu showcasing a diverse array of beverages (including red, white, sparkling, and dessert wines), as well as menus focused solely on, say, Italian wine, sake, or tea — not to mention wines paired to Mexican and Japanese dishes as well as cutting-edge New American cuisine.

So, read on and dream big!

ALINEA

Chicago, Illinois

GRANT ASCHATZ, CHEF
JOE CATTERSON, SOMMELIER

October 19, 2005

PEAR ○ celery leaf and branch, curry
Christian Drouin Pommeau de Normandie "Coeur de Lion"

CHESTNUT ○ too many garnishes to list
Vercesi del Casteliazzo "Gugiaroio" Pinot Nero Bianco

TROUT ROE ○ pineapple, cucumber, coriander
Dirler-Cade Tokay Pinot Gris, Alsace 2002

LOBSTER ○ chanterelles, ravioli of coconut powder
A. Christmann Estate Riesling, Pfalz 2004

DOVER SOLE ○ mostly traditional flavors
Movia "Veliko Bianco," Gonska Brda, Slovenia 2000

PHEASANT ○ cider, shallot, burning leaves
Albert Mann Pinot Auxerrois "Vieilles Vignes," Alsace 2003

SQUAB ○ watermelon, foie gras, black licorice
I Portali Aglianico del Vulture, Basilicata, Italy 2002

LAMB ○ fig, pernod, pillow of sassafras air
Rocche del Manzoni "La Cresta" Barbera d'Alba, Piedmont 2000

BISON ○ truffle, pistachio, sweet spices
Finca Flichman "Paisaje de Tupungato" Tinto, Argentina 2001

MATSUTAKE ○ pine nut, mastic, rosemary
Vinhos Barbetto "Charleston" Sercial Madeira

BACON ○ butterscotch, apple, thyme

CORN ○ honey, tonka bean, vanilla
Brillet Pineau des Charentes "Blanc Prestige"

PEANUT ○ frozen Pedro Ximenez

CHOCOLATE ○ avocado, lime, mint
Alto Adige Moscato Rosa with Crème de Cassis

DRY CARAMEL ○ salt

CHANTERELLE

New York, New York

DAVID WALTUCK, CHEF
ROGER DAGORN, MASTER SOMMELIER

Sake Pairing Menu, September, 2005

Amuses Bouches
Shirataki

An Assortment of Raw and Cured Fish
Shirataki Jozen "Mizunogotos"

Chilled Tomato Consommé with Crab, Chervil, and Black Caviar
Umenishiki "Sake Hitosuji"

Grilled Seafood Sausage
Urakasumi

Crispy New Zealand Snapper with Late Summer Sweet Corn and Purple Basil
Urakasumi

Grilled Turbot with Red Wine–Braised Shallots and Pistachio-Chive Vinaigrette
Umenishiki Daiginjo

Zucchini Blossoms Filled with Chicken and Black Truffles
Wakatake Ginjo "Onikoroshi"

Breast of Duck with Hot and Sour Duck Jus and Braised Duck-Leg Spring Roll
Wakatake Daiginjo "Onikoroshi"

Late-Summer Roasted Bartlett Pears with Hazelnut Streusel and Hazelnut Ice Cream
Otokoyama Fukkoshu

Coffee

Petits Fours

EMERIL'S NEW ORLEANS

New Orleans, Louisiana

MATT LIRETTE, SOMMELIER

Saturday, February 22, 2003

Bluefin Tuna with Bottarga

Black Truffle and Potato Soup
2000 Orvieto Classico Superiore "Terre Vineate," Palazzone (Umbria)

Saffron Potato Cake with Salt Cod, Tomato, and Olive Oil
2000 Greco di Tufo "San Paolo," Benito Ferrara (Campania)
1999 Verdicchio di Matelica, Castiglioni Bisci (Marche)

Sautéed Crabmeat with Gnocchi, Fried Potato, and Pancetta Carbonara
2000 Soave Classico Superiore "Salvarenza," Gini (Veneto)
2000 Chardonnay "Ciampagnis Vieris," Vie di Romans (Isonzo del Friuli)

Sliced Veal, Bluefin Tuna, and Prosciutto Smothered in Caper and Tomato Sauce
1996 Gattinara "San Francesco," Antoniolo (Piemonte)
1997 Carmignano Riserva "Le Vigne Alte Montalbiolo," Fattoria Ambra (Toscano)

Lamb and Eggplant Ragout over Spaghetti
1999 Nero d'Avola, Zenner (Sicilia)
2000 Aglianico del Vulture "La Firma," Cantine del Notaio (Bascilicata)

Zabaglione with Fresh Berries and Cookies
2002 Moscato d'Asti "Vigneto Biancospino," La Spinetta, Rivetti (Piemonte)
1994 Vin Santo "Bianco Dell'Empolese," Piazzano (Toscano)

FRONTERA GRILL / TOPOLOBAMPO

Chicago, Illinois

RICK BAYLESS, CHEF
JILL GUBESCH, SOMMELIER

Tasting Menu

FIRST COURSE

SOPES DE PAPA crispy little **potato-masa boats** filled with Sinaloa-style pork chilorio and served with three-chile salsa, grilled orange, queso añejo, and local organic baby greens
2003 Sella & Mosca, "La Cala," Vermentino, Alghero, Sardinia, Italy

SECOND COURSE

SOPA DE FLORES Y GUÍAS **rustic summer soup** of squash blossoms and young organic squash runners with smoked chicken, River Valley woodland mushrooms, and roasted tomato
2003 Quinta Dos Roques, Encruzado, Dão, Portugal

THIRD COURSE

LANGOSTA CON SALSA DE ELOTE Y CHILE CHILACA pan-roasted fresh **Maine lobster** with creamy sweet corn–chilaca chile sauce, rustic mash (potatoes, parsnips, and celeriac), fresh local morel mushrooms, and grilled zucchini-chayote salad (with local green garlic and roasted poblanos)
2003 Vincent Giradin, "Les Narvaux," Meursault, Burgundy, France

FOURTH COURSE

BIRRIA DE CHIVO chile-marinated, **slow-roasted Swan Creek Boer goat** served in a crispy potato-masa sope with rich pan juices, braised lacinato kale, and runner beans
1999 Gran Reserva, Bodegas Tarsus, Ribera del Duero, Spain

FIFTH COURSE

Best-of-the-day **dessert sampler**
1996 Marcel Deiss, Grand Cru "Altenberg de Bergheim" SGN Gewürztraminer, Alsace, France

KAI

New York, New York

HITOSHI KAGAWA, EXECUTIVE CHEF
KAI ANDERSEN AND HEIDI KOTHE-LEVIE, TEA SPECIALISTS

Fall Tea Tasting, November 7, 2004

Smoked Salmon with Ikura (Salmon Roe)
Organic Rooibos, South Africa

Watercress and Yuba in a Katsuo Broth
Honyama Yabukita, Green, Shizuoka Prefecture, Japan

Seared Tuna with Onion and Capers
Chiran Kanayamidori, Green, Kagoshima Prefecture, Japan

Ochazuke with Sliced Flounder
Uji Kabuse-cha, Green, Uji Prefecture, Japan

Shabu-Shabu of Beef with a Sesame Sauce
Aged High Mountain Oolong, Ali Shan region, Taiwan

The **rooibos,** mild with subtle notes of vanilla, was a gentle pairing
with the more pungent ikura and smoked salmon.

The **yabukita green tea** varietal is renowned for its sweeter, mild flavor,
lending itself nicely to the peppery watercress and fish-derived dashi.

Many strong flavors here: tuna, onions, and capers. This dish required a tea that could stand its own.
Chiran Kanayamidori is very vigorous, herbaceous, lively.

Kabuse-cha is a shaded like the prized gyokuro, but for a shorter period of time.
The result is a sweeter, herbaceous green tea, very easy drinking. The ochazuke here was also
prepared with the kabuse-cha, so you could see it in direct interaction with food and as a complement.

Rich flavors of beef and sesame merited a hearty oolong.
The **Aged High Mountain Oolong** — it was aged for ten years in Taiwan — was one of the
most expensive teas we've ever carried. Smooth with a prominent sweetness and strong notes
of stone fruit like apricots and peach. It seemed to make the beef seem richer and sweeter.

MARY ELAINE'S AT THE PHOENICIAN

Scottsdale, Arizona

BRADFORD THOMPSON, CHEF DE CUISINE

GREG TRESNER, MASTER SOMMELIER

Chef Table, October 15, 2004

Kumamoto Oyster and Borsht, Tuna, and Celery Parfait
Krug Grand Cuvée Brut Champagne, France, NV
Ariel Sparkling Brut, California, DA

Tempura Frog Leg, Parsley Crème Fraîche, and Garlic Chip
Jean Collet "Vaillons" 1er Cru Chablis, Burgundy, France, 2000

House-Smoked Salmon, Marinated Baby Beets, and Vodka Cream
Dr. Crusius Niederhäuser Felsenstayer Riesling Kabinet, Nahe, Germany, 1999

Clam and Pork Belly Chowder
F.E. Trimbach "Clos Ste. Hune" Riesling, Alsace, France, 1995

Lasagna of Butter-Poached Lobster, Scallop with Caviar
Ponsot "Clos des Monts Luisants" 1er Cru Morey-Saint-Denis, Burgundy, France, 2000

Dover Sole Meunière

Local Corn Fricasee and Jerusalem Artichoke
Venica Sauvignon Blanc, Collio, Friuli-Venezia Giulia, Italy, 2002

Butternut Squash Risotto

Wild Mushroom Cream, Grated Amaretti
Broadley Vineyards "Marcile Lorraine" Pinot Noir, Willamette Valley, Oregon, 1999
Navarro Pinot Noir Juice, Anderson Valley, California, 2002

Honey and Spice–Glazed Pekin Duck, Squab and Foie Gras Pastilla
Castellare "Coniale" Cabernet Sauvignon, Tuscany, Italy, 1997

Artisanal Cheeses
Alois Kracher "Nouvelle Vague" #7 Chardonnay/Welschriesling
Trockenbeerenauslese, Neusiedlersee, Austria, 1995

Strawberry and Raspberry Fruit Soup

Roasted Anjou Pear, Summer Melon

Organic Yogurt Charlotte, Peaches and Thyme
Capezzana Vin Santo, Carmignano, Italy, 1996

Petits Fours and Coffee
Barbeito Terrantez Madeira, Portugal, 1795

THE MODERN AT THE MUSEUM OF MODERN ART

New York, New York

GABRIEL KREUTHER, CHEF
KAREN KING, BEVERAGE DIRECTOR
STEPHANE COLLING, WINE DIRECTOR

The following two menus were served simultaneously at The Modern, providing an impressive showcasing of dishes matching a number of the same wines toward the end of dinner.

Signature Tasting Menu, March 19, 2005

NV Paul Goerg — Brut Absolu
Champagne, France

Foie Gras Terrine Marbled with Roasted Artichokes and Green Peppercorns
NV Domaine de Laubade
Floc de Gascone, France

Tartare of Yellow Fin Tuna and Diver Sea Scallops Seasoned with Yellowstone River Caviar
2003 De Trafford — Chenin Blanc
Walker Bay, South Africa

Roasted Maine Lobster in a "Folly of Herbs" with Asparagus and Salsify
2000 Kogl — Chardonnay
Prodravje, Slovenia

Chorizo-Crusted Chatham Cod with White Cocoa-Bean Puree and Harissa Oil
1995 Louis Jadot — Corton-Greves
Aloxe Corton, France

Buffalo Tenderloin Poached in Spiced Cabernet with Roasted Endive and Shallot-Pepper Jus
2000 Joseph Phelps — Insignia
Cabernet Sauvignon, United States

Dessert Tasting
1999 Klein Constancia
Vin de Constance, South Africa

THE MODERN AT THE MUSEUM OF MODERN ART

New York, New York

GABRIEL KREUTHER, CHEF
KAREN KING, BEVERAGE DIRECTOR
STEPHANE COLLING, WINE DIRECTOR

Spring Tasting Menu, March 19, 2005

NV Paul Goerg – Brut Absolu
Champagne, France

Chilled Maine Lobster Salad with Black Radish, Celery, and Thai Long Peppercorn Sorbet
2002 Dirler-Cade – Sylvaner Vielles Vignes
Alsace, France

Sautéed Sullivan County Foie Gras with Basil Jus, Chickweed, and Shizo
2000 Sua Sponffe
Vin de Table, France

Licorice-Poached East Coast Halibut on a Salad of New Onions, Haricots Verts, Almonds,
and Hedgehog Mushrooms
2002 Château Mont-Redon Blanc
Châteauneuf-du-Pape, France

Louisianan Crayfish Gratin
1995 Louis Jadot – Corton-Greves
Aloxe Corton, France

Milk-Fed Veal with Fresh Morels and Spring Vegetables
2000 Joseph Phelps – Insignia
Cabernet Sauvignon, United States

Dessert Tasting
1999 Klein Constancia
Vin de Constance, South Africa

SANFORD

Milwaukee, Wisconsin

SANDY D'AMATO, CHEF

Dinner, April 11, 2005

While researching this book, we asked to speak with chef **Sandy D'Amato** when we were in the Chicago area. He invited us to sit down with him and his wife **Angie** over dinner at Sanford. The restaurant blew us away with a tasting menu entitled "Drinkin' and Eatin' at Sanford," a casual moniker which belies the restaurant's seriously impressive pairing of food with not only wine, but beverages ranging from sherry to beer.

Grilled Pear and Roquefort Barquette with Caramelized Onions and Walnuts
2000 Muscat – Ottonel, Domaine Barmes Buecher, Alsace
Lustau dry Amontillado

[1]Citrus-Seared Alaskan Halibut on Morel Mushroom Risotto Cake, Asparagus Nage
2001 Grüner Veltliner–Pichier–Loibnerberg, Wachau/Osterreich, Austria
Ephemere Witbier–Unibroue: ale brewed with apple juice, coriander, and curaçao, Shelburne, Vermont

[2]Provençal Fish Soup with Rouille
2002 Vin Gris of Pinot Noir–Sanford Estate, Santa Rita Hills, Santa Barbara, California

[3]Seared Salmon on Caper Wine Potato and Sorrel Egg Salad, Caviar Vermouth Dressing
NV Col Vetoraz–Prosecco di Valdobbaidene, Brut, Italy

[4]Buckwheat Honey–Glazed Squab with Seared Foie Gras, Candied Radishes, and Spring Onions
2002 Sancerre Rouge–Domaine Vacheron, Loire Valley
1999 Sauternes–Château de Malle–Comtesse de Bournazel, France
Chambly Unibroue: wheat ale with subtle spices, Canada

[5]Black Olive–Crusted Loin of Strauss Veal with Spinach and Ricotta Gnocchi, Green Olive Dressing
2001 Cabernet Franc–Chinon, Clos du Chene Vert–Joguet, Loire Valley
Duchesse de Bourgogne: reddish-brown ale matured in oak casks, Belgium

[6]Dessert

Poppy Seed Torte, Sour Cream–Anise Ice Cream

Mango Spice Cake, Cassia Ice Cream

Tart Cherry Clafoutis, Morello Cherry Ice Cream

Banana Butterscotch Toffee Tart, Banana Rum Ice Cream

Warm Lemon Pound Cake with Lemon Curd
1997 Quarts de Chaume–Château de Suronde, F. Poirel, France (dessert Chenin Blanc)
Broadbent 10-Year-Old Mamsey Madeira, Island of Madeira
2003 Moscato d'Asti (frizzante) Nivole, M. Chiarlo, Italy
1998 Banyuls–M. Chapoutier, France
Unibroue-Quelque Chose: Belgian-style ale, Canada

1. SANDY: Belgian-style beers can be a little too much on their own, but with food they can really shine. These two beverages come at different sides of the dish. Grüner Veltliner is classic with asparagus, and the asparagus also brings out the apple in the beer.

2. SANDY: Sanford Estate makes great Pinot and Chardonnay. Their wines are all very food-friendly and also age very well. The owner brought an '88 Chardonnay to our anniversary in 2000 and, to be honest, Chardonnay is probably the last wine I like to drink because I am not that big of a fan. But his was great.

Usually we serve a rosé with this soup [bouillabaisse]. But the dish needs a touch more sweetness and fruit. The typical French rosé is too dry for my version.

ANGIE: The dish has fennel and scallops that have sweetness to them, which would erase the fruit of a rosé so all you would have left is alcohol.

SANDY: This is a hard dish to pair. You need a wine that can bring up the fish. A lot of whites can't stand up to bouillabaisse.

3. SANDY: We like to serve a sparkling wine not just at the beginning of a menu, but also later in the menu because it is refreshing.

4. SANDY: The beer [Blanche de Chambly] is great with the foie gras and rhubarb. The Sancerre worked great with the squab, which the beer did not hold up to. The Sauternes didn't fit anywhere, because it is the wrong texture. The dish is also acidic, which doesn't work with Sauternes. When we do salt and pepper cold–cured foie gras, it works great with Sauternes.

5. ANGIE: A classic Chinon smells of pencil shavings but you also get some green olive on the nose. Chinon in general is so good. We once grilled some lobster and lamb on a night off and had a Chinon and it was just spectacular. I describe this wine like a sophisticated Beaujolais.

SANDY: It is fruit forward with a nice Mediterranean vegetal quality to it. It is also lean and doesn't compete with anything.

SANDY: This is a left field pairing. The beer is sweet, rich, and has cherry qualities to it. The veal brings up the sweetness in the beer, whereas the other components of the dish mute the sweetness. This [Chinon] is my favorite wine and it is the best red wine for food.

6. SANDY: The beer with the spice cake or clafoutis is great.

ANGIE: I like the beer with the spice cake and the poppy seed tart.

SUSHISAMBA

New York, New York

TIMON BALLOO, CHEF
PAUL TANGUAY, SOMMELIER

Sake Pairing Menu, November 3, 2005

FIRST
"Hot & Cold" Blue Point Oyster Ceveche

SECOND
Frothed Uni Bisque, truffle-kirby mignonette

THIRD
"Escape from Alcatraz," yuzu truffle–broiled Alaskan king crab with escaping sawagani

FOURTH
Cornmeal-Crusted Ancas de Rana, aji panca espuma, micro green salad

FIFTH
Kobe a la Plancha, foie gras curry-yaki, and sesame tempura asparagus

SIXTH
Temari Matsu
Forbidden fruit–filled lychees, coffee salt, black sesame ice cream
Rocotto chile–dusted cake with passion fruit ice cream, puree and reduction

SAKES
Junmai, Masumi, Okuden Kansakuri, Nagano, Japan
Junmai Ginjo, Dewasansan Nama Genshu, Dewazakura, Yamagata, Japan
Gingo Oka, Dewazakura, Yamagata, Japan
Junmai Koshu, Yashiorinosake, Shimane, Japan
Junmai-Daiginjo, Kamoizumi, Hiroshima, Japan
Kome-Kome-shu, Kamoizumi, Hiroshima, Japan
Tokimeki, Blanc de Sake, Harushika, Nara, Japan

the Best *on* *the* Best

Desert Island Lists of Some of America's
Leading Beverage Experts

I'm not so much into beer and sake ... Give me a white or red wine,
and I am in heaven!

— DANIEL BOULUD, chef-owner, Daniel (NYC)

Which beverages would our distinguished experts take with them if we banished them to a proverbial desert island for the rest of their lives — and limited them to twelve (and only twelve!) bottles? It's amazing what we learned about these experts' palates, priorities, and personalities from their immediate replies. Some obviously like variety; others are obsessed by a single grape (such as the sommelier who brought along twelve bottles of red Burgundy). One brave soul admitted he couldn't bear the thought of life without Diet Coke! You'll see some wines that appear on almost every list: Most sommeliers chose to include a Riesling because of its food-pairing prowess. Several also took a bottle of Chablis because of its ability to accompany all those oysters they expected to be eating. This idea was so intriguing, we took it a step further.

Being the kind-hearted souls that we are, we decided we would offer to send along the chef of their choice to create any dish of their choosing to accompany those precious twelve bottles. We were surprised how many sommeliers thought like chefs; we assumed they'd be so wine-centric that they might brush off the idea of food, but some even said these wines would inspire them to cook for themselves. Their choices of food to pair with their wines run the gamut from family recipes to four-star feasts. You'll doubtless see echoes of your own favorite matches — like Kinkead's sommelier Michael Flynn's wish for barbecued ribs to accompany his Zinfandel, or chef Rocco DiSpirito's desire for crème brûlée for an ethereal pairing with Hungarian Tokaji Aszu.

Reading these lists is as entertaining as it is educational. You'll see for yourself what we've been saying all along: that despite all the rules and theories and principles, it still comes down to *what tastes good to you*. So, to help you on your journey to discover your own favorite flavors, we've included a tasting chart at the end of this chapter that you can use to evaluate what you like and don't like about various food and beverage pairings you encounter. (After all, we all have trouble remembering specifics after a few glasses!) We'd also encourage you to keep a food and beverage log, so that you can better recall what you ate and drank — and eventually compile your own list of favorite food and beverage pairings. Enjoy your exploration into the pleasurable life of eating and drinking.

Bon appétit, and cheers!

JOSEPH BASTIANICH

RESTAURATEUR AND OWNER,
ITALIAN WINE MERCHANTS

New York, New York

1. 1947 Vouvray le Haut Lieu, the greatest white wine ever made
DISH: **Slow-smoked king salmon** done on the barbecue, roasted over beach grass for six hours. I would serve this over the first fava beans of spring, pureed with extra-virgin olive oil.

2. 1990 Dom Pérignon Rosé
DISH: I would need Rod Mitchell [one of America's top fish purveyors] to bring me some **caviar.**

3. 1953 R.C. Richebourg or Romanée-Conti. These are the two greatest Burgundies I have ever had.
DISH: A Peter Luger **steak** for four, but shared with only one other person.

4. 1982 Bartolo Mascarello Barolo.
DISH: In Piemonte, they have **carpaccio** made from the calf when it is halfway between veal and beef, and is very pink. It is served with egg, shallot, and white truffle shaved on top.

5. 1989 Gaya Barbaresco
DISH: *Tortellini al plin*, which is a **ravioli boiled in capon stock** and served on a napkin. I'd like this from San Marco restaurant in Canelli and made by Mariuccia.

6. A magnum of Vega Sicilia from 1968, because it is my birth year
DISH: Since I would be having this on my birthday, I would have this with **hamburgers topped with Roquefort cheese and bacon.**

7. 1983 Ramonet Montrachet
It's almost a cliché, because it is one of the greatest wines in the world — as well as . . .

8. 1967 Château d'Yquem, because it is a such a great wine
DISH: **Nothing.** Each would be a meal in itself. I would want to have it while listening to bluegrass music on a ski trip in Valdezer.

9. 1947 Cheval Blanc from a magnum. This is another of the greatest wines ever made.
DISH: **Pigeon** or **squab**

10. Tocai Friulano by Bastianich, from any year
DISH: **Prosciutto San Daniele** would be a great pairing.

11. Constance de Constantia from South Africa. Any vintage.
It is one of the most elusive wines and would be interesting to drink on a desert island. This was the only non-French wine Napoleon ever drank.
DISH: I'd have this after dinner with a **crumbly blackberry bodino** made by Babbo's pastry chef, Gina De Palma.

12. Chave Hermitage Blanc 2000
DISH: This one is easy: a **lobster roll** from Pearl Oyster Bar in New York City.

STEVE BECKTA

OWNER, BECKTA DINING & WINE

Ottawa, Canada

1. Vouvray 1971 Demi-Sec Le Haut-Lieu
DISH: On my second date with Maureen [now Steve's wife], it was 112 degrees out. Because it was too hot to eat anything, we drank the best bottle of wine in my cellar by itself . . . off each other.

2. Müller-Catoir Scheurebe Spätlese
DISH: A surprise menu from an exotic East Asian country where I don't know the food well. I'd want lots of exotic fruits, spices, and herbs, because this wine has these qualities.

For wines 3, 4, and 5, I want to see how the greatest Pinot Noir in America develops after its first vintage. I will drink them all on the same night. This will be the night I say, "Screw it — I am going to live in the moment!"

3. Marcassin Pinot Noir Estate Sonoma Coast 1996

4. Marcassin Pinot Noir Estate Sonoma Coast 1997

5. Marcassin Pinot Noir Estate Sonoma Coast 1998
DISH: Wuxi-style Chinese braised, smoked, and fried pork belly. I want a simple dish. It needs to be pork, and it needs to be so fatty that it drips down your chin. This elegant Pinot Noir will be the ultimate contrast. With this pairing, the wine is the center of the show, so you want to eat the same thing all the way through so as not to throw any of them off.

6. 1989 Clos Saint-Hune Riesling from Trimbach Vendage Tardive
DISH: Smoked eel by the best chef who makes smoked eel. Now, I don't even like smoked eel, but I can imagine Mr. Trimbach himself eating it with his wine.

7. Bollinger Vielle Vignes (old vine) Françaises 1990 Champagne
DISH: Lobster with drawn butter and black truffles — and no utensils!

8. Krug Champagne NV
DISH: Fifteen courses of canapés made by Dan Barber [chef of Blue Hill at Stone Barns in Pocantico Hills, New York]

9. Egon Müller Scharzhofberger Riesling Spätlese 1995
DISH: [Chef of Eleven Madison Park restaurant] Kerry Heffernan's arctic char with pea shoots and black truffle vinaigrette with braised salsify

10. This is a fantasy wine: the Niagara Malivoire Gamay that will be made by winemaker Ann Sperling in 20 years
DISH: Seared duck breast on top of a bacon, corn, mushroom, and rosemary succotash

11. 1947 Cheval Blanc in a magnum
DISH: I just want a chair in the corner! I want eighteen hours just to smell this wine. Food would only distract you from that.

12. Guigal la Landonne Côte-Rôtie 1997. This is considered to be the greatest Syrah in the world.
DISH: A big pile of smoked salted almonds

DANIEL BOULUD

CHEF-OWNER, DANIEL

New York, New York

If I can have anything I want, I am not going to go cheap. I am going to go in style!

[We need to point out that in his enthusiasm, Boulud took the term "case of wines" rather loosely: His case worked out to thirty-one wines, not counting all the first and second growths of 1955 Bordeaux!]

1. *Krug 1990 Clos du Mesnil Champagne*
DISH: **Langoustines** cooked by [French chef] Gerard Boyer

2. *Henri Bonneau Châteauneuf-du-Pape Cuvée Special 1990. This is the greatest Rhône I have ever had.*
DISH: I'd want this wine with **beef cheeks with carrots** made by Henri Bonneau himself. He made this in his kitchen and served them to me. The last time he made this for me, he pulled out a 1955. This guy is out of control!

3. *Côte-Rôtie la Turk 1985*
DISH: **Wild saddle of hare** with two sauces made by the Belgian chef Pierre Romeyer. When I had this dish, it was the best game dish of my life. I would like one more round with it. When I had it, I was very young: I was nineteen and working for Roger Verge, and he had sent me to work for Romeyer. He was a great hunter and one of the best practitioners of game.

4. *Château d'Yquem 1921. We had this on my birthday.*
DISH: **Foie gras** by [the late chef] Jean-Louis Palladin

5. *Henri Jayer Cros Parantoux from the 1990s, just in case I need to keep it to age*
DISH: **Roast duck** done on the chimney

6. *A horizontal tasting of 1955 Bordeaux, the year I was born. I'd have a first and second growth from each Château, and then open them to compare them!*
   I will also take a vertical tasting of vintage years from 1921 to 2000. [At this point, Boulud recites vintage years off the top of his head: 1945, '49, '50, '51, '59, '61, '66, '70, '75, '82, '85, '86, '89, '90, '95, '96, and 2000.] This will just be a mixed case, but let's be sure to have a 1961 Petrus, 1945 La Tour, 1966 Palmer, 1982 Mouton, and a 1990 le Pin Cheval Blanc.
DISH: Lamb is predictable. **Red meat** in general works along with **game birds**. For the 1955, I want my grandmother to cook the dish!

7. *Giacosa Barbaresco — and I want one of his older ones.*
DISH: I will just buy a big **white truffle** and cook it for myself.

8. *Some mixed cult wines from California: Harlan, Screaming Eagle, Dalla Valle, Maya, Araujo, and Shafer*
DISH: For these wines, I will have a **different chef** cook for each: Thomas Keller, Patrick O'Connell, Michel Richard, Charlie Palmer, Christian Delouvrier — and Wolfgang Puck, who I'll have cook me some **wiener schnitzel**. I like all these chefs and their cooking because they are soulful people, and on the island you dig into the soul.

9. *Some everyday wines: red and white Châteauneuf-du-Pape from 1995*
DISH: For the white, I will have Eric Ripert cook **fish** for me. For the red, I will take Jean-Georges Vongerichten because whatever he cooks will be soulful and exotic.

RICHARD BREITKREUTZ

GENERAL MANAGER,
ELEVEN MADISON PARK

New York, New York

1. Fat Tire Beer from Colorado. This is a great beer.
DISH: **Fried and salty** anything.

2. Alsatian Riesling. Alsatian wines tend to be drier, and my favorite is the one I have in front of me. Alsatian wines in general are very versatile and go with so many foods.
DISH: A delicate **seafood** dish with Indian or Thai influences.

3. A red Rhône that is bold and spicy
DISH: **Grilled venison.** With Rhône, you can go crazy with a lot of different foods. You could have kangaroo, which I have actually had, but you have to remember that it is very lean, so you need to eat it rare.

4. A Rioja on the spicy side.
DISH: **Roast kid,** like they make in Portugal. It is simple and gorgeous and goes great with Rioja.

5. Burgundy. You'll want this for delicate moments.
DISH: The classic pairing with Burgundy is duck, so I would have **roasted duck with confit.**

6. Colhita Port, a vintage tawny port
DISH: With this, all you need is a friend. If I were to have this with food, I would have a perfect executed **sweet flan** made by my dear friend's mother.

7. Magellan gin served with a splash of tonic and lime or cucumber.
DISH: This would be good to start off the evening with a little **lobster salad canapé** on cucumber.

8. Calvados, either Gamut or Christian Drouin
DISH: Because of the apple flavor in the Calvados, I think of fall. **Bread pudding** with apples and cinnamon in front of the fire would be the thing to have with Calvados.

9. I'd want two kinds of water, one still and one sparkling: Fiji and Badoit. Water is a digestif to cleanse the system throughout the meal.

10. Old Bordeaux from Saint Julien
DISH: Beautifully executed dry-aged prime *côte de boeuf* from Eleven Madison Park.

11. Vouvray.
Loire Valley whites have a vast range — fully sparkling or *frizzante*, sweet or dry — and are incredibly versatile.
DISH: A sweeter style Vouvray Moelleux would be good with some offal, like **foie gras** or **sweetbreads.** The wine has delicate aromatics but also bracing acidity that cuts through the unctuousness of offal.

12. Billecart Salmon Rosé Champagne
DISH: I would begin my meal with some **raw tuna** or **salmon caviar** and this Champagne.

JOE CATTERSON

GENERAL MANAGER, ALINEA

Chicago, Illinois

My first question is, where is the island? Is there an abundant supply of oysters? All right then . . .

1. Guinness Stout.
Give me an endless supply of Guinness, and I'm in good shape. I want nothing else.
DISH: **Oysters** and Guinness. You have to visit Galway Bay in western Ireland where they have an oyster festival every fall. Galway oysters with Guinness is fantastic!

2. I'd want to have Champagne.
It's hard to narrow it down to just one, but if the ship sank with a huge supply of **Krug**, I'd be very happy. That would go a long way toward making my time on the desert island a more pleasant situation. DISH: I could pair the **oysters** with the Champagne, and that would work well. We should probably have some **caviar** on hand, but I'd have to do a tasting to find out which one is just right with that Krug. Different caviars go better with different Champagnes, and I have not yet had the luxury of tasting them all with Krug. We held a really interesting tasting with the cellar master from Dom Pérignon, who brought out different vintages of the Dom Pérignon which we then sampled against different caviars. It was really pretty amazing how each vintage had an affinity for different caviars.

3. A white Burgundy, such as Corton-Charlemagne
DISH: **Oak-smoked Scottish salmon,** because that could go with the Guinness, too.

4. Domaine Richebourg red Burgundy
DISH: There had better be some nice birds on this island. **Pheasant** or even some **wild turkeys** would do. I would roast them because I think one of the keys to pairing food with great wines is to keep it pretty simple—except I'd throw in some **truffles** too.

5. A great Bordeaux. I'd probably go with some Haute-Brion, an all-purpose wine.
DISH: **Grilled steaks** or **roast lamb.**

6. Palacios Priorat
DISH: I would have to have some sort of **lamb** dish with this wine. You could get a little exotic with the seasonings and herbs and go with a Mediterranean flavor.

7. Donnafugata Mille e una Notte, which translates as A Thousand and One Nights
DISH: I would go to the restaurant next door to Alinea called Boka, and I would challenge the chef Giuseppe Scurato, who is Sicilian, to come up with **a classic Sicilian dish** to serve with that wine. He would need to consult his book of recipes so he could create a very elaborate, classic nineteenth century Sicilian dish. I'm sure he's up to the challenge.

8. Domaine Zind Humbrecht Clos Windsbuhl Alsace Pinot Gris
DISH: I think a trip to Alsace is in order for this wine — I'd have to look for a great Alsatian chef to create **the perfect Alsatian dish.**

9. A great German Riesling, one of the dry Rieslings from Franz Kunstler
DISH: This wine could easily work with something that has Thai seasonings — possibly a **lighter curry** with lemongrass, coconut, peanuts, and things like that.

10. *In case I get tired of the Guinness, I'll need a light beer, which would be a classic pilsner. I used to play the French horn professionally. When I was studying music in Germany, I learned that it's very important to drink beer. I was tasting some older vintages of wine recently and it struck me, "Wow! This is from the year I moved to Germany. I don't think I ever drank this while I was there . . ." The truth is, for the three years or so I lived there, I can count on my fingers the number of times I drank wine. Even though the appreciation and interest was there at that time, the beer was just too good.*
DISH: A big bowl of **roasted peanuts.**

11. *I have to have some port. I want a vintage that holds up, so I'd choose a 1977 Fonseca.*
DISH: I'd need a nice **Stilton cheese** for that port.

12. *I don't have anything for after dinner, and I should have a digestif. I'd want Roger Groult's Doyen d'Age Calvados. It is really aromatic, tasty, and fantastic.*
DISH: I would have this **by itself** at the end of the meal. People do drink Calvados in the middle of a meal in Normandy. It is served the way someone might serve a sorbet: They'll bring you a little chilled glass of Calvados to sort of help you get the first half of the meal down, and get you ready for the rest.

BELINDA CHANG

WINE DIRECTOR,
OSTERIA VIA STATO

Chicago, Illinois

1. Salon Blanc de Blancs Champagne.
This is one of the least-released Champagnes in the world, because they are absolutely one of the pickiest houses when it comes to declaring a vintage year. It is elegant with great finesse. We call it "The Superman."
DISH: Cheesy puffs! **Gougères** from Daniel in New York City. These are perfect with Champagne.

2. Coche Dury Meursault Perrier White Burgundy.
It is so opulent and decadent — and one of the best white Burgundies in existence. Every vintage!
DISH: Charlie Trotter's **daurade** with mustard fennel sauce served on braised fennel.

3. 1971 Brauneberger Juffer-Sonnenuhr Gold Cap Riesling.
This was a legendary vintage.
DISH: **Italian crudo:** marinated hamachi with white anchovies and red onion marmelade [a la Osteria Via Stato!].

4. Henri Jayer Echezeaux 1979.
It is Grand Cru Vosne Romanée Pinot Noir. This would be in my luxury box. It is velvety, succulent, and juicy.
DISH: Anything **squab!** Scottish **grouse** that has been hung for three weeks — so long it still stands up by itself. I would like it with **white truffles.** I love the season for Scottish game — it is so yummy!

5. Penfolds Grange 1971.
When I worked at Charlie Trotter's, Charlie tried to buy every bottle in existence. It is simply phenomenal.
DISH: **Bison with a red wine boudin sauce,** which I would make myself.

6. Bryant Family Cabernet Sauvignon from Napa.
This is my favorite.
DISH: **Dry-aged Kobe beef** or Niman Ranch **dry-aged T-bone steak**

7. Merry Edwards Windsor Garden Pinot Noir from Sonoma.
It is dark and black-fruited with brown spice. Russian River Pinot Noir really screams where it is from, as it is very *terroir*-driven.
DISH: **Sea bass** with veal jus and black trumpet mushrooms made by chef Laurent Gras.

8. Hirtzberger Spitzer Singerriedel Riesling from Austria.
They were the official winemakers for the kings, and it is one of the most precise wines I have had in my life. It is amazing and ages beautifully.
DISH: This wine is amazing with caviar. I'd want the **caviar blini** at Gary Danko [restaurant in San Francisco]. This wine is harvested late and has a little richness that goes with the floralness of caviar.

9. Cuilleron Condrieu le Chaillets.
This was my first transcendent white wine experience. I used to think it was much cooler to order Merlot instead of white wine until I had this. It's sexy Viognier that has peachy, apricot, and honey perfume screaming at you from inside the glass.
DISH: This is amazing with chef Laurent Gras's **lobster cappuccino.** It is so good! I love this wine.

10. Termanthia from Spain.
We call this wine "The Terminator!"
DISH: This is ideal with something big, rich, and gamey. I'd want **braised short ribs** from our restaurant, Osteria Via Stato. We do them in the wood-burning oven so they are a little smoky, and serve them on parsnip puree. I'm mixing genres, with Spanish wine and Italian food, but it would be great.

11. Quintarelli Amarone.
This is one of my absolute favorite steakhouse wines.
DISH: No question: **osso buco** with saffron-scented orzo

12. Mouton Rothschild Bordeaux 1945.
It is the V for Victory wine. It demonstrates perseverance over great odds. This was made by women and children, so it is "girl power" wine!
DISH: I'd like this wine decanted and served in a beautiful Riedel glass — for me and six incredible friends, so we'd each get a big glass. I'd just want to sit in the salon and drink the wine, with the cigar cut and waiting to go with Armagnac afterward.

GEORGE COSSETTE

CO-OWNER, SILVERLAKE WINE

Los Angeles, California

I would definitely want to take some Grüner Veltliners:

1. Nikolaihof Grüner Veltliner.
He is a biodynamic producer and makes stellar wines. This one I would want with some age.

2. Emmerich Knoll Grüner Veltliner.

3. Jamek Grüner Veltliner.
DISH FOR ALL THREE: With these first three wines, I would like either a **schnitzel** or a **white fish with white asparagus**. Both dishes would work great.

4. Gravner "Breg" Friulian White.
DISH: This is so good I like to drink it **by itself,** but a **veal** dish would also be very nice.

5. Jacques Perrin Hommage Beaucastel Châteauneuf-du-Pape Blanc.
I have a 1998 at home now, and if I get shuffled off to an island, I am grabbing it. I really like this wine.
DISH: **Squab** or any other **game bird** works with this.

6. Sine Qua Non Syrah.
This wine would be for my more hedonistic moments. The vintner changes the names of his wines every year, but one of my favorites was his Midnight Oil.
DISH: Going against my own advice not to match rich food with rich wine, I would have *cabrito*, which is **roasted baby goat** done on a spit.

7. Alois Kracher Scheurebe dessert wine.
DISH: This should be had **all by itself.** I don't like dessert wine with food.

8. Hewitt Vineyard Vouvray from 2002.
DISH: I would let this age the longest, and then have it with **goat cheese** or a fresh **cow's milk cheese.**

9. Chambertin Red Burgundy.

10. Clos-de-Fôrets Saint-Georges, Domaine de l'Arlot.
DISH: For both of these wines, I would go with something classic like **beef with bone marrow.**

11. Yves Cuilleron Condrieu 2004
DISH: **Skate wing**

12. Emrich-Schonleber Trocken Riesling, which is a dry, not sweet, Riesling.
DISH: **Light pork dish**

TRACI DES JARDINS

CHEF-OWNER, JARDINIERE

San Francisco, California

1. Riesling
DISH: Vietnamese food

2. Raveneau Chablis
DISH: Nothing

3. Vintage Champagne
DISH: Nothing
With wines 2 and 3, sometimes even a chef does not want the food to get in the way!

4. Chave Hermitage
DISH: Anything cooked by Gerard Chave, like his **rabbit with mustard sauce**

5. Henri Jayer Burgundy
DISH: Squab

6. Txakoli
DISH: With this wine, I'd like **sardines** or **anchovies** from the coast of Spain.

7. Hungarian Tokaji
DISH: Roquefort cheese

8. Nonvintage Champagne
DISH: Almost anything works with Champagne. I had **barbecued chicken** with nonvintage rosé Champagne, and it was fun. I also like to make **broiled blue cheese toast** to eat with Champagne.

9. Late Harvest Riesling
DISH: Apple tart

10. Amontillado sherry
DISH: Spanish almonds

11. Loire Valley Sauvignon Blanc
DISH: Oysters

ROCCO DISPIRITO

CHEF

New York, New York

1. Lillet [an aperitif wine from Bordeaux, typically served with orange].
DISH: Lillet with Eli's **Parmesan Crisps** [crackers] is an ethereal pairing.

2. Krug Champagne.
DISH: **Something salty and fried** is what you want here. Caviar and Champagne is not as good a combination as many people think. I like my caviar with buckwheat blinis and cold, syrupy vodka. Vodka and buckwheat work well together.

3. 1945 Lafite Rothschild.
DISH: An **ortalan** [a tiny bird eaten whole] would be the thing to have with this wine. We got some in once at our restaurant in a big tub of duck fat. It was extremely good, like eating a foie gras bomb. If you don't have an ortalan, a great woodcock would also work with this wine.

4. Super Tuscan Montepulciano.
DISH: I'd have this with the specialty of the region, **pappardelle with wild boar sauce.**

5. Pinot Blanc.
DISH: With Pinot Blanc, I'd want **a terrine made with goat cheese, leeks, and deep-fried taro root.**

6. Grüner Veltliner.
DISH: **Taylor Bay scallops with uni and mustard oil** from Union Pacific would be the thing to have.

7. Peter Michael's Cult Cabernet Sauvignon. I recently had a bottle, and it was very good — balanced and gorgeous.
DISH: With Cabernet, I want a prime-aged **grilled rib-eye steak.**

8. Illy espresso, served in [Illy] pots.
DISH: I would want **my grandmother's biscotti** with this. She makes them good and hard, and I like to dip.

9. Côtes du Rhone.
DISH: **Buttered noodles** with a half-pound of **black truffles** shaved raw on top with a little salt. Or, a piece of **toasted country bread** with a bunch of **shaved truffles** covered with extra virgin olive oil. It would be my "tartine de truffle."

10. Hungarian Tokaji Aszu.
DISH: For an ethereal pairing with this wine, have **crème brûleé.**

BRIAN DUNCAN

WINE DIRECTOR, BIN 36

Chicago, Illinois

I have a complete meltdown when a guest asks me what my favorite wine is. It is not like trumpets sound and I then announce the "Holy Grail" answer. In truth, my answer changes every week, depending on where I am and who I am with.

1. Salon Champagne.
I am a huge Salon freak! This Champagne has a time release component to it. It is like putting a kaleidoscope in your mouth and thinking you have had that last turn or view, then something else explodes. The finish goes on and on. This wine is incredibly long-lived — you get everything from fruit to coffee to chocolate. Salon is one of the most memorable things you can taste.
DISH: **Shellfish** like lobster, oysters, and/or crab, slightly steamed and chilled.

2. Jayer Romanée-Conti.

I can not imagine being without a great red Burgundy. Since I get to pick [and this wine is one of the most exclusive and expensive in the world], this is the one I would take.

DISH: Anything with **mushrooms and truffles.**

3. Pedro Ximenez Reserva.

I would want a dessert sherry, and PX is wonderful.

DISH: This is dessert **on its own.** If I am on an island I will have **bananas,** so I will make some sugar, caramelize it, and pour it over my bananas. If I happen to have some **nuts** and **chocolate,** I'll put that on as well. It is important to keep the dessert simple, however.

4. Dr. Ernst Loosen's German Riesling.

German Rieslings are some of my favorite wines and I am a big fan of his. His Beerenauslese and Trockenbeerenauslese Rieslings are magic.

DISH: **Anything spicy,** whether it is Mexican, Vietnamese, or Korean — anything with heat! My favorite Mexican dish of all time is *chiles en nogada* [chiles in walnut sauce]. This is a roasted and peeled poblano pepper stuffed with pork shoulder that has been marinated and slow roasted with nuts, star anise, apple, pear, nectarine, and raisins. It is served with peeled nuts, and garnished with pomegranate seeds. The intensity of the heat intensifies toward the bottom because of gravity, so every bite is different. It is like fireworks with every bite and sip.

5. Comte Lafon.

I'd want a great white Burgundy. This one reminds me of swimming in an ocean because you have to move through it to experience the flavors. The wine is not something that is apparent on contact. There is a layered effect of seamlessness at the same time that you move through fruit and minerality.

DISH: When I think of this wine I think of it **by itself,** but it would certainly work with **lobster in a lemon butter.**

6. Château d'Yquem.

How could you live without d'Yquem? You're not sending me anywhere without some Sauternes!

DISH: This wine is a **meal in itself.** It would work with **Valdeon cheese** from Spain. Another choice is a dish I recently had by chef Roland Liccioni from Le Francais [in Wheeling, Illinois]. He made **ravioli with foie gras mousse,** seared foie gras, caramelized banana, and banana water. The wine would definitely stand up to this.

7. Pichon-Longueville Baron.

I need some great Bordeaux, and I am a big fan of this one. Or should I take La Tour or Margaux?

DISH: **Rack of lamb** with a simple lamb jus, shaved **truffles,** and a loaf of crusty bread.

8. Château Musar.

This is a wine from Lebanon that has an edge of sarsaparilla, which makes it unique versus any other wine.

DISH: I'd like this with **game spiced with subtle Indian flavors.**

9. Sparkling Vouvray.

DISH: **Asian food** or **sushi**

10. Bussola Amarone. It is amazing and has a time-release quality to it.

DISH: It is great with **eel,** and works with sweet-and-sour **plum sauce.**

11. Kistler Pinot Noir.

People don't realize how well Pinot Noir works with heartier dishes. The wine has a long hang time and stays focused. It is great with food.

DISH: **Tuna, game,** or **steak**

12. Beckmen Vineyards Purisima 2003 Grenache.

This wine is biodynamically farmed and has set a new standard for what Grenache can be for me. I opened a bottle, tasted it, put the cork back in, put it on a shelf in my kitchen, and forgot about it for two months. When I reopened it, it hadn't lost anything!

DISH: Simple **roasted chicken with mushrooms**

MICHAEL FLYNN

WINE DIRECTOR, KINKEAD'S

Washington, D.C.

1. Côte de Nuits Burgundy.
DISH: **Veal loin with truffles** in a red wine sauce

2. Côte de Beaune White Burgundy.
DISH: A simple **roast chicken** with tarragon and cream sauce

3. Chenin Blanc Loire Valley in a medium-dry style.
DISH: Seared **foie gras** with cranberries or loganberries

4. Dry Mosel Riesling, which I absolutely love.
DISH: Poached **salmon** with dill

5. Barolo, well-aged.
DISH: **Venison** in a rich red wine sauce with roasted chestnuts

6. Old Ridge Zinfandel from California.
DISH: **Texas BBQ ribs**

7. Taylor Fladgate Port that is at least twenty years old. I like port with power, so I'd want a vintage port.
DISH: **Soufflé with Roquefort or Stilton cheese** and walnuts

8. Grenache Shiraz blend from Barossa Valley in Australia. I love these wines.
DISH: Grenache can be a little gamey and peppery. Would it be too precious to have it with something like **grilled kangaroo?** I actually have had kangaroo in Australia and I like the spiciness of the meat. I think it actually goes pretty well.

9. Oregon Pinot Noir.
DISH: This would be good with slow-cooked **pork loin** with prunes and caramelized cipollini onions.

10. Grand Cru Chablis.
DISH: Because of the minerality of the wine, I would like a **poached oyster dish** with a little salmon roe in a light cream sauce.

11. Bollinger RD Tete de Cuvée Champagne, because I would want something from one of the good Champagne houses.
DISH: This Champagne works well with beef, and I'd have it with a simple **beef stew** with peas, carrots, and onions. I actually had a 1959 paired with a beef stew and was shocked at the time at what a great match it was.
It's that marrow-y side to a well-made Champagne that seems to work well with a red meat combination. Bollinger is one of the richest styles of Champagne, as is Krug. Once you taste it, you'll know what I'm talking about.

12. Spanish Tempranillo from the Ribera del Duero.
DISH: I would have this with rich **slow-roasted root vegetables.**

PAUL GRIECO

GENERAL MANAGER, HEARTH

New York, New York

1. Krug Champagne.
DISH: A perfect oyster from Canada.

2. Robert Weil Riesling Trockenbeerenauslese 2001.
DISH: A perfect apricot.

3. FX Pichler Grüner Veltliner.
DISH: Roasted sweetbreads.

4. Château Haut-Brion Blanc.
DISH: Game terrine.

5. Lopez de Heredia 1988 Spanish white.
DISH: Sautéed mushrooms.

6. Silvio Jermann Vintage Tunina.
DISH: Cooked sea urchin.

7. Blanck Tokay Pinot Gris Furstentum.
DISH: Pâté de foie gras.

8. Produttori del Barbaresco Ovello 1990.
DISH: Roast veal.

9. Red Burgundy.
DISH: Loin of lamb.

10. Muga Prado Enea 1994.
DISH: Short ribs.

11. Glatzer Zweigelt 2003.
DISH: A hamburger — just plain, with nothing on it.

12. Sadie Family Syrah Swartland South Africa.
DISH: Barbecued spareribs.

JILL GUBESCH

SOMMELIER, FRONTERA GRILL AND TOPOLOBAMPO

Chicago, Illinois

1. Dom Pérignon 1990 Vintage Champagne.
This wine is very focused, with balance and precision. Even the older vintages have a razor-sharp acidity and pretty fruit, and everything is intact. I just love it.
DISH: Pristine oysters on the half-shell from Pristine Bay, Alaska. There is a couple who harvests these and they are the best I have ever had.

2. Trimbach Clos Saint-Hune 1990.
I just got back from Alsace. This wine is so good! It is complex with so much power, and a great, long finish.
DISH: The fresh sardines at Auberge de I'lle [in Lyon].

3. DRC Richebourg 2002.
This is killer! I would have this to age for a little while because it is a fantastic vintage. It is so complex with so many different fruit flavors, truffle, earthiness, and amazing acidity. The finish lasts for days! Plus, if I am on an island, I'll want something to put away for a while.
DISH: Pasta with porcini mushrooms

4. Lafite 1982.
Since I can have anything I want, I want this. It is a fantastic vintage and I love Lafite as a Grand Cru Bordeaux.
DISH: Rack of lamb with rosemary and garlic

5. Vega Sicilia Unico 1962.
This is one of the best bottles of wine I have ever had. It is mainly Tempranillo blended with the Bordeaux varietals and it just ages forever. I took three pages of notes on this wine. With every sip, I was tasting twenty things.
DISH: Roast suckling pig.

6. Susan Balbo Brioso.
I would want an Argentinian wine that would be an easy-drinking, deep, rich red. This one has deep, rich concentrated fruit with velvety tannins.
DISH: The **lamb with black mole** made here at Frontera Grill and Topolobampo. Black mole is made with over thirty different ingredients, each toasted just to the point before they burn, which gives the mole a deep, caramelized flavor. It has deep dark chile flavors, sweet spices, dried fruit, and a pinch of chocolate.

7. Laurent Perrier Rosé Champagne.
This is one of my favorites right now.
DISH: **Smoked salmon** with all the typical accoutrements.

8. Beaucastel Châteauneuf-du-Pape.
DISH: Goat *birria,* which is **goat marinated in red chiles,** then roasted slowly in banana leaves. We have a farmer that raises Boer goat just for the restaurant so we only have it on the menu once a year for about four weeks. It is so good that I have it once a week.

I like to drink a lot of white wines, too:

9. Huia. I would have to have some New Zealand Sauvignon Blanc, because it is so easy to drink and so delicious.
DISH: **Eggplant goat-cheese tart** with sun-dried tomatoes or roasted red peppers.

10. J.J. Prum Wehlener Sonnenuhr 1995 Spätlese.
It is killer. As German Riesling ages, the sweetness starts to lesson. It develops this rich, complex flavor of tangerine, peach, and fresh apricot exploding in fruit. Even at the Spätlese level of ripeness, it doesn't become sweet. German Rieslings have such high acidity, it livens the fruit and minerality on the palate. Whenever you have acidity with food, it lifts the flavor of the ingredients so you taste each thing individually in a way you wouldn't taste something without acidity. More layers of flavor come out when you have a lot of acidity. If the wine is less acidic, you get a more unilateral taste. When you get an older German Riesling, you don't notice the sweetness, just the layers of flavor. It's like one of those hundred-layer pastries.
DISH: **Scallop ceviche** with tamarind and morita chile dressing on a bed of shaved fennel, orange, almonds, and orange zest

11. 1991 Côte-Rôtie la Chapoutier les Becasses.
The wine has super bacony and smoky flavor.
DISH: Either Alinea chef Grant Ashatz's or Blackbird chef Paul Kahan's current **pork belly** dish.

12. Nigl Privat Grüner Veltliner.
If I have to stab a piece of fish in the water while I'm on this desert island, I will have it with this peppery wine.
DISH: **Indian food** from Bhabi's Kitchen in Chicago, which is one of my favorite Indian/Pakistani restaurants. I'd like her **chicken** *boti* that is super spicy, and also the *mutter paneer* that is made with dried peas and Indian cheese. This wine could easily stand up to either.

GREG HARRINGTON, MS

OWNER, GRAMERCY CELLARS

Walla Walla, Washington

1. El Tesoro Tequila.
I am definitely taking a bottle of tequila!
DISH: Fresh homemade guacamole.

2. Emmerich Knoll Austrian Riesling.
His vineyard "Schutt" produces one of the most
profound wines I have ever had. People talk about
terroir and earthiness in Burgundy and Montrachet
. . . Well, I could pick this wine out of a thousand!
DISH: As it's such a dry wine, something with an
earthy sauce, like mushrooms.

3. Chave Hermitage Syrah.
His is the best Syrah in the world.
DISH: Roasted meat — lamb or duck.

4. Sagrantino de Montefalco.
This wine is local to Umbria, and just fantastic. It is
a hard grape to describe because everyone makes it
differently. It is probably closest to Tempranillo, but
a little more interesting.
DISH: Grilled sausages, or duck.

5. Bruno Giacosa Barolo.
I love Nebbiolo as a varietal. If you have a Pinot
Noir that has over thirty years of age on it, a
Nebbiolo will be far superior. I would take a 1999
and drink it when I was rescued.
DISH: Spaghetti with truffles and butter.

6. Littorai Pinot Noir from Sonoma.
I really like this winemaker for not succumbing to
the market forces and just doing what he wants.
DISH: Whole grilled fish — like black bass or redfish — with herbs.

7. Madeira.
I'd take it for the simple reason that you could keep
Madeira in the back of your trunk for thirty years at
two hundred degrees and it would not go bad! It is
by far the best value in the wine world — except for
sherry, which is a fight that is unwinnable. The law
says this wine must be aged twenty years. There is
not another wine region in the world that has to age
twenty years — it is unprecedented. The way it is
made, it is essentially cooked, so it is very hearty.
DISH: Strawberries with balsamic vinegar.

8. Egly-Ouriet Rosé Champagne.
This is the best rosé in the world.
DISH: Anything you can imagine, from canapés to
a not-very-sweet dessert.

9. Donnhoff German Riesling.
I really like his stuff.
DISH: Dim sum at Lai Wah Heen in Toronto.

10. Raveneau Chablis.
He is probably the best winemaker in Burgundy.
When the trend was to change, he stuck to his guns.
There was a trend in Chablis to put oak on the wine
and he didn't.
DISH: Fish with an earthy mushroom sauce.

11. I would take a Syrah from Waters Winery.
I want something from Washington State, where my
future is.
DISH: Some kind of smoked meat, duck, suckling
pig, or lamb.

12. Quarts de Chaumes Chenin Blanc.
This is one of the most underrated dessert wines in
the world. It is really fun, but unfortunately you
don't see it a lot.
DISH: Creme brulée with chocolate sauce.

STEVEN JENKINS

AUTHOR, *CHEESE PRIMER*, AND
CHEESEMONGER, FAIRWAY
MARKET

New York, New York

Food lovers know Steven Jenkins primarily for being a cheese authority. Yet, it turns out that over the years Jenkins has had few nice glasses of wine, among other things, while doing his research. For this list we did a slight twist and asked for Jenkins's favorite cheeses — and then his favorite drinks to pair with them.

1. VCN Camembert
WINE: Châteauneuf-du-Pape

2. Reblochon
WINE: Sauvignon Blanc from California, New Zealand, or Australia — or a Sancerre

3. Abondance from Savoie
WINE: Pinot Noir from anywhere

4. Parmigiano-Reggiano
WINE: Super Tuscan

5. Sheep's milk Pyrenees
WINE: A country wine, like Cahors

6. Pecorino from Sardinia
WINE: Sardinian country wine, nothing spectacular

7. Pecorino from Umbria
WINE: Lungarotti

8. Pecorino from Tuscany
WINE: Chianti

Why did I take three Pecorino cheeses to my desert island? I am crazy about this cheese! I hope Pecorino Romano never darkens my door, but the country ones I listed above are my passion.

You made me go too fast on my list. I must add a Corsican Pecorino! The wine that would go with this is a younger Corsican wine, or a red or pink Sancerre. You want it to be flinty dry, so all the flavors of the cheese comes through.

I love these cheeses because they are perfect foils for whatever else you are serving at the table, like the bread and the accompaniments. It is not so much the cheese but how it serves as the "sun" and everything else is celestial body that circles it and comes back to it.

9. Sicilian Ricotta
WINE: Sicilian red

10. Torta del Casar from Estreadura
WINE: Vega Sicilia or a PX sherry

11. Cabrales from Asturias
WINE: A big Bordeaux that is really complex, like a Pauillac

12. Afuega'l Pitu from Asturias
WINE: Something from nearby Rioja

13. Raw milk Epoisses
WINE: Châteauneuf-du-Pape or an old Guigal Rhône works with this cheese.

14. Middle-aged French chèvre, one that is not too soft and not rock hard
WINE: Pineau des Charentes. This is a fortified wine that is not sweet.

The Spirit of Cheese:

Genever gin is a high-end gin that is now being made in northern France and Holland, and is infused with flavors other than [the traditional] juniper. These gins are wonderful served with funky cheeses like Maroilles, which is among the oldest of the oldest cheeses and dates back 1,500 years.

Boerenkaas is a four-year-old farmer's cheese that is rock hard, fruity, and flinty-smelling, and goes beautifully with gin, Scotch whiskey or Calvados. When you taste this cheese, it burns on your tongue and has honey and Scotch whiskey flavor. This makes it *the* great cheese to serve with spirits. It will really make the lights come on for people who think they can't enjoy liquor with cheese. It is the perfect combination. This cheese would also work amazingly well with Kentucky Bourbon because of the sweetness of the Bourbon.

DANIEL JOHNNES

BEVERAGE DIRECTOR, DANIEL

New York, New York

1. Musigny
DISH: **Roasted game bird** with wild mushrooms cooked by Daniel Boulud

2. Montrachet, for nighttime
DISH: **Poached chicken** with a morel cream sauce

3. Chevalier Montrachet, for daytime
DISH: Roasted **turbot** with leeks and a beurre blanc

4. Austrian Riesling
DISH: Roasted **lobster** with butter, cream, and lemon

5. Vouvray
DISH: I'd like a white fish like **daurade with crayfish.** I would also want a little sweetness in the dish, like orange.

6. Pomerol
DISH: Standing **rib roast of beef**

[When Johnnes was chagrined too see that he only had two reds so far, we offered him half bottles of the next two wines.]

7. Côte-Rôtie
DISH: *Lievre a la Royal,* **hare** that has been boned and stuffed with **foie gras and truffles.**

Hermitage
DISH: I would have this with the same dish as the Côte-Rôtie.

8. Beaujolais, to drink on the beach
DISH: **Charcuterie and cheese plate.** On the plate I'd want country pâté, duck rillettes, dried cured sausage, and Ibérico ham from Spain. For cheese, I would like some Reblochon, a raw milk Camembert, Mont d'Or, and an aged sheep's milk cheese from the Pyrenees.

9. Clos Saint-Hune Alsatian Riesling
DISH: You could drink this on its own. I'd go with a composed dish of **poached halibut, smoked trout or bacon, fresh spring peas, baby carrots, and garlic.**

10. Vosne-Romanée Cros Parantoux
DISH: Organic free-range chicken *demi-deuil:* This is **chicken with truffles** stuffed under the skin.

11. Barolo
DISH: Venison or wild boar would work with this wine, but I am not happy with those choices. I would go with a **game bird** like wild pigeon [squab] or woodcock.

12. Premier Cru Chablis
DISH: A huge platter of **oysters:** Malpeques, West Coast, Belon, and Speciales, which are the small oysters in France. On top of my oysters, I like a small drop of lemon.

KAREN KING

BEVERAGE DIRECTOR,
THE MODERN AT THE MUSEUM OF
MODERN ART

New York, New York

1. Picq Chablis Premier Cru.
It's fermented in all stainless steel. I would be happy with the Premier Cru level of this Chablis, because it is really steely.
DISH: A delicate classic **Dover sole.**

2. Neveu Sancerre.
DISH: I'd want **oysters** from the East Coast, like Malpeques or Blue Points.

3. Larry Brundlaeyer Grüner Veltliner.
I love this wine producer — he's a very nice guy. I want this wine with a little bottle age, because when they're really young often they're just steely and they wouldn't be good with this [dish]. When the wine gets a little older, it gets rounder in texture. In the beginning they're kind of like white pepper and green vegetables. Later on, they get a little spicier, but it gets exotic — going to tropical fruit.
DISH: **Dates stuffed with almonds and wrapped in bacon.**
I would like this for my appetizer course.

4. Sori Tildin Gaja Barbaresco,
an old one, not one of his newer wines.
DISH: Of course, I would need to have **truffles.** I'd want a simple egg pasta with a really nice truffle-scented olive oil and shaved truffles on the top.

5. Mascarello Bartolo Barolo.
DISH: Same as the Barbaresco. If I need a variation on the pasta, you can throw a poached egg on the top.

6. Henri Bonneau Cuvée Celestine 1989, Chôteauneuf-du-Pape.
This is one of the best wines I've ever had.
DISH: Some kind of **lamb stew** that has black olives in it and also some Provençal herbs with thyme in it. I'd want a casserole, nothing fancy.

7. Lignier Michelot Chambolle-Musigny,
a very old red Burgundy. Or I'll take a 2002 so I can age it while I'm stuck on this island. The aging will be accelerated because it will be warm.
DISH: Not a Beef á la Bourguignonne [a classic beef dish from Burgundy], I'll tell you that. I'd like a **chicken with portobello mushrooms.**

8. Comte Lafon Meursault White Burgundy.
DISH: I'll take a **lobster** dish served in a very light lemony cream sauce, please.

9. Lopez de Heredia 1976 Rioja.
DISH: I'd like the **roast goat** from L'Impero [restaurant in New York City], which is delicious.

10. Selbach Oster German Riesling.
This wine was my first venture into German wine.
DISH: Some nice, **spicy Thai food.** Not a dish with coconut sauce — something with chicken or seafood and vegetables.

11. Barbeito Madeira.
DISH: Some kind of mild, soft cheese, like a **Taleggio.**

12. A nice old Brunello Talenti.
DISH: I would like to have some grilled **lamb chops** with rosemary-scented grilled vegetables.

TIM KOPEC

WINE DIRECTOR, VERITAS

New York, New York

1. 1990 Vosne Romanée 1er Cros Parantoux, Henri Jayer.

That is a wine that has been magic every time I have tried it throughout my career. I had it when it was $300 on release all the way to now at $2,300 a bottle, which sounds horribly expensive. Everyone knows his wines and knows that he only makes wine for his personal consumption. These wines are more sought-after than the wines of Romanée Conti.

DISH: A **poached chicken with crème fraîche, mushrooms, and fresh herbs** made by chef Scott Bryan of Veritas. It is a magical dish because it is full-flavored, but does not dominate the wine. It is all about the marriage.

2. German or pilsner-style beer.

A lighter style of crisp, refreshing beer. I am not a one-beer kind of guy, or a light-beer kind of guy. I like a 400- or 500-hundred calorie beer that says something.

DISH: **Hot dog** from Walter's in Mamaroneck, New York. Walter's is in a Chinese pagoda in the middle of a residential neighborhood, and their hot dogs are made of veal and beef. No sauerkraut, chili, or relish. He has mustard and napkins — that's it.

3. Champagne.

In my refrigerator at home, I have three types of Champagne in every format they make. For instance, I have Billecart Salmon Rosé in full bottles, half-bottles, and magnums. Magnums are for two; full bottles if I am moving on to something else to drink; and half-bottles if I have already had something to drink.

I like Dom Pérignon even though it sounds like such a luxury item. For a little over one hundred dollars, you can buy a bottle of 1996, which is an amazing Dom Pérignon. This is something you can find in the store, and you really can't do much better.

DISH: If I had to have something with the Champagne, it would be a piece of **aged Manchego cheese.**

4. Riesling Cuvée Frédéric Emile, Trimbach.

This wine costs under forty dollars. If I were indulgent, I would drink their Clos Sainte-Hune. It is a small vineyard and makes about 400 cases a year, which is not a lot considering that Kendall-Jackson probably makes 400,000 of their Chardonnay. It is a special wine, and I am sure I am not alone on this.

DISH: I would have a **cold poached lobster** cooked by me with this wine. I would serve it with a ragout of corn, bacon, tarragon, great French butter, *fleur de sel,* and a drop of Ricard.

5. Eitelsbacher Karthauserhofberg German Riesling Spätlese.

The wine is the definition of "racy Riesling." It is juicy, flinty, with lemon rind, and mouthwatering. I would take the 2001 vintage, which is a classic vintage and will last up to twenty years in the cellar.

DISH: **Thai fish dish** in the Yum [i.e., rice noodle dish] category. The dish is basically rice wine vinegar, lime juice, palm sugar, fresh cilantro, tomato, cucumber, and some chile. There are a million variations. I would have the one that is in season, whether frog legs or soft-shell crabs — you name it.

6. Green Chartreuse Tarragona.

It was made by monks after they were ousted from France and came to make this in Tarragona, Spain. It is 100 proof, and all you need just a little at the end of the night.

DISH: A **cigar** — a Partagas Series D number **4.**

7. 1990 Château Cheval Blanc, Saint-Émilion.

It is every bit the wine that the 1982 is, which every-one raves about. It is wildly complex. Unfortunately, the price has been climbing. It has the taste of Old World Bordeaux — very viscous, with wonderful texture and complexity.

DISH: **Spring lamb** with fresh cracked salt and pepper, cooked on a high heat and served rare with string beans and nothing else.

8. 1995 Château Rayas, Châteauneuf-du-Pape.

It is the best example of Grenache to me. It has a plummy, strawberry, cherry character with a long, complex finish.

DISH: **Braised short ribs** made by Veritas's chef Scott Bryan, which are amazing and so good they would work with almost any red wine. I have made them at home and it takes a few tries to get them perfect. It is all about technique — very French. [See recipe on p. 317.]

9. Edmond Vatan Sancerre.

He is in the center of Sancerre, and makes a total of 450 cases of white and red combined. Some of the co-ops around him may be making 100,000 cases, but he stays small. His wine reminds me of Ravenau Chablis in that he takes half his wine and puts in stainless steel and the other half in old natural wood. After six months, he switches them, and they become hauntingly complex. I have had them with fifteen years of bottle age and they are superb, which you don't associate with a Loire Valley wine. They are not the least expensive at thirty-five dollars a bottle when people are used to spending twelve dollars, but they are totally worth it.

DISH: **Raw oysters.** If am eating them with great wine, I eat them plain. I do like mignonette sauce, but the raw shallot is so strong it alters the taste of wine.

10. Madeira in either the Bual or Malmsey style.

They last forever and change in the glass when the air hits the wine. Decant them and let them breathe so they lose the turpentine element that comes from being in the bottle. When it opens up, it will become more youthful. Madeira is versatile — it can be served with a consommé or cold meat dish as well as to finish a meal.

DISH: Madeira works with so many things, from **roasted, pickled red peppers to chocolate** dessert as well as anything that is **caramelized** — plus **praline, nuts, marzipan, dates, apricots, and figs.**

11. 1988 Châteaux Climens, Barsac.

It is not as powerful as Château d'Yquem, but it is still plenty decadent. When you want sweet wine, it doesn't have to be the sweetest in the world.

DISH: Barsac is very versatile. If it is fall, I want **tarte Tatin.** It would also work with **Bananas Foster,** or simply ripping off the top of a pint of Häagen-Dazs **ice cream.** It would be wonderful with **biscotti** from Arthur Avenue [the Italian neighborhood in the Bronx] or even just a **butter cookie.**

12. 1990 Hermitage La Chapelle, Jaboulet.

This is a great wine with a lot of potential. It hasn't reached its peak, so if I am on this desert island for a long time, I don't want my wines to all reach their peak too soon.

DISH: You need a hearty dish for this, like a **porterhouse** grilled on the barbecue. Or the chef [Scott Bryan]'s **squab that he stuffs with foie gras** which is wrapped in Saran wrap and poached, then served with a sauce made from the organs and blood from the squab.

SCOTT BRYAN'S BRAISED SHORT RIBS WITH AROMATIC VEGETABLE AND RED WINE SAUCE

Serves 4

4 pounds short ribs, cleaned

salt and pepper

about 1 tablespoon canola oil (enough to coat pan)

1 head garlic, cloves separated and peeled

4 plum tomatoes, seeded, peeled, and diced

2 bottles red wine

2 sprigs each rosemary, thyme, and sage

6 tablespoons butter

1 cup diced onion

1 cup diced carrot

1 cup diced celery

1/2 pound fresh porcini mushrooms, sliced

1 tablespoon chopped chives (for garnish)

rosemary sprigs (for garnish)

1. Preheat oven to 350°F. Season short ribs with salt and pepper. Heat oil in a large skillet over medium-high heat. Add the ribs and cook, turn until golden. Transfer ribs to a casserole.

2. Add garlic and tomatoes to skillet and cook over medium heat, stirring occasionally, until soft. Add wine and bring to boil. Pour wine mixture over ribs and add herbs. Cover with foil and braise in the oven 2 1/2 hours, until *fork-tender*.

3. Transfer ribs to a platter. Strain cooking juices through fine strainer; discard the solids. Return strained juices and ribs to the casserole.

4. Melt 4 tablespoons butter in a large skillet over medium heat. Add the onion, carrot, and celery and sweat until tender and pale. Add to ribs. Melt remaining 2 tablespoons butter in the skillet; add the porcini and sauté until golden. Add to ribs. Adjust seasonings to taste.

5. Garnish with chopped chives and rosemary sprigs. Serve with potato puree or soft polenta.

SOMMELIER TIM KOPEC'S WINE PAIRING: *I like to pair this dish with* Châteauneuf-du-Pape. *Many versions work very well, but I particularly like 1995 Château Rayas Châteauneuf-du-Pape and 1998 Château Beaucastel Châteauneuf-du-Pape.*

JEAN-LUC LE DÛ
OWNER, LE DÛ'S WINES
New York, New York

1. Côte de Nuits Red Burgundy.
DISH: Roast rack of **veal with porcini mushrooms**. I would want this made by Chef Labelise from his restaurant in Burgundy.

2. Dry Vouvray.
DISH: **Tagliatelle with crushed tomatoes** made by chef Gray Kunz from his Manhattan restaurant Café Gray. It has a little bit of saffron in it, and I love it.

3. German Auslese.
DISH: Daniel Boulud's **crab salad with apple gelée**.

4. Northern Rhône Syrah with some age.
DISH: Grilled **woodcock**.

5. Red Priorat.
DISH: **Braised beef**.

6. Howell Mountain Cabernet Sauvignon.
DISH: Grilled **porterhouse steak** from Peter Luger in Brooklyn.

7. Côte de Beaune Chardonnay.
DISH: **Whole fish** cooked in salt crust.

8. Châteauneuf-du-Pape White Roussanne.
DISH: Handmade **ravioli with white truffle** by Borgo Antico from Alba.

9. Bosass Shiraz.
DISH: Daniel Boulud's **squab** with wild mushroom crust.

10. Saint-Julien.
DISH: Paul Bouse's **rouget** in potato crust in a red wine sauce.

11. Barolo.
DISH: **Lamb stew**.

12. Alsatian Gewürztraminer.
DISH: I'd have it with **cheese**. This is the most cheese-friendly wine in the world!

MATT LIRETTE
SOMMELIER,
EMERIL'S NEW ORLEANS
New Orleans, Louisiana

1. J.J. Prum Mosel Riesling.
Riesling is one of the noblest varietals of all, known for complexity and ageability, or even early drinking. It is very versatile on the table. I really enjoy German Riesling from many regions like Rheingau, Mosel, and Nahe, which is a hot region as well. If I had to go with one German Riesling, this is it. Something like a 1971 would be ideal. But a current vintage of 2002 or 2001, of course, would be fine. Another Riesling that would be great is by August Kessler. It's hard to choose just one!
DISH: I have a weakness for scallops. With this wine, I would have sautéed, **caramelized scallops** so they would give off their natural sweetness. Another Riesling that is off-dry or even mildly sweet from either the Mosel or Rheingau would also work.

2. Domaine des Baumard from the Loire Valley, with eight or ten years age on it
DISH: Shellfish would be good with this, but I think I'll go with a **poached freshwater bass** with a medium-bodied sauce and some bitter greens.

3. A Grand Cru Ravenau Chablis.

DISH: Oysters work really well with Chablis, so I would go with a classic **Oysters Bienvenue.** It's kind of a take on Oysters Rockefeller made with Pernod, which is how we do it in Louisiana. I think **Oysters Rockefeller** would be great, too.

4. 1988 or 1989 Bartolo Mascarello Barolo, from a magnum.

I love Barolo. It's something you almost want to drink on its own — even though people think of it as being tannic and unyielding and maybe needing food. But I go the opposite way, in that I try to enjoy the complexities of it on its own.

DISH: I would want to stick with some kind of local preparation, and **game** comes to mind. If you're in that region, you might see some kind of **rabbit in a rich sauce.** I would want something like chestnuts involved somehow.

5. Laforge Burgundy — 1993, or something even older.

DISH: A **terrine with foie gras and truffles** with some kind of cherry compote.

6. Stony Hill Chardonnay.

I've got to have something from California. If I were to start drinking white wines from California, this would be the one.

DISH: We're back to the Chablis-like quality. At the moment, we pour this by the glass so I will have a restaurant dish: **andouille-crusted Texas redfish with Creole meunière** butter sauce. The Stony Hill wines have no oak, so whatever those wines are lacking in that buttery quality, you'll get that in the sauce.

7. Prager Grüner Veltliner.

DISH: Here at Emeril's, we serve a **duck breast schnitzel** with Beluga lentils. I think this wine would stand up to something like duck or fowl or any type of poultry and the lentils.

8. Salon Clos du Mesnil Champagne in an older vintage, like a 1985. They only produce wines in great vintages, so let's go for the best. What you get in that wine is the best green apple you've ever put in your mouth.

DISH: A traditional **smoked salmon.** I'm not a huge proponent of caviar and Champagne; I think caviar needs something with some sweetness because it's so bitter and salty.

9. Cheval Blanc in a nice bold, old vintage.

DISH: **Venison** with a rich demi-glace sauce.

10. A Côte-Rôtie with a little age, like a 1995.

DISH: Why not meat and potatoes with this? I would have a nice **rib-eye steak,** I am taking into account the aromatic qualities of the wine that would go so well with the meat.

11. Taurasi from Campania. When I'm in a mood for something big, I really like a southern Italian wine, and this is a region whose wines I enjoy. Now I am thinking about Italian whites to go with the red. I'd want to include Greco di Tufo, Fiano, or a Feudi. Since it's too hard to choose just one, I'll just say a white wine from Campania.

DISH: If I'm on a desert island and I'm drinking a wine from Campania, even though I love the reds, I'd probably open one of those whites. To go with those, I'd like a **Caprese salad** (of tomatoes, basil, and fresh mozzarella).

12. Any wine made by Alvaro Palacios from the Priorato. This would be my obscure choice.

DISH: A rustic **beef stew.** These are big, sturdy wines and just huge for food.

PHILIPPE MARCHAL

SOMMELIER, DANIEL

New York, New York

1. Condrieu.
DISH: **Sautéed frogs' legs,** on top of Alsatian pasta with fresh mushrooms and a little cream.

2. 1966 Dom Pérignon Rosé.
DISH: With some **smoked salmon** served with toasted bread, cream, and onions, I'm happy!

3. Domaine Ostertag Tokay Pinot Gris 2003.
DISH: I'd want this with a traditional Alsatian **tarte flambée** — thin dough topped with cream, cheese, onion, and bacon — like the one [made by Alsatian chef Olivier Muller] I plan to have on my first day off in a month, over lunch next Tuesday at DB Bistro Moderne [also owned by Daniel Boulud].

4. 2002 Altenbourg Domaine Paul Blanc Gewürztraminer.
DISH: **Seared foie gras,** a little salad, and a reduction sauce made with some of the wine.

5. 2003 Hogl Grüner Veltliner.
DISH: **Creamy mushroom soup.**

6. Romanée-Conti Montrachet.
DISH: A **green salad with scallops,** shaved black truffle, and a drizzle of olive oil.

7. Albert Mann Pinot Noir, from Alsace.
DISH: **Roasted pigeon with foie gras** over mashed potatoes with cauliflower gratin.

8. La Tache Romanée Conti.
DISH: Something gamey — like **oven-roasted grouse** *à la Française* (i.e., roasted with bacon, carrots, etc.).

9. Guigal Côte-Rôte la Landonne.
DISH: It's a big wine, so I love this with a nice, **high-acid cheese** like Camembert or Brie.

10. Château La Tour.
DISH: **Herb-crusted lamb** with French fries and green beans.

11. Château Palmer [Bordeaux] — one of my very favorite wines. Growing up in Alsace, I only drank white wines. In 1989, this was essentially the first red wine I ever tasted, a 1982 and a 1983.
DISH: It's so amazing, I like to drink it **by itself.**

12. Bonnezeaux from the Loire Valley.
DISH: **Tarte Tatin** [caramelized apple tart] with whipped cream *and* vanilla ice cream — all the way!

MAX McCALMAN

MAÎTRE FROMAGER, PICHOLINE
RESTAURANT AND ARTISANAL
CHEESE CENTER

New York, New York

We asked Max to take along a dozen of his favorite cheeses, and then beverages to go with them.

1. Sbrinz.
WINE: This cheese goes with **everything**.

2. Roquefort. If I sit down to a cheese tasting, I can taste a lot of different cheeses but I can only handle one blue. So if I am having blue, make it the zenith: A Roquefort that is not oversalted but sweet, crisp, refreshing, and creamy.
WINE: **Château d'Yquem**, which is nectar of the gods. This is a classic pairing, and I'll point out that it is not *terroir*-driven. With Roquefort, you could also go with **Zinfandel**, **PX sherry**, a fruity **Cabernet Sauvignon** from Sonoma, or **Barbeito Madeira**.

3. Montenebro from Spain.
WINE: **Moscato d'Asti**, **Muscat**, **sherry**, **Muscatel**, **Château d'Yquem**, or a wine that isn't sweet, like a **Tempranillo**.

I now have sheep, goat, and cow's milk cheeses.

4. Gruyère. A good, aged, crunchy, sweet one.
WINE: **Krug 1990 Brut Champagne** or another sparkling wine.

5. Aged sweet Gouda.
WINE: **Corton Charlemagne**, because this cheese works well with an Old World Chardonnay.

6. Serra or Serena or Torta del Casar, whichever looks best that day. They are thistle-rennetted cheeses from Spain and Portugal.
WINE: **Chenin Blanc**, **Pinot Noir**, or a **Rhône red wine**.

7. Pyrenees-style sheep's milk cheese: Vermont Shepherd or Spenwood from England.
WINE: Tannat varietal like a **Madiran** or a dry **Riesling** both work with this style of cheese.

8. Selles-sur-Cher goat cheese.
WINE: A dry **Chenin Blanc** or a drier **Sauvignon Blanc**.

9. Krummenswiler Forsterkase, a lovely washed-rind cheese.
WINE: **Riesling** or **Pinot Noir** from Côte de Nuits, **Gamay**, or **Vouvray Sec**.

10. Montgomery's Cheddar.
WINE: **Pinot Noir** from Sonoma or Oregon, **red Rhône**, **Chardonnay** with a little oak, **Amarone**, **Gamay**, **Shiraz**, or **Champagne**.

11. Le Petit Fiancier. This is one of the "Holy Grail" of cheeses. It is a washed-rind cheese from near the Pyrenees. It is smooth, creamy, semi-soft, semi-pungent, and refreshing. It is the closest thing you could get to milk just out of the goat. I had this in St. Malo and it was so good I actually decided not to bring one home because I knew it would never be as good.
WINE: **Vouvray Demi-Sec**, **Riesling**, or **Late Harvest Sauvignon Blanc**.

12. Saint-Felicien.
You can't find this in the United States, unfortunately. It is a lot of fun — I can eat a four-ounce disk in one sitting and smile for hours.
WINE: **Vouvray Sec**, **Chenin Blanc**, drier **Sauvignon Blanc**, or **Syrah**.

RON MILLER

MAÎTRE D'HOTEL, SOLERA

New York, New York

I would take mostly Spanish wines, because that has been my focus for the last twelve years. My first four choices are perfect for a desert island climate. Though I love white Burgundy, I think it might be too heavy.

1. Las Brisas from Rueda, which is a crisp, white wine.
DISH: **Ceviche** made from a lighter fish.

2. Albarino.
DISH: Steamed **mussels** with a pinch of pimenton; **raw oysters** and boiled **cracked crab** with a sauce made from the entrails.

3. Ribeiro made from Treixadura grapes.
DISH: **Grilled prawns.**

4. Txakoli.
DISH: **Bacalao** [salt cod].

5. Calvario from Rioja.
DISH: Richly flavored **rabbit** or **game.**

6. Sierra Cantabria Reserva Especial.
DISH: This works with many things: **paella, pork, beef,** or **meaty fish** or even **sole..**

7. San Vicente.
DISH: This is a wine for all seasons that is just as versatile as number 6. Last night, I had this with **chicken, roasted beets, and garlic,** and it was fantastic.

8. Finca Sandoval, which is a Syrah-based wine.
DISH: This needs something hearty, and **rabbit** would be a natural because there are so many in the region. A **lamb chop** with some barbecue sauce and tomatoes certainly works with Syrah. I would want our Moroccan barbecue sauce that we make here at Solera with the lamb.

9. Alion from Ribera del Duero.
DISH: Baby **lamb chops** would be fantastic, with **beef** as a second choice.

10. Emilio Moro Malleolus.
This is a new wave producer that is extremely accessible.
DISH: **Rib-eye steak** with some fat.

11. Clos de l'Obac from the Priorato.
DISH: This wine is the Spanish equivalent of Barolo and perfect with **grilled vegetables.** *Calcotada* onions are second-generation onions that you can't find in the United States, and I would have them with Romesco sauce. They are roasted over a wood fire, and you slip the skins off and dip the onions in the sauce.

12. Ribas de Cabrera from Mallorca.
This is a wonderful wine that is rich without being heavy.
DISH: Good with fresh **seafood** or even **beef.**

ALAN MURRAY, MS

WINE DIRECTOR, MASA'S

San Francisco, California

1. Krug Clos du Mesnil 1986.

This is for the quality as well as sentimental reasons: I had this wine with fellow students and [mentor] Larry Stone as a thank-you for his mentorship the night I passed my advanced wine exam.

DISH: **Crab salad** served by chef Gregory Short. He is doing it in a gazpacho style with tomatoes and cucumber.

2. Coche-Dury 1996 Corton Charlemagne White Burgundy.

It is absolutely delicious. This is the wine I had the day I passed my Master Sommelier exam. I took some over to Larry [Stone] and blind-tasted it on him.

DISH: **Dover sole with a beurre blanc.** It would be simply ethereal.

3. Leflaive 2000 Chevalier-Montrachet White Burgundy.

This is an overlooked year for the wine, and it is outstanding.

DISH: **Lobster** that has been poached in butter, served on a sunchoke puree à la Ron Siegal, the former chef of Masa's.

4. Herman Donnhoff Auslese 2003.

Riesling is probably the greatest white wine varietal, and Donnhoff is a genius.

DISH: **Carpaccio of hamachi** from chef Ron Siegal, dressed with a light soy vinaigrette.

5. Fred Prinz Riesling Kabinett, bought at auction.

In Germany, producers hold back their best barrels for auction. This wine is absolutely stunning, with layers of flavor.

DISH: **Roasted beet salad** with hazelnuts and hazelnut vinaigrette. Roasted beets and Riesling is a beautiful match.

6. Vosne-Romanée 1978.

Once I got into wine, I got into Burgundy Pinot Noir pretty quickly.

DISH: Serve this wine with pan-roasted **quail with a truffle sauce,** and everyone goes home happy!

7. Henri Jayer Richbourg 1962.

DISH: **Roasted Scottish pheasant** made by chef Thomas Keller [of the French Laundry] with hen of the woods mushrooms.

8. Guigal Côte Roti la Turk 1985.

It is made with young vines and is great.

DISH: **Slow-cooked pork belly** with a light mustard jus would be so good with this wine.

9. Penfolds Grange 1966.

This wine is brilliant. It is in the older style, which has a more bacony, smoked meat character to it. The new ones are more focused on fruit.

DISH: The gaminess of **roasted squab** would be a great match.

10. Harlan Estate Napa Valley Cabernet 1994.

It is one of the first Cabernets I ever had. It was at a cult Cabernet tasting at Rubicon, where I first worked after moving to San Francisco from Australia. This wine showed me how great California Cabernet could be.

DISH: **Rib-eye steak** is a great cut of beef, and with some Cabernet Sauvignon, you're a happy boy.

11. Château Rayas Châteauneuf-du-Pape 1976.

Raj [Parr] gave this wine to me twice. The first time I called it Burgundy. The second time I called it Château Rayas 1976.

DISH: **Duck confit** done in a summer style with haricot verts and hen of the woods mushrooms, with a sherry vinaigrette.

12. Raveneau le Clos 1986 Chablis.

Drinking this wine is like visiting the seashore every time you have it. It is seashells and ocean, along with apple and passion fruit. It is stunning stuff.

DISH: **Scallops with a light butter sauce** with a slight fruit element, like passion fruit.

GARRETT OLIVER

BREWMASTER,
BROOKLYN BREWERY

Brooklyn, New York

We asked Oliver which dozen beers he would take to his island. (We do want to note that beer is not his only passion and that he is a avid wine collector as well). He added, "By the way, this would also make a good, short beer list at a restaurant."

1. Saison du Fond
DISH: A spicy Goan **seafood bouillabaisse** cooked by chef Floyd Cardoz of Tabla [in New York City]

2. Schneider Weis
This wheat beer from Germany is dark and has some weight to it.
DISH: I would go down south for **double-smoked bacon** with fresh just-laid **eggs** and **cornbread** for **breakfast.** The beer has a smoky component that would go with the bacon.

3. Brooklyn Brown Ale.
DISH: A **medium-rare steak** from Peter Luger restaurant [in Brooklyn].

4. Brooklyn Black Chocolate Stout.
DISH: Osteria Veglio in Italy makes the most amazing raw-milk **panna cotta** you have ever had in your life. It is hard to eat panna cotta for six months afterward. I would have one with a little espresso poured around it.

5. Adnams Bitter Cast Beer from England.
DISH: Fresh **fish and chips** at the seaside in Southwald, England.

6. Achel Extra Brun.
This beer is from a Trappist brewery and is really stunning.
DISH: The restaurant Ambassade de Verne in Paris does a dish of *saucisson with aligot,* which is **mashed potato with Cantal cheese and garlic.** This dish is so good it just blows your head off!

7. Christophle Blond.
This is an unfiltered pilsner-style beer from Holland.
DISH: **Soft-shell crabs** made by Jean-Georges Vongerichten at Jean Georges [in New York City].

8. Sierra Nevada Pale Ale.
It is a great standard for pale ale and always nicely done.
DISH: **Fish tacos** made with the fresh fish at a fish shack called Velasquez located ten miles outside Cancún. Get the Pescado Especial which is: the boat pulls up, Grandma goes and gets the fish that is still wiggling, and ten minutes later you have the special.

9. Belgian wheat beer.
This style is bright, fluffy, yeasty, earthy, and refreshing.
DISH: At the Spaniard restaurant in Amsterdam, they serve an open-faced sandwich made with **salmon and melted cheese, and lemon** on the side. The combination is one of those that make you think, "There is nothing on the face of the earth I would rather be eating or drinking at this moment!"

10. Ayinger Double Bock Celebrator.
DISH: The **pork with pipian** [pumpkin seed sauce] at La Palapa restaurant [in New York City].

11. J.W. Lees Barley Wine.
I was at a tasting of barley wine and the youngest was from 1935 and the oldest was from 1869. They were mind-boggling.
DISH: **Stilton cheese.**
Since I have an endless supply, I am going to bring something I drink only occasionally:

12. Hanson's Oude Gueueze.
This is a Lambic beer that is somewhat acidic, really bright and funky, sort of "the blue cheese of beer." It is shocking when you taste it, but it goes well with ceviche.
DISH: **Ceviche** made by Rick Bayless [chef-owner of Frontera Grill and Topolobampo restaurants in Chicago] — one with gutsy seafood flavor and some avocado.

RAJAT PARR, MS

WINE DIRECTOR,
THE MINA GROUP

San Francisco, California

1. Krug Champagne
— any vintage is great, but let's say 1979. Krug is one of my favorites. It has power: it's almost like a still wine with bubbles. It is very fermented, Pinot-predominant, rich, unctuous, and smoky. It's got all the flavors of a big Champagne. It's consistently absolutely phenomenal.
DISH: I would want a **cold cauliflower soup with black truffles** and some **seared bay scallops.**

I would take German and Austrian **Rieslings.** If I am on a desert island, it's going to be hot. You've got to have some Riesling as an afternoon drink for on the beach:

2. Gunderloch Spätlese.
He is one of my favorite producers in the Rheinhessen.
DISH: I would like something very simple, like chef Michael Mina's famous **tuna tartare.** He puts in mint, pine nuts, hot pepper, sesame oil, and a little quail egg on top. That's a nice lunch on the beach. He can just go fish, get the tuna, then make a little tartare from the belly. Perfect!

3. A dry Prager Austrian Riesling.
Prager is my favorite Austrian producer, and I would take a 2001.
DISH: **Seared scallops** on a potato shallot cake with a simple lemon caviar beurre blanc.

I would take three **white Burgundies.** I'd like them from a single producer: Anne-Claude Leflaive of Domaine Leflaive. All are Grand Cru wines and I would want to take the 2000 vintage. The three vineyards are all on the same hill, but each has very different flavor components:

4. Batard Montrachet is at the bottom of the hill.
The vines grow in dense soil, so the wine is heavier, more buttery, and more dense. You can drink it younger and softer.

5. Chevalier Montrachet is at the middle of the hill.
Chevalier Montrachet grows in soil that has limestone, chalk, and a lot of minerals. The wines are firm and high-acid, and also take the longest time to evolve.

6. Le Montrachet is at the top of the hill.
Le Montrachet has the perfect exposure to sunlight, and the soil has a mix of limestone and clay. The wines are rich, dense, and minerally and combine these qualities the best. It is also the most expensive white wine in the world, going for over $1,000 a bottle. They make only about thirty or forty cases a year.
DISH: (for all three white Burgundies): All three wines have similar aromatics, even though their density is different. The Batard is the richest and most opulent. The Chevalier is lean, minerally, and nervy with high acid. The Montrachet is perfectly balanced. It has these amazing aromatic white truffle, corn, and praline notes to it. The weight is very different even though the aromas are very similar.

If they were older, I would have said different dishes. But the wines are so young, they haven't evolved.

If I had said 1992, then I would eat very different food. The Batard would work with a more buttery dish, and the Chevalier would be with a cleaner or crisper dish, while the Montrachet would be with something like light-roasted foie gras with a little gnocchi and white truffle or something like that — something richer and more opulent.

I would like a **potato-crusted** John Dory, very simply done. Just crush a potato and sear it off, so it is just a little crusty. Since these wines are opulent and rich but have a leanness that is only five years old, I would want a little roasted corn, and a little bit of saffron cream sauce with fresh vanilla. These wines have corn and coconut and vanilla to them.

My last six bottles are all going to be **red Burgundies:**

7. La Tache 1985.
DISH: I remember having this wine once with an incredible dish made by one of the chefs at Rubicon: an amazing **squab breast** with a squab jus. With the squab, he took a potato and he made a cup out of it. He then stuffed the cup with all the innards of the squab and shaved some black truffles on top.

8. Romanée-Conti 1978.
DISH: I would serve this with a dish I have made of farm-raised **chicken with black truffle and foie gras** baked in parchment. Under the chicken was a puree of roasted chestnuts with more black truffle and foie gras fat.

For the sauce, I reduced chicken stock to an essence. I finished the sauce with the same Romanée Conti we were drinking for just a few seconds, so the fruit was preserved. With one last shaving of black truffle on top of the sauced chicken, the dish had the same aromas of the Romanée Conti.

9. Henri Jayer Richebourg 1962.
DISH: This is a big, dense wine. I would like a sous-vide **duck breast** cooked slowly, no skin, served on top of a little cinnamon-flavored couscous. The wine is delicate but has some weight, so I would go with a very simple Pinot Noir sauce. That's it.

10. Roumier Musigny 1945. This is a big monster wine that is impossible to find.
DISH: I would want to serve something traditional like a beef bourguignon made with **Kobe beef short ribs** cooked in a nice Pinot Noir sauce, braised and very simply prepared. I would have some roasted vegetables and potatoes, keeping it all very simple because the wine is so dense and so opulent.

11. Romanée Saint-Vivant from Domain Leroy 1990.
DISH: **Sottocenere truffle cheese.** This is a big opulent wine with a lot of rhubarb and strawberry flavors. It is very earthy, very dense, and still young. We did a blind tasting with all the top 1990 producers and it just blew everything else away. I remember the wine was so dense, sweet, and opulent, and that it worked so well with this cheese.
Last but not least, I'd take:

12. Clos de la Roche, 1978 Domaine Dujac. This is a magical wine, which is very hard to get.
DISH: **Quail** with a little bit of red wine and mustard. When I made this dish previously, I simply grilled the quail and served it sitting on a bed of shaved raw porcini mushrooms. On top of the porcinis, we had a little porcini risotto and the whole quail. We just took a little demi-glace and finished it with the Dujac.

I like finishing the sauce with same wine. You just finish it, not cook it — that way, you get just the fresh fruit flavor. That was a very straightforward dish. This wine is very earthy, very sherry-like with truffle-like aromas.

PAUL ROBERTS, MS

SOMMELIER, PER SE AND THE FRENCH LAUNDRY

New York, New York and Yountville, California

The first thing I would ask for is a six-pack of beer in case it is a *hot* desert island. Since am a boy from Texas and still a classicist, I would want a six-pack of **Tecate** in cans with lime and salt. It is still one of the greatest things! I'm sure people think I should be drinking Chimay or something, but if I am on a desert island, hot, and sitting on the beach, this is what I would want. I know I am not going any-where, so I don't need reflection — I need intoxica-tion.

So what would Roberts want with his can of Tecate on the beach?

I would make a **butter sauce** with garlic, lime, chilcostle chile, and a splash of tequila which would be spooned over **shrimp** and tossed on the grill. This dish would also work with a margarita!

1. Savennieres.

DISH: **Poached halibut with shaved coconut and fresh green apple** made by chef Jean-Georges Vongerichten. I had this dish when we came to New York for the James Beard Awards. It was one of those moments that I felt so proud of my career direction and what I was doing. I was no longer just "crazy" "liquor boy." We were sitting in the middle of the dining room at Jean Georges [restaurant] on a perfect New York spring day and all around us was the Who's Who of food: Charlie Trotter eating with Fredy Girardet, Gale Gand and Rick Tramonto, Wolfgang Puck, and on and on.

Jean-Georges walked this dish out to our table and then-sommelier Kurt Eckert brought out a Soucherie Savennieres Clos de Perrier. Between the room, the sunlight, Central Park, and being served this incredible dish, I thought my life could have ended right there.

2. *I am debating between wine and a margarita — but then again, I equate Mosel Riesling and a margarita because they have a similar structure, taste, and flavor. The margarita has high-acid, lemon-lime, salty-mineral qualities and perfume that comes from the Cointreau. Still, I think I'd take Mosel Riesling Kabinett by Fritz Haag. He is not only one of my favorite people in the business, but his wines are very special.*

DISH: **Smoked salmon.** I used to always have Champagne with smoked salmon, but I had this combination in Germany and it was great. I could also easily go with **guacamole!**

3. Chambolle-Musigny.

DISH: Perfect **rotisserie chicken** with crispy skin made with a Four Story Farm chicken. Chickens are lactose intolerant, but Four Story has found a way to feed them powdered milk that makes the flesh really juicy. This is the "Holy Grail" of chicken.

I would want chefs Thomas Keller [of the French Laundry and Per Se] and chef Robert Del Grande [of Café Annie] to make this dish together because I would want Thomas to supply the bird and Robert to season it. The chicken comes from Thomas's supplier but Robert used to do a pheasant rubbed with cinnamon. After it was cooked, we could all sit and eat and drink together.

4. Ciacci Piccolomini Brunello.

DISH: Easy — *bistecca alla Fiorentina.* Fresh arugula, medium-rare steak, balsamic vinegar, Tuscan olive oil, sea salt, crushed garlic, and shaved Parmesan.

5. Krug Clos du Mesnil.

It is rich, but if you are not going anywhere, this would be it. This Champagne is all about sense of place. It is on a little three-acre vineyard and it is so precise.

DISH: I am **not eating anything** with this. I will sit and watch the sun set with my wife, sipping and saying, "Aren't we glad we are stranded on a desert island?"

6. *Raveneau Chablis.*
DISH: This will be my spring dish: **roasted halibut with pickled ramps.** It would also go well with **whole-roasted striped bass.**

7. *Mendocino County Syrah.*
This a remarkable place. In the middle of the forest with crazy people growing marijuana, there are these farmers working on these steeps hills growing this wine with a true sense of place.
DISH: Simply **grilled lamb.**

8. *Domaine Weinbach Gewürztraminer Furstentum.*
DISH: On the Silverado Trail [a road that goes around the Napa Valley] is a Vietnamese family that moved there in the 1970s during all the turmoil in Vietnam. They have about eight acres that are probably worth millions of dollars and they grow strawberries. In Napa Valley, people get so excited that when their stand opens cell phones start ringing.

I would have their **strawberries** in simple syrup with **brioche** and a wedge of Thomas Keller's torchon of **foie gras.**

9. *Lafitte Rothschild Bordeaux, any year — they are all my favorites.*
DISH: This wine is like the Krug; it is meant for reflection. That said, it would be great with a Robert Del Grande dish. He makes a whole center-cut piece of **tenderloin** and rolls it in **adobo paste and coffee,** roasting it and serving it with cèpes from Oregon that are tossed in a mild mole.

The first time we made this dish, we served it to Eric de Rothschild, the owner of Lafitte and one of the most esteemed winemakers in the world. When he tasted the dish he said, "I might have just had the greatest match to my wine in my life." I ran into the kitchen and yelled, "Cook one for me!"

10. *Modicum Cabernet Sauvignon that [Thomas Keller] and I made.*
DISH: An old **aged Cheddar.**

11. *Manzanilla sherry that has a little age.*
DISH: Thomas Keller's **cured shad roe with shaved bottarga.** When you have these together, you think you are in southern Spain and all is well with the world.

12. *Armand Rousseau Chambertin Clos de Ves.*
DISH: Roasted **wild bird** like a partridge or pheasant, followed by **Abby de Citeaux cheese** from Burgundy. It is similar to an Epoisses, but not as stinky or runny.

CHARLES SCICOLONE
WINE DIRECTOR, I TRULLI AND
ENOTECA RESTAURANTS

New York, New York

1. Rufino Chianti Classico Reserva 1990.
Sangiovese is a perfect wine with food.
DISH: **Chianina beef, grilled.** This is the beef used
to make *bistecca alla Fiorentina.*

2. Ovello Barbaresco Reserva 1996.
This is one of the oldest co-ops in Italy. The wine
has undertones of faded roses, tobacco, cherries, and
occasionally white truffles.
DISH: **Risotto with mushrooms or truffles,** or any
game like quail.

3. Vietti Barbera d'Alba.
This wine is elegant with good acidity and drinks so
well.
DISH: This wine would go with almost anything.
If I had to choose a dish, it would have to be **rabbit.**

4. Litina Cascina Castlet.
DISH: This is another wine that is a fabulous food
wine and goes with almost anything. I'd have **pasta
with a nice ragu sauce.**

5. Maria Borio Barbera d'Asti.
DISH: This is a light red and would go well with
tuna.

6. Il Falcone Castel del Monte Riserva 2001.
This is a very elegant wine.
DISH: Osso buco made with **veal shank,** which in
Italy is called *Stinko.*

7. Tenuta de Portale Aglianico del Vulture 2001.
DISH: **Grilled sausages.**

*8. Ezio Voyat Vino da Tavola Rosso "Le
Muralie."*
DISH: **Roasted Cornish hen.**

9. Lungarotti Rubesco Vigna Monticcino.
This is a very big wine.
DISH: **Roast pork.**

10. Castel de Paolis I Quattro Mori.
This wine has a leathery taste to it that is very inter-
esting.
DISH: **Roast leg of lamb.**

11. Montepulciano d'Abruzzo Emidio Pepe.
I would want a 1985 or older. This is a very special
wine and all the grapes are crushed by hand.
DISH: A plain **steak,** because you don't want to get
in the way of this wine.

12. Edwardo Valnetini Trebbiano d'Abruzzo.
This is a great white wine that is big and rich and
close to a white Burgundy. [It was the only white
wine Scicolone brought along.]
DISH: **Swordfish.**

I TRULLI RESTAURANT *New York, New York*

NICOLA MARZOVILLA'S GNOCCHI AL RAGU DI AGNELLO
Gnocchi with Lamb Ragu

Serves 6 to 8

2 tablespoons olive oil

1 medium onion, finely chopped

2 garlic cloves, finely chopped

1 pound lean ground lamb

1 (28- to 35-ounce) can Italian tomatoes with their juice, chopped

1 tablespoon tomato paste

1 bay leaf

salt to taste

freshly ground pepper to taste

Gnocchi (recipe follows)

1/2 cup freshly grated Pecorino Romano or Parmigiano-Reggiano

1. In a large skillet, heat the olive oil over medium heat. Add the onion and sauté, 10 minutes, or until the onion is tender. Add the garlic and cook 1 minute more.

2. Stir in the lamb and cook 15 minutes, stirring frequently to break up any lumps, until it is no longer pink. Stir in the tomatoes. Add the tomato paste, bay leaf, salt, and pepper to taste.

3. Bring the sauce to a simmer and reduce the heat to low. Cook, stirring occasionally, until the sauce is thickened, about 1 1/2 hours.

4. Serve with gnocchi and grated cheese.

SOMMELIER CHARLES SCICOLONE'S WINE PAIRING: *Aglianico del Vulture DOC Riserva 1999, Tenuta del Portale (Basilicata)*

GNOCCHI (POTATO DUMPLINGS)

Serves 4

2 1/2 pounds baking potatoes (about 4)

3 large eggs

3 teaspoons salt

pinch nutmeg

2 1/2 cups all-purpose flour, plus more as needed

1. Cook the potatoes in a large pot of boiling water until a fork easily pierces the centers. Peel the potatoes. (To make the peeling of the hot potatoes a little easier, hold the potato with an oven mitt or kitchen towel and scrape out the flesh with a spoon.) Pass the potato flesh through a ricer or food mill. As you are ricing the potatoes, let them fall evenly in one layer onto a large pan; this helps the potatoes cool and reduces excess moisture. Let cool, about 15 minutes.

2. Transfer the potatoes to a clean workspace and pull them together, making a well in the center. Crack the eggs into the center; add 1 teaspoon of salt and the nutmeg. With your fingertips, work the potato and egg together to make rough dough. Sprinkle 1 cup of flour over the potato mix and gently combine. If the dough feels wet, add a bit more flour (up to 1 1/2 cups). Knead the dough until it is smooth and uniform, 3 to 4 minutes. If you are uncertain about the dough, pinch off a 1-inch piece and boil it. If it is mushy you will need to add a bit more flour.

3. Form the dough into a rectangle and cut it into 8 equal pieces. On a flat workspace, roll each piece into a ropelike cylinder, about 18 inches long and the width of your finger. This can be awkward at first, but glide your fingers out over the dough, working it back and forth while gently pulling outward. Lightly dust each piece with flour.

4. Place 2 lengths of dough horizontally in front of you. With a knife, cut across the dough to make 3/4-inch pieces. Repeat with the remaining lengths. Spread the gnocchi in a single layer on a tray so they don't stick together.

5. To cook the gnocchi, bring a large pot of water to a boil with the remaining 2 teaspoons of salt. Gently add the gnocchi to the lightly boiling water and cook until the gnocchi float back up to the surface, 2 to 3 minutes.

PIERO SELVAGGIO

OWNER, VALENTINO

Los Angeles, California

1. Barolo.
DISH: This is a wine for **truffles.**

2. Passito de Pantelleria. This is a robust, sweet wine from a little island near Sicily.
DISH: **Foie gras,** of course.

3. A young Chianti, from 2002 or 2003. I want to be able to taste the freshness of the cherry and the subtle forwardness of a red wine.
DISH: I love this wine with pasta that has not been overly sauced. I like an artisanal **pasta with vegetables** — like asparagus and great mushrooms — or anything in the cabbage family, such as rapini or broccoli tossed with garlic olive oil and chile peppers.

4. Pinot Noir from the Russian River, or Central Coast, which we now call the "Sideways" area. The rich, robust yet not overpowering fruit of a Pinot Noir makes for a very good thing.
DISH: **Pork loin** with dried fruit paired with Pinot Noir is one of the great matches of all time. I also like pork with a compote made of apples and figs.

5. Nero d'Avola from Sicily.
DISH: I'd have this with **rice croquettes** also known as *arancini,* to keep the tradition alive.

6. Chardonnay. I have a hard time with Chardonnay because it can be overly oaky and have too much vanilla for me.
DISH: That said, if there is a great *fritto misto,* a big California Chardonnay is a wonderful match. I don't want only seafood in my *fritto misto,* but also vegetables like zucchini, mushrooms, squash, and some offal, like sweetbreads or brains. I like them all fried with lemon zest.

7. Brunello di Montalcino.
DISH: With this wine, you want power against power! Strength with strength, richness with richness . . . Being Italian, I need to think of the ultimate marriage, which is **gamey risotto** with quail, pheasant, or lamb meatballs.

8. Lambrusco, which is a wine too many people have forgotten about.
DISH: I will not be a good Italian if I don't have my share of **salumi.** The Lambrusco would be the traditional match, because most of the salumi comes from Emilia-Romagna and it is a good marriage.

9. Syrah. This is for good American food. The wine works like spice on spice, or rich on rich.
DISH: Any kind of **ribs** are good with any kind of Syrah.

10. A Sauvignon Blanc with some crispness.
DISH: This is the wine I would have with my **cheese.**

11. An old Amarone that is powerful and bold, for when I'd want to treat myself.
DISH: I would have this with any **creamy or aged cheese.**

12. The oldest bottle of wine in the cellar and bread.
DISH: If you have an old bottle of wine and you are wondering what will work with it, don't work so hard. Have it with a great piece of **bread.** There is one thing I never have enough and that is a little panini with lardo, ricotta, and tomato.

Bonus wine and cheese:

If I could take a thirteenth wine to my island, I would add **Vin Santo.** Vin Santo is good by itself, but with a **hazelnut cookie,** it is heaven! Another taste of heaven is a dash of **Marsala with ricotta cheese.** It is like a sauce: you can eat and drink it at the same time.

PIERO SELVAGGIO'S INVOLTINI DI PESCE SPADA CON COUSCOUS TRAPANESE
Swordfish Involtini with Couscous
Serves 4

1/2 cup couscous

2 tablespoons butter

3 tablespoons olive oil

2 teaspoons finely chopped garlic

8 large prawns, shelled, deveined, and roughly chopped

1/4 cup finely chopped red bell pepper

1/4 cup finely chopped yellow bell pepper

1/4 cup finely chopped zucchini

1/4 cup finely chopped celery

1/4 cup finely chopped carrots

1/2 cup dry white wine

salt and pepper, to taste

8 (4-ounce) swordfish steaks, pounded to 1/8-inch thickness

baby lettuce (for garnish)

1 tablespoon white wine vinegar

1. Preheat the oven to 500°F. In a small saucepan, bring 1 1/2 cups of salted water to a boil. Add the couscous, cover, and remove from heat. Let sit until all water has been absorbed, 5 to 7 minutes.

2. Heat 1 tablespoon butter and 1 tablespoon oil in a skillet over medium heat. Add 1 teaspoon of the garlic and sauté until golden. Add the prawns and vegetables. Add the wine and cook until the wine is reduced and vegetables are tender. Stir in the couscous and season with salt and pepper.

3. Lay the swordfish slices on a clean surface, divide the stuffing evenly on top of the slices, and roll up. Secure with toothpicks if necessary. Put the swordfish rolls in a shallow roasting pan, add 1 tablespoon of the remaining olive oil and the remaining 1 tablespoon butter and 1 teaspoon garlic; season with salt and pepper. Bake 7 to 10 minutes, until the swordfish is lightly colored and the swordfish and prawns are cooked through. Place the swordfish rolls on a bed of baby lettuce.

4. Transfer the cooking juices to a small pan, places over high heat, and reduce for a few minutes. Stir in the remaining 1 tablespoon olive oil and the vinegar; drizzle the sauce over the swordfish rolls and lettuce.

SELVAGGIO'S WINE PAIRING: *Choose a full-bodied white, rich in citrus, tartar, and dry fruits — a* California Chardonnay *that is not too oaky, like Littorai or Iron Horse, with just a touch of austerity.* Champagne *is a richer choice — a Blanc de Blancs or even a wonderful rosé.*

ALPANA SINGH, MS

SOMMELIER, EVEREST

Chicago, Illinois

I love all "my children" — how am I supposed to choose just a few favorites?

1. Sauvignon Blanc.
This is what I like to drink while I'm cooking.

2. Pinot Gris.
This is my go-to wine. I love it because it has a softness of texture, it is not too full and void of any oak characteristic, and has just enough of a tropical fruit element. It is a no-brainer — it automatically contrasts savoriness, especially against the smokiness of **bacon.** Texturally, it works with a large variety of foods and is pleasing to the palate.

3. Burgundy.
With Burgundy, you really use your sense of smell. I find when people smell Burgundy, they close their eyes. You need to take a moment, return to yourself and ask, "What is this wine trying to say to me? What am I experiencing and feeling?" This wine is the art of seduction in the purest sense. You give yourself to this wine. It is very primal.

4. Zinfandel.
This is my favorite gratuitous wine. I don't have to think about it. It hits me without looking for it — it is fun, inexpensive, and sassy. I love the bright fruity jammy notes. It is America's grape varietal. I have almost twenty on our list and it doesn't even go with our food that well, other than with the **cheese course,** since it is similar to port but not as sweet.

5. Riesling.
If I am going be on an island for a long time, this wine will hold up best. It ages forever. I like it with my **Vietnamese food,** which is a gorgeous combination.

6. Champagne.
Bollinger is my number one Champagne. I like a good nutty, toasty one. It is consistently fabulous and it comes in many different flavors.

7. Grenache.
I love it! It is Pinot Noir, but kicked up a notch. I like it with roast meat like **osso buco** and **stews.**

8. Rioja.
This is probably my biggest "wow" factor, because it teaches me what technology and determination can do in a region. When I first started, I hated Riojas for being tired and over-oaked. A few years later, they were great and not overpriced. They are comparable to California Cabernets, but if you spend sixty dollars on a Spanish wine it is a lot and very special, while for that same amount you'd get just an average Cabernet.

CARLOS SOLIS

FOOD AND BEVERAGE
DIRECTOR/CHEF, FOUR POINTS
SHERATON/LAX

Los Angeles, California

Instead of having a chef come to cook my food, I would rather cook it myself. If you could send someone do the dishes, that would be great.

1. Chimay — my favorite beers in the world. They are the fine wine of beer.
DISH: I would love Chimay with **leftover stew.**

2. New Belgium Beer from Colorado.
This beer is a cross between American and Belgium beer. The brewmaster was formerly the assistant brewer of Chimay.
DISH: **Grilled salmon** or fresh **steamed mussels** for lunch.

3. Lambic beer.
I like the fruity styles, but I would take a plain one. A plain style is a little sour and has a wonderful aftertaste.
DISH: An egg **dish** or **fruit salad** with melon and berries, something not too sweet, for breakfast.

4. Imperial Stout Porter from the North Coast Brewery.
This beer has sweetness and variety of flavor and is robust.
DISH: This goes well with dessert. I would like it with **cheesecake with raspberries.**

5. Fisher Amber.
DISH: I'd drink this with the **Cobb salad** that we serve in our restaurant, which is made with blue cheese, caramelized walnuts, and bacon, and dressed in a coriander vinaigrette.

6. Sunny Claus.
I would take this Swedish beer to put me to sleep at night. This beer is like drinking a brandy; it is 14 percent alcohol, so it is like an after-dinner drink.
DISH: I'd have this with a **cigar** to end the day. I'd want the cigar to be milder with soft sweetness for a great pairing.

7. Double Chocolate Stort from England.
It is brewed with cocoa, so it would serve as dessert.
DISH: **Chocolate-dipped strawberries,** because the sour fruit and bitter chocolate would go great with this beer.

8. Cantillon Rosé de Gambrinus.
It is like wine from the beer family, in that it has bitterness, sourness, acidity, and is sparkling.
DISH: This is an **aperitif** that you would drink like Champagne before the meal to use for your toast. It also is a nice "Sunday morning" beer. It is also good at the end of the night if you have had one too many, because it will put you right to sleep.

9. Biere de Garde.
This is a French beer that is so herbal, it almost is like an Asian tea. The beer is so refreshing that you can drink it at room temperature and it has the same flavor as if it were cold, which is very unusual. This beer is also great for picnics.
DISH: Because it is herbal, it pairs well with a **spring salad** with young leaves.

10. Keg of wheat beer from B. J.'s Brew Pub called Hefeweissen.
This is a restaurant out of Chicago and is big in L.A. Their wheat beer is fruity and refreshing.
DISH: You can drink it by itself, but I also like it with **Thai red or yellow curry with beef.** Another direction you could go is **spicy Asian or Mediterranean food.**

LARRY STONE, MS

WINEMAKER, RUBICON

San Francisco, California

1. DRC Romanée-Conti 1934, Burgundy.

2. Petrus 1921, Pomerol.

3. Château Cheval Blanc 1947, Saint-Émilion.

4. Inglenook Reserve Cabernet 1941, Napa Valley.

5. Château d'Yquem 1847, Sauternes.

6. Abudarham Terrantez Madeira 1795.

7. Prager "Bodenstein" Riesling Smaragd 2001, Wachau (Austria).

8. Kracher Trockenbeerenauslese #8 2001, Burgenland (Austria).

9. Rubicon 2001, Napa Valley.

10. Guigal Côte-Rôtie "La Mouline" 1985.

11. Remirez de Ganuza 2001, Rioja.

12. L'Eremita 2001, Priorat.

DISH: Most of these wines make eating irrelevant . . . Besides, I do believe that I could just catch live **crabs and shrimp** and eat them with about any of the wines. If there were a **wild goat** or two roaming around and something to spit roast them with (following sustainable farming and harvesting principles, of course, to perpetuate the species), then I wouldn't need to have any worries for the rest of my life (and there would be no need to rescue me). These complex wines are best with very simple food.

BERNARD SUN

BEVERAGE DIRECTOR, JEAN-GEORGES MANAGEMENT

New York, New York

I would take twelve Burgundy wines. My background, after all, is four and a half years at Montrachet [restaurant], so I have tasted some of the greatest Burgundies in the world. To me, there is no other wine like a great Burgundy. I won't turn down a glass of 1929 La Tour or 1961 Petrus, but give me a bottle of Old Vines Musigny Bouchard and I am happy as a clam. I don't need anything else.

I have tasted so many great wines I could never pick twelve. I have tasted 1929 Musigny and 1900 Château d'Yquem. I was reading a publication that had a list of the greatest wines ever made and I was saying to myself, "had it, had it, had it." I have tasted the 1945 Mouton — from a 750-liter, Magnum, and Double Magnum — which is one of the greatest classic wines ever made. I have been very lucky to work at Le Cirque, Montrachet, and Lespinasse which all had award-winning wine lists and the clientele for them.

I also never forget that a great-tasting nice little Pinot Noir from the Central Coast or from Oregon has a winemaker working just as hard.

You find when you meet someone who has been bitten by the Burgundy bug there is no other wine.

PAUL TANGUAY

BEVERAGE DIRECTOR,
SUSHI SAMBA

New York, New York

1. Pilsner beer — either a Pilsner Urquell or an Einbecker.
DISH: **Simple pizza** with a little basil and oregano sprinkled on top.

2. Riesling Kabinett.
DISH: A plate of assorted **sushi.**

3. Riesling Spätlese.
DISH: I would have this with some **Pad Thai** or **chicken curry.**

4. Grüner Veltliner.
DISH: The **Blue Ribbon Royal** from Blue Ribbon restaurant in New York, which has oysters, clams, lobster, shrimp, and other seafood. It is fantastic!

5. Ice Wine.
DISH: I would have this with some **foie gras with toro tuna** underneath it, and would save it to eat and drink on cooler nights.

6. Viognier.
DISH: **Moqueca Mista,** which is a stew we serve at Sushi Samba. The stew has shellfish and a little coconut milk in it, so it is a little rich and a little sweet. Viognier would be great with this stew.

7. Pierre Ferrand Cognac.
DISH: I would like this on its own or with a **crème brûlée.**

8. A good bottle of water: either Fiji or Saratoga.
DISH: I'd like this with a **light salad** with some arugula and cucumber.

9. Oka sake. This is my go-to sake!
DISH: This sake is so versatile that I would have it with **shrimp** done five ways: raw, grilled, ceviche, tempura-fried, and stir-fried.

10. Daiginjo sake.
DISH: I'd like this with some **fresh vegetables,** or a **tomato, basil and mozzarella salad,** or even a **fruit salad.**

11. Super daiginjo sake Masumi Yumedono.
DISH: This sake is so good that you could just sit and sip it! However, it would definitely work with **miso-glazed sea bass.**

12. A great Pinot Noir from Burgundy.
DISH: I'd keep it simple with **lamb chops.**

DEREK TODD

SOMMELIER,
BLUE HILL AT STONE BARNS

Pocantico Hills, New York

1. Hogarten Wheat Beer.
This beer is so refreshing.
DISH: *Moules frites* [mussels and French fries]
made by a Belgian chef.

2. Volnay Red Burgundy.
This is my first love of wine, and I like an earthier
appellation.
DISH: Something with mushrooms, like Stone
Barns' **lobster with mushroom broth.**

3. White Burgundy.
It is a magical expression of *terrior.*
DISH: A **poached fish** dish from Per Se [restaurant
in New York City].

4. Diet Coke.
It is refreshing after a night of drinking wine.
DISH: **Salt and vinegar potato chips.** I particularly
like Cape Cod chips.

5. Rioja.
DISH: Stone Barns' **lamb with horseradish broth.**

6. Fiano from Campania.
I love a crisp Italian white.
DISH: **Grilled prawns** on a salad.

7. Beaucastel Châteauneuf-du-Pape.
I have a weakness for this wine!
DISH: I like this wine with almost anything,
including a **strip steak** with a Provençal herb butter.

*8. Giacomo Conterno Monfortino Barolo from any
great vintage.*
DISH: Almost anything from Babbo [restaurant in
New York City] — their **lamb's tongue salad** comes
to mind in particular. This is about the dish and the
wine from the region just hooking up. You want a
woodsy, earthy dish with this wine.

9. Jean-Louis Chave Hermitage.
I am fan of the Northern Rhône 1983. There really
is no question among professionals that he is the
king of Northern Rhône.
DISH: A **pork** dish that is a touch tangy and
smoky.

*10. Late Harvest Chenin Blanc from Coteaux du
Layon.*
You need to have something for after dinner.
DISH: Definitely an aged **goat cheese** or a **Spanish
white cheese.**

*11. Dönnhoff Niederhauser Hermannshohle
Riesling.*
It is a great wine that is fun to pronounce!
DISH: **Anything.** This is an incredibly versatile
wine. I'd like to have it with **scallops** with a slightly
sweet preparation.

Now it is really tough. This is the point where I
am thinking people are going to read this and say,
"Hey, he didn't include . . ."

*12. Roger Sabon White Châteauneuf-du-Pape
Cuvée Renaissance.*
DISH: Something nutty, like a rich **lobster salad
with hazelnuts.**

GREG TRESNER, MS

SOMMELIER, MARY ELAINE'S AT THE PHOENICIAN

Scottsdale, Arizona

I am going to bring a cooler!

1. Krug Champagne, vintage 1998.
DISH: A series of **appetizers:** tuna tartare, Kumamoto oysters with caviar, and celery parfait.

2. Venica e Venica or Edi Kante Sauvignon from Italy.
DISH: **Dover sole** in a meunière sauce.

3. L'Ermita from Spain.
DISH: **Cassoulet** made by our chef Brad Thompson with braised lamb shoulder, garlic sausage, duck confit, and pork belly.

4. Vega Sicilia from Spain.
DISH: **Roast pork** tenderloin.

5. Domaine Romanée-Conti La Tache from any good vintage.
DISH: An herb-crusted **rack of lamb** with garlic, spring vegetables, and pancetta.

6. Comte Lafon Meursault.
DISH: **Turbot with mushrooms,** because this wine is very full-bodied.

7. Hirtzberger Grüner Veltliner.
DISH: This is a great fish wine! I'd want it with **lobster poached in butter** with a pinch of curry.

8. Domaine Weinbach Riesling from Alsace.
DISH: **Hamachi.**

9. White Coat by Turley Vineyards.
DISH: **Sea bass.**

10. Domaine Serene from Oregon.
DISH: **Duck** with a honey and spice glaze.

11. Penfolds Grange from Australia.
Since they are all so good, I'll take a 1996 or else I will never be able to choose.
DISH: A **grilled steak.**

12. Antinori Masseto, which is an Italian Merlot.
DISH: This wine is great with **cheese.** I would have this with Parmigiano-Reggiano, Vella Dried Jack, and Laguiole from France.

13. 1982 Château La Tour Bordeaux.
DISH: This is a great beef wine. Have this with **beef and a bordelaise sauce,** and one taste of the combination will take all the new-wave cutting-cdge desires out of you. After one bite of this classic pairing, it will be all you want to eat.

MADELINE TRIFFON, MS

DIRECTOR OF WINE, MATT
PRENTICE RESTAURANT GROUP

Detroit, Michigan

1. Blanc de Blancs Champagne.
DISH: **Cracker-crust pizza** with herbs and salt (no tomato sauce), or buttery **mashed potatoes.**

2. Sauvignon Blanc, unoaked, from the Loire Valley (Sancerre), or South Africa.
DISH: **Salad** of fresh vegetables with great olive oil, lemon, and salt — or **soba noodles** with sesame oil.

3. Mosel Riesling, Kabinett or Trocken or Spätlese.
DISH: **Triple-crème cheese.**

4. White Burgundy in a traditional style with some bottle age.
DISH: Fresh **pasta** tossed with brown butter or **roasted chicken.**

5. A Côte-Rôtie from northern Rhône — and make it a meaty, peppery one.
DISH: **Roast leg of lamb** with oregano.

6. Napa Valley Cabernet — I'd like one that is big, edgy, tannic, extracted, and young.
DISH: **Grilled sirloin steak** with Detroit Zip Sauce (soy, garlic, olive oil, and pepper). I would have this on a baked potato with the Zip Sauce while my friends enjoyed their steaks.

7. Chianti Classico Riserva or a 100 percent Sangiovese.
DISH: **Pasta Bolognese.**

8. Monastrell from southeast Spain, which has a little Rhône character.
DISH: **Manchego cheese** and little green olives.

9. Lager beer. I like beer in general, and I enjoy a nice clean lager.
DISH: **Deep-fried anything** — such as fries or zucchini sticks.

10. Tea. I like really good black tea, iced or hot.
DISH: I especially like black tea with spicy **sambar and potato dosa** (from southern India).

11. Water. Tons of water — and I would like it from the Great Lakes.
DISH: **Nothing.**

12. Pinot Noir from Oregon, or a modern red Burgundy.
DISH: **Swiss chard or wild greens,** simply steamed, braised, or sautéed — or a homemade **spinach pie.**

13. Coteaux du Layon Bonnezeaux dessert-level Chenin Blanc from the Loire Valley.
DISH: **Pear pastry** with fresh whipped cream.

SCOTT TYREE

SOMMELIER, TRU

Chicago, Illinois

The first thing I need to know is; Will there be proper refrigeration and do I get a corkscrew? Yes. OK, then I'm going to request an island in the South Pacific, and I am going to need wine that goes with tropical fruit.

I must have German Riesling. In fact, this will be selections 1 through 3, as I will need all levels of sweetness for my Riesling. It will be hot on my island, and these wines have low alcohol and lots of refreshing acidity which is good because I am going to be parched. They will also have plenty of ripe fruit flavors that will go with the lovely mangoes and papayas I will eat.

I don't mean to sound like I am joking, because I would take three Rieslings with me for sure:

1. Kabinett. This is the driest.
DISH: **Root vegetable terrine** with coriander, roasted garlic, and crispy taro root made by chef Paul Kahan of Blackbird [in Chicago].

2. Spätlese — a little sweeter than the Kabinett.
DISH: **Rare bluefin tuna** with sunchokes, caviar, and crème fraîche made by chef Eric Ripert of Le Bernardin [in New York City].

3. Auslese — fairly sweet, verging on dessert sweetness.
DISH: **Foie gras torchon** with a quince compote made by chef Koren Grieveson of Avec restaurant [in Chicago].

Several producers make wonderful **Riesling: Donnhoff, Robert Veil,** and **Gunderloch** are just a few to consider.

4. I would also have to have Champagne — a Blanc de Blancs or Rosé Billecart Salmon 1982.
DISH: **Hot buttered popcorn** made by Orville Redenbacher.

5. 1990 Jean-Francois Coche-Dury Meursault Rougeots.
DISH: I would pair this wine with a dish from my favorite chef of all time: my grandmother Nora Tyree of Nora's Cafe in Thayer, Missouri. Her **southern fried chicken** with mashed potatoes and chicken gravy would make this the best wine and food pairing *ever*.

6. Palliser Estate Sauvignon Blanc from New Zealand.
I love its vibrancy, acidity, and tropical fruit flavor. I was on a panel where we blind-tasted twenty-five Sauvignon Blancs from New Zealand, and this wine was the unanimous choice for number one. It is the purest expression of New Zealand Sauvignon Blanc. It also happened to be the only wine with a screw top.
DISH: **Hearts of palm salad** with mango and truffle vinaigrette made by chef Laurent Gras.

7. Vosne-Romanée Burgundy.
François Gros or any other producer. Wines from this region are the quintessential expressions of Pinot Noir from Burgundy. They are the most concentrated, balanced, and silkiest.
DISH: **Pulled pork sandwich** from the Cuban lady on the corner of my block.

8. Hermitage made by Jean-Louis Chave.
To me, these are the most elegant Syrah-based wines. Syrah can be tannic, dark, brooding, reticent, and overpowering. However his wine has a lot of finesse and when I taste it, I think, "This is the perfect expression of Hermitage made by Jean-Louis Chave." It is a fairly hard wine to find from a small appellation, so it is not inexpensive.
DISH: Whole **roasted squab with Perigord truffles,** made by chef Gabrielle Hamilton of Prune [in New York City].

9. Pinot Noir from the Russian River Valley.
A wine by Merry Edwards for their suppleness and generous fruit; which is a lot like Merry herself. She is a warm, generous, lovely person. Her passion is Pinot Noir and you can taste her passion! Her wines have wonderful berry flavor and silky texture.
DISH: **Venison with hen of the woods mushrooms** and French lentils, prepared by Jonathan Benno of Per Se in New York City.

10. Classic Bordeaux.
I would take something from my birth year, so it would be 1961 La Tour. It is the perfect example of Paulliac from one of the best vintages ever produced. This would be the last wine I drink. I would take it on the boat and share it with my rescuers! It is not a wine that I could savor on my own: I would have to share it with my friends!
DISH: **A double cheese hamburger** from the Billy Goat Tavern in Chicago.

11. My uncle's wine.
If I were on a desert island, I would be lonely and would want something to remind me of home. My uncle used to make wine from grapes he would buy locally — I am from the South, and the grapes were probably the Catawba grapes that grow wild — and ferment in the bottle. It was really bad, almost like moonshine. It was a sweet red and he would bring it over to my grandparents' house for Christmas and everyone would have a nip of it. In my family no one drank wine, but to me it was such a treat to have this big fancy awful wine. I was underage and thought I was so sophisticated to have wine with my turkey and stuffing. It was my first taste of fermented grape juice, so this wine would keep me grounded and take me back to my roots.
DISH: **Christmas dinner.**

12. Le Chapelle Jabolet 1961. This is the most amazing wine I have ever tasted.
DISH: Smoky **grilled mushrooms** with herb butter.

DAVID WALTUCK AND ROGER DAGORN, MS

CHEF-OWNER AND MAÎTRE D'HOTEL, CHANTERELLE

New York, New York

We had a side-by-side discussion with chef David Waltuck and sommelier Roger Dagorn at Chanterelle on this question. Most of the time, they took turns choosing the wines and the dishes. Other times, they would discuss and negotiate . . . or simply decide to bring whatever the heck they wanted:

1. Dagorn: 1989 Romanée-Conti.
DISH: **Squab stuffed with foie gras.**

2. Waltuck: Meursault.
DISH: A classic fish dish. I would have it with one of my own dishes: **scallops sautéed in duck fat.** **Lobster salad** or **quenelles** would also be good.

3. Dagorn: Bourbon or rum — Maker's Mark Bourbon or St. James Rum.
DISH, WALTUCK: **Cohiba** [Cuban] **cigars.**

4. Dagorn: If my wife Cheryl is with me, I must have some Champagne, either Krug or Dom Pérignon Rosé.
DISH (FOR CHERYL): **Caviar with blini** served with sour cream and chopped egg.

5. Waltuck: Karen [his wife] is not much of a white wine drinker — she is more of a Bordeaux person.

Dagorn chimes in: **Château La Tour** 1961 or 1966, what else?

DISH (FOR KAREN): **Rack of lamb** in light lamb jus.

6. Dagorn: A Saint-Joseph Côte-Rôtie, because I need a solid Rhône.

DISH, WALTUCK: **Beef, lamb,** or **Epoisses cheese.**

DISH, DAGORN: **Reblochon** or **Levroux cheese.**

7. Dagorn: Clos des Truffiers from the Languedoc. This wine is a rich, ruby color with spice. It is soft and silky with hints of clove and cassis.

DISH, WALTUCK: A **stew** of some sort, or a **lamb shank.**

DISH, DAGORN: **Braised oxtail** with red wine sauce and turnips.

8. Waltuck: Yves Cuilleron Condrieu.

I have a sentimental attachment to this wine, as it was the house wine of La Pyramide [the legendary restaurant over which legendary French chef Fernand Point presided].

DISH, DAGORN: **Seafood sausage** [one of the signature dishes at Chanterelle].

9. Waltuck: Château d'Yquem is the only sweet wine I would consider.

DAGORN: The best bottle was an 1893. It is similar to the 1967 and 1983. It was sweet without being cloying, it had a fair amount of body to it, and it was perfectly balanced. The older wines can get dried out, but this one was not. We have a customer who is collector and shares them with us, and we have had one from every decade.

DISH, WALTUCK: **Just by itself.**

DISH, DAGORN: **Fontainebleau cheese.**

10. Dagorn: Harlan Cabernet Sauvignon, because we need something from the New World. It is a classic Cabernet with a fair amount of body, a forward nose, and tannin that is there for structure. It could easily be mistaken for Bordeaux.

DISH, DAGORN: **Grilled skirt steak** with shallot butter.

DISH, WALTUCK: I'm in — I could eat that!

11. Dagorn: Shea Wine Cellars Pinot Noir Estate 2001 (Oregon).

He grows grapes and sells them to other vintners, but this is the wine he makes for himself.

DISH: **Wild salmon** that is poached and served with creamed leeks.

12. Waltuck: Let's bring some Beaujolais in case we want a picnic on the beach.

DAGORN: **Potel Aviron** is a very good wine.

DISH, DAGORN: **Sandwiches: Grilled cheese, BLT, po' boy,** or **lobster roll.**

DISH, WALTUCK: **Steak** *frites.*

JOSHUA WESSON

OWNER, BEST CELLARS

New York, New York

1. Müller-Catoir Scheurebe Kabinett from the Pfalz in Germany.
DISH: **Grilled day-boat scallops** in a Tahitian vanilla–tinged beurre blanc.

2. Blanc de Blancs Champagne.
DISH: **White truffle crostini with Parmigiano-Reggiano** cheese.

3. Dupont sparkling cider from Normandy, a dry cider that is world class.
DISH: A selection of **stinky cheeses**: Livarot, Pont l'Évêque, and a real Muenster.

4. Vermentino from Sardinia.
DISH: This is a wine for seafood like **grilled sea bass with wild herbs.**

5. Santorini white from Greece.
DISH: A delicate fish, like **sole in parchment** with an herb lemon butter.

6. Margan Saignee Rosé Shiraz from Australia. This wine has just a little sweetness to it.
DISH: **Peking duck** or **barbecued ribs** or a **pulled pork sandwich.** Or road-kill **kangaroo**, field dressed and grilled.

7. Chardonnay from New Zealand, unoaked.
DISH: Wood-grilled **spiny lobster,** drizzled with anise butter.

8. Cabernet Merlot blend from the Columbia Valley in Washington State.
DISH: **Grilled lamb chops.**

9. Côtes du Rhône Villages.
DISH: Hearty **oxtail ragout over pappardelle.** Or Chef Cesare Casella's **wild boar and chocolate ragout** over pappardelle from Maremma [restaurant in New York City].

10. Pinot Noir from the California Central Coast.
DISH: **Grilled squab** with sour cherries.

11. Pinot Blanc from Niagara Peninsula. This wine is like liquid chicken; it goes with everything.
DISH: **Chicken salad** with homemade mayonnaise. I love a good chicken salad sandwich. I don't go to sleep in fear of mayonnaise like so many people do. I embrace mayonnaise, and even make it from scratch. A fresh mayo is a thing of beauty. Homemade mayonnaise with French fries is off the charts! It is like sex — the umami factor is over the top.

12. Argentinian Malbec blend or Syrah.
DISH: **Lombardi's pizza** [the first pizzeria in New York City], with mushrooms and sausage.

FOOD AND BEVERAGE TASTING CHART

Today's Date _____

BEVERAGE

Vintage _____

Maker (Country/Region) _____

Grape _____

Other _____

Use an X to indicate your assessment of the beverage on the following spectrums:

AROMA:	None ⟷ Fragrant
WEIGHT:	Light-Bodied ⟷ Full-Bodied
FLAVOR VOLUME:	Quiet ⟷ Loud
TEXTURE:	Still ⟷ Boldly Sparkling
SWEETNESS:	Dry ⟷ Sweet
ACIDITY:	Low Acidity ⟷ Highly Acidic
TANNIN:	None ⟷ Highly Tannic
OAK:	None ⟷ Heavily Oaked
COMPLEXITY:	Straightforward ⟷ Nuanced

FOOD

DESCRIPTION OF DISH _____

KEY FLAVOR COMPONENTS _____

COOKING TECHNIQUE USED _____ raw _____ steamed _____ sautéed

_____ roasted _____ grilled _____ braised

DOMINANT CHARACTERISTICS *(circle all that apply)*:

Weight	LIGHT	MEDIUM	HEAVY	
Texture	CREAMY	CRISPY	CRUNCHY	
Flavors	SALTY	SWEET	TART	BITTER

PAIRING ASSESSMENT   *Best*   +2   +1   0   −1   −2   *Worst*

Pairing Notes _____

_____

_____

_____

ABOUT THE EXPERTS

Colin Alevras is the chef and sommelier of the Tasting Room in New York City. He and his wife and partner, Renee (who runs the dining room), opened the twenty-five-seat restaurant in 1999 after working in restaurant kitchens following their graduation from Peter Kump's New York Cooking School (now known as the Institute for Culinary Education) and apprenticeship at the Michelin three-star L'Arpège in Paris. Alevras previously worked as a private chef to a United Nations ambassador. www.thetastingroomnyc.com

Kai Andersen is the marketing manager for Ito En, a tea purveyor that includes the tea restaurant Kai on Madison Avenue in New York City. Kai restaurant was awarded two stars by the *New York Times* in 2004 and rated New York's number one tea destination in the 2006 *Zagat Survey*. Originally from Honolulu, Andersen became interested in tea while studying French literature in Paris. In 2002 he joined Ito En, where he discovers new teas and develops new blends. Both an expert and educator regarding all aspects of Japanese tea, Andersen has taught a workshop, the Art of Sencha, at the Brooklyn Botanic Garden. www.itoen.com/kai

CHRISTOPHER TRACY

Michael Anthony is opening his own restaurant in New York. Previously, he was executive chef at Blue Hill at Stone Barns in Pocantico Hills, New York, and Blue Hill in New York City. After graduating from École Supérieure de Cuisine Françaises in Paris with a CAP de cuisine, Anthony trained in some of France's finest restaurants, including L'Arpège, Les Prés d'Eugénie, and L'Astrance. It was during his tenure with Restaurant Jacques Cagna that he met and worked with Dan Barber. In 1995, the opportunity to work at Daniel brought Anthony back to the United States. Two years later, he joined March Restaurant as sous chef and was later promoted to chef de cuisine. www.bluehillstonebarns.com

Dan Barber is executive chef at Blue Hill at Stone Barns in Pocantico Hills, New York, and Blue Hill in New York City. Barber began farming and cooking for family and friends at Blue Hill Farm in the Berkshires where he was first introduced to and gained respect for locally grown and seasonal produce. Blue Hill was nominated for a 2001 James Beard Foundation award for Best New Restaurant and was most recently named one of America's Best Restaurants by *Gourmet* magazine. In the summer of 2002, *Food & Wine* magazine featured Barber as one of the country's Best New Chefs. He was also named one of the Next Generation of great chefs in *Bon Appétit* magazine's tenth annual restaurant issue. www.bluehillstonebarns.com

Joseph Bastianich is the co-owner (with Mario Batali) of Babbo, Bar Jamon, Casa Mono, Del Posto, Esca, Lupa, and Otto Enoteca Pizzeria, all in New York City. Bastianich is also a partner with Sergio Esposito and Mario Batali in Italian Wine Merchants. In Italy, he started the wine estate Azienda Agricola Bastianich in Friuli and is bottling olive oil from groves in Colli Orientali and Trieste. He is partner in Becco and Felidia with his mother, chef Lidia Bastianich. He is also the coauthor, along with David Lynch, of two books on Italian wines, *Vino Italiano* and *Vino Italiano Buying Guide*. The James Beard Foundation honored him in 2005 with its Outstanding Wine and Spirits Professional award and he is a member of the Who's Who in Food and Beverage in America. www.italianwinemerchant.com

Stephen Beckta is the owner-sommelier of Beckta Dining & Wine in Ottawa. Beckta Dining & Wine was named the fourth Best New Restaurant in Canada by *enRoute* magazine (2003) and won five stars from the *Ottawa Sun* (2003) and four diamonds from Canada's AAA (2005). He worked as a sommelier in New York City at Daniel Boulud's Café Boulud. During the two years he spent there, Café Boulud won two *Wine Spectator* Awards of Excellence. While in New York, Beckta also worked with Danny Meyer and Richard Coraine at Eleven Madison Park. He is a graduate of the sommelier program at Ottawa's Algonquin College and was previously the wine director for the Ritz restaurant group in Ottawa. www.beckta.com

Daniel Boulud is the executive chef and owner of the *New York Times* four-star Daniel (New York City), along with Café Boulud (New York City and Palm Beach), DB Bistro Moderne (New York City), and Daniel Boulud Brasserie (Las Vegas). Originally from a farm near Lyon, he is now one of the world's premiere chefs. He won James Beard Foundation awards for Best Chef: New York in 1992 and Outstanding Chef in 1994 and was named Chef of the Year by *Bon Appétit* magazine. Daniel was rated "one of the ten best restaurants in the world" by the *International Herald Tribune*, and also earned top ratings from *Gourmet* magazine, *Wine Spectator* magazine (Grand Award), and the *Zagat Survey*. Boulud is the author of five cookbooks and has been a guest chef on many television programs, including *Today*, *The Late Show with David Letterman*, and *Martha Stewart Living*. www.danielnyc.com

Richard Breitkreutz is at Hudson Yards Catering in New York City. Previously he was the general manager of Eleven Madison Park in New York City. He studied with the Wine and Spirits Education Trust and the Court of Master Sommeliers. Breitkreutz was part of the opening team at Eleven Madison Park. In July 2000, he left to run the beverage program and service in the main dining room at Tabla, the Indian-inspired fine dining restaurant next door. He returned to Eleven Madison Park in October 2002 as the service and beverage director, and was promoted to general manager in 2004. www.hycnyc.com

Scott Calvert is the sommelier at the Inn at Little Washington in Washington, Virginia. He won *Wine Spectator's* Grand Award in 2003, 2004, and 2005. He was previously a wine consultant for Ilo, Rick Laakonnen's restaurant at the Bryant Park Hotel, which won three stars from the *New York Times*.

Calvert began his sommelier training at the River Café in Brooklyn under wine director Joe Delissio and became the restaurant's first sommelier. He also started an educational wine program for staff and created the restaurant's first wine pairing menus. www.theinnatlittlewashington.com

Kathy Casey is the chef-owner of Kathy Casey Food Studios in Seattle. She wrote *Pacific Northwest: The Beautiful Cookbook*, which was nominated for the Julia Child Cookbook Award. Her most recent books are *Dishing with Kathy Casey* and *Kathy Casey Cooks Favorites*. She also coauthored both *Best Places Seattle Cookbook* and *Star Palate*. She and her husband, John Casey, are the owners of Dish D'Lish, a combination retail store and catering business in Pike Place Market, and an outpost in Seattle's Sea-Tac airport. She also writes the column Dishing for the *Seattle Times*. www.kathycasey.com

Joe Catterson is the general manager and wine director at Alinea in Chicago. He previously designed the wine program for Trio restaurant in Evanston, Illinois, where he first worked with Alinea's chef Grant Achatz. *Chicago* magazine awarded Trio its Best Wine Program honors in its 2002 and 2003 restaurant issues and recognized Catterson as Best Sommelier in 2003. Before working with Achatz, Catterson was named sommelier at Le Francais in Wheeling, Illinois, and later at Les Nomades in Chicago. He has traveled and lived abroad pursuing his work as a classical musician. www.alinearestaurant.com

Belinda Chang is the wine director of Osteria Via Stato and Big Bowl, both Lettuce Entertain You restaurants in Chicago. Previously, Chang spent two years as both the wine director and general manager of the Fifth Floor in San Francisco. She was nominated for the 2004 James Beard Foundation award for Outstanding Wine Service. Prior to this, Chang was at Charlie Trotter's in Chicago, where she was trained in the wine program developed by master sommeliers Larry Stone and Joseph Spellman and served as the restaurant's sommelier for three years. While at Rice University, she worked in the kitchen at Houston's famed Cafe Annie. www.leye.com

Rebecca Charles is the owner and executive chef of Pearl Oyster Bar in Greenwich Village in New York City. Charles was awarded four stars at the White Barn Inn in Kennebunkport, and later at her own Café 74. She returned to Manhattan in 1987 to work as sous chef at Anne Rosenzweig's Arcadia. After serving as executive chef at several New York City restaurants, she opened Pearl Oyster Bar in

1997 to enormous critical and popular acclaim. In 2003, Charles chronicled her family's experiences in Maine and her time in the kitchen in the memoir cookbook, *Lobster Rolls & Blueberry Pie*. www.pearloysterbar.com

Stephane Colling has been the wine director at The Modern at the Museum of Modern Art in New York City since its 2004 opening. In 1998, Colling studied at Oxford University while working at the three-star Waterside Inn in Bray, England. In 1999, he moved to New York to become head sommelier at the Castle at Tarrytown. In 2002 he moved on to become wine director at Compass in New York City, earning *Wine Spectator*'s Best of Award of Excellence. Eventually, Colling became assistant head sommelier at Alain Ducasse at the Essex House and won *Wine Spectator*'s Grand Award. At The Modern, he has created a list of over nine hundred wines to complement the menu of chef Gabriel Kreuther, a fellow Alsatian. www.themodernnyc.com

George Cossette is the co-owner of Silverlake Wine in Los Angeles. He was formerly the wine director at Campanile. While there, he received a 2003 James Beard Foundation nomination for Best Wine Service. He has designed wine lists for other area restaurants, including Lucques and Jar. He also worked on the wine list at the East Coast Grill in Cambridge, Massachusetts. His partners in Silverlake Wine are Randy Clement (also formerly of Campanile) and April Langford (formerly of the Park Hyatt Los Angeles). www.silverlakewine.com

Roger Dagorn, MS, has been the maître d' and sommelier at Chanterelle in New York City since 1993. In 1996 Chanterelle was recognized by the James Beard Foundation with its Outstanding Wine Service award. Dagorn represented the United States as a contestant in the international Concours Mondial des Sommeliers VI; then, for the Concours VIII in Japan, he served as a judge. In both 1987 and 1988 he was first runner-up in the national finals of the Best Sommelier of French Wine and Spirits. Prior to joining Chanterelle, he was the sommelier at Tse Yang, restaurant director at L'École, and the sommelier at the Hotel Parker Meridien in New York. Currently, Dagorn is an adjunct professor of wine education at the New York Technical College. www.chanterellenyc.com

Sanford D'Amato is the chef-owner of Sanford restaurant, Coquette Café, and Harlequin bakery, all in Milwaukee. After being nominated for six consec-

utive years, D'Amato won the 1996 James Beard Foundation award for Best Chef: Midwest. In the October 2001 issue of *Gourmet* magazine, Sanford was listed as number twenty-one of the fifty best restaurants in America. Sanford has also consistently received four diamonds from AAA, four stars from the *Mobil Travel Guide*, and the highest ratings for food (29) and service (29) awarded by the *Zagat Survey*. In November 1992, D'Amato was one of twelve chefs chosen by Julia Child to cook for her eightieth birthday celebration in her hometown of Boston. www.sanfordrestaurant.com

Traci Des Jardins is the executive chef and partner in Jardiniere, Acme Chophouse, and Mijita restaurants in San Francisco. In 1995, she was awarded the James Beard Foundation's Rising Star Chef award and she has since been nominated for its Best Chef: California award. She was also named one of *Food & Wine* magazine's Best New Chefs, *San Francisco* magazine's Chef of the Year for two consecutive years, and one of the top three chefs in the Bay Area by the *San Francisco Chronicle* each year since opening. She apprenticed in Europe with many of the French greats, including Michel and Pierre Troisgros, Lucas Carton, Alain Ducasse, and Alain Passard. She cooked at Montrachet in New York City before returning to Los Angeles as opening chef de cuisine of Joachim Splichal's Patina. www.tracidesjardins.com

Rocco DiSpirito is a chef and radio host in New York City. He was previously chef-partner at Union Pacific and Rocco's 22nd Street, the debut of which was featured in the NBC television show *The Restaurant* from 2003 to 2004. He is the author of three cookbooks, including a 2004 James Beard Cookbook Award winner, *Flavor*. DiSpirito also has his own line of cookware and hosts a wine club on wine.com. In 1999 DiSpirito was named *Food & Wine* magazine's Best New Chef and in 2000 *Gourmet* magazine called him America's Most Exciting Young Chef. He graduated from the Culinary Institute of America in 1986 and from Boston University with a degree in business in 1990. www.roccodispirito.com

Brian Duncan is wine director and partner in Bin 36 Restaurant, Wine Bar & Market in Chicago and Bin 36 Lincolnshire in Lincolnshire, Illinois. In 2003, he won a *Chicago Tribune* Good Eating award. He has also consulted on the wine lists for Frontera Grill/Topolobampo, Spruce, Erwin, and Zinfandel restaurants. Duncan has created about a dozen of his own wine blends and is passionate about educating both his staff and his customers about wine and food pairings. He developed the Discovery Series, an interactive series of seminars with executive training on a variety of food and wine subjects. www.bin36.com

Michael Flynn is the wine director and sommelier at Kinkead's in Washington, DC. In 1988 he was named sommelier at Le Pavillon, where he presided over a *Wine Spectator* Grand Award–winning cellar of over sixty-five thousand bottles. Kinkead's has earned four stars from Mobil, *Washingtonian* magazine's Blue Ribbon award ten years in a row, and seven *Wine Spectator* Awards of Excellence. Flynn has been described as Washington's "best known, best loved sommelier" (*Washingtonian* magazine) and "one of America's finest sommeliers" (Robert Parker's *Wine Advocate*). He has been nominated multiple times for the James Beard Foundation award for Outstanding Wine Service. www.kinkead.com

Philippe Gouze is the general manager of Blue Hill at Stone Barns in Pocantico Hills, New York, and its resident cocktail expert. A native of Provence, he spent a summer in New York to celebrate the completion of his MBA in marketing; he fell in love with the city and never left. After taking an introductory position with a Greenwich Village restaurant, Gouze decided to enter the restaurant business and quickly rose to a management position within the Jean-Georges Vongerichten organization. Since 1993, Gouze has served as general manager at Vong as well as at 66. www.bluehill stonebarns.com

Paul Grieco is the general manager and cocreator (with chef Marco Canora) of Hearth in New York City. Grieco's lessons in fine dining began in Toronto at La Scala, his family's grand Italian restaurant, and continued in Italy, where he first studied wine. He came to New York in 1991, where he worked at Remi, Gotham Bar & Grill, and Judson Grill, which he opened with Chris Cannon in 1994. Later, Grieco managed the beverage program at Gramercy Tavern, which won the 2002 James Beard Foundation award for Outstanding Wine Service. The same year, Grieco placed eighth in the American Sommelier Association's competition to name the best sommelier in the country. www.restauranthearth.com

Jill Gubesch is the sommelier at Frontera Grill / Topolobampo in Chicago, where she started as the restaurants' first sommelier. In 2005, Gubesch was nominated for the Jean Banchet Award for Culinary Excellence. Gubesch developed a class with chef Rick Bayless that teaches wine pairing with Mexican food and Bayless has called her "the best wine-and-food pairer I've ever met." A graduate of Illinois Wesleyan University and a certified sommelier since 2001, Gubesch's wine advice has been featured in *Wine Enthusiast* magazine, in *Restaurant Hospitality*, and on Starchefs.com. She has also served as a judge for *Food & Wine*'s American Wine Awards. www.fronterakitchens.com

Greg Harrington, MS, is the owner and winemaker of Gramercy Cellars, a boutique winery in Walla Walla, Washington, focusing on small-lot, *terroir*-based wines, primarily Syrah. In 1996, at the age of twenty-six, he became the youngest American to pass the master sommelier exam. Previously, Harrington was a partner and director of beverage for B. R. Guest and James Hotels, overseeing fifteen restaurants and hotels in New York, Las Vegas, Scottsdale, and Chicago. Previously, he served as wine director and associate partner for the Wolfgang Puck Fine Dining Group, as wine director for Emeril Lagasse's restaurants in New Orleans and Las Vegas, and as sommelier for Joyce Goldstein's Square One in San Francisco.

Willard "Dub" Hay is the senior vice president of coffee and global procurement at Starbucks in Seattle. He oversees the green coffee buying, roasting, blending, and recipe development of Starbucks coffees. Hay is also responsible for educating Starbucks employees about coffee. He joined Starbucks in 2002 as a senior vice president of coffee. As part of the 2005 expansion of his role, he now works with both coffee and tea. He came to Starbucks from UBS PaineWebber in Sonoma. He also worked as a vice president at Nestlé, where he was responsible for the quality of its coffee blends. www.starbucks.com

Robert Hess, founder of DrinkBoy.com and a director at Microsoft in Seattle, traces his interest in cocktails to a childhood fascination with bartenders who effortlessly transformed the contents of the bottles around them into gleaming jewels of refreshment. Eventually, he took action on these early memories, absorbing all he could about the classic art of mixology. Using his culinary training as a canvas, he views cocktails as a cuisine with the same artistic flavor potentials as that of any French chef. He has since become a ceaseless evangelist of quality cocktails, working with restaurants, bartenders, and consumers to increase recognition and respect for this undervalued art. www.drinkboy.com

Hiromi Iuchi is the chief operating officer and vice president of Jizake, Inc., formerly known as the Sake Service Institute. She received a BA in English from Kansai University of Foreign Studies in Osaka and came to the United States on an internship, teaching Japanese culture in New Hampshire. She moved to New York in 1993 and studied painting at the Art Students League. In 1997, she joined Jizake as their East Coast sales manager. In 2000, she was promoted to national sales manager and then in 2004 to her present positions. Iuchi educates people about sake and is known as a sake sommelier. www.sakejapan.com

Steven Jenkins is the master cheesemonger at Fairway Markets in New York City. In 1996 Jenkins published *The Cheese Primer,* which won a James Beard Book Award in 1997. He began his cheese career at Dean & DeLuca. He has been a member of France's Guilde de St. Uguzon since 1976. Jenkins is a board member of the American Cheese Society. The *New York Times* called him "the enfant terrible of the fancy food business," while *New York* magazine cited him as the city's "highest-profile grocer." He hosts "The Jenkins Chronicles," which can be heard on National Public Radio's *The Splendid Table* with Lynn Rossetto Kasper. www.fairwaymarket.com

Daniel Johnnes is the wine director for the Dinex Group, which includes Daniel, in New York, Café Boulud in New York City and Palm Beach, DB Bistrot Moderne in New York City, and Boulud Brasserie in Las Vegas. Before that, he was the wine director at Montrachet. He founded Jeroboam Wines, an importing company. In 2004, Johnnes introduced his Petit Chapeau line of wines. He also wrote *Daniel Johnnes's Top 200 Wines.* The James Beard Foundation nominated him for the Wine and Spirits Professional of the Year award for three consecutive years (2002, 2003, and 2004). In 2000 he was named Wine and Spirits Professional of the Year by *Santé* magazine. Wine writer Robert Parker describes Johnnes as "our nation's finest (and nicest) sommelier." www.danielnyc.com and www.danieljohnneswines.com

Karen King is the beverage director at the Museum of Modern Art's restaurant, The Modern, in New York City. She is an advanced sommelier by the Court of Sommeliers. In 2003, she was hired as the wine director at Gramercy Tavern. Before coming to Gramercy, she was the wine director at Union Square Cafe. In 1998 Union Square Cafe was nominated by the James Beard Foundation for the Best Wine Service award and in 1999 USC won the Outstanding Wine Service award from the foundation. In 2001, 2002, and 2003 *Wine Spectator* gave Union Square Cafe's wine list its Best of Award of Excellence. King has taught at New York University, the French Culinary Institute, and the American Sommelier Association. www.themodernnyc.com

Tim Kopec has been the wine director of Veritas restaurant in New York City since 1999. He was awarded the 2005 James Beard Foundation award for Outstanding Wine Service. Kopec's ongoing efforts to raise the bar and enhance the restaurant's reputation as a world-class wine destination quickly earned Veritas the industry's top honor: the coveted Grand Award from *Wine Spectator* in 2000. This prestigious award was also granted to restaurant Montrachet from 1994 to 1999, when Kopec played an instrumental role in advancing the three-star restaurant's distinctive standing. Kopec is a graduate of the Culinary Institute of America in Hyde Park, New York, and a member in good standing of the Sommelier Society of America. www.veritas-nyc.com

James Labe owns and operates Teahouse Kuan Yin in Seattle, through which he is taster and buyer for his own brand, Teahouse Choice teas. In 1998, he became the nation's first tea sommelier when the position was created for him at the opening of the flagship W Hotel in New York City. Since then he has become world renowned as a master of tea tasting and preparation. As instructor, lecturer, taster, and sommelier, he has been the subject of hundreds of news pieces around the globe. He consults for the world's largest tea concerns and collaborates with great chefs for special tea tasting dinners and afternoon teas. Labe's tea selections and original chai recipes are featured at India's Taj Hotels, for which he is currently engaged in building the world's first tea cellar. www.teahousechoice.com

Lisane Lapointe is the lead brand ambassador for Dom Pérignon in the United States. Lapointe is responsible for public relations and educational activities for Dom Pérignon in California on behalf of Moët Hennessy USA, one of the leading luxury wine importers in the United States. Before becoming Dom Pérignon ambassador, Lapointe was the entertainment marketing manager for brands such as Hennessy Cognac, Grand Marnier, Johnnie Walker

Scotch Whisky, and Tanqueray Gin. Lapointe attended HEC Montréal (École des Hautes Études Commerciales), where she graduated with a bachelor's degree. Lapointe has taken a course with the Court of Master Sommeliers and the New School of Cooking. She also has certificates 1 and 2 from the International Sommelier Guild. www.moet.com

Jean-Luc Le Dû is the owner of Le Dû's Wines in New York City. He was previously head sommelier at Daniel, a position he held with distinction until December 2004. During his tenure, he expanded the wine list to almost two thousand selections from around the world and established one of the best wine programs in the United States while also creating wine lists for all the new restaurants opened under the Daniel Boulud banner (DB Bistro Moderne in New York City and Café Boulud in New York City and Palm Beach). While at Daniel, Le Dû won the title of Best Sommelier Northeast America in the 1997 Sopexa competition. In August 2002, Le Dû's wine list was awarded *Wine Spectator*'s Grand Award, as one of the best in the world. Shortly afterwards, in 2003, after having been nominated in 2000, he was awarded the James Beard Foundation award for Outstanding Wine Service. www.leduwines.com

Matt Lirette is the sommelier at Emeril's New Orleans. In 1996, he joined Emeril Lagasse's team at Emeril's and was quickly promoted to assistant sommelier, when he was able to study the wines as he stocked and learned from the extensive wine list. After a year, Lirette was promoted to sommelier at NOLA Restaurant, Lagasse's second restaurant, where he gained knowledge in wine buying, inventory, and further increasing the wine appeal. In 2002, after a short stint as sommelier at Emeril's Delmonico, he returned to the flagship restaurant, Emeril's New Orleans, as sommelier. The restaurant has received *Wine Spectator*'s Grand Award since 1999. Lirette was also nominated for the James Beard Foundation's Outstanding Wine Service award in 2005. www.emerils.com

Ryan Magarian is the master mixologist at Kathy Casey Food Studios in Seattle. *Food & Wine* magazine gave him a 2004 Tastemaker Award and described him as a "fierce young talent." He was named Best Bartender in Seattle by *Seattle* magazine in 2002 and Best Bartender in Portland, Oregon, in 2000. Some of his cocktail recipes are included in *The Joy of Mixology* by Gary Regan and *Food & Wine Cocktails 2005*. He has written for *Mixologist* and *NW Stir* magazines. He is

designing a bar/mixology program for Holland America Cruise Lines and does cocktail development for the Marriott Hotel Group. He is also the spokesperson for Fris Vodka. www.kathycasey.com

Philippe Marchal is the sommelier at Daniel in New York City. Marchal oversees Daniel's wine list, spanning fifteen countries and including over 1,500 selections carefully chosen for their utmost quality—including the restaurant's own cuvées, Cuvée Daniel, a 1999 Graves red Bordeaux, and Champagne Cuvée Daniel. The restaurant is proud that its wine list offers something for everyone, ranging from a twenty-five-dollar bottle of Palha-Canas, a robust and flavorful Portuguese red wine from the Estremadurra region, to a bottle of the legendary Château Lafite-Rothschild that sells for more than five thousand dollars. www.danielnyc.com

Dr. Michael Mascha is the founder and publisher of FineWaters.com, launched in 2003 and based in Los Angeles. Mascha has been a passionate devotee of the culinary arts for more than twenty years and first explored various ways to expand his culinary experiences via fine bottled waters after he developed a heart condition which prohibited him from drinking alcohol. Prior to this, Mascha was cofounder of CrownPeak Technology, the leader in hosted content management. He was previously assistant professor for visual anthropology at the University of Southern California and the first director of the E-Lab, where he worked with Dr. Jane Goodall on developing innovative interactive media projects. While at USC, Mascha cofounded the ground-breaking Mercury Project, hailed by the *London Times* as a "piece of computer history." www.finewaters.com

Max McCalman is dean of curriculum and maître fromager at the Artisanal Cheese Center in New York City. As America's first restaurant-based maître fromager and a Garde et Jure as designated by France's exclusive Guilde des Fromagers, McCalman established the critically acclaimed cheese programs at New York City's Picholine and Artisanal restaurants over the past decade and has become a highly visible advocate for artisanal cheese production around the world. McCalman's first book, *The Cheese Plate*, was a finalist for both the James Beard Foundation and the International Association of Culinary Professionals cookbook awards. *Cheese: A Connoisseur's Guide to the World's Best* was published in 2005. McCalman lives in Manhattan with his daughter, Scarlett. www.artisanalcheese.com

Danny Meyer is the owner of some of New York City's most successful and award-winning restaurants, including Union Square Cafe, Gramercy Tavern, Eleven Madison Park, Tabla, Blue Smoke, Shake Shack, and The Modern at the Museum of Modern Art. In his effort to fight hunger, he serves on several hunger relief organization boards and in 1996 won the James Beard Foundation award for Humanitarian of the Year. Meyer is the coauthor of *The Union Square Cafe Cookbook* and *Second Helpings from Union Square Cafe* with his longtime partner, chef Michael Romano. Among his proudest honors are the 2000 IFMA Gold Plate Award, Share Our Strength's Humanitarian Award, and the twelve James Beard Foundation awards won by his restaurants and chefs. www.ushg.org

Ron Miller is the maître d'hôtel at Solera Restaurant and Tapas Bar in New York City, having joined the restaurant in 1993. Solera has been featured in *New York* magazine as Best Small Plates and Ruth Reichl wrote of Solera in the *New York Times*, "prepare to be seduced by the food and wine of Spain." Solera is known for its wine list, which is composed solely of Spanish wines. The restaurant won *Wine Spectator*'s Award of Excellence. Miller has served on the *New York Times*'s wine-tasting panels led by Eric Asimov and teaches classes on sherry and other Spanish wines. www.solerany.com

Alan Murray, MS, joined Masa's in San Francisco as sommelier and wine director in 2001. In 1997, after taking a couple of wine courses and working at a Sydney restaurant with a serious wine program, Murray and his American wife came to the United States. With the encouragement of Larry Stone while working under him at Rubicon, Murray took the certificate course at the Court of Master Sommeliers and, two years later, earned his advanced certificate. After moving to Masa's in 2001, Murray passed the advanced exam for the Wine & Spirits Education Trust with distinction, and in February 2005 he completed his exams to qualify as master sommelier, becoming the first Australian to earn the title. www.masasrestaurant.com

Michael Obnowlenny is the former tea sommelier at Epic restaurant at the Fairmont Royal York Hotel in Toronto. In that position, he received national media attention as Canada's first tea sommelier, certified by the Tea Association of Canada and the Tea Council of Canada. Obnowlenny brought his extensive knowledge and passion to the tea program, developing ways to appeal to a wide range of tastes. Each day that he was on duty he guided guests through the tea experience, answering questions, suggesting pairing items, and sharing his expertise on this dearly loved ritual. Obnowlenny believes the right food and tea combination should "dance on your tongue and be a mouth-watering experience."

Patrick O'Connell is the chef-owner of the Inn at Little Washington in Virginia. In 1972, he and his partner, Reinhardt Lynch, settled in the mountains of Virginia to begin a catering business which ultimately evolved into the Inn at Little Washington, now considered one of America's most renowned country retreats. The Inn has won Mobil's Five Star Award for the past fifteen years. O'Connell and the Inn have also won several James Beard Foundation awards, including Best Chef: Mid-Atlantic, Outstanding Restaurant, Outstanding Service, and Outstanding Chef. *Travel + Leisure* magazine rated the Inn number one in North America and number two in the Top Hotels for Food category. O'Connell currently serves as President of the North American Relais Gourmands, part of Relais & Châteaux. www.theinnatlittlewashington.com

Garrett Oliver is the brewmaster and part-owner of the Brooklyn Brewery in Brooklyn, New York. He won the Russell Scherer Award for Innovation and Excellence in Brewing from the Institute for Brewing Studies in 1998, the highest award in the United States for brewing excellence. He also won the Semper Ardens Award for Beer Culture in Denmark in 2003. He began his brewing career at The Manhattan Brewing Company in 1989. He became brewmaster there in 1993 and in 1994 joined the Brooklyn Brewery. He is the author of two books, *The Good Beer Book*, cowritten with Timothy Harper, and *The Brewmaster's Table*, which won an International Association of Culinary Professionals award in 2004. www.garrettoliver.com

Rajat Parr, MS, is the wine director for the Mina Group in San Francisco. He oversees wine programs at Michael Mina Bellagio (formerly Aqua Bellagio, Las Vegas), Arcadia (San Jose Marriott), Nobhill and SeaBlue (MGM Grand, Las Vegas), and most recently, Michael Mina (San Francisco). Parr began his wine career at Rubicon in San Francisco. In 1999, he went to Fifth Floor in San Francisco. He is a graduate of the Welcomgroup Graduate School of Hotel Administration and the Culinary Institute of America. Restaurant Michael Mina, where he designed the wine list, won *Wine Spectator*'s Grand Award in 2005, the first Grand Award given to a restaurant open for less than a year. www.westinstfrancis.com

Gary Regan is a recognized cocktail connoisseur, spirits expert, author, and bartending and restaurant consultant based in Croton-on-Hudson, New York. He is author of the 2003 book, *The Joy of Mixology*. Prior to that, he wrote *The Bartender's Bible*. With his wife, Mardee Haidin Regan, he has coauthored such books as *The Martini Companion, New Classic Cocktails*, and *The Book of Bourbon and Other Fine American Whiskeys*. www.ardentspirits.com

Eric Renaud is the senior sommelier at Bern's Steak House in Tampa. He started as a part-time wine steward at Bern's in 1995 and in 1998 was promoted to sommelier. Renaud catalogues the 6,500-bottle inventory and works with two other sommeliers, advising diners on wine selections. Bern's also has 184 Armagnacs (dating back to the 1830s), 196 cognacs (going back to 1785), 206 Scotches, and 111 eaux-de-vie. Renaud passed the introductory Court of Master Sommeliers course and also teaches wine classes at Bern's Steak House. www.bernssteakhouse.com

Maximilian Riedel is the chief executive officer of Riedel Crystal of America, based in Edison, New Jersey. The company is the world's largest manufacturer of fine wine glasses. Representing the eleventh generation of the glassmaking family, Riedel joined the family business in 1997 at the age of twenty, first training in sales and administration. Riedel also leads tasting seminars at major wine events around the country, showing consumers that the right wine glass does make a difference in the aroma, taste, and perception of a wine. www.riedel.com

Paul Roberts, MS, is the director of wine and beverage for the Thomas Keller Restaurant Group in Napa Valley. In this role, he oversees fourteen full-time sommeliers, divided between the French Laundry (Yountville, California), Per Se (New York City), and Bouchon (Yountville and Las Vegas). Previously, Roberts was the wine director at Cafe Annie in Houston. Both *Food & Wine* and *Gourmet* magazines awarded him a Best Wine List distinction. In addition, the James Beard Foundation nominated him for the 2001 Outstanding Wine Service Award. A master sommelier, he was also awarded the Krug Cup by the Court of Master Sommeliers for passing all three parts of the master sommelier exam on the first try and with the highest combined score. He was the sixth person ever to be awarded the Krug Cup. www.frenchlaundry.com

David Rosengarten is the editor in chief of www.DavidRosengarten.com in New York City. He also edits *The Rosengarten Report*, which covers the most exciting, undiscovered food products, restaurants, wines, and travel destinations in the world and won the 2003 James Beard Foundation award for best food and wine newsletter. Rosengarten is the author of the award-winning cookbook, *Taste*, based on his television cooking show of the same name. He is also the author of *The Dean & DeLuca Cookbook*, a five-hundred-recipe book devoted to the food and food ideas of America's most famous grocery. He holds a doctorate in dramatic literature from Cornell University. www.davidrosengarten.com

Suvir Saran is the executive chef of Devi restaurant in New York City. With tandoori master Hemant Mathur, with whom he had worked for more than a decade, he opened Devi in 2004. Saran's first cookbook, *Indian Home Cooking*, with veteran food writer Stephanie Lyness, was published in 2004. He has taught at New York University's Department of Food and Nutrition, and has served as a contributing authority to *Food Arts* magazine and the Indian Forum of eGullet.com. www.suvir.com

Arthur Schwartz is the author of *Arthur Schwartz's New York City Food*. One of the first male newspaper food editors in the country and a former restaurant critic, Schwartz is now a cookbook author, cooking teacher, and host of *The Food Maven*, a weekly radio program heard on New York's WWRL Radio. His previous books include *Cooking in a Small Kitchen, What to Cook When You Think There's Nothing in the House to Eat, Soup Suppers*, and *Naples at Table: Cooking in Campania*. www.thefoodmaven.com

Charles Scicolone is the wine director of I Trulli Restaurant and Enoteca, a restaurant/wine bar with an all-Italian wine list, both in New York City. He has been nominated multiple times for the James Beard Foundation award for Outstanding Wine Service, most recently in 2006. Scicolone also consults for Vino, an Italian wine and spirits store in Manhattan. He cowrote *Pizza — Any Way You Slice It* with his wife, Italian food expert Michele Scicolone. He has also written for *Eating Well, House Beautiful, McCall's, Gourmet, Epicurean* and *Wine Enthusiast* magazines. He is a member of the Wine Media Guild. www.vinosite.com

Piero Selvaggio is the owner of Valentino in Santa Monica and Las Vegas, and Caffe Giorgio in Las Vegas. Selvaggio was the first to bring treasures like fresh buffalo mozzarella to the West Coast and amassed what wine enthusiasts have called "one of the greatest cellars of them all." Valentino has won a number of James Beard Foundation awards, including Outstanding Wine Service (1994), Outstanding

Service (1996), and Outstanding Restaurant (2000). The restaurant has been cited as the country's number one restaurant in *Forbes* and as having one of the country's ten best wine lists by *Wine Spectator*. Selvaggio is the author of *The Valentino Cookbook*. www.welovewine.com

Craig Shelton is the chef-owner of the Ryland Inn in Whitehouse, New Jersey. He received the 2000 James Beard Foundation award for Best Chef: Mid-Atlantic. The restaurant was rated "extraordinary" by the *New York Times* and as "arguably America's best country French restaurant" by Bob Lape of *Crain's New York Business*. *Gourmet* magazine named the Inn "one of the top 10 country restaurants in America." The Ryland Inn's wine list was voted the Best French Wine List of America by *Restaurant Hospitality* at the Eighth Annual World of Wines Festival. When not cooking, Shelton tends to his several-acre vegetable and herb garden on the fifty-acre property of the Ryland Inn. www.theryland inn.com

Alpana Singh, MS, for years the sommelier at Everest restaurant in Chicago, was recently promoted to corporate wine sommelier for Lettuce Entertain You Enterprises. Called a "sommelier prodigy" by *Food & Wine* magazine, Singh became the youngest master sommelier in the United States at age twenty-six — she was also one of only fourteen women in the world to hold the title. Before playing a role in Everest's winning the James Beard Foundation award for Outstanding Wine Service, Singh gave up college and waitressing to pass the advanced test of the Court of Master Sommeliers at the age of twenty-one. She has also served as host of the television show *Check, Please!* on WTTW in Chicago. www.leye.com

Carlos Solis is the food and beverage director and executive chef of T. H. Brewster's at the Sheraton Four Points at the Los Angeles Airport (LAX). There, he oversees a beer selection numbering more than seventy-five hard-to-find bottles from around the world and offers a series of beer dinners in which each course is paired with a different beer. He studied culinary arts at University of California, Los Angeles, and the Culinary Institute of America at Greystone in Napa Valley and food and beverage management at Cornell University. His hobbies include outdoor barbecuing and brewing his own beer. www.fourpointslax.com

Joseph Spellman, MS, is the director of education at Joseph Phelps Vineyards, in Spring Valley, California. In 1996, he earned his Master Sommelier diploma. The following year, he won the French Sommelier Competition in Paris sponsored by Sopexa and the title Best International Sommelier in French Wines and Spirits. In 1998, he was named *Bon Appétit* magazine's Wine and Spirits Professional of the Year. Having passed the Certified Wine Educator exam, he is now a teacher and examiner in the Court of Master Sommeliers and serves as the chairman of its American chapter. He has written for *Wine & Spirits*, *Wine Enthusiast*, *Santé*, *Decanter*, and *Appellation* magazines. Spellman also wrote the wine notes for Charlie Trotter's books, having previously served as the restaurant's sommelier. www.jpvwines.com

Larry Stone, MS, is the general manager of Rubicon Estate in Napa Valley. He became the first American to win the title of Best International Sommelier in French Wines and Spirits in Paris, and remains the only American to have earned the title of French Master Sommelier from the Union de la Sommellerie Française. Stone is also a master sommelier under the English Court of Master Sommeliers. He has won Grand Awards from *Wine Spectator* magazine for his work at Charlie Trotter's in Chicago and at Rubicon in San Francisco and earned both restaurants the James Beard Foundation award for Outstanding Wine Service. Stone sits on the board of the Court of Master Sommeliers and is a trustee of the James Beard Foundation. He also makes Cabernet Sauvignon, Cabernet Franc, and Merlot in Napa Valley under his own Sirita label. www.rubiconestate.com

Bernard Sun is the corporate beverage director for Jean-Georges Vongerichten's four-star restaurant group, overseeing the beverage programs at all sixteen Jean-Georges restaurants from Shanghai to New York and composing wine lists, creating cocktails, training staff, and managing the financials. Sun's wine knowledge and palate are the result of years of study and work in New York's top restaurants. Before joining Jean-Georges in January 2005, he was sommelier at Gray Kunz's four-star Lespinasse, Sirio Maccioni's famed Le Cirque 2000, and Drew Nieporent's legendary Montrachet. Sun donates his time and talents to numerous causes close to his heart, including the Jackson Hole Wine Auction and the Windows of Hope Family Relief Fund. www.jean-georges.com

Paul Tanguay is the corporate beverage director for Sushi Samba, headquartered in New York City with four locations in Manhattan, Chicago, and Miami. From 2003 to 2005, Tanguay served as a judge at the United States National Sake Appraisal. At the event, he tasted and judged aromas, flavors, and balances of 150 sakes. Tanguay was also instrumental in bringing the Joy of Sake, the largest sake-tasting event outside of Japan, to New York City. In 2004, Tanguay was honored to be one of a handful of Americans to attend the public tasting of the Zenkoku Shinshu Kampyokai in Hiroshima, the largest sake-tasting event in the world. www.sushisamba.com

Don Tillman is co-owner (with his wife, Chika) and sommelier of ChikaLicious, a dessert-only restaurant in New York City. ChikaLicious earned a food rating of 25 in the 2006 *Zagat Survey*, which described the restaurant as "a brilliant concept" featuring "'sublime' sweets plus 'perfect wine pairings.'" A native of Hershey, Pennsylvania, Tillman previously worked at Prime, Tom Tom, and Tavern at Phipps. On his days off, he can be found playing his saxophone in the Union Square Green Market. www.chikalicious.com

Derek Todd is the sommelier at Blue Hill at Stone Barns in Pocantico Hills, New York. A native of Vancouver, Canada, Todd developed a love of cooking at an early age in his mother's kitchen. He moved to New York over twenty years ago to pursue a career in theater and started a symbiotic relationship with the restaurant industry. At a certain point he realized he was more inclined to spend his nights off at wine tastings or new restaurants than at the theater and so chose to focus on his passion for food and wine. He has worked in numerous New York restaurants, most recently as manager at the Red Cat and general manager and wine director at Vanderbilt Station. www.bluehillstonebarns.com

Christopher Tracy is the winemaker and chef at Channing Daughters Winery in Bridgehampton, New York. He earned his Sommelier Certificate from the Sommelier Society of America, as well as the Higher Certificate and the Diploma from the Wine & Spirits Education Trust. Since 2001, Tracy has been developing prestige cuvées and other products. Tracy graduated from the French Culinary Institute in Manhattan. He was previously the pastry sous chef at March, and executive chef of Robbins Wolfe Eventeurs. www.channingdaughters.com

Corinne Trang, an award-winning New York–based author, has written and worked for such publications as *Food & Wine, Health, Cooking Light, Bottom Line Personal, Organic Style,* and *Saveur,* where she held the positions of test kitchen director and producing editor from 1996 to 1998. She is the author of *Authentic Vietnamese Cooking, Essentials of Asian Cuisine,* and *The Asian Grill.* The *Washington Post* dubbed Trang "the Julia Child of Asian cuisine." www.corinnetrang.com

Greg Tresner, MS, is the sommelier at Mary Elaine's at the Phoenician in Scottsdale, Arizona. Tresner joined the Phoenician in 1998 after twenty years in the restaurant industry. He was named Arizona's first master sommelier by the American chapter of the Court of Master Sommeliers. Tresner helped design the wine list and purchase the wines for Mary Elaine's, resulting in its first *Wine Spectator* Grand Award in 2000. He also helped earn Mary Elaine's wine service five diamonds from AAA, five stars from Mobil, and several James Beard Foundation award nominations for Outstanding Wine Service. Mary Elaine's earned the Grand Award from *Wine Spectator* magazine for the sixth consecutive year in 2005. www.thephoenician.com

Madeline Triffon, MS, is the director of wine for the Matt Prentice Restaurant Group in Detroit. She is responsible for development of all wine lists and beverage programs for five fine dining and three casual venues, four of which have won *Wine Spectator* Awards of Excellence. Triffon also coordinates food and wine events and serves as corporate wine educator. In 1987, she was awarded the title of master sommelier and became the eighth American to win the title and one of only two female master sommeliers in the world at the time. In 1999, *Santé* magazine named Triffon its Wine and Spirits Professional of the Year and in 2002 *Restaurant Hospitality* magazine awarded her its Vanguard Award for industry leadership and vision. www.mattprenticerg.com

Scott Tyree is the sommelier at Tru restaurant in Chicago. He is a graduate of Northwestern University's School of Speech with a degree in Radio, Television, and Film. While studying in the Bordeaux region of France, he developed a fascination with wine and viniculture. In 1996 Tyree accepted the position of sommelier at Lettuce Entertain You's bustling Shaw's Crab House. He became wine director at Tru in 1999, where his wine program has received accolades from such publications as *Food & Wine* (Top Ten Best New Wine Lists in the United States, 2000) and *Wine Spectator* (Best of Award of Excellence, 2000 and 2001). He has passed the Certificate and Advanced Examinations of the Court of Master Sommeliers. www.leye.com

David Waltuck is the chef-owner of Chanterelle restaurant in New York City. Chanterelle has received numerous awards, including James Beard Foundation awards for Outstanding Service in 2000 and Outstanding Restaurant in 2004. In a characteristically trailblazing style, Waltuck opened Chanterelle at the age of twenty-four with his wife, Karen, in a then-remote section of Manhattan inhabited mostly by artists. He has long taken advantage of the best ingredients available, seeking out small producers and the finest suppliers of fresh seafood, domestic and imported game, and, of course, wild mushrooms. Waltuck's book, *Staff Meals from Chanterelle*, was published in 2000. www.chanterellenyc.com

Joshua Wesson is cofounder and wine director of Best Cellars, Inc. In 2003, he won the Ambassador's Award from the European Wine Council. He co-authored *Red Wine with Fish* with David Rosengarten, which won the 1990 International Association of Culinary Professionals Silver Medal and the 1989 Duboeuf Wine Book of the Year. He has contributed wine recommendations to *Our Latin Table* by Fernando Saralegui, *Arcadia Seasonal Mural and Cookbook* by Anne Rosenzweig, and *Bistro Fare* by Betty Fussell. In 1984, he won the title of Best French Wine Sommelier in the United States. In 1986, he was named one of the top five sommeliers worldwide by Sopexa Food and Wines from France. He is a commentator on National Public Radio's *The Splendid Table*. www.bestcellars.com

Janos Wilder is the chef-owner of Janos in Tucson. In 2000, he was named the Best Chef: Southwest by the James Beard Foundation. He wrote *Janos: Recipes and Tales from a Southwest Restaurant*, which was published in 1990. In 1998, the restaurant relocated to its present home in a free-standing building on the grounds of the Westin La Paloma Resort overlooking the entire Tucson Valley. In 1999, under the same roof as Janos, J Bar was opened as a casual, less expensive alternative featuring the foods of Southern Arizona, Latin America, Mexico, and the Caribbean in a style emphasizing the conviviality of the shared table. www.janos.com